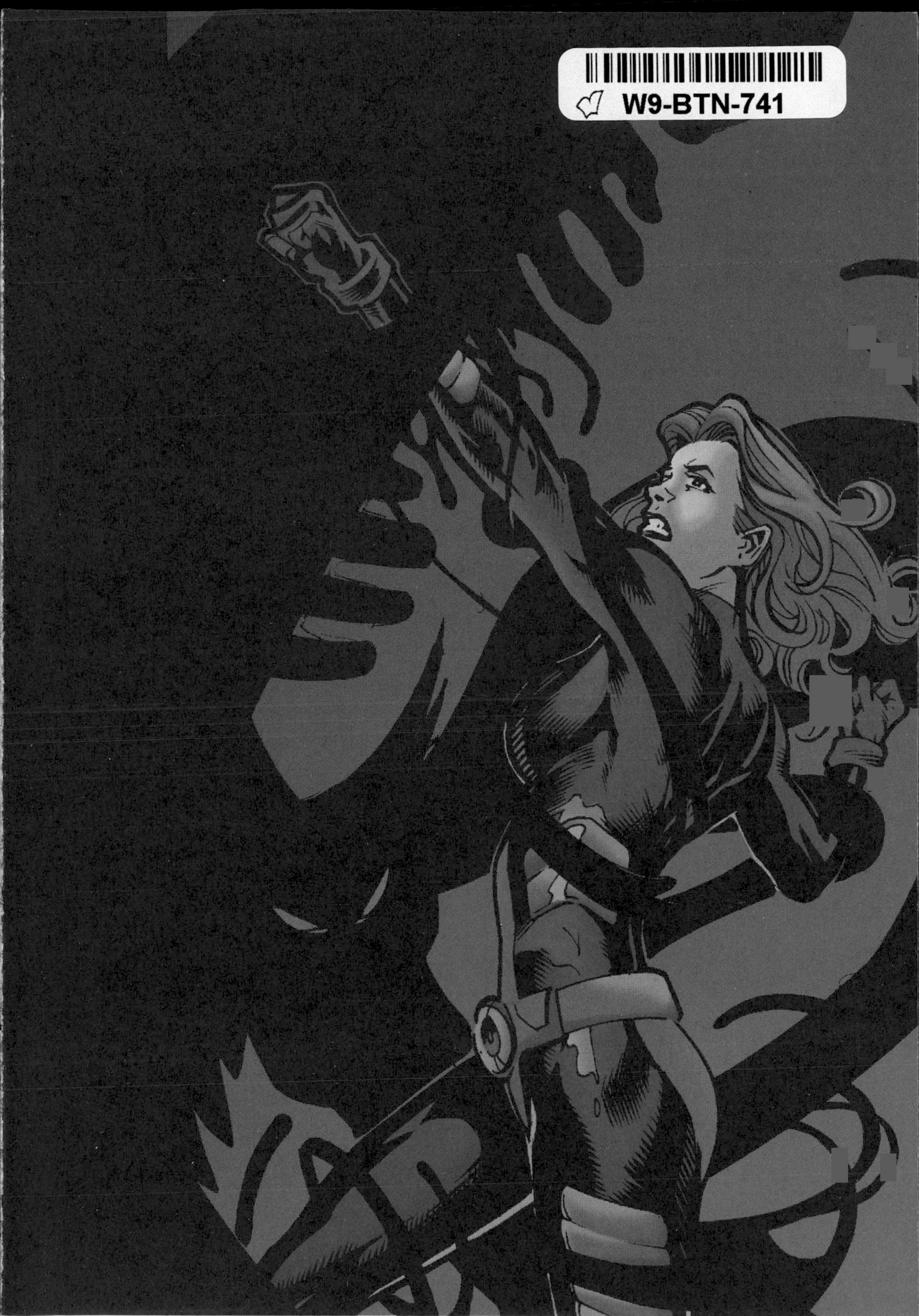

JSA DARKNESS FALLS

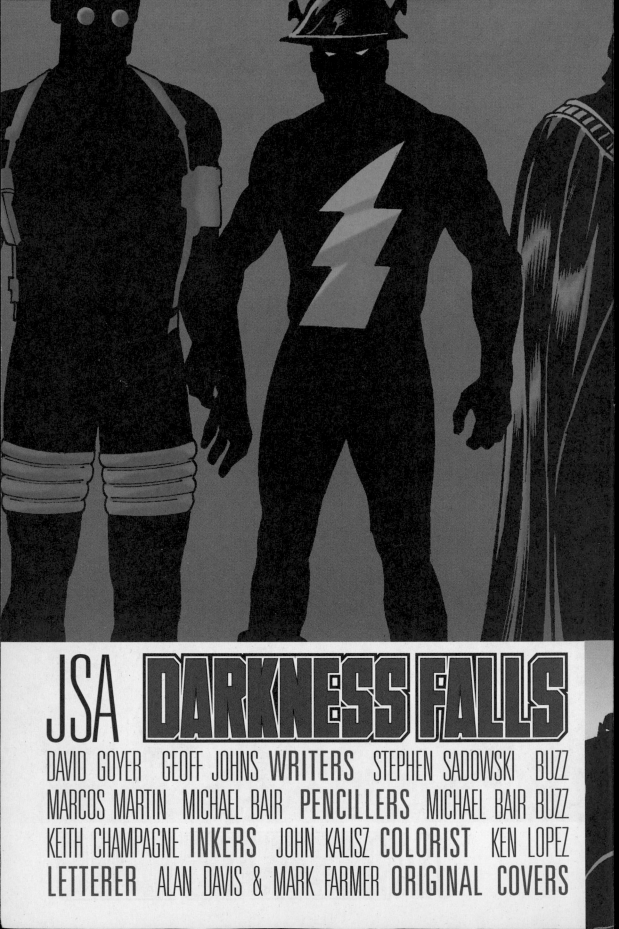

JSA DARKNESS FALLS

DAVID GOYER GEOFF JOHNS WRITERS STEPHEN SADOWSKI BUZZ

MARCOS MARTIN MICHAEL BAIR PENCILLERS MICHAEL BAIR BUZZ

KEITH CHAMPAGNE INKERS JOHN KALISZ COLORIST KEN LOPEZ

LETTERER ALAN DAVIS & MARK FARMER ORIGINAL COVERS

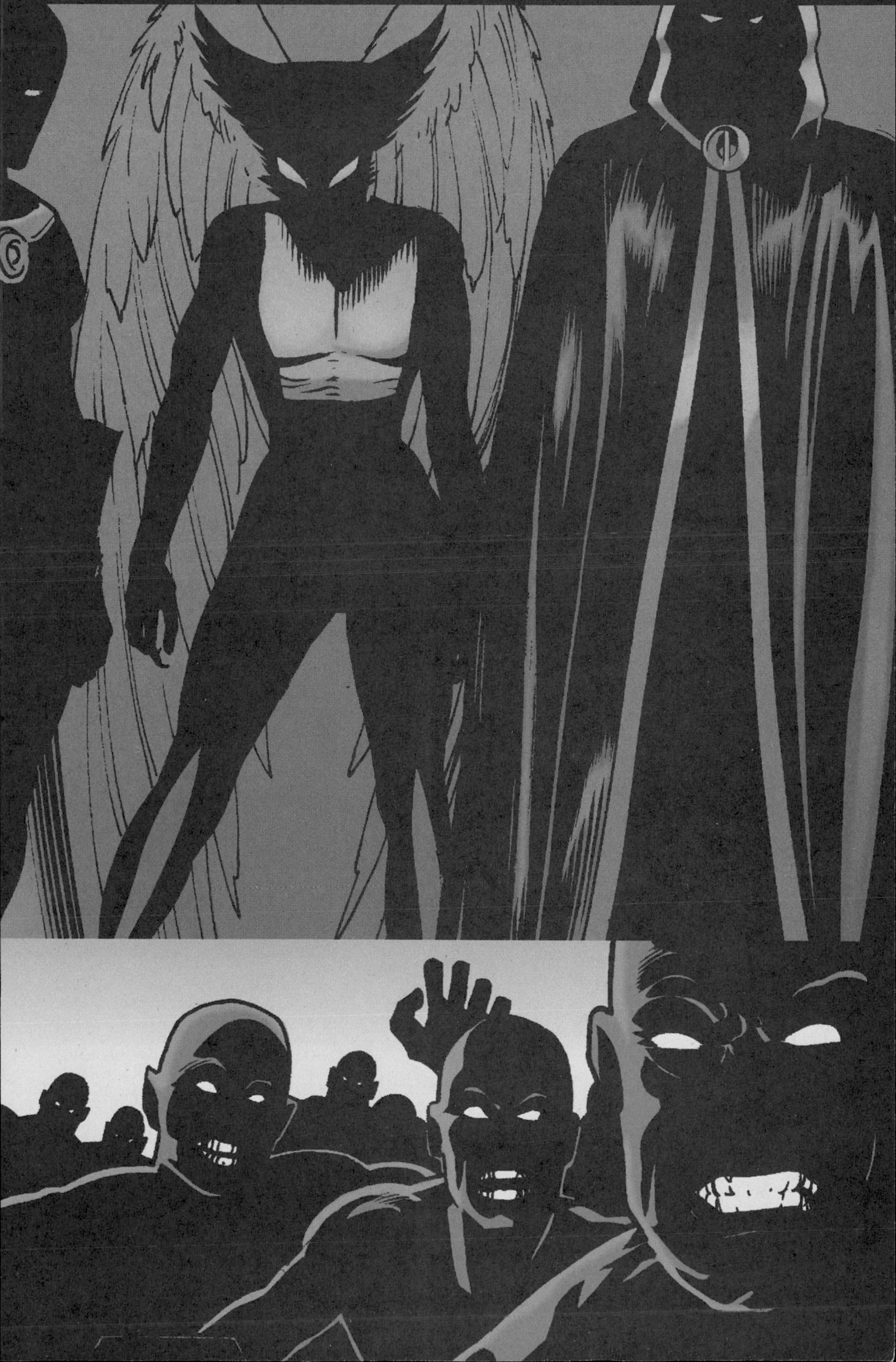

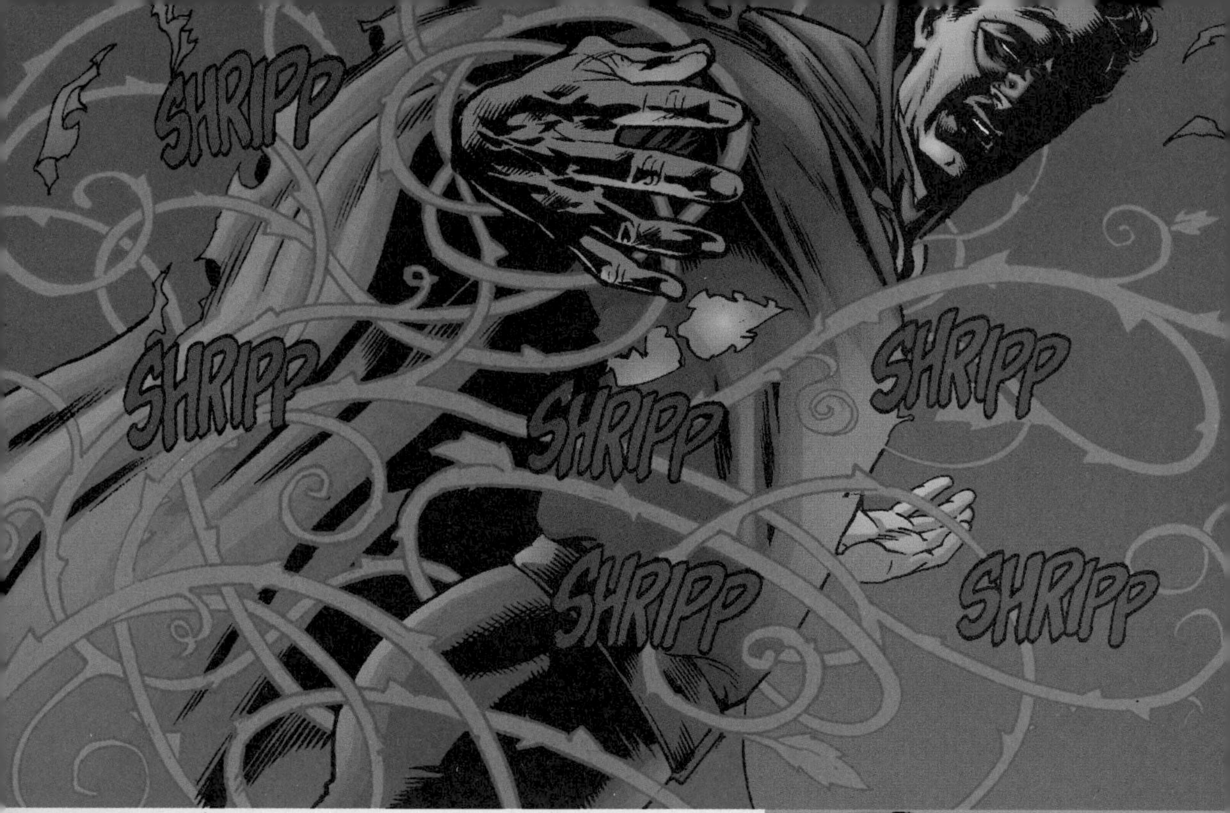
SHRIPP
SHRIPP
SHRIPP
SHRIPP
SHRIPP
SHRIPP

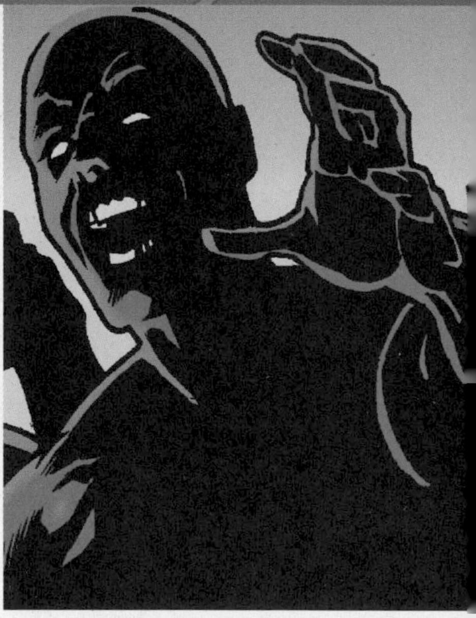

JSA: DARKNESS FALLS. Published by DC Comics. Cover and compilation copyright © 2002 DC Comics. All Rights Reserved. Originally published in single magazine form as JSA 6-15. Copyright © 2000 DC Comics. All Rights Reserved. All characters, their distinctive likenesses and related indicia featured in this publication are trademarks of DC Comics. The stories, characters, and incidents featured in this publication are entirely fictional. DC Comics does not read or accept unsolicited submissions of ideas, stories or artwork. DC Comics, 1700 Broadway, New York, NY 10019. A division of Warner Bros. – An AOL Time Warner Company. Printed in Canada. First Printing. ISBN: 1-56389-739-3. Cover illustration by Stephen Sadowski & Mark Farmer. Cover color by John Kalisz. Publication design by Louis Prandi.

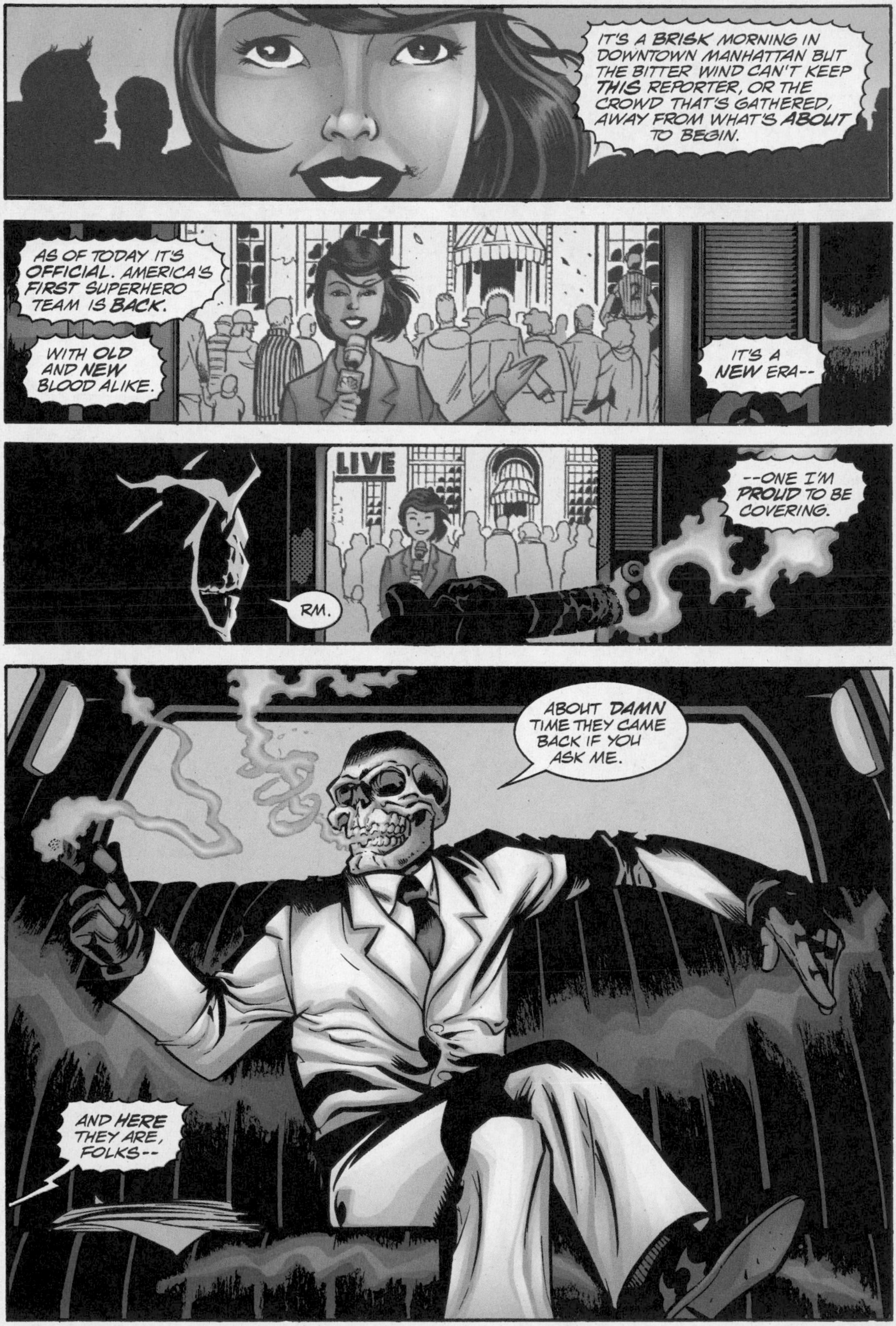
IT'S A BRISK MORNING IN DOWNTOWN MANHATTAN BUT THE BITTER WIND CAN'T KEEP THIS REPORTER, OR THE CROWD THAT'S GATHERED, AWAY FROM WHAT'S ABOUT TO BEGIN.
AS OF TODAY IT'S OFFICIAL. AMERICA'S FIRST SUPERHERO TEAM IS BACK.
WITH OLD AND NEW BLOOD ALIKE.
IT'S A NEW ERA--
LIVE
--ONE I'M PROUD TO BE COVERING.
RM.
ABOUT DAMN TIME THEY CAME BACK IF YOU ASK ME.
AND HERE THEY ARE, FOLKS--

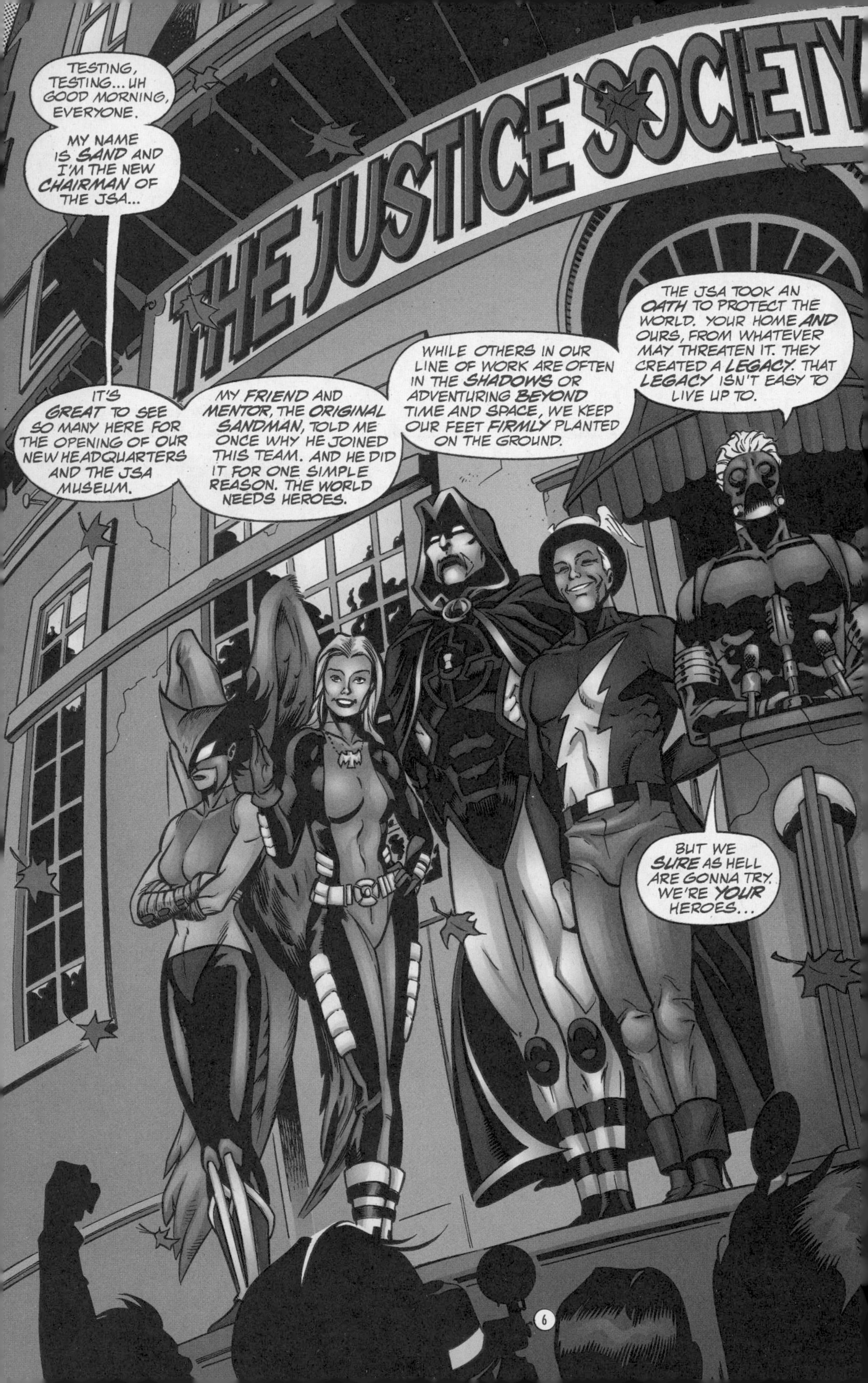

THE JUSTICE SOCIETY
TESTING, TESTING... UH GOOD MORNING, EVERYONE.
MY NAME IS SAND AND I'M THE NEW CHAIRMAN OF THE JSA...
IT'S GREAT TO SEE SO MANY HERE FOR THE OPENING OF OUR NEW HEADQUARTERS AND THE JSA MUSEUM.
MY FRIEND AND MENTOR, THE ORIGINAL SANDMAN, TOLD ME ONCE WHY HE JOINED THIS TEAM. AND HE DID IT FOR ONE SIMPLE REASON. THE WORLD NEEDS HEROES.
WHILE OTHERS IN OUR LINE OF WORK ARE OFTEN IN THE SHADOWS OR ADVENTURING BEYOND TIME AND SPACE, WE KEEP OUR FEET FIRMLY PLANTED ON THE GROUND.
THE JSA TOOK AN OATH TO PROTECT THE WORLD. YOUR HOME AND OURS, FROM WHATEVER MAY THREATEN IT. THEY CREATED A LEGACY. THAT LEGACY ISN'T EASY TO LIVE UP TO.
BUT WE SURE AS HELL ARE GONNA TRY. WE'RE YOUR HEROES...

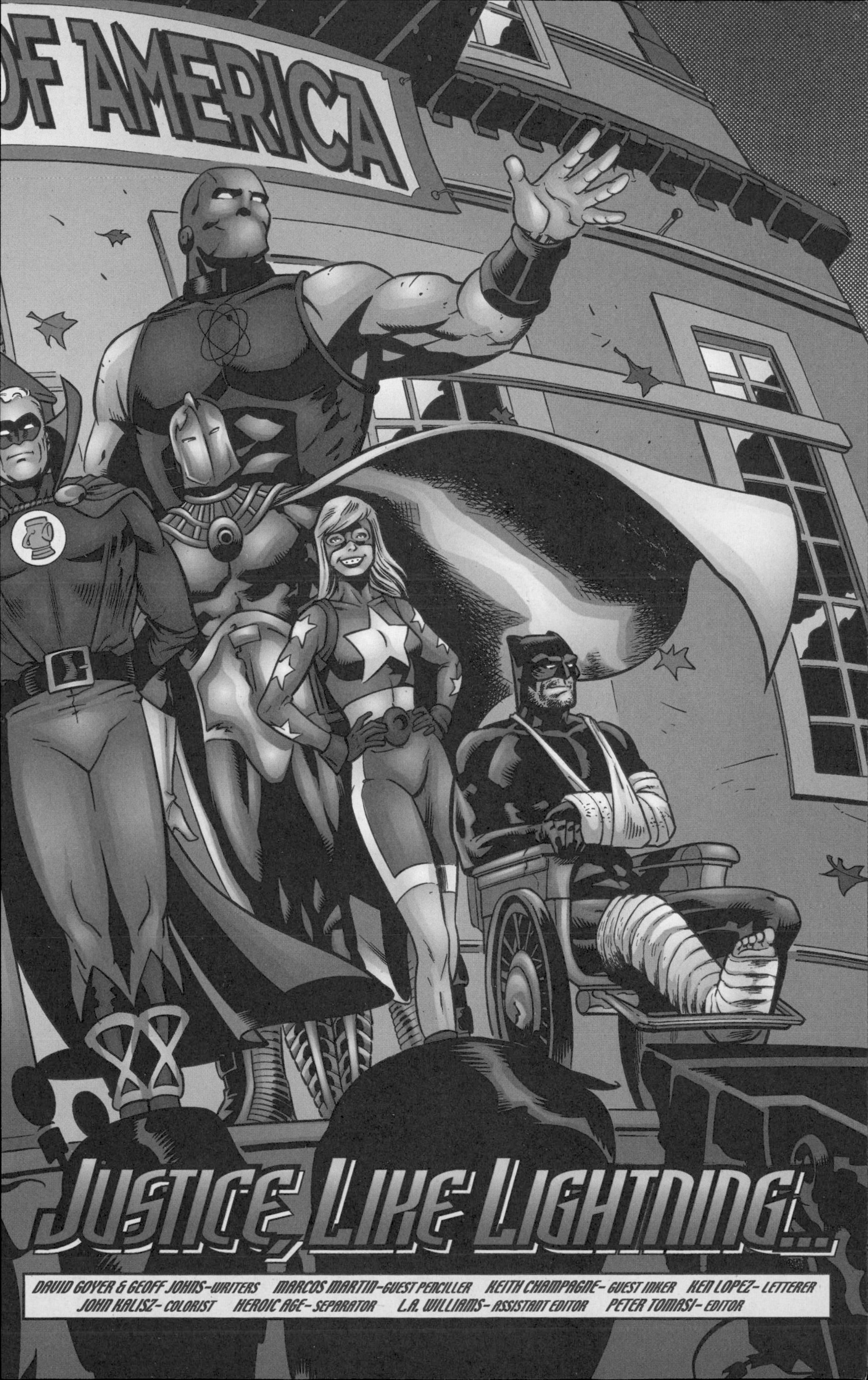
OF AMERICA
JUSTICE, LIKE LIGHTNING...
DAVID GOYER & GEOFF JOHNS-WRITERS MARCOS MARTIN-GUEST PENCILLER KEITH CHAMPAGNE- GUEST INKER KEN LOPEZ- LETTERER
JOHN KALISZ- COLORIST HEROIC AGE- SEPARATOR L.A. WILLIAMS- ASSISTANT EDITOR PETER TOMASI- EDITOR

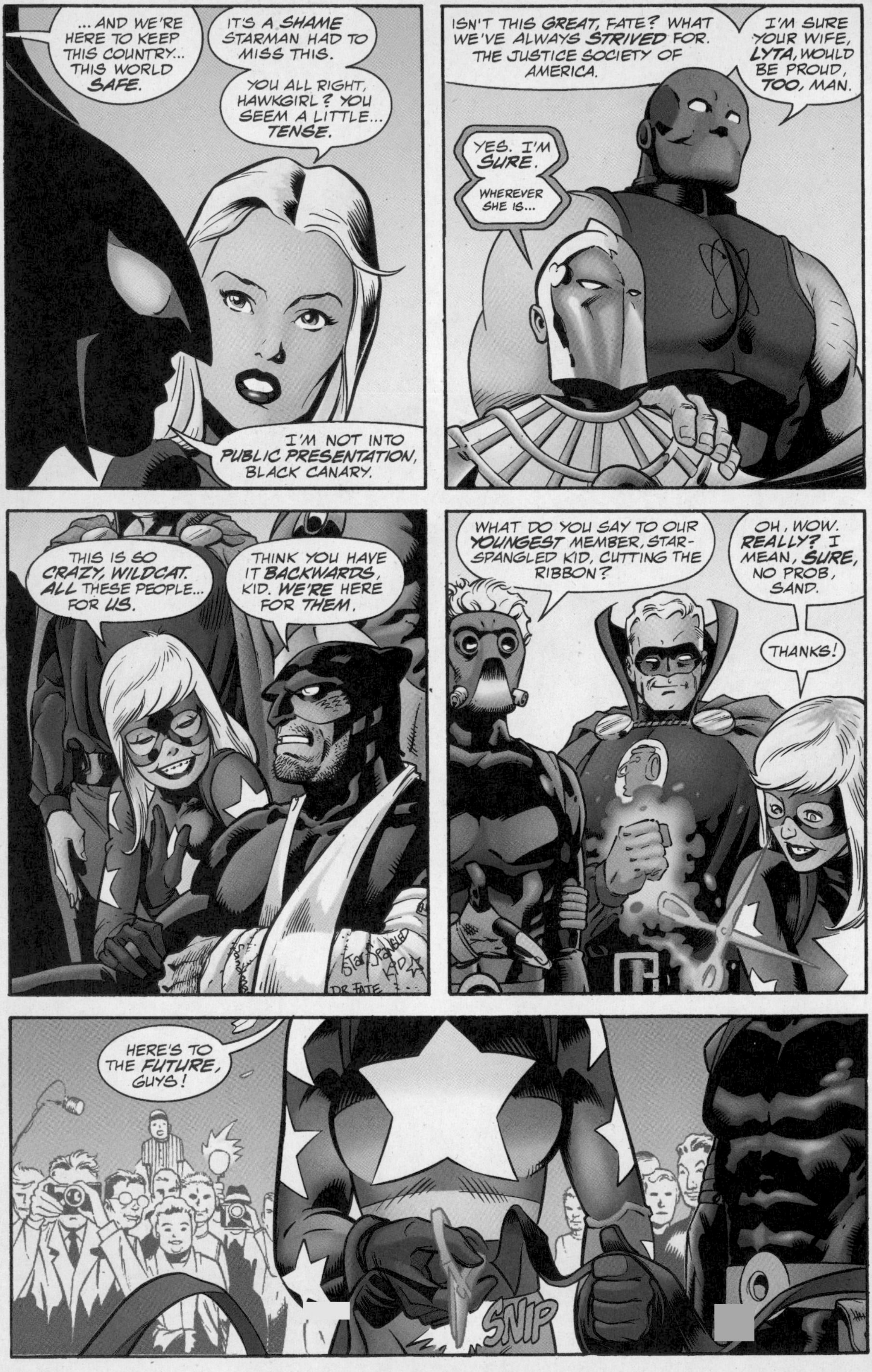
... AND WE'RE HERE TO KEEP THIS COUNTRY... THIS WORLD *SAFE*.
IT'S A *SHAME* STARMAN HAD TO MISS THIS.
YOU ALL RIGHT, HAWKGIRL? YOU SEEM A LITTLE... *TENSE*.
I'M NOT INTO *PUBLIC PRESENTATION*, BLACK CANARY.
ISN'T THIS *GREAT*, FATE? WHAT WE'VE ALWAYS *STRIVED* FOR. THE JUSTICE SOCIETY OF AMERICA.
I'M SURE YOUR WIFE, *LYTA*, WOULD BE PROUD, *TOO*, MAN.
YES. I'M *SURE*.
WHEREVER SHE IS...
THIS IS SO *CRAZY, WILDCAT*. *ALL* THESE PEOPLE... FOR *US*.
THINK YOU HAVE IT *BACKWARDS*, KID. *WE'RE* HERE FOR *THEM*.
WHAT DO YOU SAY TO OUR *YOUNGEST* MEMBER, STAR-SPANGLED KID, CUTTING THE RIBBON?
OH, WOW. *REALLY?* I MEAN, *SURE*, NO PROB, SAND.
THANKS!
HERE'S TO THE *FUTURE*, GUYS!
SNIP

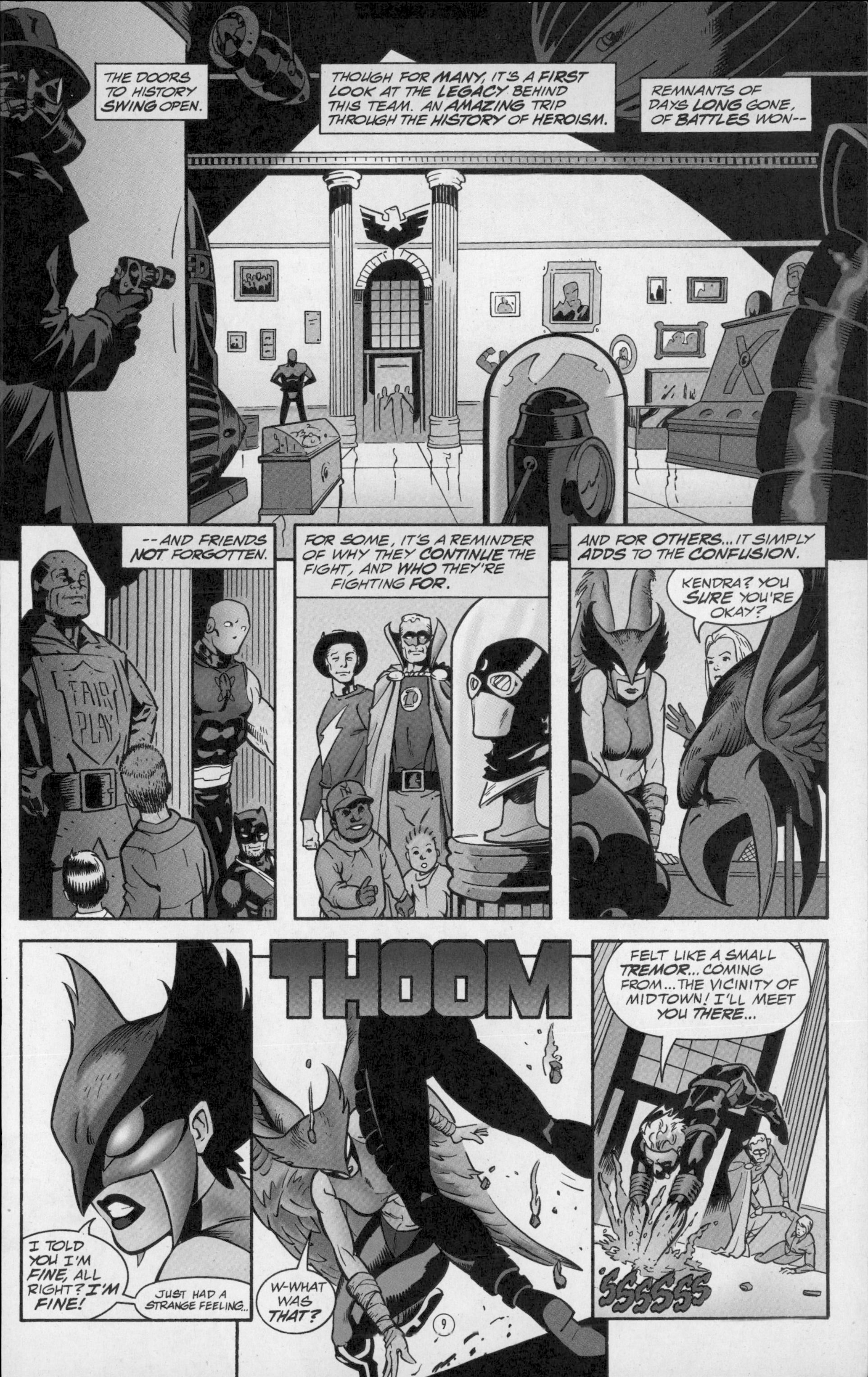
THE DOORS TO HISTORY SWING OPEN.
THOUGH FOR MANY, IT'S A FIRST LOOK AT THE LEGACY BEHIND THIS TEAM. AN AMAZING TRIP THROUGH THE HISTORY OF HEROISM.
REMNANTS OF DAYS LONG GONE, OF BATTLES WON--
--AND FRIENDS NOT FORGOTTEN.
FAIR PLAY
FOR SOME, IT'S A REMINDER OF WHY THEY CONTINUE THE FIGHT, AND WHO THEY'RE FIGHTING FOR.
AND FOR OTHERS... IT SIMPLY ADDS TO THE CONFUSION.
KENDRA? YOU SURE YOU'RE OKAY?
I TOLD YOU I'M FINE, ALL RIGHT? I'M FINE!
JUST HAD A STRANGE FEELING...
THOOM
W-WHAT WAS THAT?
FELT LIKE A SMALL TREMOR... COMING FROM... THE VICINITY OF MIDTOWN! I'LL MEET YOU THERE...
SSSSSS
9

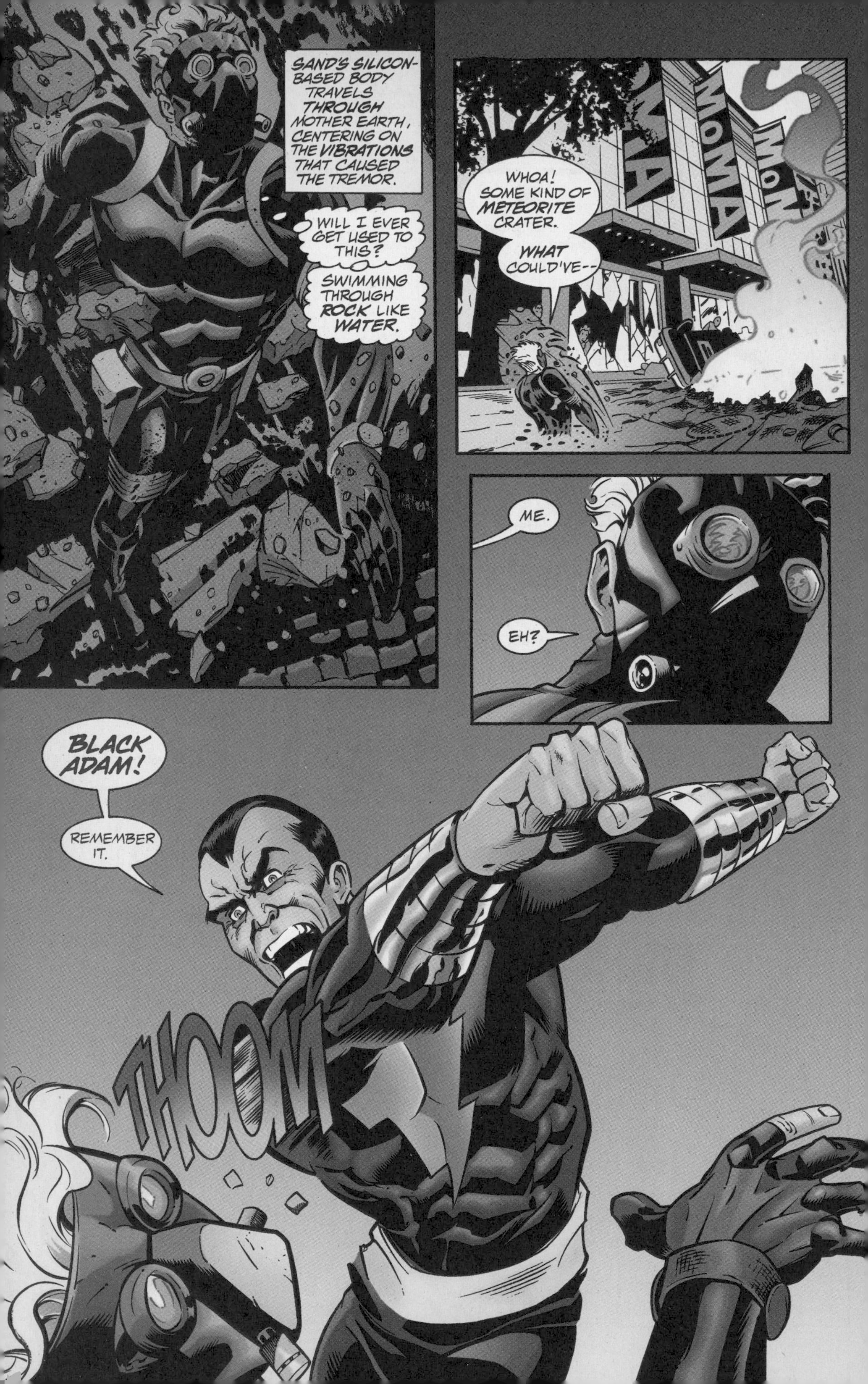
SAND'S SILICON-BASED BODY TRAVELS THROUGH MOTHER EARTH, CENTERING ON THE VIBRATIONS THAT CAUSED THE TREMOR.
WILL I EVER GET USED TO THIS?
SWIMMING THROUGH ROCK LIKE WATER.
MOMA
WHOA! SOME KIND OF METEORITE CRATER.
WHAT COULD'VE--
ME.
EH?
BLACK ADAM!
REMEMBER IT.
THOOM

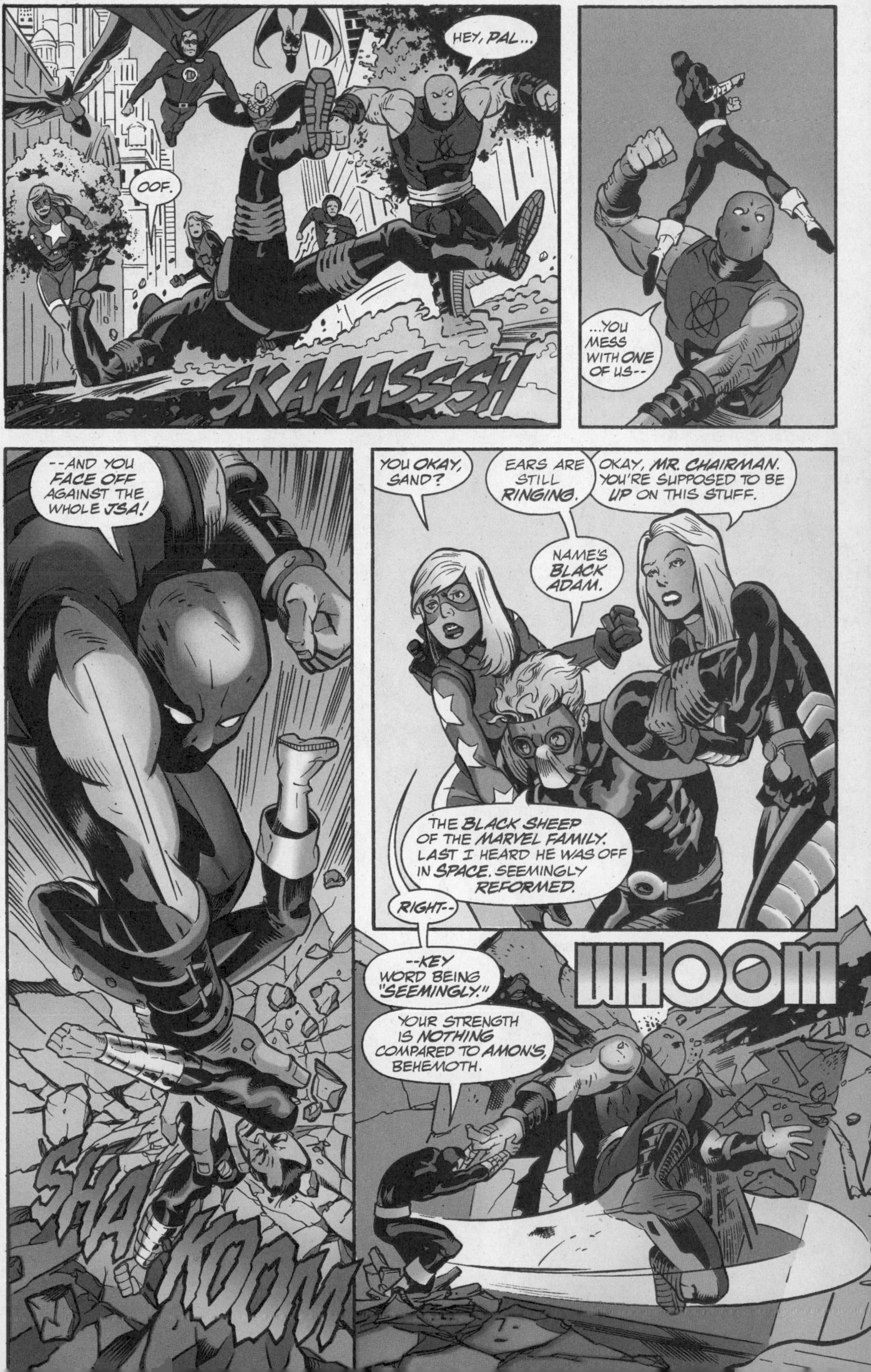

HEY, PAL...
OOF.
SKAAASSSH
...YOU MESS WITH ONE OF US--
--AND YOU FACE OFF AGAINST THE WHOLE JSA!
YOU OKAY, SAND?
EARS ARE STILL RINGING.
OKAY, MR. CHAIRMAN. YOU'RE SUPPOSED TO BE UP ON THIS STUFF.
NAME'S BLACK ADAM.
THE BLACK SHEEP OF THE MARVEL FAMILY. LAST I HEARD HE WAS OFF IN SPACE. SEEMINGLY REFORMED.
RIGHT--
--KEY WORD BEING "SEEMINGLY."
WHOOM
YOUR STRENGTH IS NOTHING COMPARED TO AMON'S, BEHEMOTH.
SHA KOOM

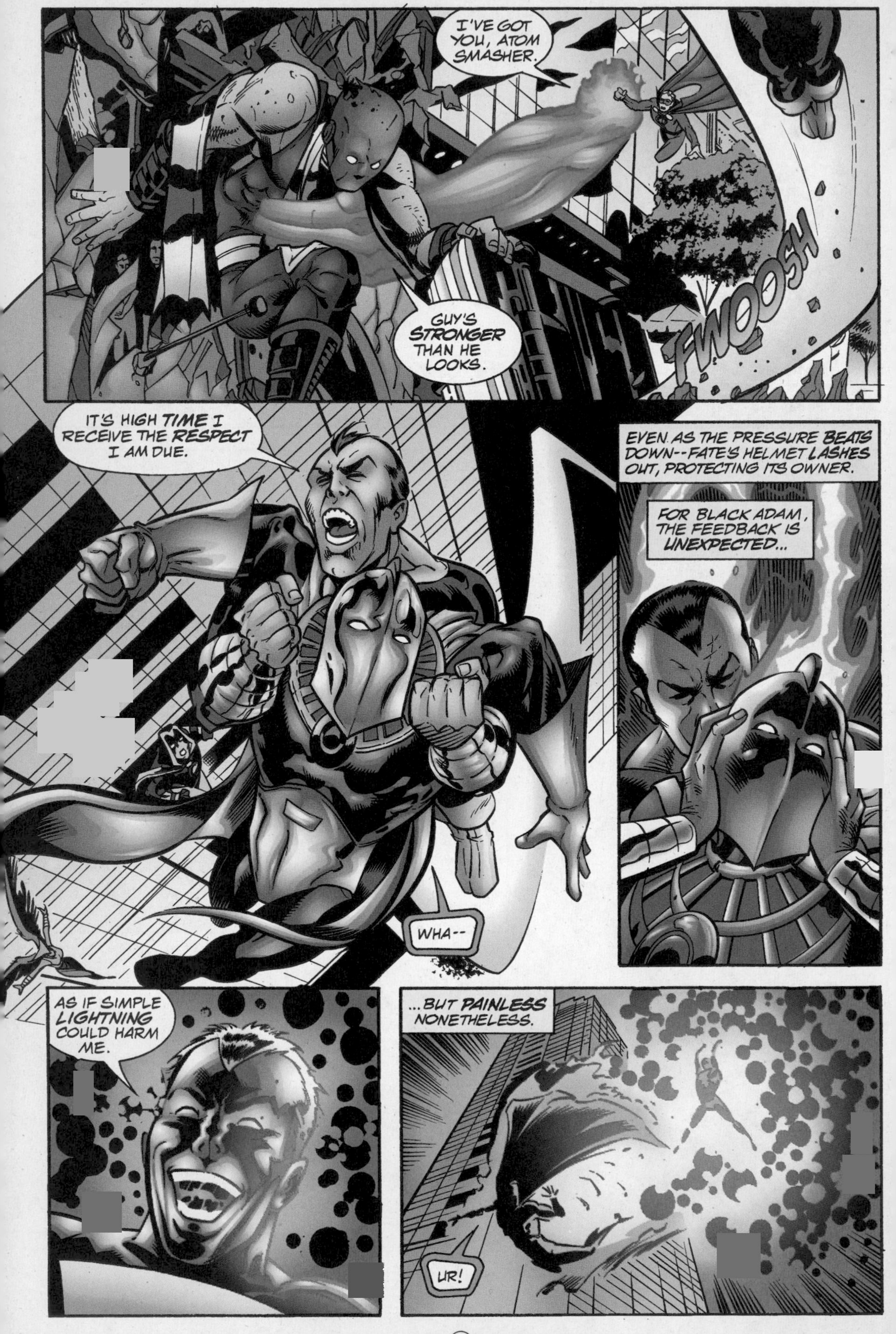
I'VE GOT YOU, ATOM SMASHER.
GUY'S STRONGER THAN HE LOOKS.
FWOOSH
IT'S HIGH TIME I RECEIVE THE RESPECT I AM DUE.
WHA--
EVEN AS THE PRESSURE BEATS DOWN--FATE'S HELMET LASHES OUT, PROTECTING ITS OWNER.
FOR BLACK ADAM, THE FEEDBACK IS UNEXPECTED...
AS IF SIMPLE LIGHTNING COULD HARM ME.
...BUT PAINLESS NONETHELESS.
UR!

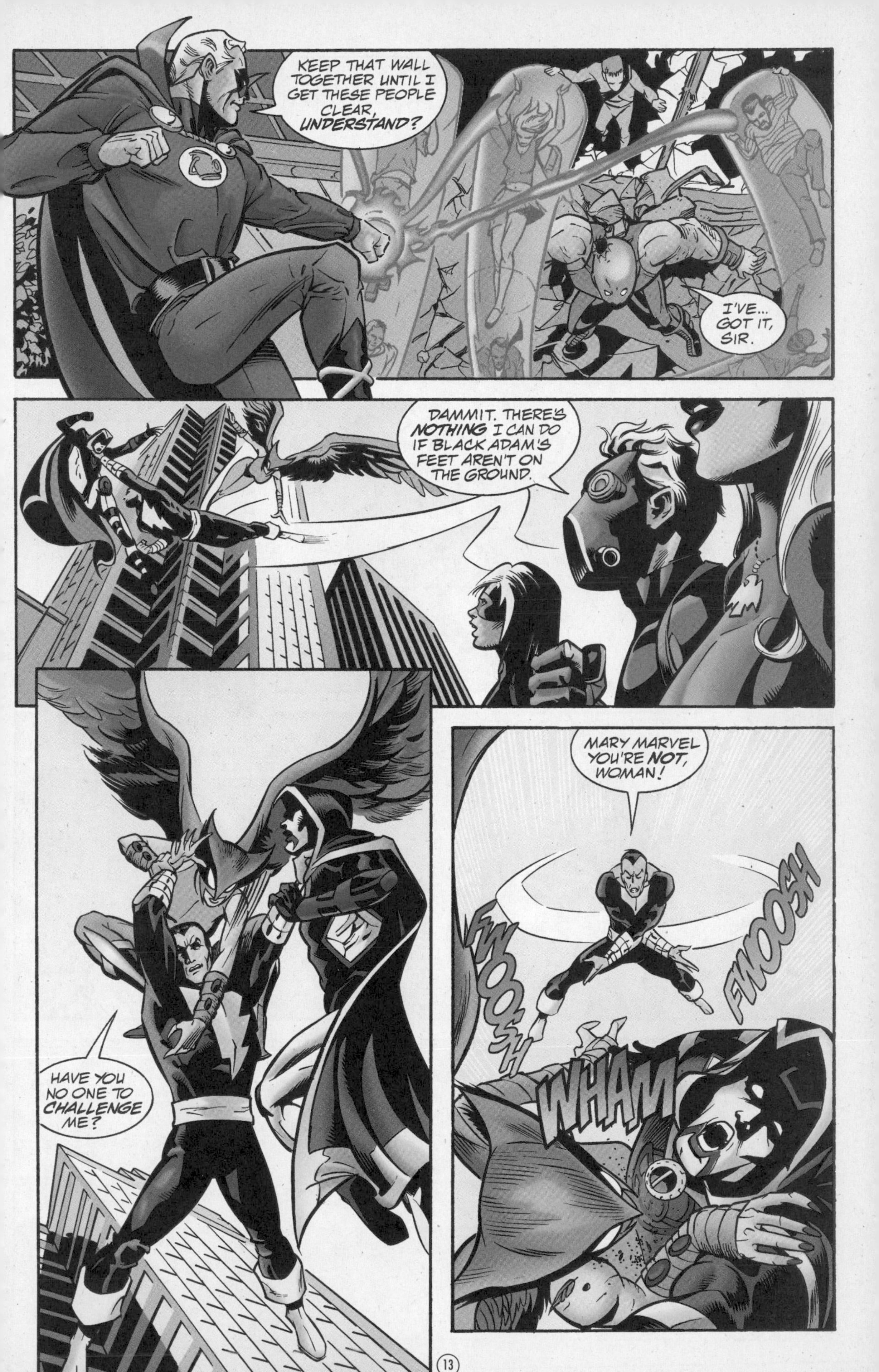
KEEP THAT WALL TOGETHER UNTIL I GET THESE PEOPLE CLEAR, UNDERSTAND?
I'VE... GOT IT, SIR.
DAMMIT. THERE'S NOTHING I CAN DO IF BLACK ADAM'S FEET AREN'T ON THE GROUND.
HAVE YOU NO ONE TO CHALLENGE ME?
MARY MARVEL YOU'RE NOT, WOMAN!
FWOOSH
FWOOSH
WHAM

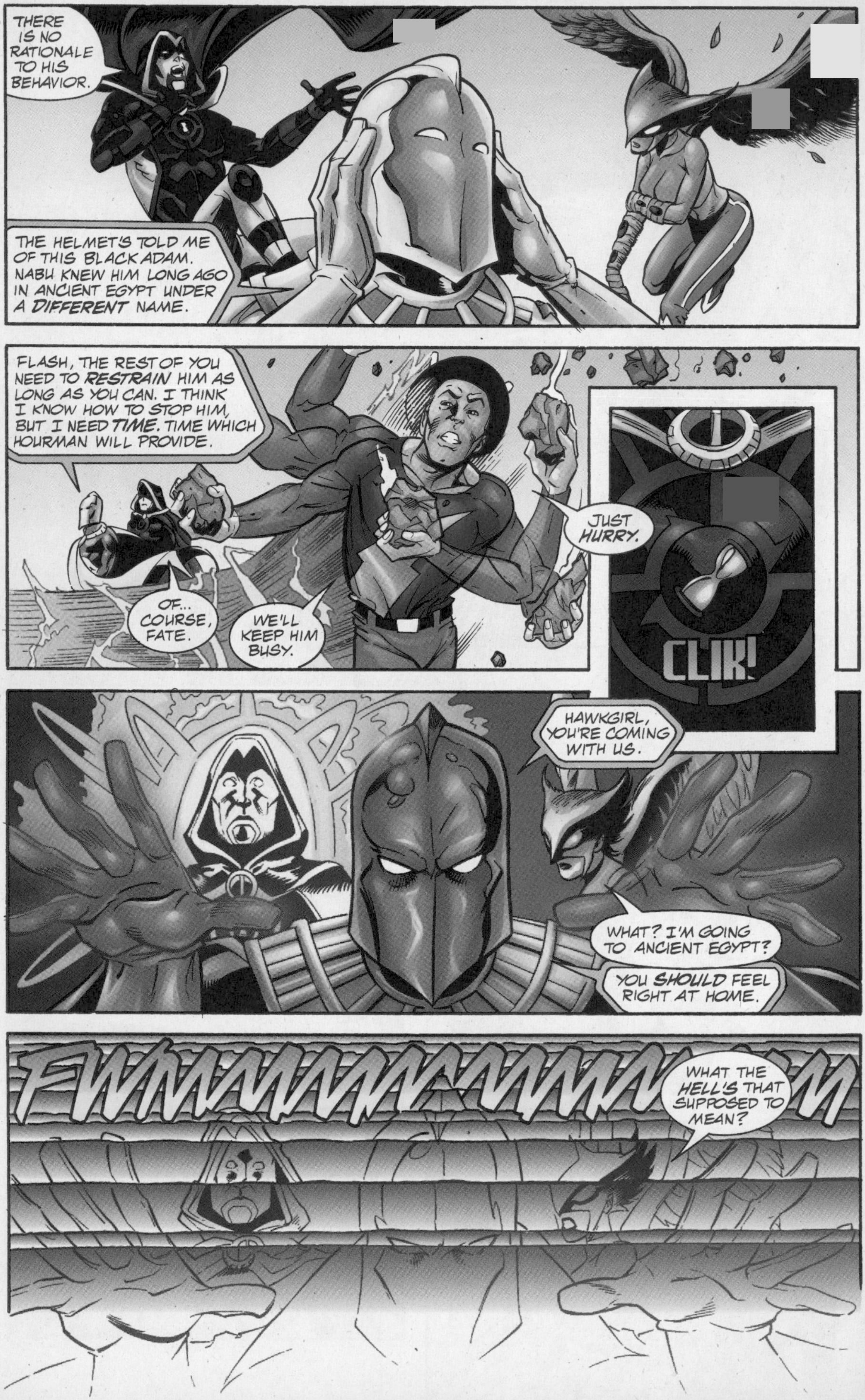
THERE IS NO RATIONALE TO HIS BEHAVIOR.
THE HELMET'S TOLD ME OF THIS BLACK ADAM. NABU KNEW HIM LONG AGO IN ANCIENT EGYPT UNDER A DIFFERENT NAME.
FLASH, THE REST OF YOU NEED TO RESTRAIN HIM AS LONG AS YOU CAN. I THINK I KNOW HOW TO STOP HIM, BUT I NEED TIME. TIME WHICH HOURMAN WILL PROVIDE.
JUST HURRY.
OF... COURSE, FATE.
WE'LL KEEP HIM BUSY.
CLIK!
HAWKGIRL, YOU'RE COMING WITH US.
WHAT? I'M GOING TO ANCIENT EGYPT?
YOU SHOULD FEEL RIGHT AT HOME.
FWMMMMMMMMMMMM
WHAT THE HELL'S THAT SUPPOSED TO MEAN?

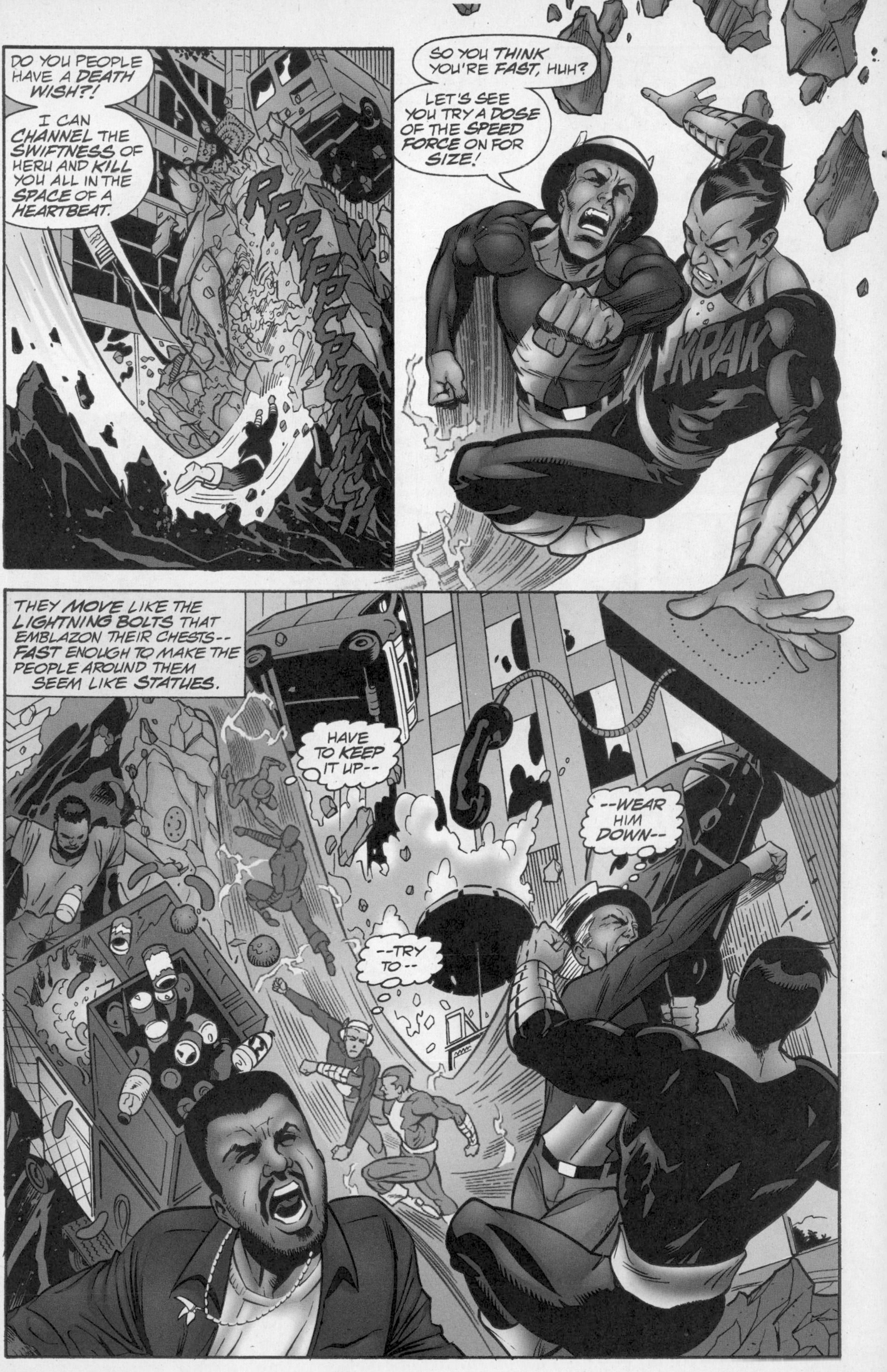
DO YOU PEOPLE HAVE A DEATH WISH?!
I CAN CHANNEL THE SWIFTNESS OF HERU AND KILL YOU ALL IN THE SPACE OF A HEARTBEAT.
RRRIPPCRUNNSH
SO YOU THINK YOU'RE FAST, HUH?
LET'S SEE YOU TRY A DOSE OF THE SPEED FORCE ON FOR SIZE!
KRAK
THEY MOVE LIKE THE LIGHTNING BOLTS THAT EMBLAZON THEIR CHESTS-- FAST ENOUGH TO MAKE THE PEOPLE AROUND THEM SEEM LIKE STATUES.
HAVE TO KEEP IT UP--
--WEAR HIM DOWN--
--TRY TO--

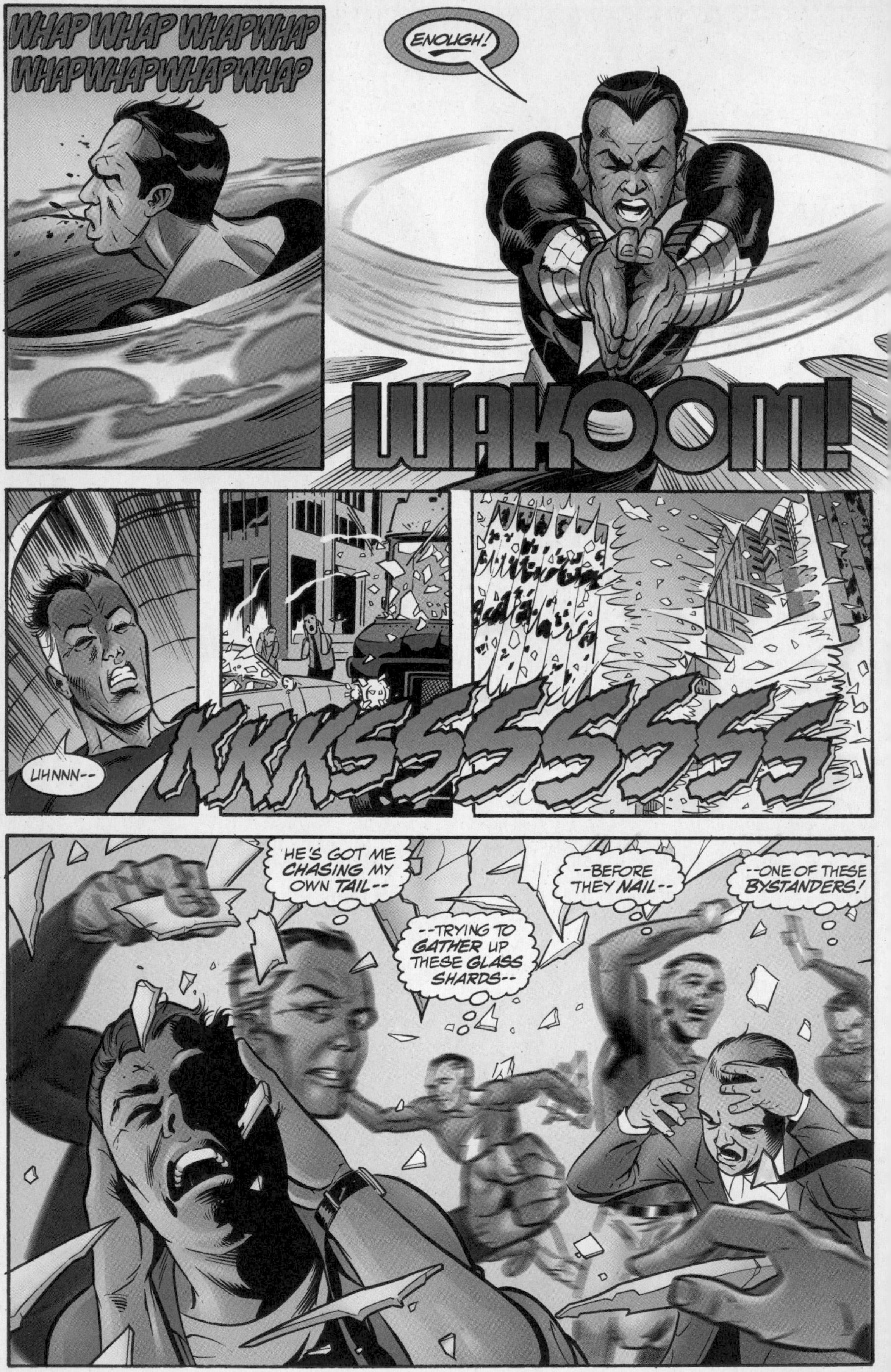
WHAP WHAP WHAPWHAP
WHAPWHAPWHAPWHAP
ENOUGH!
WAKOOM!
UHNNN--
KKKSSSSSSSS
HE'S GOT ME CHASING MY OWN TAIL--
--TRYING TO GATHER UP THESE GLASS SHARDS--
--BEFORE THEY NAIL--
--ONE OF THESE BYSTANDERS!

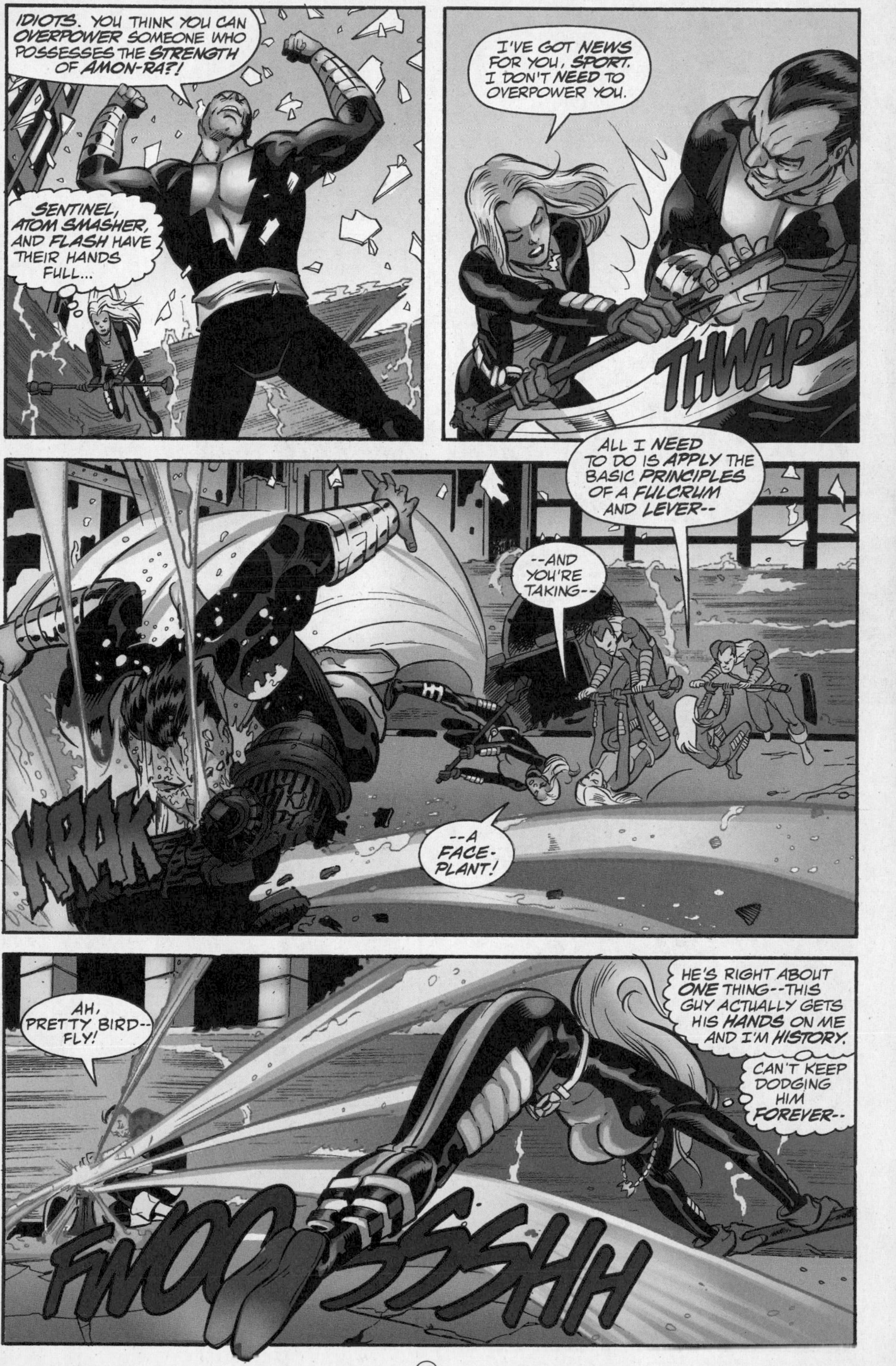
IDIOTS. YOU THINK YOU CAN OVERPOWER SOMEONE WHO POSSESSES THE STRENGTH OF AMON-RA?!
SENTINEL, ATOM SMASHER, AND FLASH HAVE THEIR HANDS FULL...
I'VE GOT NEWS FOR YOU, SPORT. I DON'T NEED TO OVERPOWER YOU.
THWAP
ALL I NEED TO DO IS APPLY THE BASIC PRINCIPLES OF A FULCRUM AND LEVER--
--AND YOU'RE TAKING--
--A FACE-PLANT!
KRAK
AH, PRETTY BIRD--FLY!
HE'S RIGHT ABOUT ONE THING--THIS GUY ACTUALLY GETS HIS HANDS ON ME AND I'M HISTORY.
CAN'T KEEP DODGING HIM FOREVER--
FWOOOSSHH

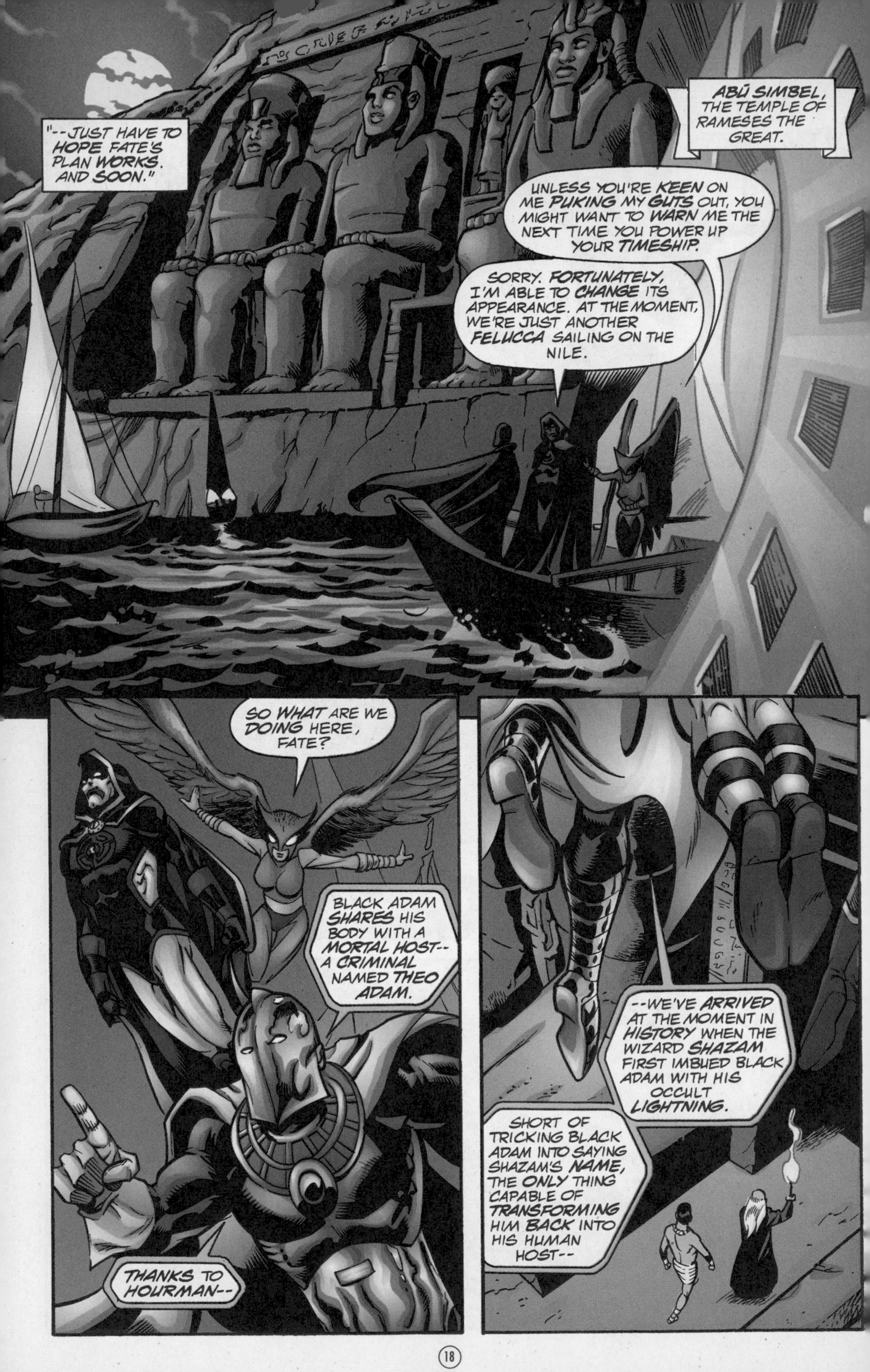
"--JUST HAVE TO HOPE FATE'S PLAN WORKS. AND SOON."
ABŪ SIMBEL, THE TEMPLE OF RAMESES THE GREAT.
UNLESS YOU'RE KEEN ON ME PUKING MY GUTS OUT, YOU MIGHT WANT TO WARN ME THE NEXT TIME YOU POWER UP YOUR TIMESHIP.
SORRY. FORTUNATELY, I'M ABLE TO CHANGE ITS APPEARANCE. AT THE MOMENT, WE'RE JUST ANOTHER FELUCCA SAILING ON THE NILE.
SO WHAT ARE WE DOING HERE, FATE?
BLACK ADAM SHARES HIS BODY WITH A MORTAL HOST-- A CRIMINAL NAMED THEO ADAM.
THANKS TO HOURMAN--
--WE'VE ARRIVED AT THE MOMENT IN HISTORY WHEN THE WIZARD SHAZAM FIRST IMBUED BLACK ADAM WITH HIS OCCULT LIGHTNING.
SHORT OF TRICKING BLACK ADAM INTO SAYING SHAZAM'S NAME, THE ONLY THING CAPABLE OF TRANSFORMING HIM BACK INTO HIS HUMAN HOST--

"--IS THE WIZARD'S MAGIC LIGHTNING WHICH FIRST IMBUED HIM WITH HIS POWERS."

WHAT'S THIS? NOW YOU'RE SENDING CHILDREN AGAINST ME?

HE'S BACK ON TERRA FIRMA. TIME TO RATTLE HIS CAGE A LITTLE.

RRRUUMMMMBLE

HE'S ALL YOURS, SANDY!

WHA--?!?

KKRRZAAAKKK

WHAKOOM

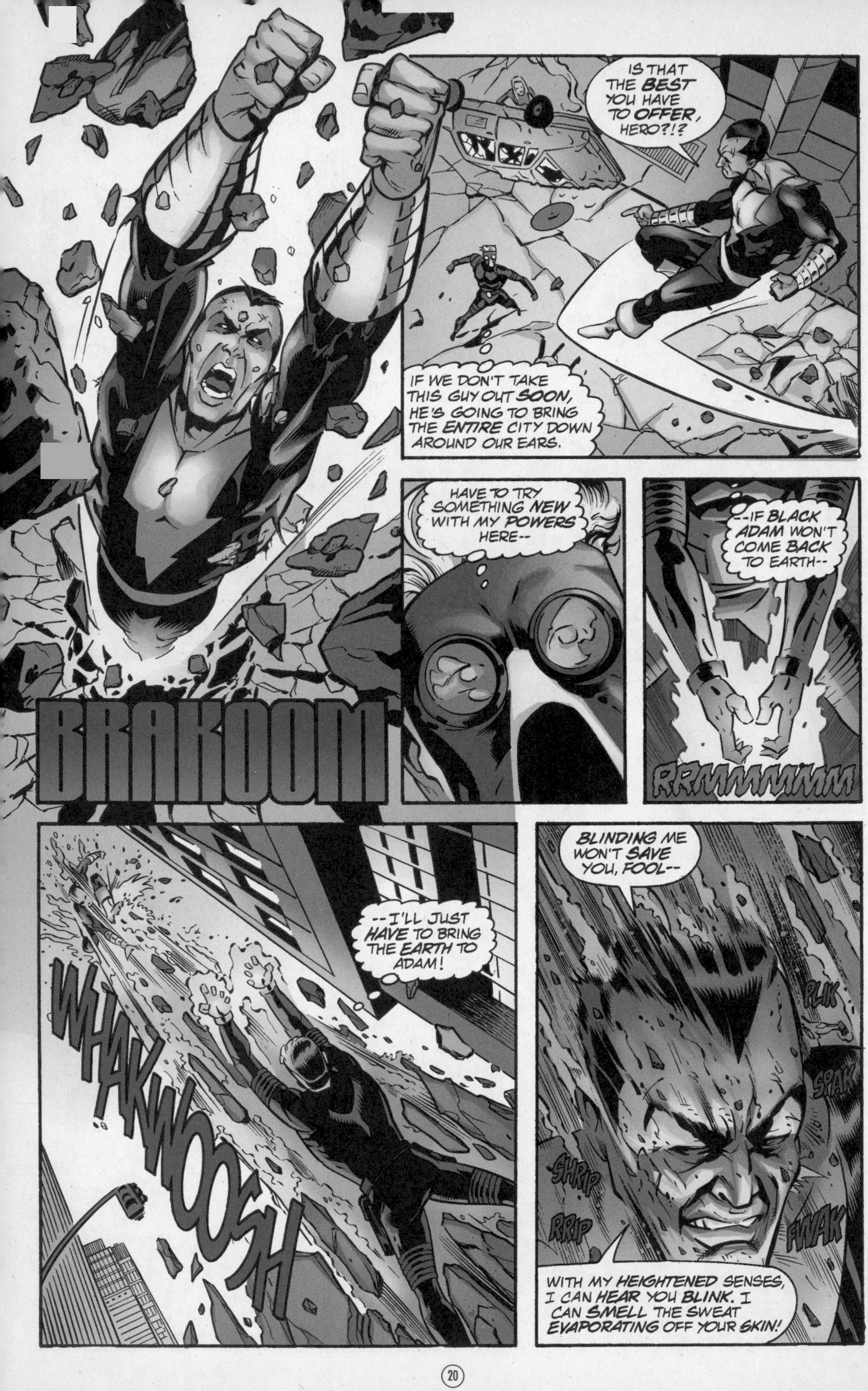
BRAKOOM
IS THAT THE BEST YOU HAVE TO OFFER, HERO?!?
IF WE DON'T TAKE THIS GUY OUT SOON, HE'S GOING TO BRING THE ENTIRE CITY DOWN AROUND OUR EARS.
HAVE TO TRY SOMETHING NEW WITH MY POWERS HERE--
--IF BLACK ADAM WON'T COME BACK TO EARTH--
RRMMMMMM
--I'LL JUST HAVE TO BRING THE EARTH TO ADAM!
WHAKWOOSH
BLINDING ME WON'T SAVE YOU, FOOL--
PLIK
SPAK
SHRIP
RRIP
FWAK
WITH MY HEIGHTENED SENSES, I CAN HEAR YOU BLINK. I CAN SMELL THE SWEAT EVAPORATING OFF YOUR SKIN!

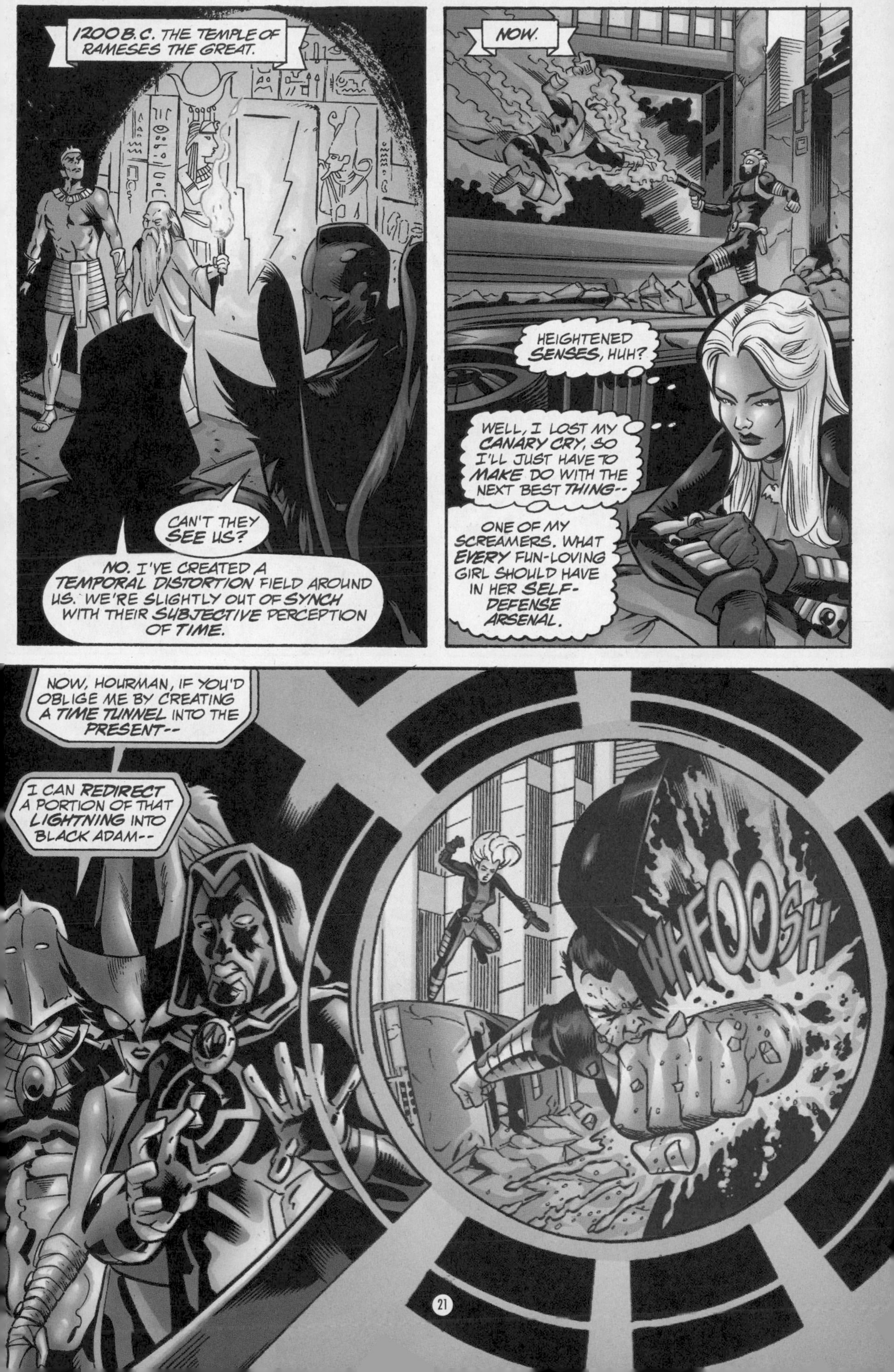
1200 B.C. THE TEMPLE OF RAMESES THE GREAT.
CAN'T THEY SEE US?
NO. I'VE CREATED A TEMPORAL DISTORTION FIELD AROUND US. WE'RE SLIGHTLY OUT OF SYNCH WITH THEIR SUBJECTIVE PERCEPTION OF TIME.
NOW.
HEIGHTENED SENSES, HUH?
WELL, I LOST MY CANARY CRY, SO I'LL JUST HAVE TO MAKE DO WITH THE NEXT BEST THING--
ONE OF MY SCREAMERS. WHAT EVERY FUN-LOVING GIRL SHOULD HAVE IN HER SELF-DEFENSE ARSENAL.
NOW, HOURMAN, IF YOU'D OBLIGE ME BY CREATING A TIME TUNNEL INTO THE PRESENT--
I CAN REDIRECT A PORTION OF THAT LIGHTNING INTO BLACK ADAM--
WHFOOSH

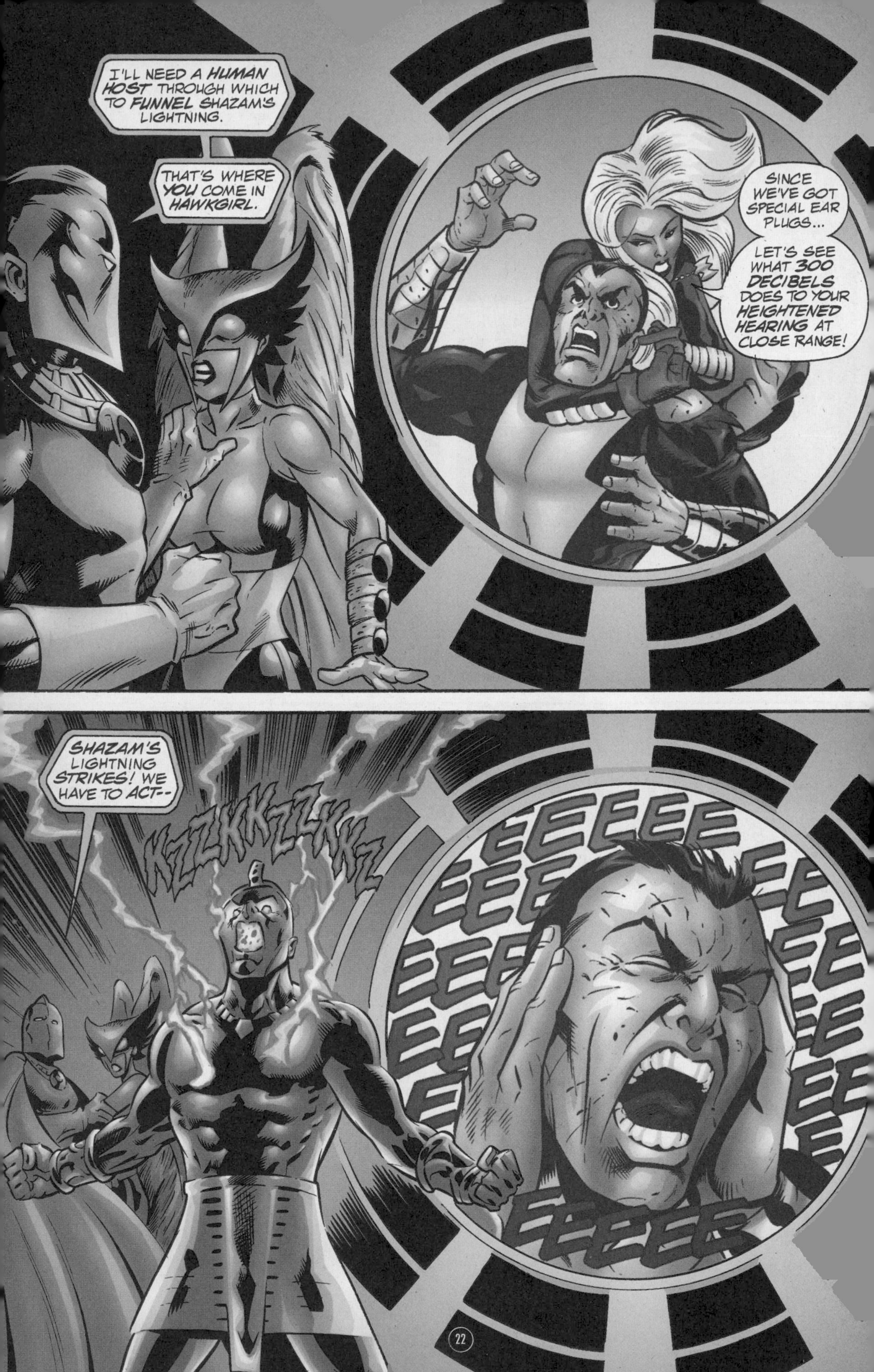
I'LL NEED A HUMAN HOST THROUGH WHICH TO FUNNEL SHAZAM'S LIGHTNING.
THAT'S WHERE YOU COME IN HAWKGIRL.
SINCE WE'VE GOT SPECIAL EAR PLUGS...
LET'S SEE WHAT 300 DECIBELS DOES TO YOUR HEIGHTENED HEARING AT CLOSE RANGE!
SHAZAM'S LIGHTNING STRIKES! WE HAVE TO ACT--
KZZKKZZZKKZ
EEEEE
EEEEE

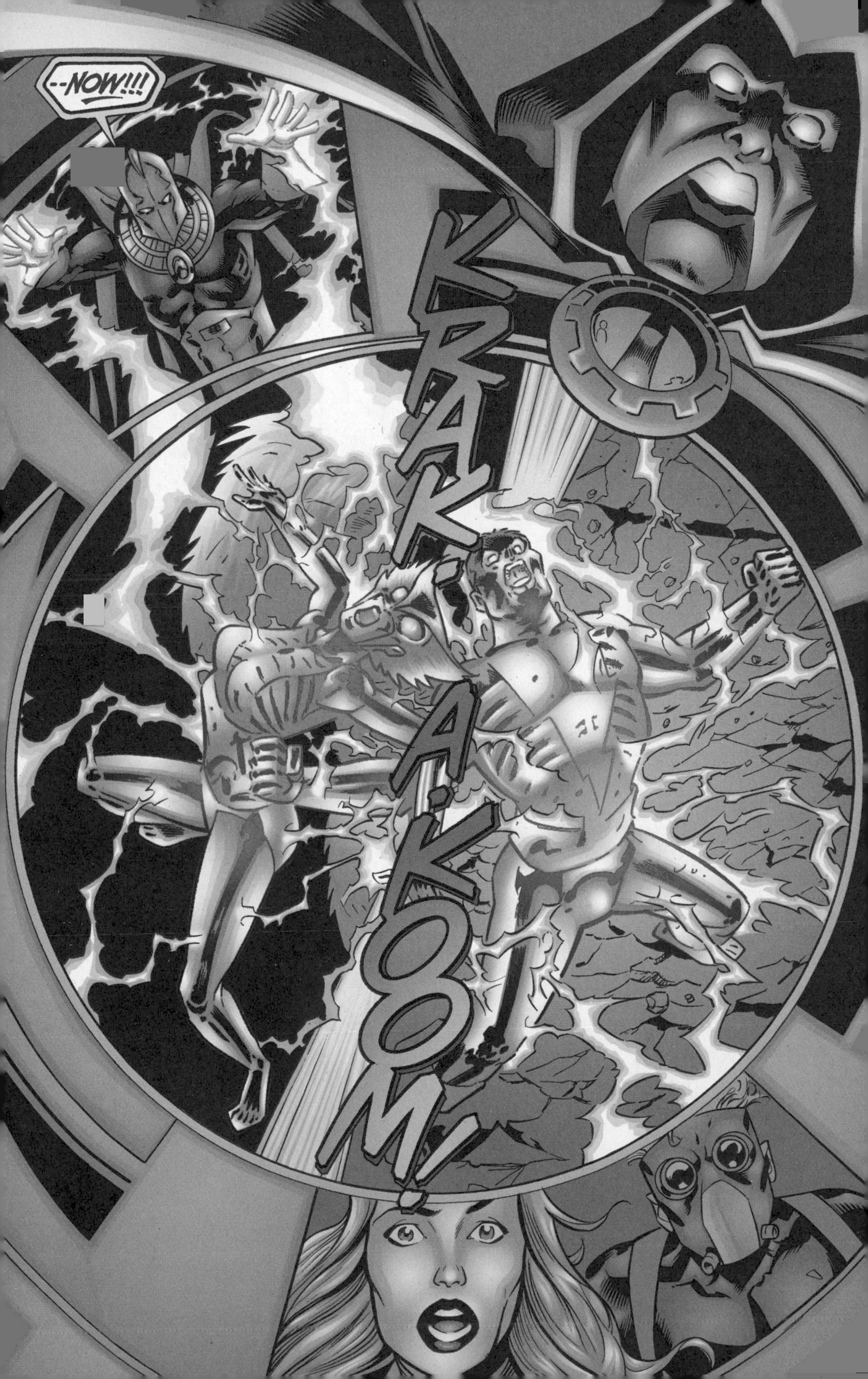
--NOW!!!
KRAKA-KOOM!

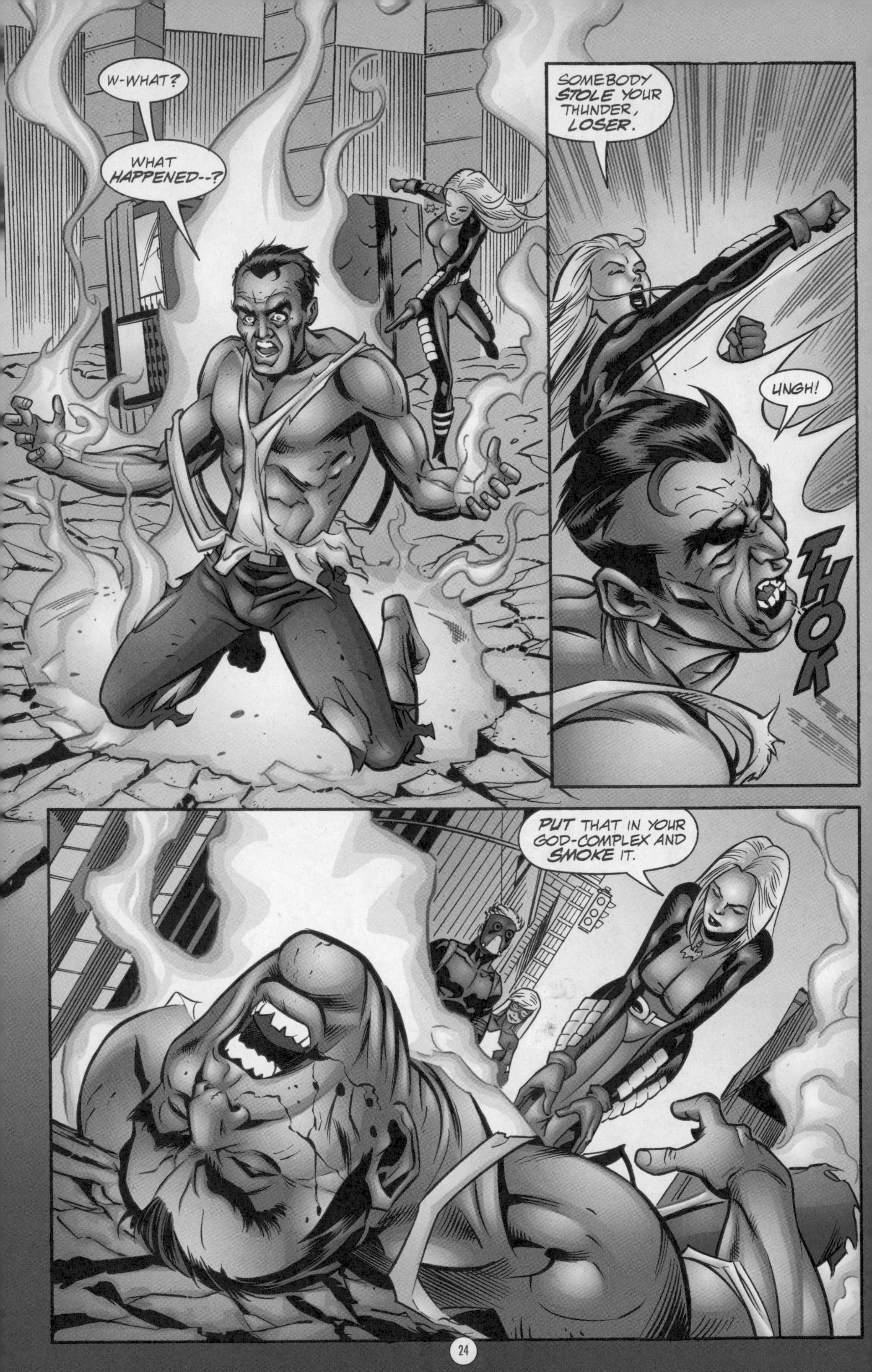
W-WHAT?
WHAT HAPPENED--?
SOMEBODY STOLE YOUR THUNDER, LOSER.
UNGH!
THOK
PUT THAT IN YOUR GOD-COMPLEX AND SMOKE IT.

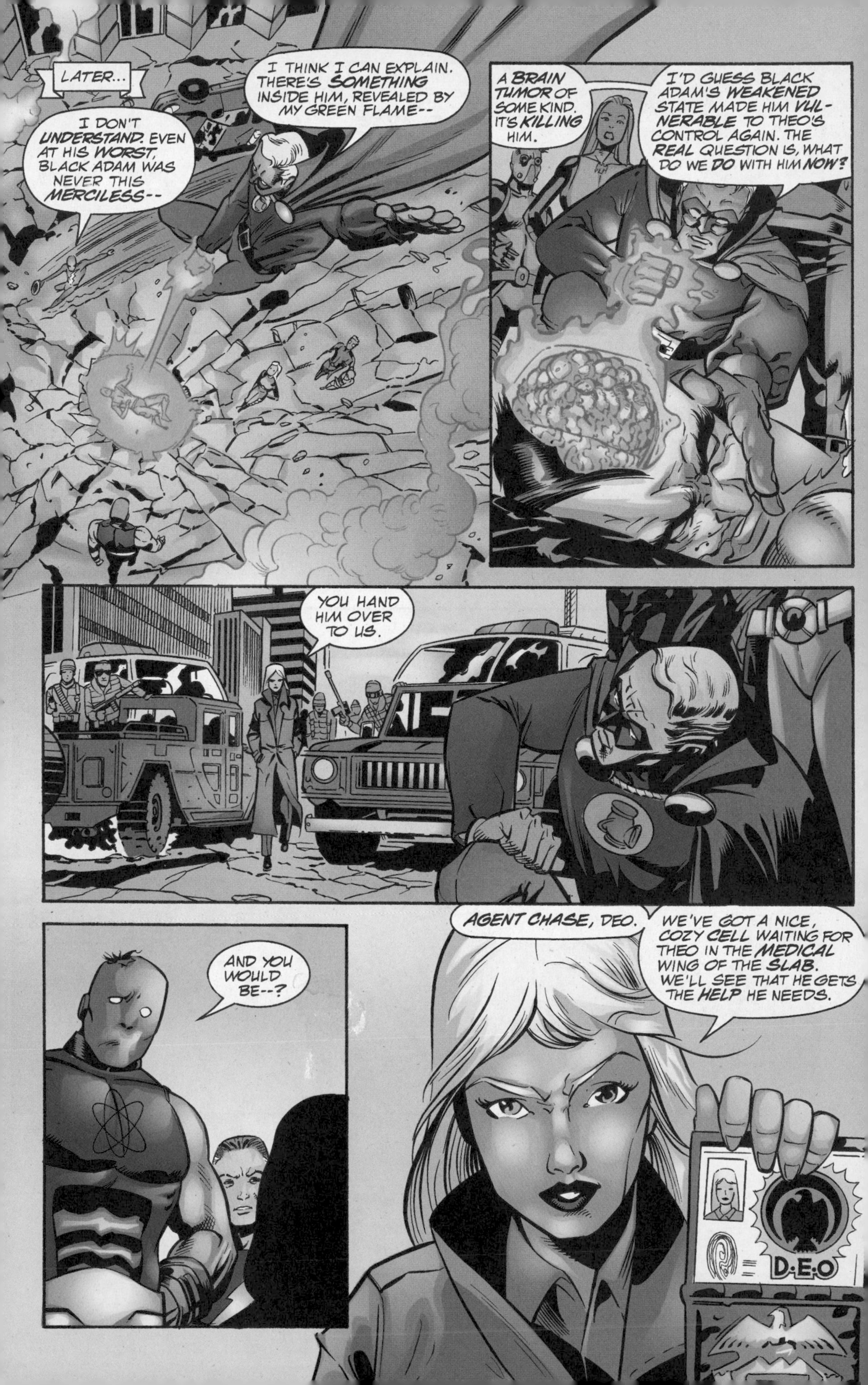
LATER...
I DON'T UNDERSTAND. EVEN AT HIS WORST, BLACK ADAM WAS NEVER THIS MERCILESS--
I THINK I CAN EXPLAIN. THERE'S SOMETHING INSIDE HIM, REVEALED BY MY GREEN FLAME--
A BRAIN TUMOR OF SOME KIND. IT'S KILLING HIM.
I'D GUESS BLACK ADAM'S WEAKENED STATE MADE HIM VULNERABLE TO THEO'S CONTROL AGAIN. THE REAL QUESTION IS, WHAT DO WE DO WITH HIM NOW?
YOU HAND HIM OVER TO US.
AND YOU WOULD BE--?
AGENT CHASE, DEO.
WE'VE GOT A NICE, COZY CELL WAITING FOR THEO IN THE MEDICAL WING OF THE SLAB. WE'LL SEE THAT HE GETS THE HELP HE NEEDS.
D.E.O

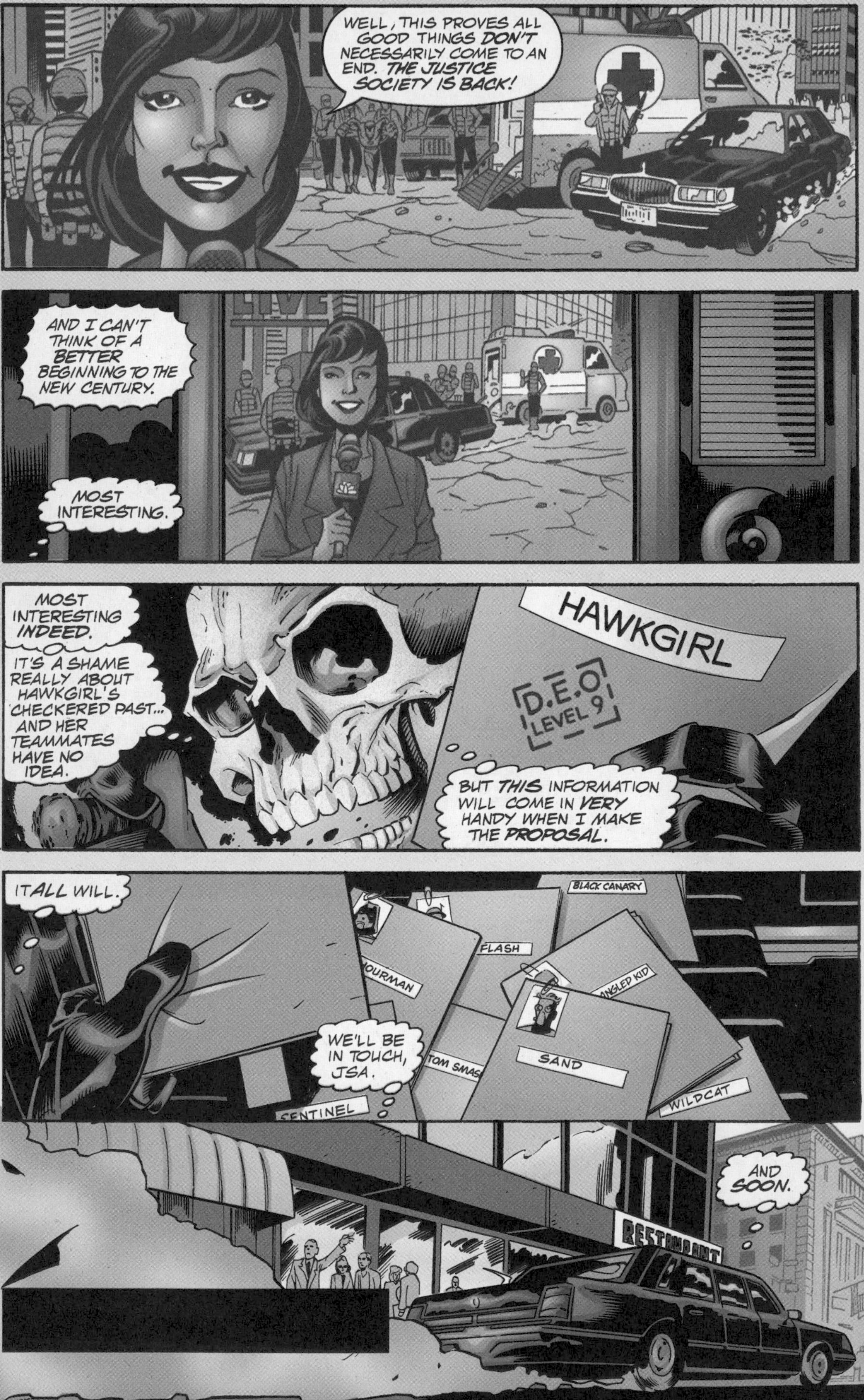

WELL, THIS PROVES ALL GOOD THINGS DON'T NECESSARILY COME TO AN END. THE JUSTICE SOCIETY IS BACK!
AND I CAN'T THINK OF A BETTER BEGINNING TO THE NEW CENTURY.
MOST INTERESTING.
MOST INTERESTING INDEED.
IT'S A SHAME REALLY ABOUT HAWKGIRL'S CHECKERED PAST... AND HER TEAMMATES HAVE NO IDEA.
HAWKGIRL
D.E.O LEVEL 9
BUT THIS INFORMATION WILL COME IN VERY HANDY WHEN I MAKE THE PROPOSAL.
IT ALL WILL.
BLACK CANARY
FLASH
SAND
WILDCAT
WE'LL BE IN TOUCH, JSA.
AND SOON.

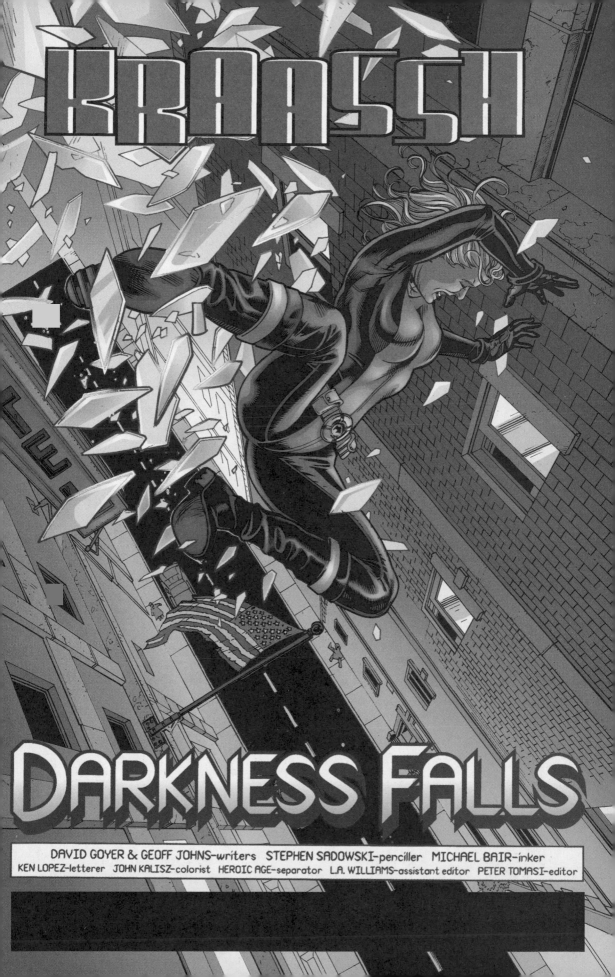

KRAASSH

DARKNESS FALLS

DAVID GOYER & GEOFF JOHNS–writers STEPHEN SADOWSKI–penciller MICHAEL BAIR–inker

KEN LOPEZ–letterer JOHN KALISZ–colorist HEROIC AGE–separator L.A. WILLIAMS–assistant editor PETER TOMASI–editor

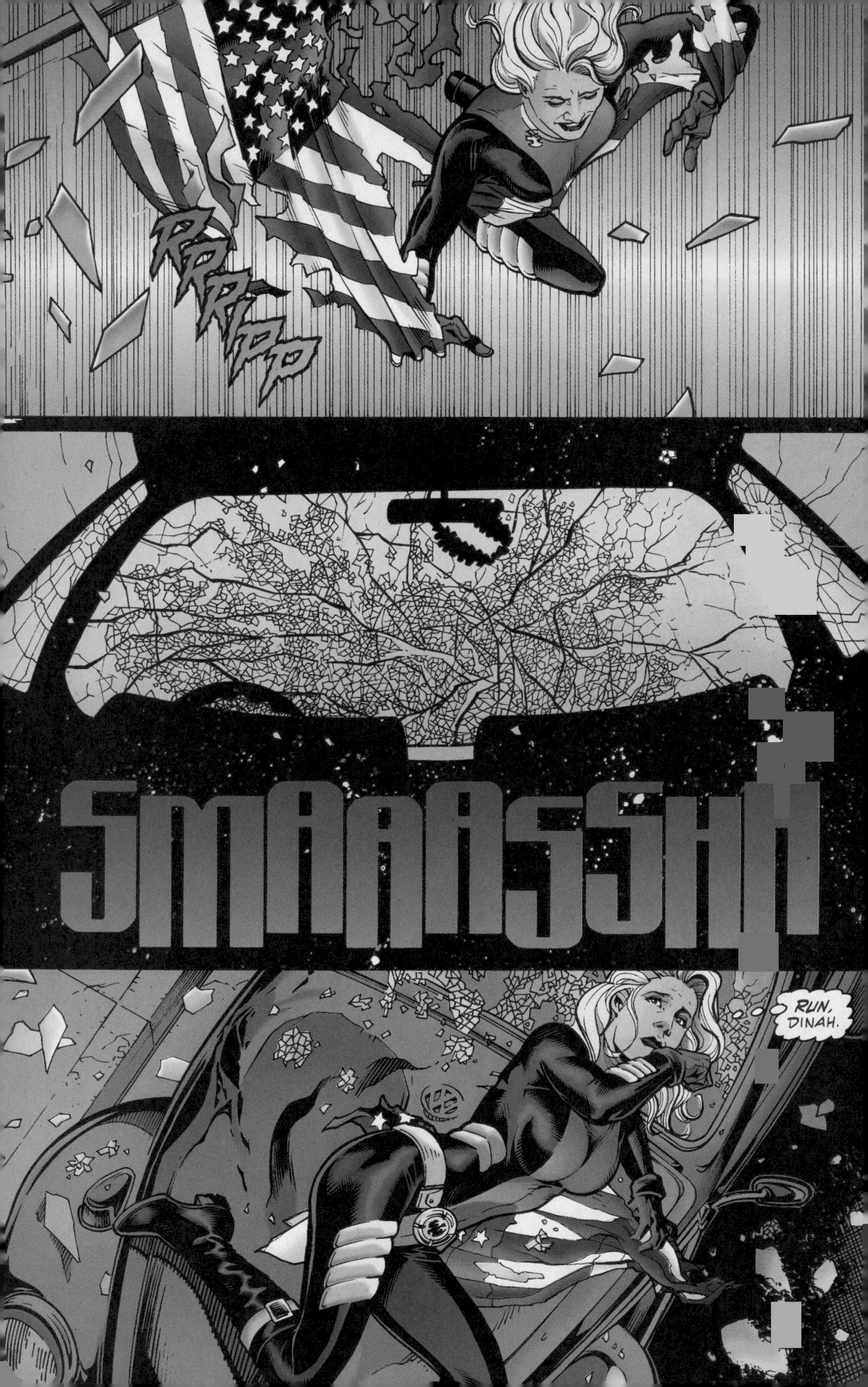
RRRIPP
SMAAASSHH
RUN, DINAH.

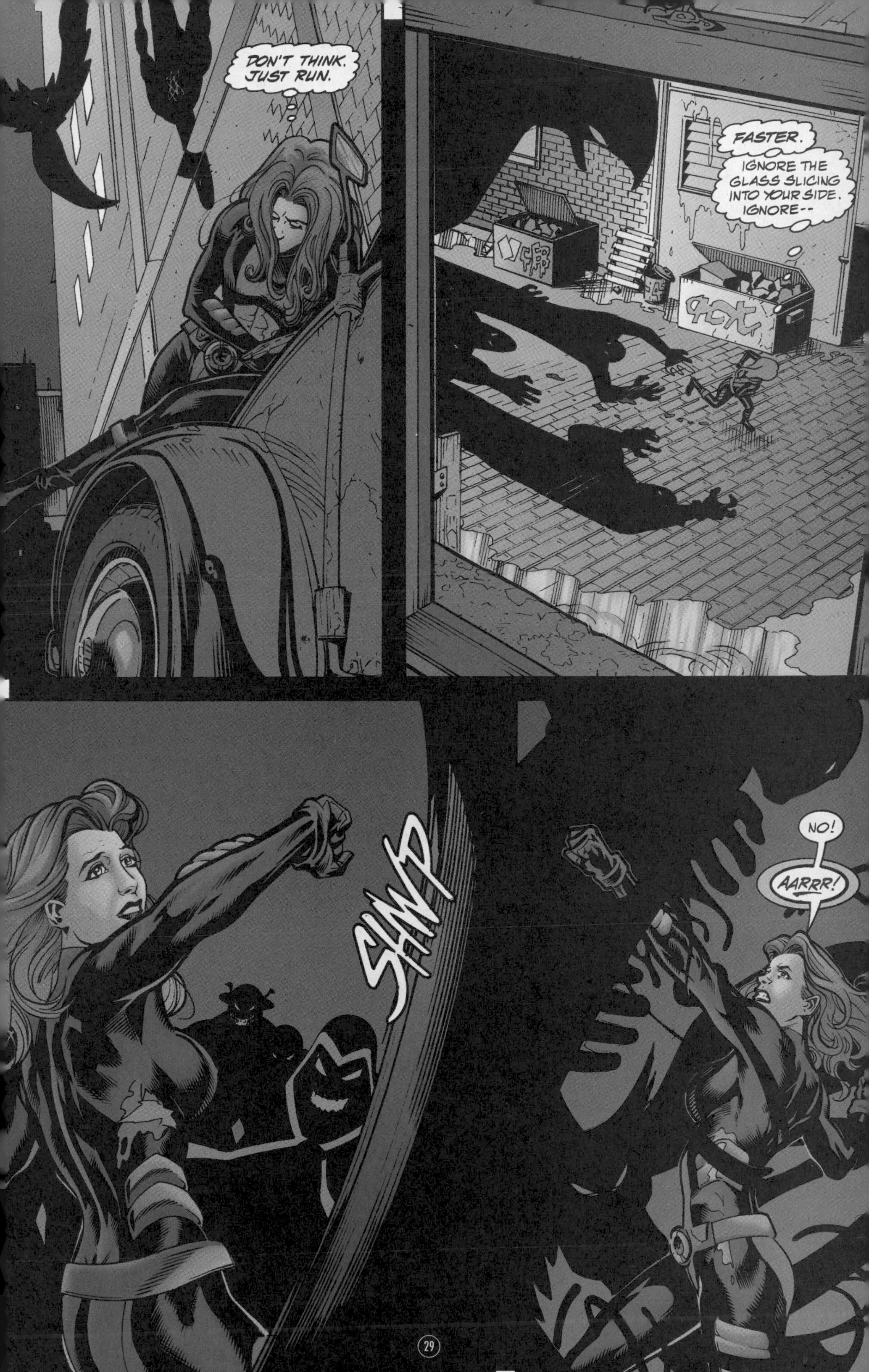
DON'T THINK. JUST RUN.
FASTER.
IGNORE THE GLASS SLICING INTO YOUR SIDE. IGNORE--
SHNP
NO!
AARRR!

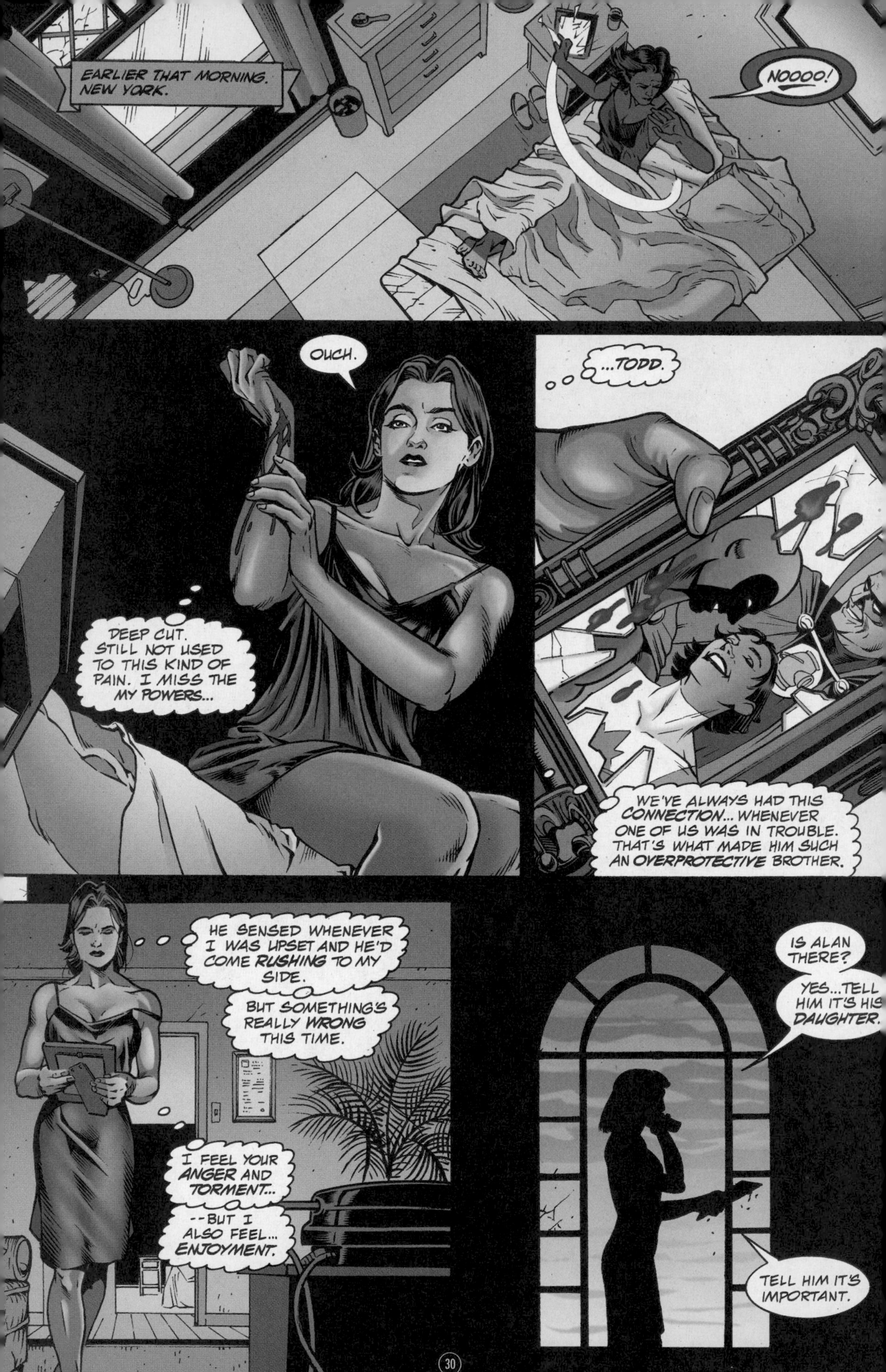
EARLIER THAT MORNING. NEW YORK.
NOOOO!
OUCH.
DEEP CUT. STILL NOT USED TO THIS KIND OF PAIN. I MISS THE MY POWERS...
...TODD.
WE'VE ALWAYS HAD THIS CONNECTION... WHENEVER ONE OF US WAS IN TROUBLE. THAT'S WHAT MADE HIM SUCH AN OVERPROTECTIVE BROTHER.
HE SENSED WHENEVER I WAS UPSET AND HE'D COME RUSHING TO MY SIDE.
BUT SOMETHING'S REALLY WRONG THIS TIME.
I FEEL YOUR ANGER AND TORMENT...
--BUT I ALSO FEEL... ENJOYMENT.
IS ALAN THERE?
YES...TELL HIM IT'S HIS DAUGHTER.
TELL HIM IT'S IMPORTANT.

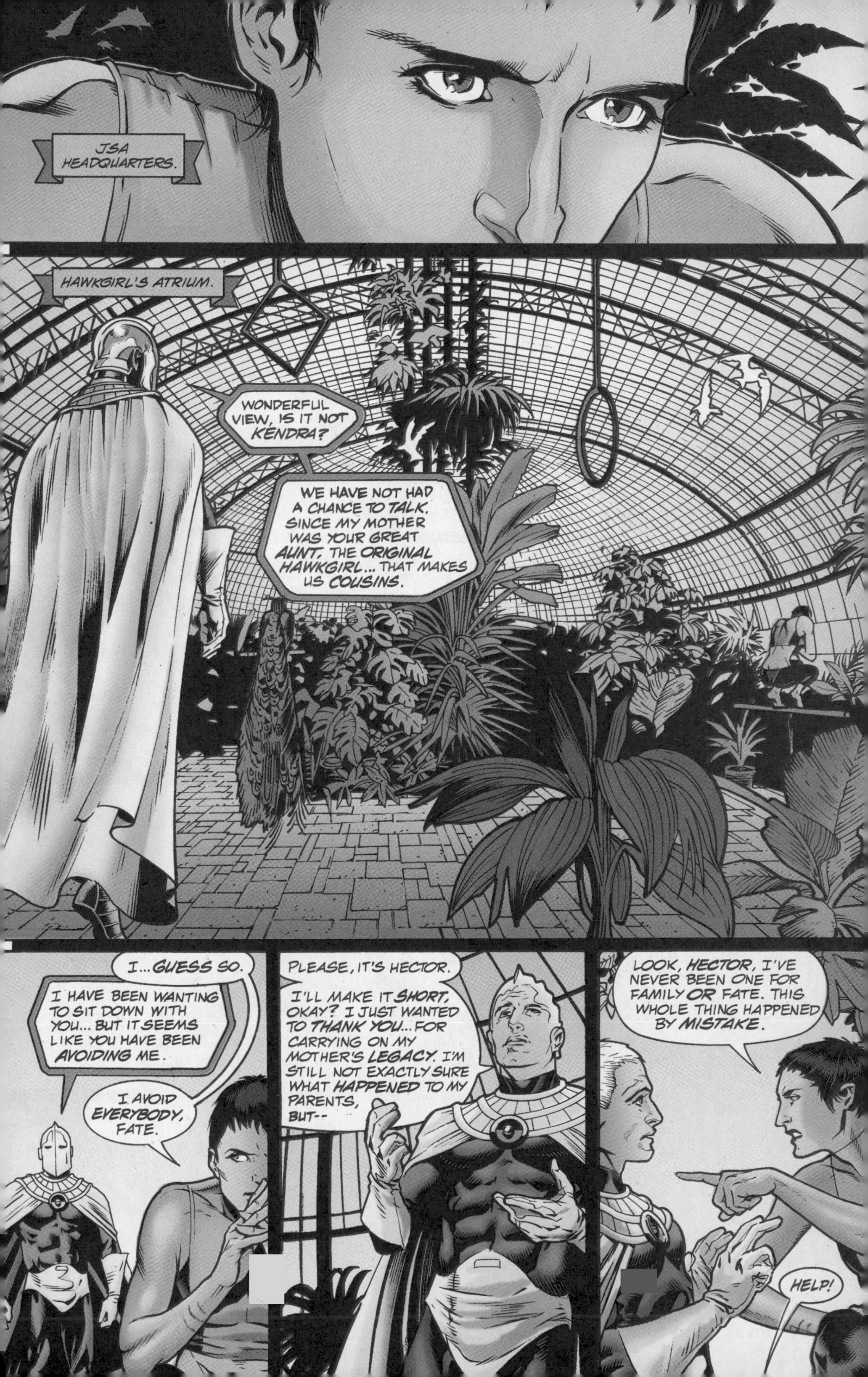
JSA HEADQUARTERS.
HAWKGIRL'S ATRIUM.
WONDERFUL VIEW, IS IT NOT KENDRA?
WE HAVE NOT HAD A CHANCE TO TALK. SINCE MY MOTHER WAS YOUR GREAT AUNT, THE ORIGINAL HAWKGIRL... THAT MAKES US COUSINS.
I HAVE BEEN WANTING TO SIT DOWN WITH YOU... BUT IT SEEMS LIKE YOU HAVE BEEN AVOIDING ME.
I... GUESS SO.
I AVOID EVERYBODY, FATE.
PLEASE, IT'S HECTOR.
I'LL MAKE IT SHORT, OKAY? I JUST WANTED TO THANK YOU... FOR CARRYING ON MY MOTHER'S LEGACY. I'M STILL NOT EXACTLY SURE WHAT HAPPENED TO MY PARENTS, BUT--
LOOK, HECTOR, I'VE NEVER BEEN ONE FOR FAMILY OR FATE. THIS WHOLE THING HAPPENED BY MISTAKE.
HELP!

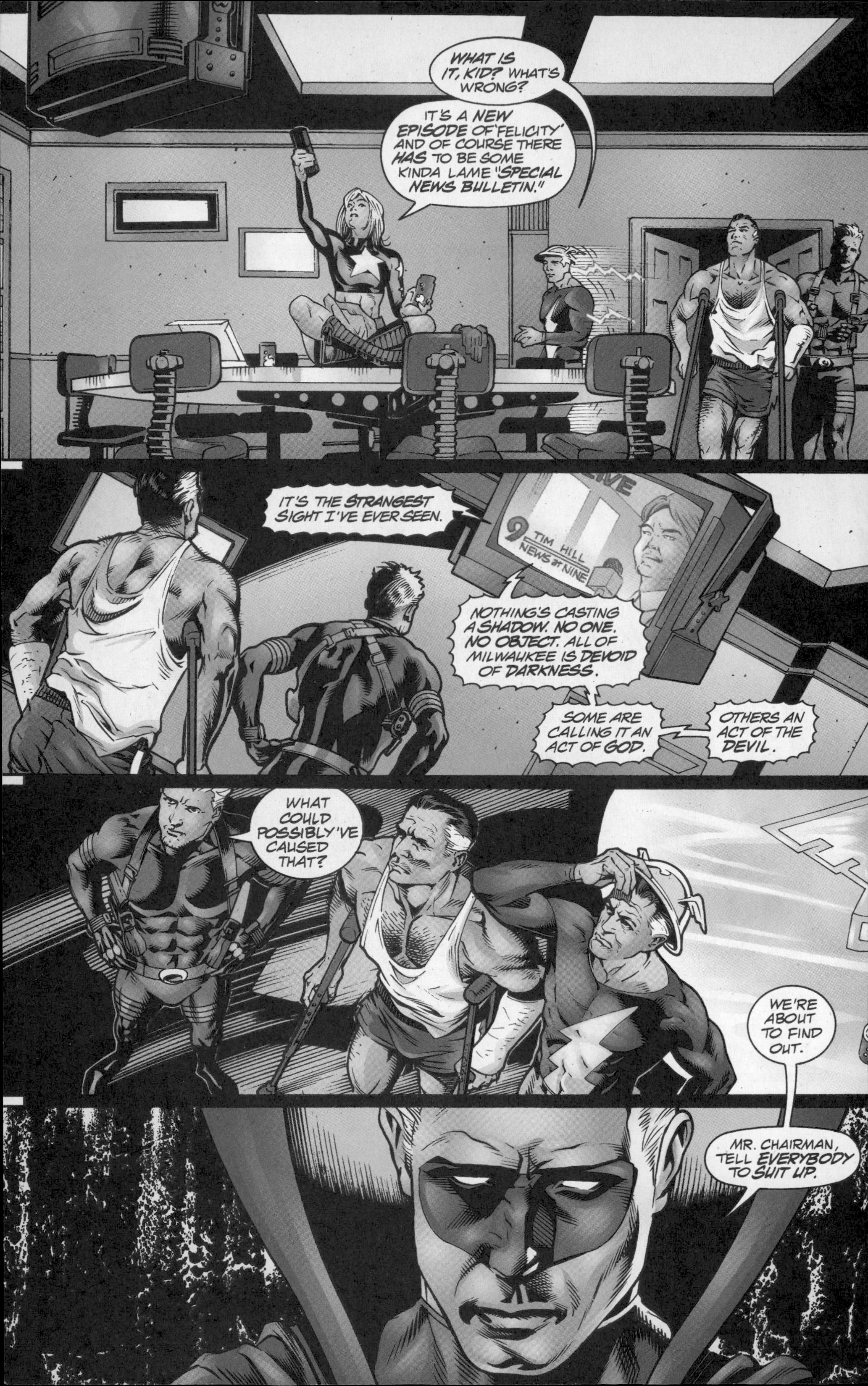
WHAT IS IT, KID? WHAT'S WRONG?
IT'S A NEW EPISODE OF 'FELICITY' AND OF COURSE THERE HAS TO BE SOME KINDA LAME "SPECIAL NEWS BULLETIN."
IT'S THE STRANGEST SIGHT I'VE EVER SEEN.
9 TIM HILL NEWS at NINE
NOTHING'S CASTING A SHADOW. NO ONE. NO OBJECT. ALL OF MILWAUKEE IS DEVOID OF DARKNESS.
SOME ARE CALLING IT AN ACT OF GOD.
OTHERS AN ACT OF THE DEVIL.
WHAT COULD POSSIBLY'VE CAUSED THAT?
WE'RE ABOUT TO FIND OUT.
MR. CHAIRMAN, TELL EVERYBODY TO SUIT UP.

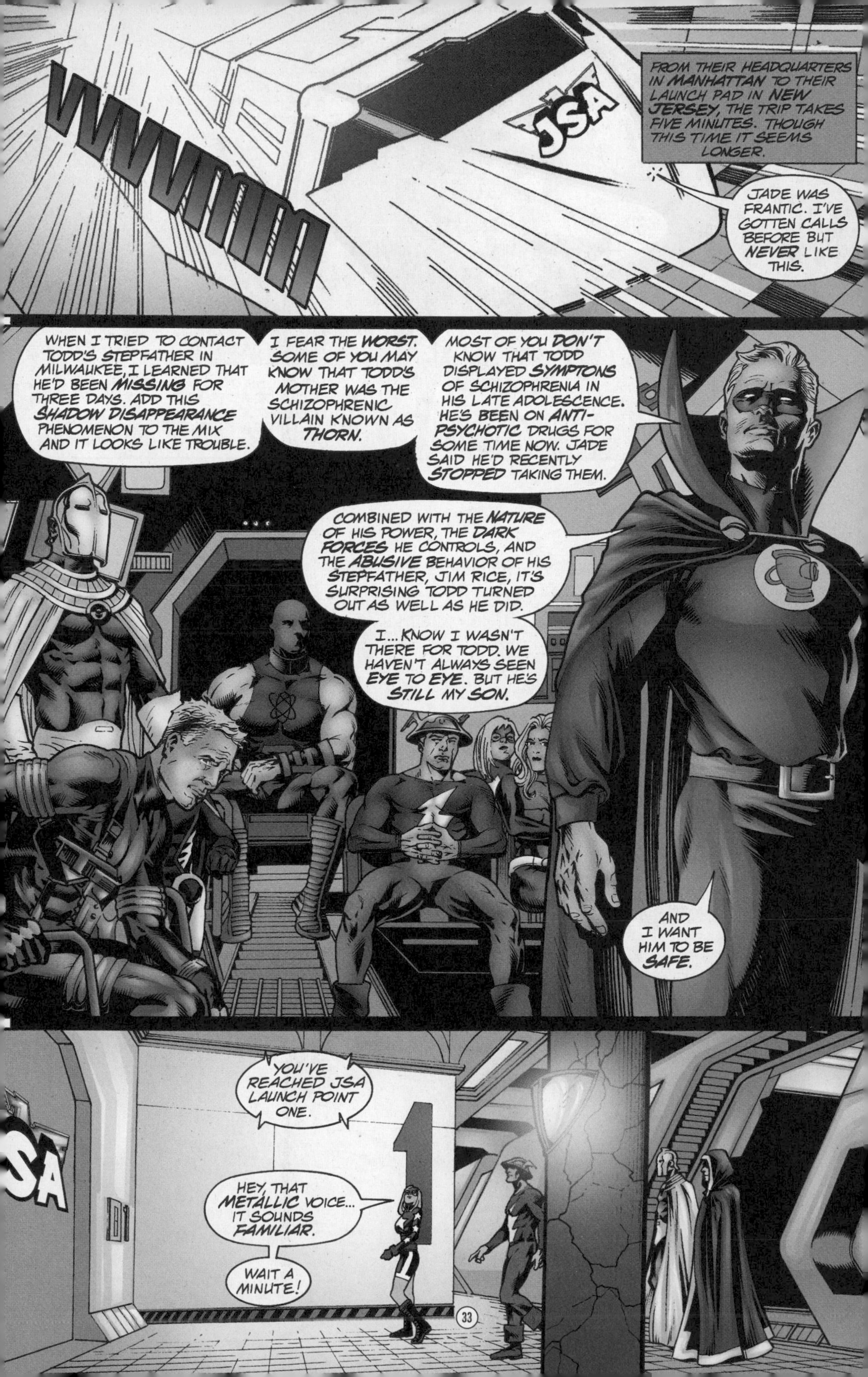
VVVVMMM
JSA
FROM THEIR HEADQUARTERS IN MANHATTAN TO THEIR LAUNCH PAD IN NEW JERSEY, THE TRIP TAKES FIVE MINUTES. THOUGH THIS TIME IT SEEMS LONGER.
JADE WAS FRANTIC. I'VE GOTTEN CALLS BEFORE BUT NEVER LIKE THIS.
WHEN I TRIED TO CONTACT TODD'S STEPFATHER IN MILWAUKEE, I LEARNED THAT HE'D BEEN MISSING FOR THREE DAYS. ADD THIS SHADOW DISAPPEARANCE PHENOMENON TO THE MIX AND IT LOOKS LIKE TROUBLE.
I FEAR THE WORST. SOME OF YOU MAY KNOW THAT TODD'S MOTHER WAS THE SCHIZOPHRENIC VILLAIN KNOWN AS THORN.
MOST OF YOU DON'T KNOW THAT TODD DISPLAYED SYMPTONS OF SCHIZOPHRENIA IN HIS LATE ADOLESCENCE. HE'S BEEN ON ANTI-PSYCHOTIC DRUGS FOR SOME TIME NOW. JADE SAID HE'D RECENTLY STOPPED TAKING THEM.
COMBINED WITH THE NATURE OF HIS POWER, THE DARK FORCES HE CONTROLS, AND THE ABUSIVE BEHAVIOR OF HIS STEPFATHER, JIM RICE, IT'S SURPRISING TODD TURNED OUT AS WELL AS HE DID.
I... KNOW I WASN'T THERE FOR TODD. WE HAVEN'T ALWAYS SEEN EYE TO EYE. BUT HE'S STILL MY SON.
AND I WANT HIM TO BE SAFE.
YOU'VE REACHED JSA LAUNCH POINT ONE.
HEY, THAT METALLIC VOICE... IT SOUNDS FAMILIAR.
WAIT A MINUTE!

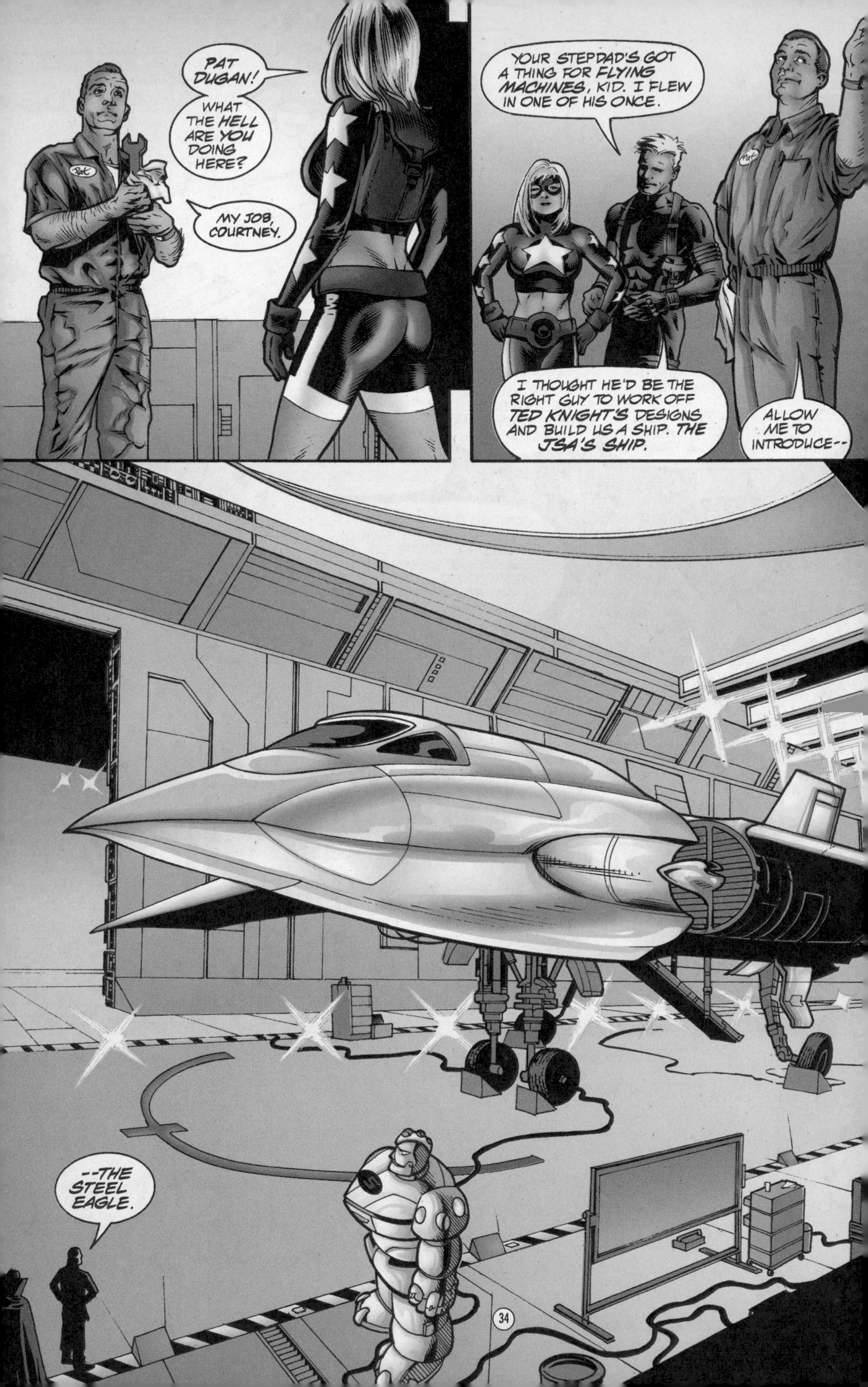
PAT DUGAN!
WHAT THE HELL ARE YOU DOING HERE?
MY JOB, COURTNEY.
YOUR STEPDAD'S GOT A THING FOR FLYING MACHINES, KID. I FLEW IN ONE OF HIS ONCE.
I THOUGHT HE'D BE THE RIGHT GUY TO WORK OFF TED KNIGHT'S DESIGNS AND BUILD US A SHIP. THE JSA'S SHIP.
ALLOW ME TO INTRODUCE--
--THE STEEL EAGLE.

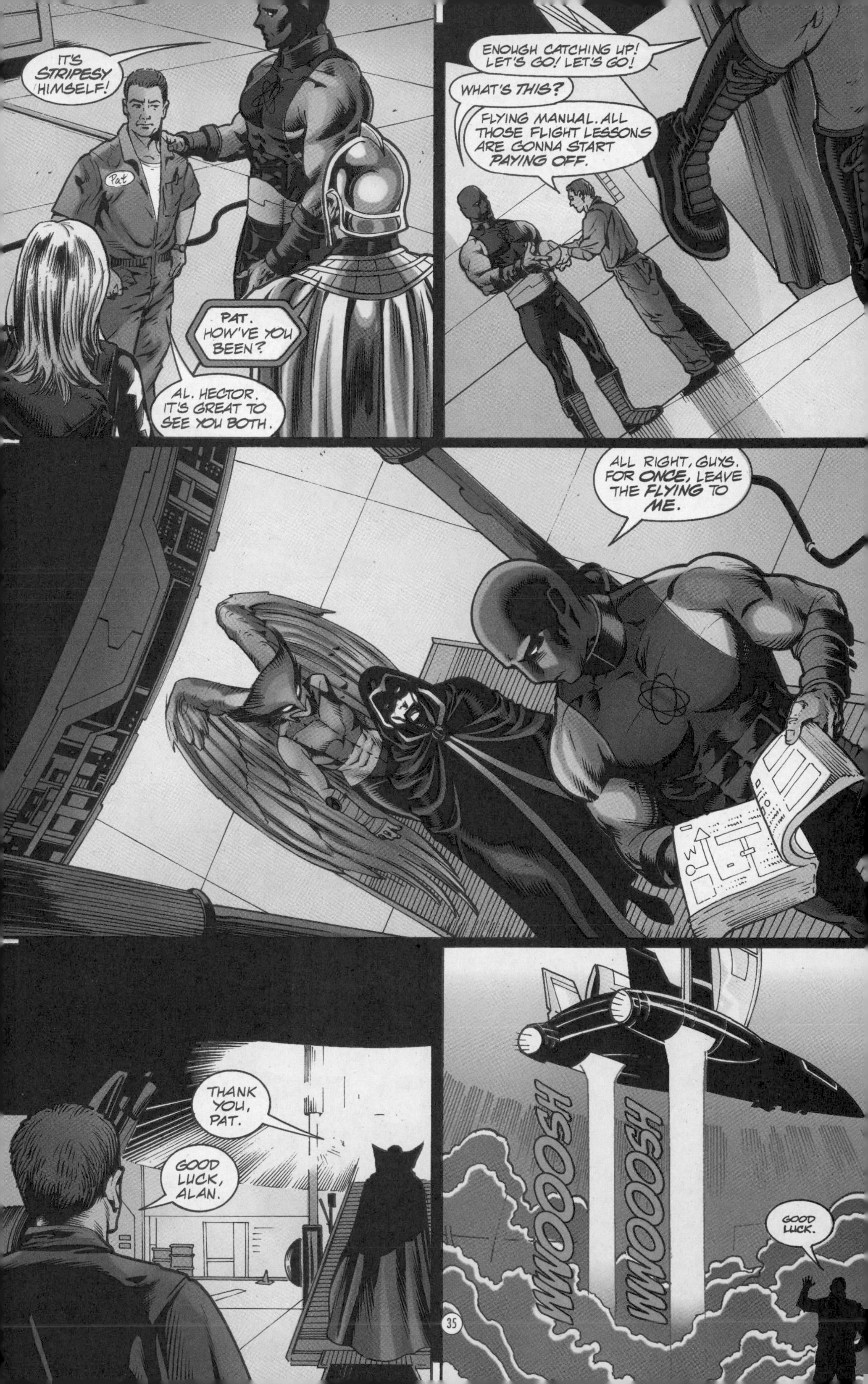
IT'S STRIPESY HIMSELF!
PAT. HOW'VE YOU BEEN?
AL. HECTOR. IT'S GREAT TO SEE YOU BOTH.
ENOUGH CATCHING UP! LET'S GO! LET'S GO!
WHAT'S THIS?
FLYING MANUAL. ALL THOSE FLIGHT LESSONS ARE GONNA START PAYING OFF.
ALL RIGHT, GUYS. FOR ONCE, LEAVE THE FLYING TO ME.
THANK YOU, PAT.
GOOD LUCK, ALAN.
WHOOOOSH
WHOOOOSH
GOOD LUCK.

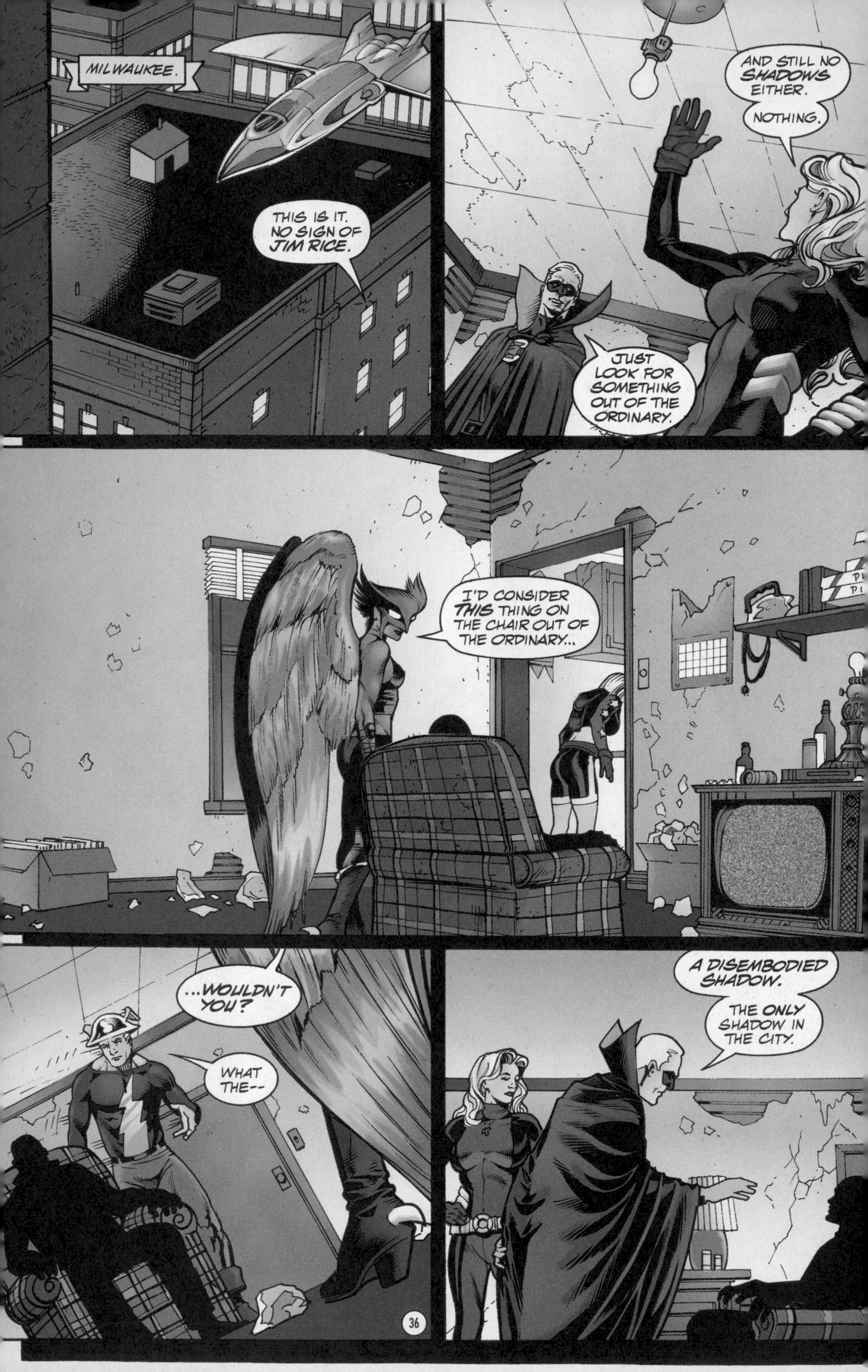
MILWAUKEE.
THIS IS IT. NO SIGN OF JIM RICE.
AND STILL NO SHADOWS EITHER.
NOTHING.
JUST LOOK FOR SOMETHING OUT OF THE ORDINARY.
I'D CONSIDER THIS THING ON THE CHAIR OUT OF THE ORDINARY...
...WOULDN'T YOU?
WHAT THE--
A DISEMBODIED SHADOW.
THE ONLY SHADOW IN THE CITY.

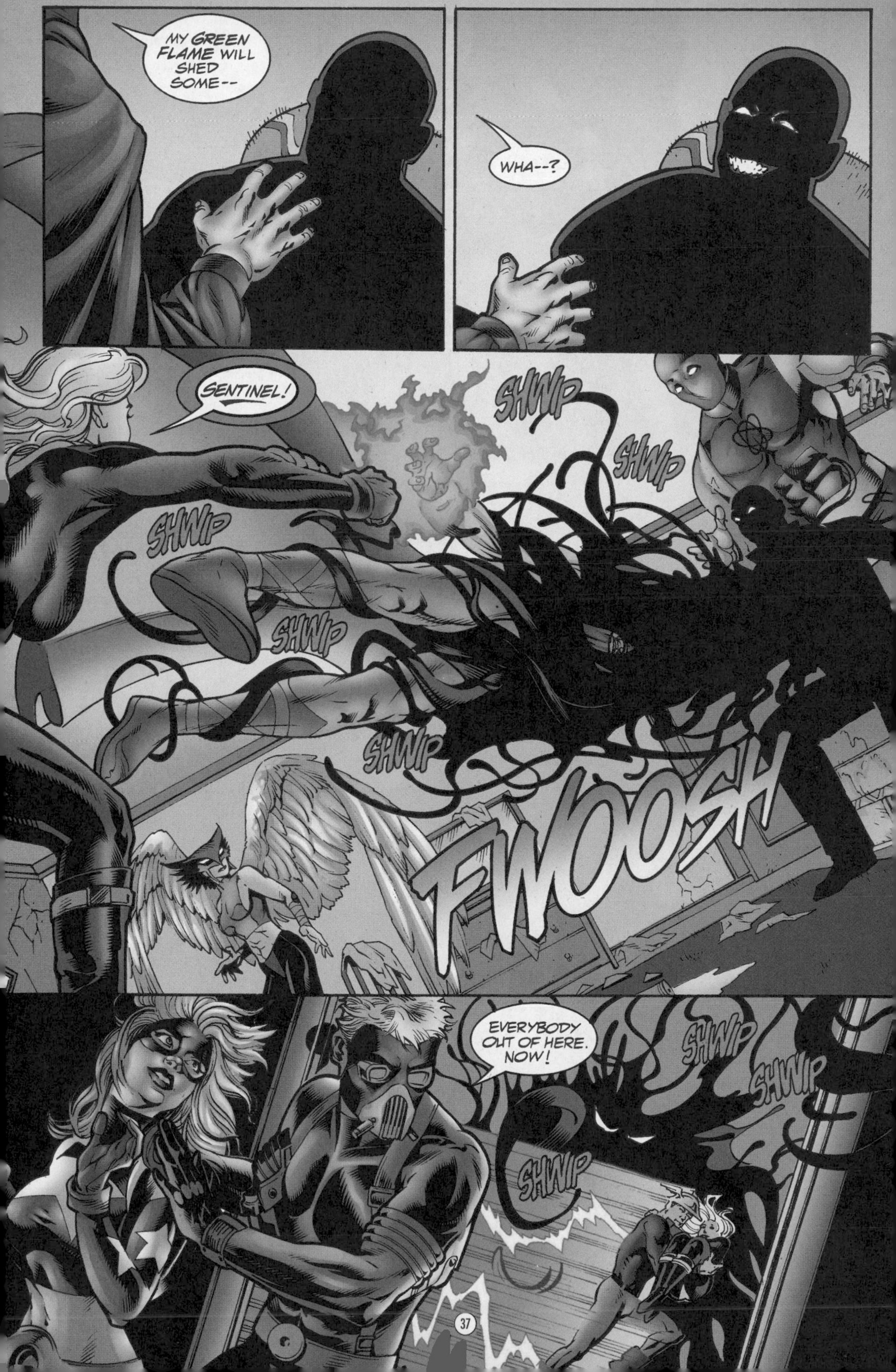
MY GREEN FLAME WILL SHED SOME--
WHA--?
SENTINEL!
SHWIP
SHWIP
SHWIP
SHWIP
SHWIP
FWOOSH
EVERYBODY OUT OF HERE. NOW!
SHWIP
SHWIP
SHWIP

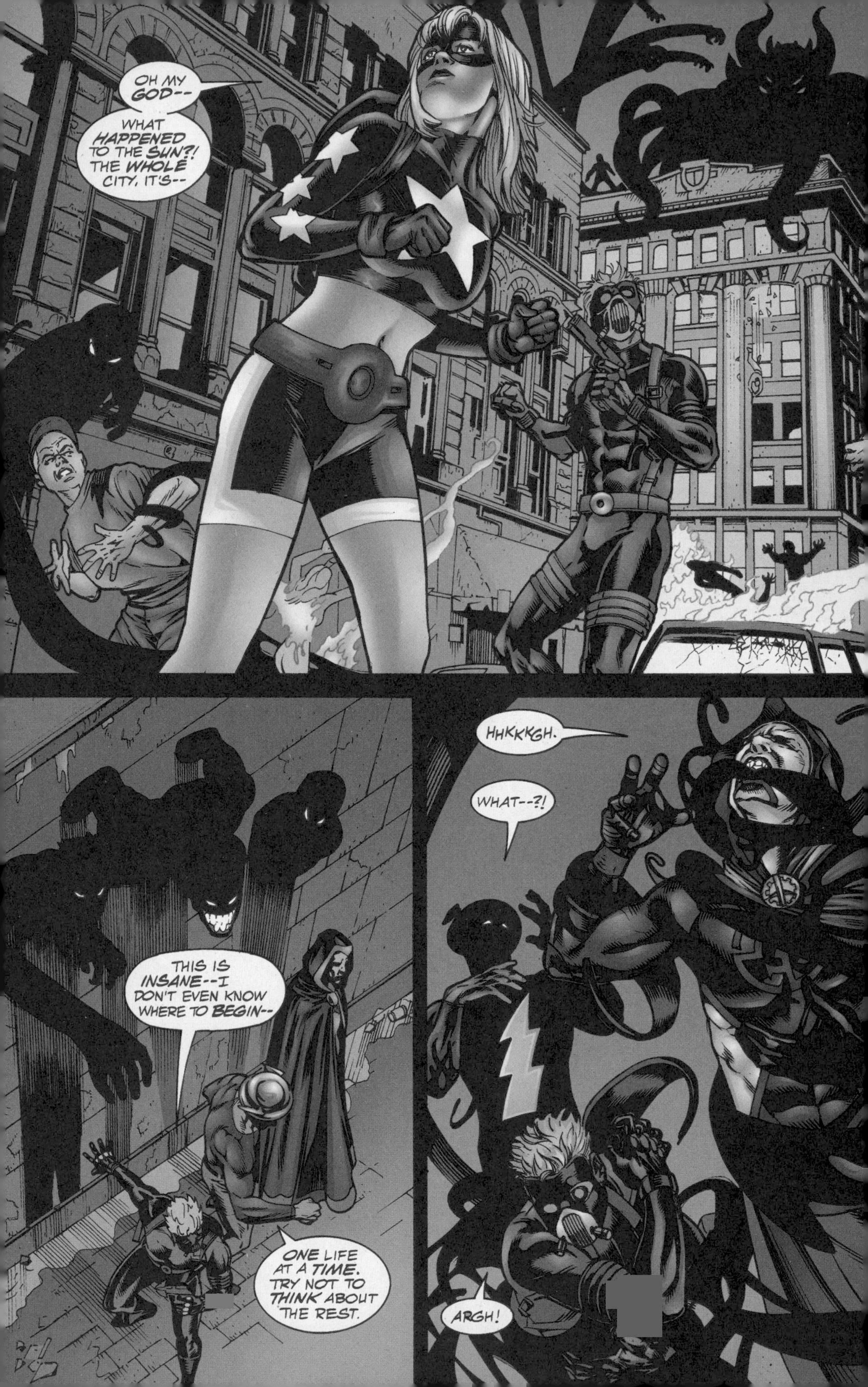
OH MY GOD--
WHAT HAPPENED TO THE SUN?! THE WHOLE CITY, IT'S--
THIS IS INSANE--I DON'T EVEN KNOW WHERE TO BEGIN--
ONE LIFE AT A TIME. TRY NOT TO THINK ABOUT THE REST.
HHKKKGH.
WHAT--?!
ARGH!

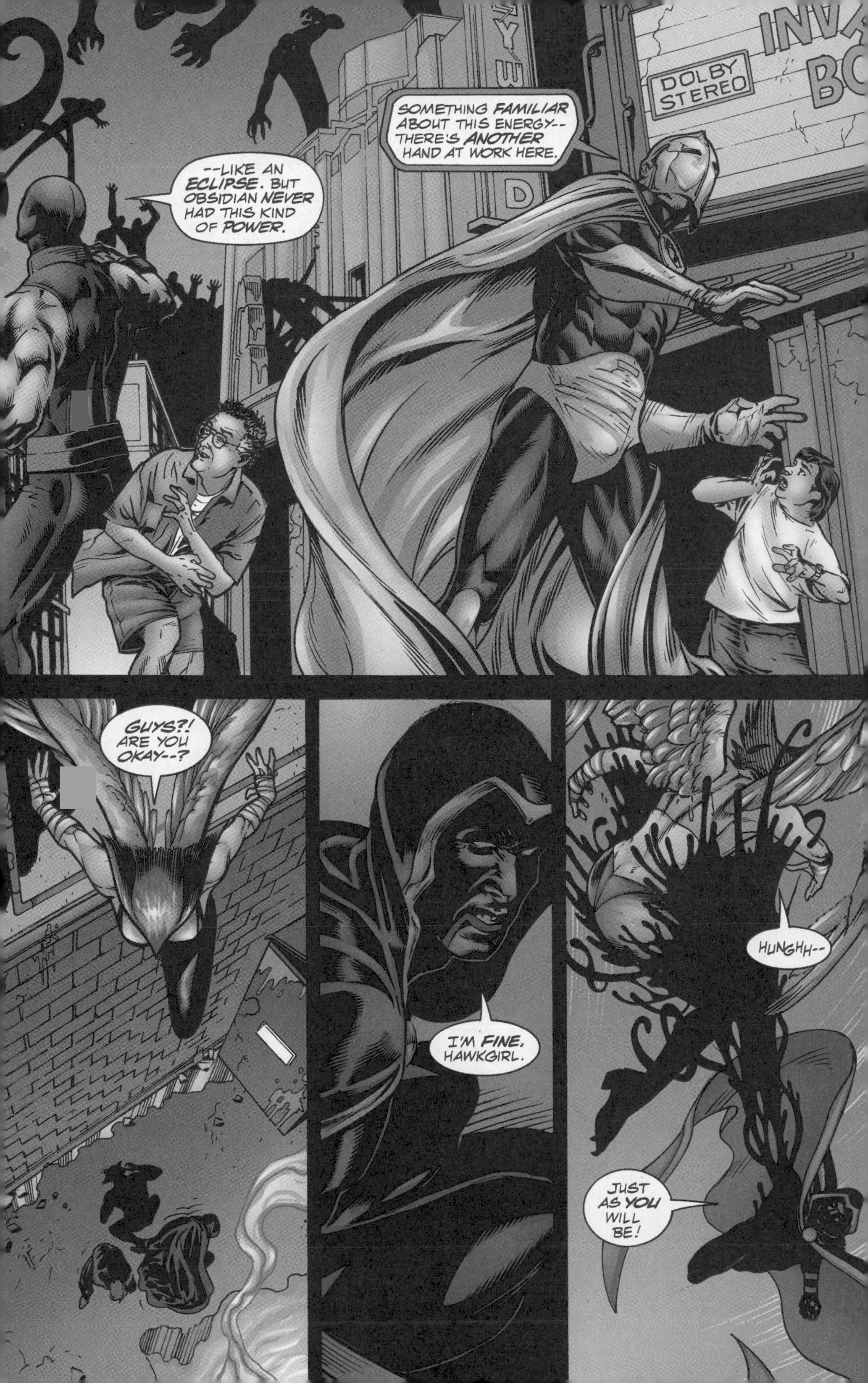
--LIKE AN ECLIPSE. BUT OBSIDIAN NEVER HAD THIS KIND OF POWER.
SOMETHING FAMILIAR ABOUT THIS ENERGY-- THERE'S ANOTHER HAND AT WORK HERE.
DOLBY STEREO
GUYS?! ARE YOU OKAY--?
I'M FINE, HAWKGIRL.
HUNGHH--
JUST AS YOU WILL BE!

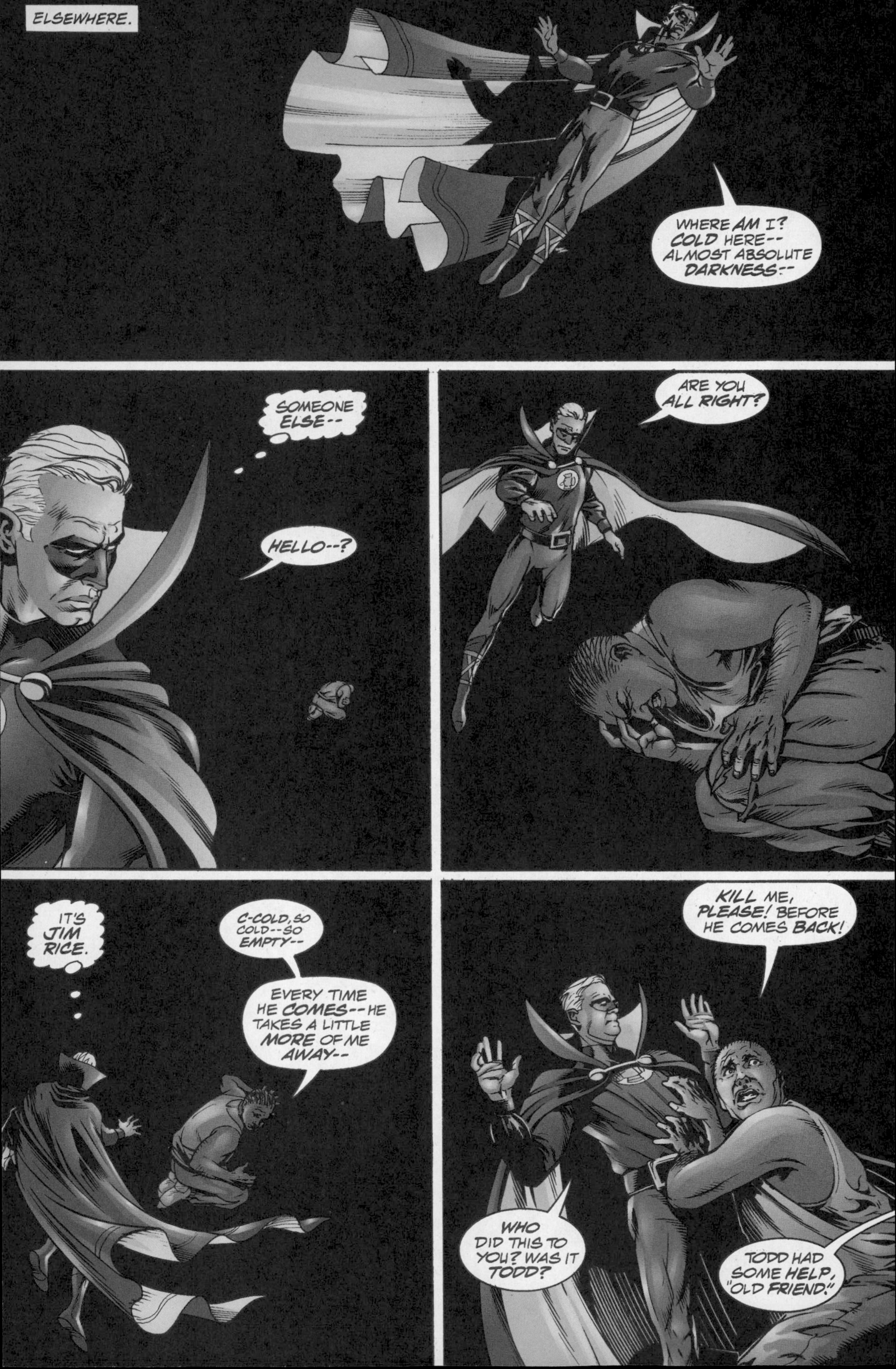
ELSEWHERE.
WHERE AM I? COLD HERE-- ALMOST ABSOLUTE DARKNESS--
SOMEONE ELSE--
HELLO--?
ARE YOU ALL RIGHT?
IT'S JIM RICE.
C-COLD, SO COLD--SO EMPTY--
EVERY TIME HE COMES--HE TAKES A LITTLE MORE OF ME AWAY--
KILL ME, PLEASE! BEFORE HE COMES BACK!
WHO DID THIS TO YOU? WAS IT TODD?
TODD HAD SOME HELP, "OLD FRIEND."

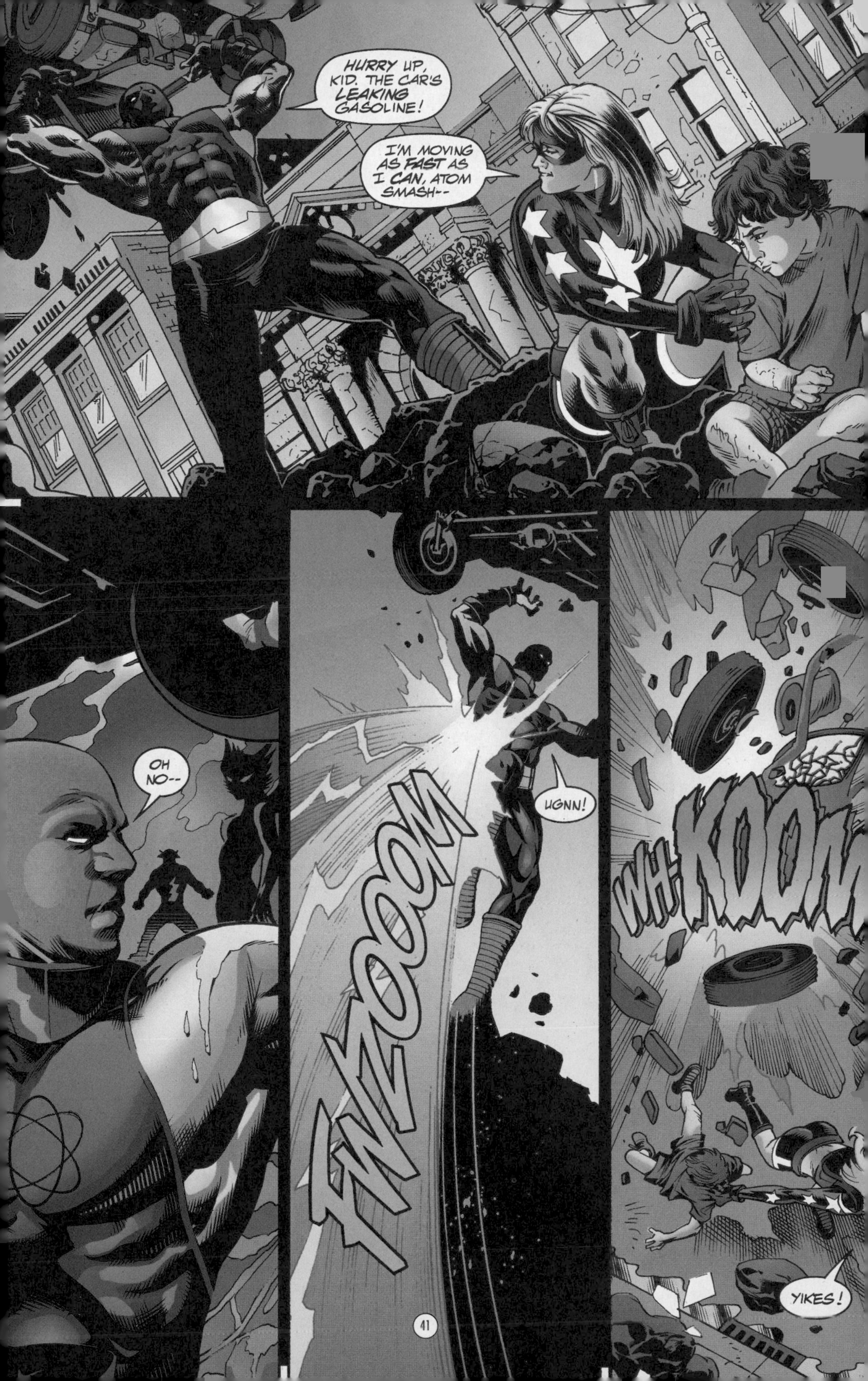
HURRY UP, KID. THE CAR'S LEAKING GASOLINE!
I'M MOVING AS FAST AS I CAN, ATOM SMASH--
OH NO--
FWZOOOM
UGNN!
WH-KOOM
YIKES!

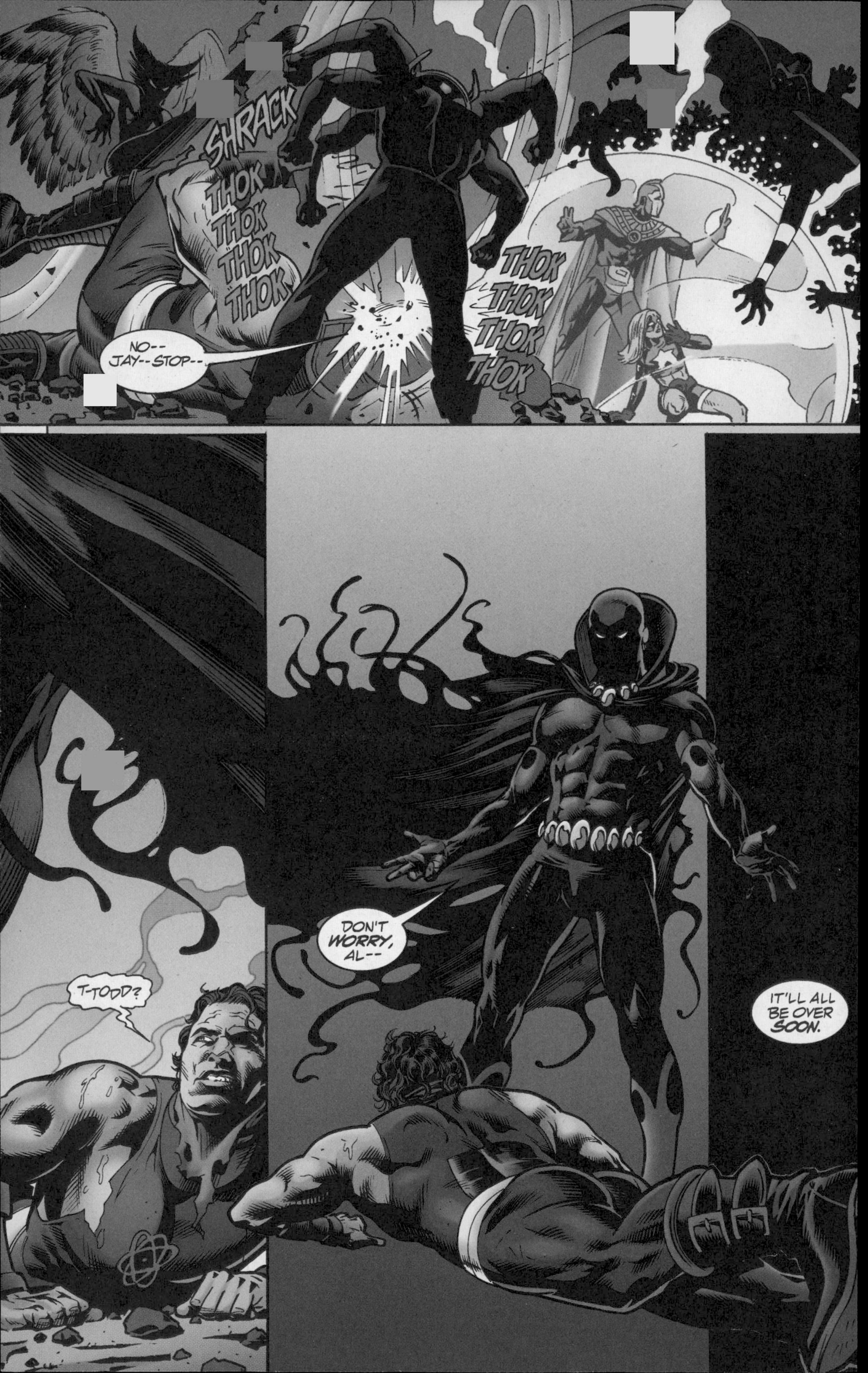
SHRACK
THOK THOK THOK THOK
NO-- JAY--STOP--
THOK THOK THOK THOK
T-TODD?
DON'T WORRY, AL--
IT'LL ALL BE OVER SOON.

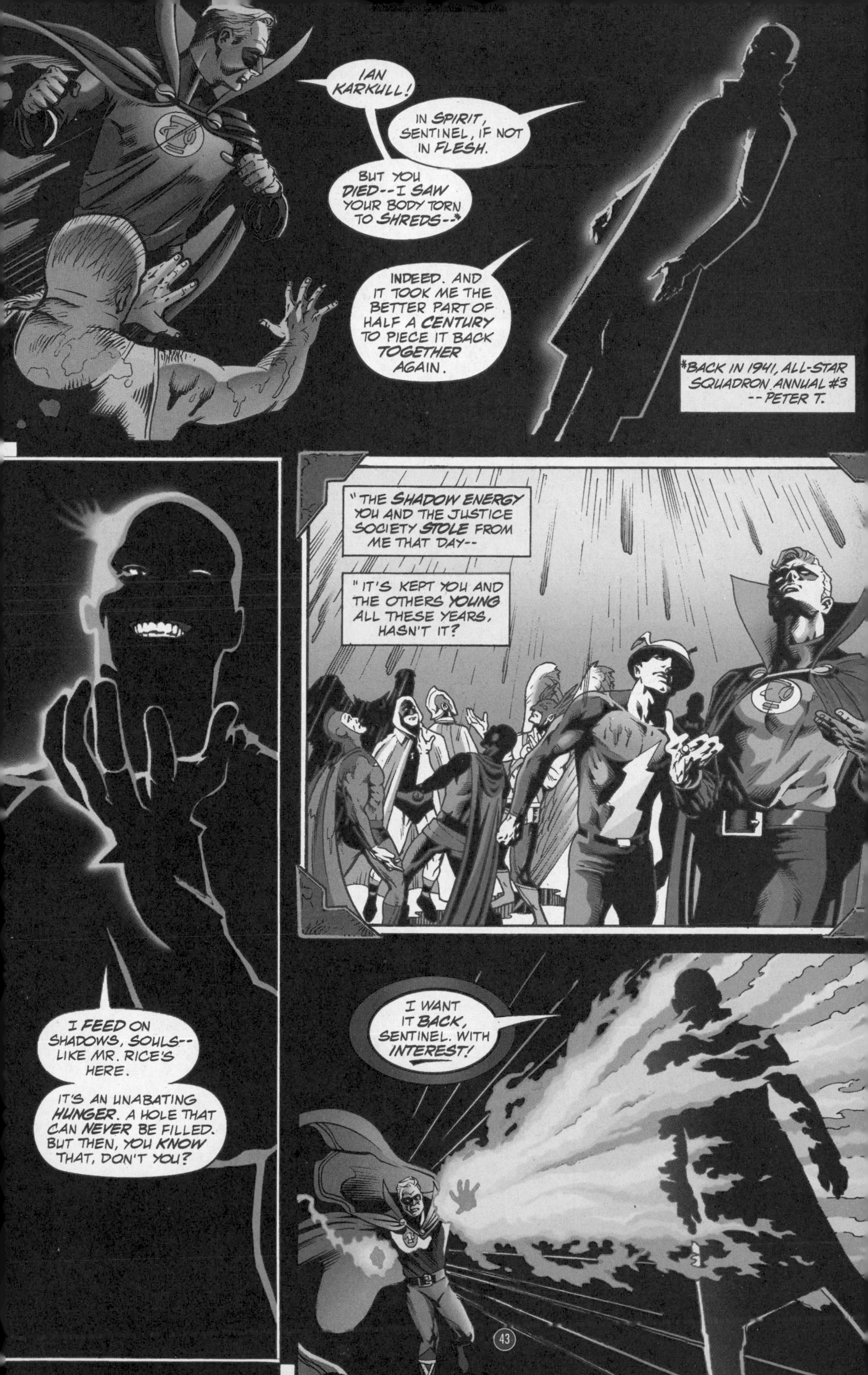

IAN KARKULL!
IN SPIRIT, SENTINEL, IF NOT IN FLESH.
BUT YOU DIED--I SAW YOUR BODY TORN TO SHREDS--*
INDEED. AND IT TOOK ME THE BETTER PART OF HALF A CENTURY TO PIECE IT BACK TOGETHER AGAIN.
*BACK IN 1941, ALL-STAR SQUADRON ANNUAL #3 --PETER T.
I FEED ON SHADOWS, SOULS-- LIKE MR. RICE'S HERE.
IT'S AN UNABATING HUNGER. A HOLE THAT CAN NEVER BE FILLED. BUT THEN, YOU KNOW THAT, DON'T YOU?
"THE SHADOW ENERGY YOU AND THE JUSTICE SOCIETY STOLE FROM ME THAT DAY--
"IT'S KEPT YOU AND THE OTHERS YOUNG ALL THESE YEARS, HASN'T IT?
I WANT IT BACK, SENTINEL. WITH INTEREST!

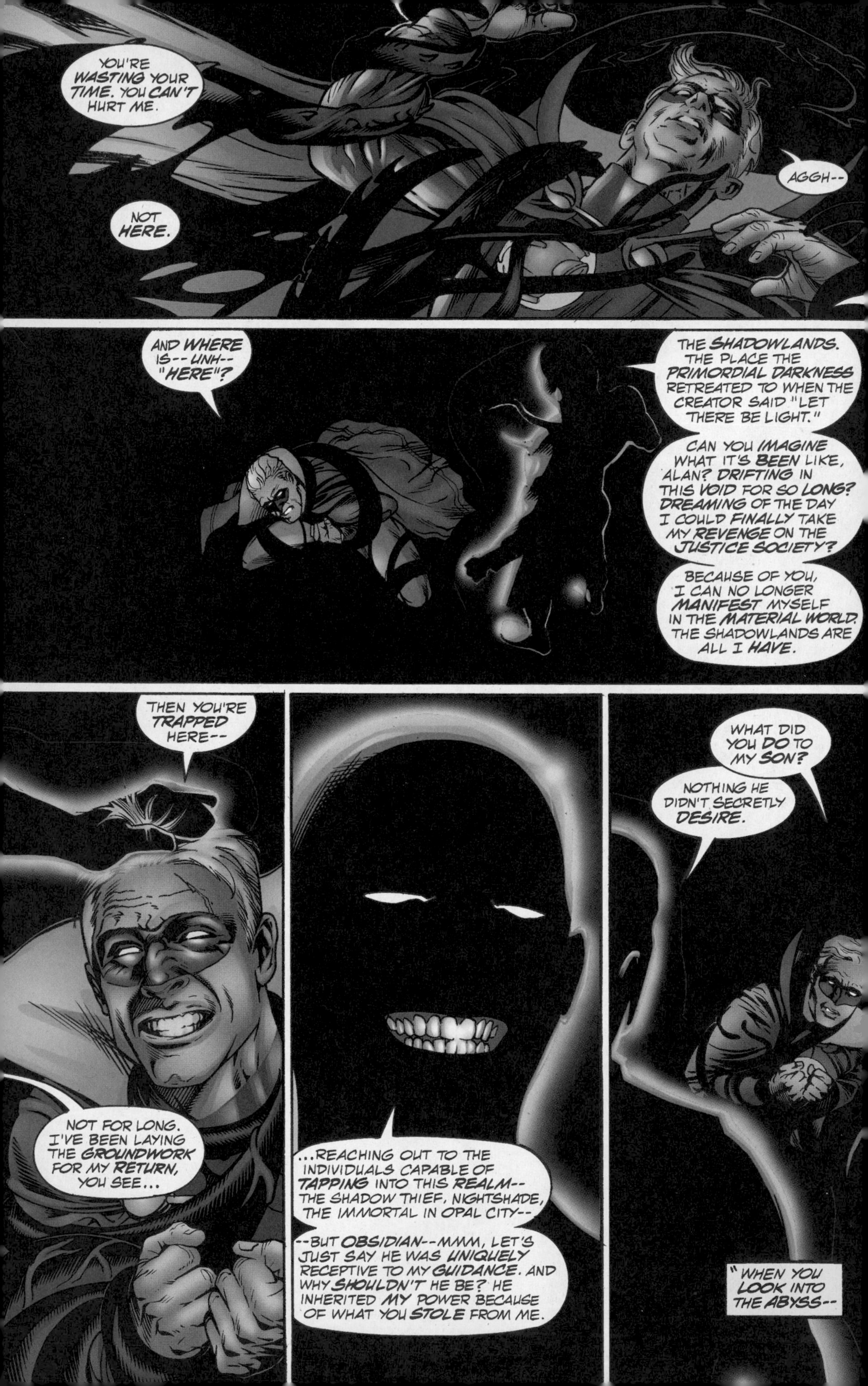
YOU'RE WASTING YOUR TIME. YOU CAN'T HURT ME.
AGGH--
NOT HERE.
AND WHERE IS-- UNH-- "HERE"?
THE SHADOWLANDS. THE PLACE THE PRIMORDIAL DARKNESS RETREATED TO WHEN THE CREATOR SAID "LET THERE BE LIGHT."
CAN YOU IMAGINE WHAT IT'S BEEN LIKE, ALAN? DRIFTING IN THIS VOID FOR SO LONG? DREAMING OF THE DAY I COULD FINALLY TAKE MY REVENGE ON THE JUSTICE SOCIETY?
BECAUSE OF YOU, I CAN NO LONGER MANIFEST MYSELF IN THE MATERIAL WORLD. THE SHADOWLANDS ARE ALL I HAVE.
THEN YOU'RE TRAPPED HERE--
NOT FOR LONG. I'VE BEEN LAYING THE GROUNDWORK FOR MY RETURN, YOU SEE...
...REACHING OUT TO THE INDIVIDUALS CAPABLE OF TAPPING INTO THIS REALM-- THE SHADOW THIEF, NIGHTSHADE, THE IMMORTAL IN OPAL CITY--
--BUT OBSIDIAN--MMM, LET'S JUST SAY HE WAS UNIQUELY RECEPTIVE TO MY GUIDANCE. AND WHY SHOULDN'T HE BE? HE INHERITED MY POWER BECAUSE OF WHAT YOU STOLE FROM ME.
WHAT DID YOU DO TO MY SON?
NOTHING HE DIDN'T SECRETLY DESIRE.
"WHEN YOU LOOK INTO THE ABYSS--

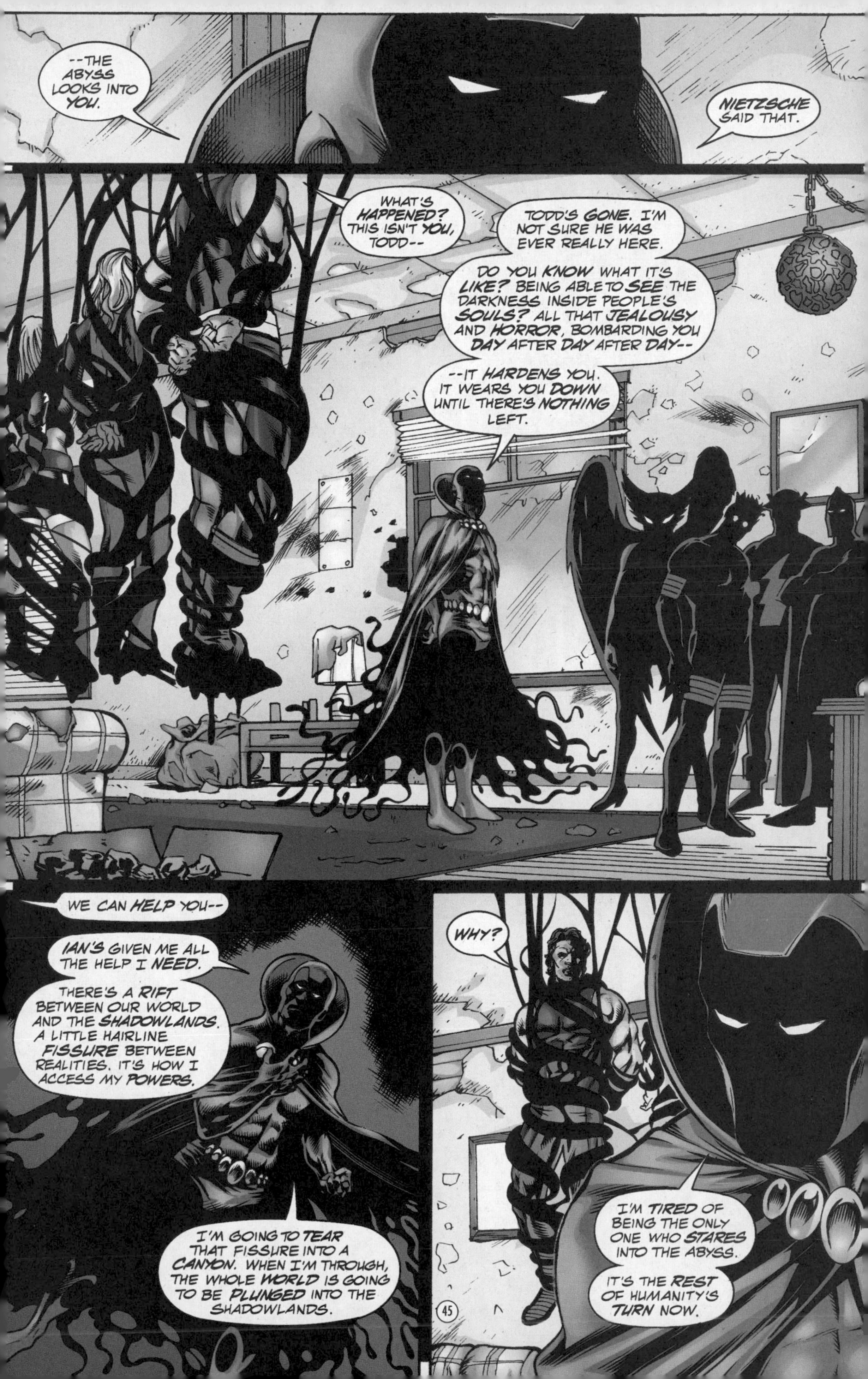

--THE ABYSS LOOKS INTO YOU.
NIETZSCHE SAID THAT.
WHAT'S HAPPENED? THIS ISN'T YOU, TODD--
TODD'S GONE. I'M NOT SURE HE WAS EVER REALLY HERE.
DO YOU KNOW WHAT IT'S LIKE? BEING ABLE TO SEE THE DARKNESS INSIDE PEOPLE'S SOULS? ALL THAT JEALOUSY AND HORROR, BOMBARDING YOU DAY AFTER DAY AFTER DAY--
--IT HARDENS YOU. IT WEARS YOU DOWN UNTIL THERE'S NOTHING LEFT.
WE CAN HELP YOU--
IAN'S GIVEN ME ALL THE HELP I NEED.
THERE'S A RIFT BETWEEN OUR WORLD AND THE SHADOWLANDS. A LITTLE HAIRLINE FISSURE BETWEEN REALITIES. IT'S HOW I ACCESS MY POWERS.
I'M GOING TO TEAR THAT FISSURE INTO A CANYON. WHEN I'M THROUGH, THE WHOLE WORLD IS GOING TO BE PLUNGED INTO THE SHADOWLANDS.
WHY?
I'M TIRED OF BEING THE ONLY ONE WHO STARES INTO THE ABYSS.
IT'S THE REST OF HUMANITY'S TURN NOW.

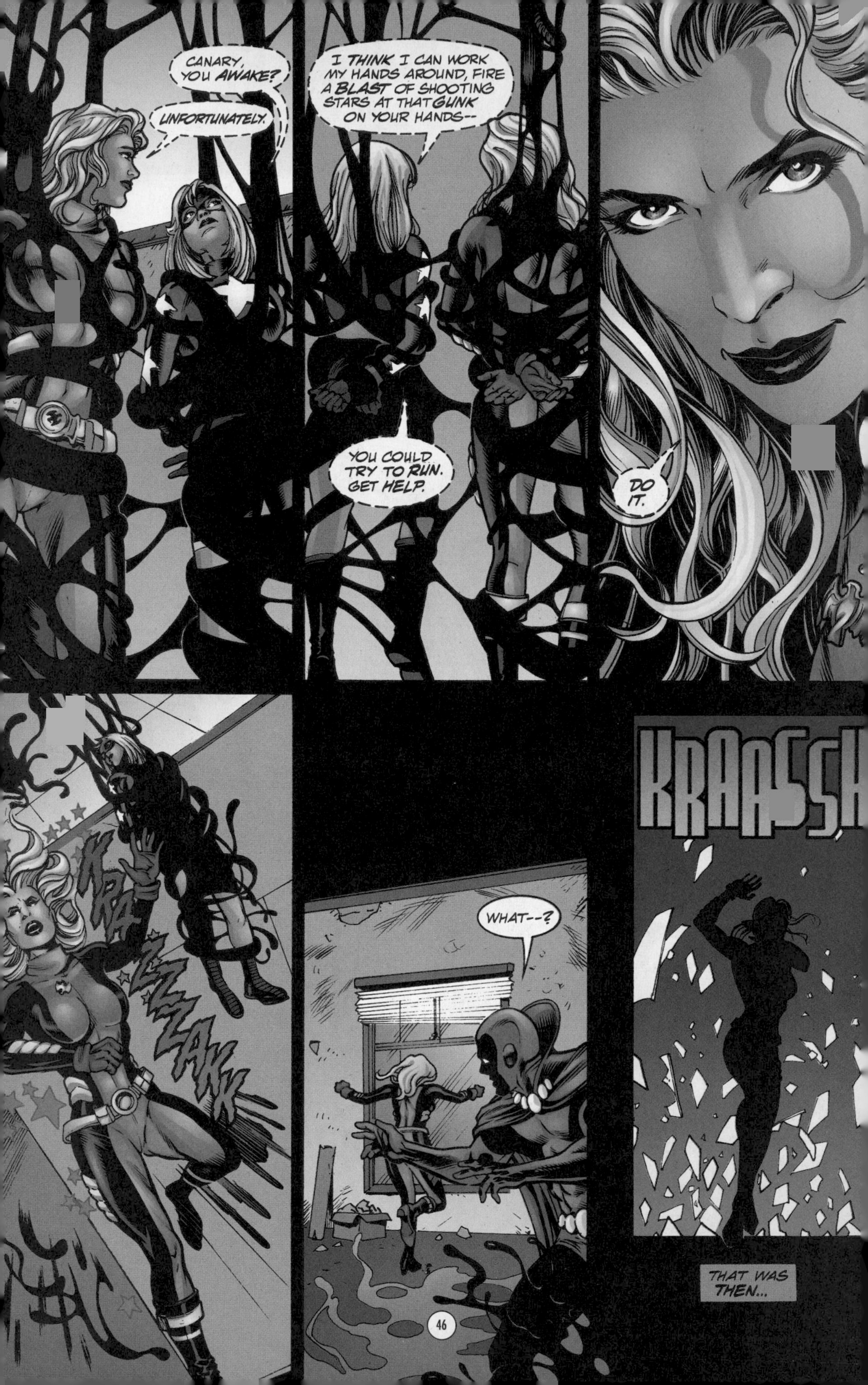
CANARY, YOU AWAKE?
UNFORTUNATELY.
I THINK I CAN WORK MY HANDS AROUND, FIRE A BLAST OF SHOOTING STARS AT THAT GUNK ON YOUR HANDS--
YOU COULD TRY TO RUN. GET HELP.
DO IT.
KRA
ZZZAKK
WHAT--?
KRAASSH
THAT WAS THEN...

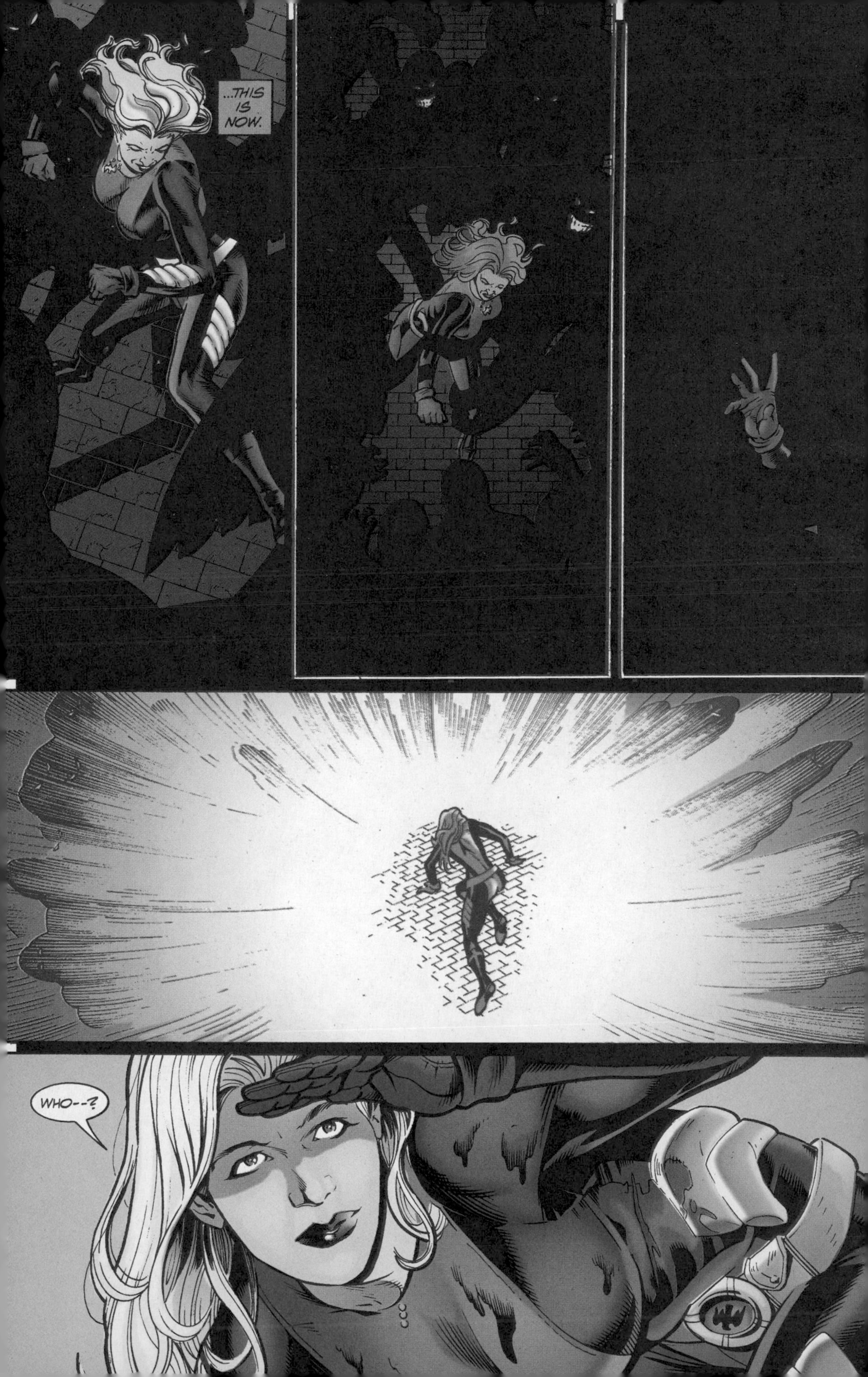
...THIS IS NOW.
WHO--?

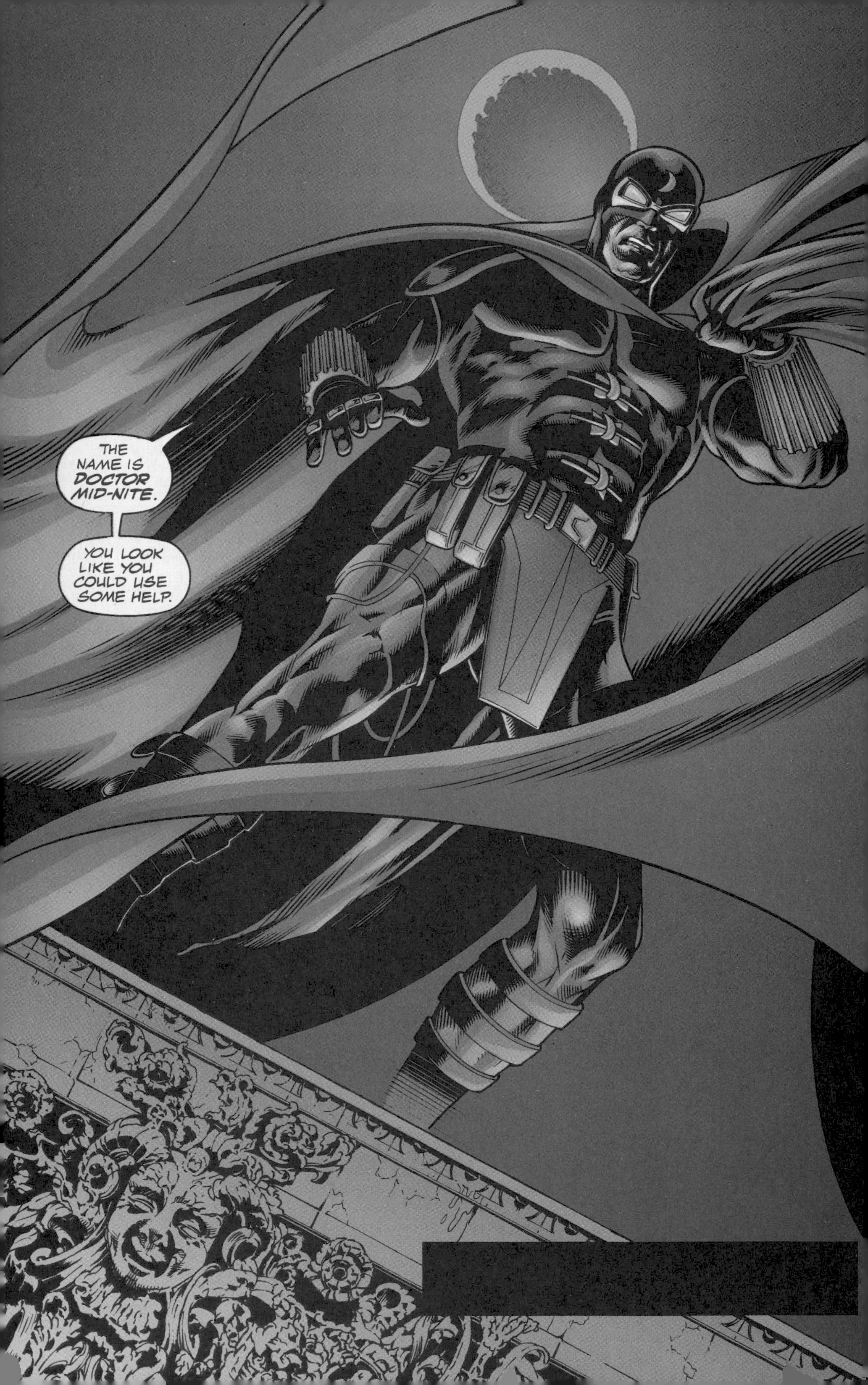
THE NAME IS DOCTOR MID-NITE.
YOU LOOK LIKE YOU COULD USE SOME HELP.
[redacted]

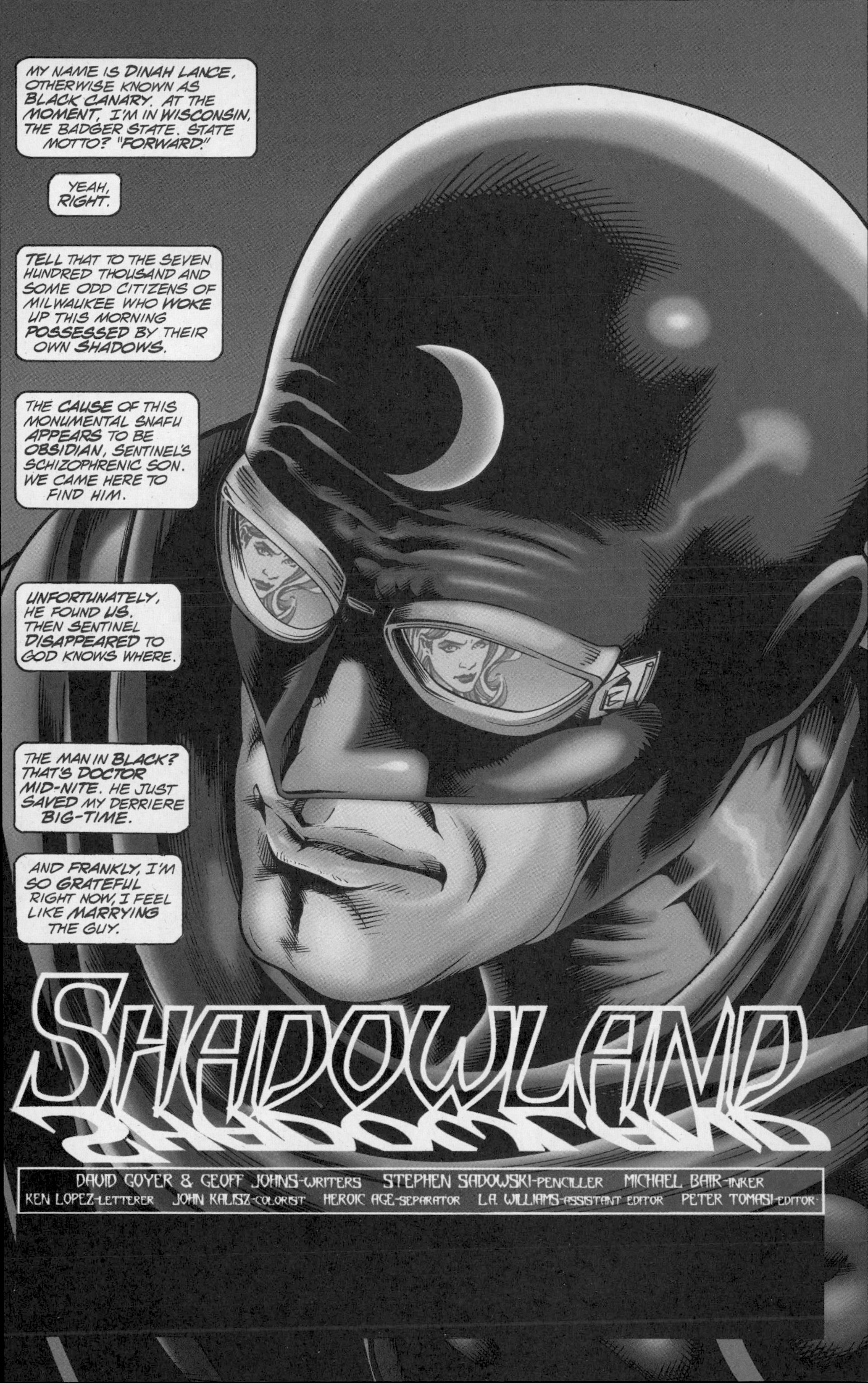
MY NAME IS DINAH LANCE, OTHERWISE KNOWN AS BLACK CANARY. AT THE MOMENT, I'M IN WISCONSIN, THE BADGER STATE. STATE MOTTO? "FORWARD."
YEAH, RIGHT.
TELL THAT TO THE SEVEN HUNDRED THOUSAND AND SOME ODD CITIZENS OF MILWAUKEE WHO WOKE UP THIS MORNING POSSESSED BY THEIR OWN SHADOWS.
THE CAUSE OF THIS MONUMENTAL SNAFU APPEARS TO BE OBSIDIAN, SENTINEL'S SCHIZOPHRENIC SON. WE CAME HERE TO FIND HIM.
UNFORTUNATELY, HE FOUND US. THEN SENTINEL DISAPPEARED TO GOD KNOWS WHERE.
THE MAN IN BLACK? THAT'S DOCTOR MID-NITE. HE JUST SAVED MY DERRIERE BIG-TIME.
AND FRANKLY, I'M SO GRATEFUL RIGHT NOW, I FEEL LIKE MARRYING THE GUY.
SHADOWLAND
DAVID GOYER & GEOFF JOHNS-WRITERS STEPHEN SADOWSKI-PENCILLER MICHAEL BAIR-INKER
KEN LOPEZ-LETTERER JOHN KALISZ-COLORIST HEROIC AGE-SEPARATOR L.A. WILLIAMS-ASSISTANT EDITOR PETER TOMASI-EDITOR

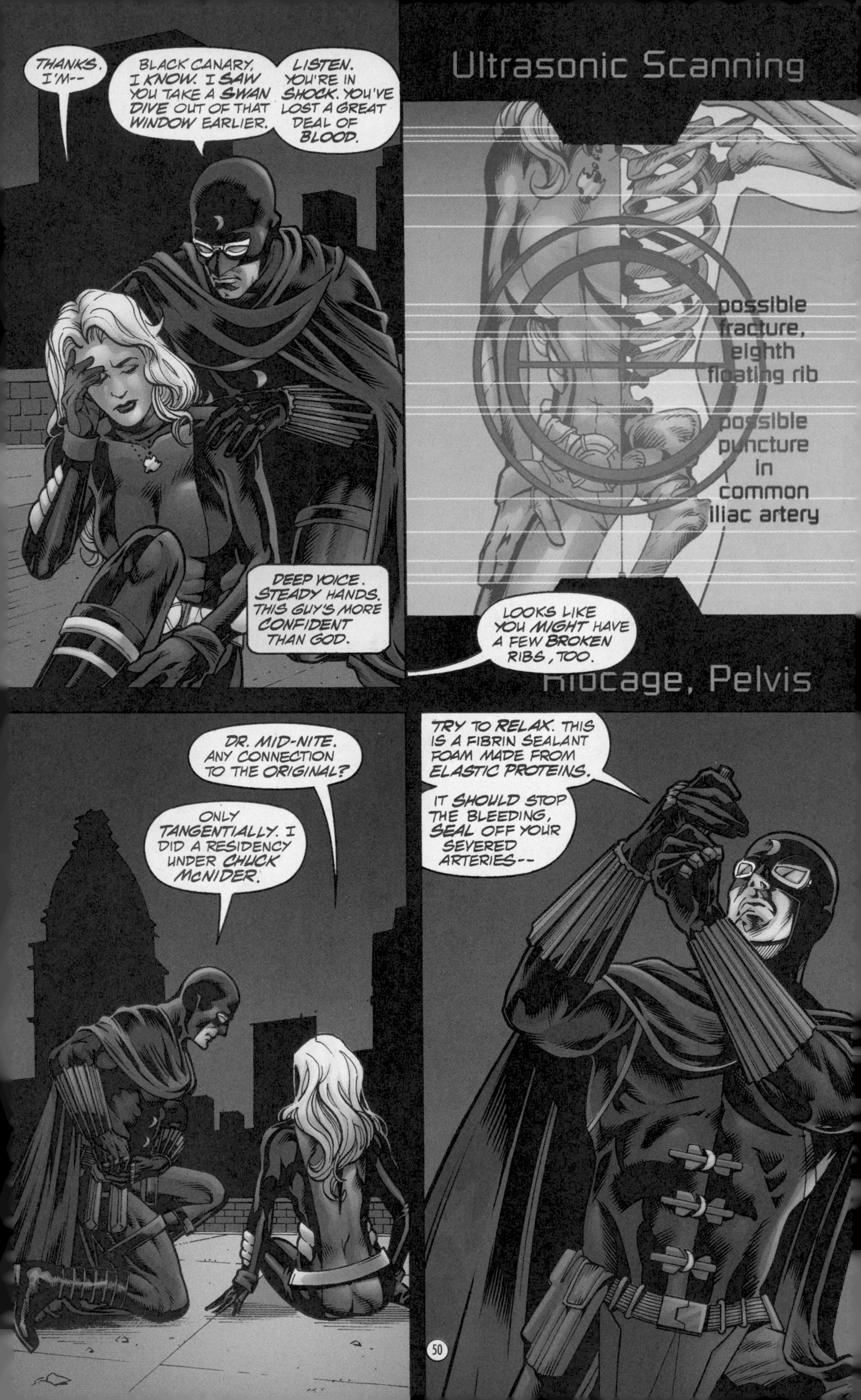
THANKS. I'M--
BLACK CANARY, I KNOW. I SAW YOU TAKE A SWAN DIVE OUT OF THAT WINDOW EARLIER.
LISTEN. YOU'RE IN SHOCK. YOU'VE LOST A GREAT DEAL OF BLOOD.
DEEP VOICE. STEADY HANDS. THIS GUY'S MORE CONFIDENT THAN GOD.
Ultrasonic Scanning
possible fracture, eighth floating rib
possible puncture in common iliac artery
LOOKS LIKE YOU MIGHT HAVE A FEW BROKEN RIBS, TOO.
Ribcage, Pelvis
DR. MID-NITE. ANY CONNECTION TO THE ORIGINAL?
ONLY TANGENTIALLY. I DID A RESIDENCY UNDER CHUCK MCNIDER.
TRY TO RELAX. THIS IS A FIBRIN SEALANT FOAM MADE FROM ELASTIC PROTEINS.
IT SHOULD STOP THE BLEEDING, SEAL OFF YOUR SEVERED ARTERIES--

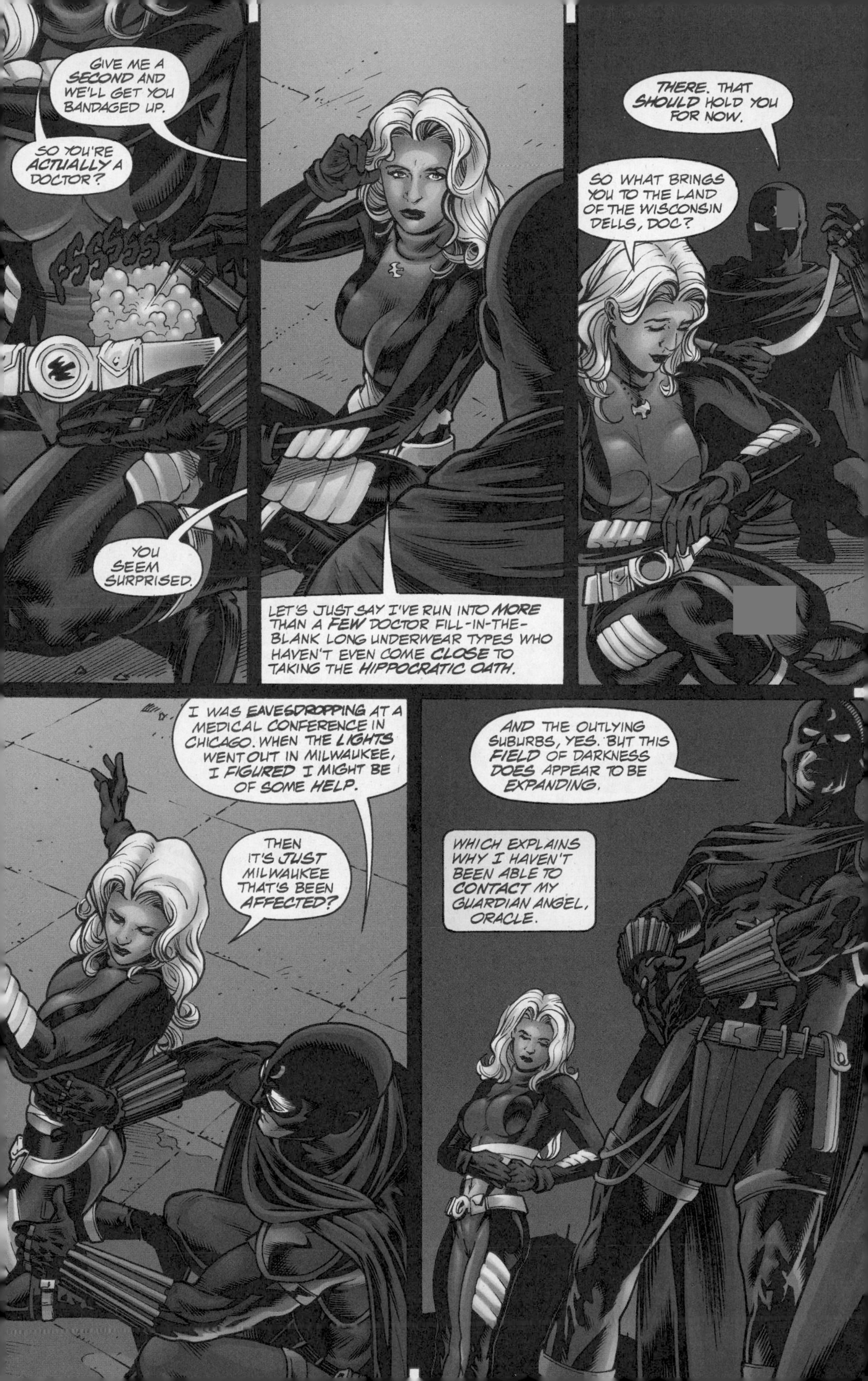
GIVE ME A SECOND AND WE'LL GET YOU BANDAGED UP.
SO YOU'RE ACTUALLY A DOCTOR?
FSSSSS
YOU SEEM SURPRISED.
LET'S JUST SAY I'VE RUN INTO MORE THAN A FEW DOCTOR FILL-IN-THE-BLANK LONG UNDERWEAR TYPES WHO HAVEN'T EVEN COME CLOSE TO TAKING THE HIPPOCRATIC OATH.
THERE. THAT SHOULD HOLD YOU FOR NOW.
SO WHAT BRINGS YOU TO THE LAND OF THE WISCONSIN DELLS, DOC?
I WAS EAVESDROPPING AT A MEDICAL CONFERENCE IN CHICAGO. WHEN THE LIGHTS WENT OUT IN MILWAUKEE, I FIGURED I MIGHT BE OF SOME HELP.
THEN IT'S JUST MILWAUKEE THAT'S BEEN AFFECTED?
AND THE OUTLYING SUBURBS, YES. BUT THIS FIELD OF DARKNESS DOES APPEAR TO BE EXPANDING.
WHICH EXPLAINS WHY I HAVEN'T BEEN ABLE TO CONTACT MY GUARDIAN ANGEL, ORACLE.

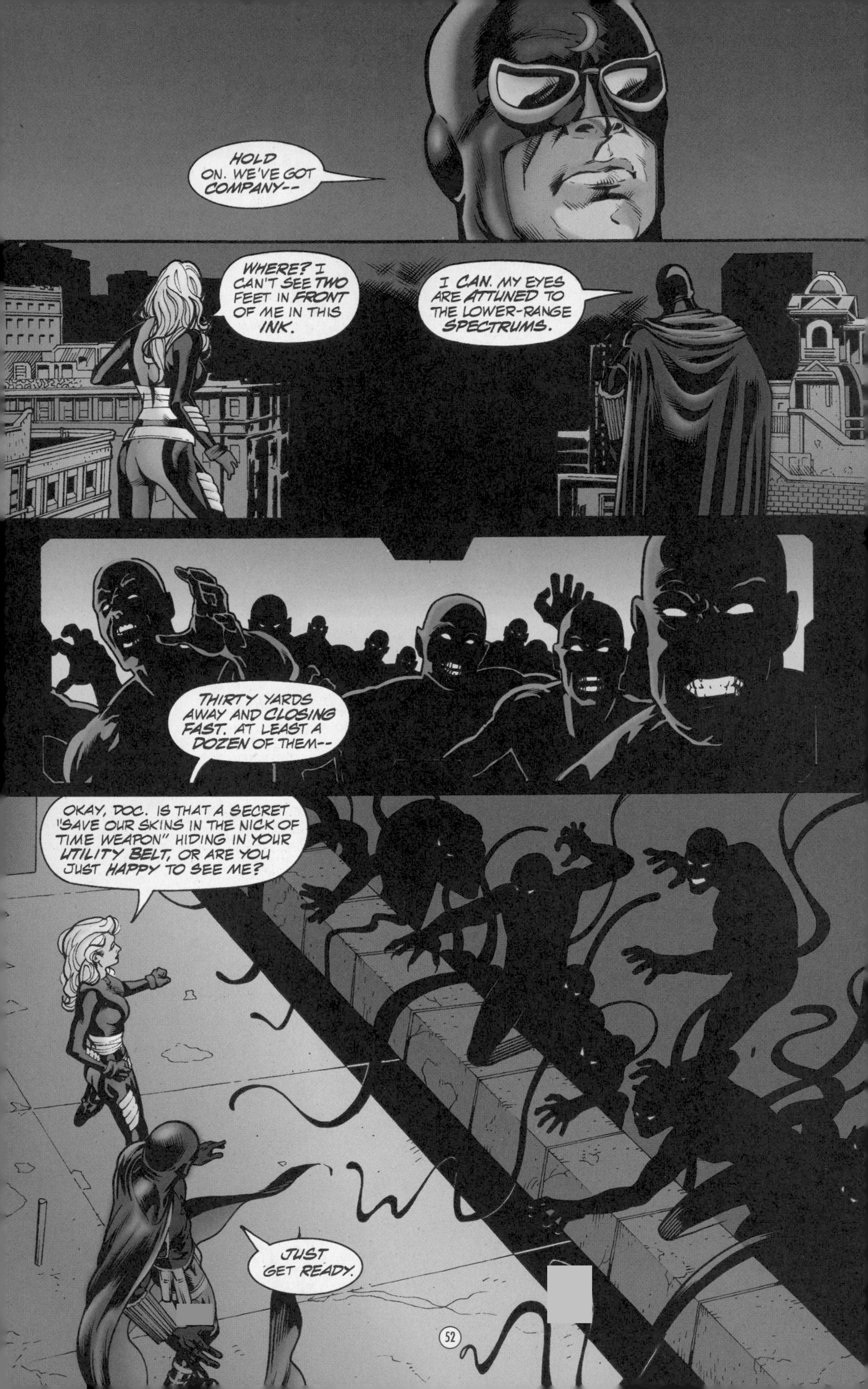
HOLD ON. WE'VE GOT COMPANY--
WHERE? I CAN'T SEE TWO FEET IN FRONT OF ME IN THIS INK.
I CAN. MY EYES ARE ATTUNED TO THE LOWER-RANGE SPECTRUMS.
THIRTY YARDS AWAY AND CLOSING FAST. AT LEAST A DOZEN OF THEM--
OKAY, DOC. IS THAT A SECRET "SAVE OUR SKINS IN THE NICK OF TIME WEAPON" HIDING IN YOUR UTILITY BELT, OR ARE YOU JUST HAPPY TO SEE ME?
JUST GET READY.

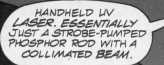

HANDHELD UV *LASER.* ESSENTIALLY JUST A *STROBE-PUMPED* PHOSPHOR ROD WITH A *COLLIMATED BEAM.*

FZZZAAASSSHH

--IT SHOULD *MORE* THAN DO THE *TRICK!*

AAAAAAAAA!!!

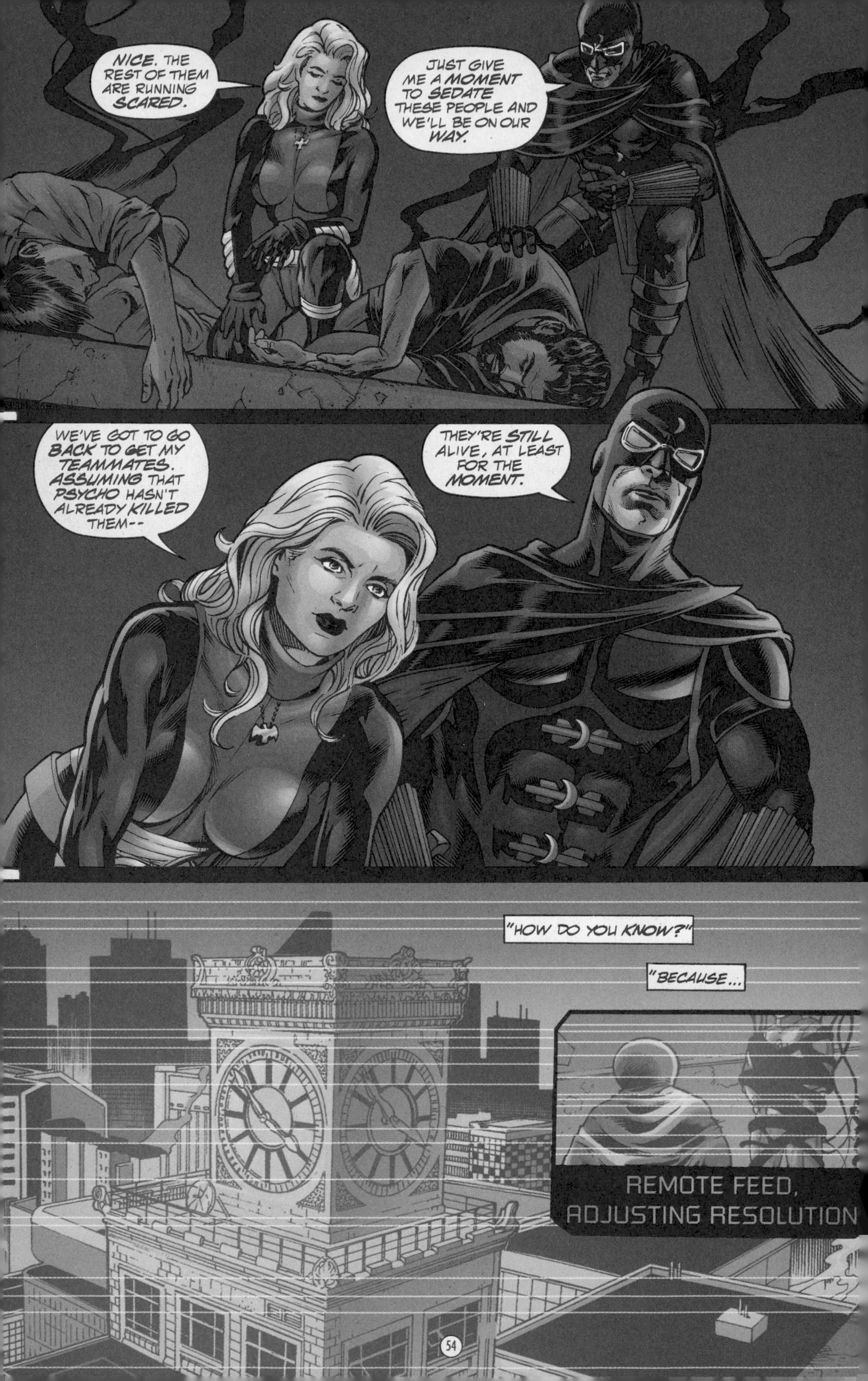
NICE. THE REST OF THEM ARE RUNNING SCARED.
JUST GIVE ME A MOMENT TO SEDATE THESE PEOPLE AND WE'LL BE ON OUR WAY.
WE'VE GOT TO GO BACK TO GET MY TEAMMATES. ASSUMING THAT PSYCHO HASN'T ALREADY KILLED THEM--
THEY'RE STILL ALIVE, AT LEAST FOR THE MOMENT.
"HOW DO YOU KNOW?"
"BECAUSE...
REMOTE FEED, ADJUSTING RESOLUTION

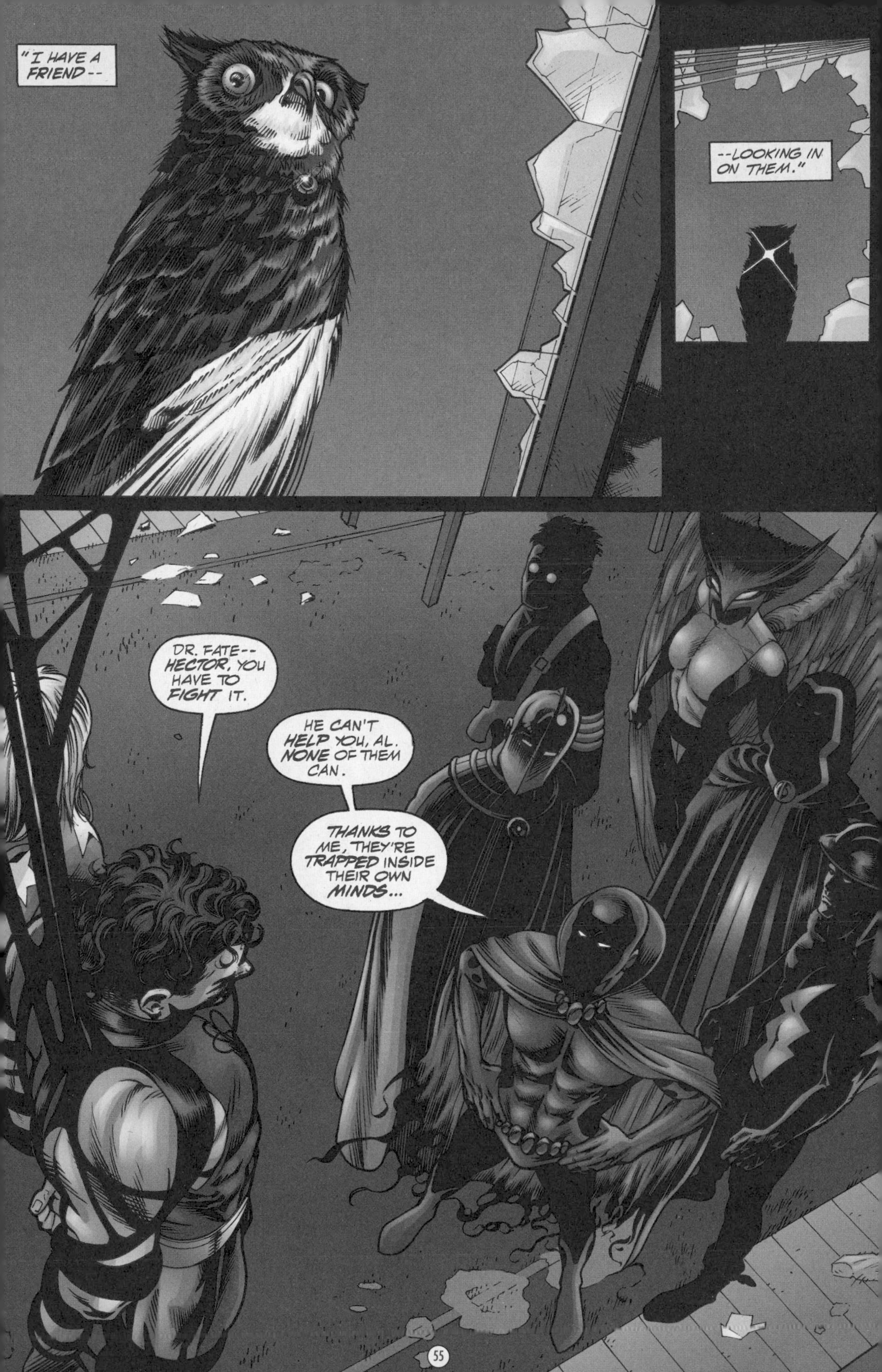
"I HAVE A FRIEND--
--LOOKING IN ON THEM."
DR. FATE-- HECTOR, YOU HAVE TO FIGHT IT.
HE CAN'T HELP YOU, AL. NONE OF THEM CAN.
THANKS TO ME, THEY'RE TRAPPED INSIDE THEIR OWN MINDS...

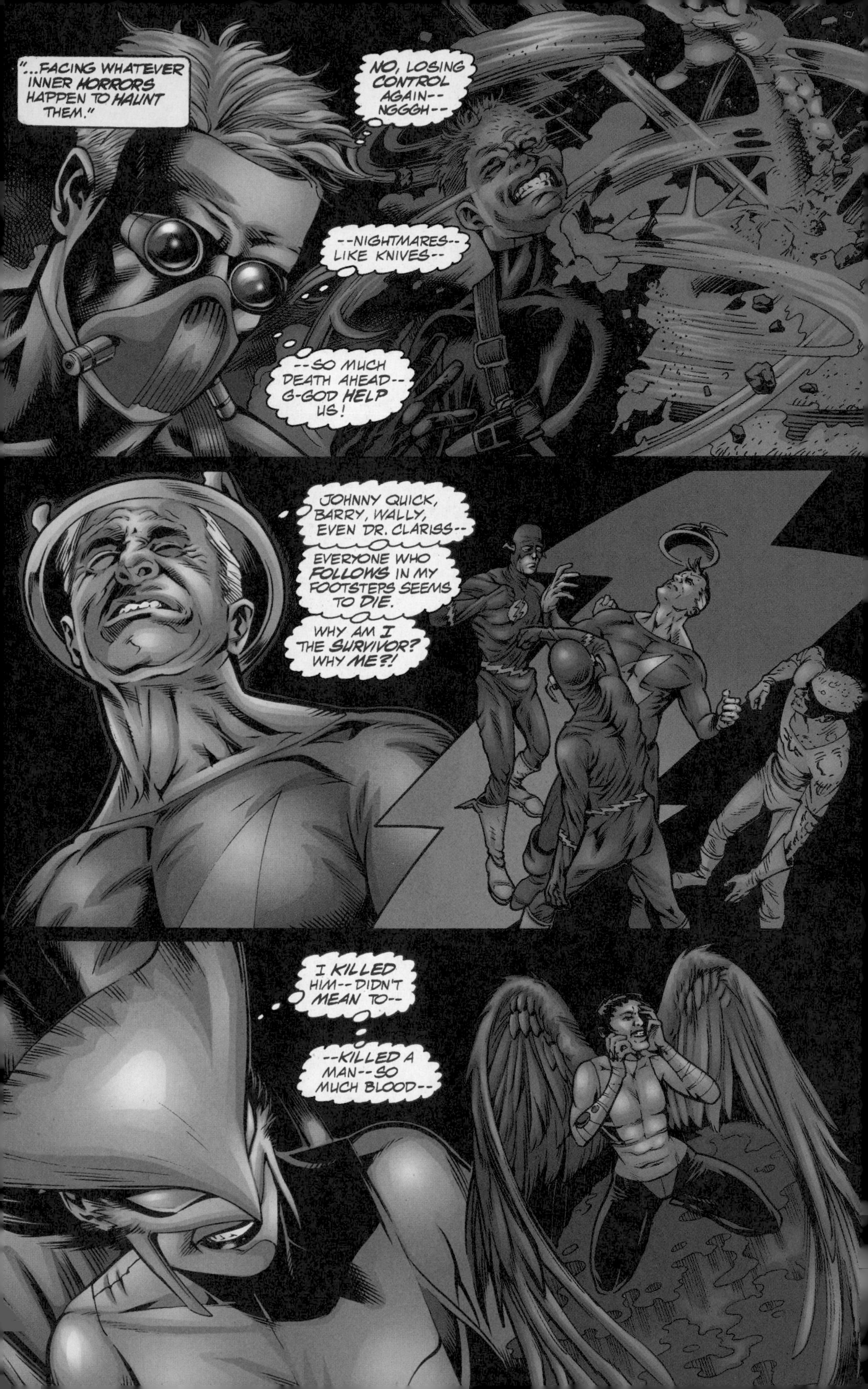
"...FACING WHATEVER INNER HORRORS HAPPEN TO HAUNT THEM."
NO, LOSING CONTROL AGAIN-- NGGGH--
--NIGHTMARES-- LIKE KNIVES--
--SO MUCH DEATH AHEAD-- G-GOD HELP US!
JOHNNY QUICK, BARRY, WALLY, EVEN DR. CLARISS--
EVERYONE WHO FOLLOWS IN MY FOOTSTEPS SEEMS TO DIE.
WHY AM I THE SURVIVOR? WHY ME?!
I KILLED HIM--DIDN'T MEAN TO--
--KILLED A MAN--SO MUCH BLOOD--

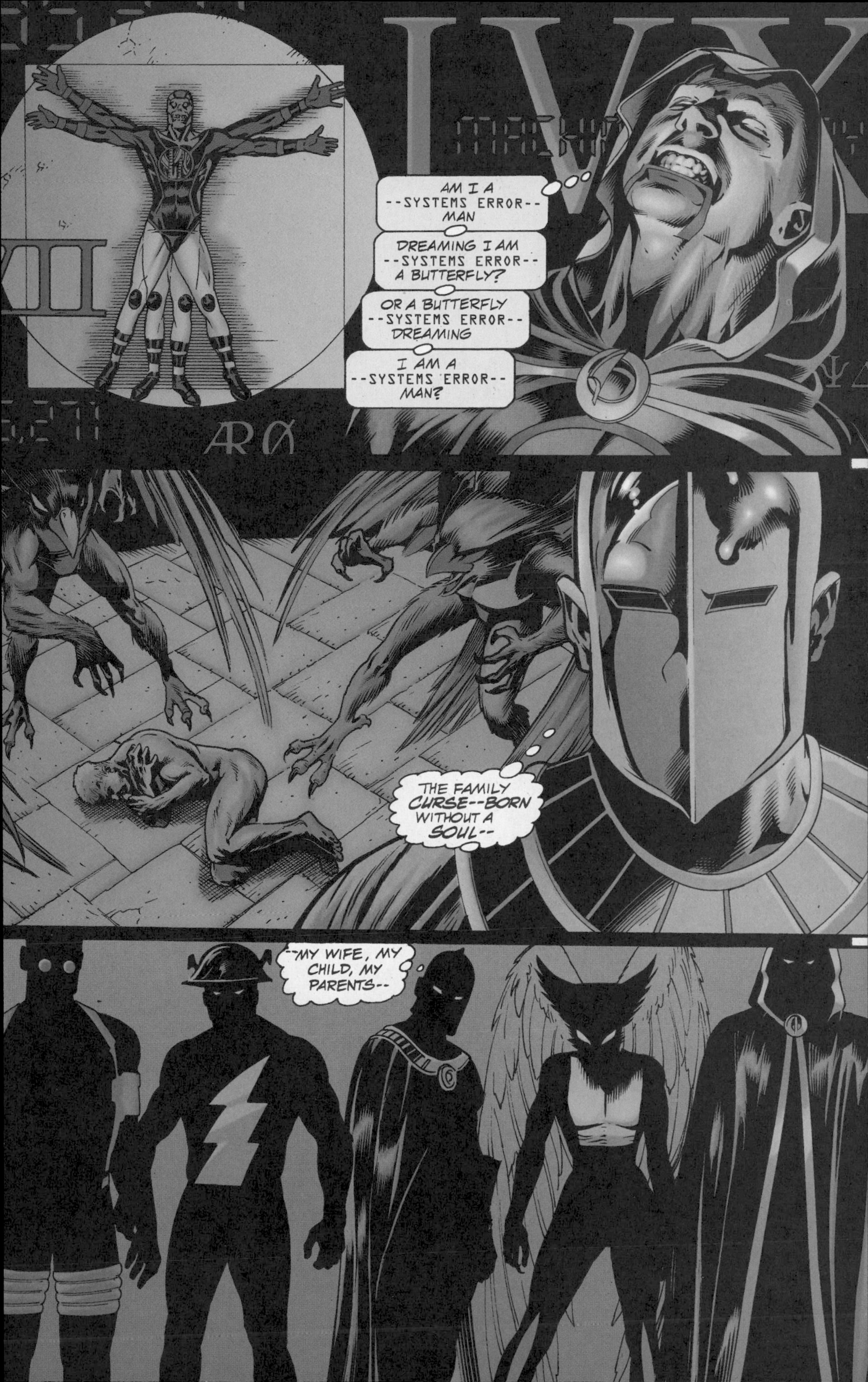
AM I A --SYSTEMS ERROR-- MAN
DREAMING I AM --SYSTEMS ERROR-- A BUTTERFLY?
OR A BUTTERFLY --SYSTEMS ERROR-- DREAMING
I AM A --SYSTEMS ERROR-- MAN?
THE FAMILY CURSE--BORN WITHOUT A SOUL--
--MY WIFE, MY CHILD, MY PARENTS--

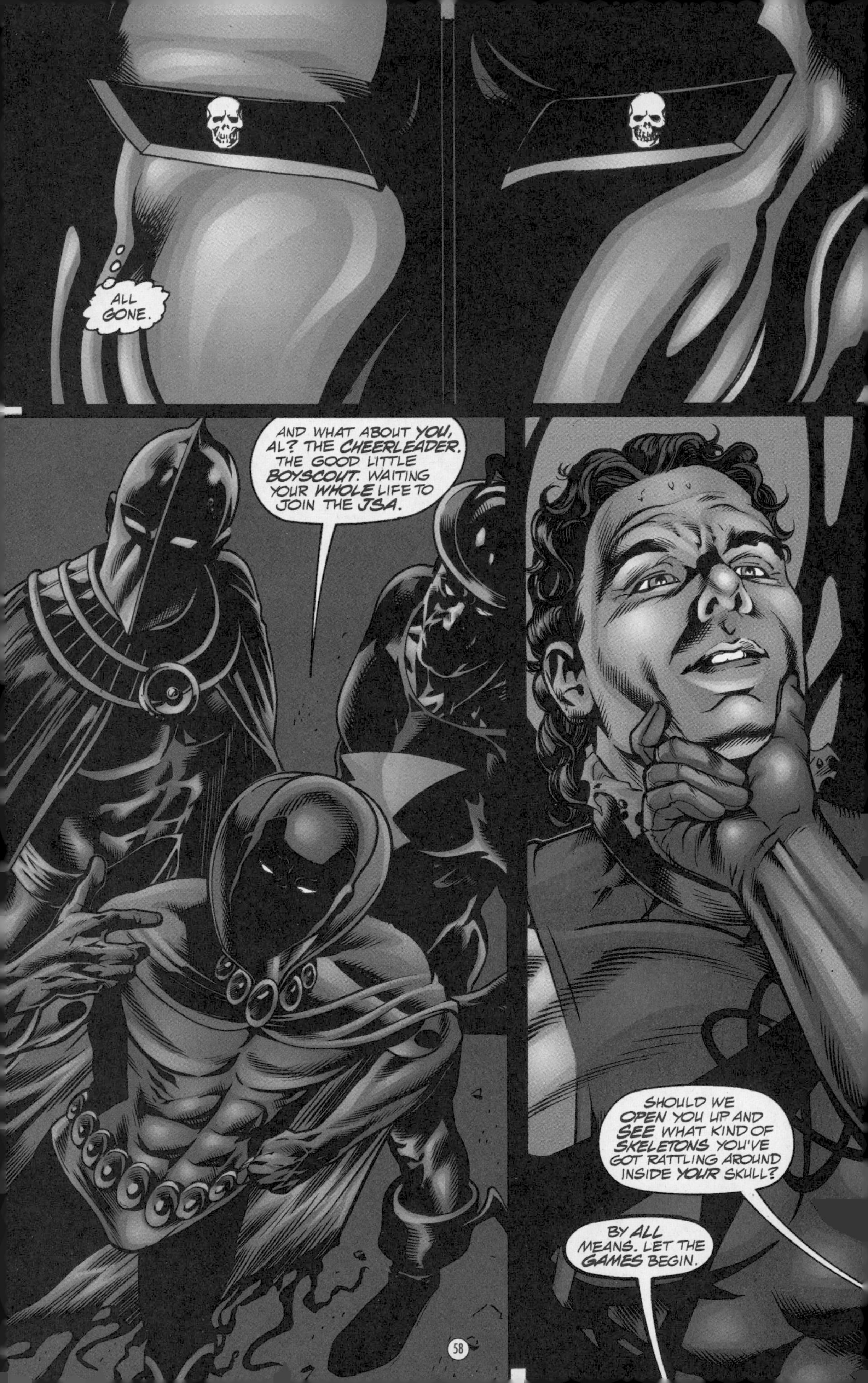
ALL GONE.
AND WHAT ABOUT YOU, AL? THE CHEERLEADER. THE GOOD LITTLE BOYSCOUT. WAITING YOUR WHOLE LIFE TO JOIN THE JSA.
SHOULD WE OPEN YOU UP AND SEE WHAT KIND OF SKELETONS YOU'VE GOT RATTLING AROUND INSIDE YOUR SKULL?
BY ALL MEANS. LET THE GAMES BEGIN.

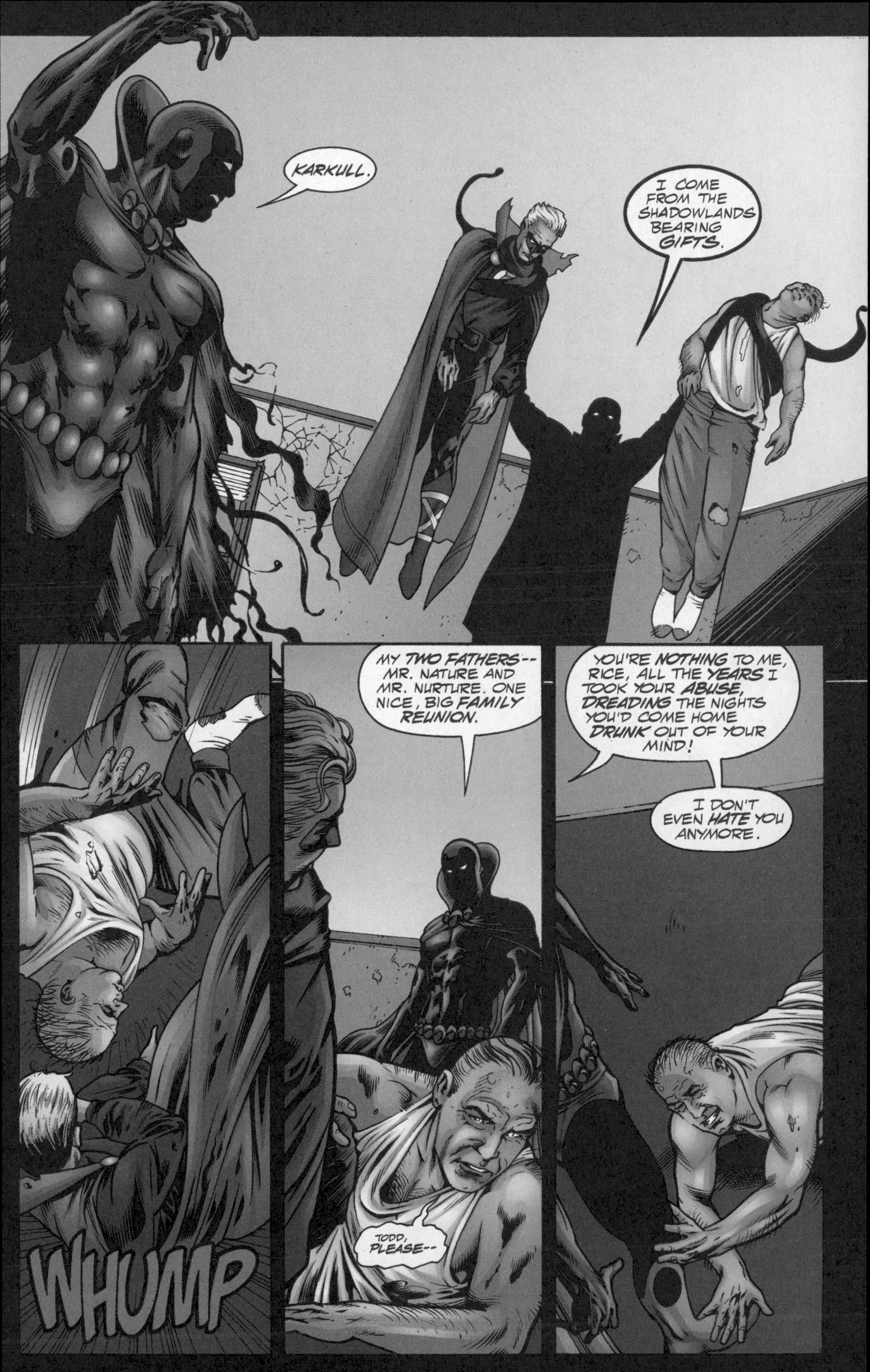
KARKULL.
I COME FROM THE SHADOWLANDS BEARING GIFTS.
WHUMP
MY TWO FATHERS--MR. NATURE AND MR. NURTURE. ONE NICE, BIG FAMILY REUNION.
TODD, PLEASE--
YOU'RE NOTHING TO ME, RICE, ALL THE YEARS I TOOK YOUR ABUSE, DREADING THE NIGHTS YOU'D COME HOME DRUNK OUT OF YOUR MIND!
I DON'T EVEN HATE YOU ANYMORE.

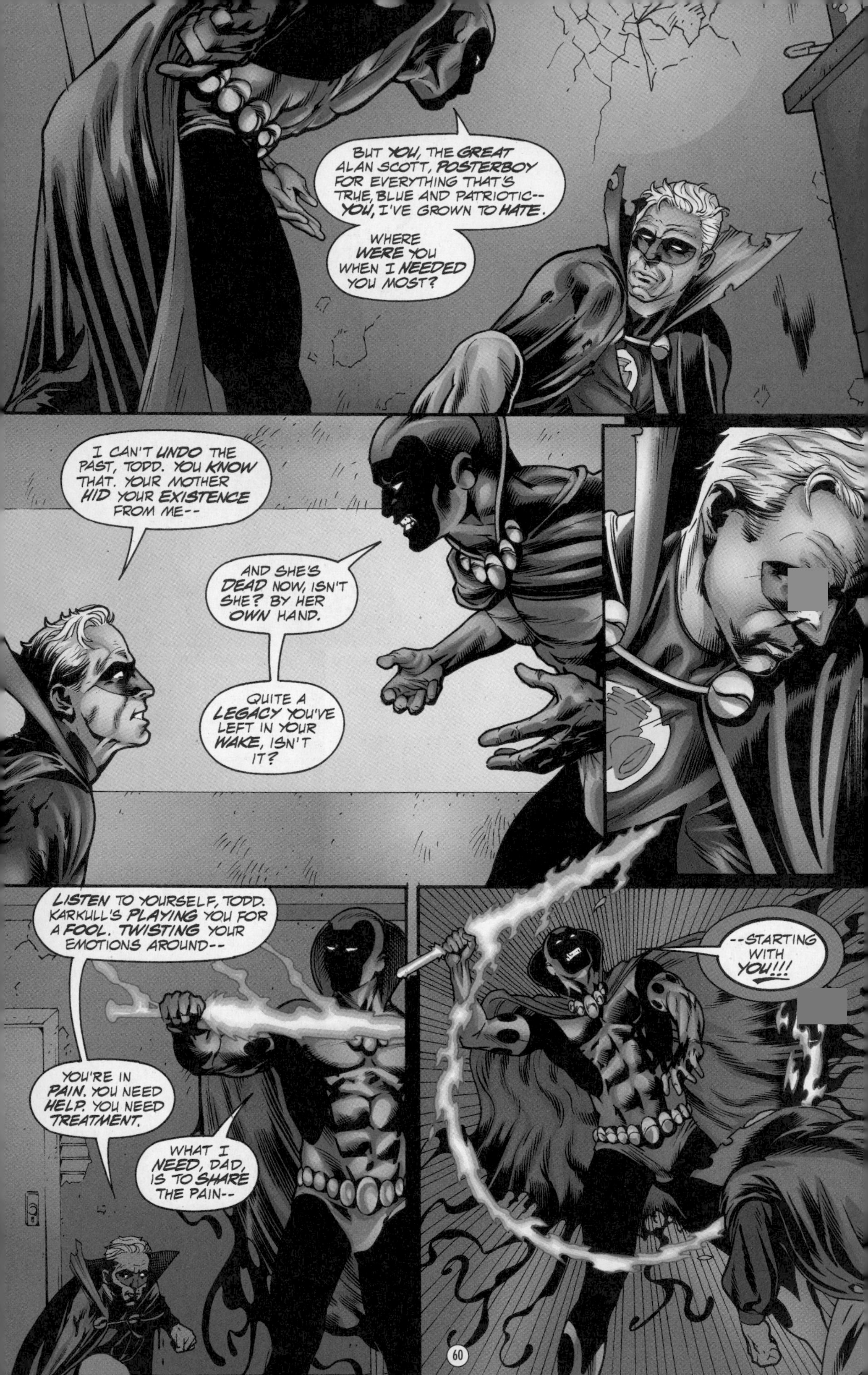

BUT YOU, THE GREAT ALAN SCOTT, POSTERBOY FOR EVERYTHING THAT'S TRUE, BLUE AND PATRIOTIC-- YOU, I'VE GROWN TO HATE.
WHERE WERE YOU WHEN I NEEDED YOU MOST?
I CAN'T UNDO THE PAST, TODD. YOU KNOW THAT. YOUR MOTHER HID YOUR EXISTENCE FROM ME--
AND SHE'S DEAD NOW, ISN'T SHE? BY HER OWN HAND.
QUITE A LEGACY YOU'VE LEFT IN YOUR WAKE, ISN'T IT?
LISTEN TO YOURSELF, TODD. KARKULL'S PLAYING YOU FOR A FOOL. TWISTING YOUR EMOTIONS AROUND--
YOU'RE IN PAIN. YOU NEED HELP. YOU NEED TREATMENT.
WHAT I NEED, DAD, IS TO SHARE THE PAIN--
--STARTING WITH YOU!!!

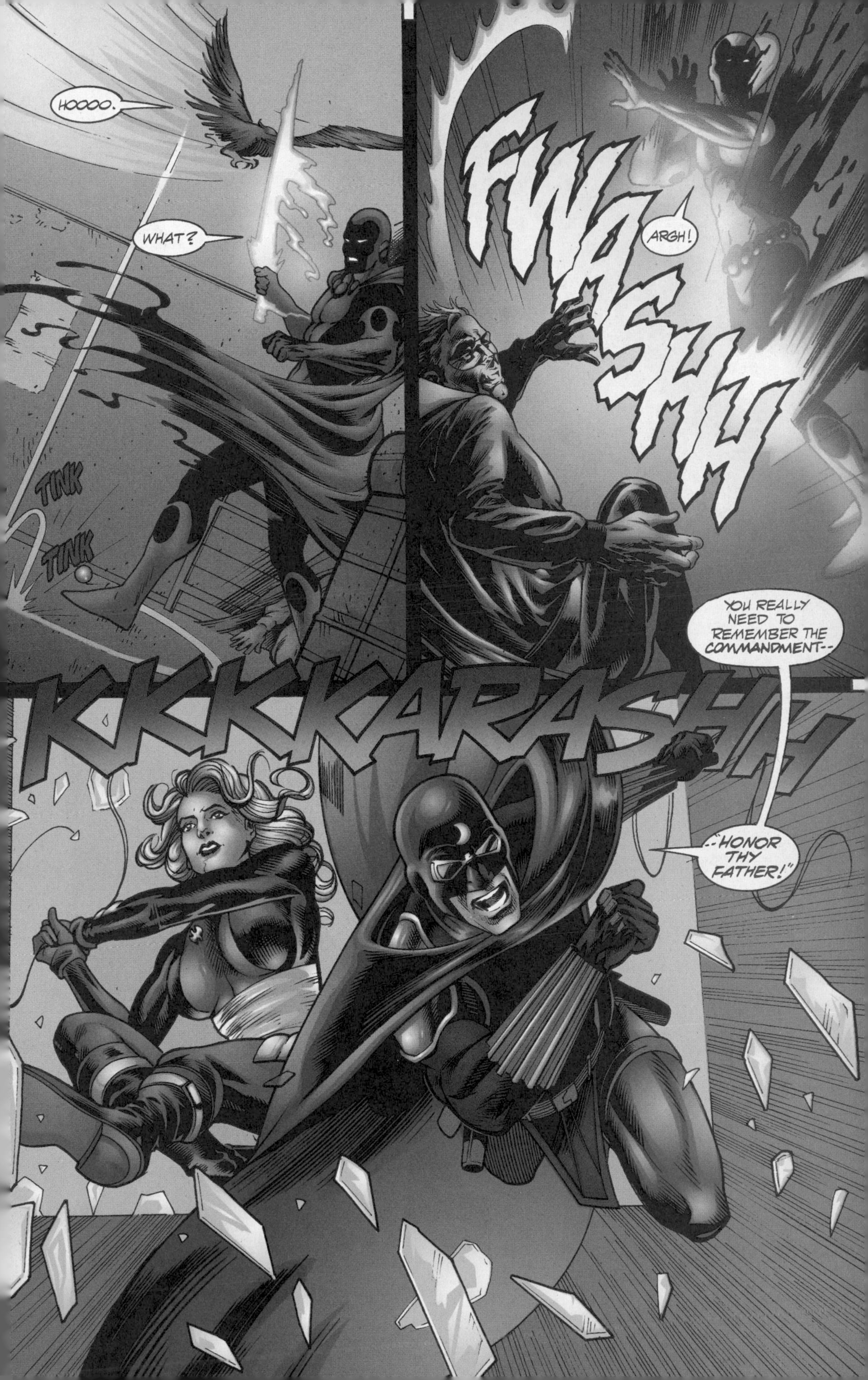
HOOOO.
WHAT?
TINK
TINK
FWASHH
ARGH!
YOU REALLY NEED TO REMEMBER THE COMMANDMENT--
KKKKARASHH
--"HONOR THY FATHER!"

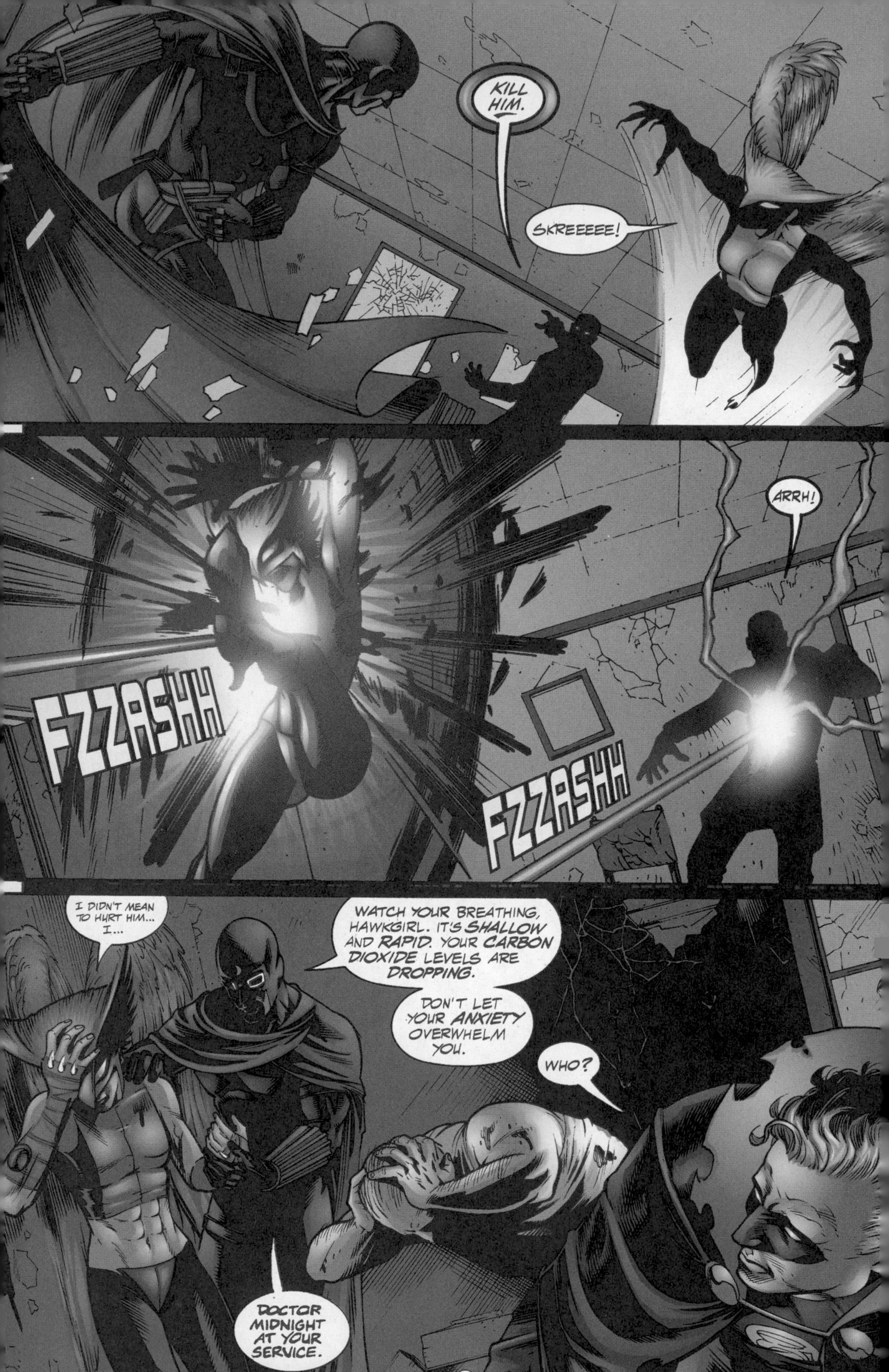

KILL HIM.
SKREEEEEE!
ARRH!
FZZASHH
FZZASHH
I DIDN'T MEAN TO HURT HIM... I...
WATCH YOUR BREATHING, HAWKGIRL. IT'S SHALLOW AND RAPID. YOUR CARBON DIOXIDE LEVELS ARE DROPPING.
DON'T LET YOUR ANXIETY OVERWHELM YOU.
WHO?
DOCTOR MIDNIGHT AT YOUR SERVICE.

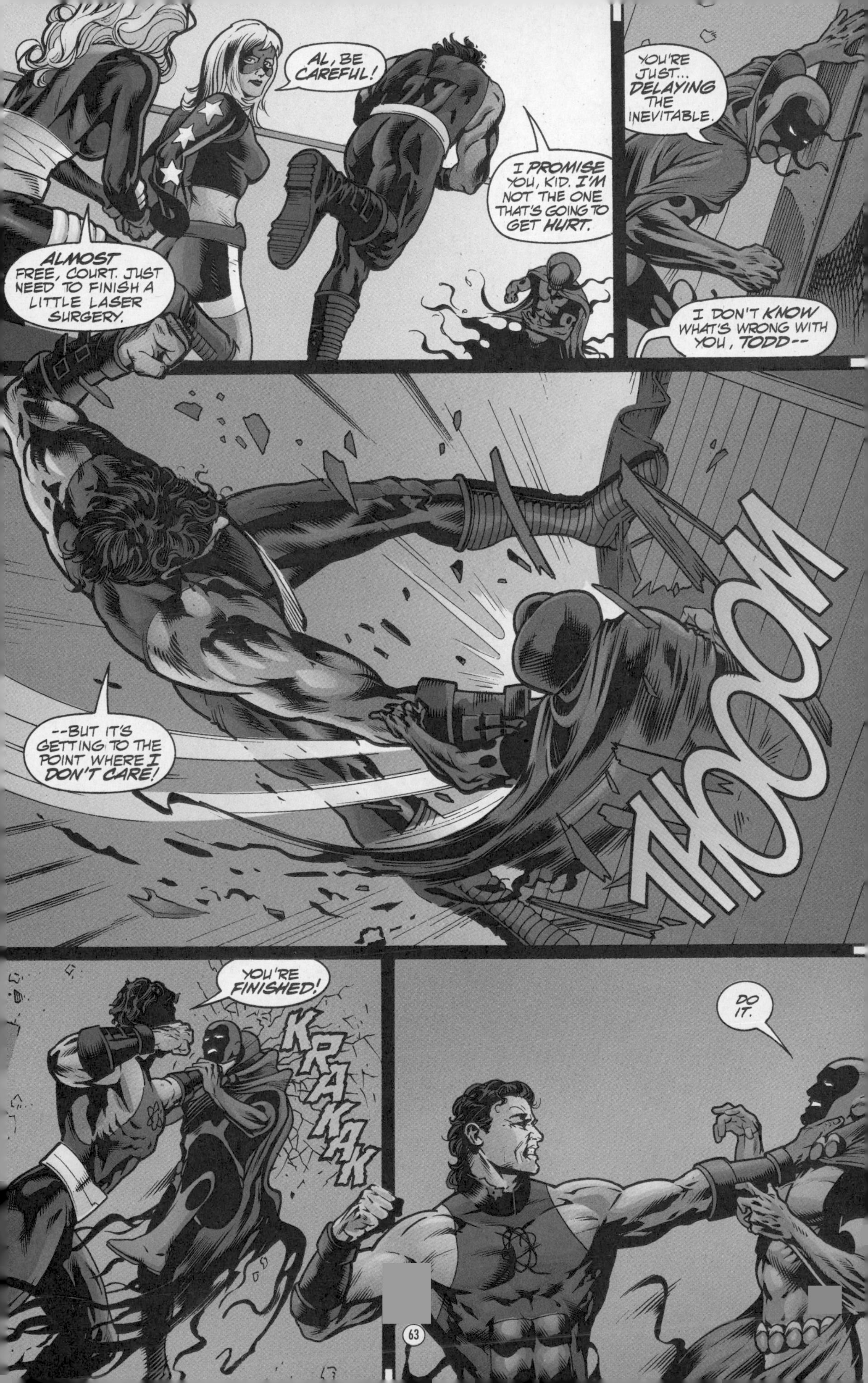
ALMOST FREE, COURT. JUST NEED TO FINISH A LITTLE LASER SURGERY.
AL, BE CAREFUL!
I PROMISE YOU, KID. I'M NOT THE ONE THAT'S GOING TO GET HURT.
YOU'RE JUST... DELAYING THE INEVITABLE.
I DON'T KNOW WHAT'S WRONG WITH YOU, TODD--
--BUT IT'S GETTING TO THE POINT WHERE I DON'T CARE!
THOOOM
YOU'RE FINISHED!
KRAKAK
DO IT.

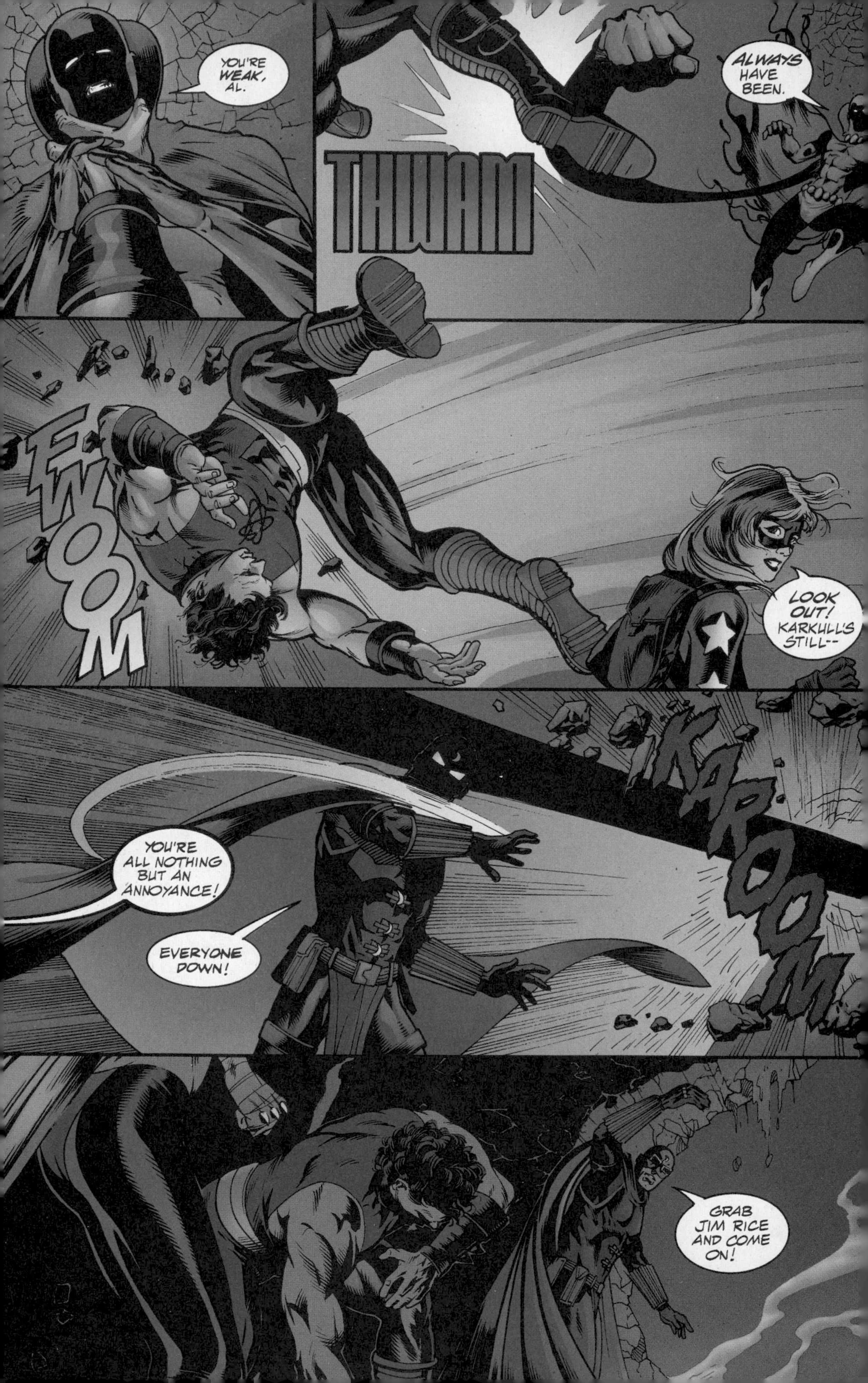
YOU'RE WEAK, AL.
THWAM
ALWAYS HAVE BEEN.
FWOOM
LOOK OUT! KARKULL'S STILL--
KAROOOM
YOU'RE ALL NOTHING BUT AN ANNOYANCE!
EVERYONE DOWN!
GRAB JIM RICE AND COME ON!

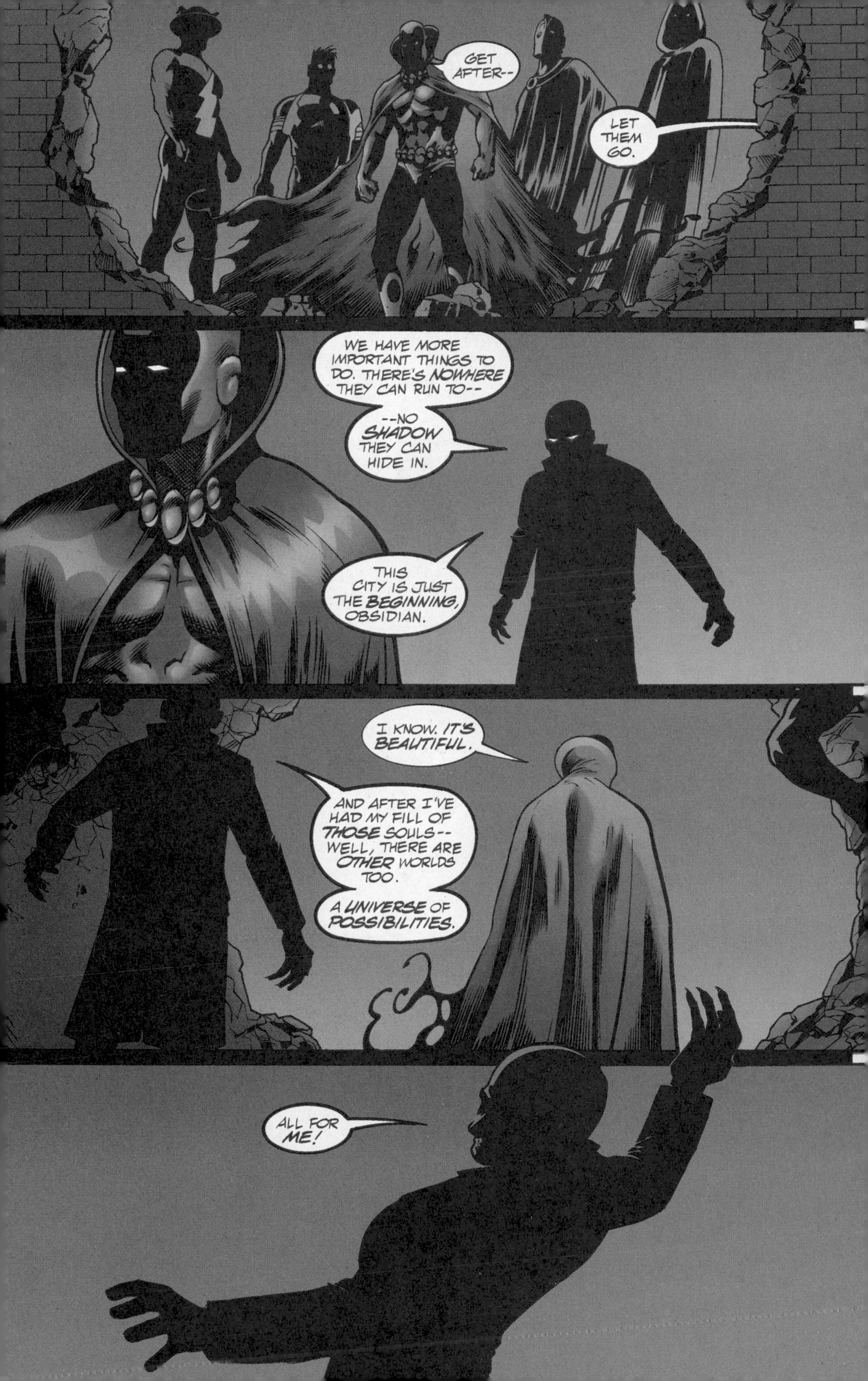
GET AFTER--
LET THEM GO.
WE HAVE MORE IMPORTANT THINGS TO DO. THERE'S NOWHERE THEY CAN RUN TO--
--NO SHADOW THEY CAN HIDE IN.
THIS CITY IS JUST THE BEGINNING, OBSIDIAN.
I KNOW. IT'S BEAUTIFUL.
AND AFTER I'VE HAD MY FILL OF THOSE SOULS-- WELL, THERE ARE OTHER WORLDS TOO.
A UNIVERSE OF POSSIBILITIES.
ALL FOR ME!

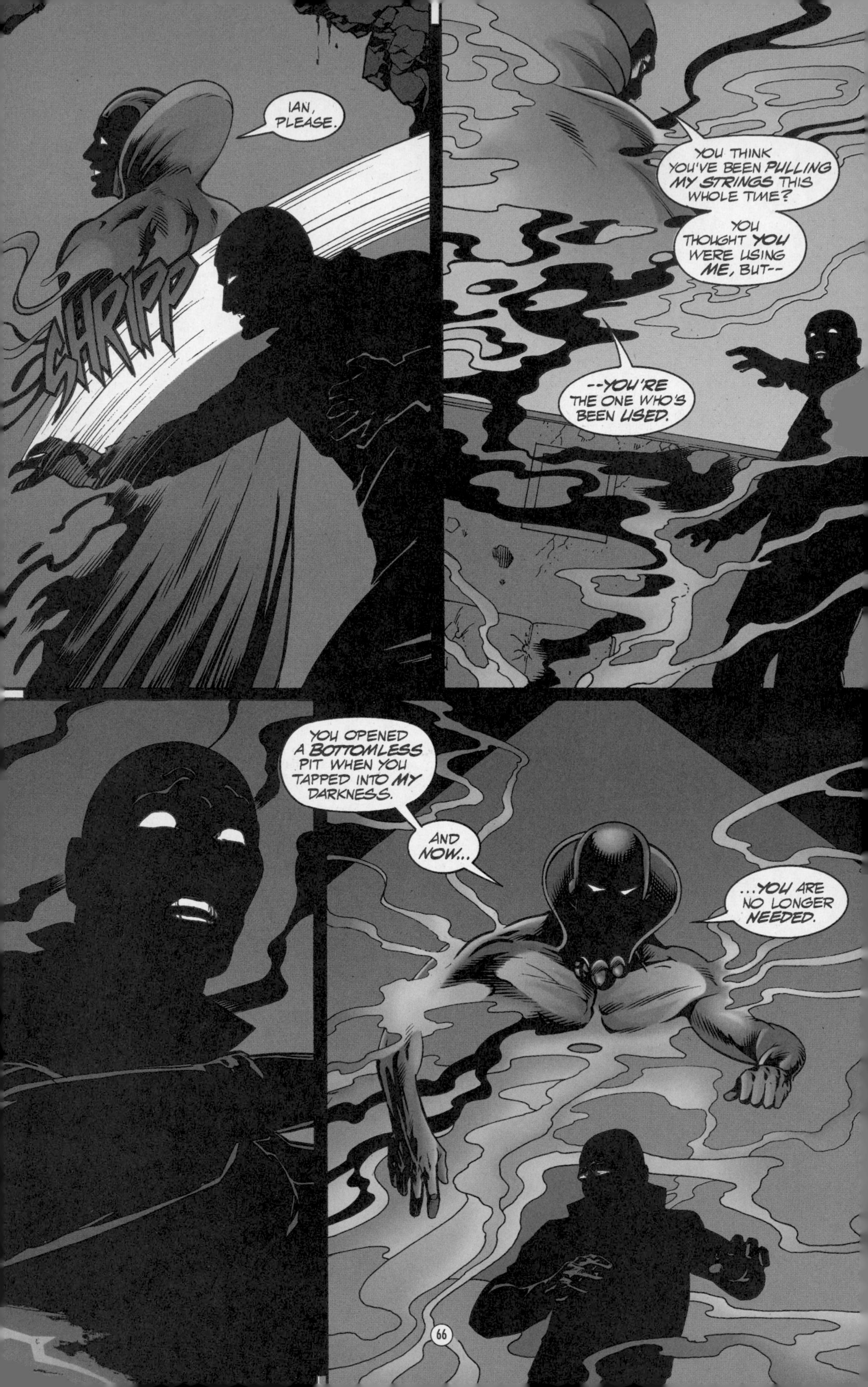
IAN, PLEASE.
SHRIPP
YOU THINK YOU'VE BEEN PULLING MY STRINGS THIS WHOLE TIME?
YOU THOUGHT YOU WERE USING ME, BUT--
--YOU'RE THE ONE WHO'S BEEN USED.
YOU OPENED A BOTTOMLESS PIT WHEN YOU TAPPED INTO MY DARKNESS.
AND NOW...
...YOU ARE NO LONGER NEEDED.

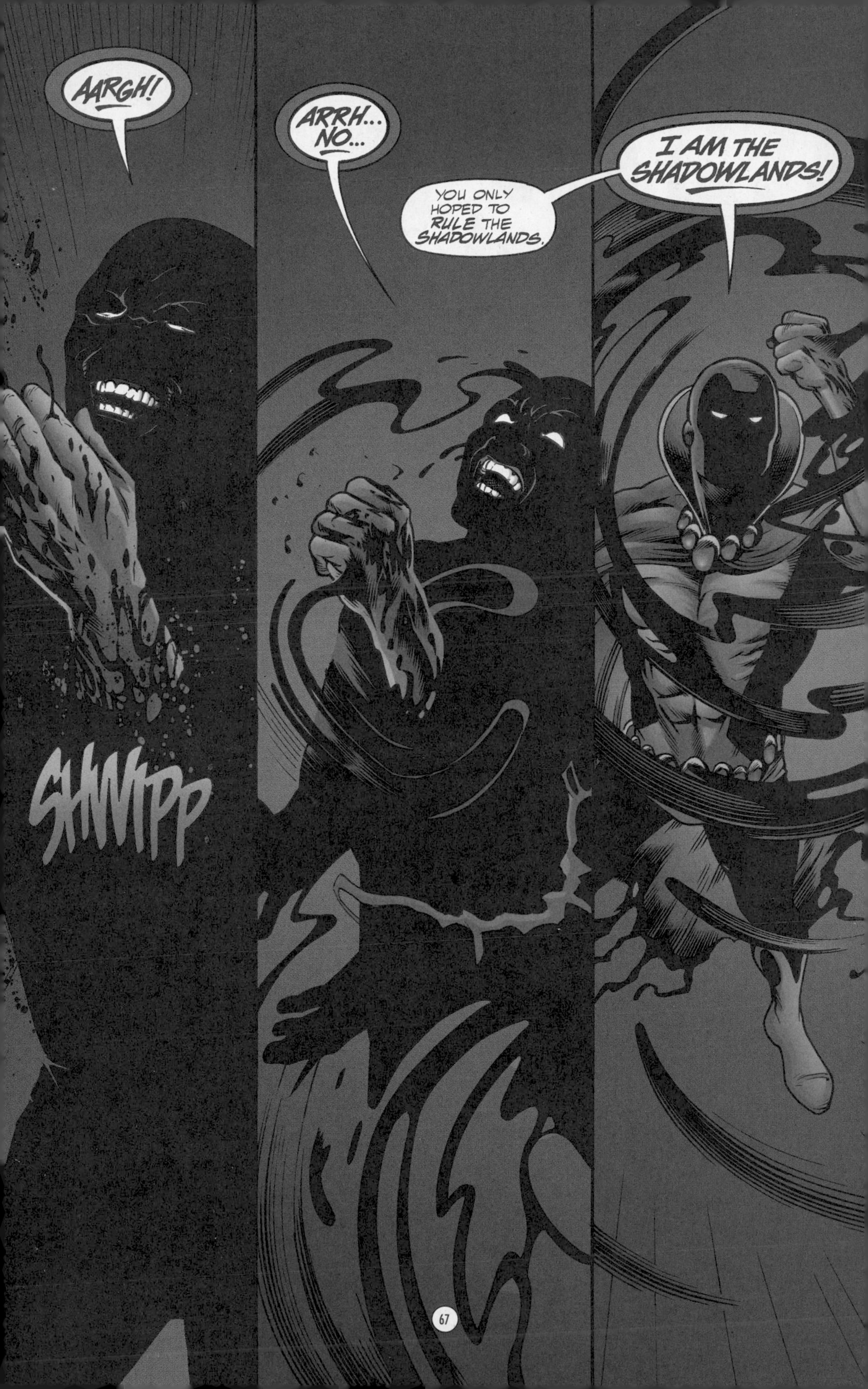
AARGH!
SHWIPP
ARRH... NO...
YOU ONLY HOPED TO RULE THE SHADOWLANDS.
I AM THE SHADOWLANDS!

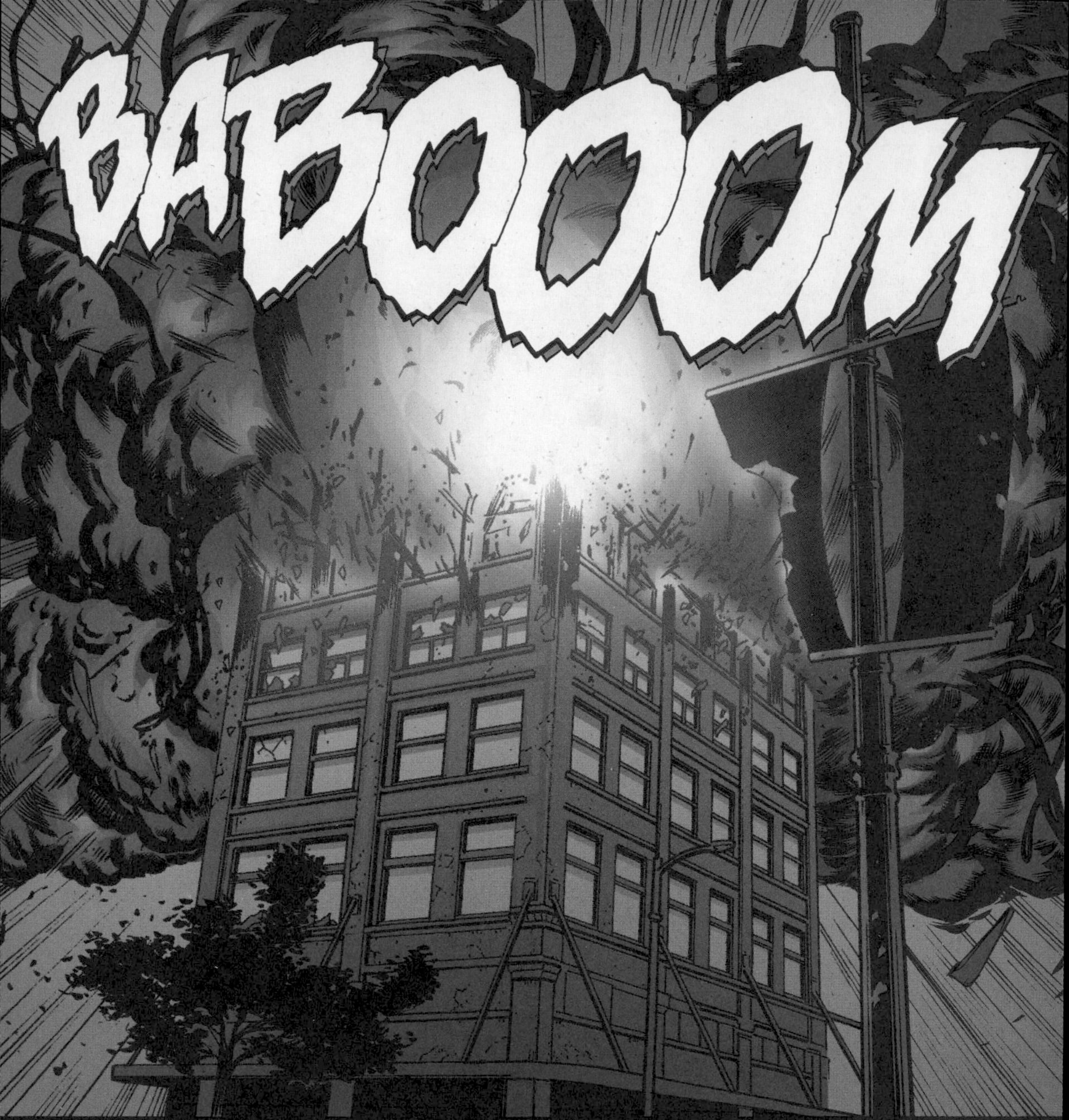
BABOOOM

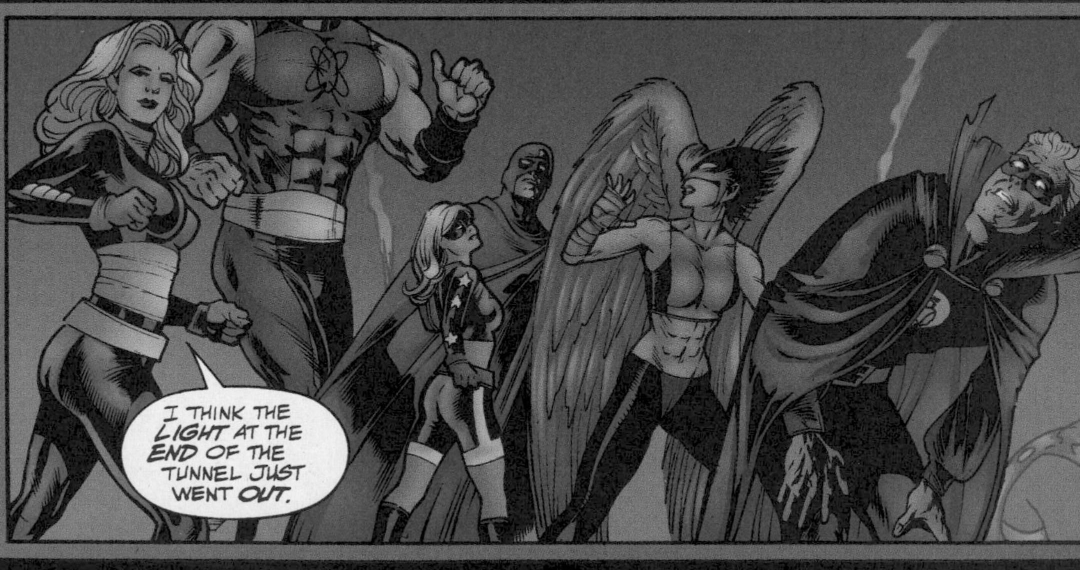
I THINK THE LIGHT AT THE END OF THE TUNNEL JUST WENT OUT.

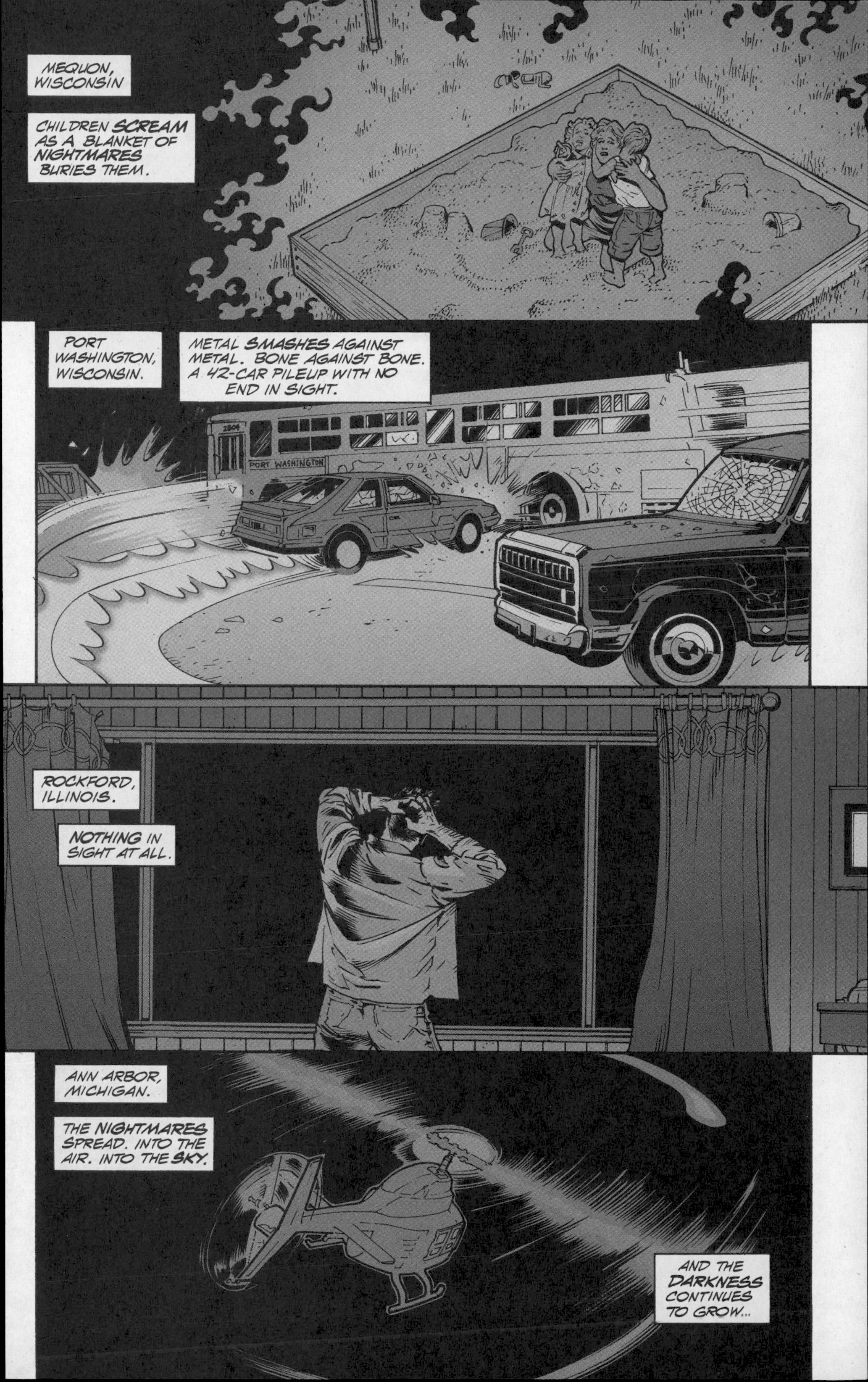
MEQUON, WISCONSIN
CHILDREN SCREAM AS A BLANKET OF NIGHTMARES BURIES THEM.
PORT WASHINGTON, WISCONSIN.
METAL SMASHES AGAINST METAL. BONE AGAINST BONE. A 42-CAR PILEUP WITH NO END IN SIGHT.
PORT WASHINGTON
ROCKFORD, ILLINOIS.
NOTHING IN SIGHT AT ALL.
ANN ARBOR, MICHIGAN.
THE NIGHTMARES SPREAD. INTO THE AIR. INTO THE SKY.
AND THE DARKNESS CONTINUES TO GROW...

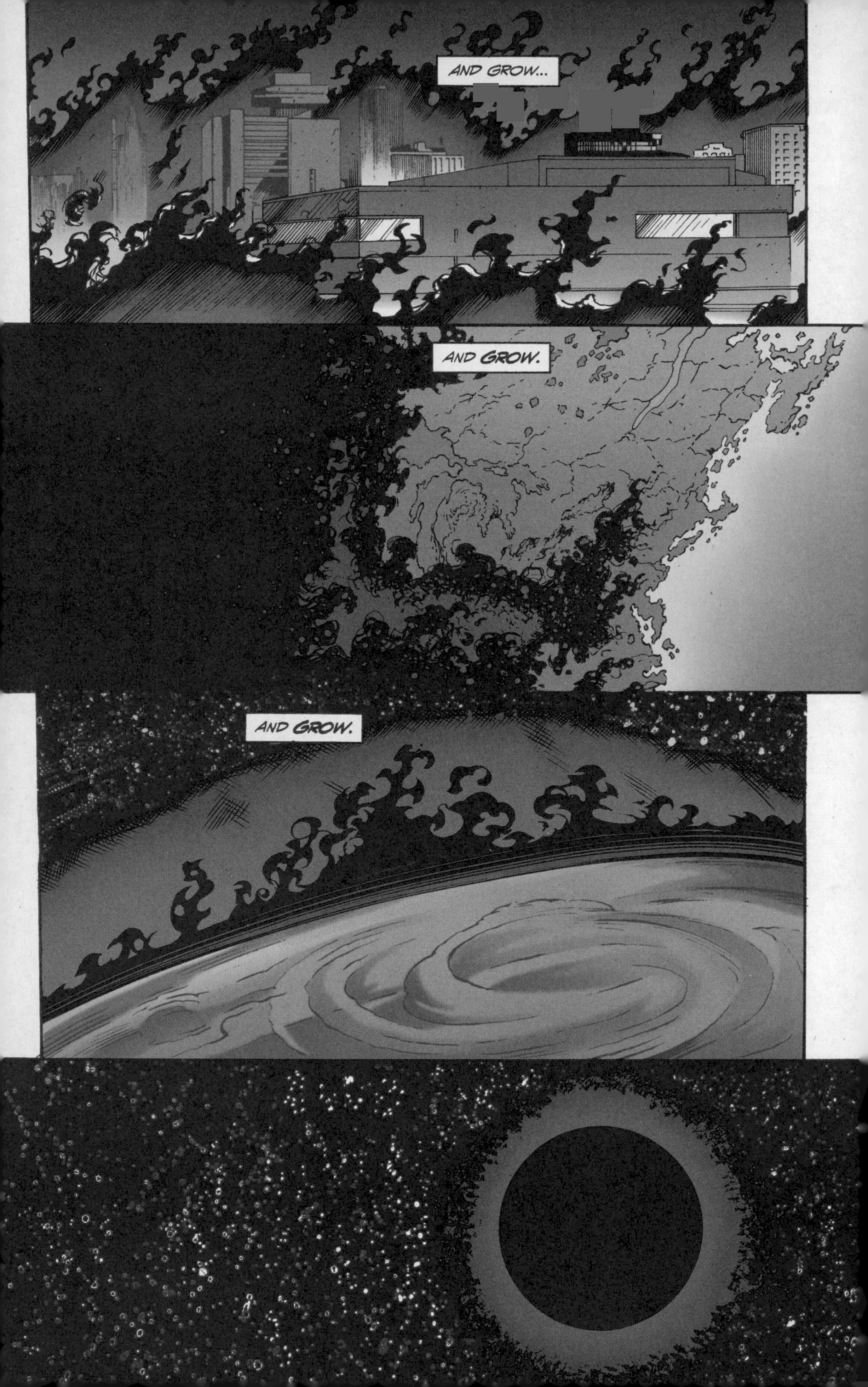
AND GROW...
AND GROW.
AND GROW.

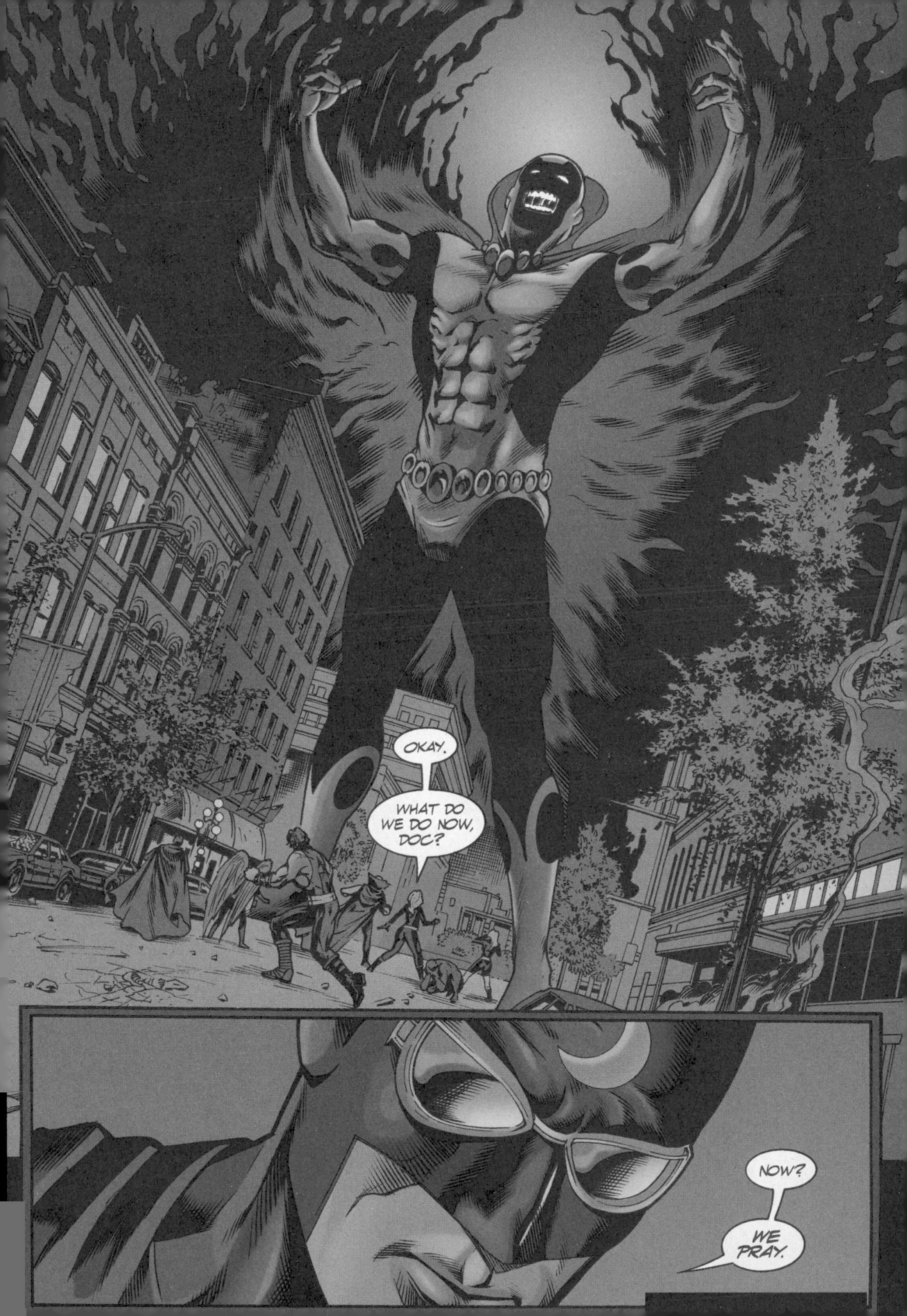
OKAY.
WHAT DO WE DO NOW, DOC?
NOW?
WE PRAY.

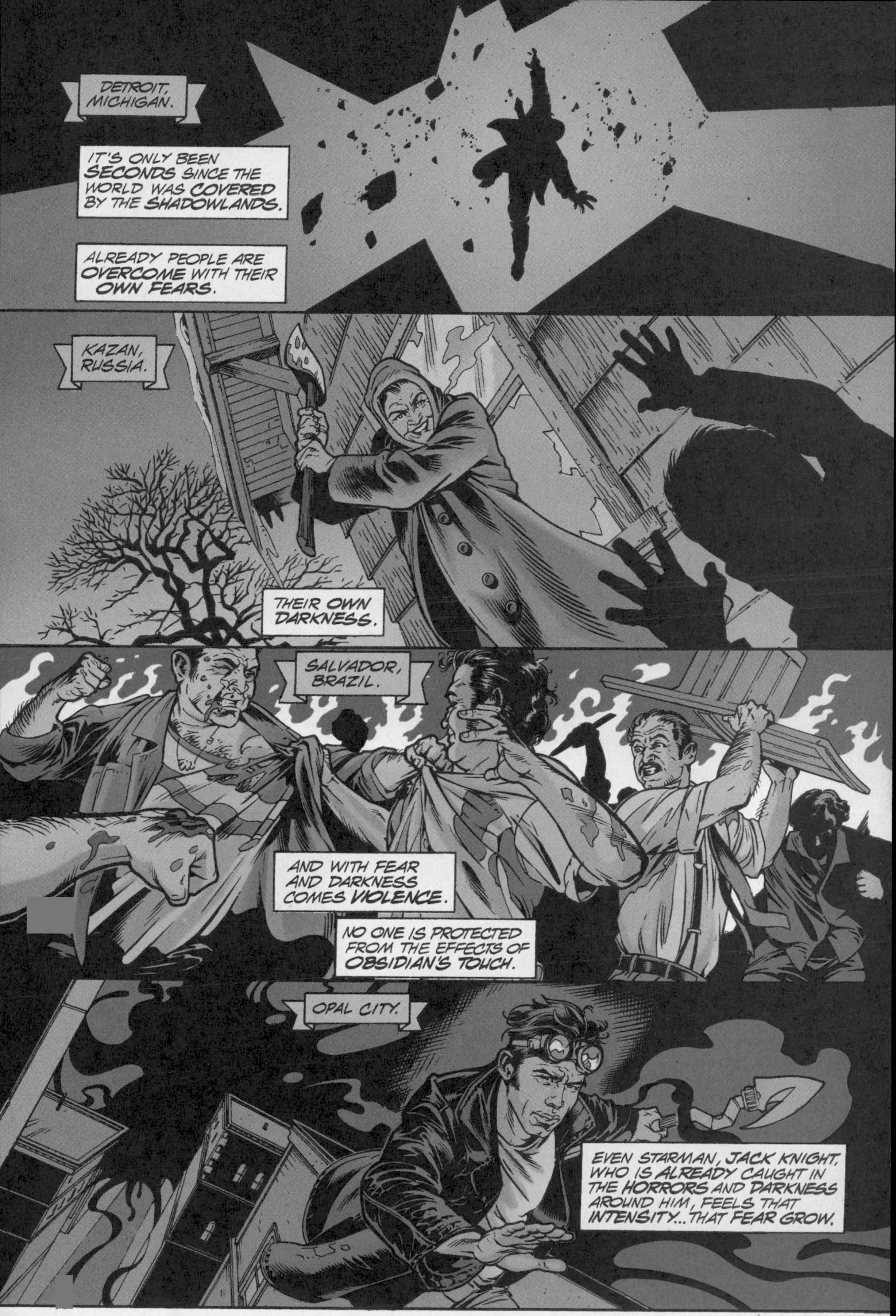
DETROIT, MICHIGAN.
IT'S ONLY BEEN SECONDS SINCE THE WORLD WAS COVERED BY THE SHADOWLANDS.
ALREADY PEOPLE ARE OVERCOME WITH THEIR OWN FEARS.
KAZAN, RUSSIA.
THEIR OWN DARKNESS.
SALVADOR, BRAZIL.
AND WITH FEAR AND DARKNESS COMES VIOLENCE.
NO ONE IS PROTECTED FROM THE EFFECTS OF OBSIDIAN'S TOUCH.
OPAL CITY.
EVEN STARMAN, JACK KNIGHT, WHO IS ALREADY CAUGHT IN THE HORRORS AND DARKNESS AROUND HIM, FEELS THAT INTENSITY... THAT FEAR GROW.

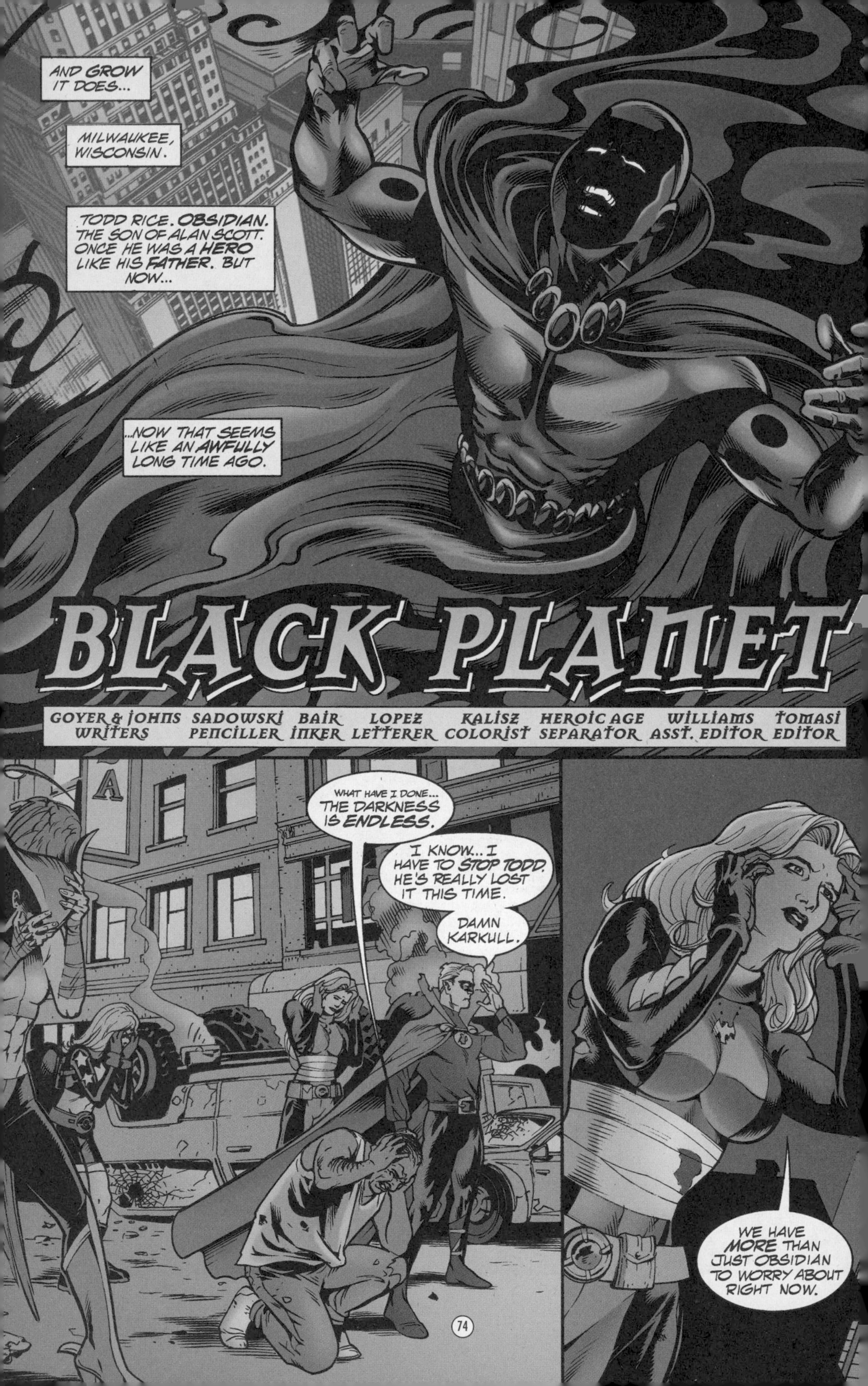
AND GROW IT DOES...
MILWAUKEE, WISCONSIN.
TODD RICE. OBSIDIAN. THE SON OF ALAN SCOTT. ONCE HE WAS A HERO LIKE HIS FATHER. BUT NOW...
...NOW THAT SEEMS LIKE AN AWFULLY LONG TIME AGO.
BLACK PLANET
GOYER & JOHNS WRITERS
SADOWSKI PENCILLER
BAIR INKER
LOPEZ LETTERER
KALISZ COLORIST
HEROIC AGE SEPARATOR
WILLIAMS ASST. EDITOR
TOMASI EDITOR
WHAT HAVE I DONE... THE DARKNESS IS ENDLESS.
I KNOW... I HAVE TO STOP TODD. HE'S REALLY LOST IT THIS TIME.
DAMN KARKULL.
WE HAVE MORE THAN JUST OBSIDIAN TO WORRY ABOUT RIGHT NOW.

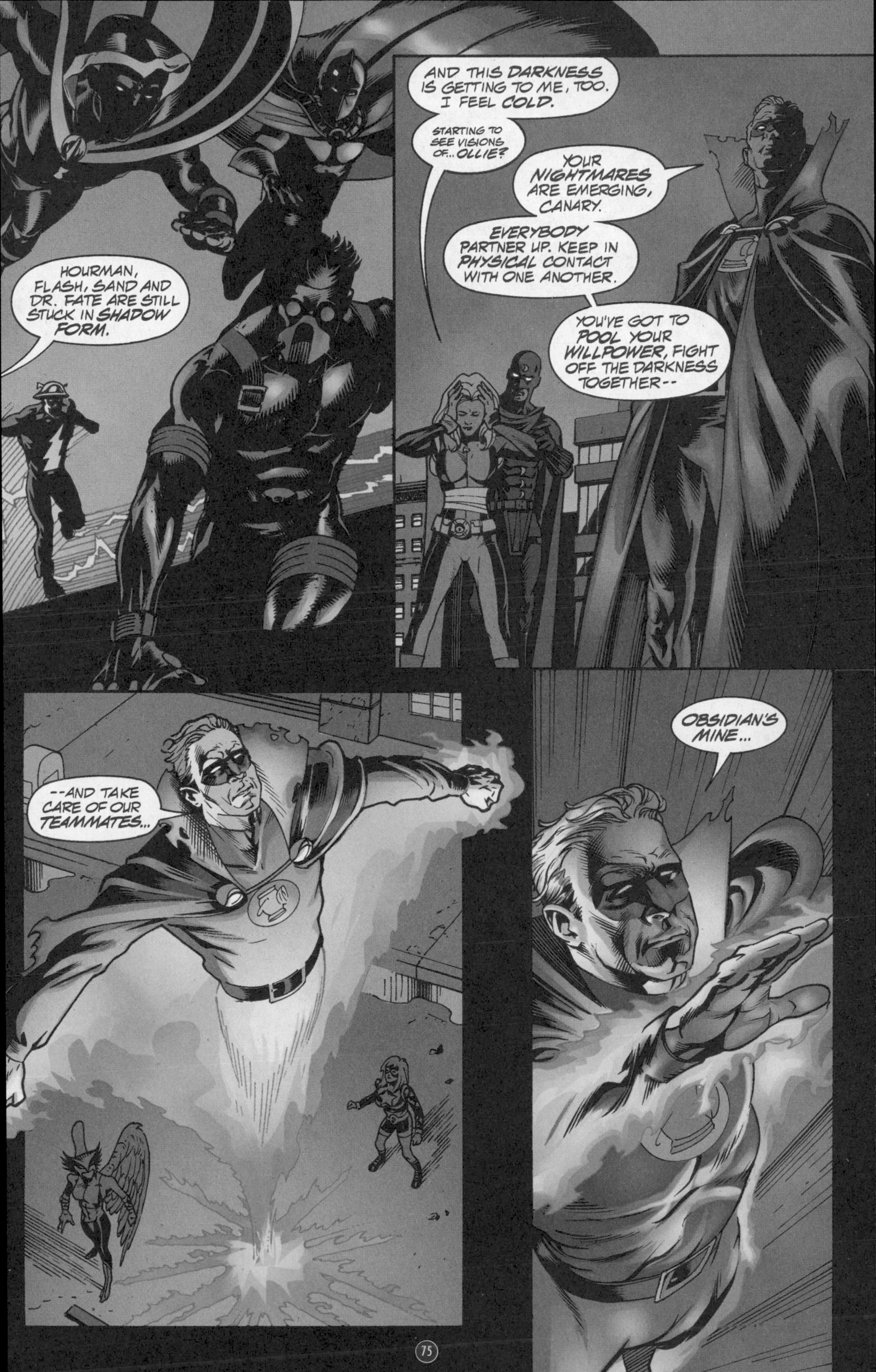
HOURMAN, FLASH, SAND AND DR. FATE ARE STILL STUCK IN SHADOW FORM.
AND THIS DARKNESS IS GETTING TO ME, TOO. I FEEL COLD.
STARTING TO SEE VISIONS OF... OLLIE?
YOUR NIGHTMARES ARE EMERGING, CANARY.
EVERYBODY PARTNER UP. KEEP IN PHYSICAL CONTACT WITH ONE ANOTHER.
YOU'VE GOT TO POOL YOUR WILLPOWER, FIGHT OFF THE DARKNESS TOGETHER--
--AND TAKE CARE OF OUR TEAMMATES...
OBSIDIAN'S MINE...

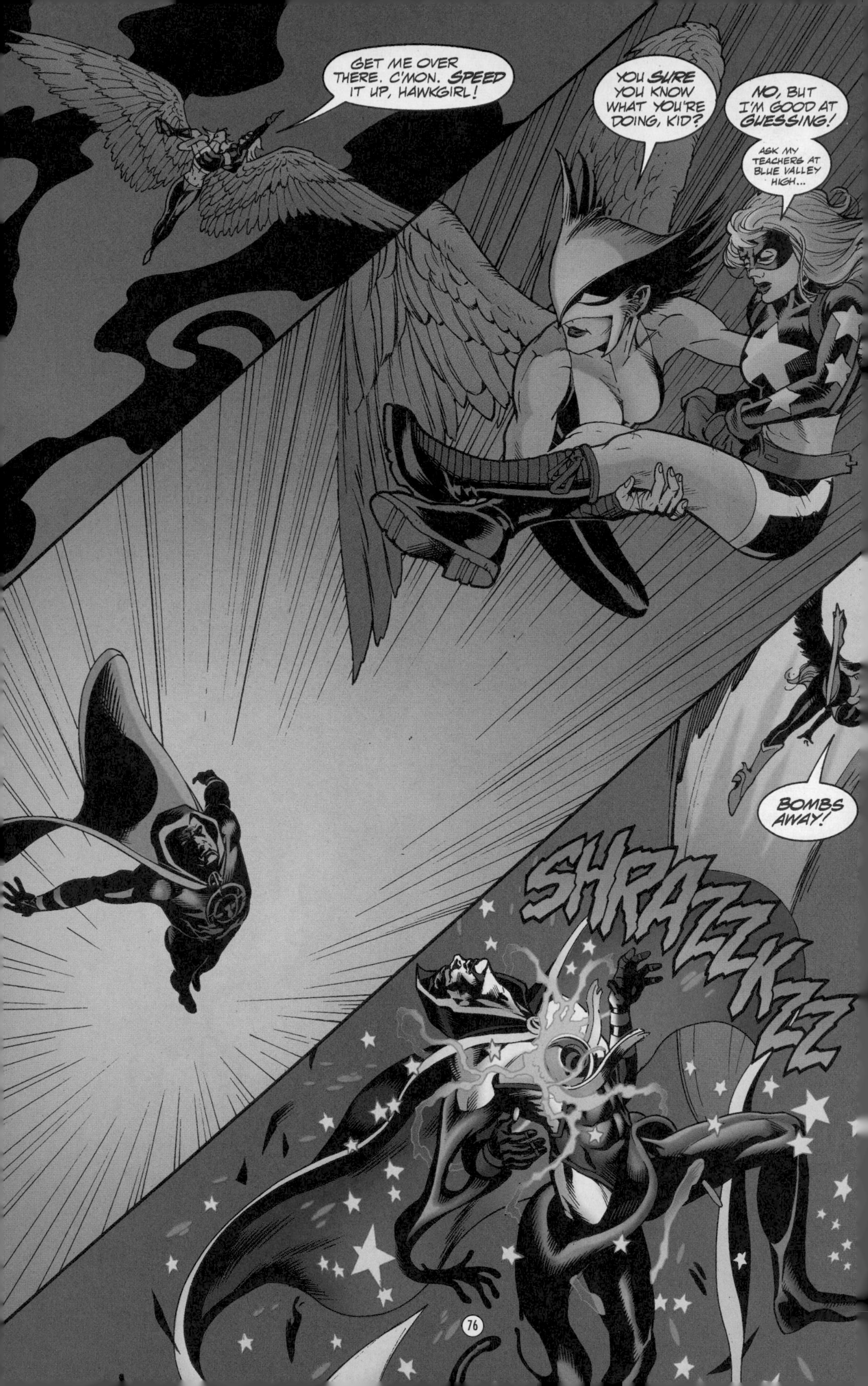
GET ME OVER THERE. C'MON. SPEED IT UP, HAWKGIRL!
YOU SURE YOU KNOW WHAT YOU'RE DOING, KID?
NO, BUT I'M GOOD AT GUESSING!
ASK MY TEACHERS AT BLUE VALLEY HIGH...
BOMBS AWAY!
SHRAZZKZZ

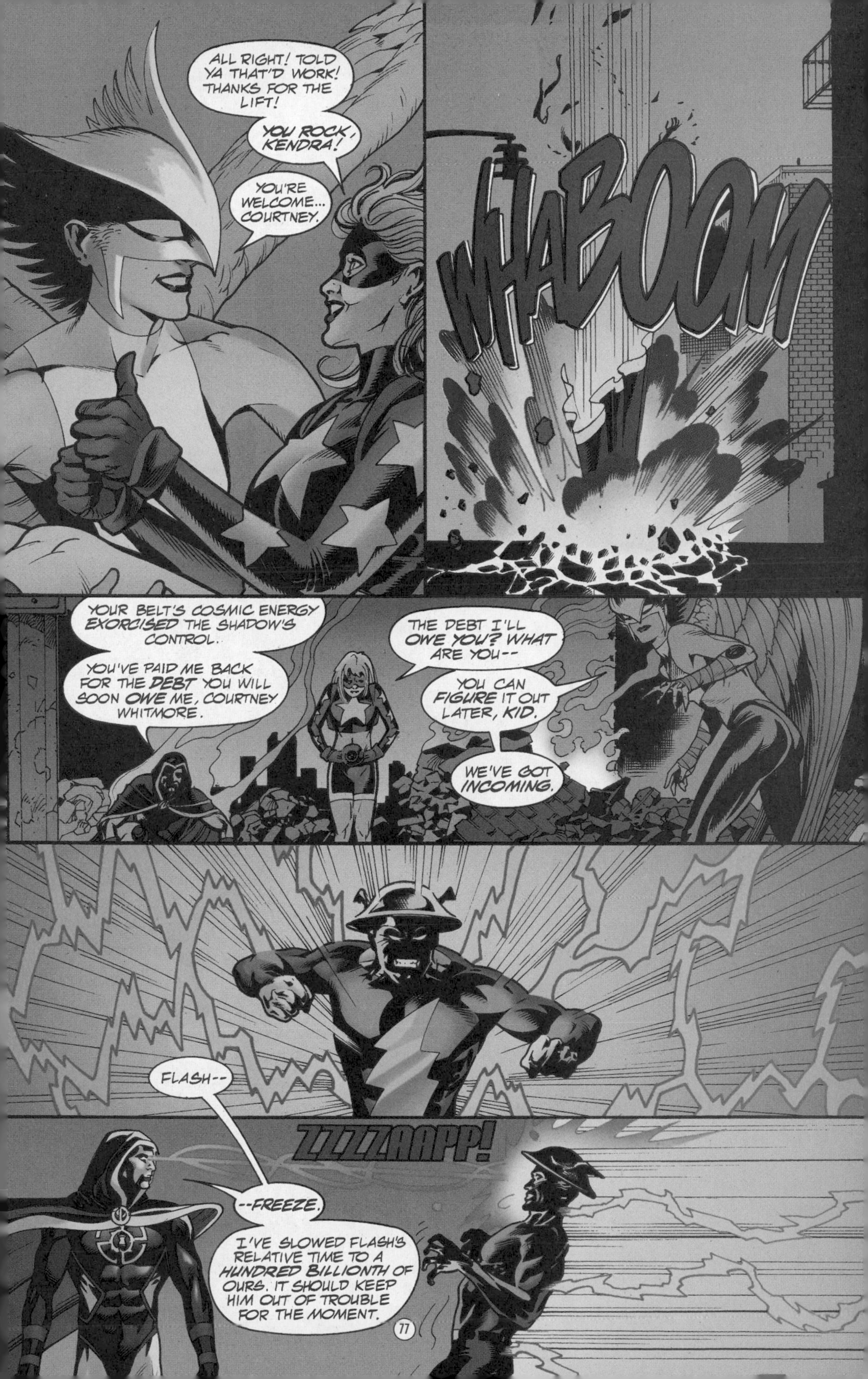
ALL RIGHT! TOLD YA THAT'D WORK! THANKS FOR THE LIFT!
YOU ROCK, KENDRA!
YOU'RE WELCOME... COURTNEY.
WHABOOM
YOUR BELT'S COSMIC ENERGY EXORCISED THE SHADOW'S CONTROL.
YOU'VE PAID ME BACK FOR THE DEBT YOU WILL SOON OWE ME, COURTNEY WHITMORE.
THE DEBT I'LL OWE YOU? WHAT ARE YOU--
YOU CAN FIGURE IT OUT LATER, KID.
WE'VE GOT INCOMING.
FLASH--
ZZZZZAAPP!
--FREEZE.
I'VE SLOWED FLASH'S RELATIVE TIME TO A HUNDRED BILLIONTH OF OURS. IT SHOULD KEEP HIM OUT OF TROUBLE FOR THE MOMENT.

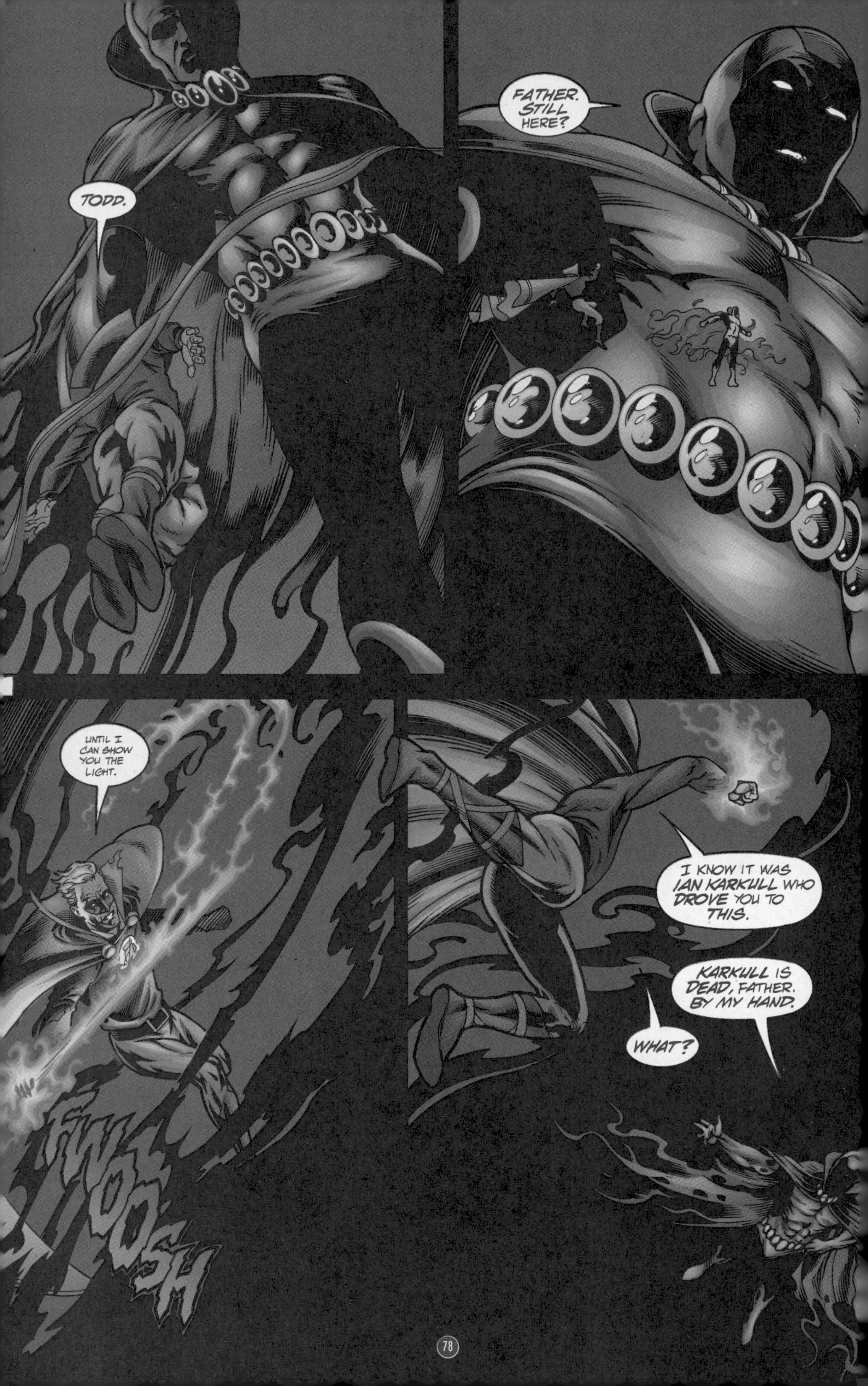
TODD.
FATHER. STILL HERE?
UNTIL I CAN SHOW YOU THE LIGHT.
FWOOSH
I KNOW IT WAS IAN KARKULL WHO DROVE YOU TO THIS.
KARKULL IS DEAD, FATHER. BY MY HAND.
WHAT?

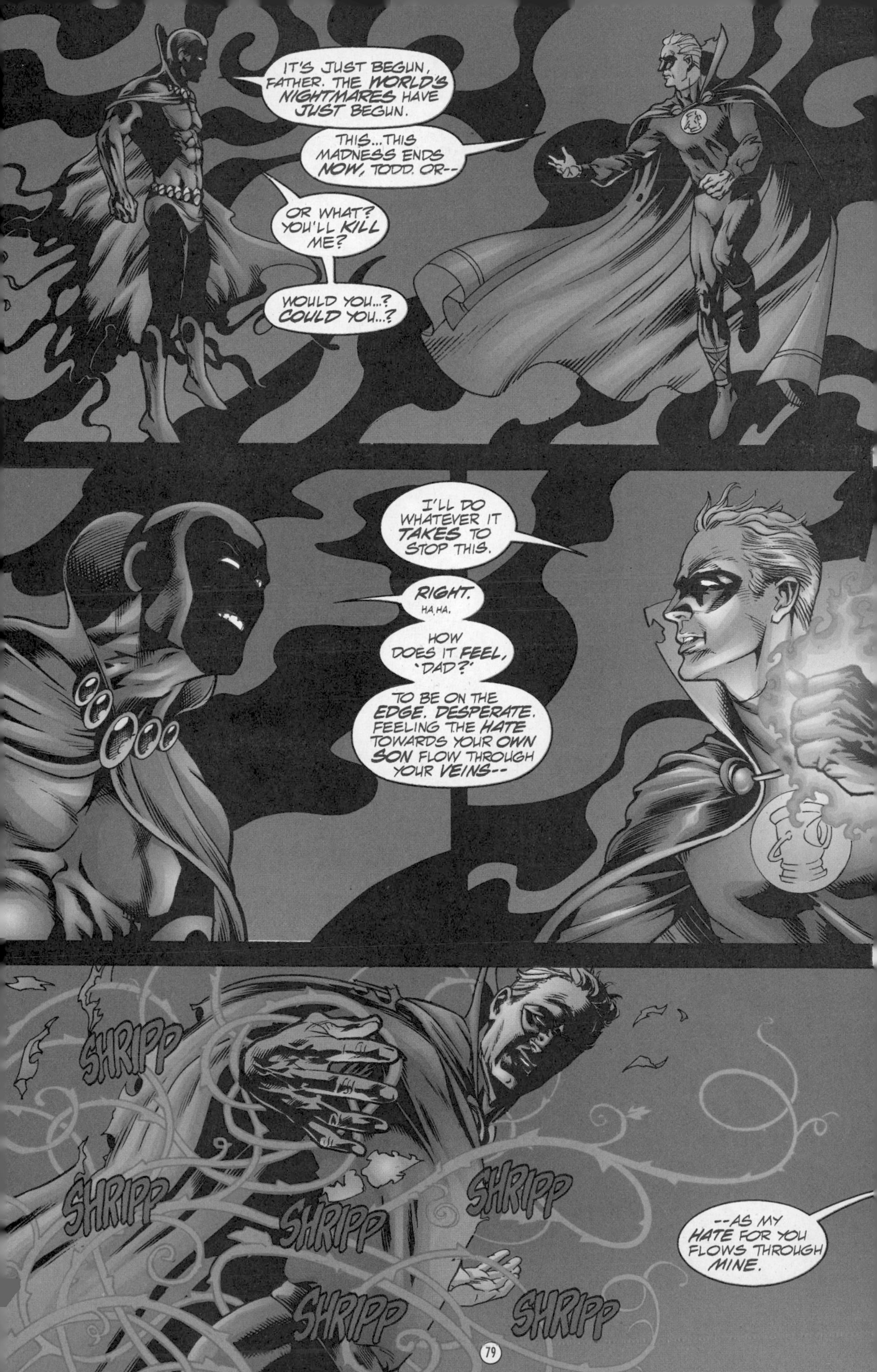
IT'S JUST BEGUN, FATHER. THE WORLD'S NIGHTMARES HAVE JUST BEGUN.
THIS...THIS MADNESS ENDS NOW, TODD. OR--
OR WHAT? YOU'LL KILL ME?
WOULD YOU...? COULD YOU...?
I'LL DO WHATEVER IT TAKES TO STOP THIS.
RIGHT. HA HA.
HOW DOES IT FEEL, 'DAD?'
TO BE ON THE EDGE. DESPERATE. FEELING THE HATE TOWARDS YOUR OWN SON FLOW THROUGH YOUR VEINS--
SHRIPP
SHRIPP
SHRIPP
SHRIPP
SHRIPP
SHRIPP
--AS MY HATE FOR YOU FLOWS THROUGH MINE.

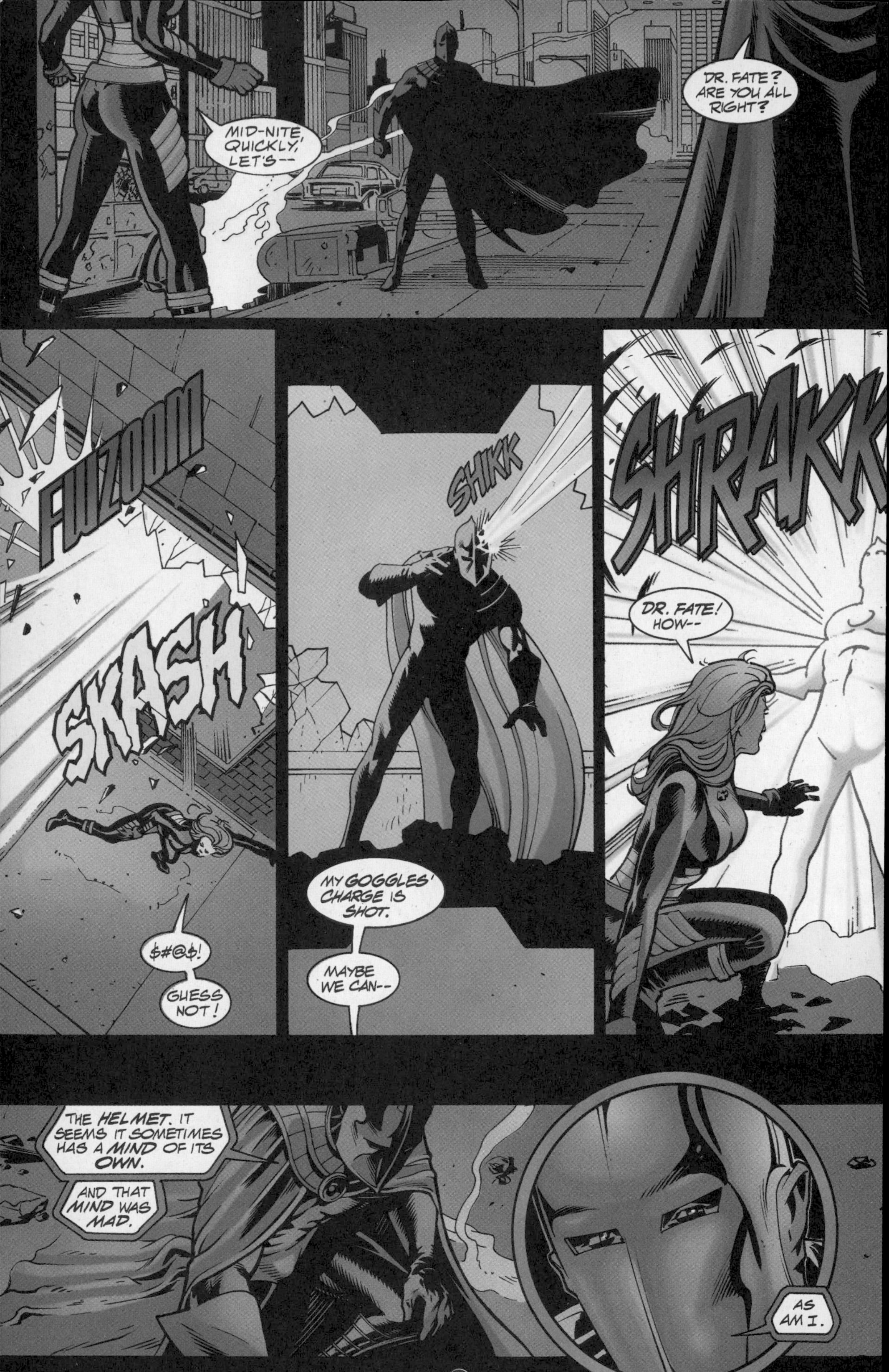

MID-NITE QUICKLY, LET'S--
DR. FATE? ARE YOU ALL RIGHT?
FWZOOM
SKASH
$#@$!
GUESS NOT!
SHIKK
MY GOGGLES' CHARGE IS SHOT.
MAYBE WE CAN--
SHRAKK
DR. FATE! HOW--
THE HELMET. IT SEEMS IT SOMETIMES HAS A MIND OF ITS OWN.
AND THAT MIND WAS MAD.
AS AM I.

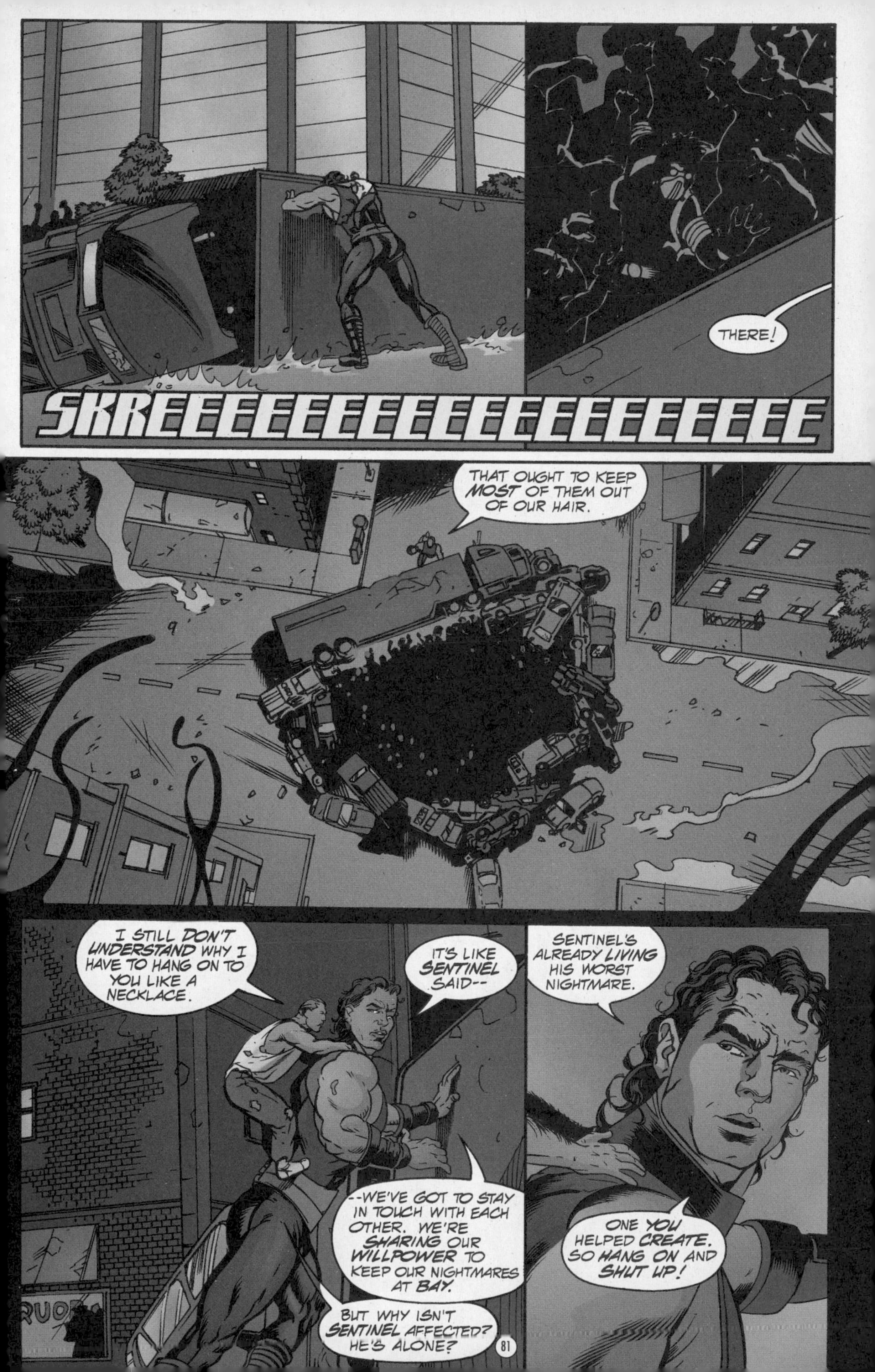
THERE!
SKREEEEEEEEEEEEEEEEEEEEEE
THAT OUGHT TO KEEP MOST OF THEM OUT OF OUR HAIR.
I STILL DON'T UNDERSTAND WHY I HAVE TO HANG ON TO YOU LIKE A NECKLACE.
IT'S LIKE SENTINEL SAID--
--WE'VE GOT TO STAY IN TOUCH WITH EACH OTHER. WE'RE SHARING OUR WILLPOWER TO KEEP OUR NIGHTMARES AT BAY.
BUT WHY ISN'T SENTINEL AFFECTED? HE'S ALONE?
SENTINEL'S ALREADY LIVING HIS WORST NIGHTMARE.
ONE YOU HELPED CREATE. SO HANG ON AND SHUT UP!

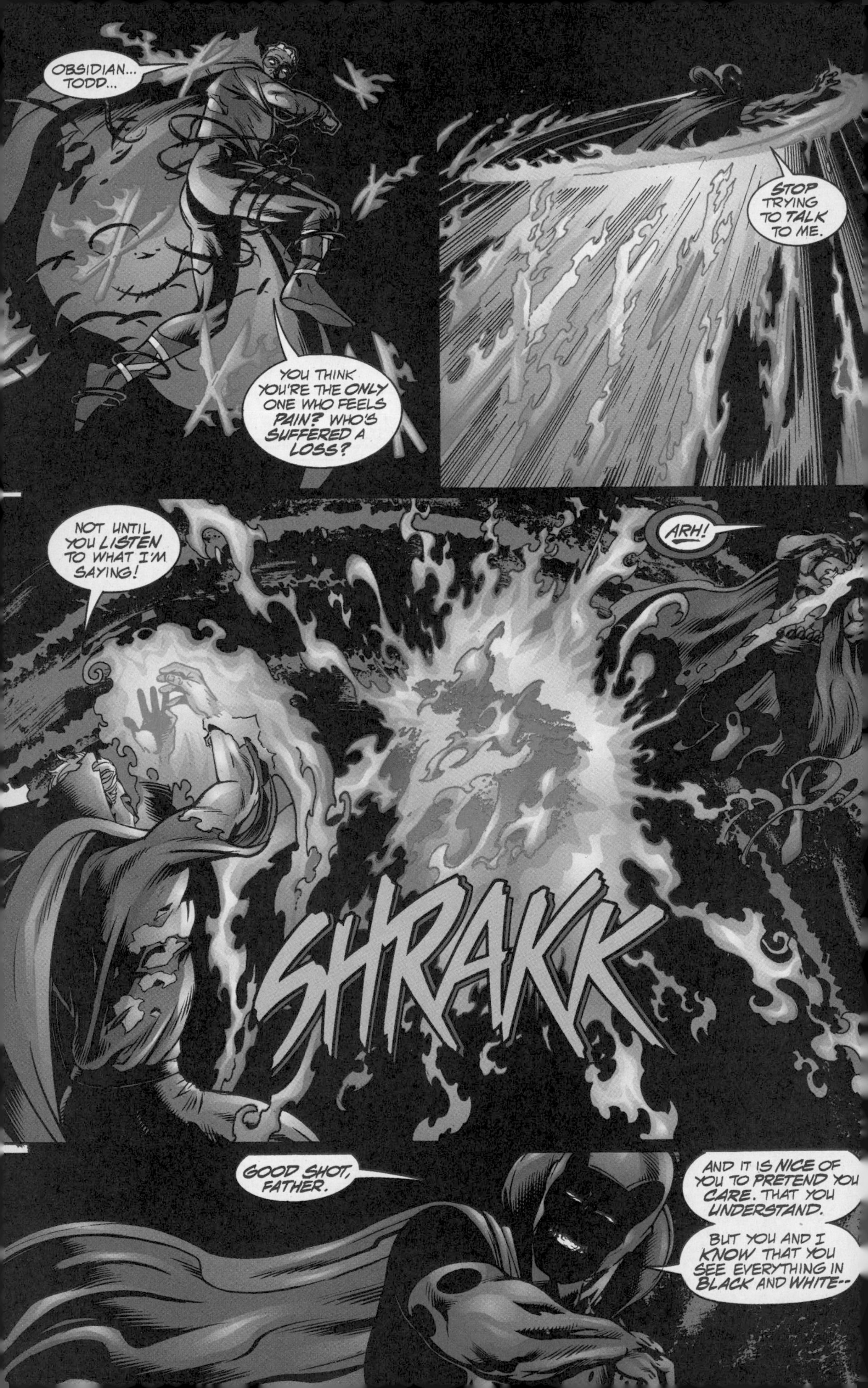
OBSIDIAN... TODD...
YOU THINK YOU'RE THE ONLY ONE WHO FEELS PAIN? WHO'S SUFFERED A LOSS?
STOP TRYING TO TALK TO ME.
NOT UNTIL YOU LISTEN TO WHAT I'M SAYING!
ARH!
SHRAKK
GOOD SHOT, FATHER.
AND IT IS NICE OF YOU TO PRETEND YOU CARE. THAT YOU UNDERSTAND.
BUT YOU AND I KNOW THAT YOU SEE EVERYTHING IN BLACK AND WHITE--

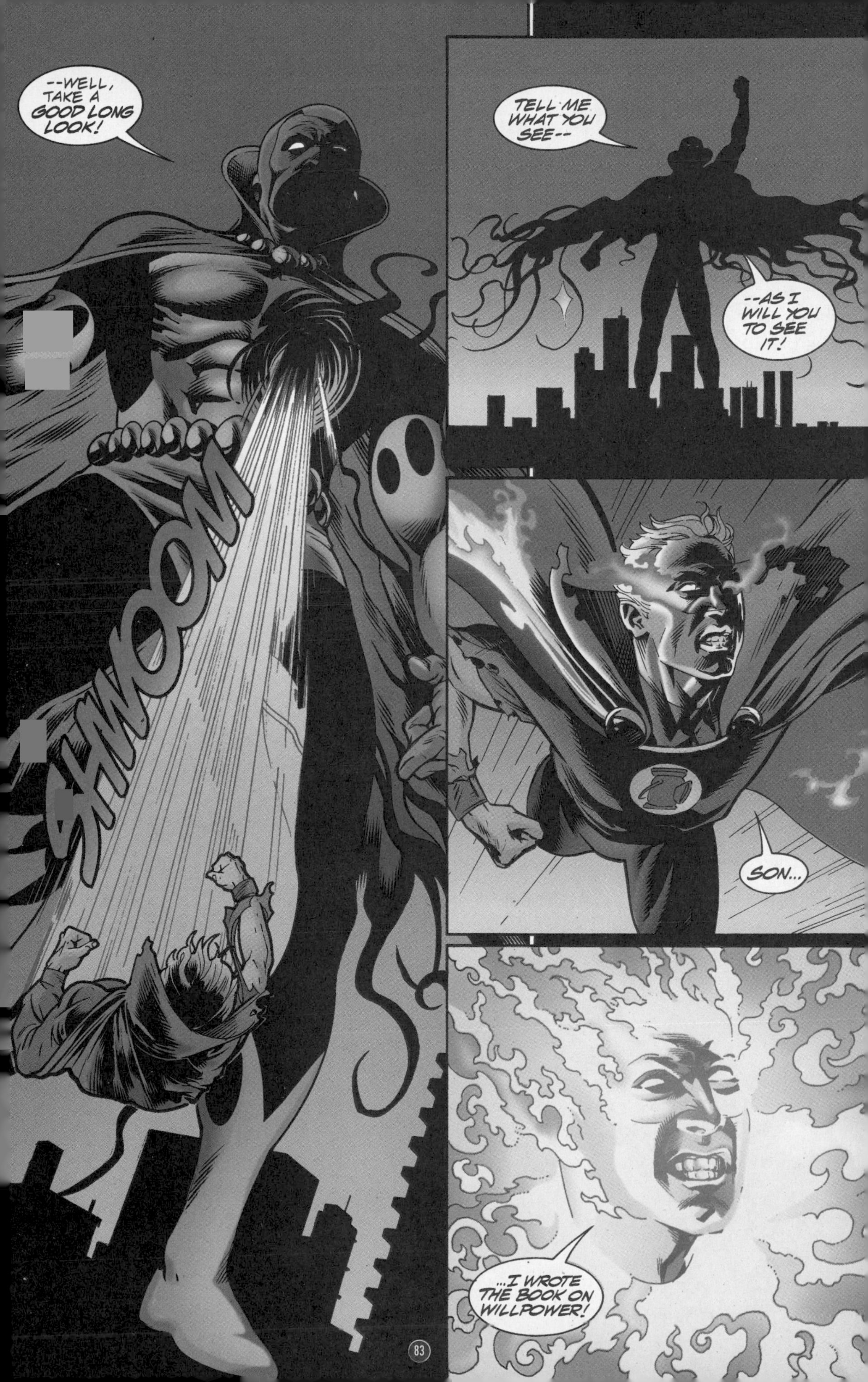
--WELL, TAKE A GOOD LONG LOOK!
SHWOOM
TELL ME WHAT YOU SEE--
--AS I WILL YOU TO SEE IT!
SON...
...I WROTE THE BOOK ON WILLPOWER!

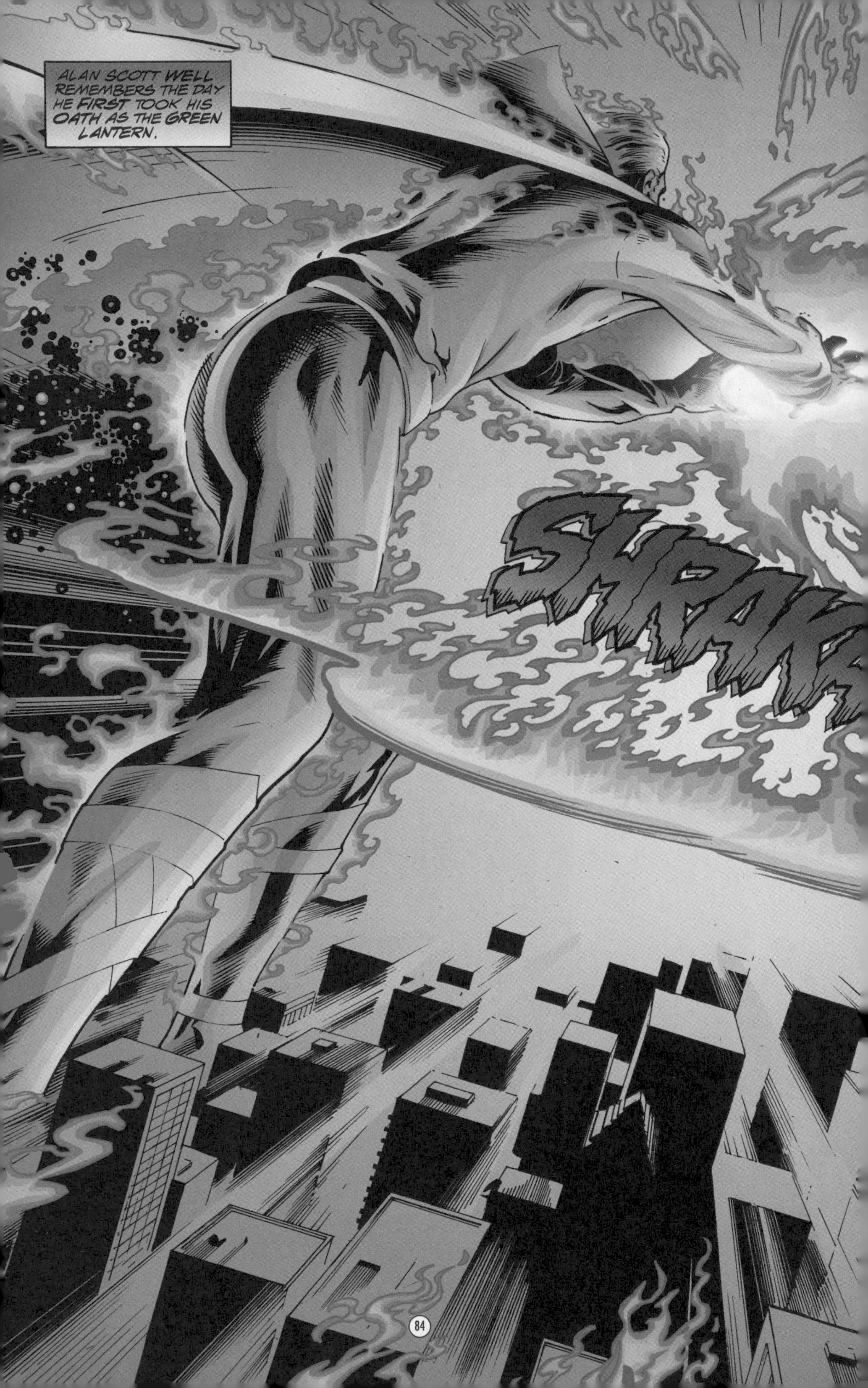
ALAN SCOTT WELL REMEMBERS THE DAY HE FIRST TOOK HIS OATH AS THE GREEN LANTERN.

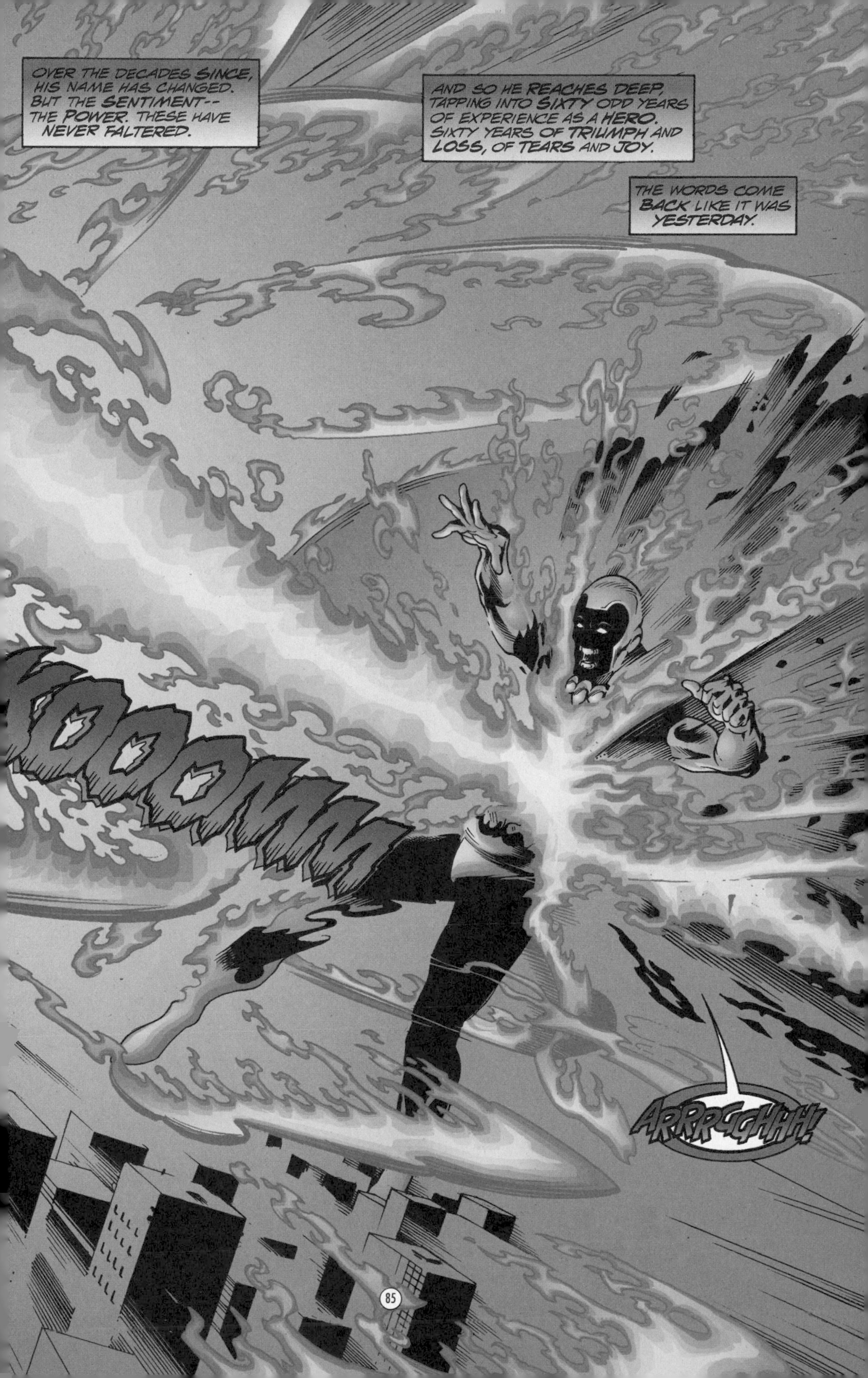
OVER THE DECADES SINCE, HIS NAME HAS CHANGED. BUT THE SENTIMENT-- THE POWER. THESE HAVE NEVER FALTERED.
AND SO HE REACHES DEEP, TAPPING INTO SIXTY ODD YEARS OF EXPERIENCE AS A HERO. SIXTY YEARS OF TRIUMPH AND LOSS, OF TEARS AND JOY.
THE WORDS COME BACK LIKE IT WAS YESTERDAY.
KOOOOMM
ARRRGGHHH!

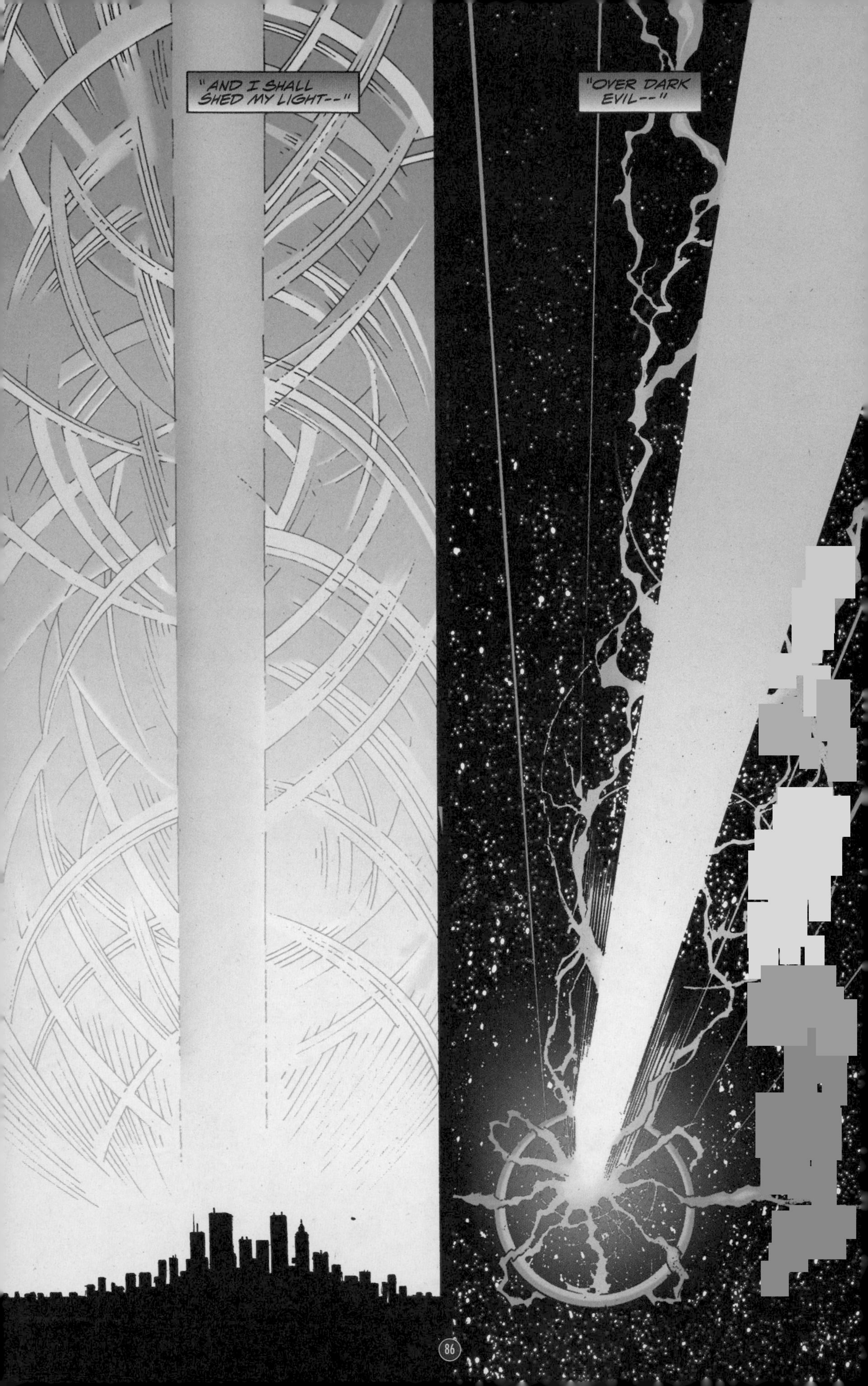
"AND I SHALL SHED MY LIGHT--"
"OVER DARK EVIL--"

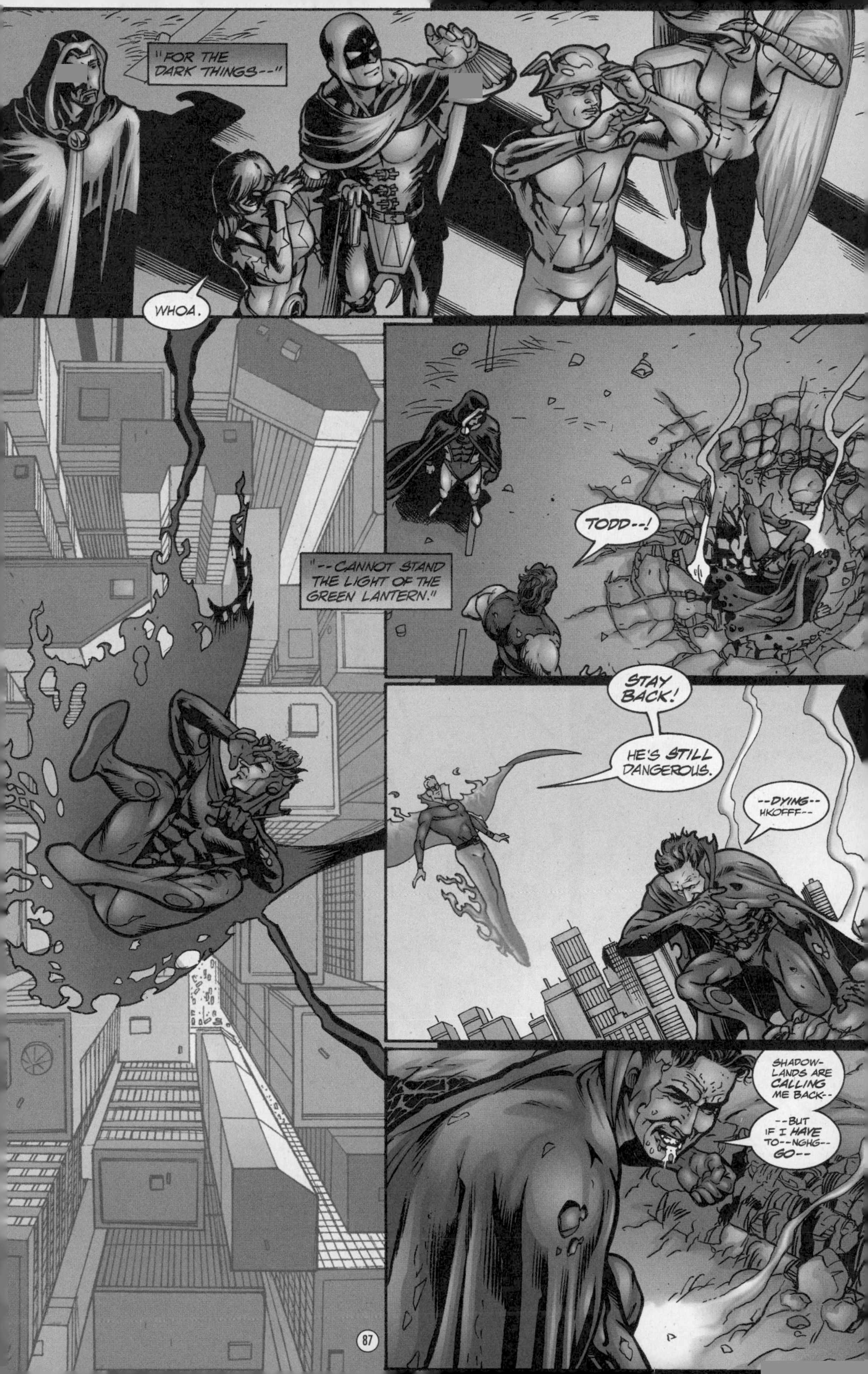
"FOR THE DARK THINGS--"
WHOA.
"--CANNOT STAND THE LIGHT OF THE GREEN LANTERN."
TODD--!
STAY BACK!
HE'S STILL DANGEROUS.
--DYING-- HKOFFF--
SHADOW-LANDS ARE CALLING ME BACK--
--BUT IF I HAVE TO--NGHG--GO--

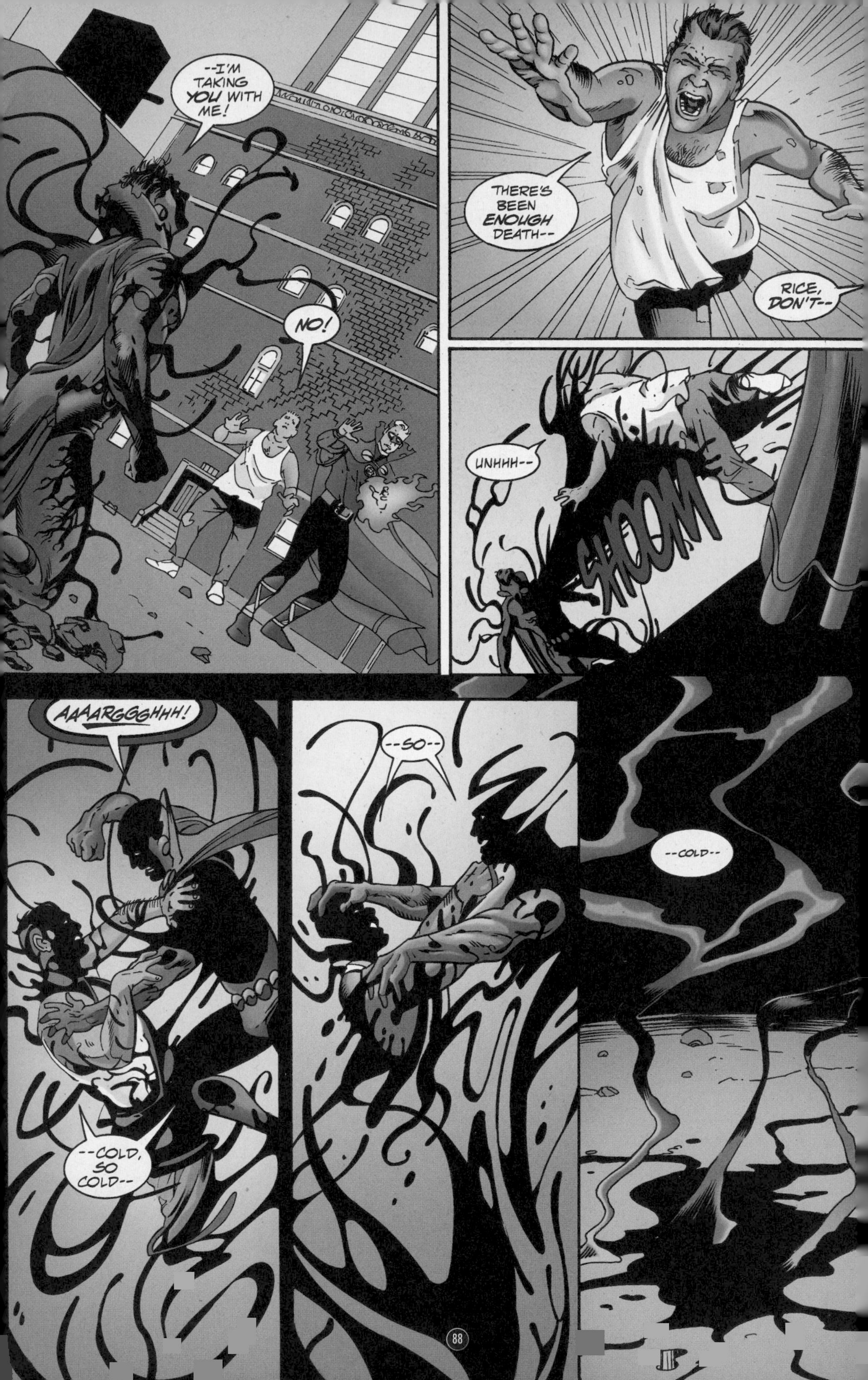
--I'M TAKING YOU WITH ME!
NO!
THERE'S BEEN ENOUGH DEATH--
RICE, DON'T--
UNHHH--
SHOOM
AAAARGGGHHH!
--COLD, SO COLD--
--SO--
--COLD--

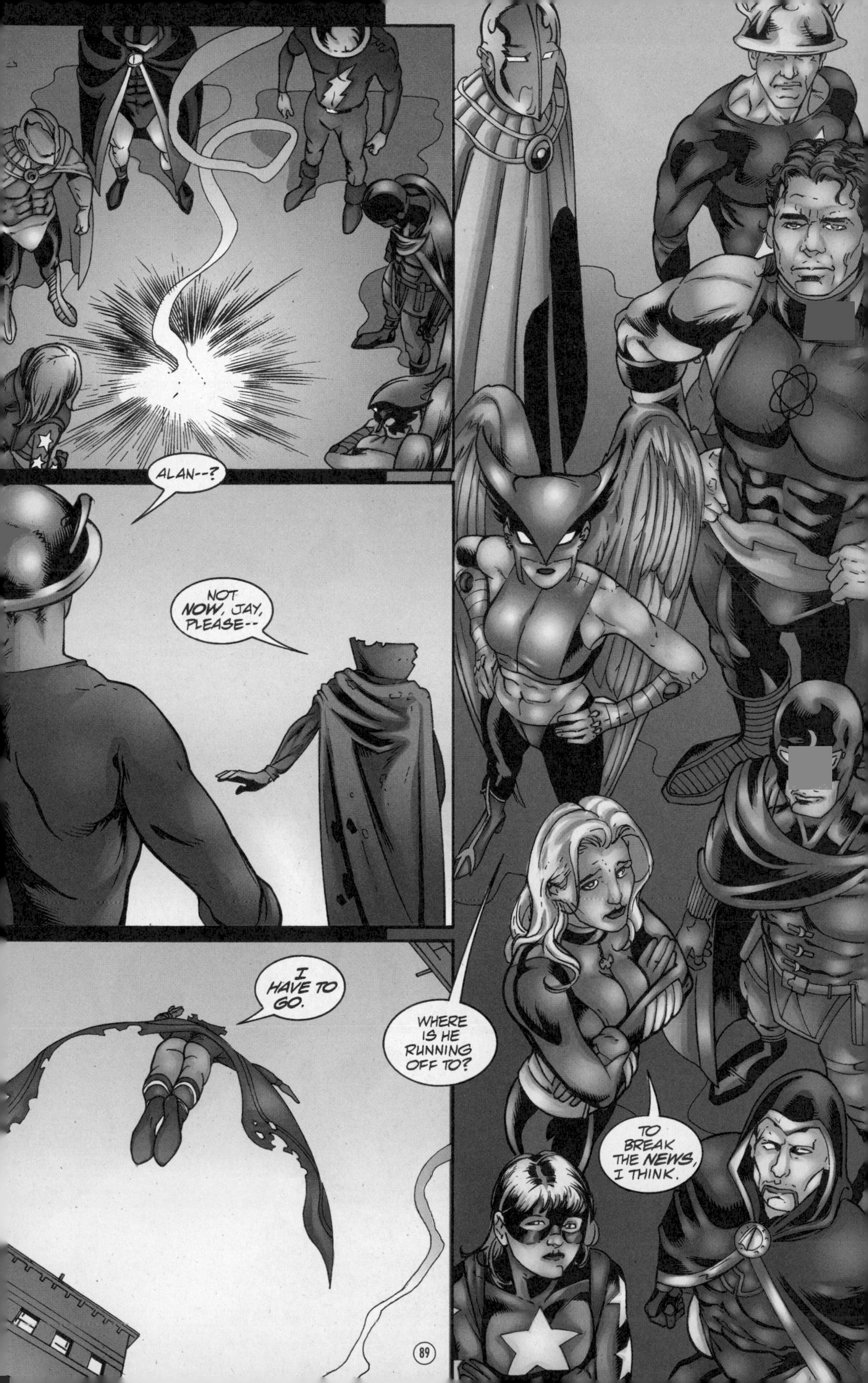
ALAN--?
NOT NOW, JAY, PLEASE--
I HAVE TO GO.
WHERE IS HE RUNNING OFF TO?
TO BREAK THE NEWS, I THINK.

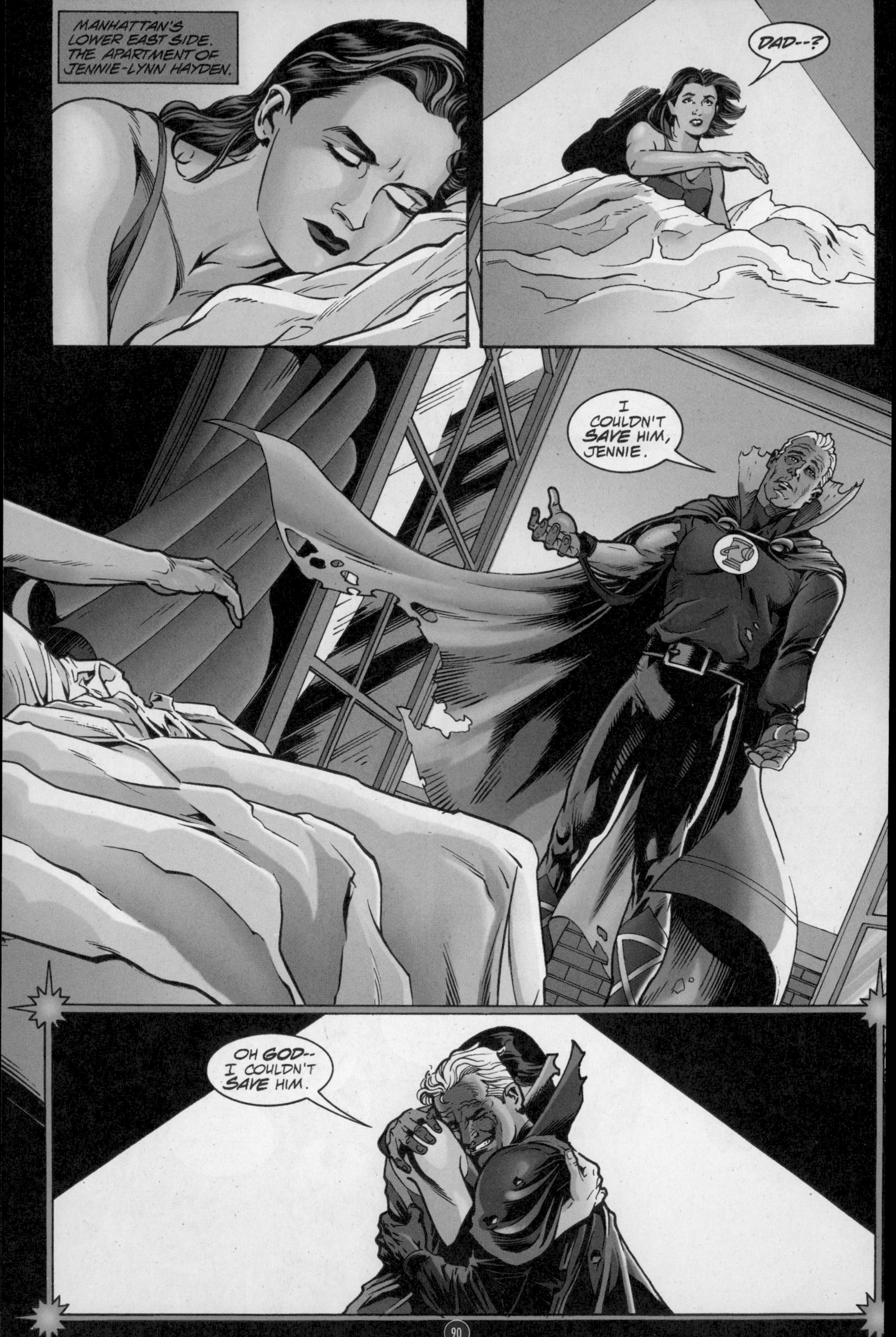
MANHATTAN'S LOWER EAST SIDE. THE APARTMENT OF JENNIE-LYNN HAYDEN.
DAD--?
I COULDN'T SAVE HIM, JENNIE.
OH GOD-- I COULDN'T SAVE HIM.

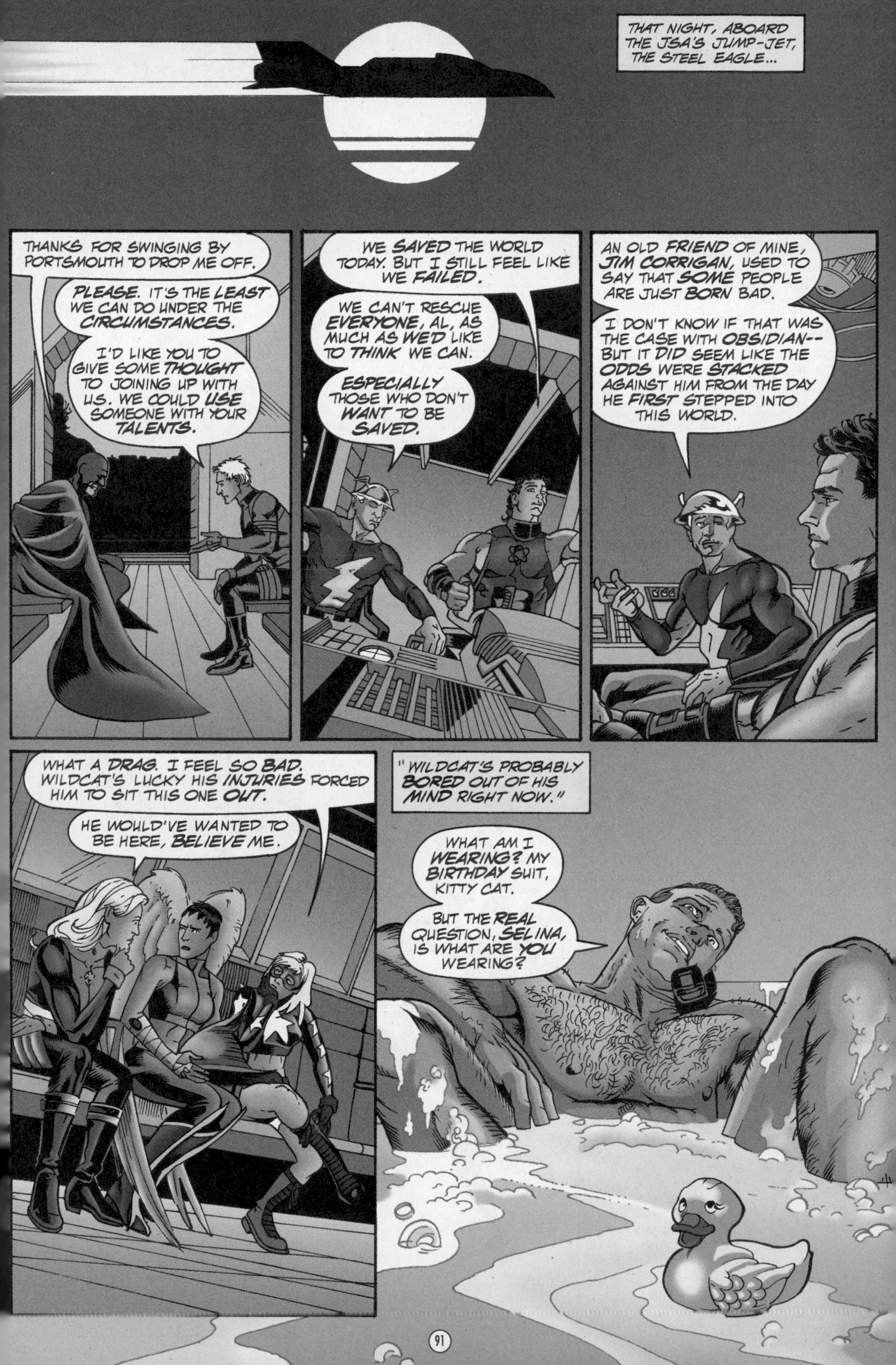
THAT NIGHT, ABOARD THE JSA'S JUMP-JET, THE STEEL EAGLE...
THANKS FOR SWINGING BY PORTSMOUTH TO DROP ME OFF.
PLEASE. IT'S THE LEAST WE CAN DO UNDER THE CIRCUMSTANCES.
I'D LIKE YOU TO GIVE SOME THOUGHT TO JOINING UP WITH US. WE COULD USE SOMEONE WITH YOUR TALENTS.
WE SAVED THE WORLD TODAY. BUT I STILL FEEL LIKE WE FAILED.
WE CAN'T RESCUE EVERYONE, AL, AS MUCH AS WE'D LIKE TO THINK WE CAN.
ESPECIALLY THOSE WHO DON'T WANT TO BE SAVED.
AN OLD FRIEND OF MINE, JIM CORRIGAN, USED TO SAY THAT SOME PEOPLE ARE JUST BORN BAD.
I DON'T KNOW IF THAT WAS THE CASE WITH OBSIDIAN-- BUT IT DID SEEM LIKE THE ODDS WERE STACKED AGAINST HIM FROM THE DAY HE FIRST STEPPED INTO THIS WORLD.
WHAT A DRAG. I FEEL SO BAD. WILDCAT'S LUCKY HIS INJURIES FORCED HIM TO SIT THIS ONE OUT.
HE WOULD'VE WANTED TO BE HERE, BELIEVE ME.
"WILDCAT'S PROBABLY BORED OUT OF HIS MIND RIGHT NOW."
WHAT AM I WEARING? MY BIRTHDAY SUIT, KITTY CAT.
BUT THE REAL QUESTION, SELINA, IS WHAT ARE YOU WEARING?

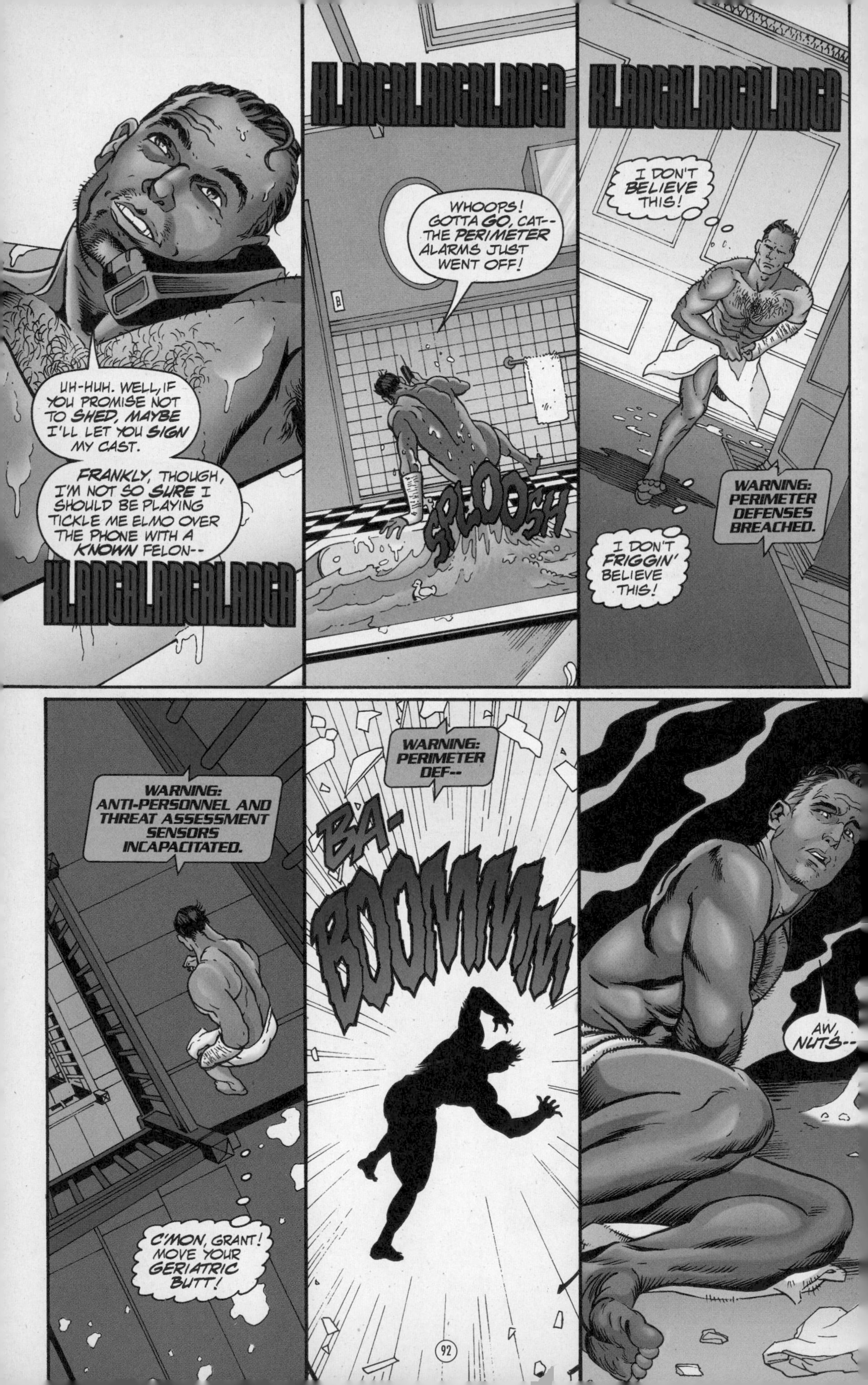
UH-HUH. WELL, IF YOU PROMISE NOT TO SHED, MAYBE I'LL LET YOU SIGN MY CAST.
FRANKLY, THOUGH, I'M NOT SO SURE I SHOULD BE PLAYING TICKLE ME ELMO OVER THE PHONE WITH A KNOWN FELON--
KLANGALANGALANGA
KLANGALANGALANGA
WHOOPS! GOTTA GO, CAT-- THE PERIMETER ALARMS JUST WENT OFF!
SPLOOSH
KLANGALANGALANGA
I DON'T BELIEVE THIS!
WARNING: PERIMETER DEFENSES BREACHED.
I DON'T FRIGGIN' BELIEVE THIS!
WARNING: ANTI-PERSONNEL AND THREAT ASSESSMENT SENSORS INCAPACITATED.
C'MON, GRANT! MOVE YOUR GERIATRIC BUTT!
WARNING: PERIMETER DEF--
BA-BOOMMM
AW, NUTS--

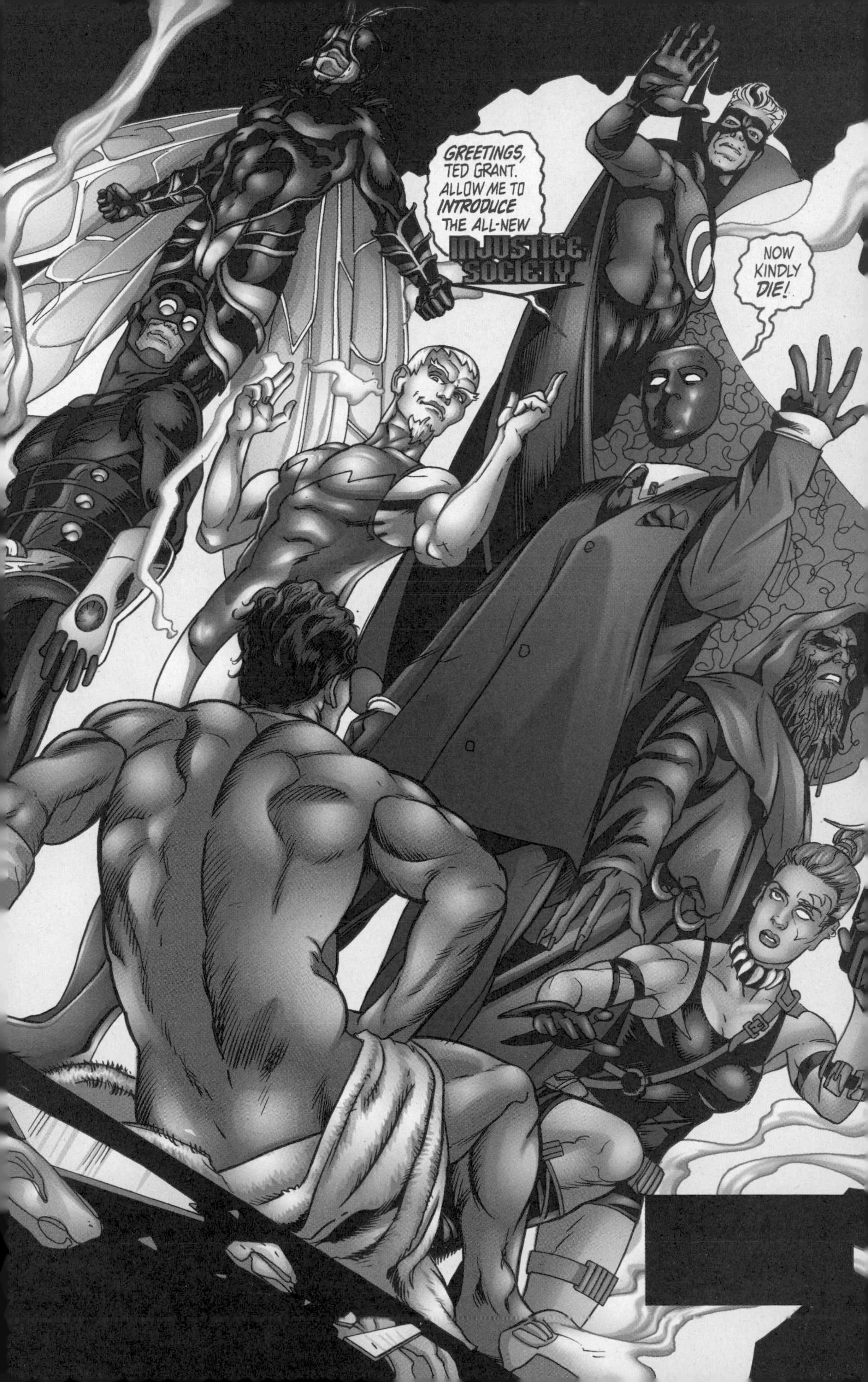
GREETINGS, TED GRANT. ALLOW ME TO INTRODUCE THE ALL-NEW
INJUSTICE SOCIETY
NOW KINDLY DIE!

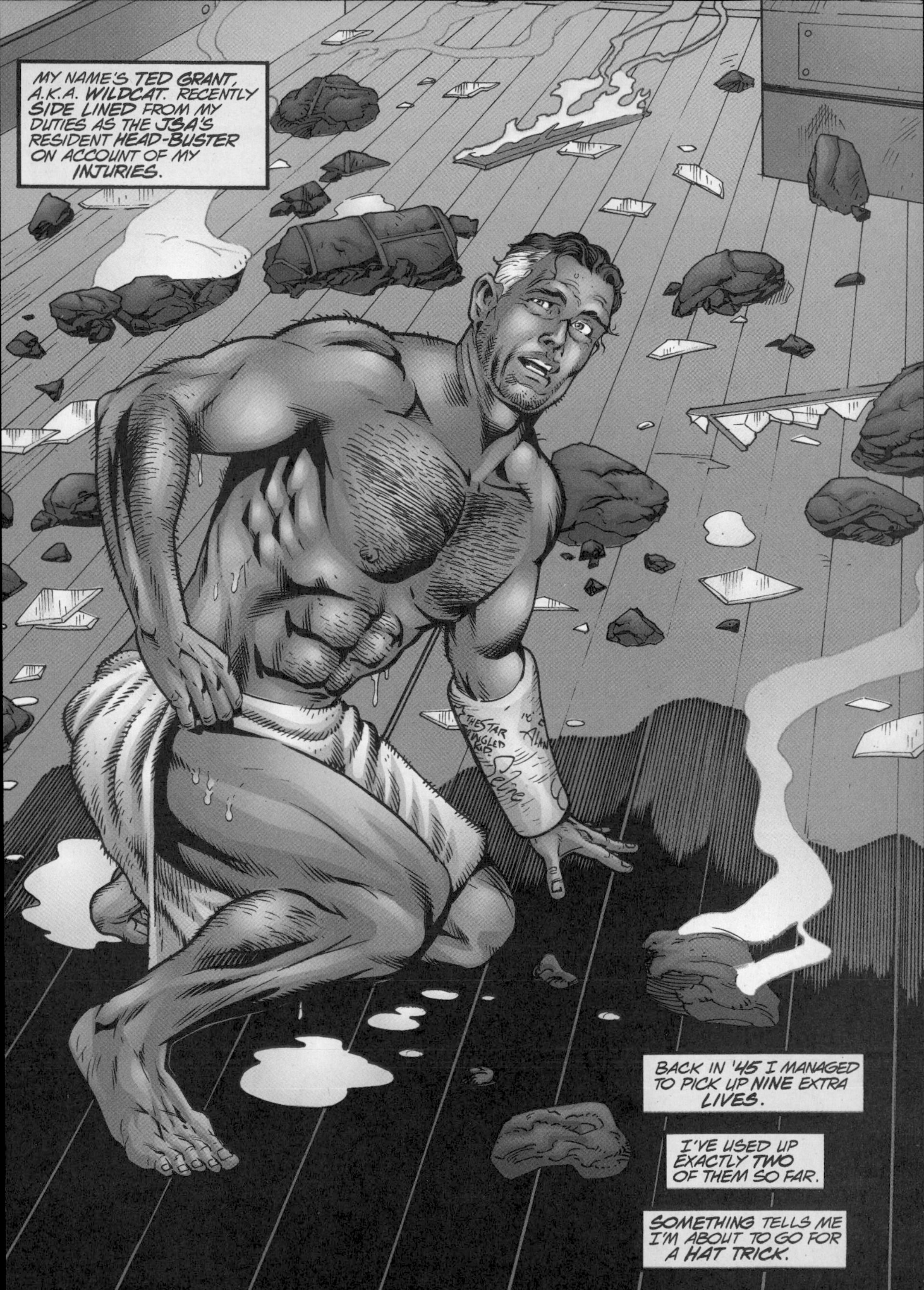
MY NAME'S TED GRANT, A.K.A. WILDCAT. RECENTLY SIDE LINED FROM MY DUTIES AS THE JSA'S RESIDENT HEAD-BUSTER ON ACCOUNT OF MY INJURIES.
BACK IN '45 I MANAGED TO PICK UP NINE EXTRA LIVES.
I'VE USED UP EXACTLY TWO OF THEM SO FAR.
SOMETHING TELLS ME I'M ABOUT TO GO FOR A HAT TRICK.

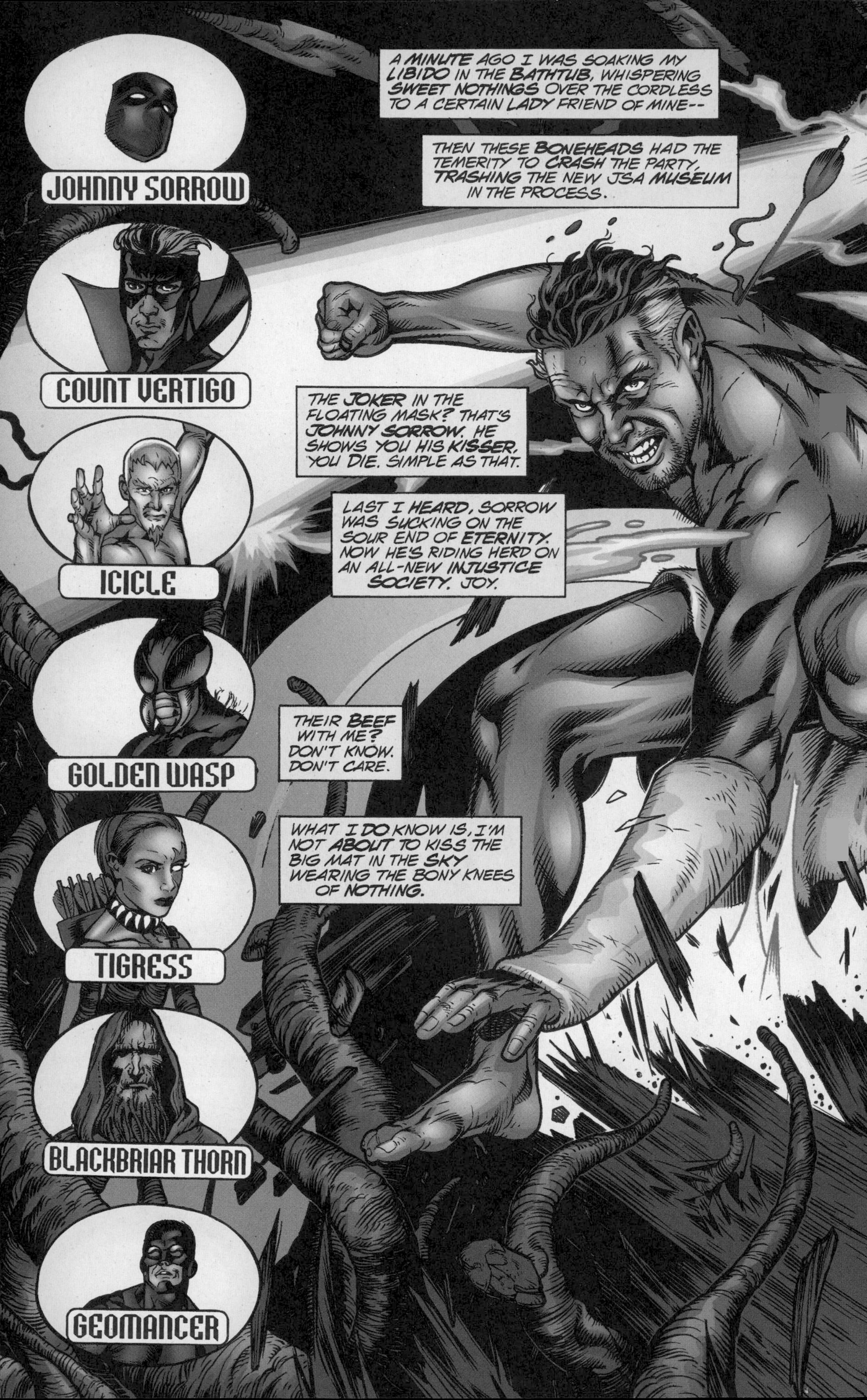
A MINUTE AGO I WAS SOAKING MY LIBIDO IN THE BATHTUB, WHISPERING SWEET NOTHINGS OVER THE CORDLESS TO A CERTAIN LADY FRIEND OF MINE--
THEN THESE BONEHEADS HAD THE TEMERITY TO CRASH THE PARTY, TRASHING THE NEW JSA MUSEUM IN THE PROCESS.
JOHNNY SORROW
COUNT VERTIGO
ICICLE
GOLDEN WASP
TIGRESS
BLACKBRIAR THORN
GEOMANCER
THE JOKER IN THE FLOATING MASK? THAT'S JOHNNY SORROW. HE SHOWS YOU HIS KISSER, YOU DIE. SIMPLE AS THAT.
LAST I HEARD, SORROW WAS SUCKING ON THE SOUR END OF ETERNITY. NOW HE'S RIDING HERD ON AN ALL-NEW INJUSTICE SOCIETY. JOY.
THEIR BEEF WITH ME? DON'T KNOW. DON'T CARE.
WHAT I DO KNOW IS, I'M NOT ABOUT TO KISS THE BIG MAT IN THE SKY WEARING THE BONY KNEES OF NOTHING.

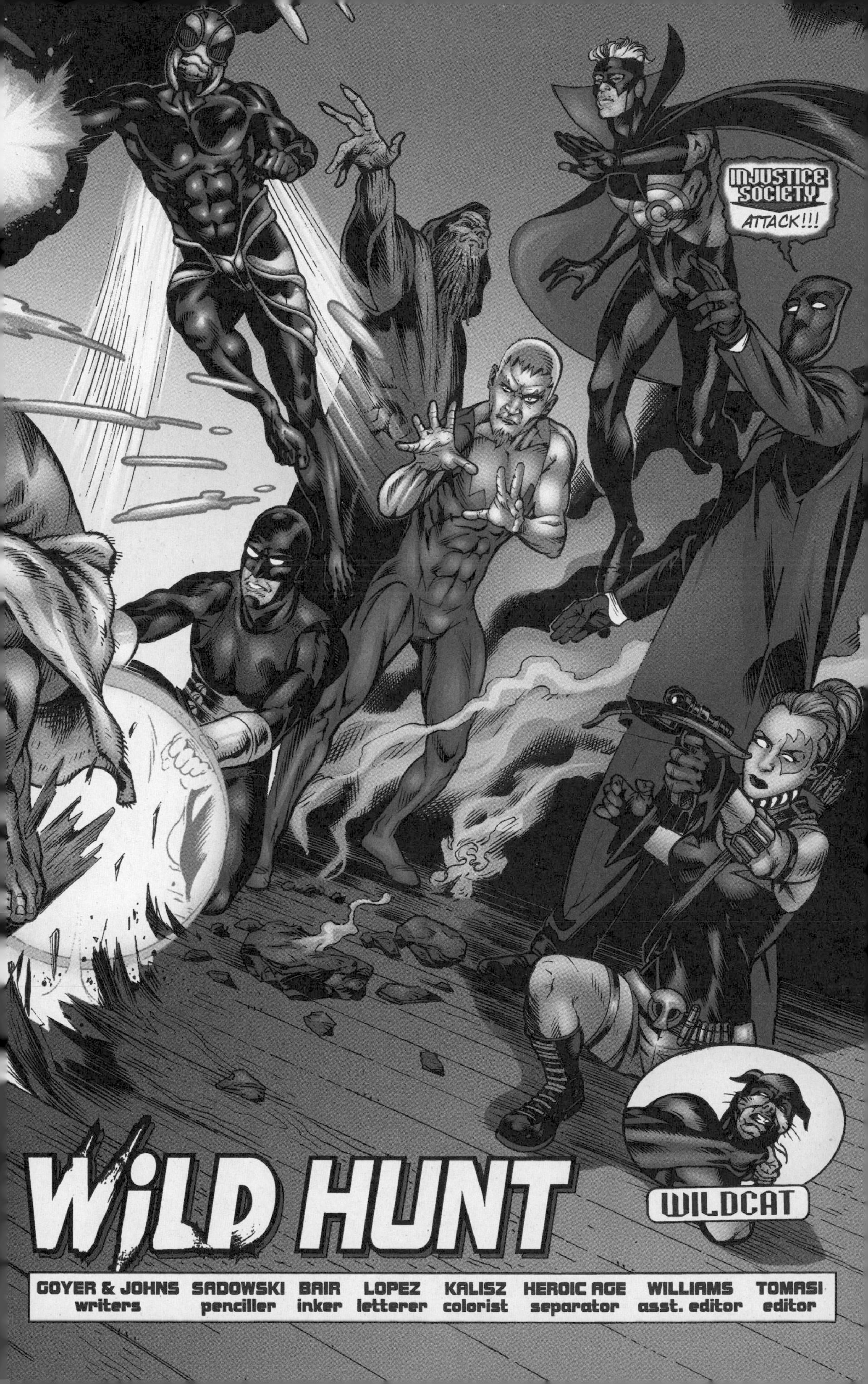
INJUSTICE SOCIETY ATTACK!!!
WILDCAT
WILD HUNT
GOYER & JOHNS writers
SADOWSKI penciller
BAIR inker
LOPEZ letterer
KALISZ colorist
HEROIC AGE separator
WILLIAMS asst. editor
TOMASI editor

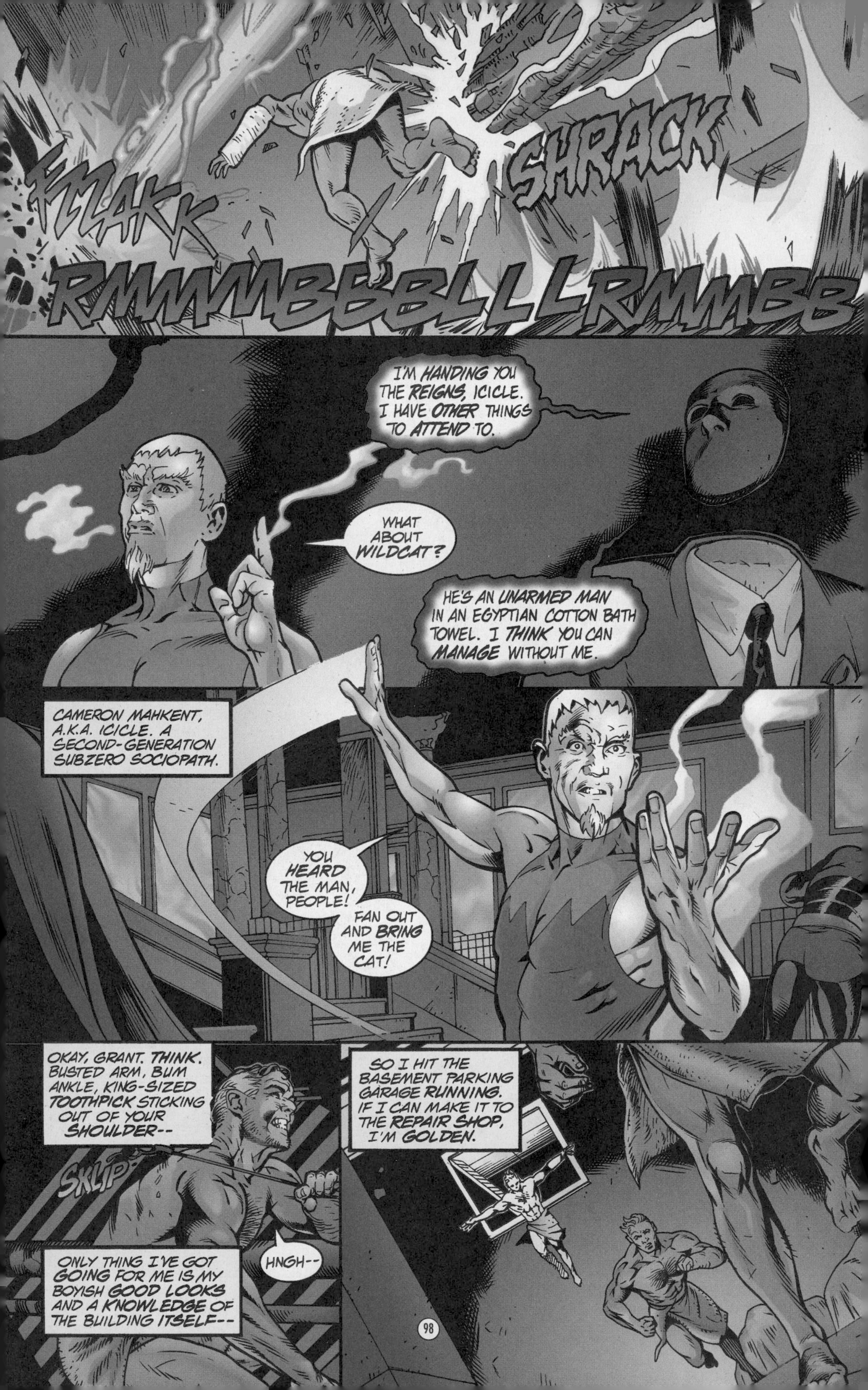
FLAKK
SHRACK
RMMMBBBLLLRMMMBB
I'M HANDING YOU THE REIGNS, ICICLE. I HAVE OTHER THINGS TO ATTEND TO.
WHAT ABOUT WILDCAT?
HE'S AN UNARMED MAN IN AN EGYPTIAN COTTON BATH TOWEL. I THINK YOU CAN MANAGE WITHOUT ME.
CAMERON MAHKENT, A.K.A. ICICLE. A SECOND-GENERATION SUBZERO SOCIOPATH.
YOU HEARD THE MAN, PEOPLE!
FAN OUT AND BRING ME THE CAT!
OKAY, GRANT. THINK. BUSTED ARM, BUM ANKLE, KING-SIZED TOOTHPICK STICKING OUT OF YOUR SHOULDER--
SKLIP
HNGH--
ONLY THING I'VE GOT GOING FOR ME IS MY BOYISH GOOD LOOKS AND A KNOWLEDGE OF THE BUILDING ITSELF--
SO I HIT THE BASEMENT PARKING GARAGE RUNNING. IF I CAN MAKE IT TO THE REPAIR SHOP, I'M GOLDEN.

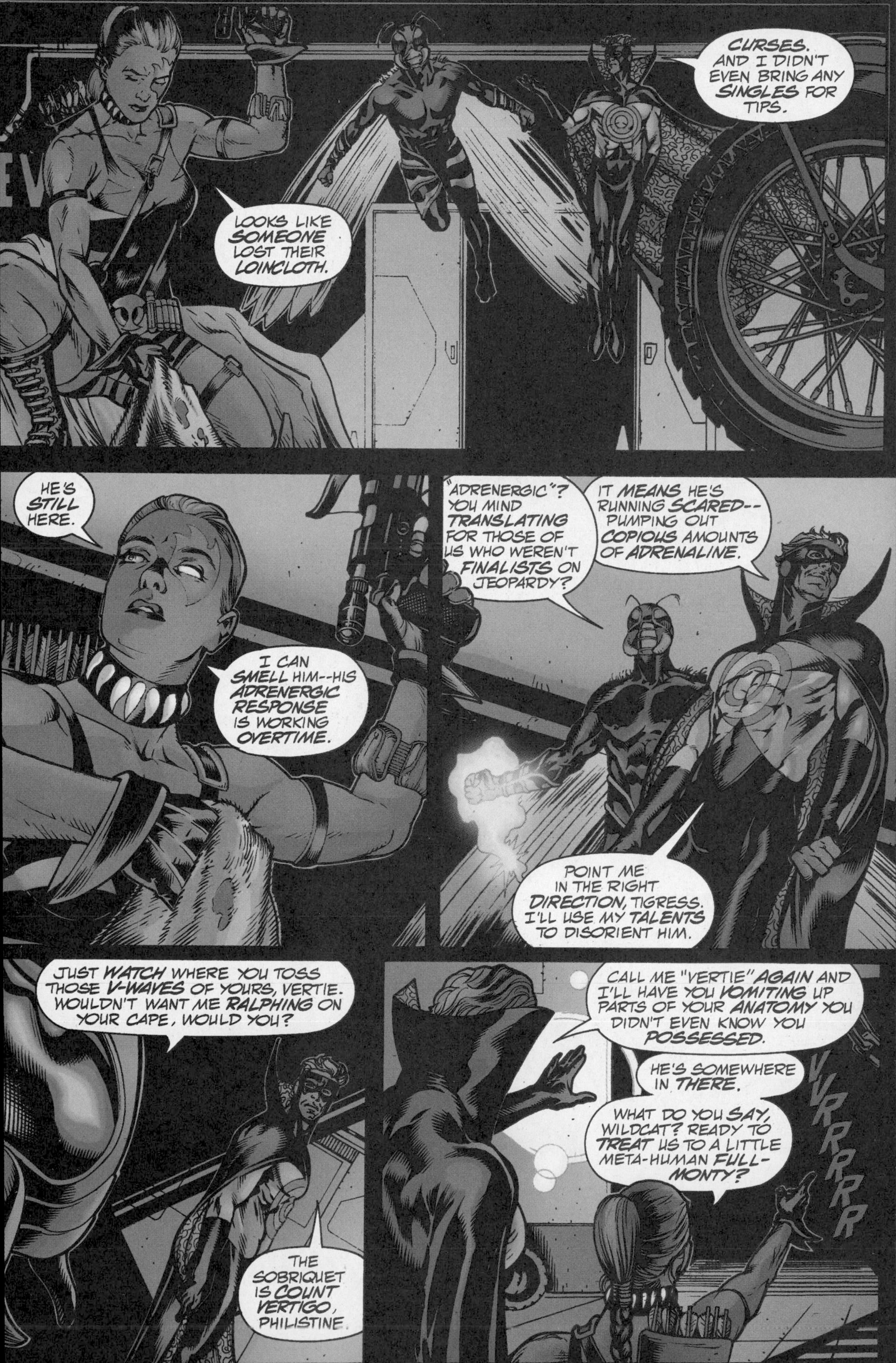
LOOKS LIKE SOMEONE LOST THEIR LOINCLOTH.
CURSES. AND I DIDN'T EVEN BRING ANY SINGLES FOR TIPS.
HE'S STILL HERE.
I CAN SMELL HIM--HIS ADRENERGIC RESPONSE IS WORKING OVERTIME.
"ADRENERGIC"? YOU MIND TRANSLATING FOR THOSE OF US WHO WEREN'T FINALISTS ON JEOPARDY?
IT MEANS HE'S RUNNING SCARED-- PUMPING OUT COPIOUS AMOUNTS OF ADRENALINE.
POINT ME IN THE RIGHT DIRECTION, TIGRESS. I'LL USE MY TALENTS TO DISORIENT HIM.
JUST WATCH WHERE YOU TOSS THOSE V-WAVES OF YOURS, VERTIE. WOULDN'T WANT ME RALPHING ON YOUR CAPE, WOULD YOU?
THE SOBRIQUET IS COUNT VERTIGO, PHILISTINE.
CALL ME "VERTIE" AGAIN AND I'LL HAVE YOU VOMITING UP PARTS OF YOUR ANATOMY YOU DIDN'T EVEN KNOW YOU POSSESSED.
HE'S SOMEWHERE IN THERE.
WHAT DO YOU SAY, WILDCAT? READY TO TREAT US TO A LITTLE META-HUMAN FULL-MONTY?
VVRRRR

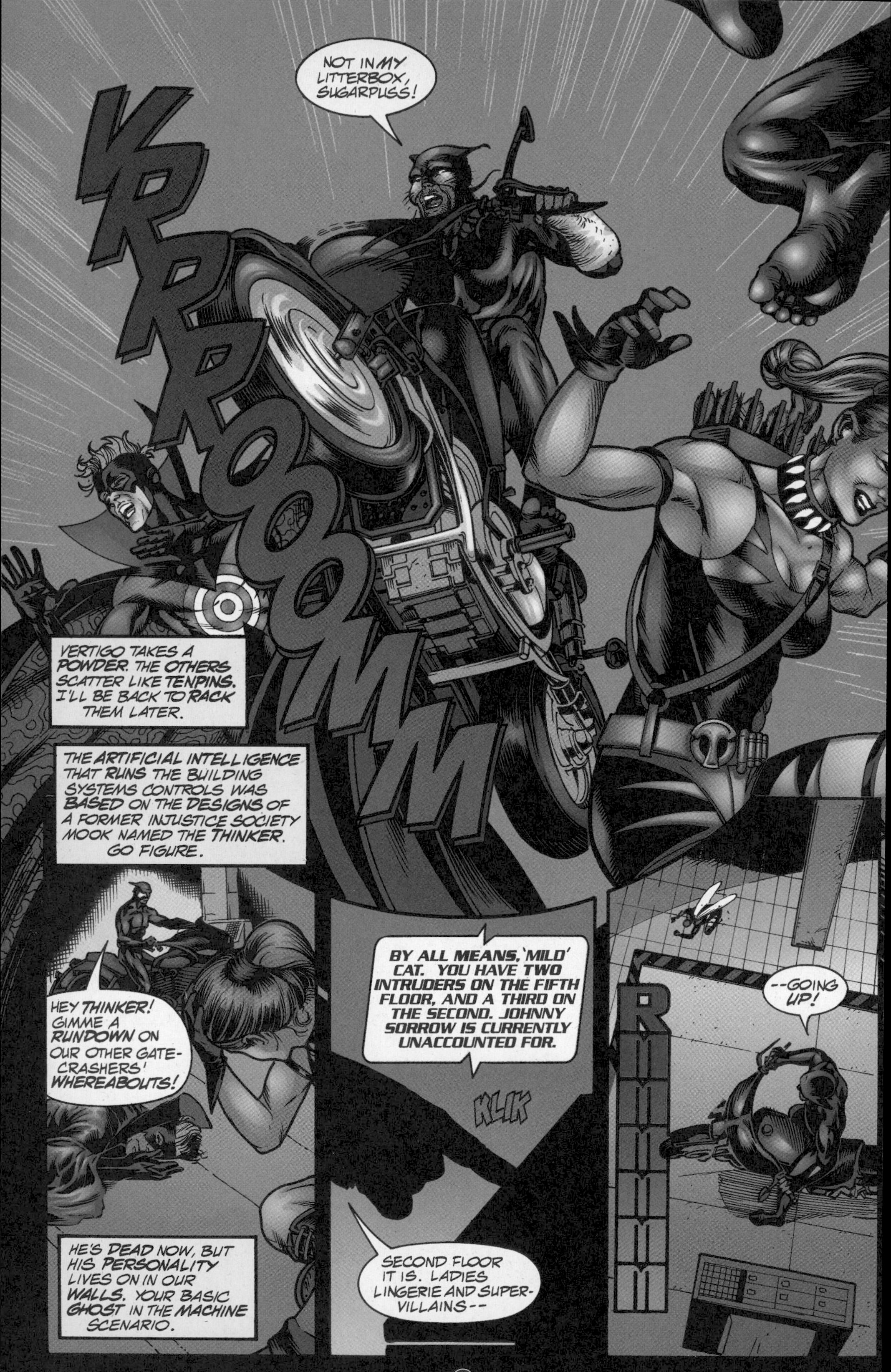

VRRROOOOMMM
NOT IN MY LITTERBOX, SUGARPUSS!
VERTIGO TAKES A POWDER. THE OTHERS SCATTER LIKE TENPINS. I'LL BE BACK TO RACK THEM LATER.
THE ARTIFICIAL INTELLIGENCE THAT RUNS THE BUILDING SYSTEMS CONTROLS WAS BASED ON THE DESIGNS OF A FORMER INJUSTICE SOCIETY MOOK NAMED THE THINKER. GO FIGURE.
HEY THINKER! GIMME A RUNDOWN ON OUR OTHER GATE-CRASHERS' WHEREABOUTS!
HE'S DEAD NOW, BUT HIS PERSONALITY LIVES ON IN OUR WALLS. YOUR BASIC GHOST IN THE MACHINE SCENARIO.
BY ALL MEANS, 'MILD' CAT. YOU HAVE TWO INTRUDERS ON THE FIFTH FLOOR, AND A THIRD ON THE SECOND. JOHNNY SORROW IS CURRENTLY UNACCOUNTED FOR.
KLIK
SECOND FLOOR IT IS. LADIES LINGERIE AND SUPER-VILLAINS--
RMMMMMM
--GOING UP!

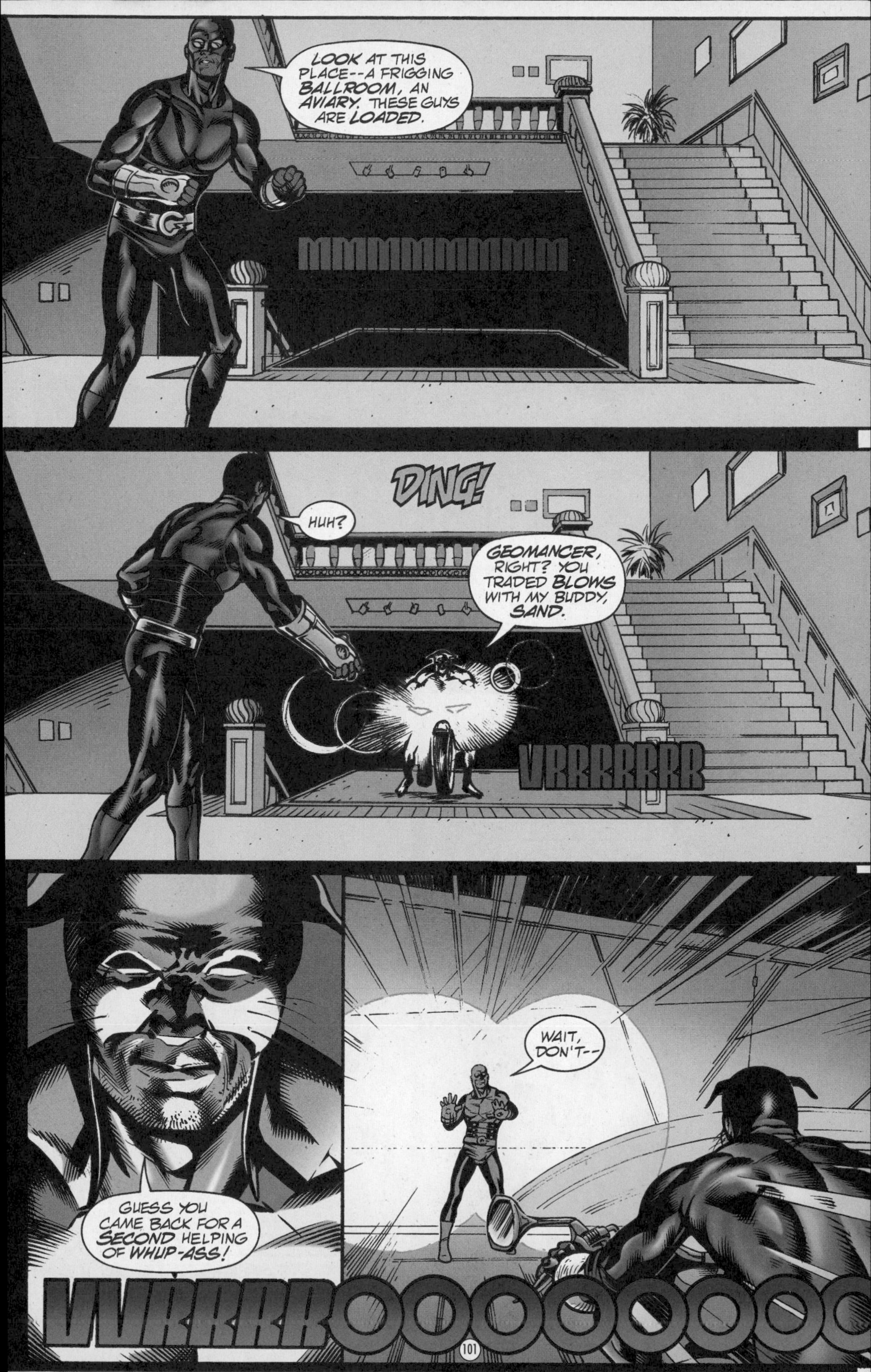
LOOK AT THIS PLACE--A FRIGGING BALLROOM, AN AVIARY. THESE GUYS ARE LOADED.
MMMMMMMMMM
DING!
HUH?
GEOMANCER, RIGHT? YOU TRADED BLOWS WITH MY BUDDY, SAND.
VRRRRRRR
GUESS YOU CAME BACK FOR A SECOND HELPING OF WHUP-ASS!
WAIT, DON'T--
VVRRRROOOOOOOOOO

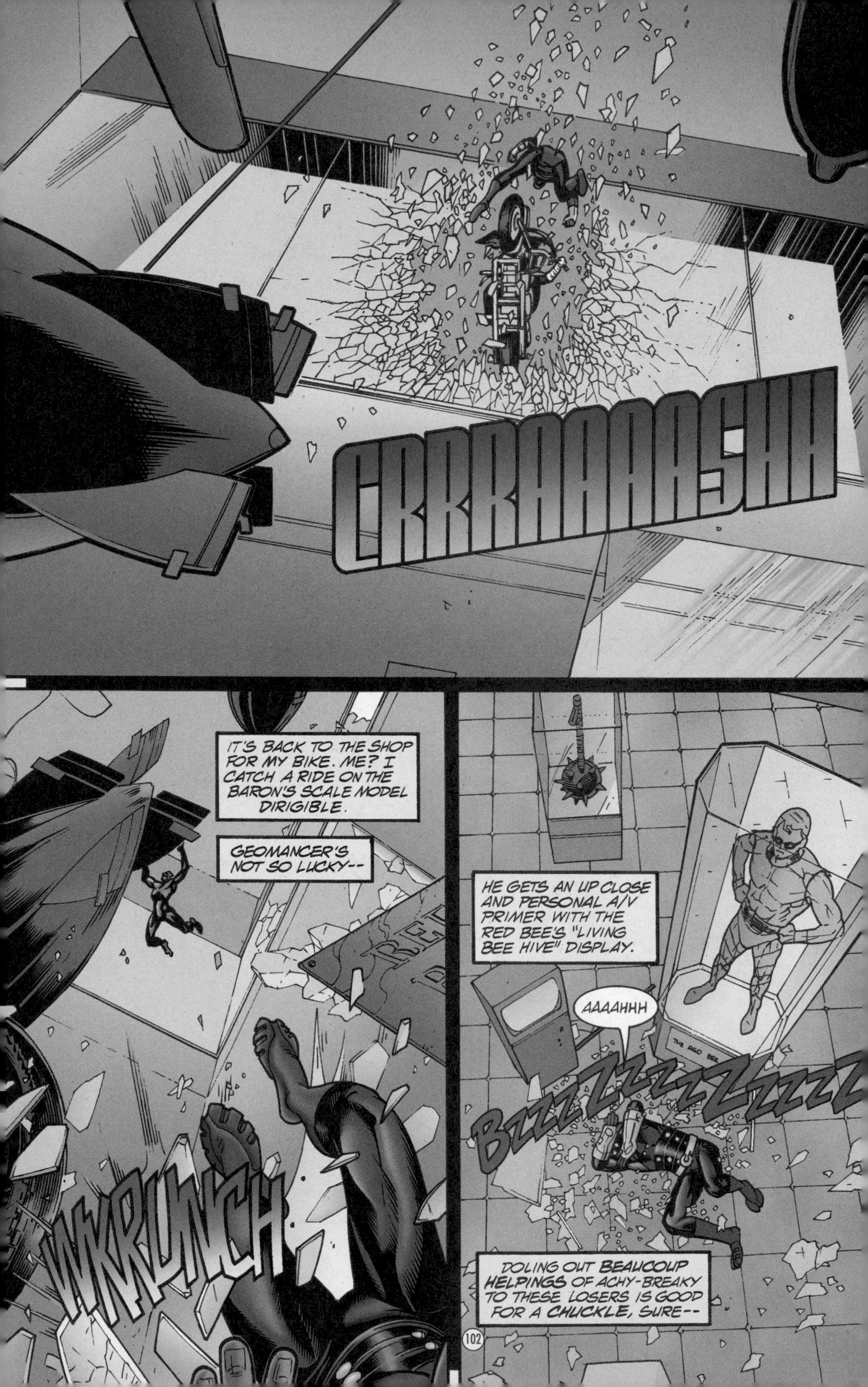
CRRAAAAASHH
IT'S BACK TO THE SHOP FOR MY BIKE. ME? I CATCH A RIDE ON THE BARON'S SCALE MODEL DIRIGIBLE.
GEOMANCER'S NOT SO LUCKY--
WKRUNCH
HE GETS AN UP CLOSE AND PERSONAL A/V PRIMER WITH THE RED BEE'S "LIVING BEE HIVE" DISPLAY.
AAAAHHH
BZZZZZZZZZZZZZ
DOLING OUT BEAUCOUP HELPINGS OF ACHY-BREAKY TO THESE LOSERS IS GOOD FOR A CHUCKLE, SURE--

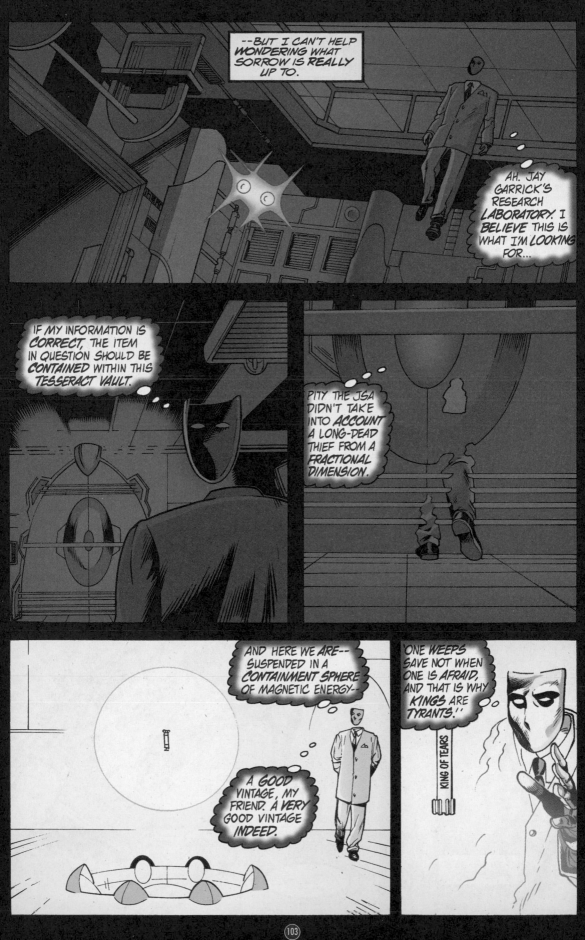

--BUT I CAN'T HELP WONDERING WHAT SORROW IS REALLY UP TO.

AH. JAY GARRICK'S RESEARCH LABORATORY. I BELIEVE THIS IS WHAT I'M LOOKING FOR...

IF MY INFORMATION IS CORRECT, THE ITEM IN QUESTION SHOULD BE CONTAINED WITHIN THIS TESSERACT VAULT.

PITY THE JSA DIDN'T TAKE INTO ACCOUNT A LONG-DEAD THIEF FROM A FRACTIONAL DIMENSION.

AND HERE WE ARE-- SUSPENDED IN A CONTAINMENT SPHERE OF MAGNETIC ENERGY--

A GOOD VINTAGE, MY FRIEND. A VERY GOOD VINTAGE INDEED.

'ONE WEEPS SAVE NOT WHEN ONE IS AFRAID, AND THAT IS WHY KINGS ARE TYRANTS.'

KING OF TEARS

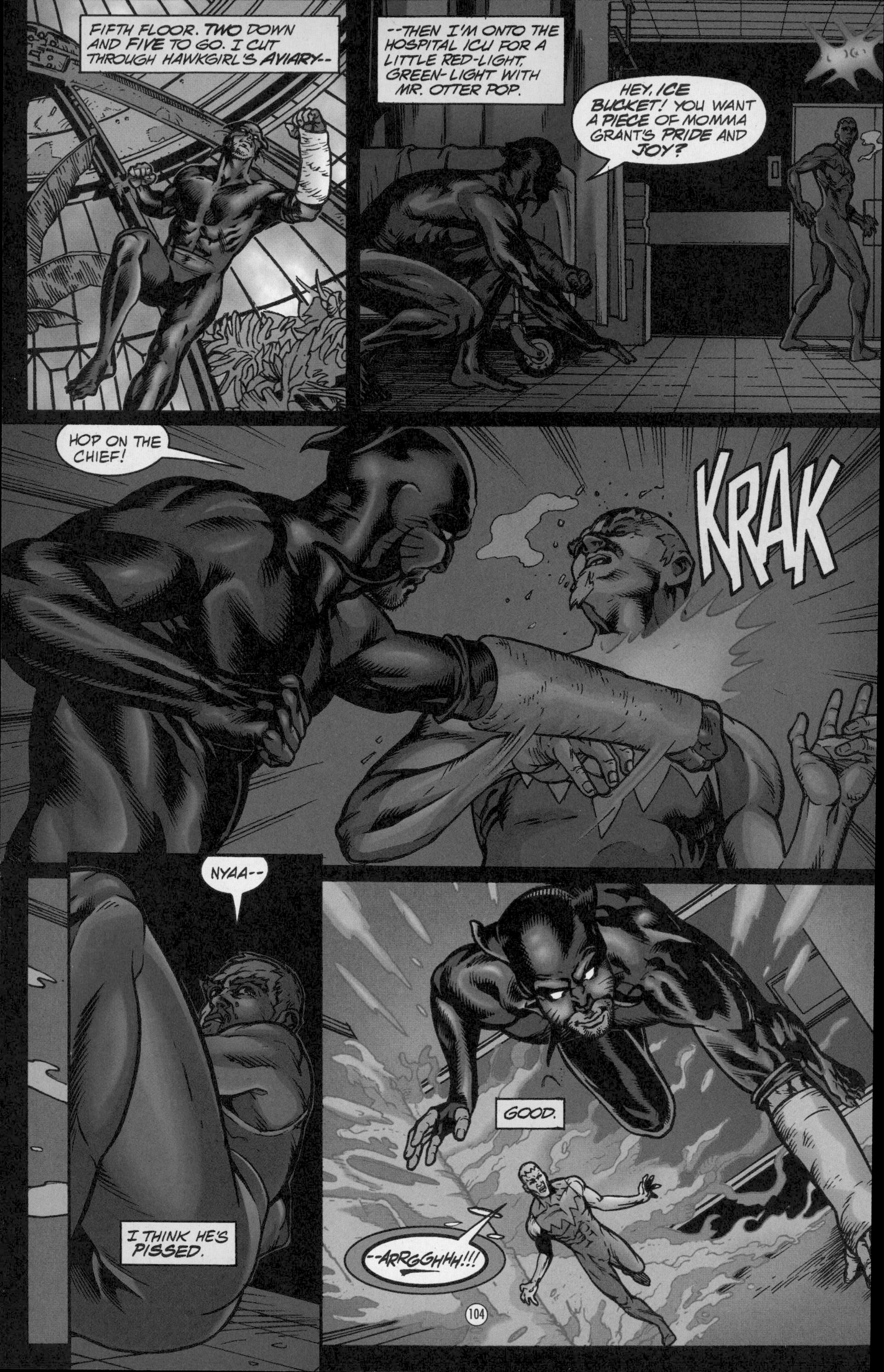
FIFTH FLOOR. TWO DOWN AND FIVE TO GO. I CUT THROUGH HAWKGIRL'S AVIARY--
--THEN I'M ONTO THE HOSPITAL ICU FOR A LITTLE RED-LIGHT, GREEN-LIGHT WITH MR. OTTER POP.
HEY, ICE BUCKET! YOU WANT A PIECE OF MOMMA GRANT'S PRIDE AND JOY?
HOP ON THE CHIEF!
KRAK
NYAA--
I THINK HE'S PISSED.
GOOD.
--ARRGGHHH!!!

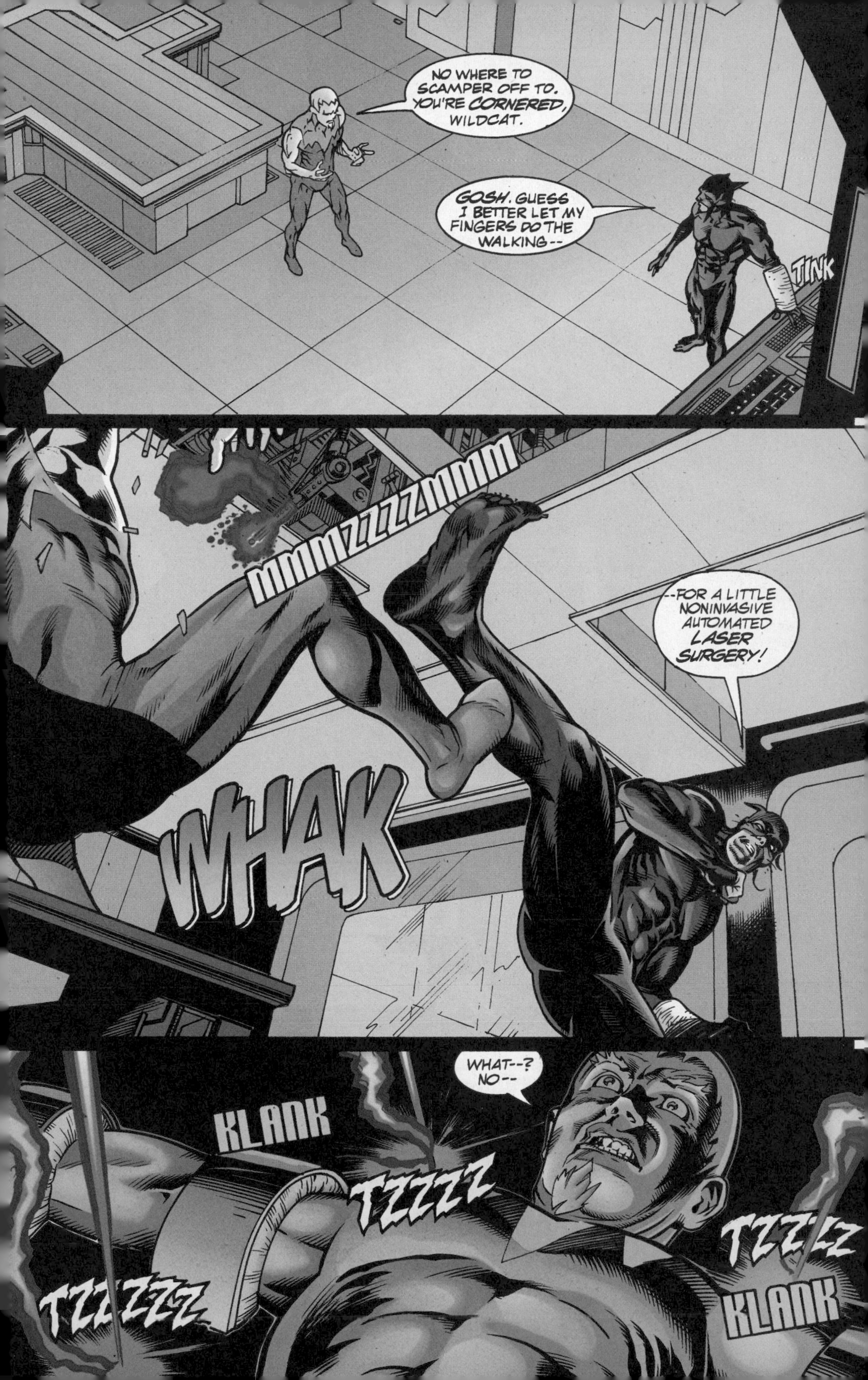
NO WHERE TO SCAMPER OFF TO. YOU'RE CORNERED, WILDCAT.
GOSH. GUESS I BETTER LET MY FINGERS DO THE WALKING--
TINK
MMMZZZZMMM
--FOR A LITTLE NONINVASIVE AUTOMATED LASER SURGERY!
WHAK
WHAT--? NO--
KLANK
TZZZZ
TZZZ
TZZZZZZ
KLANK

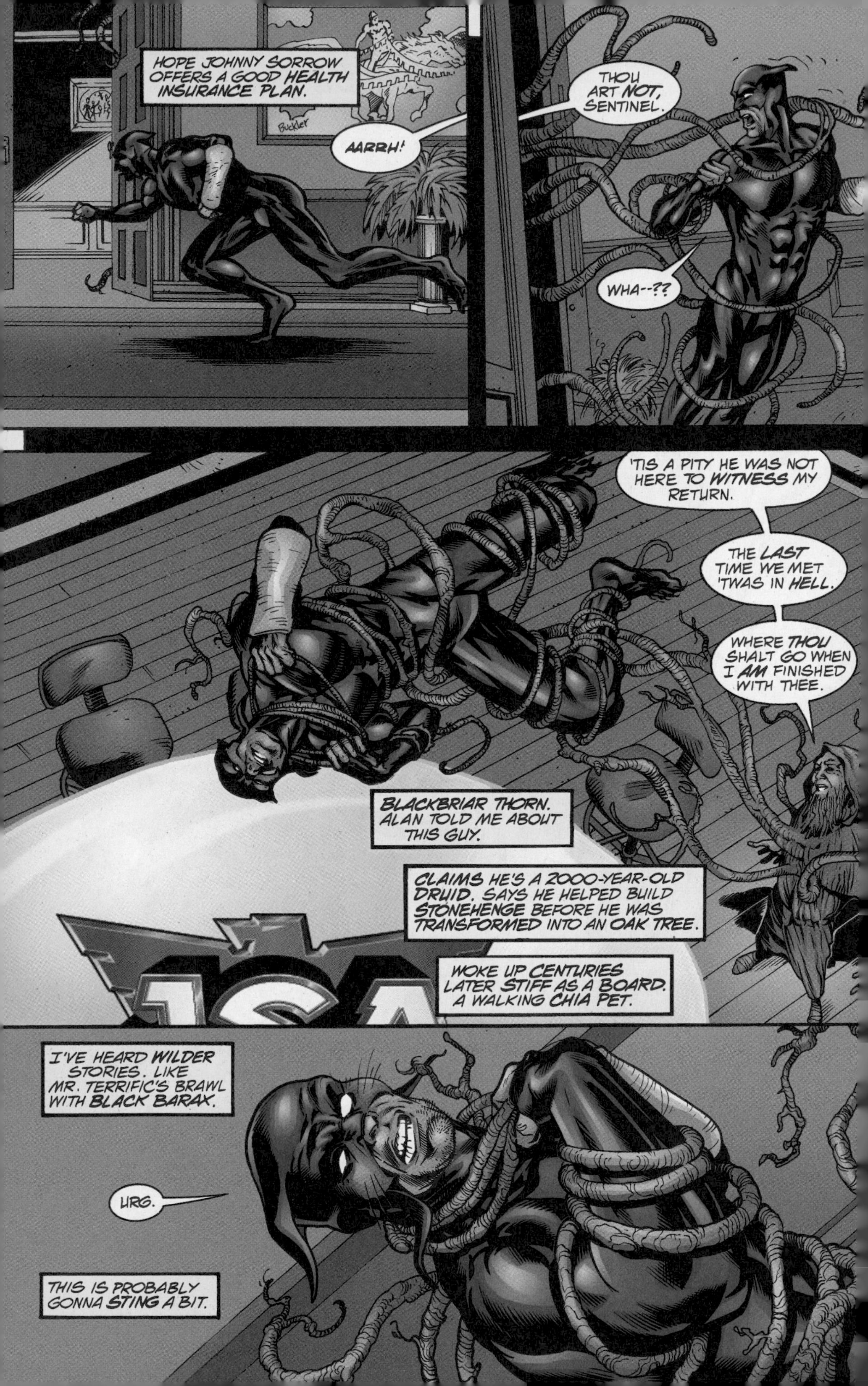

HOPE JOHNNY SORROW OFFERS A GOOD HEALTH INSURANCE PLAN.
Buckler
AARRH!
THOU ART NOT, SENTINEL.
WHA--??
'TIS A PITY HE WAS NOT HERE TO WITNESS MY RETURN.
THE LAST TIME WE MET 'TWAS IN HELL.
WHERE THOU SHALT GO WHEN I AM FINISHED WITH THEE.
BLACKBRIAR THORN. ALAN TOLD ME ABOUT THIS GUY.
CLAIMS HE'S A 2000-YEAR-OLD DRUID. SAYS HE HELPED BUILD STONEHENGE BEFORE HE WAS TRANSFORMED INTO AN OAK TREE.
WOKE UP CENTURIES LATER STIFF AS A BOARD. A WALKING CHIA PET.
I'VE HEARD WILDER STORIES. LIKE MR. TERRIFIC'S BRAWL WITH BLACK BARAX.
URG.
THIS IS PROBABLY GONNA STING A BIT.

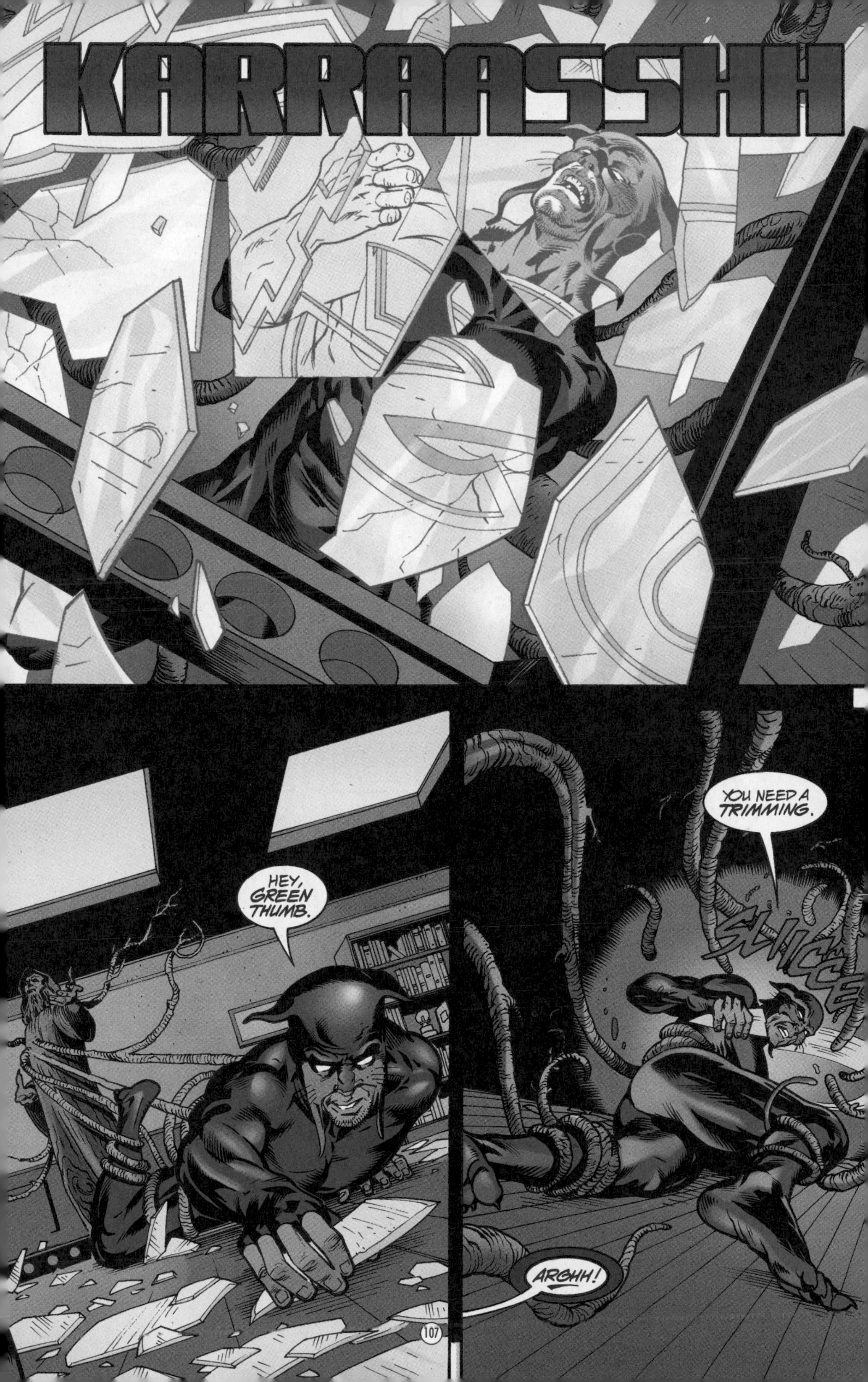
KARRAASSHH
HEY, GREEN THUMB.
YOU NEED A TRIMMING.
SLICCE
ARGHH!

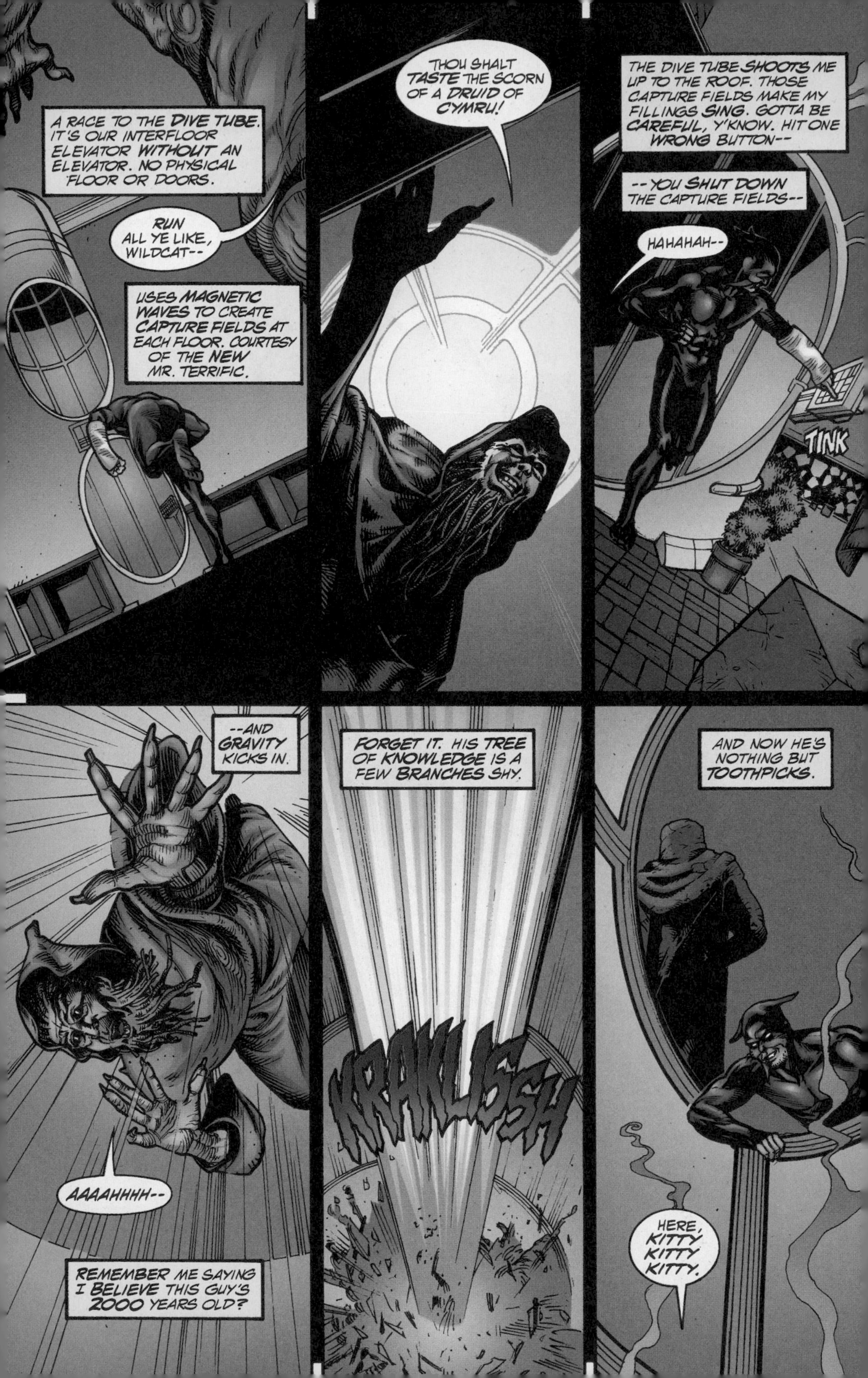
A RACE TO THE DIVE TUBE. IT'S OUR INTERFLOOR ELEVATOR WITHOUT AN ELEVATOR. NO PHYSICAL FLOOR OR DOORS.
RUN ALL YE LIKE, WILDCAT--
USES MAGNETIC WAVES TO CREATE CAPTURE FIELDS AT EACH FLOOR. COURTESY OF THE NEW MR. TERRIFIC.
THOU SHALT TASTE THE SCORN OF A DRUID OF CYMRU!
THE DIVE TUBE SHOOTS ME UP TO THE ROOF. THOSE CAPTURE FIELDS MAKE MY FILLINGS SING. GOTTA BE CAREFUL, Y'KNOW. HIT ONE WRONG BUTTON--
--YOU SHUT DOWN THE CAPTURE FIELDS--
HAHAHAH--
TINK
--AND GRAVITY KICKS IN.
AAAAHHHH--
REMEMBER ME SAYING I BELIEVE THIS GUY'S 2000 YEARS OLD?
FORGET IT. HIS TREE OF KNOWLEDGE IS A FEW BRANCHES SHY.
KRAKLISSH
AND NOW HE'S NOTHING BUT TOOTHPICKS.
HERE, KITTY KITTY KITTY.

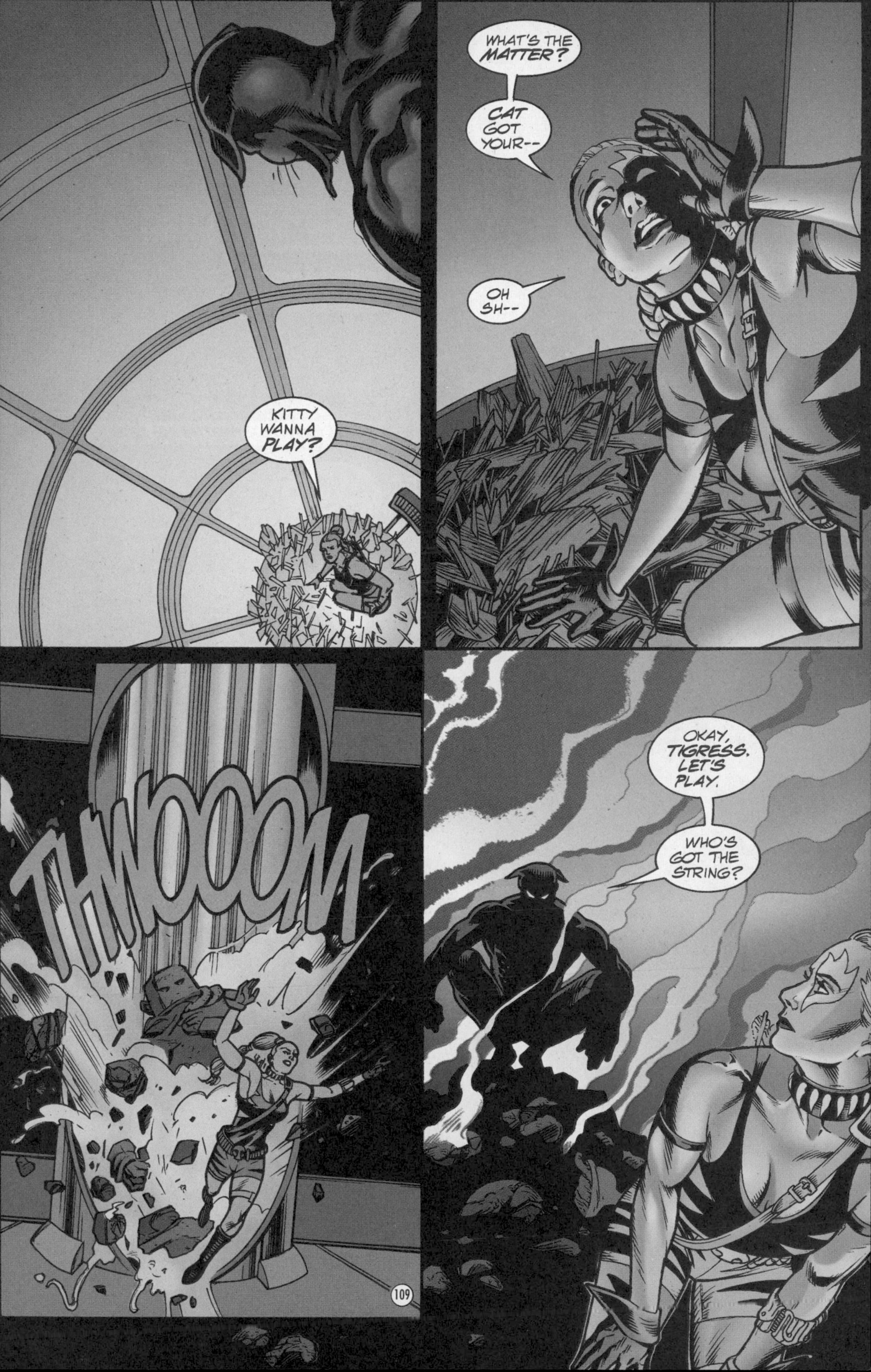
KITTY WANNA PLAY?
WHAT'S THE MATTER?
CAT GOT YOUR--
OH SH--
THWOOOM
OKAY, TIGRESS. LET'S PLAY.
WHO'S GOT THE STRING?

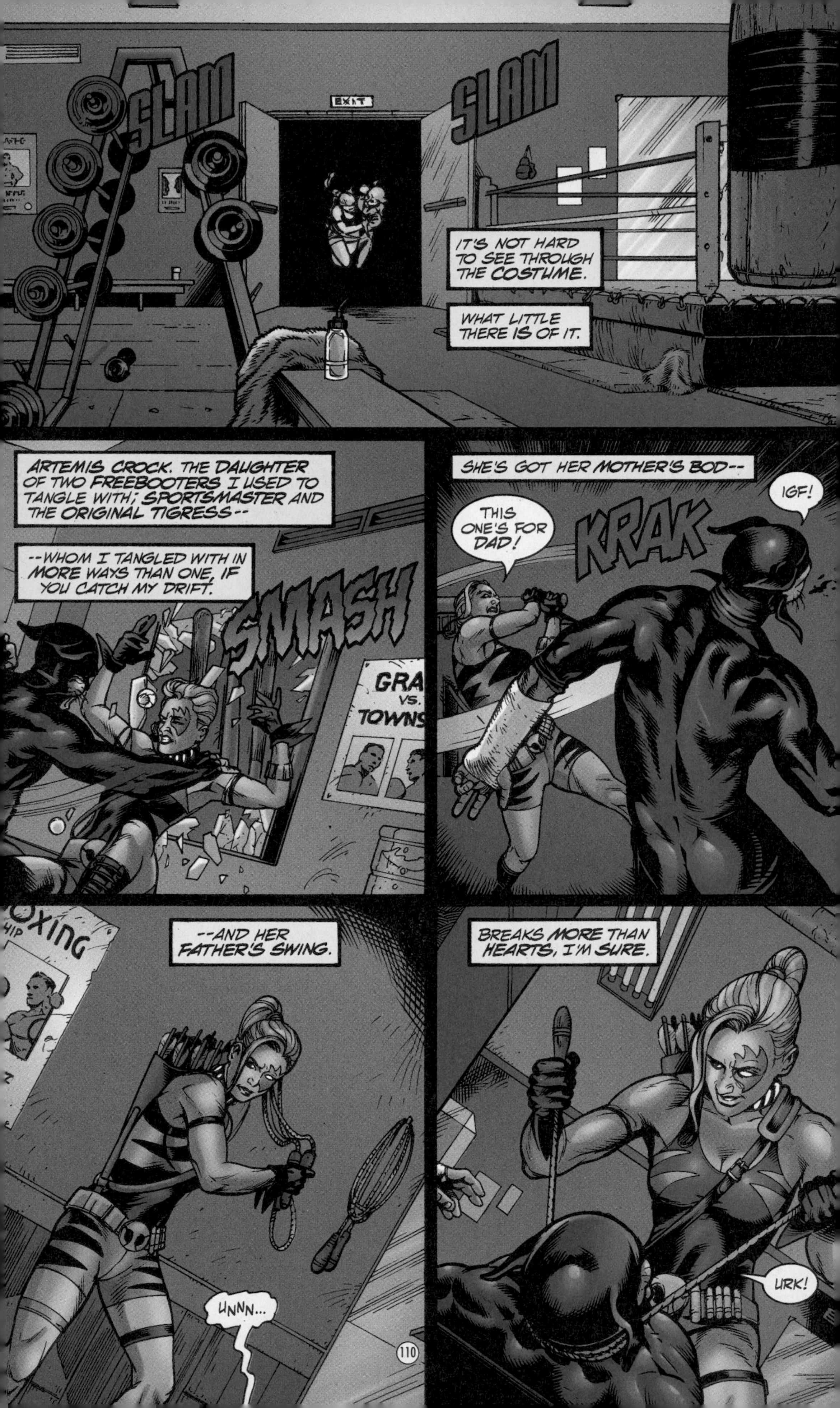
SLAM
EXIT
SLAM
IT'S NOT HARD TO SEE THROUGH THE COSTUME.
WHAT LITTLE THERE IS OF IT.
ARTEMIS CROCK. THE DAUGHTER OF TWO FREEBOOTERS I USED TO TANGLE WITH; SPORTSMASTER AND THE ORIGINAL TIGRESS--
--WHOM I TANGLED WITH IN MORE WAYS THAN ONE, IF YOU CATCH MY DRIFT.
SMASH
GRA
VS.
TOWNS
SHE'S GOT HER MOTHER'S BOD--
THIS ONE'S FOR DAD!
KRAK
IGF!
OXING
--AND HER FATHER'S SWING.
UNNN...
BREAKS MORE THAN HEARTS, I'M SURE.
URK!

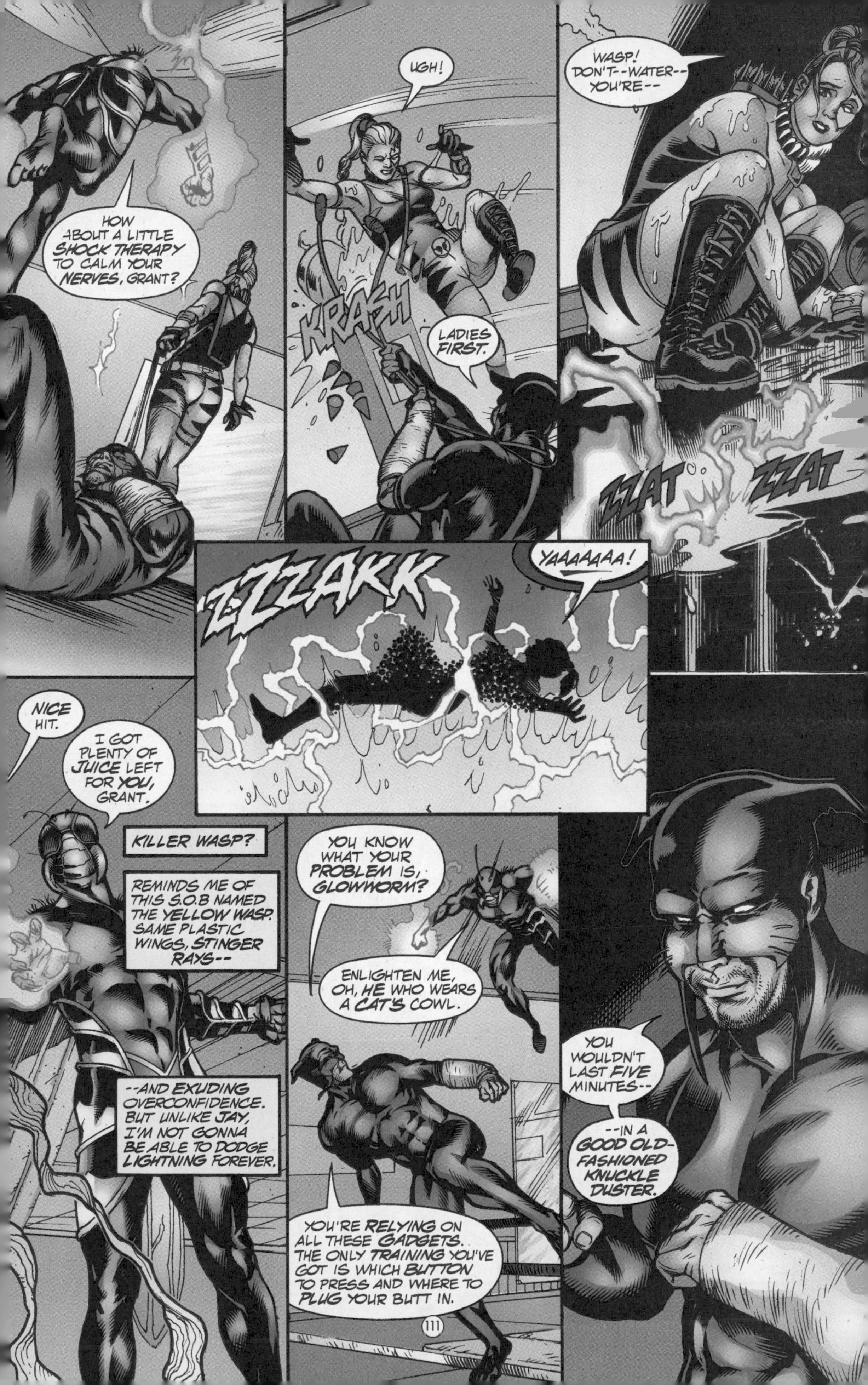
HOW ABOUT A LITTLE SHOCK THERAPY TO CALM YOUR NERVES, GRANT?
UGH!
KRASH
LADIES FIRST.
WASP! DON'T--WATER--YOU'RE--
ZZAT ZZAT
ZZZAKK
YAAAAAAA!
NICE HIT.
I GOT PLENTY OF JUICE LEFT FOR YOU, GRANT.
KILLER WASP?
REMINDS ME OF THIS S.O.B NAMED THE YELLOW WASP. SAME PLASTIC WINGS, STINGER RAYS--
--AND EXUDING OVERCONFIDENCE. BUT UNLIKE JAY, I'M NOT GONNA BE ABLE TO DODGE LIGHTNING FOREVER.
YOU KNOW WHAT YOUR PROBLEM IS, GLOWWORM?
ENLIGHTEN ME, OH, HE WHO WEARS A CAT'S COWL.
YOU'RE RELYING ON ALL THESE GADGETS. THE ONLY TRAINING YOU'VE GOT IS WHICH BUTTON TO PRESS AND WHERE TO PLUG YOUR BUTT IN.
YOU WOULDN'T LAST FIVE MINUTES--
--IN A GOOD OLD-FASHIONED KNUCKLE DUSTER.

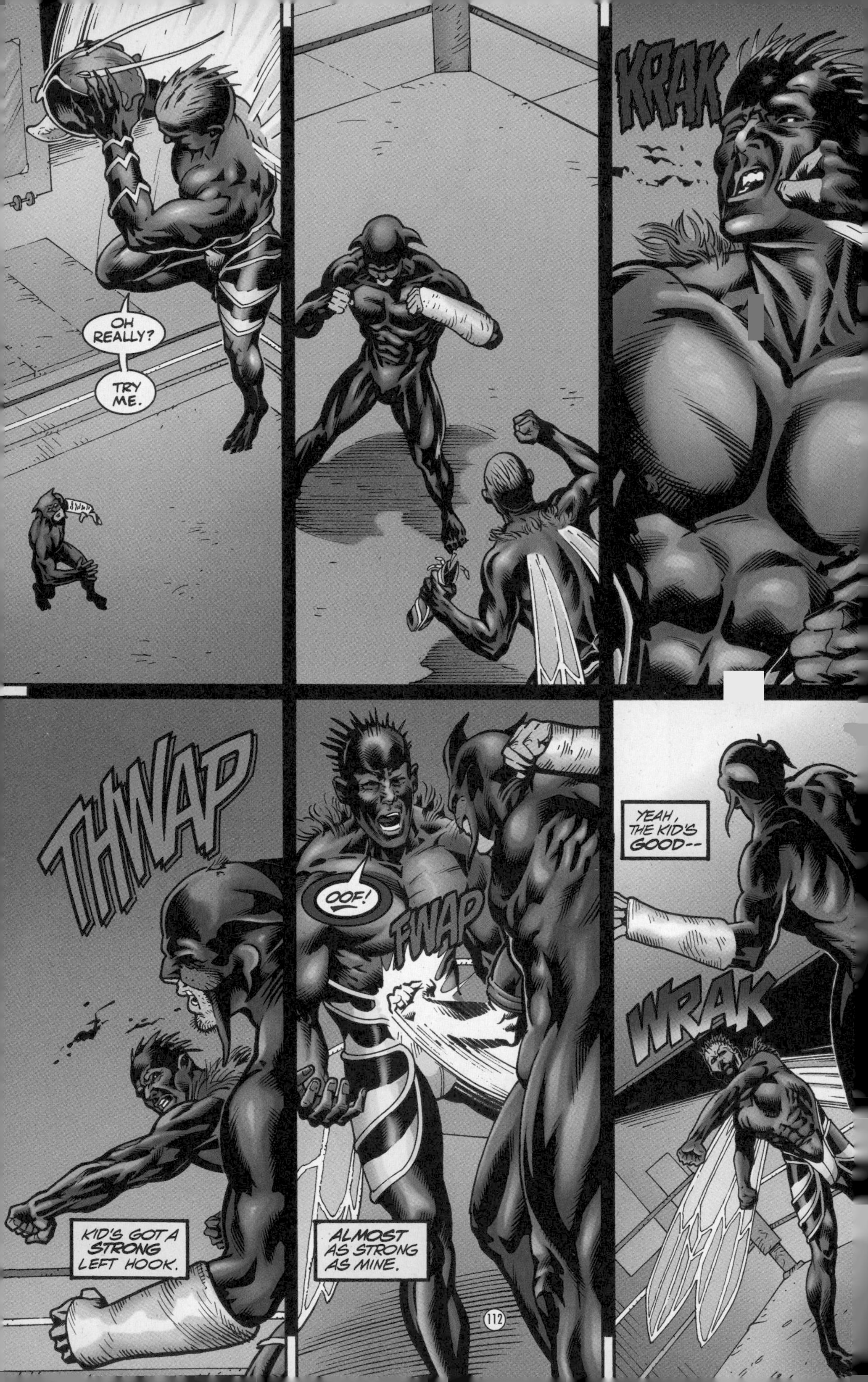
OH REALLY?
TRY ME.
KRAK
THWAP
KID'S GOT A STRONG LEFT HOOK.
OOF!
FWAP
ALMOST AS STRONG AS MINE.
YEAH, THE KID'S GOOD--
WRAK

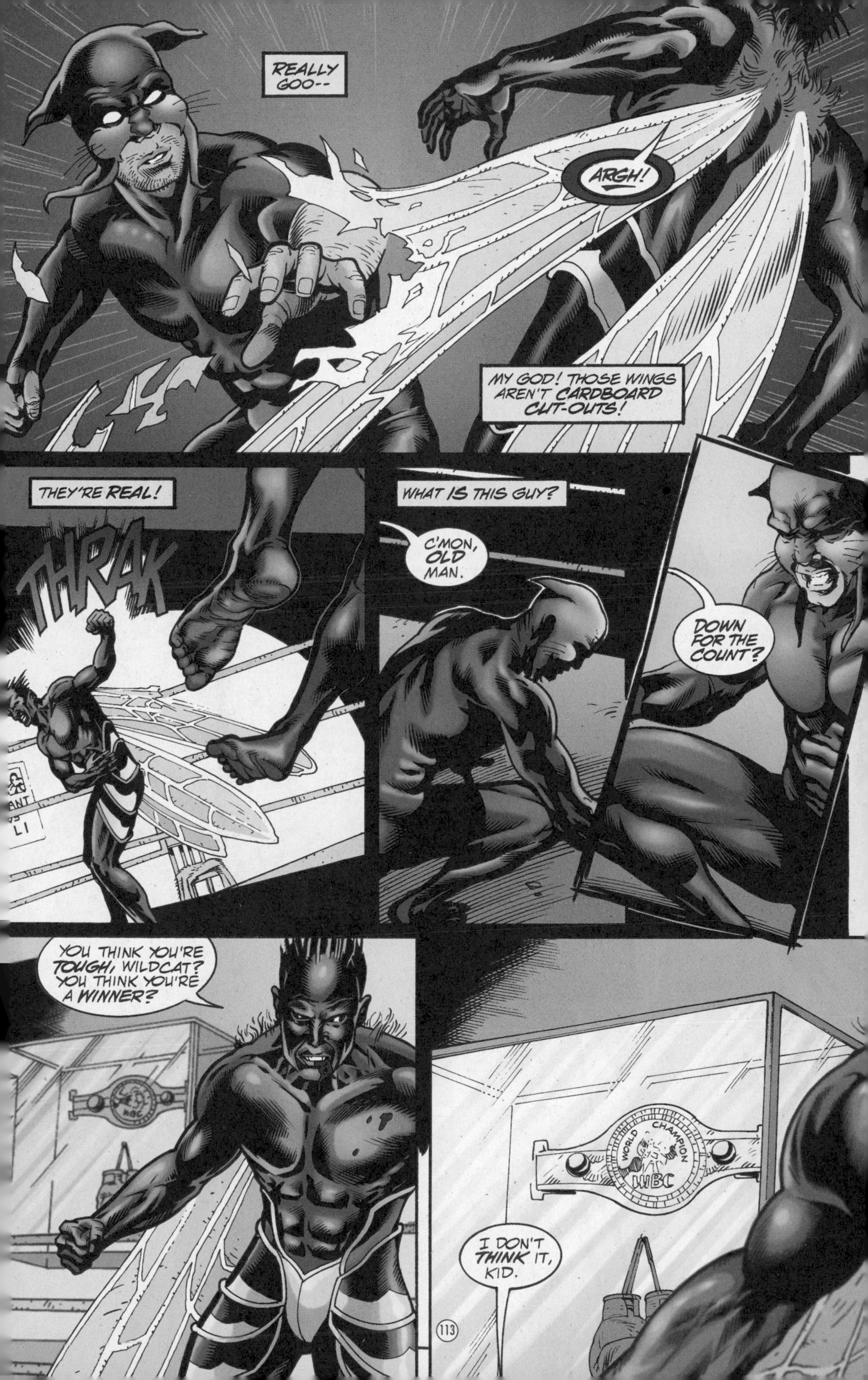
REALLY GOO--
ARGH!
MY GOD! THOSE WINGS AREN'T CARDBOARD CUT-OUTS!
THEY'RE REAL!
THRAK
WHAT IS THIS GUY?
C'MON, OLD MAN.
DOWN FOR THE COUNT?
YOU THINK YOU'RE TOUGH, WILDCAT? YOU THINK YOU'RE A WINNER?
WORLD CHAMPION
WBC
I DON'T THINK IT, KID.

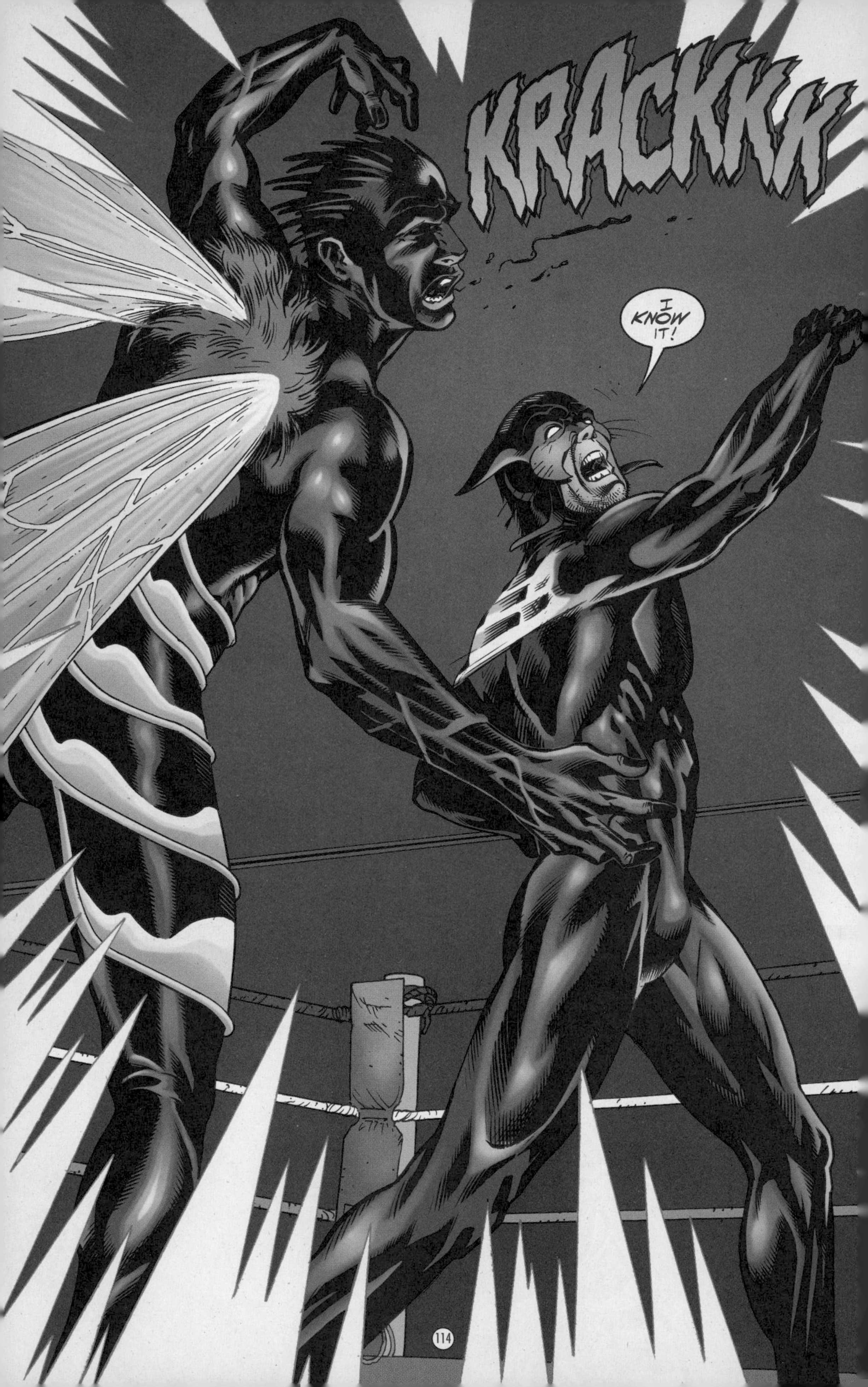
KRACKKK
I KNOW IT!

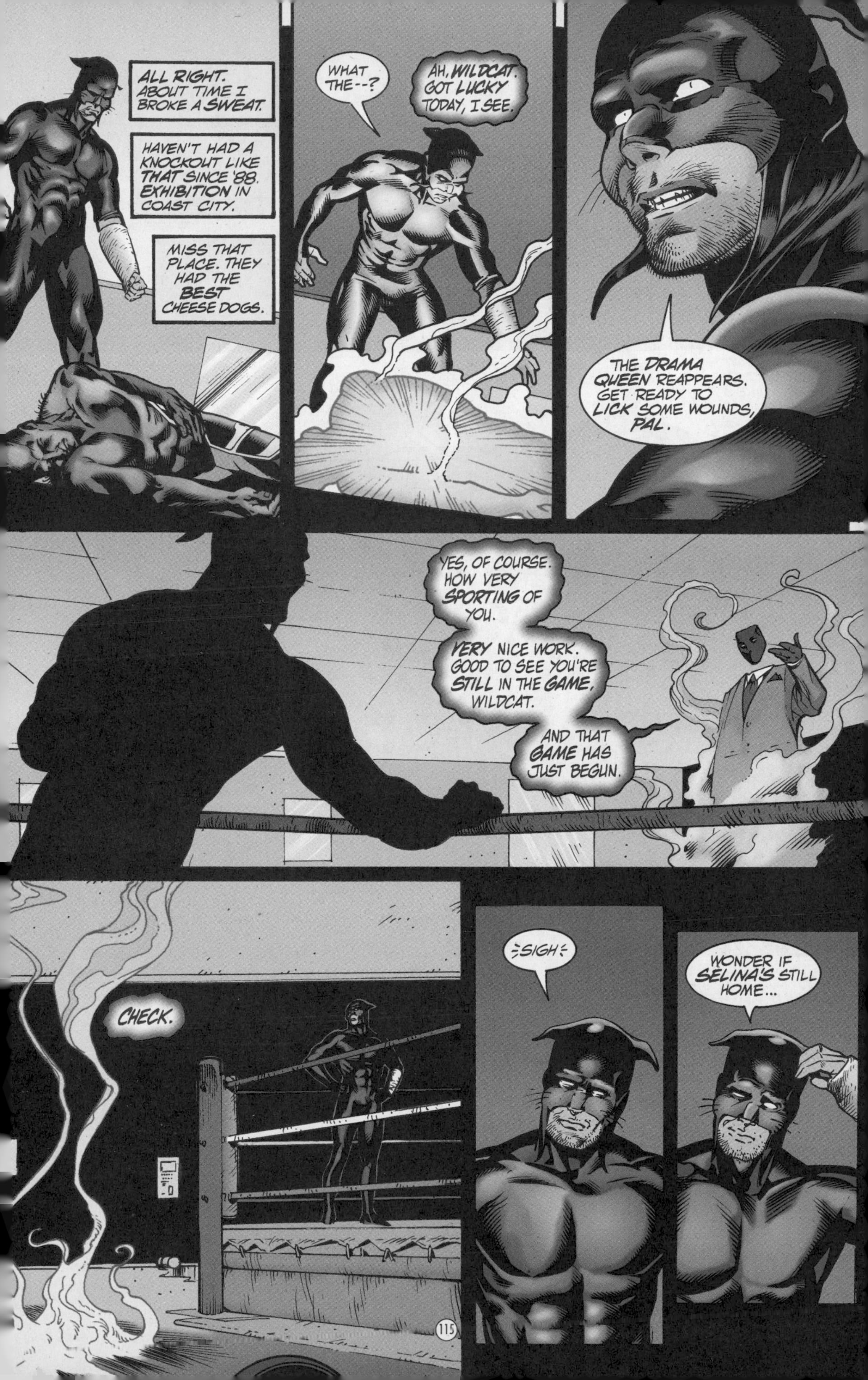

ALL RIGHT. ABOUT TIME I BROKE A SWEAT.
HAVEN'T HAD A KNOCKOUT LIKE THAT SINCE '88. EXHIBITION IN COAST CITY.
MISS THAT PLACE. THEY HAD THE BEST CHEESE DOGS.
WHAT THE--?
AH, WILDCAT. GOT LUCKY TODAY, I SEE.
THE DRAMA QUEEN REAPPEARS. GET READY TO LICK SOME WOUNDS, PAL.
YES, OF COURSE. HOW VERY SPORTING OF YOU.
VERY NICE WORK. GOOD TO SEE YOU'RE STILL IN THE GAME, WILDCAT.
AND THAT GAME HAS JUST BEGUN.
CHECK.
:SIGH:
WONDER IF SELINA'S STILL HOME...

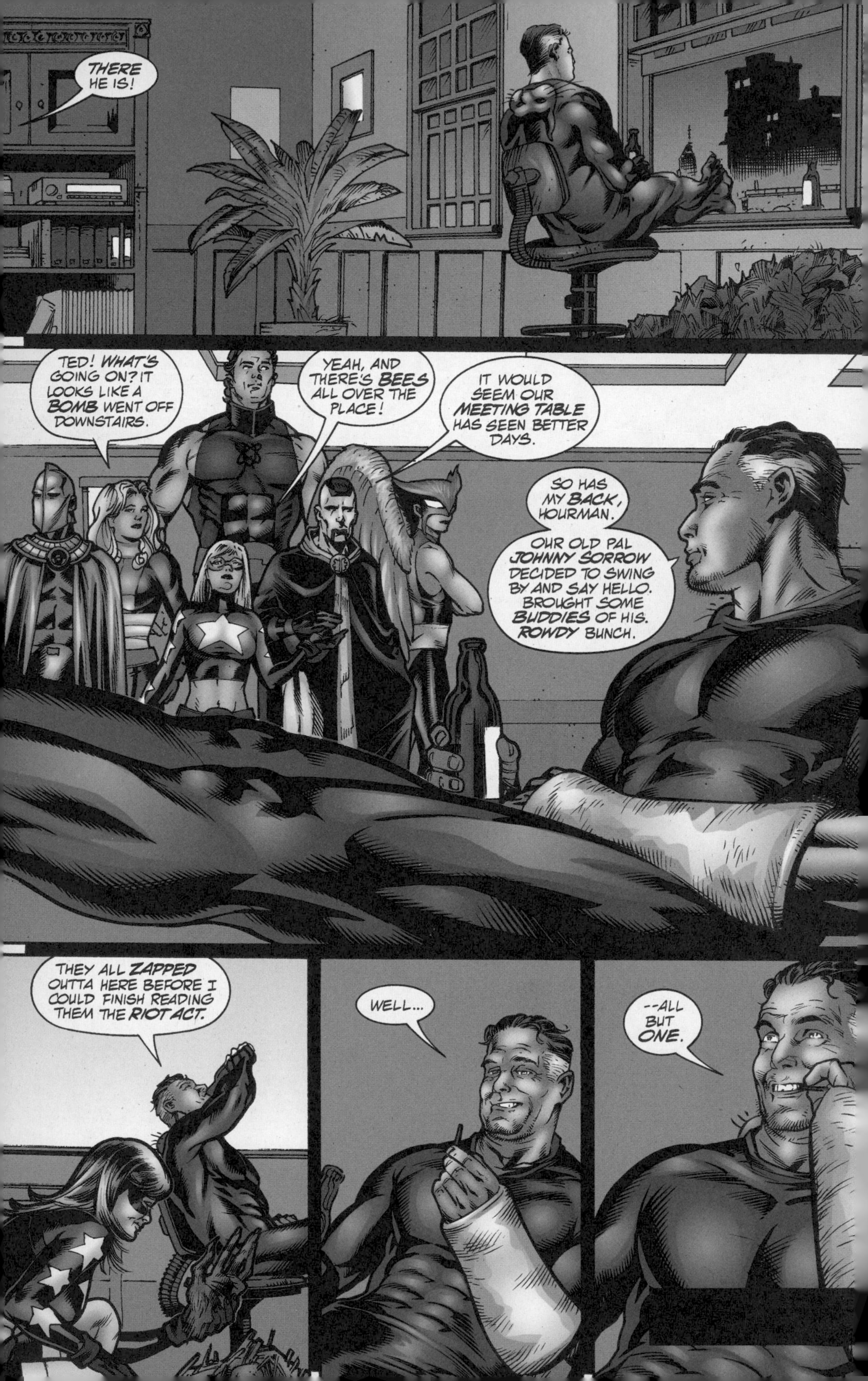
THERE HE IS!
TED! WHAT'S GOING ON? IT LOOKS LIKE A BOMB WENT OFF DOWNSTAIRS.
YEAH, AND THERE'S BEES ALL OVER THE PLACE!
IT WOULD SEEM OUR MEETING TABLE HAS SEEN BETTER DAYS.
SO HAS MY BACK, HOURMAN.
OUR OLD PAL JOHNNY SORROW DECIDED TO SWING BY AND SAY HELLO. BROUGHT SOME BUDDIES OF HIS. ROWDY BUNCH.
THEY ALL ZAPPED OUTTA HERE BEFORE I COULD FINISH READING THEM THE RIOT ACT.
WELL...
--ALL BUT ONE.

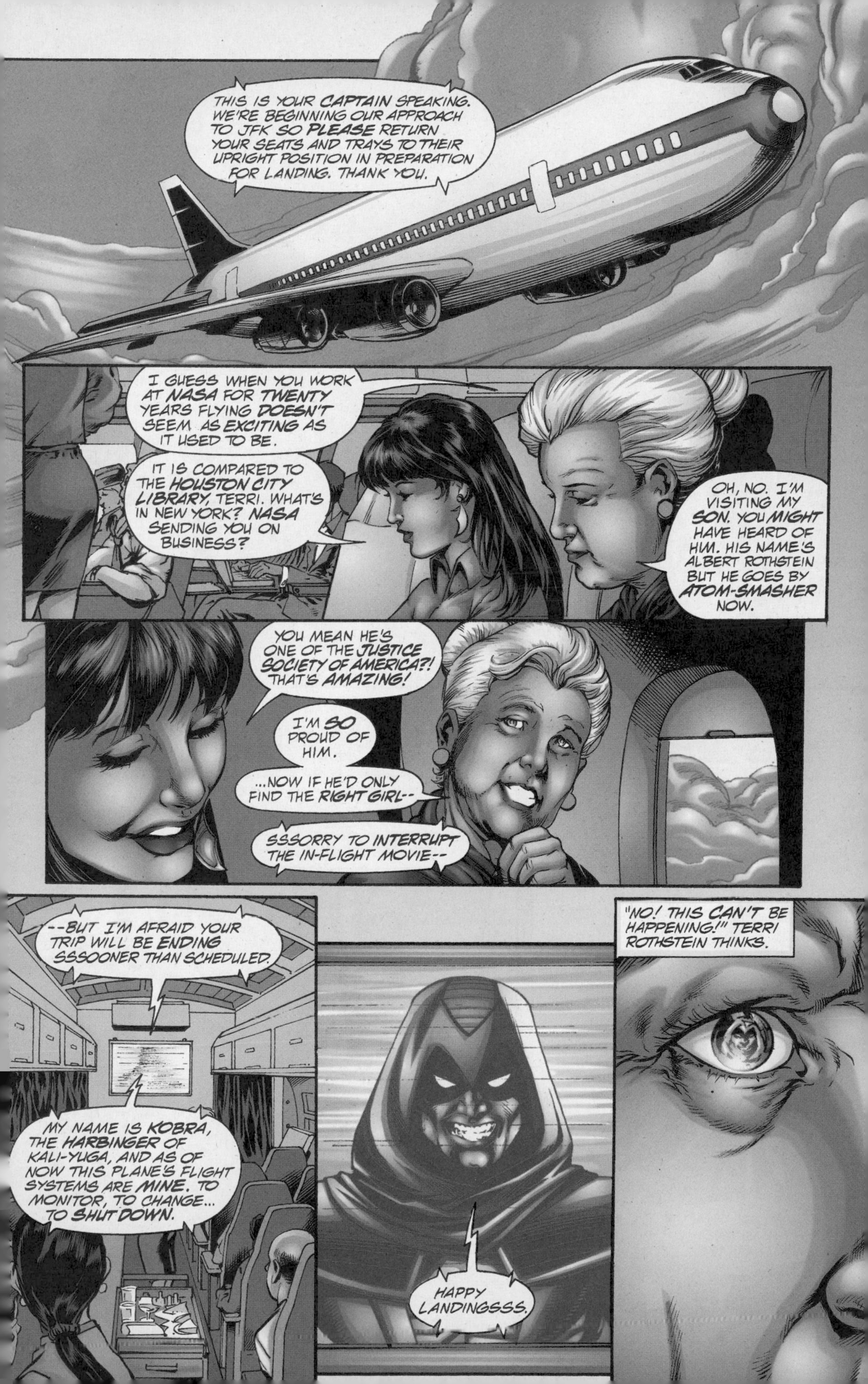
THIS IS YOUR CAPTAIN SPEAKING. WE'RE BEGINNING OUR APPROACH TO JFK SO PLEASE RETURN YOUR SEATS AND TRAYS TO THEIR UPRIGHT POSITION IN PREPARATION FOR LANDING. THANK YOU.
I GUESS WHEN YOU WORK AT NASA FOR TWENTY YEARS FLYING DOESN'T SEEM AS EXCITING AS IT USED TO BE.
IT IS COMPARED TO THE HOUSTON CITY LIBRARY, TERRI. WHAT'S IN NEW YORK? NASA SENDING YOU ON BUSINESS?
OH, NO. I'M VISITING MY SON. YOU MIGHT HAVE HEARD OF HIM. HIS NAME'S ALBERT ROTHSTEIN BUT HE GOES BY ATOM-SMASHER NOW.
YOU MEAN HE'S ONE OF THE JUSTICE SOCIETY OF AMERICA?! THAT'S AMAZING!
I'M SO PROUD OF HIM.
...NOW IF HE'D ONLY FIND THE RIGHT GIRL--
SSSORRY TO INTERRUPT THE IN-FLIGHT MOVIE--
--BUT I'M AFRAID YOUR TRIP WILL BE ENDING SSSOONER THAN SCHEDULED.
MY NAME IS KOBRA, THE HARBINGER OF KALI-YUGA, AND AS OF NOW THIS PLANE'S FLIGHT SYSTEMS ARE MINE. TO MONITOR, TO CHANGE... TO SHUT DOWN.
HAPPY LANDINGSSS.
"NO! THIS CAN'T BE HAPPENING!" TERRI ROTHSTEIN THINKS.

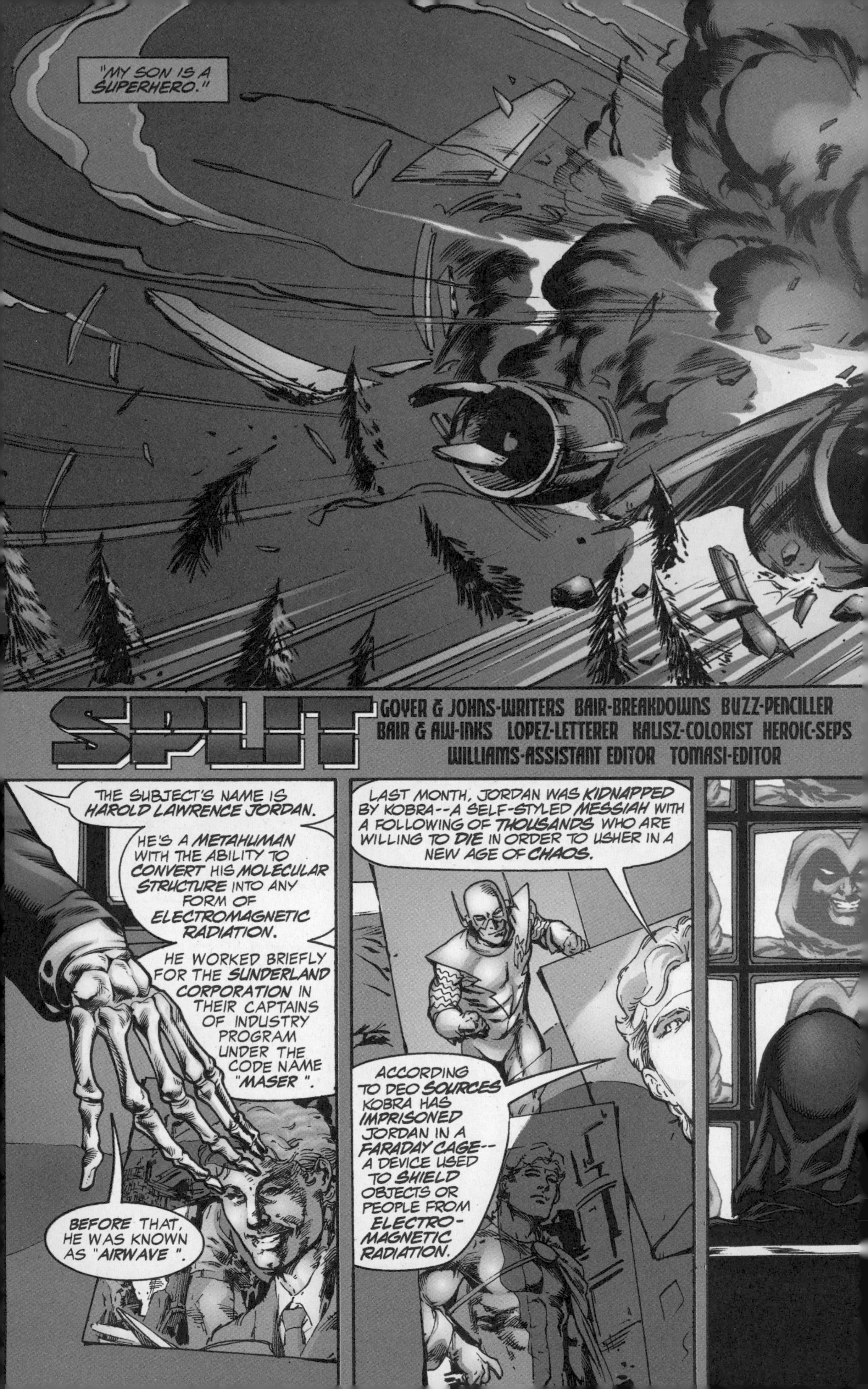
"MY SON IS A SUPERHERO."
SPLIT
GOYER & JOHNS-WRITERS BAIR-BREAKDOWNS BUZZ-PENCILLER BAIR & AW-INKS LOPEZ-LETTERER KALISZ-COLORIST HEROIC-SEPS WILLIAMS-ASSISTANT EDITOR TOMASI-EDITOR
THE SUBJECT'S NAME IS HAROLD LAWRENCE JORDAN.
HE'S A METAHUMAN WITH THE ABILITY TO CONVERT HIS MOLECULAR STRUCTURE INTO ANY FORM OF ELECTROMAGNETIC RADIATION.
HE WORKED BRIEFLY FOR THE SUNDERLAND CORPORATION IN THEIR CAPTAINS OF INDUSTRY PROGRAM UNDER THE CODE NAME "MASER".
BEFORE THAT, HE WAS KNOWN AS "AIRWAVE".
LAST MONTH, JORDAN WAS KIDNAPPED BY KOBRA--A SELF-STYLED MESSIAH WITH A FOLLOWING OF THOUSANDS WHO ARE WILLING TO DIE IN ORDER TO USHER IN A NEW AGE OF CHAOS.
ACCORDING TO DEO SOURCES KOBRA HAS IMPRISONED JORDAN IN A FARADAY CAGE-- A DEVICE USED TO SHIELD OBJECTS OR PEOPLE FROM ELECTRO-MAGNETIC RADIATION.

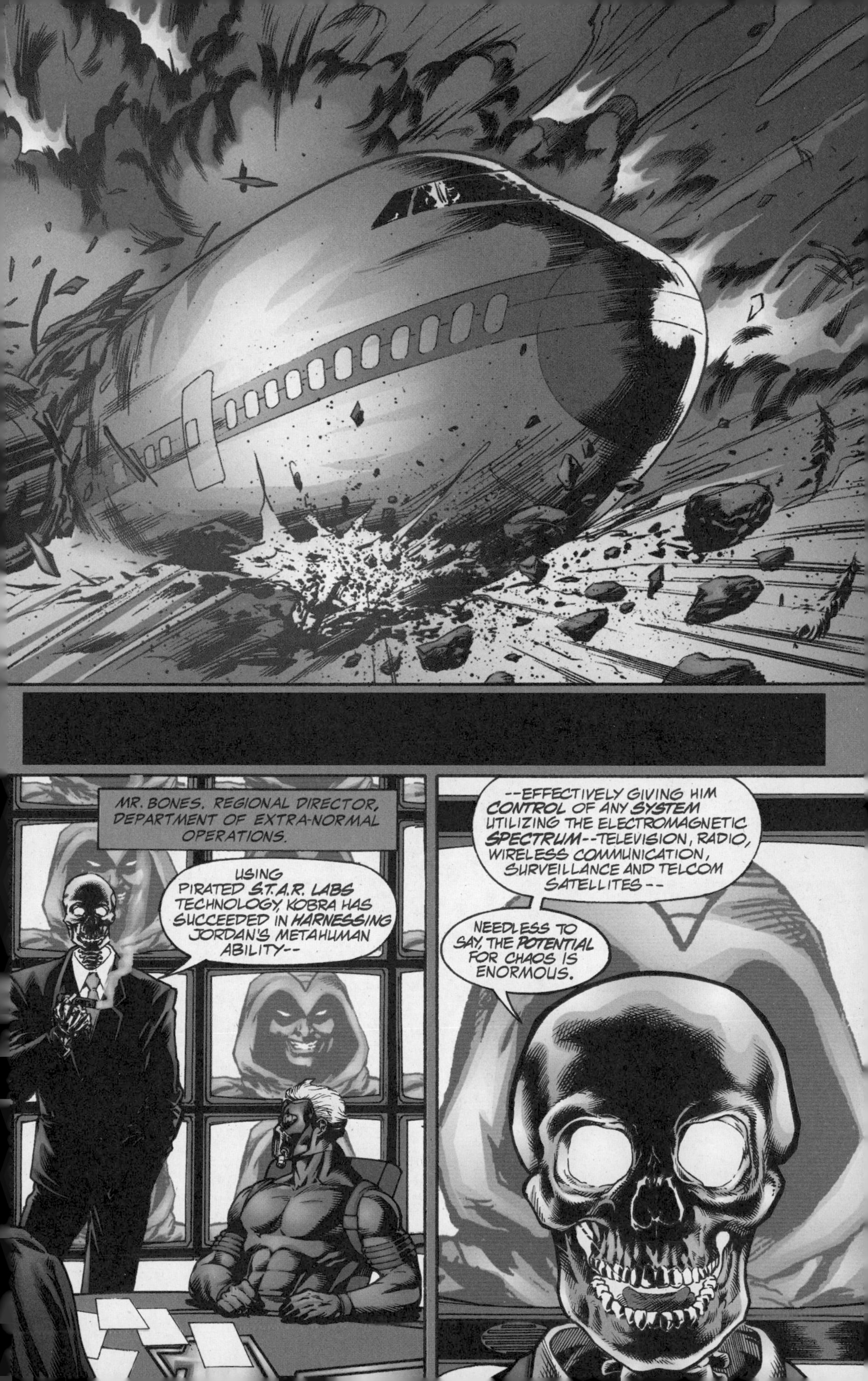
MR. BONES. REGIONAL DIRECTOR, DEPARTMENT OF EXTRA-NORMAL OPERATIONS.
USING PIRATED S.T.A.R. LABS TECHNOLOGY, KOBRA HAS SUCCEEDED IN HARNESSING JORDAN'S METAHUMAN ABILITY--
--EFFECTIVELY GIVING HIM CONTROL OF ANY SYSTEM UTILIZING THE ELECTROMAGNETIC SPECTRUM--TELEVISION, RADIO, WIRELESS COMMUNICATION, SURVEILLANCE AND TELCOM SATELLITES--
NEEDLESS TO SAY, THE POTENTIAL FOR CHAOS IS ENORMOUS.

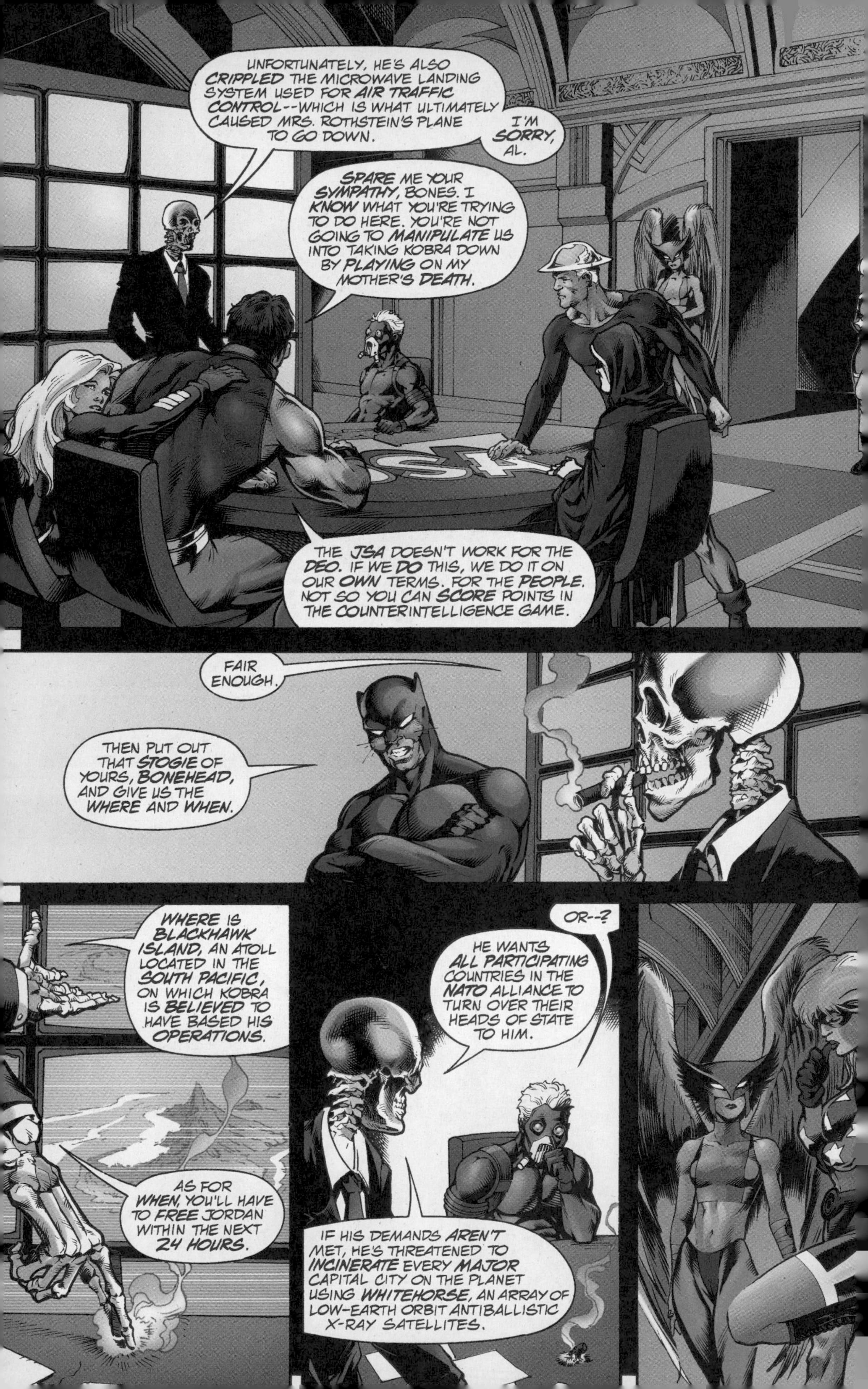

UNFORTUNATELY, HE'S ALSO CRIPPLED THE MICROWAVE LANDING SYSTEM USED FOR AIR TRAFFIC CONTROL--WHICH IS WHAT ULTIMATELY CAUSED MRS. ROTHSTEIN'S PLANE TO GO DOWN.
I'M SORRY, AL.
SPARE ME YOUR SYMPATHY, BONES. I KNOW WHAT YOU'RE TRYING TO DO HERE. YOU'RE NOT GOING TO MANIPULATE US INTO TAKING KOBRA DOWN BY PLAYING ON MY MOTHER'S DEATH.
THE JSA DOESN'T WORK FOR THE DEO. IF WE DO THIS, WE DO IT ON OUR OWN TERMS. FOR THE PEOPLE. NOT SO YOU CAN SCORE POINTS IN THE COUNTERINTELLIGENCE GAME.
FAIR ENOUGH.
THEN PUT OUT THAT STOGIE OF YOURS, BONEHEAD, AND GIVE US THE WHERE AND WHEN.
WHERE IS BLACKHAWK ISLAND, AN ATOLL LOCATED IN THE SOUTH PACIFIC, ON WHICH KOBRA IS BELIEVED TO HAVE BASED HIS OPERATIONS.
AS FOR WHEN, YOU'LL HAVE TO FREE JORDAN WITHIN THE NEXT 24 HOURS.
HE WANTS ALL PARTICIPATING COUNTRIES IN THE NATO ALLIANCE TO TURN OVER THEIR HEADS OF STATE TO HIM.
OR--?
IF HIS DEMANDS AREN'T MET, HE'S THREATENED TO INCINERATE EVERY MAJOR CAPITAL CITY ON THE PLANET USING WHITEHORSE, AN ARRAY OF LOW-EARTH ORBIT ANTIBALLISTIC X-RAY SATELLITES.

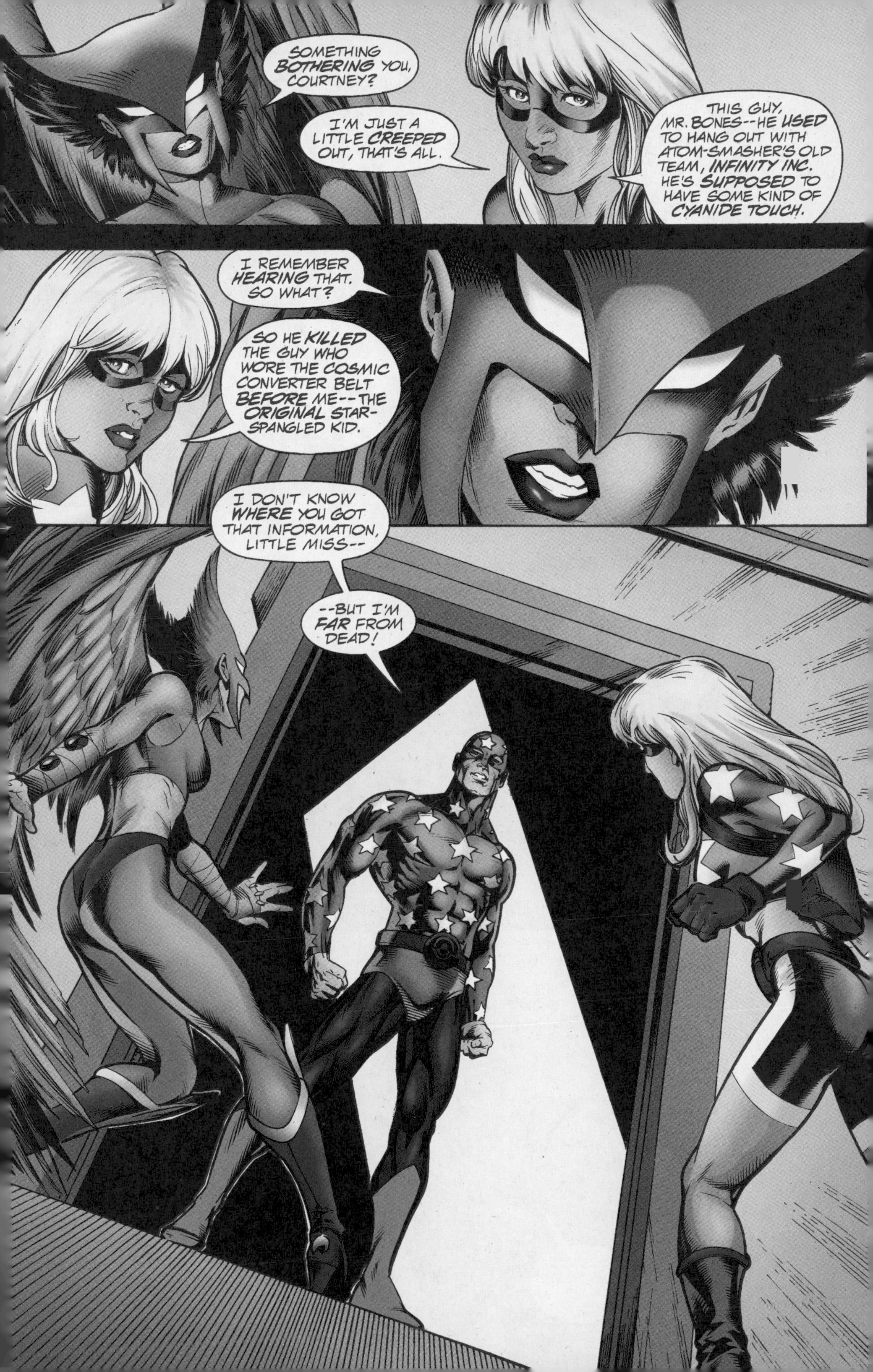
SOMETHING BOTHERING YOU, COURTNEY?
I'M JUST A LITTLE CREEPED OUT, THAT'S ALL.
THIS GUY, MR. BONES--HE USED TO HANG OUT WITH ATOM-SMASHER'S OLD TEAM, INFINITY INC. HE'S SUPPOSED TO HAVE SOME KIND OF CYANIDE TOUCH.
I REMEMBER HEARING THAT. SO WHAT?
SO HE KILLED THE GUY WHO WORE THE COSMIC CONVERTER BELT BEFORE ME--THE ORIGINAL STAR-SPANGLED KID.
I DON'T KNOW WHERE YOU GOT THAT INFORMATION, LITTLE MISS--
--BUT I'M FAR FROM DEAD!

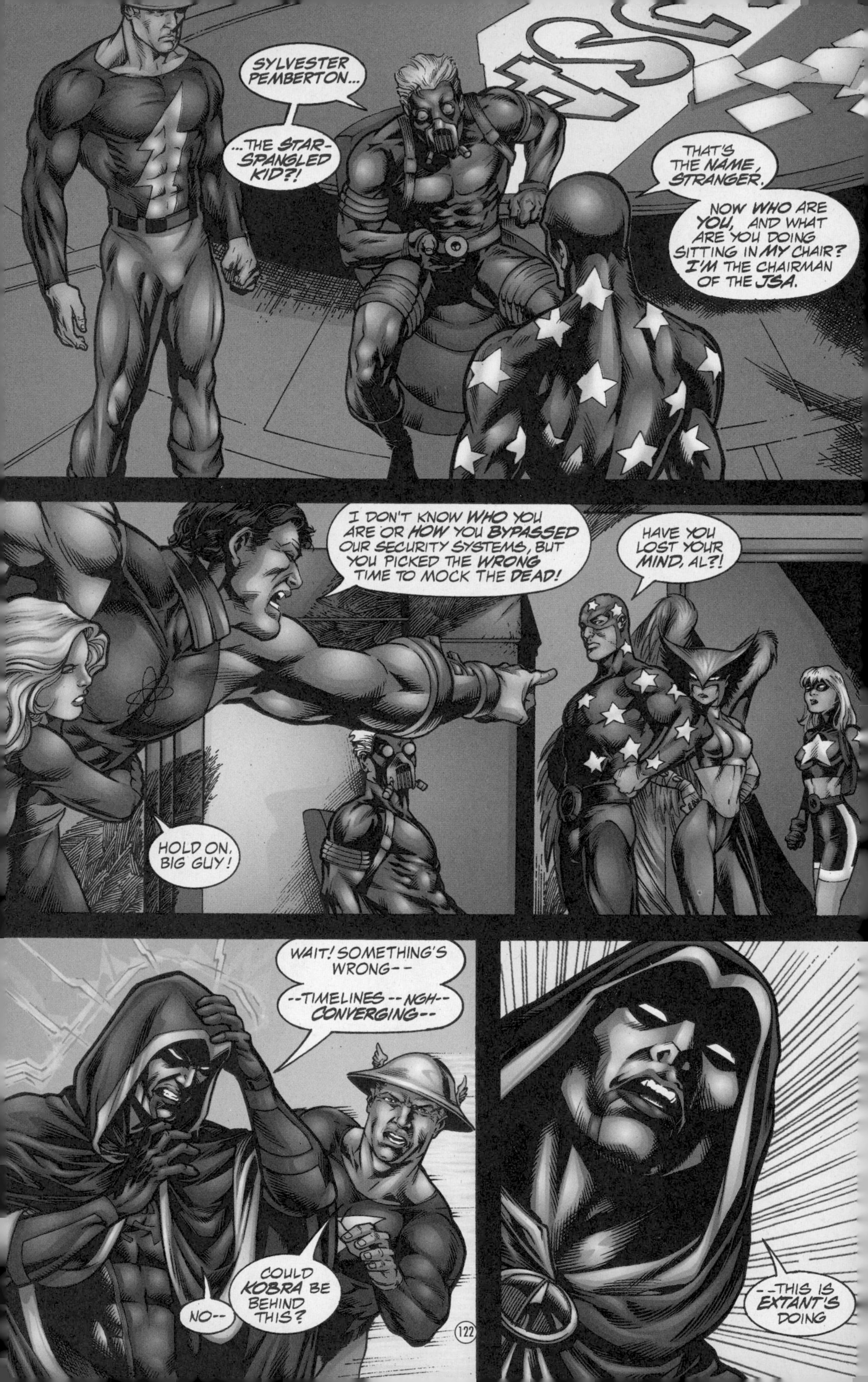
SYLVESTER PEMBERTON...
...THE STAR-SPANGLED KID?!
THAT'S THE NAME, STRANGER.
NOW WHO ARE YOU, AND WHAT ARE YOU DOING SITTING IN MY CHAIR? I'M THE CHAIRMAN OF THE JSA.
I DON'T KNOW WHO YOU ARE OR HOW YOU BYPASSED OUR SECURITY SYSTEMS, BUT YOU PICKED THE WRONG TIME TO MOCK THE DEAD!
HOLD ON, BIG GUY!
HAVE YOU LOST YOUR MIND, AL?!
WAIT! SOMETHING'S WRONG--
--TIMELINES--NGH--CONVERGING--
COULD KOBRA BE BEHIND THIS?
NO--
--THIS IS EXTANT'S DOING

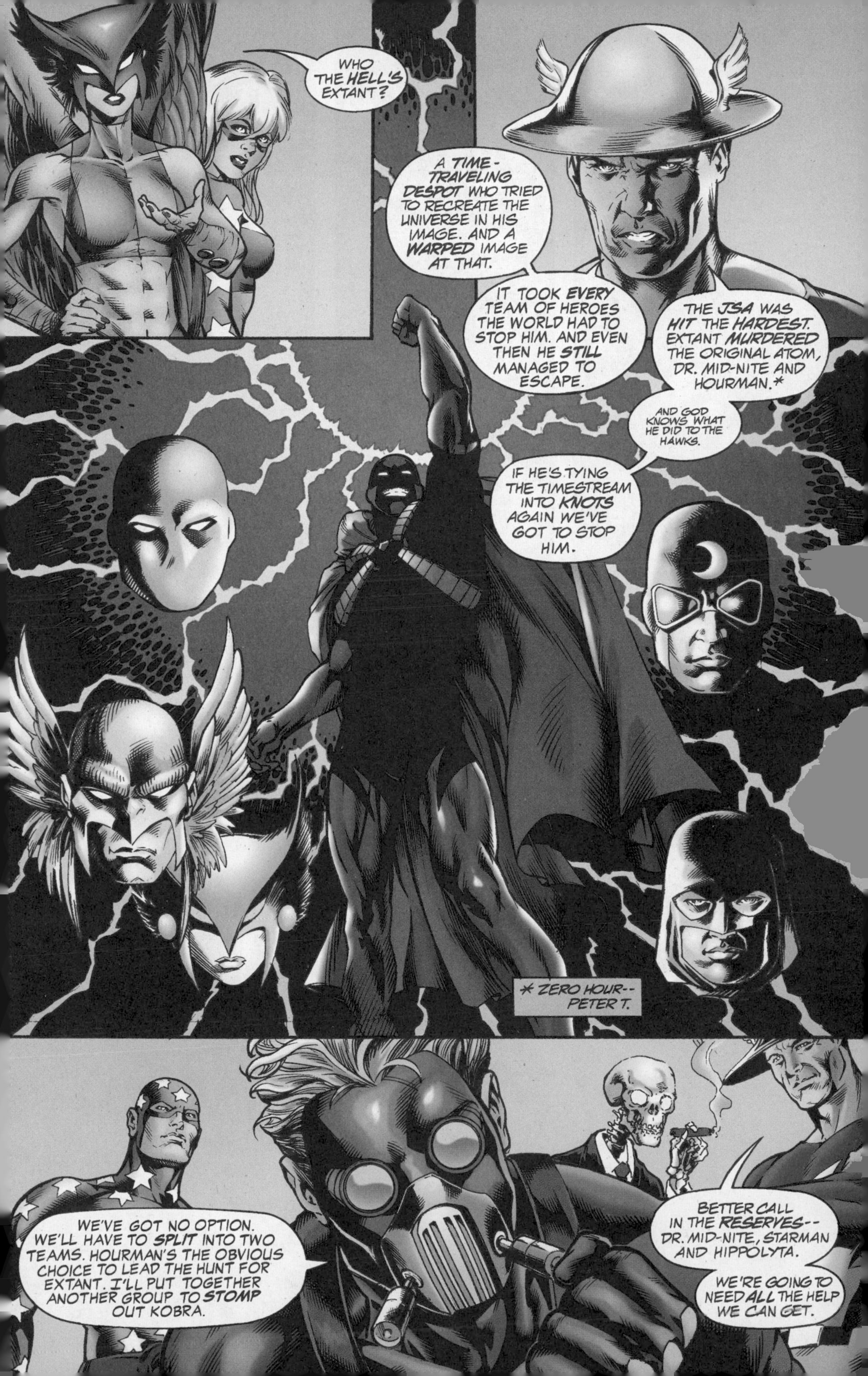
WHO THE HELL'S EXTANT?
A TIME-TRAVELING DESPOT WHO TRIED TO RECREATE THE UNIVERSE IN HIS IMAGE. AND A WARPED IMAGE AT THAT.
IT TOOK EVERY TEAM OF HEROES THE WORLD HAD TO STOP HIM. AND EVEN THEN HE STILL MANAGED TO ESCAPE.
THE JSA WAS HIT THE HARDEST. EXTANT MURDERED THE ORIGINAL ATOM, DR. MID-NITE AND HOURMAN.*
AND GOD KNOWS WHAT HE DID TO THE HAWKS.
IF HE'S TYING THE TIMESTREAM INTO KNOTS AGAIN WE'VE GOT TO STOP HIM.
* ZERO HOUR-- PETER T.
WE'VE GOT NO OPTION. WE'LL HAVE TO SPLIT INTO TWO TEAMS. HOURMAN'S THE OBVIOUS CHOICE TO LEAD THE HUNT FOR EXTANT. I'LL PUT TOGETHER ANOTHER GROUP TO STOMP OUT KOBRA.
BETTER CALL IN THE RESERVES-- DR. MID-NITE, STARMAN AND HIPPOLYTA.
WE'RE GOING TO NEED ALL THE HELP WE CAN GET.

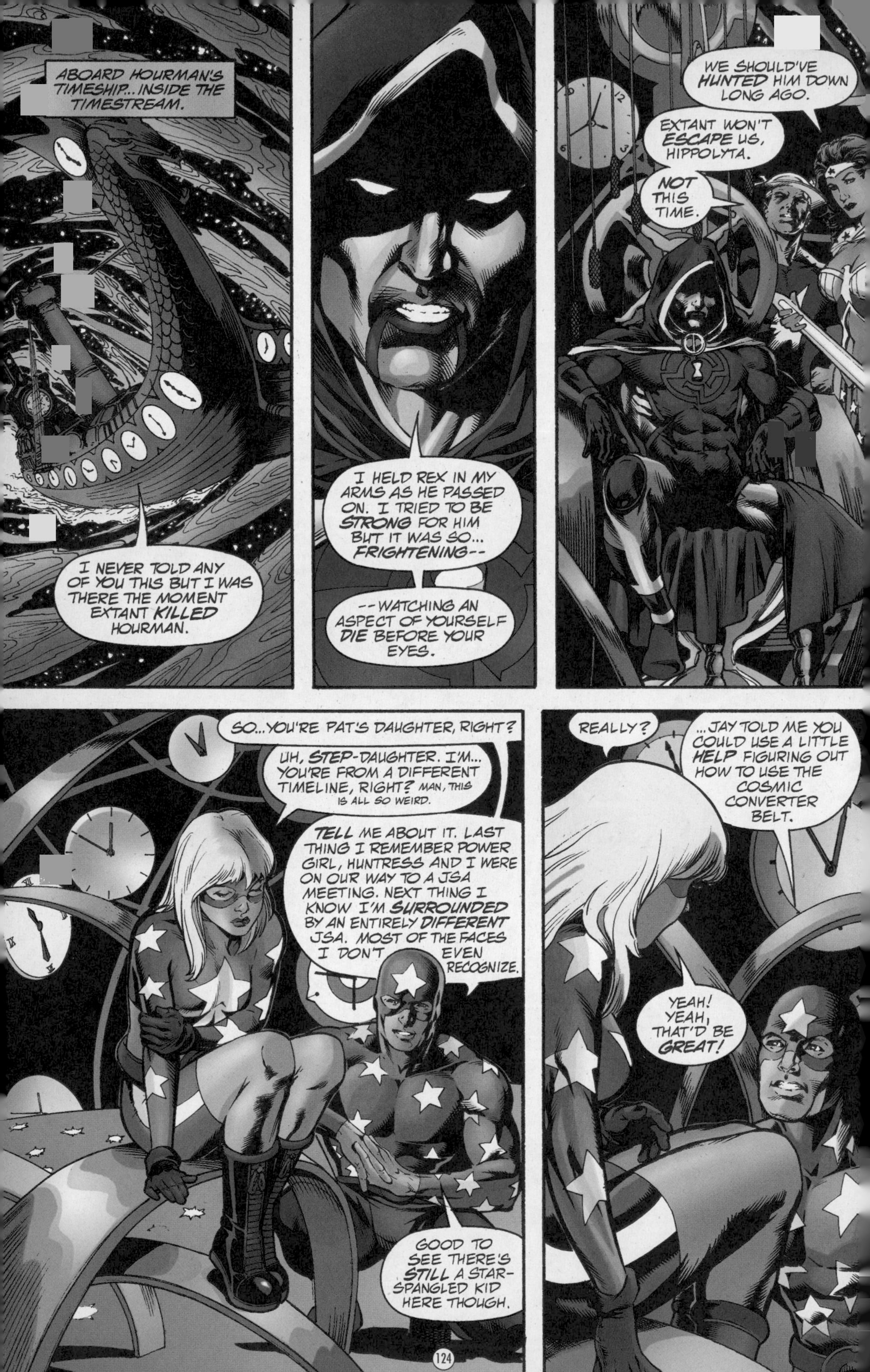
ABOARD HOURMAN'S TIMESHIP...INSIDE THE TIMESTREAM.
I NEVER TOLD ANY OF YOU THIS BUT I WAS THERE THE MOMENT EXTANT KILLED HOURMAN.
I HELD REX IN MY ARMS AS HE PASSED ON. I TRIED TO BE STRONG FOR HIM BUT IT WAS SO... FRIGHTENING--
--WATCHING AN ASPECT OF YOURSELF DIE BEFORE YOUR EYES.
WE SHOULD'VE HUNTED HIM DOWN LONG AGO.
EXTANT WON'T ESCAPE US, HIPPOLYTA.
NOT THIS TIME.
SO...YOU'RE PAT'S DAUGHTER, RIGHT?
UH, STEP-DAUGHTER. I'M... YOU'RE FROM A DIFFERENT TIMELINE, RIGHT? MAN, THIS IS ALL SO WEIRD.
TELL ME ABOUT IT. LAST THING I REMEMBER POWER GIRL, HUNTRESS AND I WERE ON OUR WAY TO A JSA MEETING. NEXT THING I KNOW I'M SURROUNDED BY AN ENTIRELY DIFFERENT JSA. MOST OF THE FACES I DON'T EVEN RECOGNIZE.
GOOD TO SEE THERE'S STILL A STAR-SPANGLED KID HERE THOUGH.
REALLY?
...JAY TOLD ME YOU COULD USE A LITTLE HELP FIGURING OUT HOW TO USE THE COSMIC CONVERTER BELT.
YEAH! YEAH, THAT'D BE GREAT!

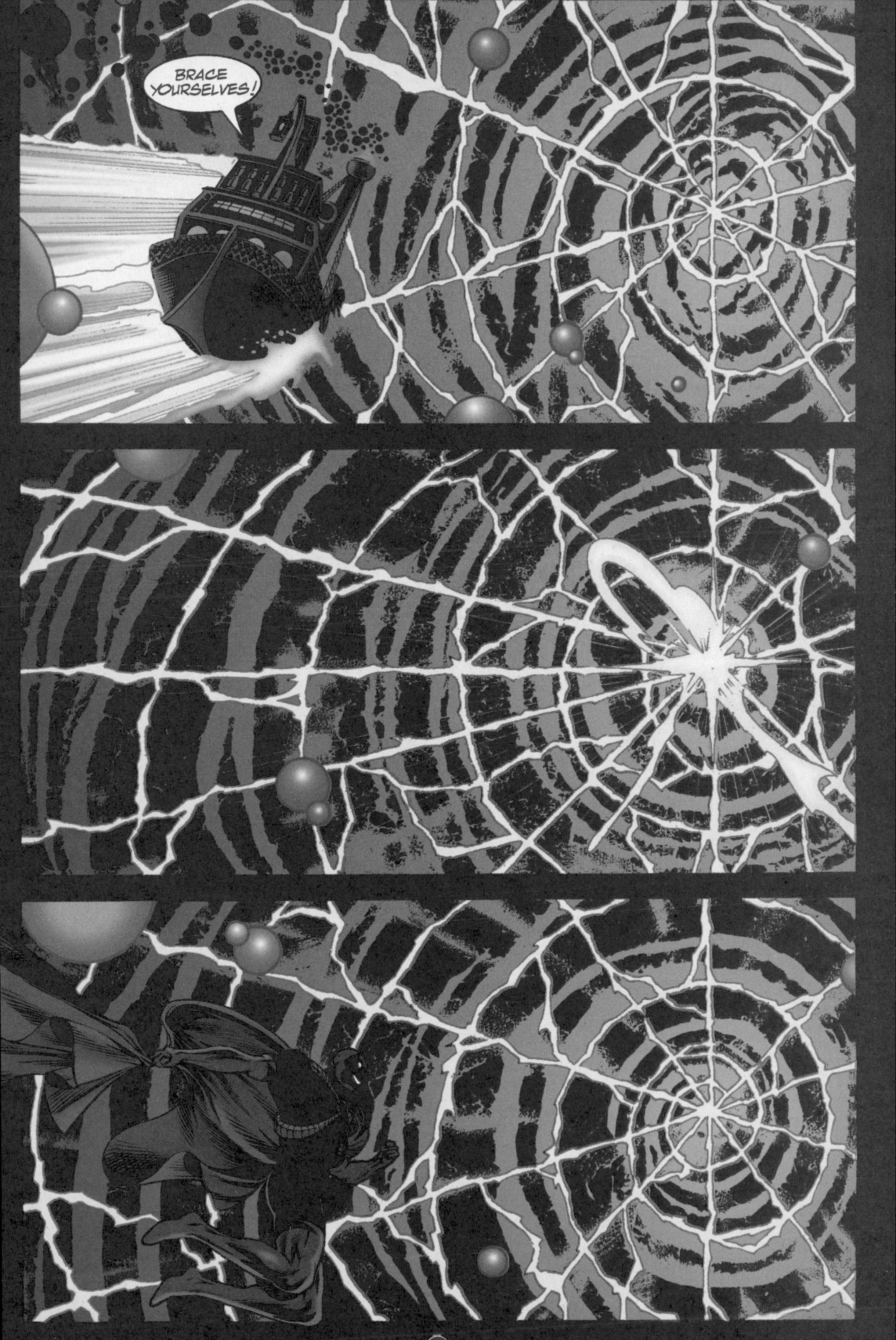
BRACE YOURSELVES!

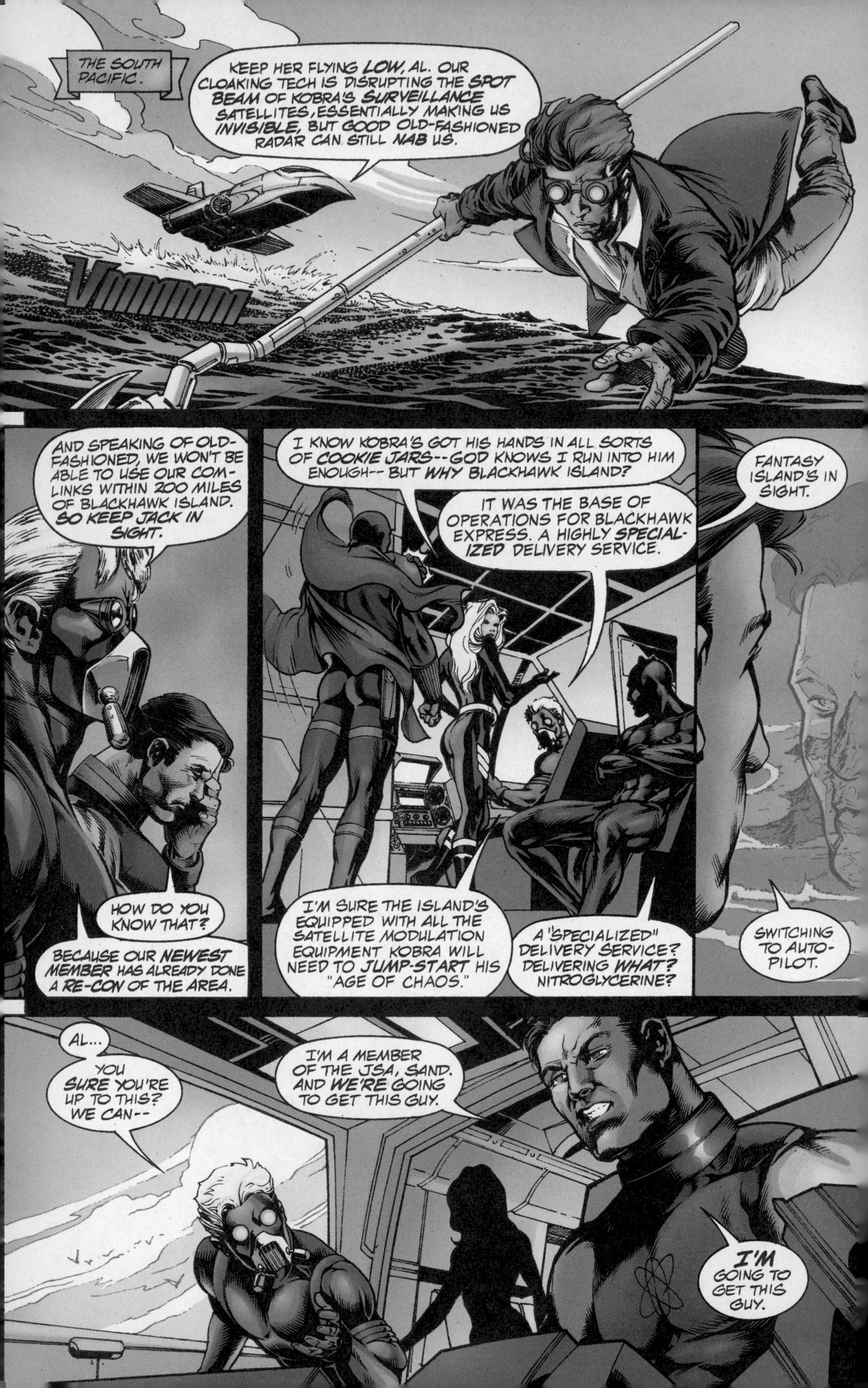
THE SOUTH PACIFIC.
KEEP HER FLYING LOW, AL. OUR CLOAKING TECH IS DISRUPTING THE SPOT BEAM OF KOBRA'S SURVEILLANCE SATELLITES, ESSENTIALLY MAKING US INVISIBLE, BUT GOOD OLD-FASHIONED RADAR CAN STILL NAB US.
VMMMMM
AND SPEAKING OF OLD-FASHIONED, WE WON'T BE ABLE TO USE OUR COM-LINKS WITHIN 200 MILES OF BLACKHAWK ISLAND. SO KEEP JACK IN SIGHT.
HOW DO YOU KNOW THAT?
BECAUSE OUR NEWEST MEMBER HAS ALREADY DONE A RE-CON OF THE AREA.
I KNOW KOBRA'S GOT HIS HANDS IN ALL SORTS OF COOKIE JARS--GOD KNOWS I RUN INTO HIM ENOUGH-- BUT WHY BLACKHAWK ISLAND?
IT WAS THE BASE OF OPERATIONS FOR BLACKHAWK EXPRESS. A HIGHLY SPECIALIZED DELIVERY SERVICE.
I'M SURE THE ISLAND'S EQUIPPED WITH ALL THE SATELLITE MODULATION EQUIPMENT KOBRA WILL NEED TO JUMP-START HIS "AGE OF CHAOS."
A "SPECIALIZED" DELIVERY SERVICE? DELIVERING WHAT? NITROGLYCERINE?
FANTASY ISLAND'S IN SIGHT.
SWITCHING TO AUTO-PILOT.
AL... YOU SURE YOU'RE UP TO THIS? WE CAN--
I'M A MEMBER OF THE JSA, SAND. AND WE'RE GOING TO GET THIS GUY.
I'M GOING TO GET THIS GUY.

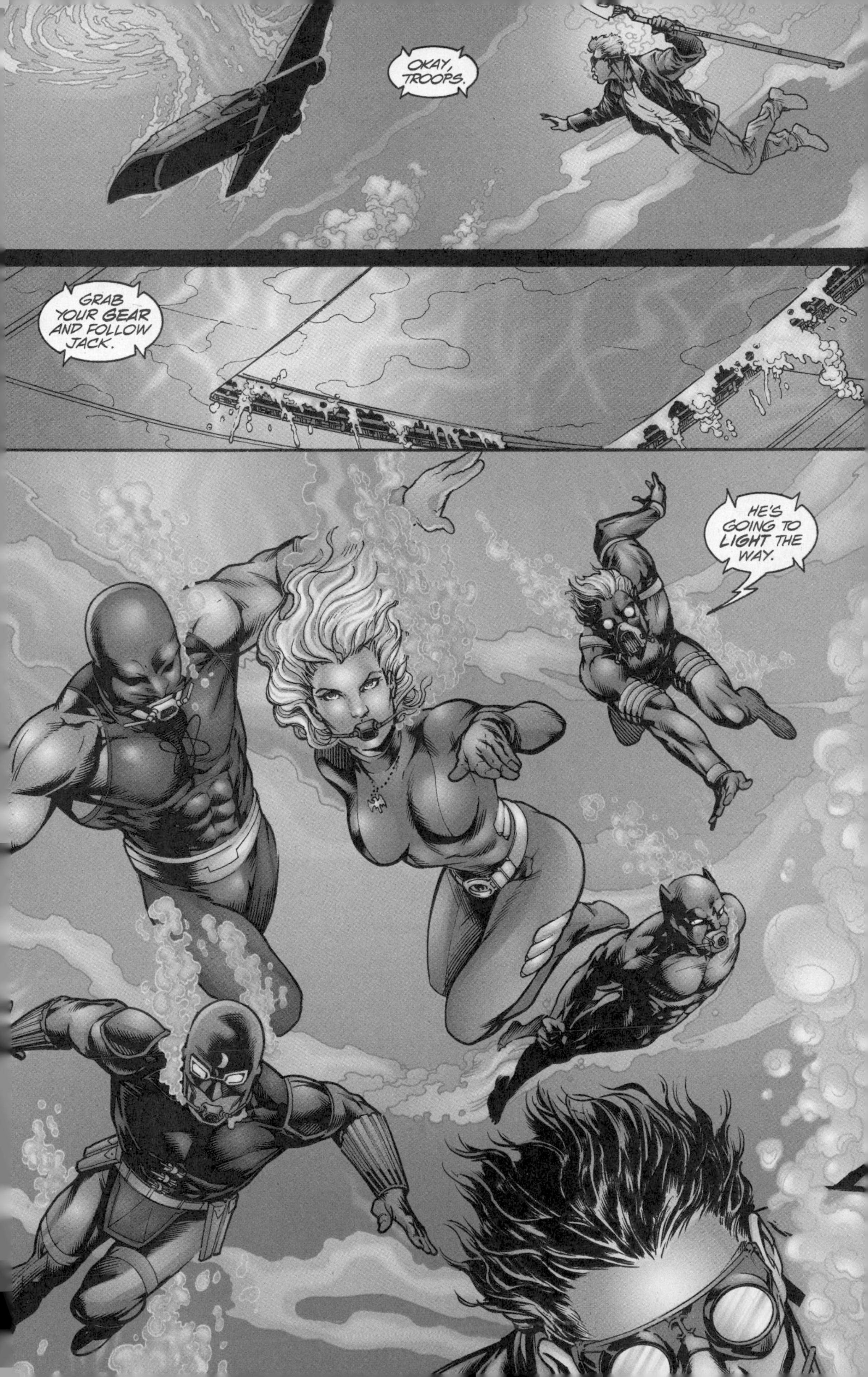
OKAY, TROOPS.
GRAB YOUR GEAR AND FOLLOW JACK.
HE'S GOING TO LIGHT THE WAY.

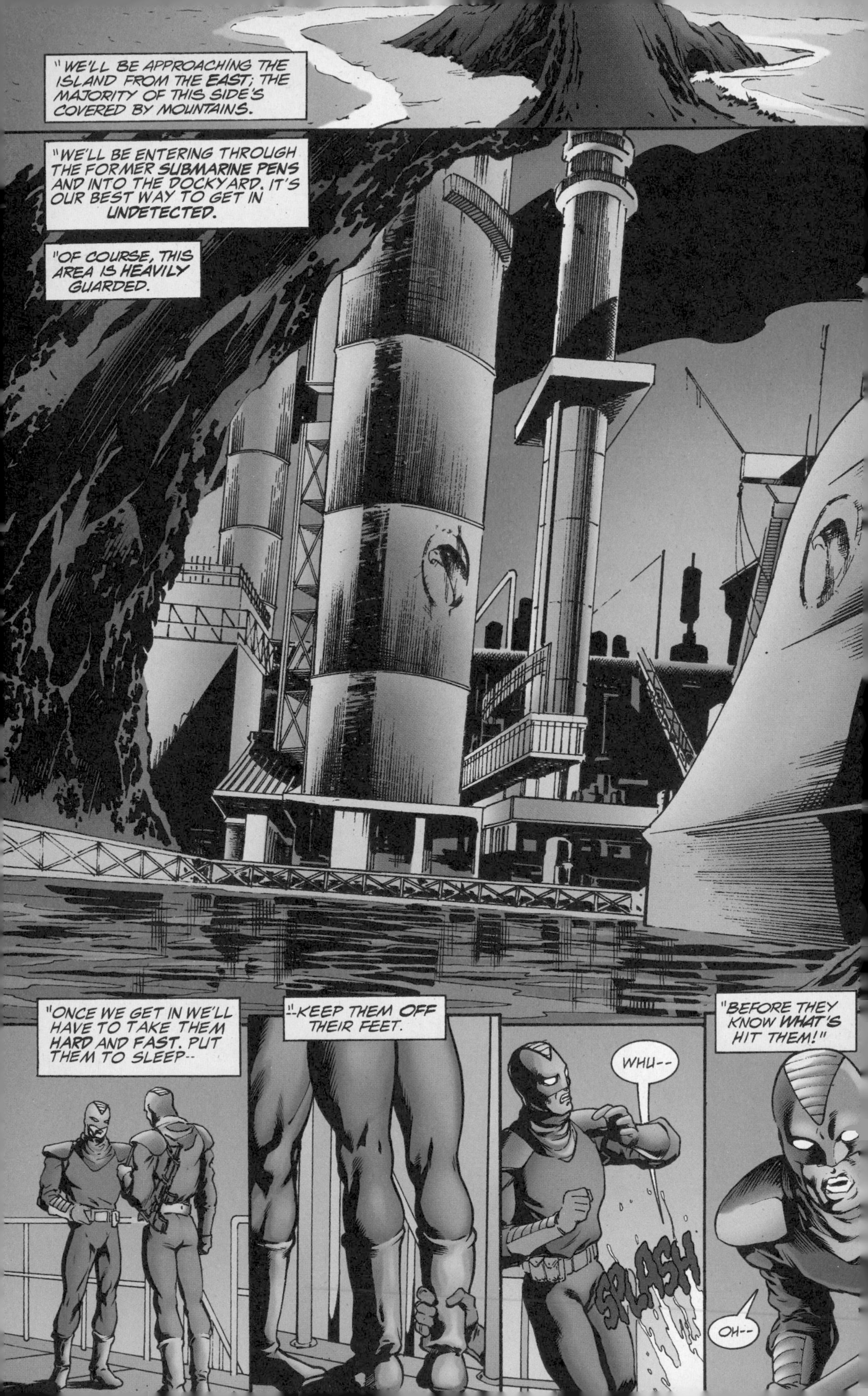
"WE'LL BE APPROACHING THE ISLAND FROM THE EAST; THE MAJORITY OF THIS SIDE'S COVERED BY MOUNTAINS.
"WE'LL BE ENTERING THROUGH THE FORMER SUBMARINE PENS AND INTO THE DOCKYARD. IT'S OUR BEST WAY TO GET IN UNDETECTED.
"OF COURSE, THIS AREA IS HEAVILY GUARDED.
"ONCE WE GET IN WE'LL HAVE TO TAKE THEM HARD AND FAST. PUT THEM TO SLEEP--
--KEEP THEM OFF THEIR FEET.
WHU--
SPLASH
"BEFORE THEY KNOW WHAT'S HIT THEM!"
OH--

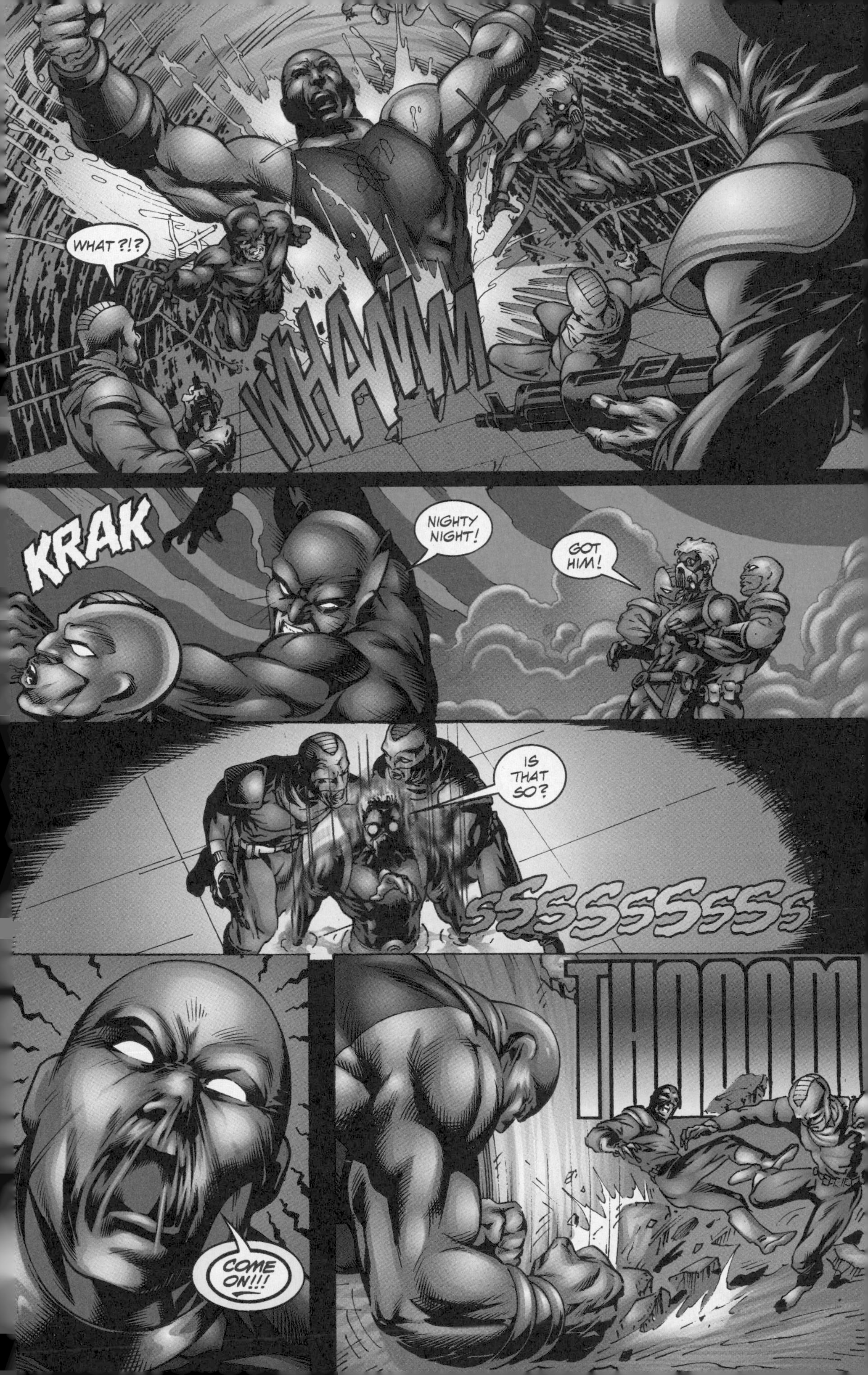
WHAT ?!?
WHAMM
KRAK
NIGHTY NIGHT!
GOT HIM!
IS THAT SO?
SSSSSSSSSS
COME ON!!!
THOOOM

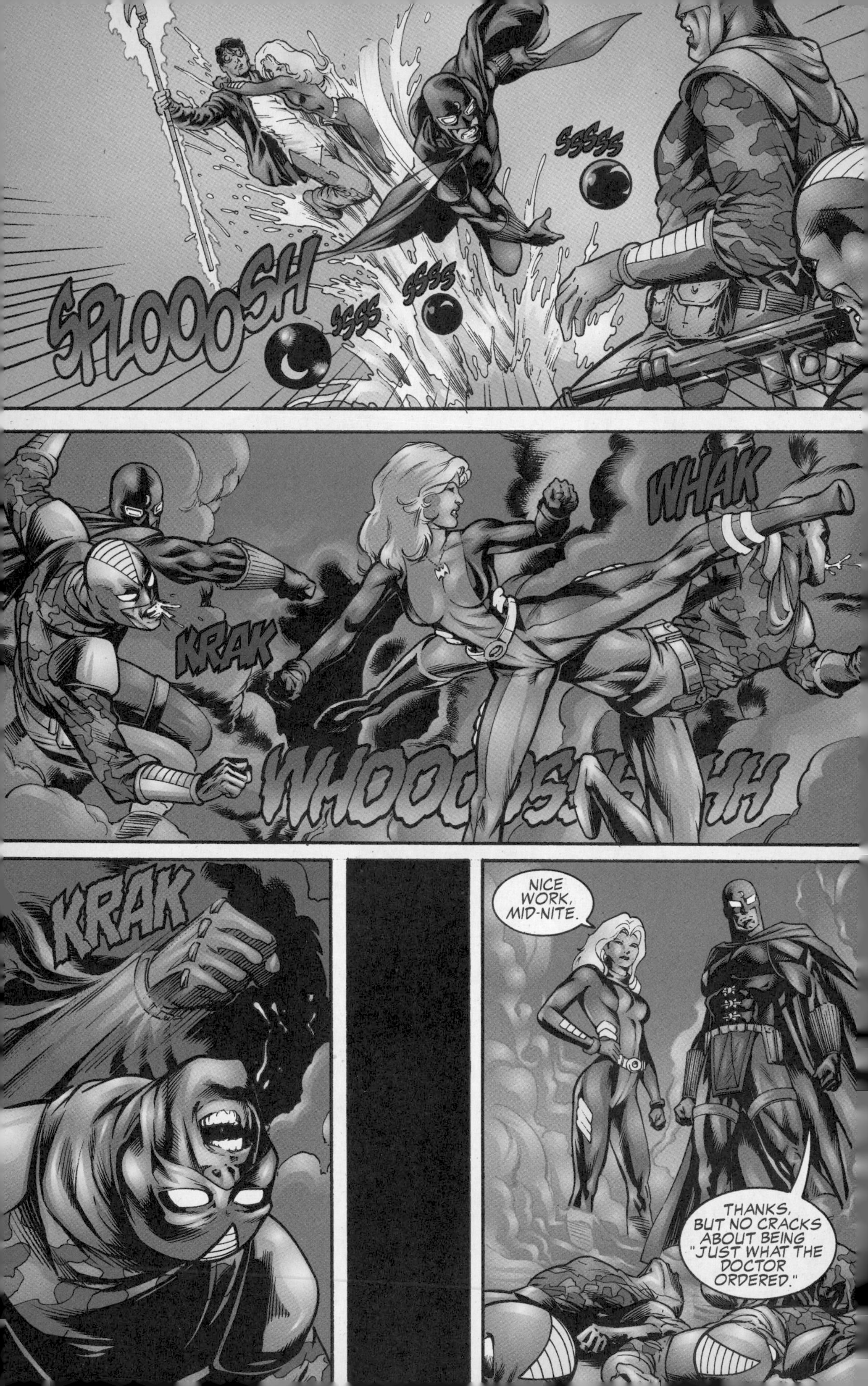
SSSSS
SPLOOOSH
SSSS
SSSS
WHAK
KRAK
WHOOOSSSHH
KRAK
NICE WORK, MID-NITE.
THANKS, BUT NO CRACKS ABOUT BEING "JUST WHAT THE DOCTOR ORDERED."

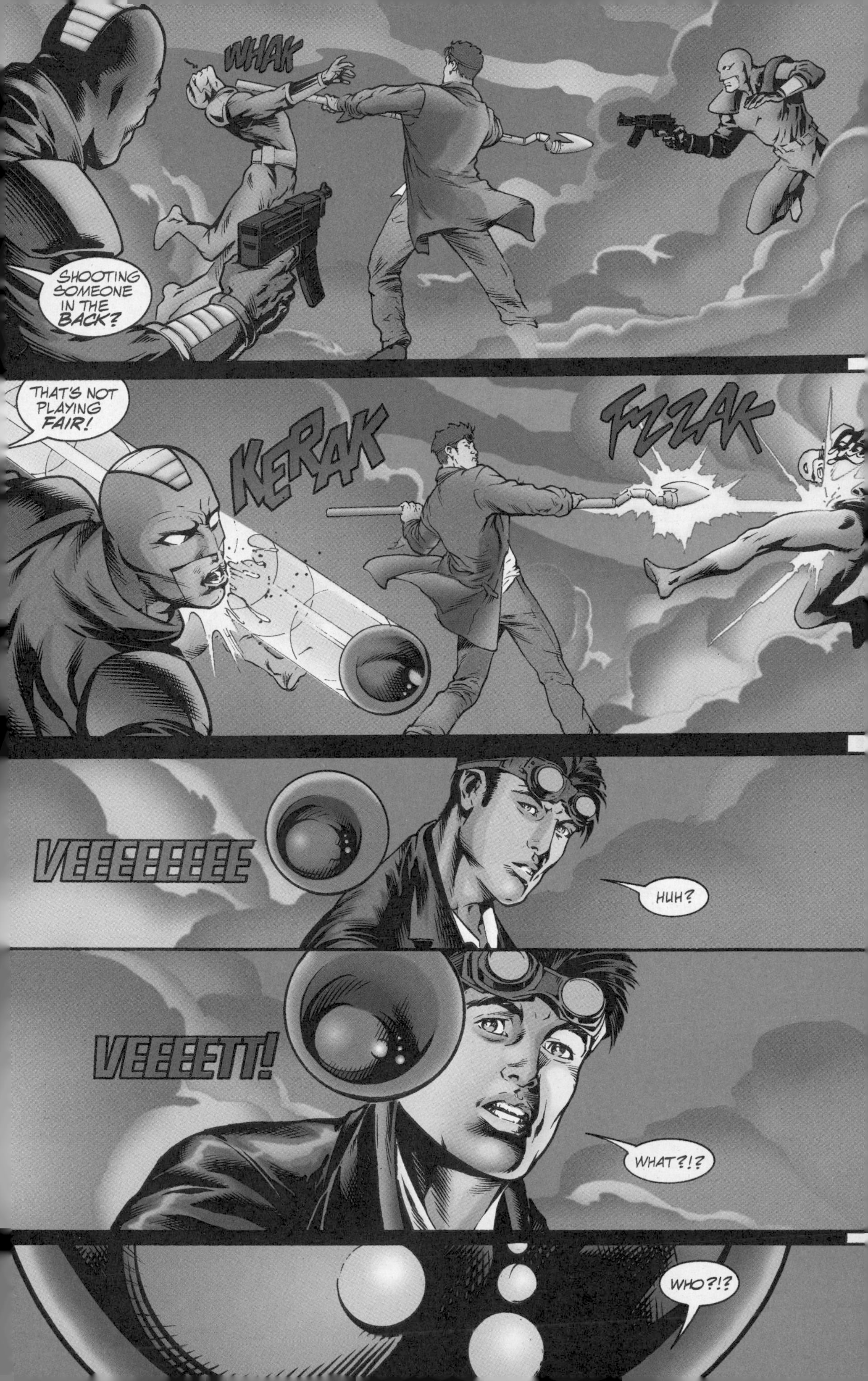
WHAK
SHOOTING SOMEONE IN THE BACK?
THAT'S NOT PLAYING FAIR!
KERAK
FZZAK
VEEEEEEEE
HUH?
VEEEETT!
WHAT?!?
WHO?!?

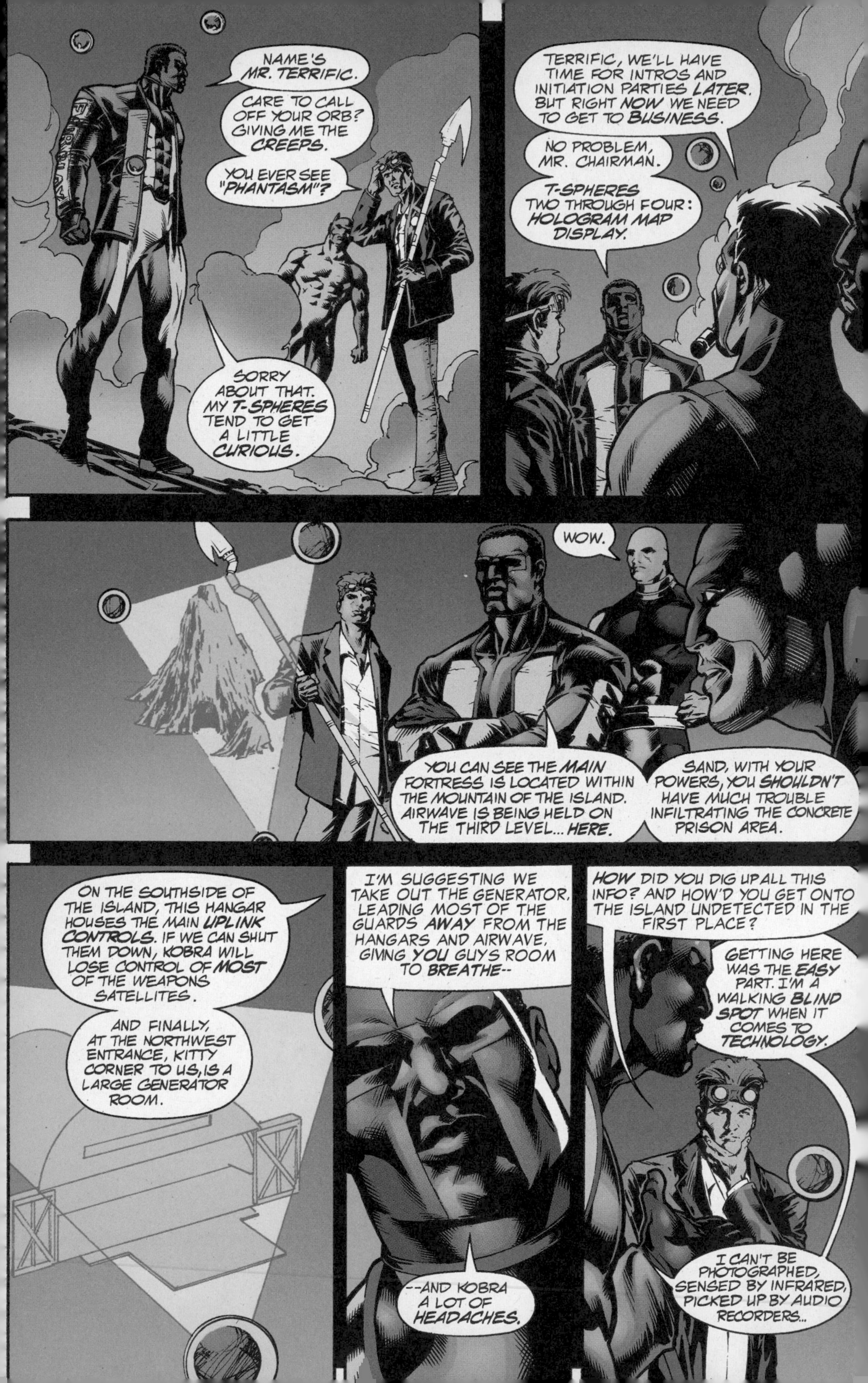
NAME'S MR. TERRIFIC.
CARE TO CALL OFF YOUR ORB? GIVING ME THE CREEPS.
YOU EVER SEE "PHANTASM"?
SORRY ABOUT THAT. MY T-SPHERES TEND TO GET A LITTLE CURIOUS.
TERRIFIC, WE'LL HAVE TIME FOR INTROS AND INITIATION PARTIES LATER. BUT RIGHT NOW WE NEED TO GET TO BUSINESS.
NO PROBLEM, MR. CHAIRMAN.
T-SPHERES TWO THROUGH FOUR: HOLOGRAM MAP DISPLAY.
WOW.
YOU CAN SEE THE MAIN FORTRESS IS LOCATED WITHIN THE MOUNTAIN OF THE ISLAND. AIRWAVE IS BEING HELD ON THE THIRD LEVEL... HERE.
SAND, WITH YOUR POWERS, YOU SHOULDN'T HAVE MUCH TROUBLE INFILTRATING THE CONCRETE PRISON AREA.
ON THE SOUTHSIDE OF THE ISLAND, THIS HANGAR HOUSES THE MAIN UPLINK CONTROLS. IF WE CAN SHUT THEM DOWN, KOBRA WILL LOSE CONTROL OF MOST OF THE WEAPONS SATELLITES.
AND FINALLY, AT THE NORTHWEST ENTRANCE, KITTY CORNER TO US, IS A LARGE GENERATOR ROOM.
I'M SUGGESTING WE TAKE OUT THE GENERATOR, LEADING MOST OF THE GUARDS AWAY FROM THE HANGARS AND AIRWAVE, GIVING YOU GUYS ROOM TO BREATHE--
--AND KOBRA A LOT OF HEADACHES.
HOW DID YOU DIG UP ALL THIS INFO? AND HOW'D YOU GET ONTO THE ISLAND UNDETECTED IN THE FIRST PLACE?
GETTING HERE WAS THE EASY PART. I'M A WALKING BLIND SPOT WHEN IT COMES TO TECHNOLOGY.
I CAN'T BE PHOTOGRAPHED, SENSED BY INFRARED, PICKED UP BY AUDIO RECORDERS...

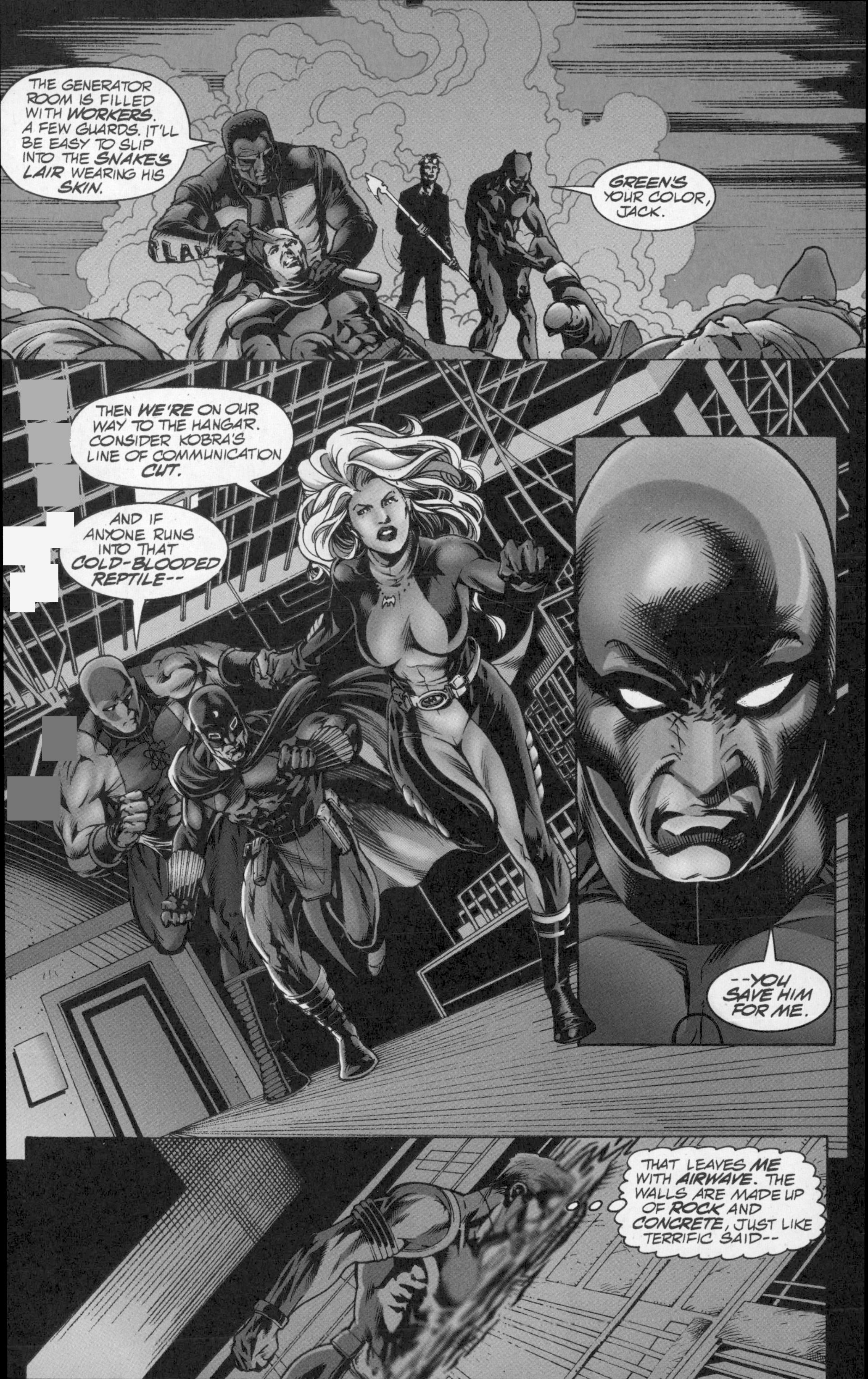
THE GENERATOR ROOM IS FILLED WITH WORKERS. A FEW GUARDS. IT'LL BE EASY TO SLIP INTO THE SNAKE'S LAIR WEARING HIS SKIN.
GREEN'S YOUR COLOR, JACK.
THEN WE'RE ON OUR WAY TO THE HANGAR. CONSIDER KOBRA'S LINE OF COMMUNICATION CUT.
AND IF ANYONE RUNS INTO THAT COLD-BLOODED REPTILE--
--YOU SAVE HIM FOR ME.
THAT LEAVES ME WITH AIRWAVE. THE WALLS ARE MADE UP OF ROCK AND CONCRETE, JUST LIKE TERRIFIC SAID--

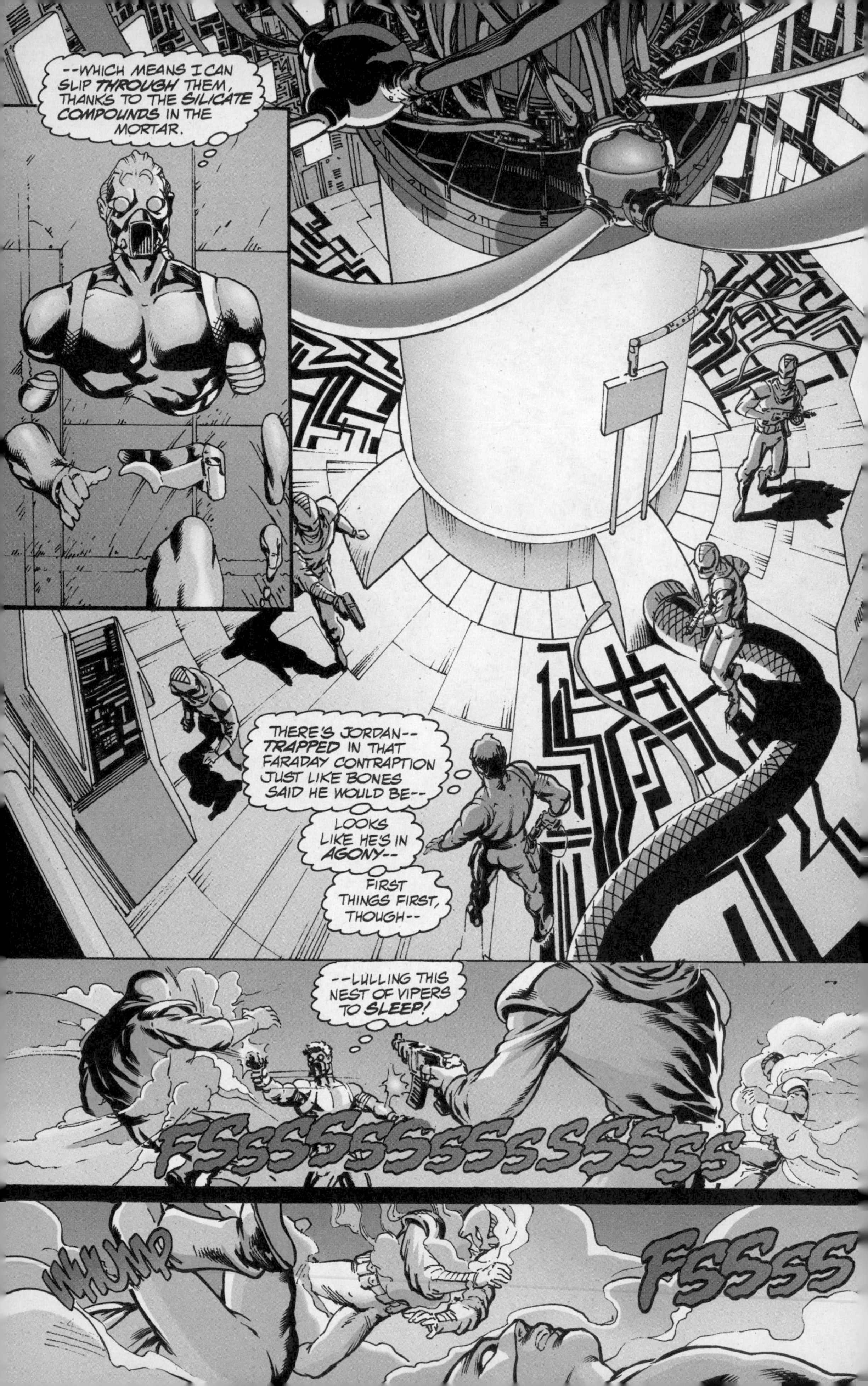
--WHICH MEANS I CAN SLIP THROUGH THEM, THANKS TO THE SILICATE COMPOUNDS IN THE MORTAR.
THERE'S JORDAN-- TRAPPED IN THAT FARADAY CONTRAPTION JUST LIKE BONES SAID HE WOULD BE--
LOOKS LIKE HE'S IN AGONY--
FIRST THINGS FIRST, THOUGH--
--LULLING THIS NEST OF VIPERS TO SLEEP!
FSSSSSSSSSSSSSSS
WHUMP
FSSSS

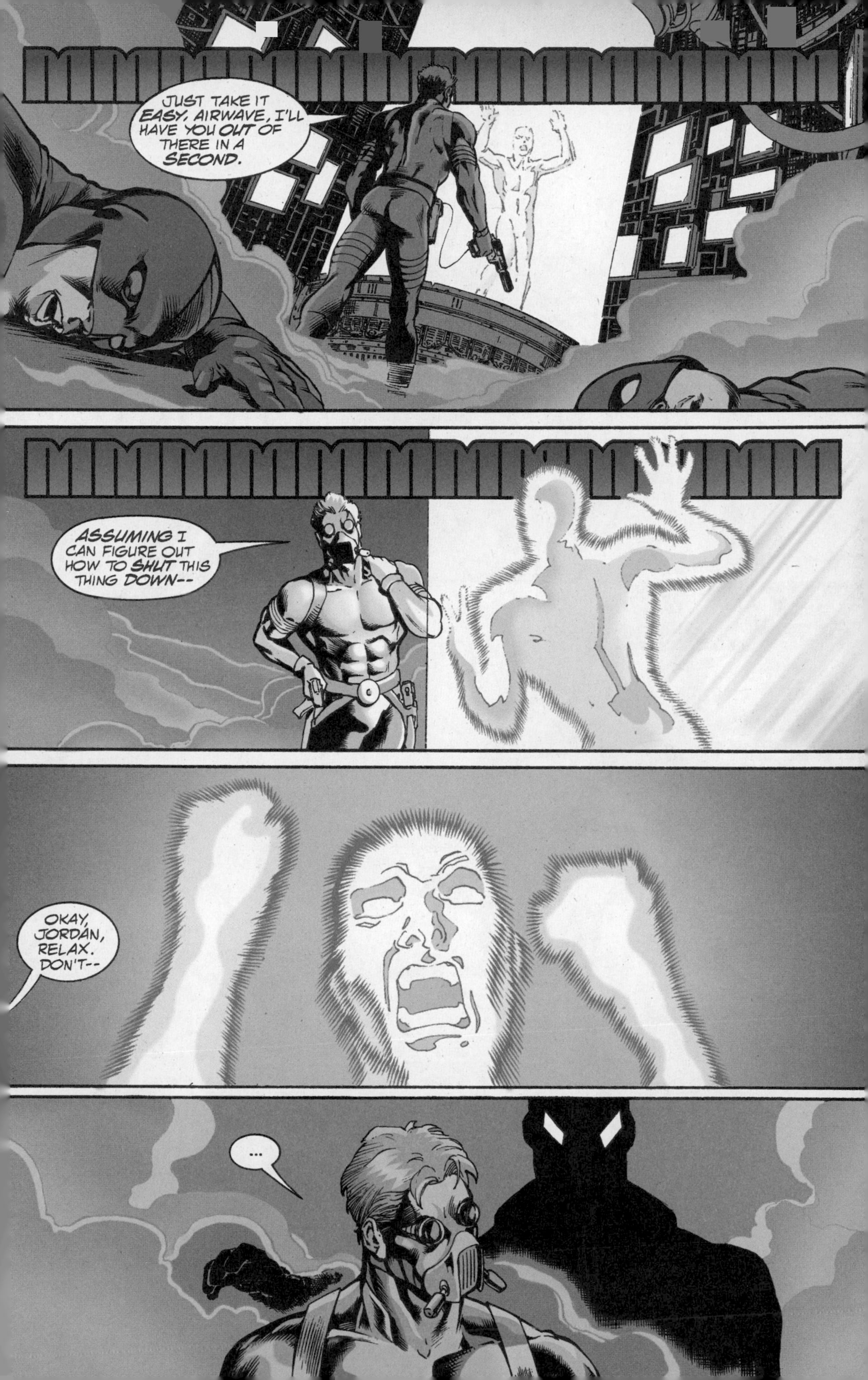
MMMMMMMMMMMMMMMMMMMMMM
JUST TAKE IT EASY, AIRWAVE, I'LL HAVE YOU OUT OF THERE IN A SECOND.
MMMMMMMMMMMMMMMMMMMMMM
ASSUMING I CAN FIGURE OUT HOW TO SHUT THIS THING DOWN--
OKAY, JORDAN, RELAX. DON'T--
...

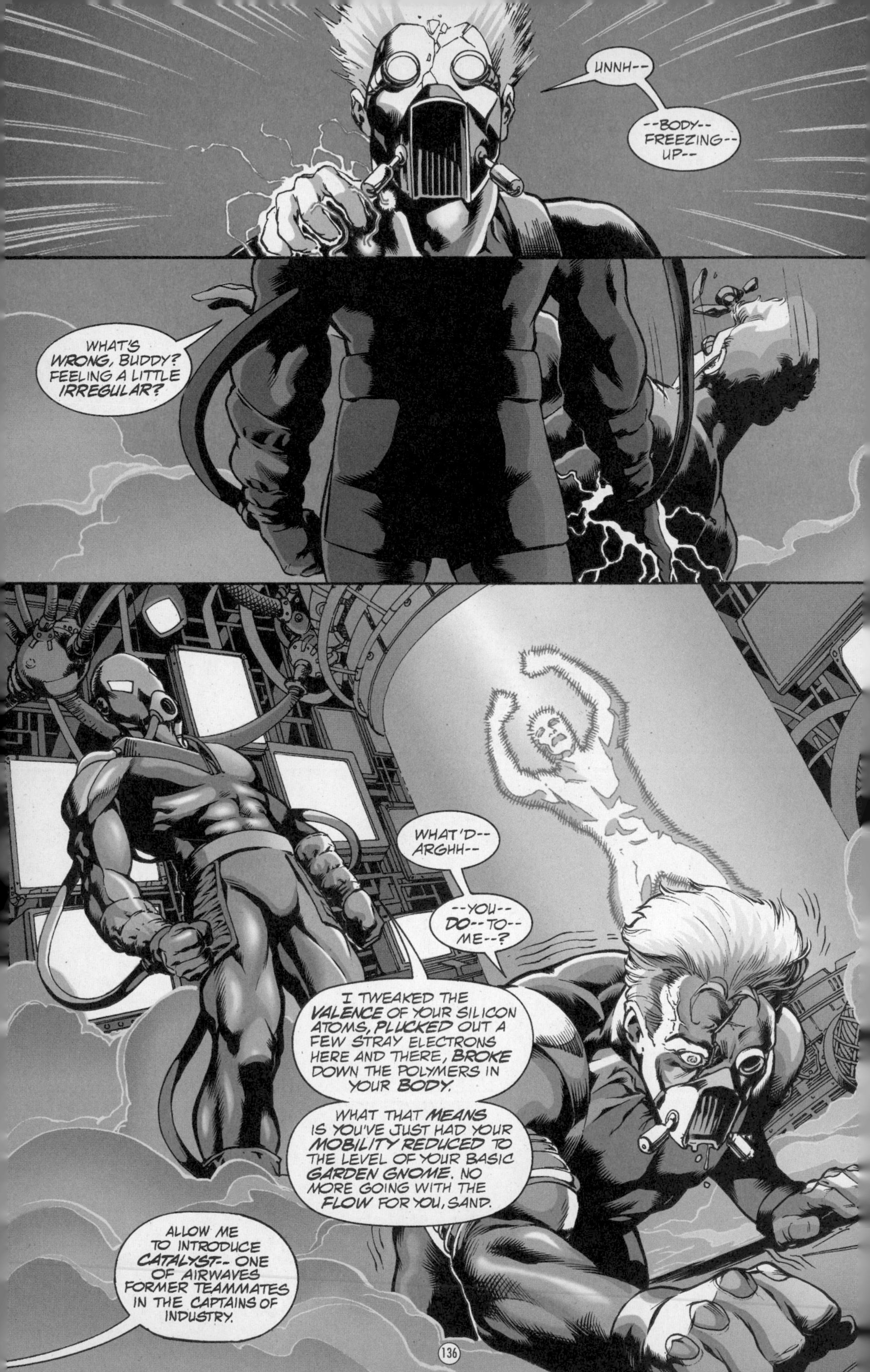
UNNH--
--BODY-- FREEZING-- UP--
WHAT'S WRONG, BUDDY? FEELING A LITTLE IRREGULAR?
WHAT'D-- ARGHH--
--YOU-- DO-- TO-- ME--?
I TWEAKED THE VALENCE OF YOUR SILICON ATOMS, PLUCKED OUT A FEW STRAY ELECTRONS HERE AND THERE, BROKE DOWN THE POLYMERS IN YOUR BODY.
WHAT THAT MEANS IS YOU'VE JUST HAD YOUR MOBILITY REDUCED TO THE LEVEL OF YOUR BASIC GARDEN GNOME. NO MORE GOING WITH THE FLOW FOR YOU, SAND.
ALLOW ME TO INTRODUCE CATALYST-- ONE OF AIRWAVES FORMER TEAMMATES IN THE CAPTAINS OF INDUSTRY.

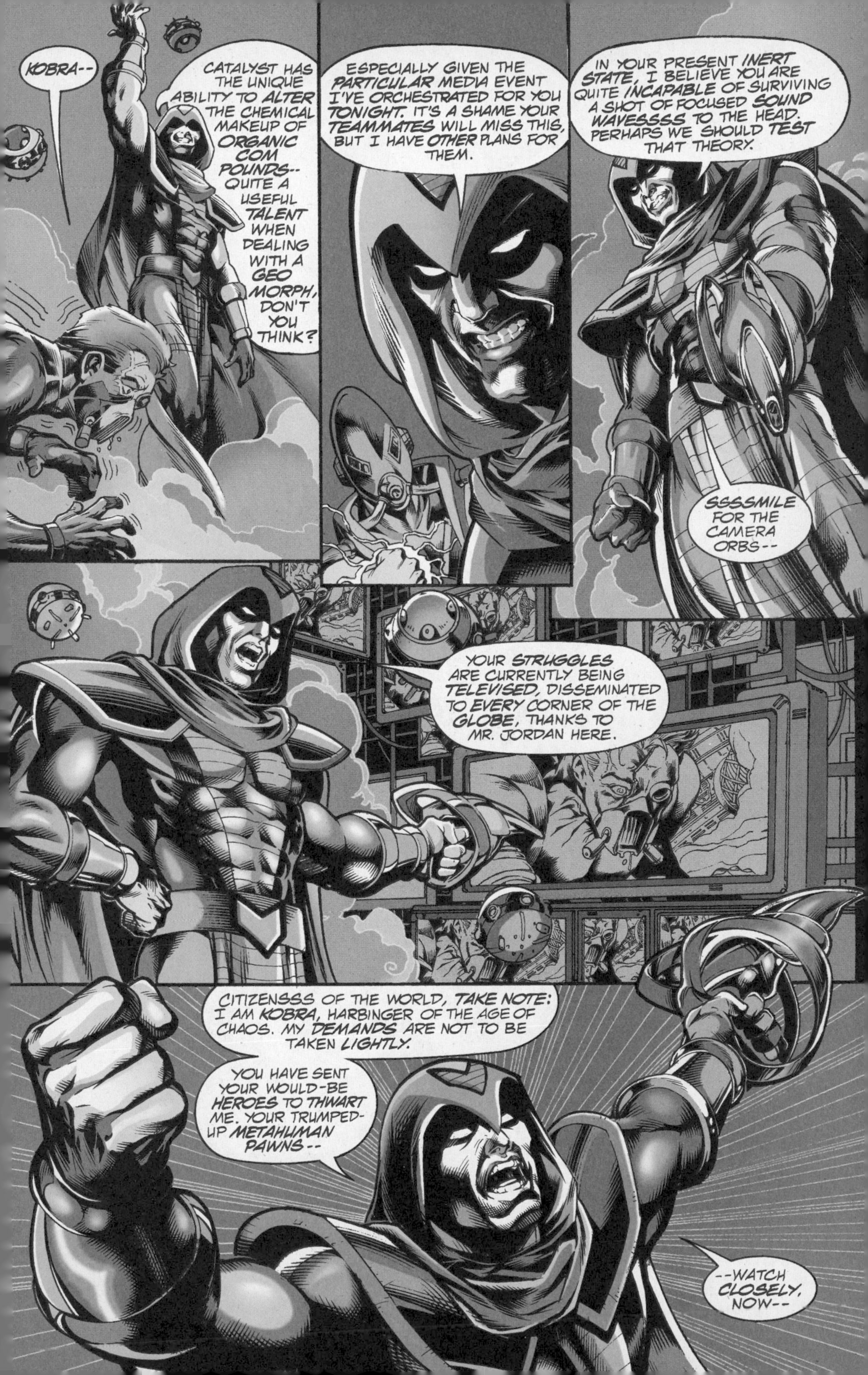
KOBRA--
CATALYST HAS THE UNIQUE ABILITY TO ALTER THE CHEMICAL MAKEUP OF ORGANIC COM POUNDS-- QUITE A USEFUL TALENT WHEN DEALING WITH A GEO MORPH, DON'T YOU THINK?
ESPECIALLY GIVEN THE PARTICULAR MEDIA EVENT I'VE ORCHESTRATED FOR YOU TONIGHT. IT'S A SHAME YOUR TEAMMATES WILL MISS THIS, BUT I HAVE OTHER PLANS FOR THEM.
IN YOUR PRESENT INERT STATE, I BELIEVE YOU ARE QUITE INCAPABLE OF SURVIVING A SHOT OF FOCUSED SOUND WAVESSSS TO THE HEAD. PERHAPS WE SHOULD TEST THAT THEORY.
SSSSMILE FOR THE CAMERA ORBS--
YOUR STRUGGLES ARE CURRENTLY BEING TELEVISED, DISSEMINATED TO EVERY CORNER OF THE GLOBE, THANKS TO MR. JORDAN HERE.
CITIZENSSS OF THE WORLD, TAKE NOTE: I AM KOBRA, HARBINGER OF THE AGE OF CHAOS. MY DEMANDS ARE NOT TO BE TAKEN LIGHTLY.
YOU HAVE SENT YOUR WOULD-BE HEROES TO THWART ME. YOUR TRUMPED-UP METAHUMAN PAWNS--
--WATCH CLOSELY, NOW--

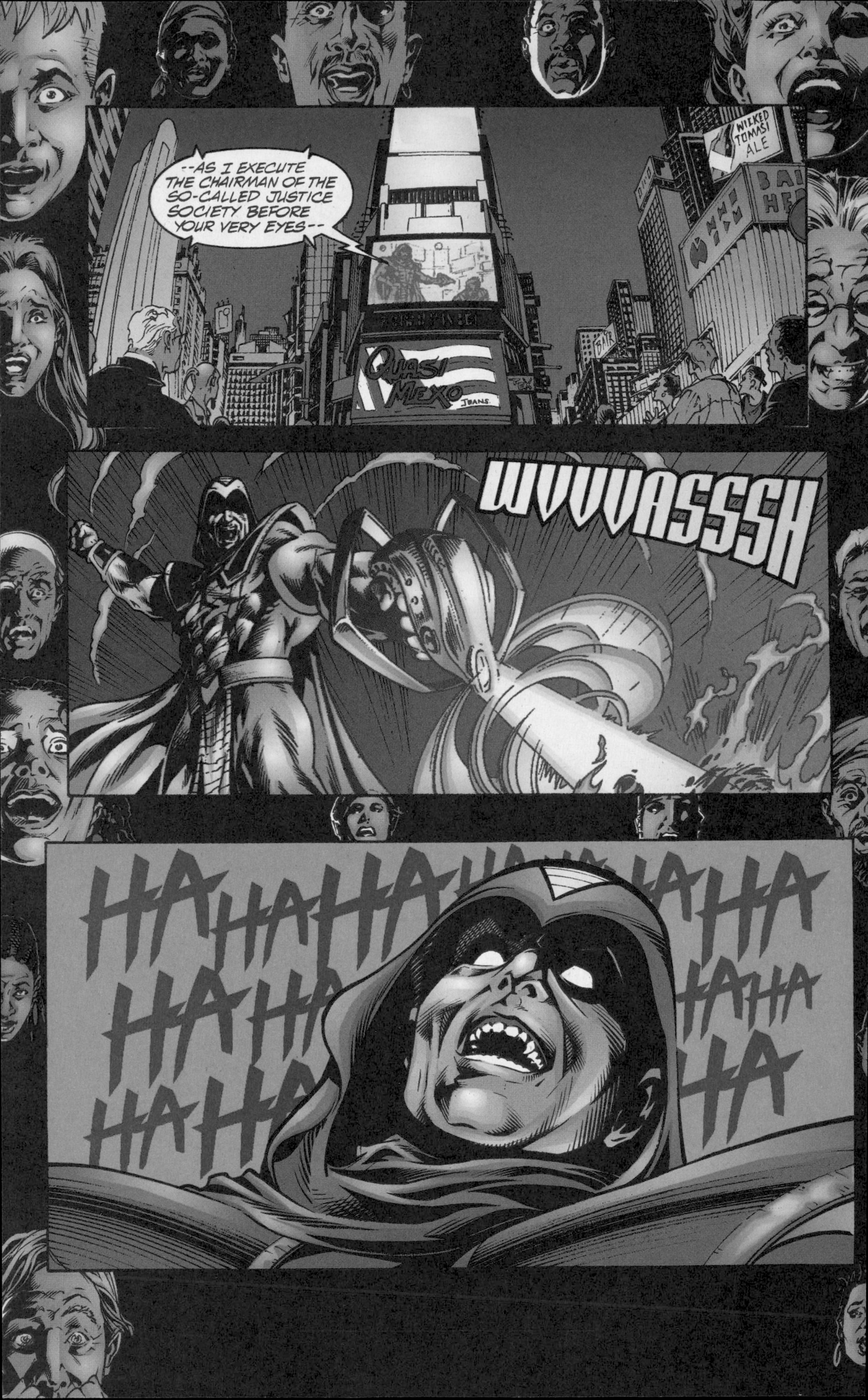

--AS I EXECUTE THE CHAIRMAN OF THE SO-CALLED JUSTICE SOCIETY BEFORE YOUR VERY EYES--
WICKED TOMASI ALE
QUASI MEXO JEANS
WVVVASSSH
HAHAHAHAHAHAHA
HAHA HAHA
HAHA HA

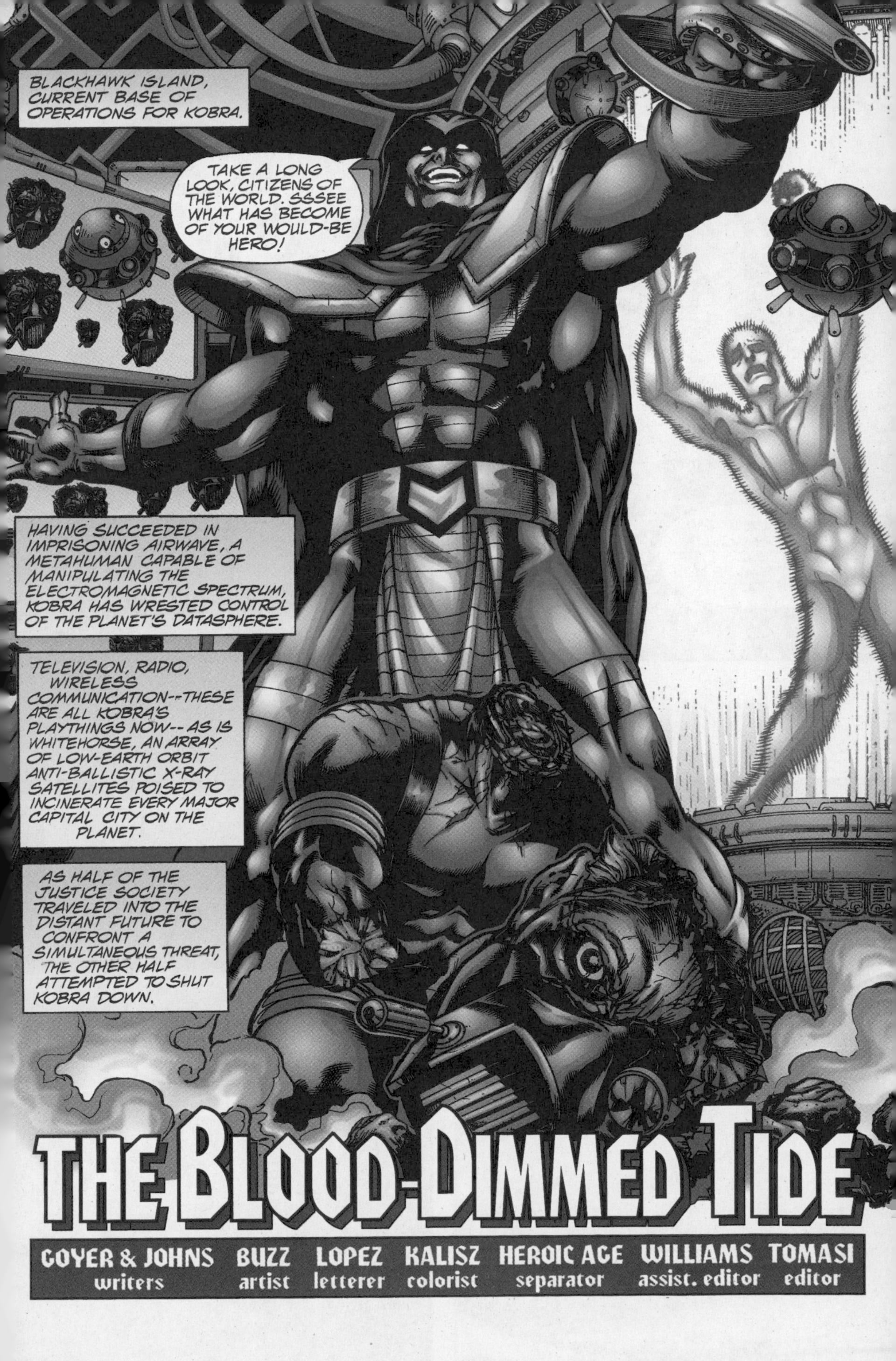
BLACKHAWK ISLAND, CURRENT BASE OF OPERATIONS FOR KOBRA.
TAKE A LONG LOOK, CITIZENS OF THE WORLD. SSSEE WHAT HAS BECOME OF YOUR WOULD-BE HERO!
HAVING SUCCEEDED IN IMPRISONING AIRWAVE, A METAHUMAN CAPABLE OF MANIPULATING THE ELECTROMAGNETIC SPECTRUM, KOBRA HAS WRESTED CONTROL OF THE PLANET'S DATASPHERE.
TELEVISION, RADIO, WIRELESS COMMUNICATION--THESE ARE ALL KOBRA'S PLAYTHINGS NOW-- AS IS WHITEHORSE, AN ARRAY OF LOW-EARTH ORBIT ANTI-BALLISTIC X-RAY SATELLITES POISED TO INCINERATE EVERY MAJOR CAPITAL CITY ON THE PLANET.
AS HALF OF THE JUSTICE SOCIETY TRAVELED INTO THE DISTANT FUTURE TO CONFRONT A SIMULTANEOUS THREAT, THE OTHER HALF ATTEMPTED TO SHUT KOBRA DOWN.
THE BLOOD-DIMMED TIDE
GOYER & JOHNS writers
BUZZ artist
LOPEZ letterer
KALISZ colorist
HEROIC AGE separator
WILLIAMS assist. editor
TOMASI editor

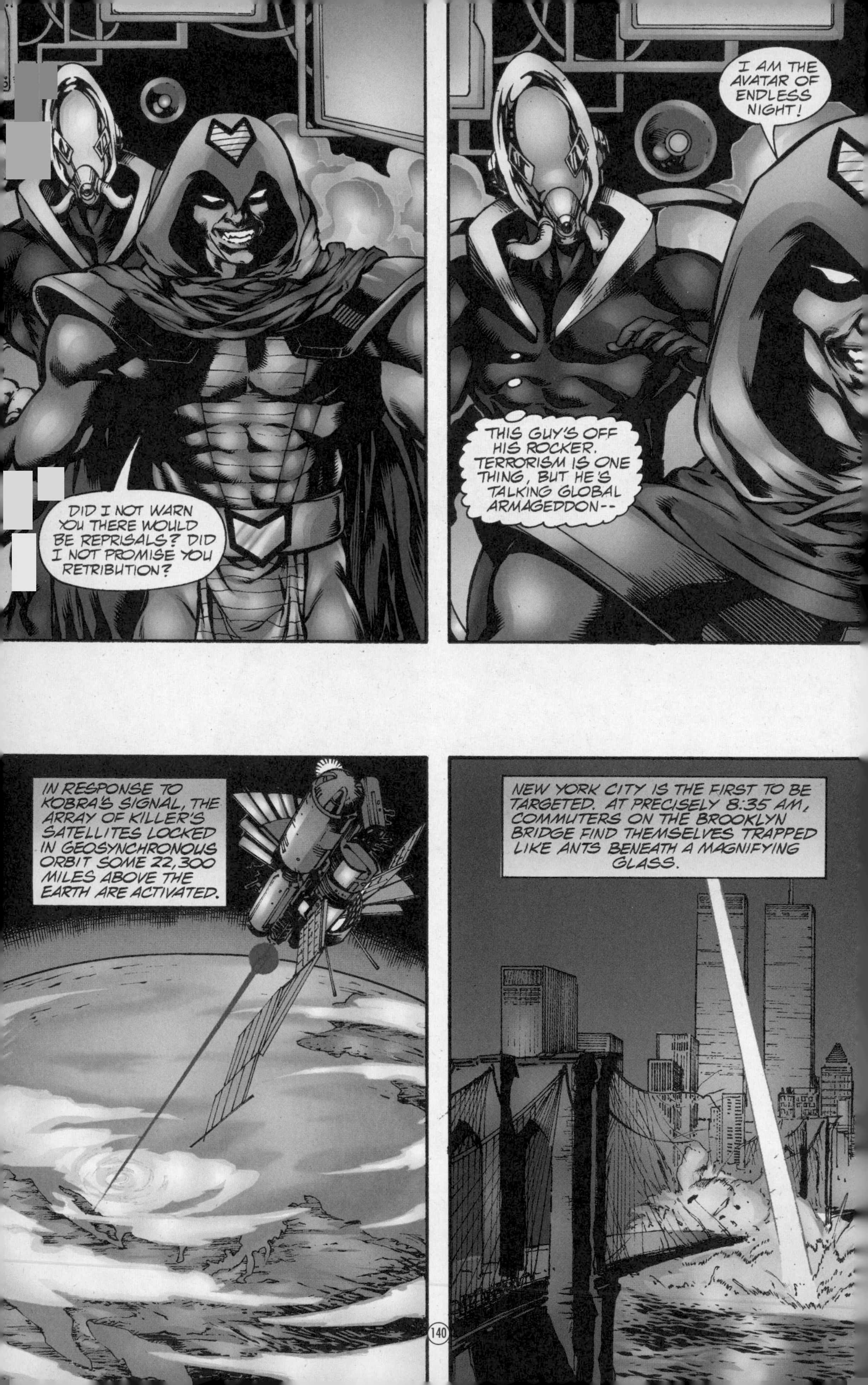
DID I NOT WARN YOU THERE WOULD BE REPRISALS? DID I NOT PROMISE YOU RETRIBUTION?
I AM THE AVATAR OF ENDLESS NIGHT!
THIS GUY'S OFF HIS ROCKER. TERRORISM IS ONE THING, BUT HE'S TALKING GLOBAL ARMAGEDDON--
IN RESPONSE TO KOBRA'S SIGNAL, THE ARRAY OF KILLER'S SATELLITES LOCKED IN GEOSYNCHRONOUS ORBIT SOME 22,300 MILES ABOVE THE EARTH ARE ACTIVATED.
NEW YORK CITY IS THE FIRST TO BE TARGETED. AT PRECISELY 8:35 AM, COMMUTERS ON THE BROOKLYN BRIDGE FIND THEMSELVES TRAPPED LIKE ANTS BENEATH A MAGNIFYING GLASS.

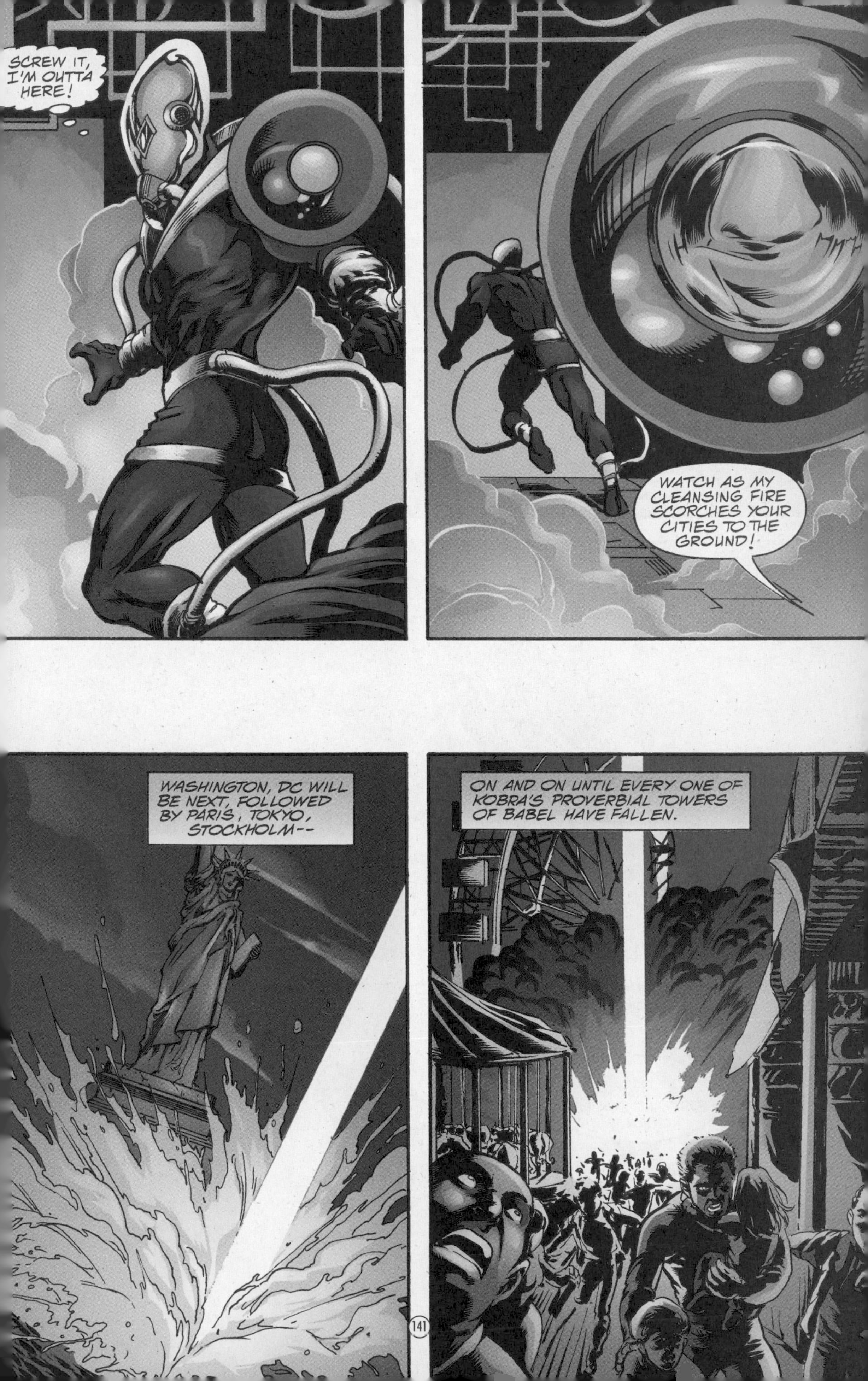
SCREW IT, I'M OUTTA HERE!
WATCH AS MY CLEANSING FIRE SCORCHES YOUR CITIES TO THE GROUND!
WASHINGTON, DC WILL BE NEXT, FOLLOWED BY PARIS, TOKYO, STOCKHOLM--
ON AND ON UNTIL EVERY ONE OF KOBRA'S PROVERBIAL TOWERS OF BABEL HAVE FALLEN.

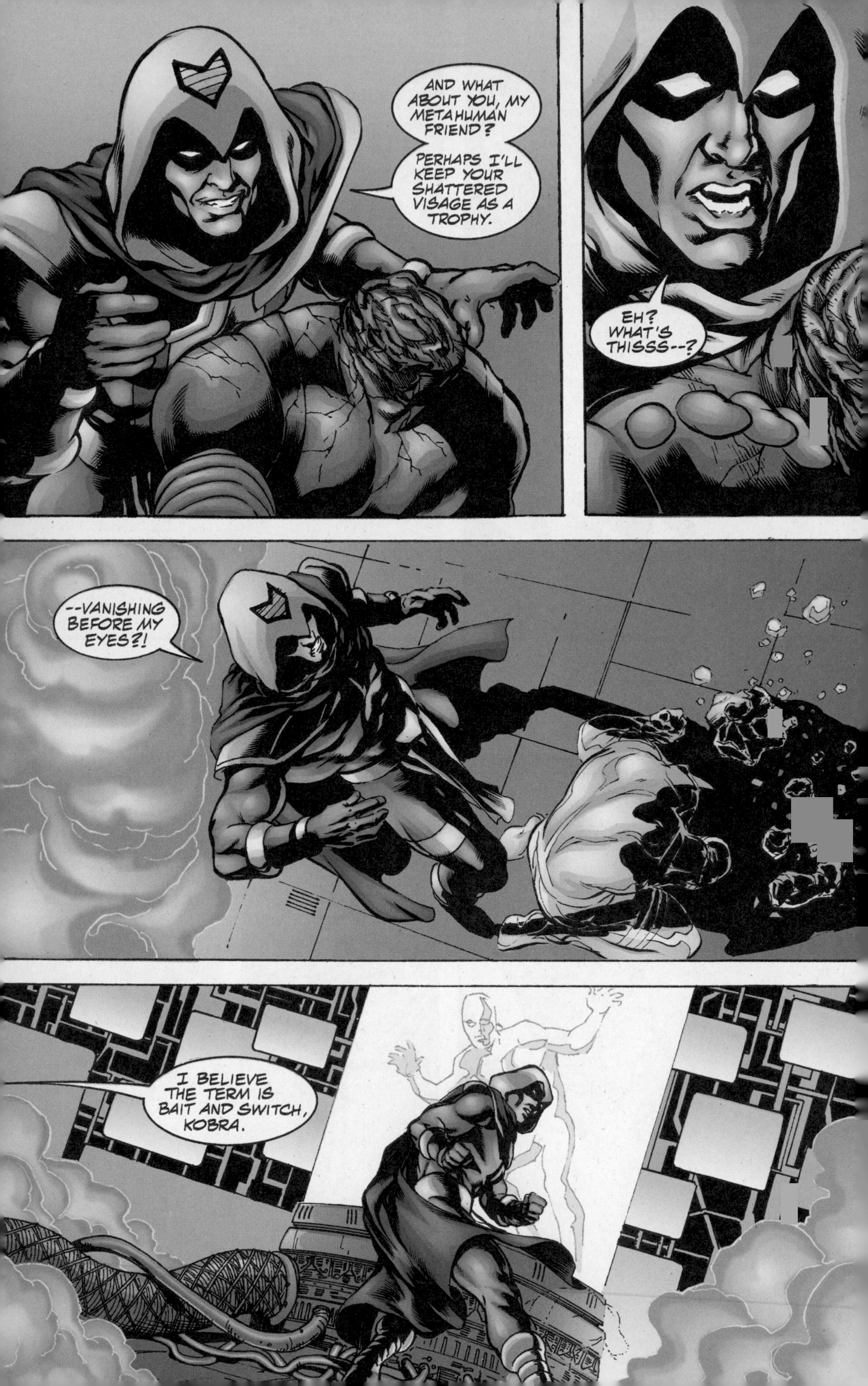
AND WHAT ABOUT YOU, MY METAHUMAN FRIEND?
PERHAPS I'LL KEEP YOUR SHATTERED VISAGE AS A TROPHY.
EH? WHAT'S THISSS--?
--VANISHING BEFORE MY EYES?!
I BELIEVE THE TERM IS BAIT AND SWITCH, KOBRA.

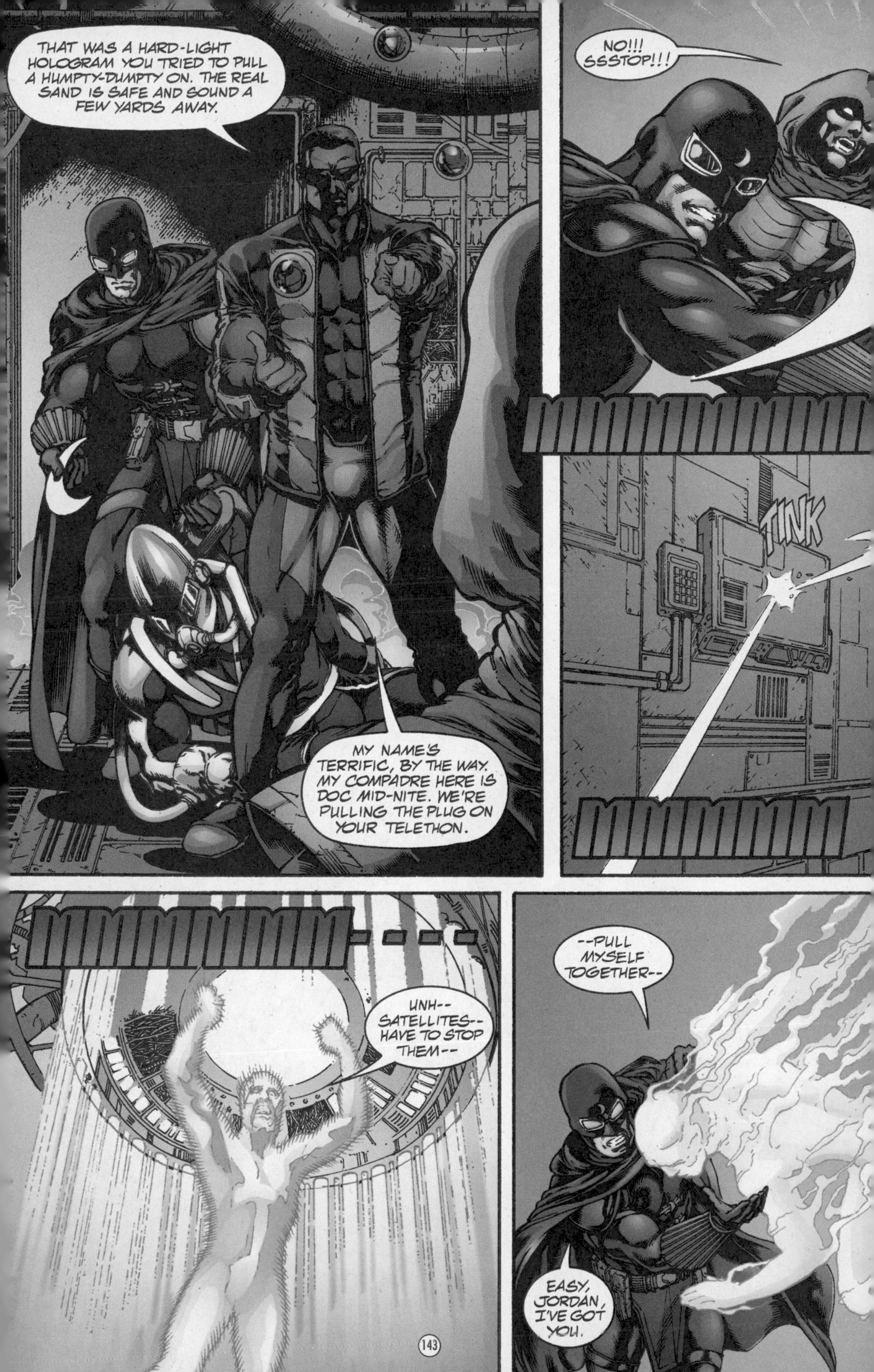
THAT WAS A HARD-LIGHT HOLOGRAM YOU TRIED TO PULL A HUMPTY-DUMPTY ON. THE REAL SAND IS SAFE AND SOUND A FEW YARDS AWAY.
MY NAME'S TERRIFIC, BY THE WAY. MY COMPADRE HERE IS DOC MID-NITE. WE'RE PULLING THE PLUG ON YOUR TELETHON.
NO!!! SSSTOP!!!
MMMMMMMMM
TINK
MMMMMMMM
MMMMMMMM----
UNH-- SATELLITES-- HAVE TO STOP THEM--
--PULL MYSELF TOGETHER--
EASY, JORDAN, I'VE GOT YOU.

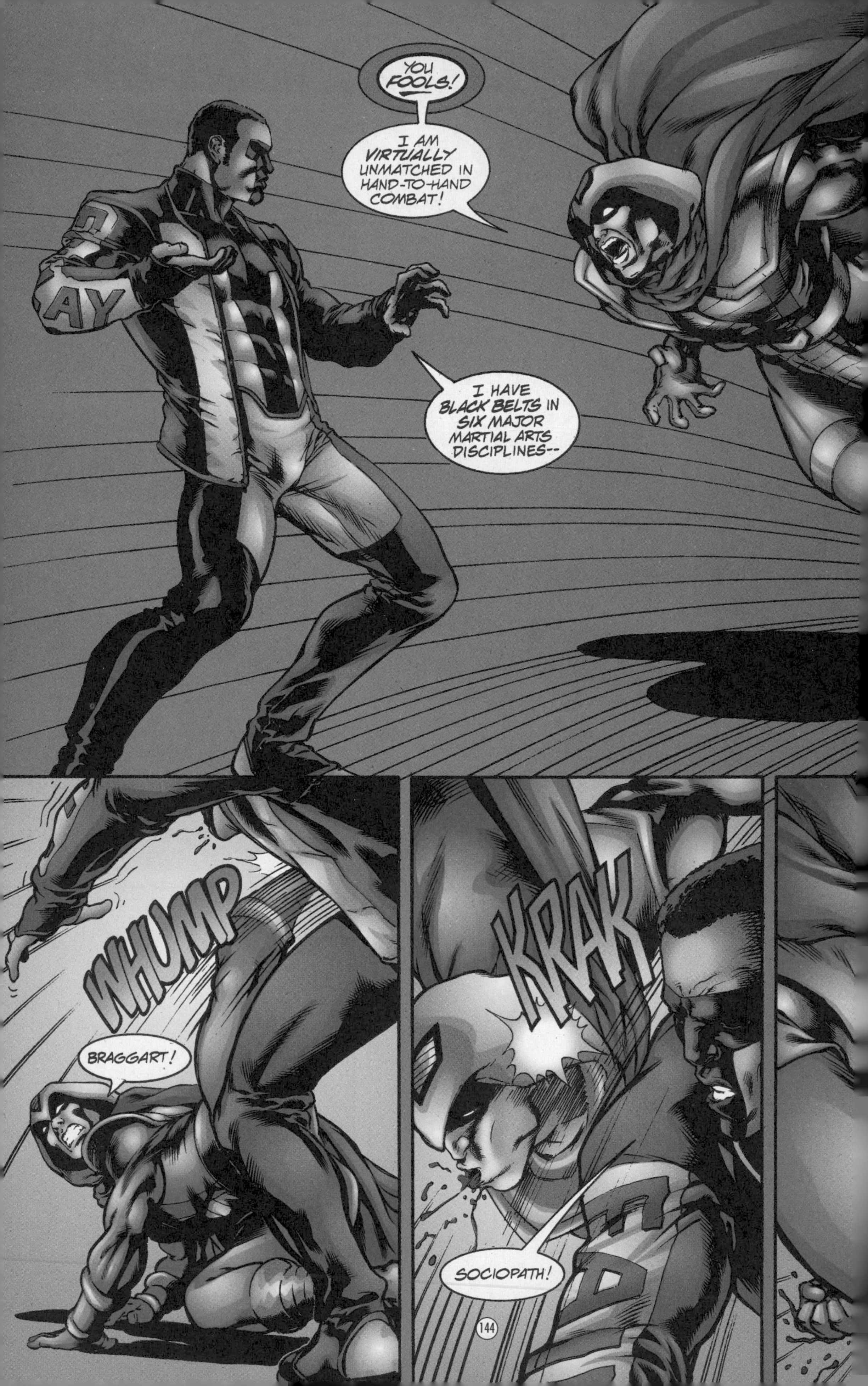
YOU FOOLS!
I AM VIRTUALLY UNMATCHED IN HAND-TO-HAND COMBAT!
I HAVE BLACK BELTS IN SIX MAJOR MARTIAL ARTS DISCIPLINES--
WHUMP
BRAGGART!
KRAK
SOCIOPATH!

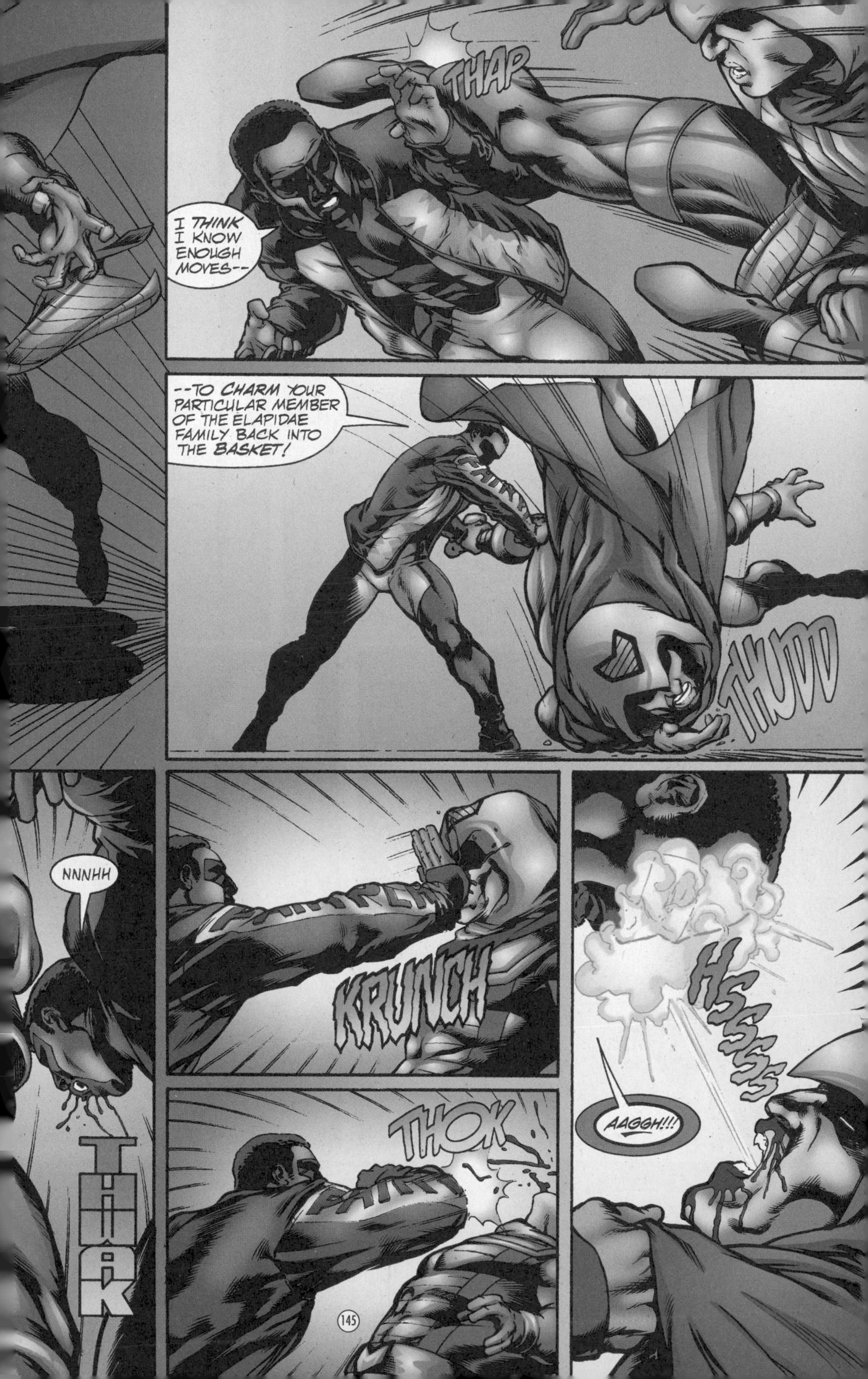
THAP
I THINK I KNOW ENOUGH MOVES--
--TO CHARM YOUR PARTICULAR MEMBER OF THE ELAPIDAE FAMILY BACK INTO THE BASKET!
THUDD
NNNHH
THWAK
KRUNCH
THOK
HSSSSS
AAGGH!!!

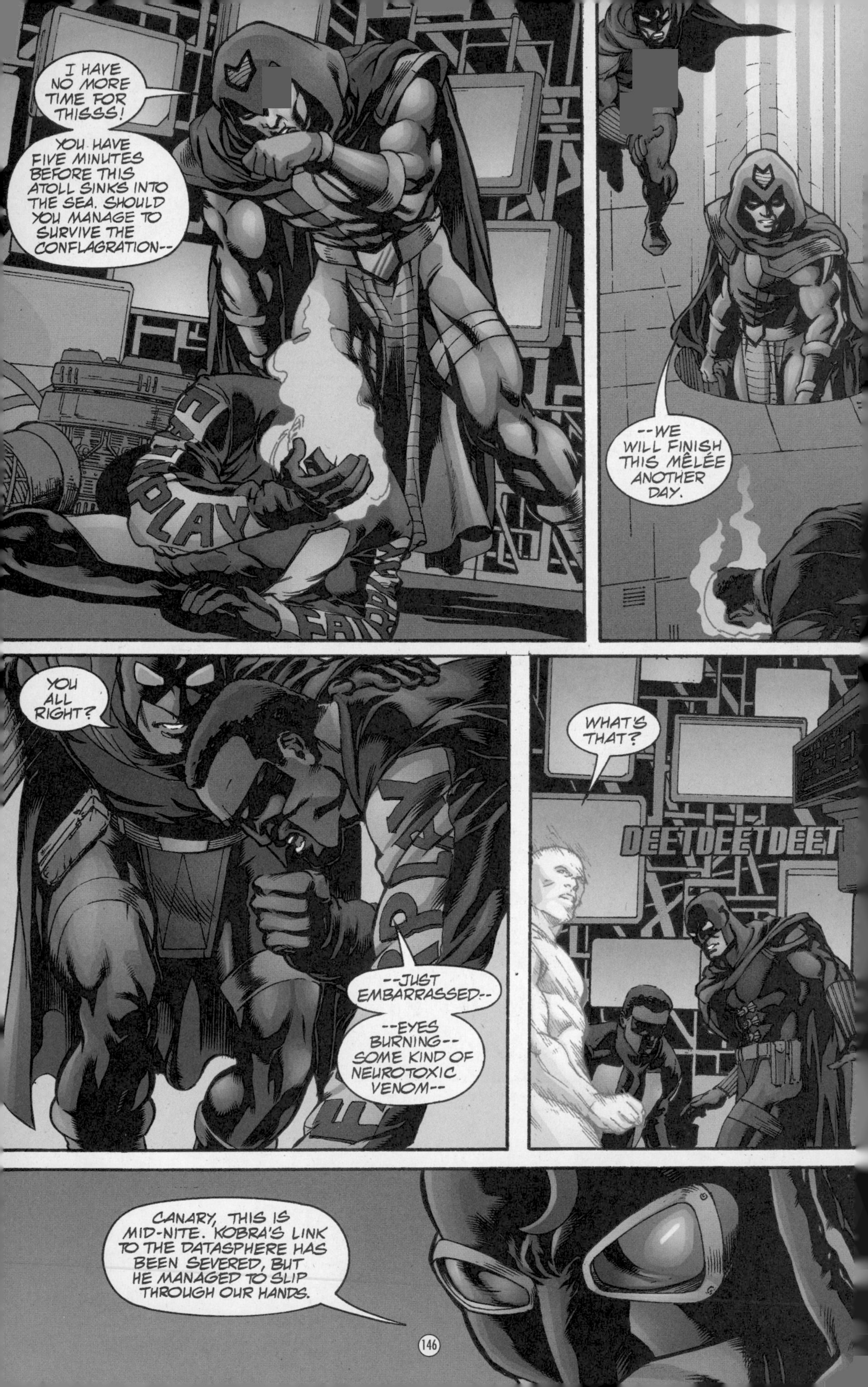
I HAVE NO MORE TIME FOR THISSS!
YOU HAVE FIVE MINUTES BEFORE THIS ATOLL SINKS INTO THE SEA. SHOULD YOU MANAGE TO SURVIVE THE CONFLAGRATION--
--WE WILL FINISH THIS MÊLÉE ANOTHER DAY.
YOU ALL RIGHT?
--JUST EMBARRASSED--
--EYES BURNING-- SOME KIND OF NEUROTOXIC VENOM--
WHAT'S THAT?
DEETDEETDEET
CANARY, THIS IS MID-NITE. KOBRA'S LINK TO THE DATASPHERE HAS BEEN SEVERED, BUT HE MANAGED TO SLIP THROUGH OUR HANDS.

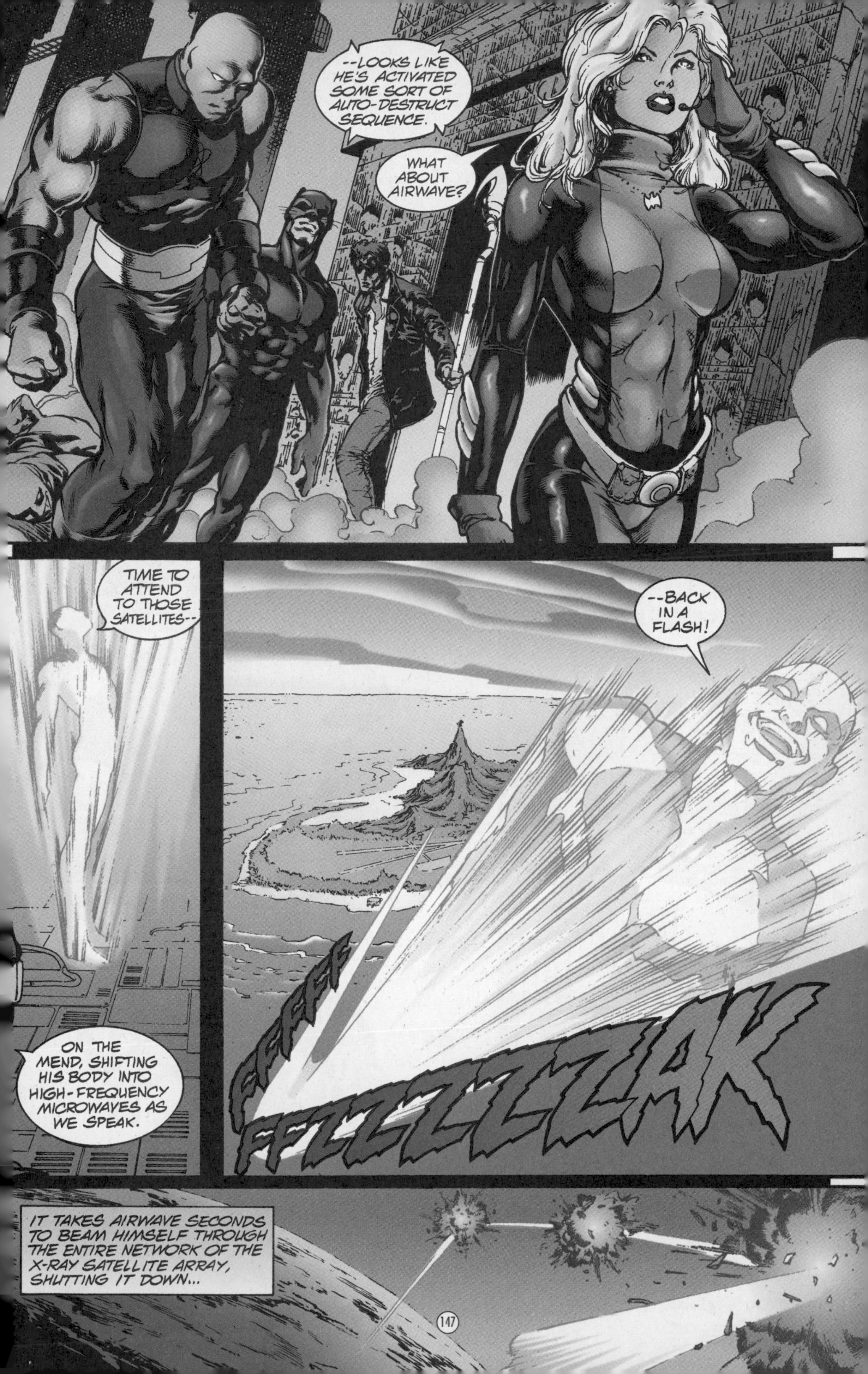
--LOOKS LIKE HE'S ACTIVATED SOME SORT OF AUTO-DESTRUCT SEQUENCE.
WHAT ABOUT AIRWAVE?
TIME TO ATTEND TO THOSE SATELLITES--
ON THE MEND, SHIFTING HIS BODY INTO HIGH-FREQUENCY MICROWAVES AS WE SPEAK.
--BACK IN A FLASH!
FFFFFF
FFZZZZZAK
IT TAKES AIRWAVE SECONDS TO BEAM HIMSELF THROUGH THE ENTIRE NETWORK OF THE X-RAY SATELLITE ARRAY, SHUTTING IT DOWN...

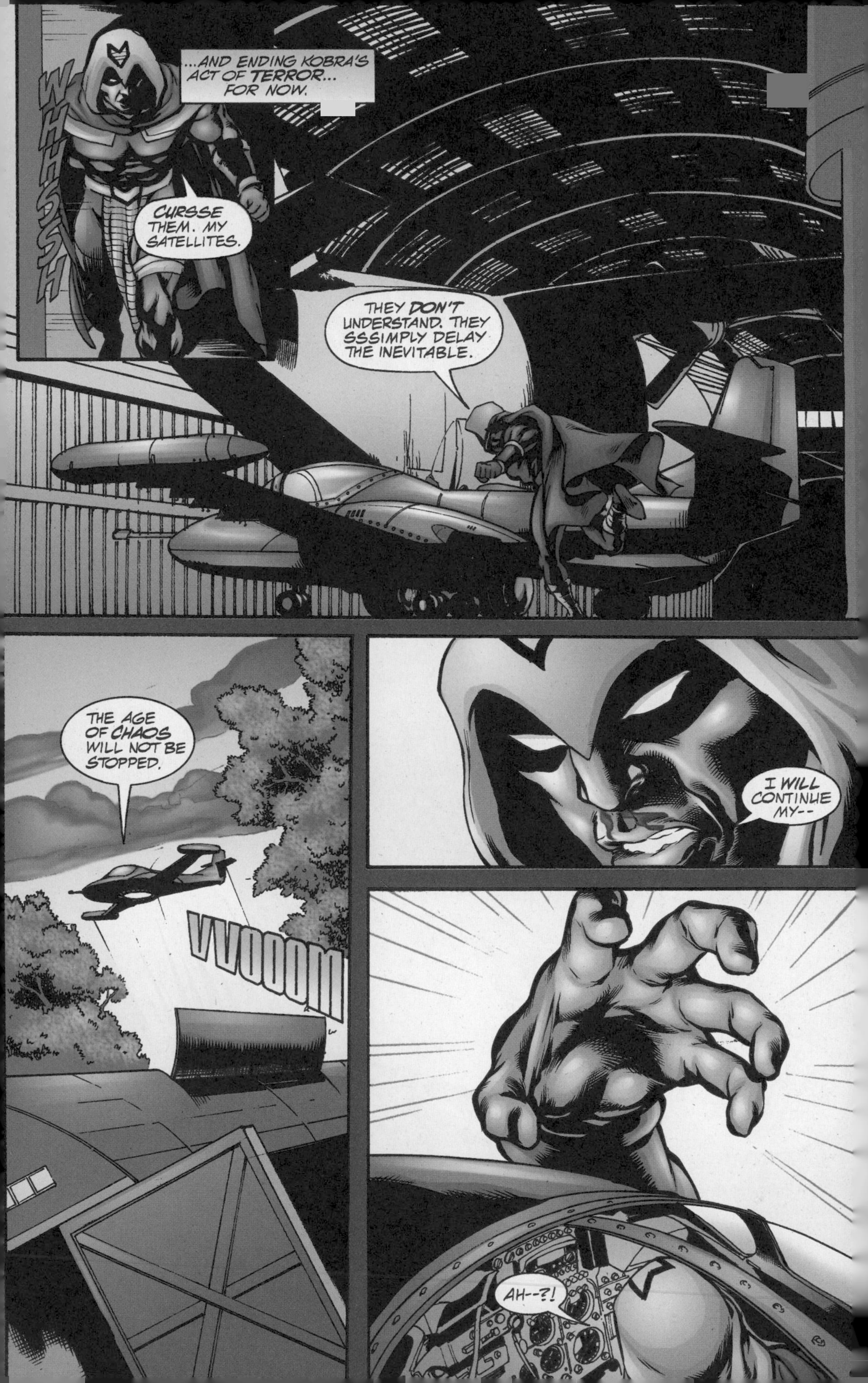
...AND ENDING KOBRA'S ACT OF TERROR... FOR NOW.
WHHSSH
CURSSE THEM. MY SATELLITES.
THEY DON'T UNDERSTAND. THEY SSSIMPLY DELAY THE INEVITABLE.
THE AGE OF CHAOS WILL NOT BE STOPPED.
VVOOOM
I WILL CONTINUE MY--
AH--?!

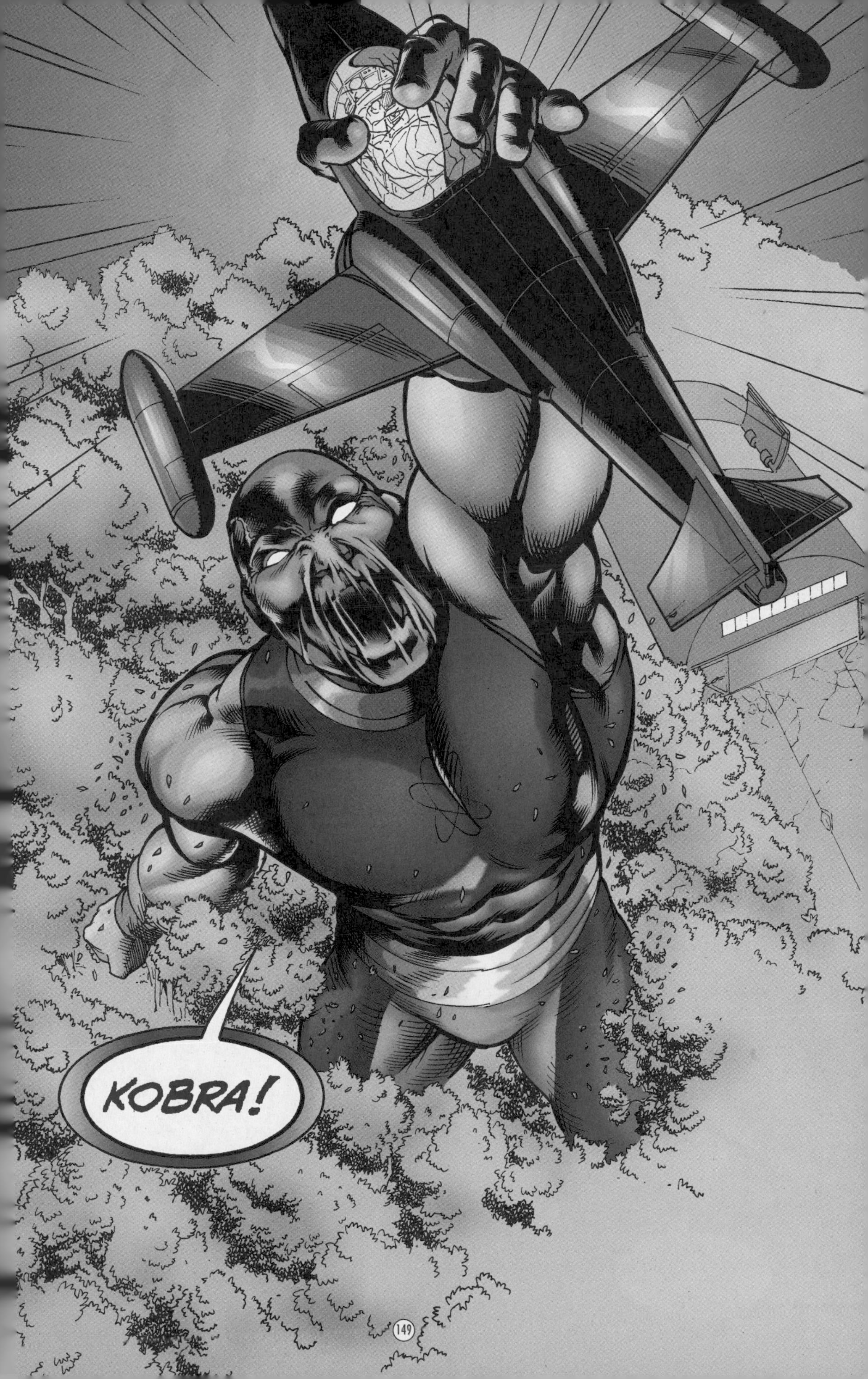
KOBRA!

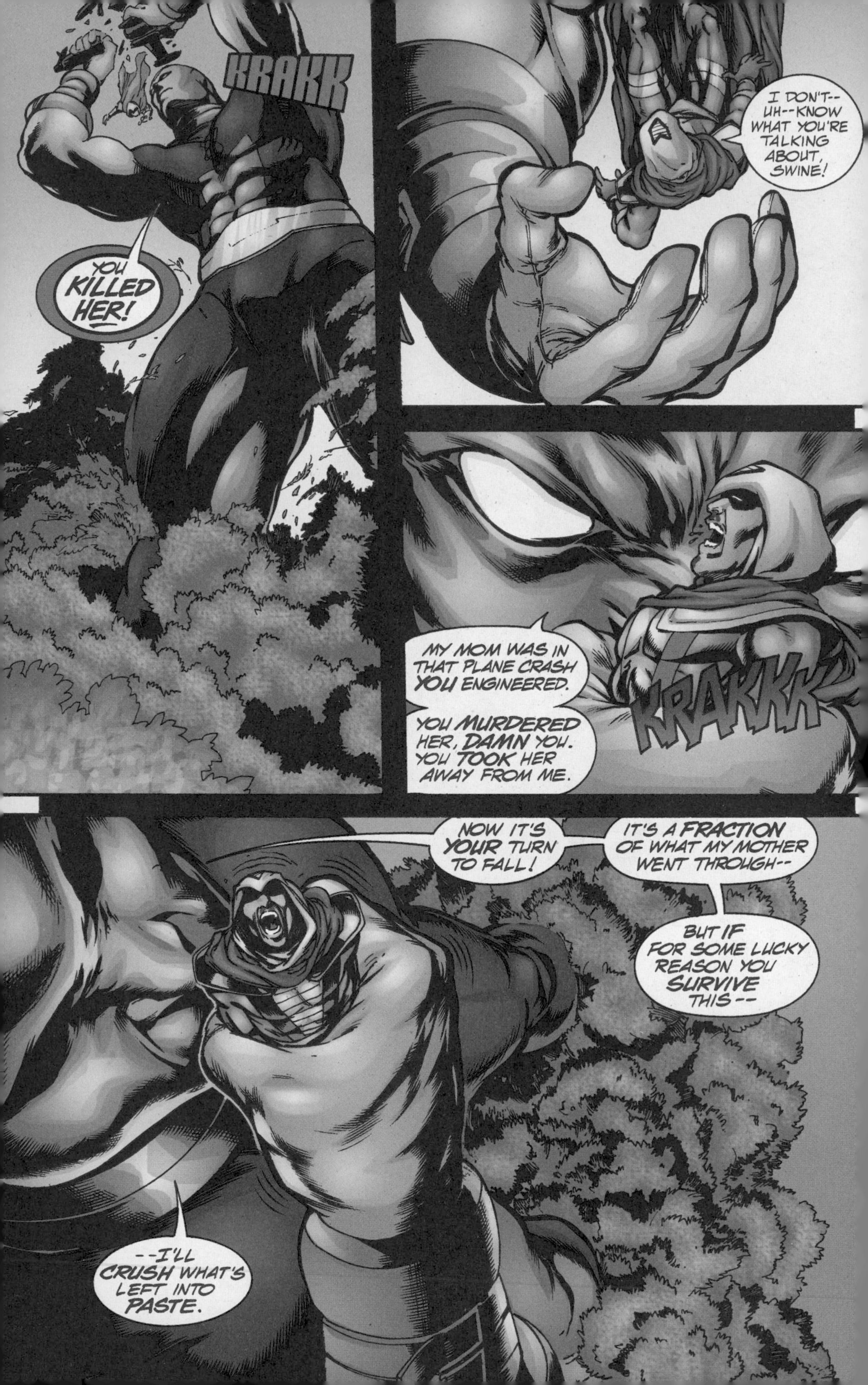
KRAKK
YOU KILLED HER!
I DON'T-- UH--KNOW WHAT YOU'RE TALKING ABOUT, SWINE!
MY MOM WAS IN THAT PLANE CRASH YOU ENGINEERED.
YOU MURDERED HER, DAMN YOU. YOU TOOK HER AWAY FROM ME.
KRAKKK
NOW IT'S YOUR TURN TO FALL!
IT'S A FRACTION OF WHAT MY MOTHER WENT THROUGH--
BUT IF FOR SOME LUCKY REASON YOU SURVIVE THIS--
--I'LL CRUSH WHAT'S LEFT INTO PASTE.

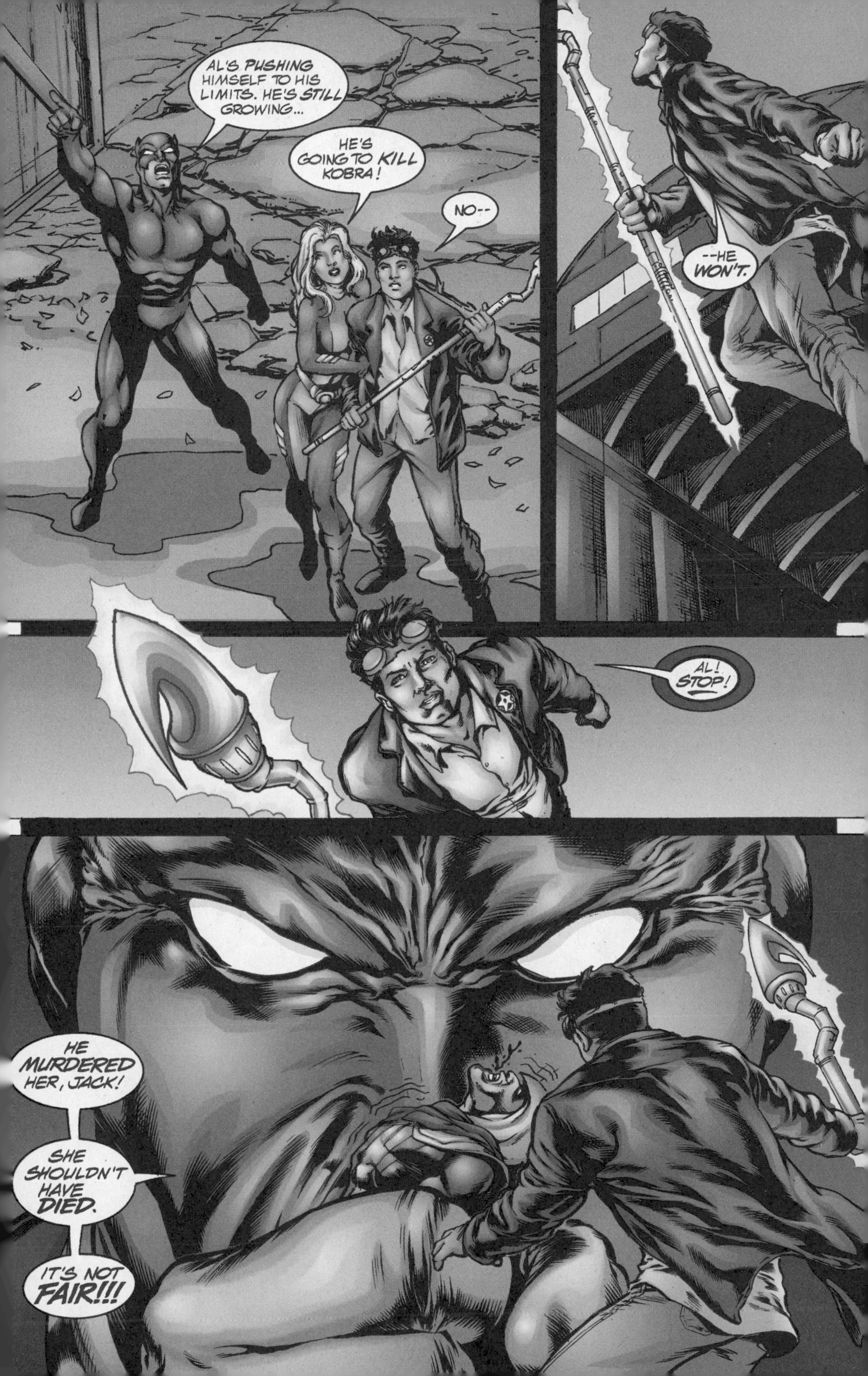
AL'S PUSHING HIMSELF TO HIS LIMITS. HE'S STILL GROWING...
HE'S GOING TO KILL KOBRA!
NO--
--HE WON'T.
AL! STOP!
HE MURDERED HER, JACK!
SHE SHOULDN'T HAVE DIED.
IT'S NOT FAIR!!!

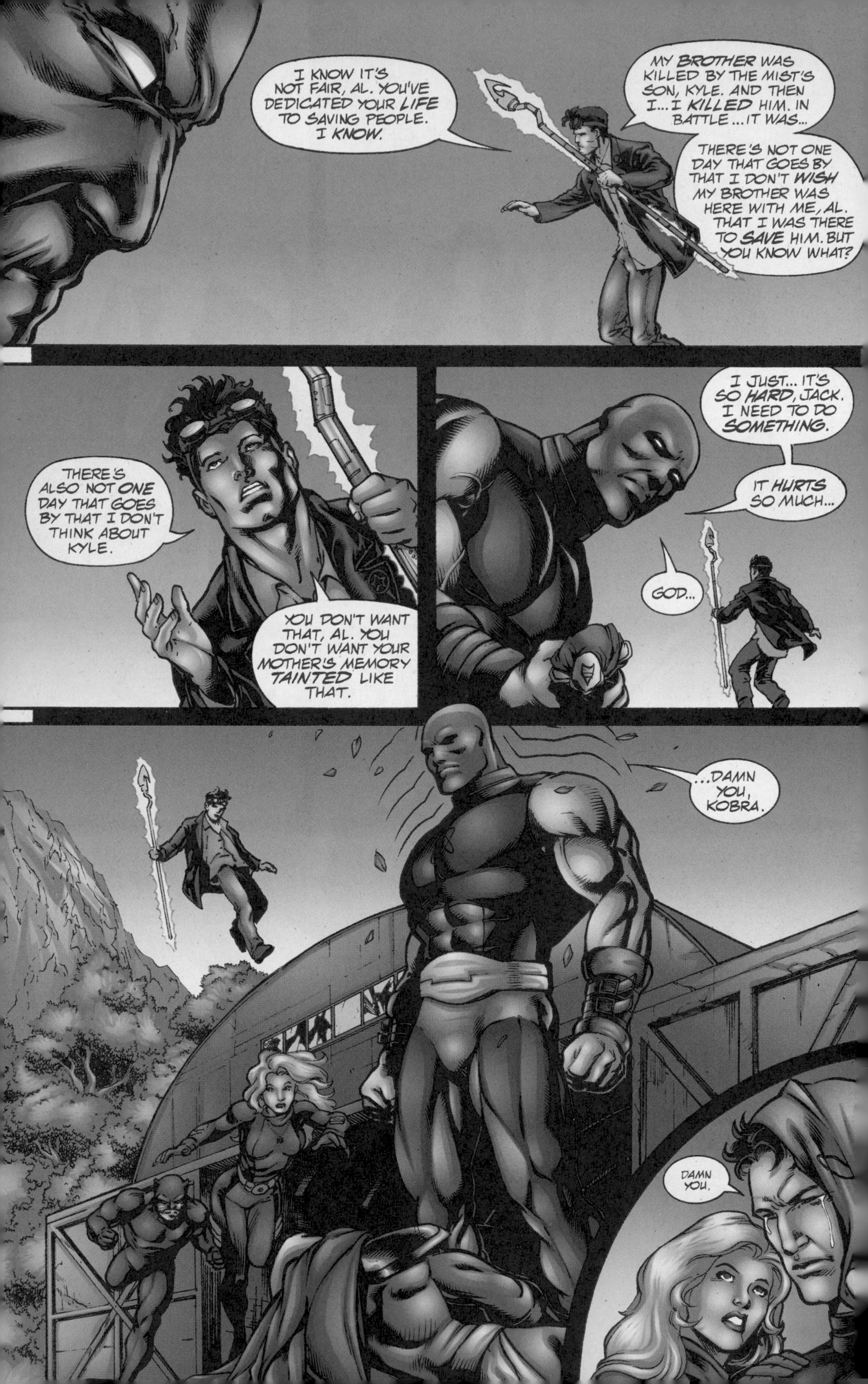
I KNOW IT'S NOT FAIR, AL. YOU'VE DEDICATED YOUR LIFE TO SAVING PEOPLE. I KNOW.
MY BROTHER WAS KILLED BY THE MIST'S SON, KYLE. AND THEN I... I KILLED HIM. IN BATTLE... IT WAS...
THERE'S NOT ONE DAY THAT GOES BY THAT I DON'T WISH MY BROTHER WAS HERE WITH ME, AL. THAT I WAS THERE TO SAVE HIM. BUT YOU KNOW WHAT?
THERE'S ALSO NOT ONE DAY THAT GOES BY THAT I DON'T THINK ABOUT KYLE.
YOU DON'T WANT THAT, AL. YOU DON'T WANT YOUR MOTHER'S MEMORY TAINTED LIKE THAT.
I JUST... IT'S SO HARD, JACK. I NEED TO DO SOMETHING.
IT HURTS SO MUCH...
GOD...
...DAMN YOU, KOBRA.
DAMN YOU.

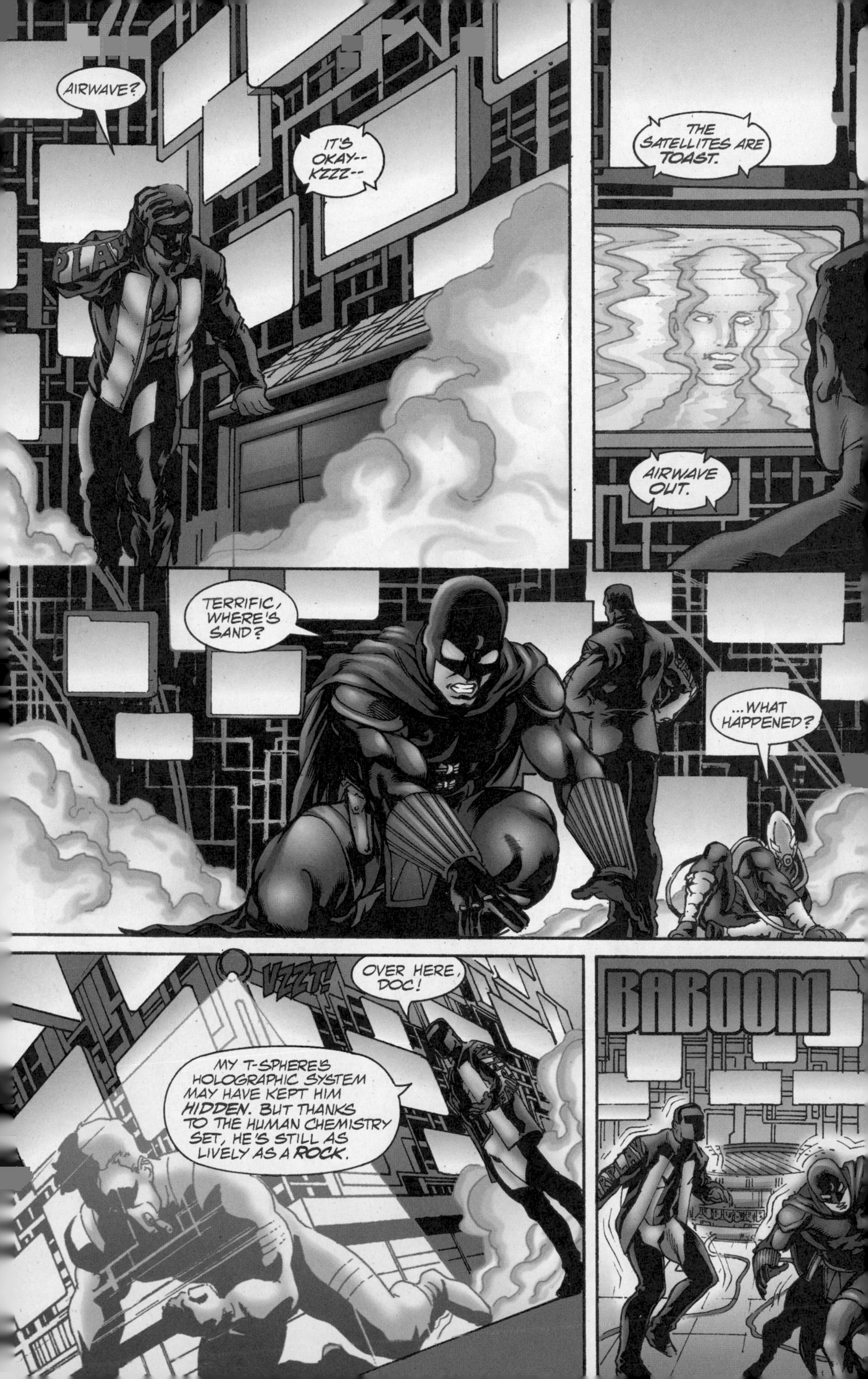
AIRWAVE?
IT'S OKAY-- KZZZ--
THE SATELLITES ARE TOAST.
AIRWAVE OUT.
TERRIFIC, WHERE'S SAND?
...WHAT HAPPENED?
VZZT!
OVER HERE, DOC!
MY T-SPHERE'S HOLOGRAPHIC SYSTEM MAY HAVE KEPT HIM HIDDEN. BUT THANKS TO THE HUMAN CHEMISTRY SET, HE'S STILL AS LIVELY AS A ROCK.
BABOOM

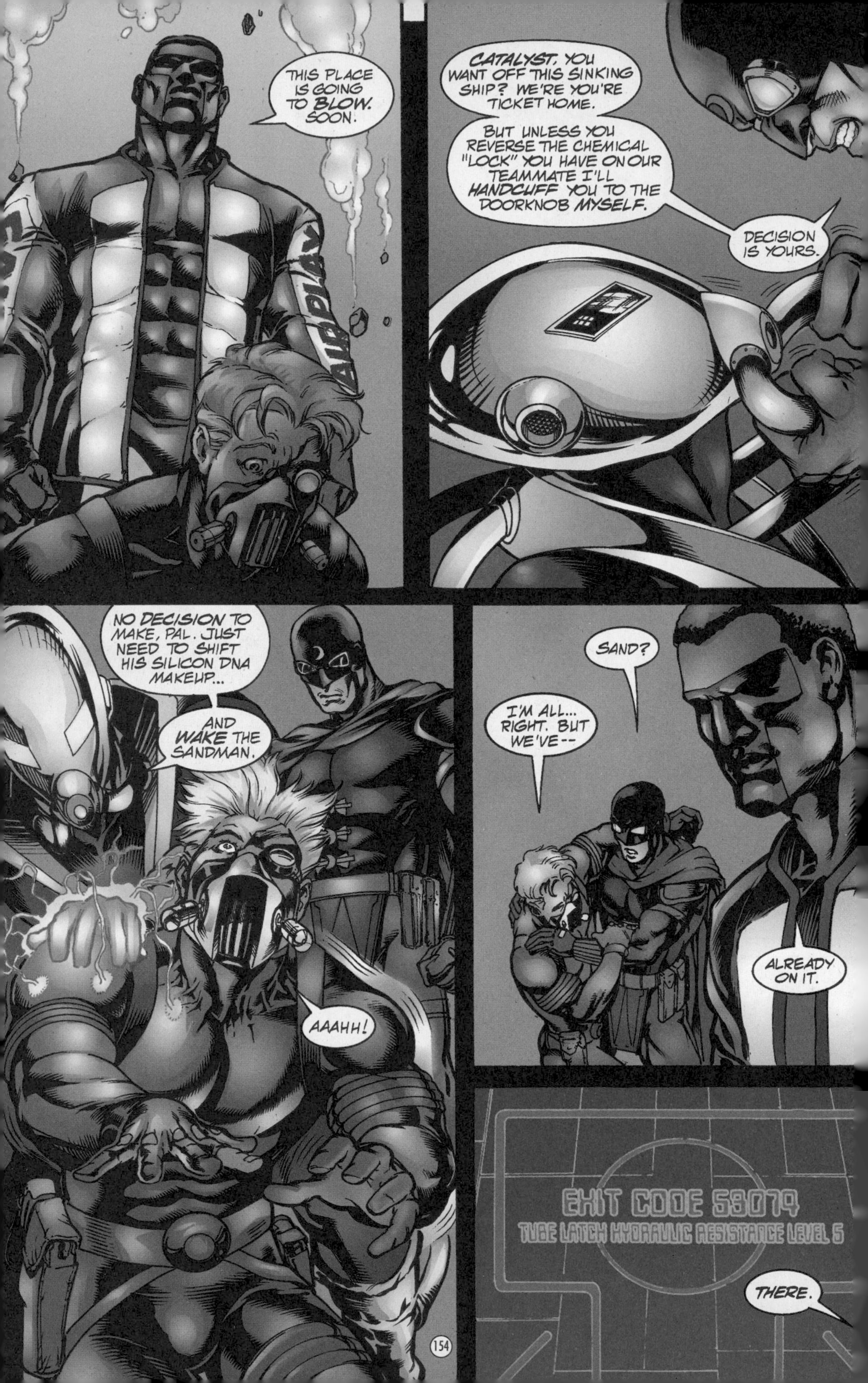
THIS PLACE IS GOING TO BLOW. SOON.
AIRPLAY
CATALYST. YOU WANT OFF THIS SINKING SHIP? WE'RE YOU'RE TICKET HOME.
BUT UNLESS YOU REVERSE THE CHEMICAL "LOCK" YOU HAVE ON OUR TEAMMATE I'LL HANDCUFF YOU TO THE DOORKNOB MYSELF.
DECISION IS YOURS.
NO DECISION TO MAKE, PAL. JUST NEED TO SHIFT HIS SILICON DNA MAKEUP...
AND WAKE THE SANDMAN.
AAAHH!
SAND?
I'M ALL... RIGHT. BUT WE'VE--
ALREADY ON IT.
EXIT CODE 53074
TUBE LATCH HYDRAULIC RESISTANCE LEVEL 5
THERE.

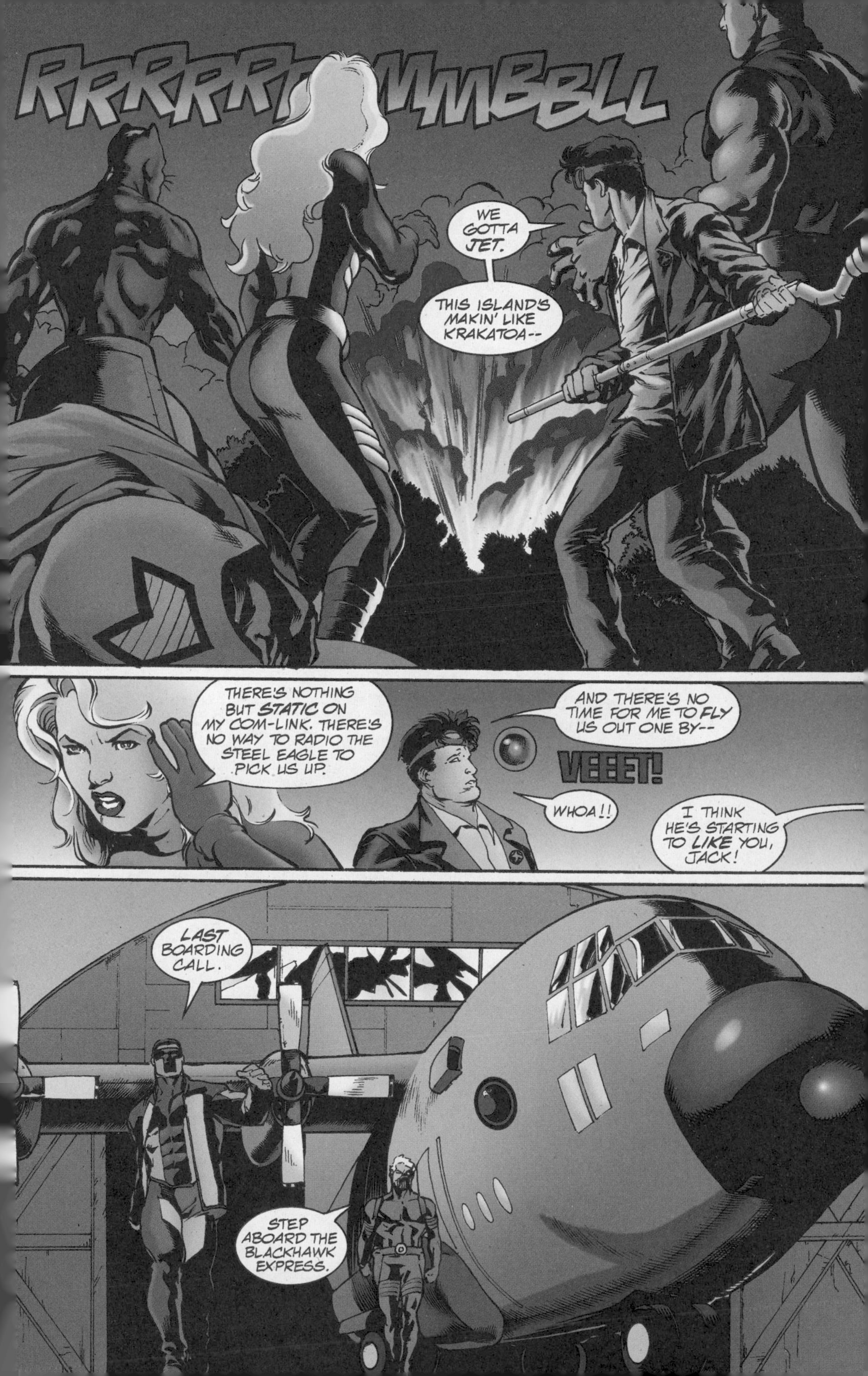
RRRRRRMMMBBLL
WE GOTTA JET.
THIS ISLAND'S MAKIN' LIKE KRAKATOA--
THERE'S NOTHING BUT STATIC ON MY COM-LINK. THERE'S NO WAY TO RADIO THE STEEL EAGLE TO PICK US UP.
AND THERE'S NO TIME FOR ME TO FLY US OUT ONE BY--
VEEEET!
WHOA!!
I THINK HE'S STARTING TO LIKE YOU, JACK!
LAST BOARDING CALL.
STEP ABOARD THE BLACKHAWK EXPRESS.

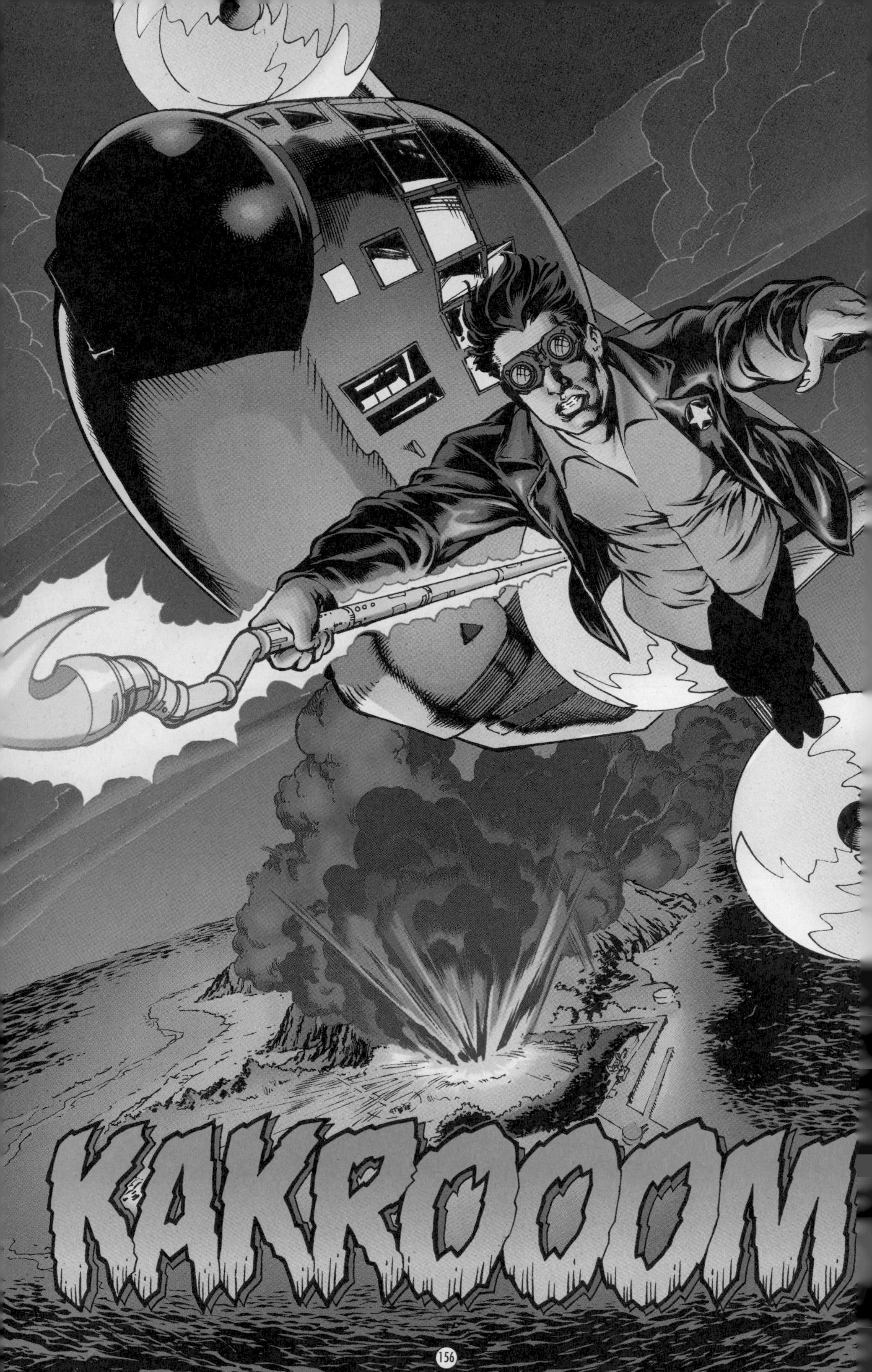
KAKROOOM

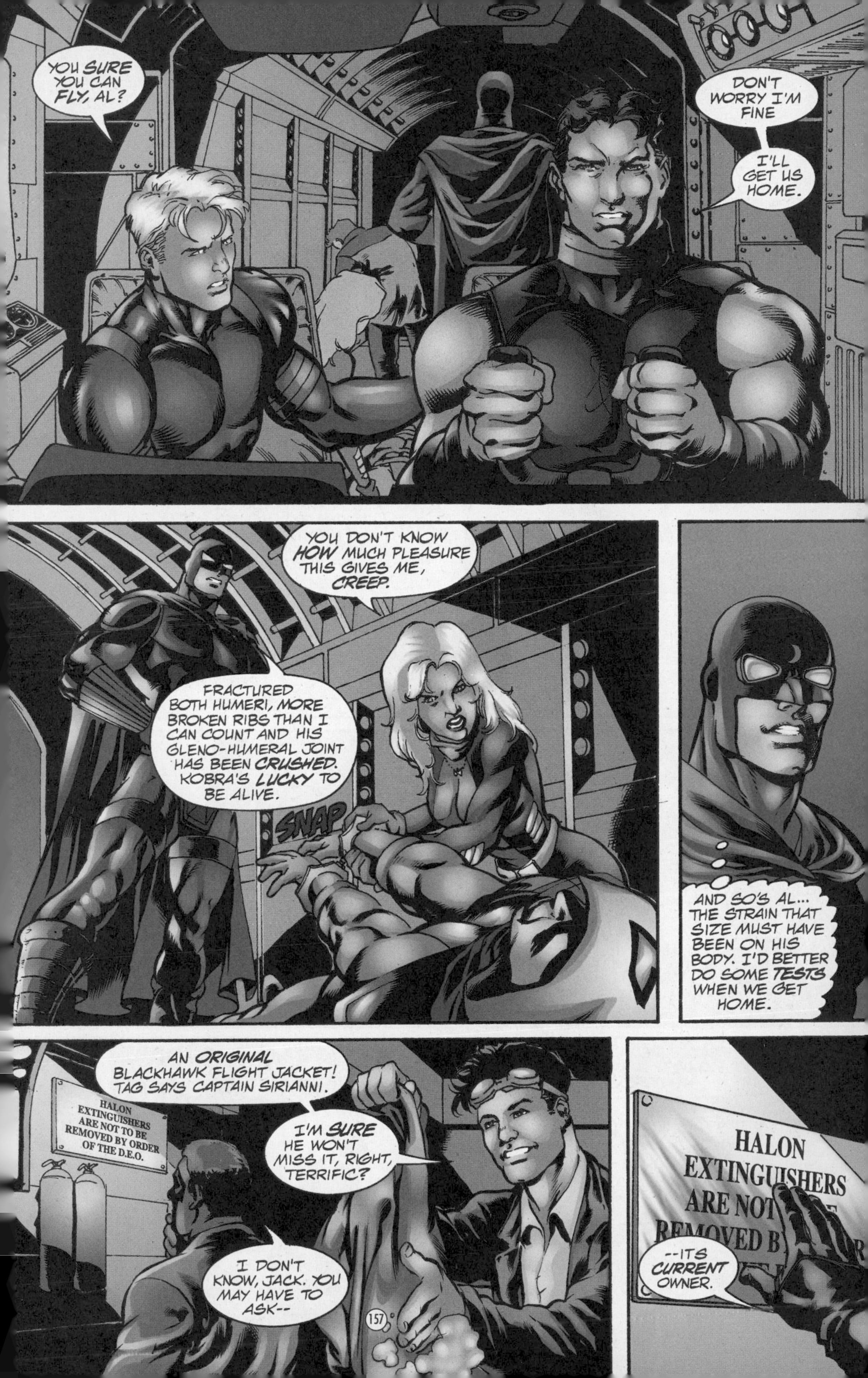
YOU SURE YOU CAN FLY, AL?
DON'T WORRY I'M FINE
I'LL GET US HOME.
YOU DON'T KNOW HOW MUCH PLEASURE THIS GIVES ME, CREEP.
FRACTURED BOTH HUMERI, MORE BROKEN RIBS THAN I CAN COUNT AND HIS GLENO-HUMERAL JOINT HAS BEEN CRUSHED. KOBRA'S LUCKY TO BE ALIVE.
SNAP
AND SO'S AL... THE STRAIN THAT SIZE MUST HAVE BEEN ON HIS BODY. I'D BETTER DO SOME TESTS WHEN WE GET HOME.
HALON EXTINGUISHERS ARE NOT TO BE REMOVED BY ORDER OF THE D.E.O.
AN ORIGINAL BLACKHAWK FLIGHT JACKET! TAG SAYS CAPTAIN SIRIANNI.
I'M SURE HE WON'T MISS IT, RIGHT, TERRIFIC?
I DON'T KNOW, JACK. YOU MAY HAVE TO ASK--
HALON EXTINGUISHERS ARE NOT
--ITS CURRENT OWNER.

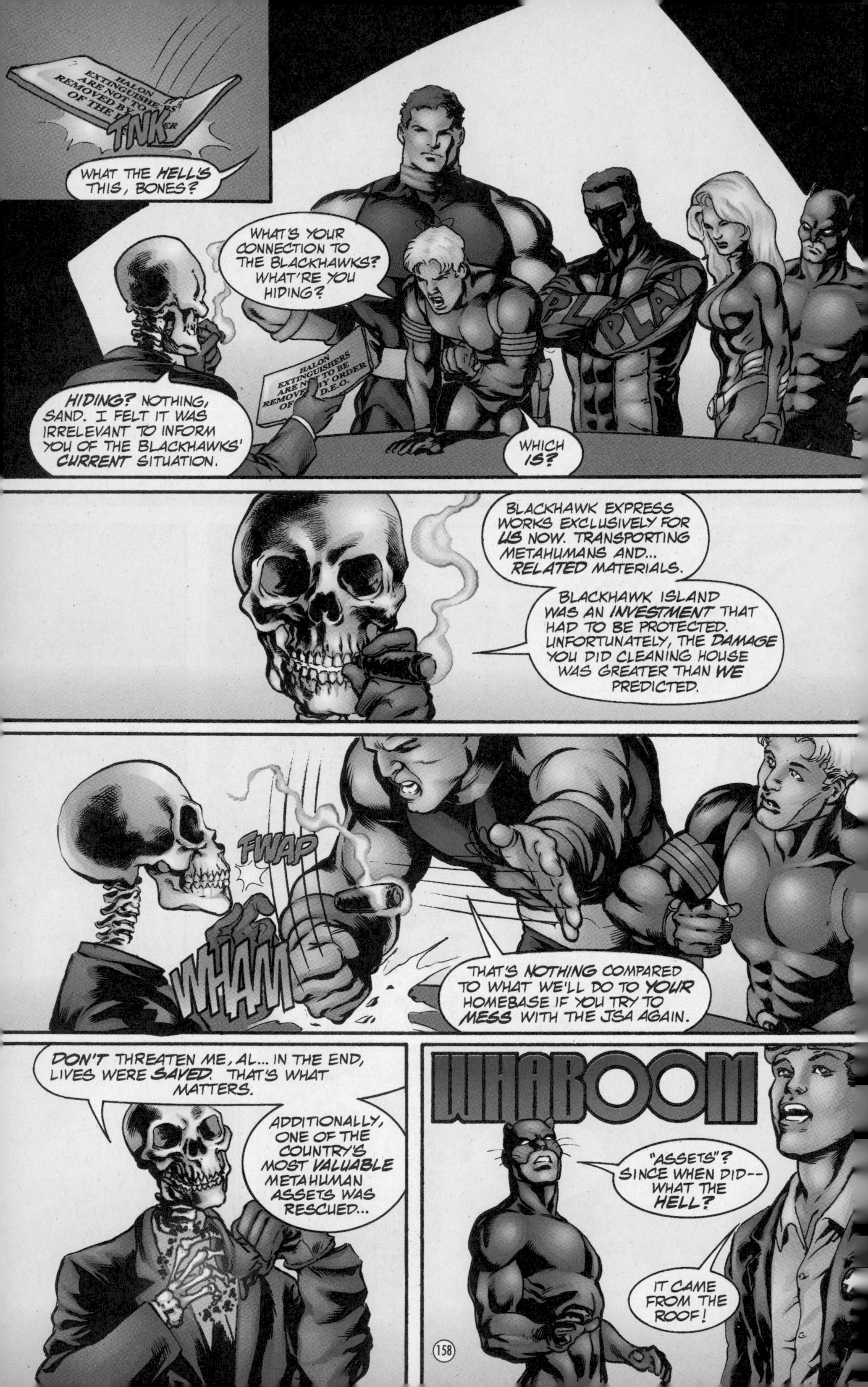

TNK
WHAT THE HELL'S THIS, BONES?
WHAT'S YOUR CONNECTION TO THE BLACKHAWKS? WHAT'RE YOU HIDING?
HIDING? NOTHING, SAND. I FELT IT WAS IRRELEVANT TO INFORM YOU OF THE BLACKHAWKS' CURRENT SITUATION.
WHICH IS?
BLACKHAWK EXPRESS WORKS EXCLUSIVELY FOR US NOW. TRANSPORTING METAHUMANS AND... RELATED MATERIALS.
BLACKHAWK ISLAND WAS AN INVESTMENT THAT HAD TO BE PROTECTED. UNFORTUNATELY, THE DAMAGE YOU DID CLEANING HOUSE WAS GREATER THAN WE PREDICTED.
FWAP
WHAM
THAT'S NOTHING COMPARED TO WHAT WE'LL DO TO YOUR HOMEBASE IF YOU TRY TO MESS WITH THE JSA AGAIN.
DON'T THREATEN ME, AL... IN THE END, LIVES WERE SAVED. THAT'S WHAT MATTERS.
ADDITIONALLY, ONE OF THE COUNTRY'S MOST VALUABLE METAHUMAN ASSETS WAS RESCUED...
WHABOOM
"ASSETS"? SINCE WHEN DID-- WHAT THE HELL?
IT CAME FROM THE ROOF!

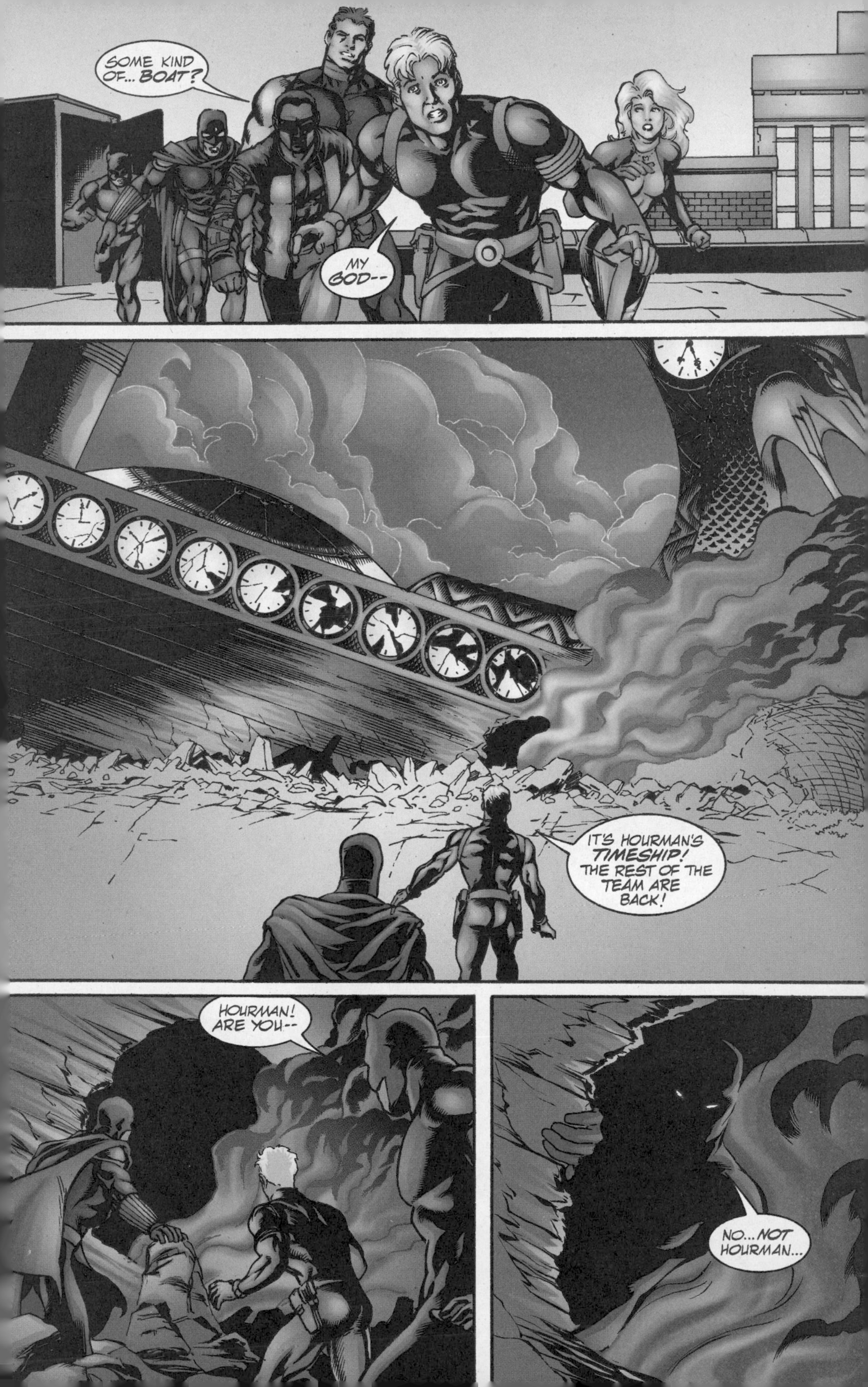
SOME KIND OF... BOAT?
MY GOD--
IT'S HOURMAN'S TIMESHIP! THE REST OF THE TEAM ARE BACK!
HOURMAN! ARE YOU--
NO... NOT HOURMAN...

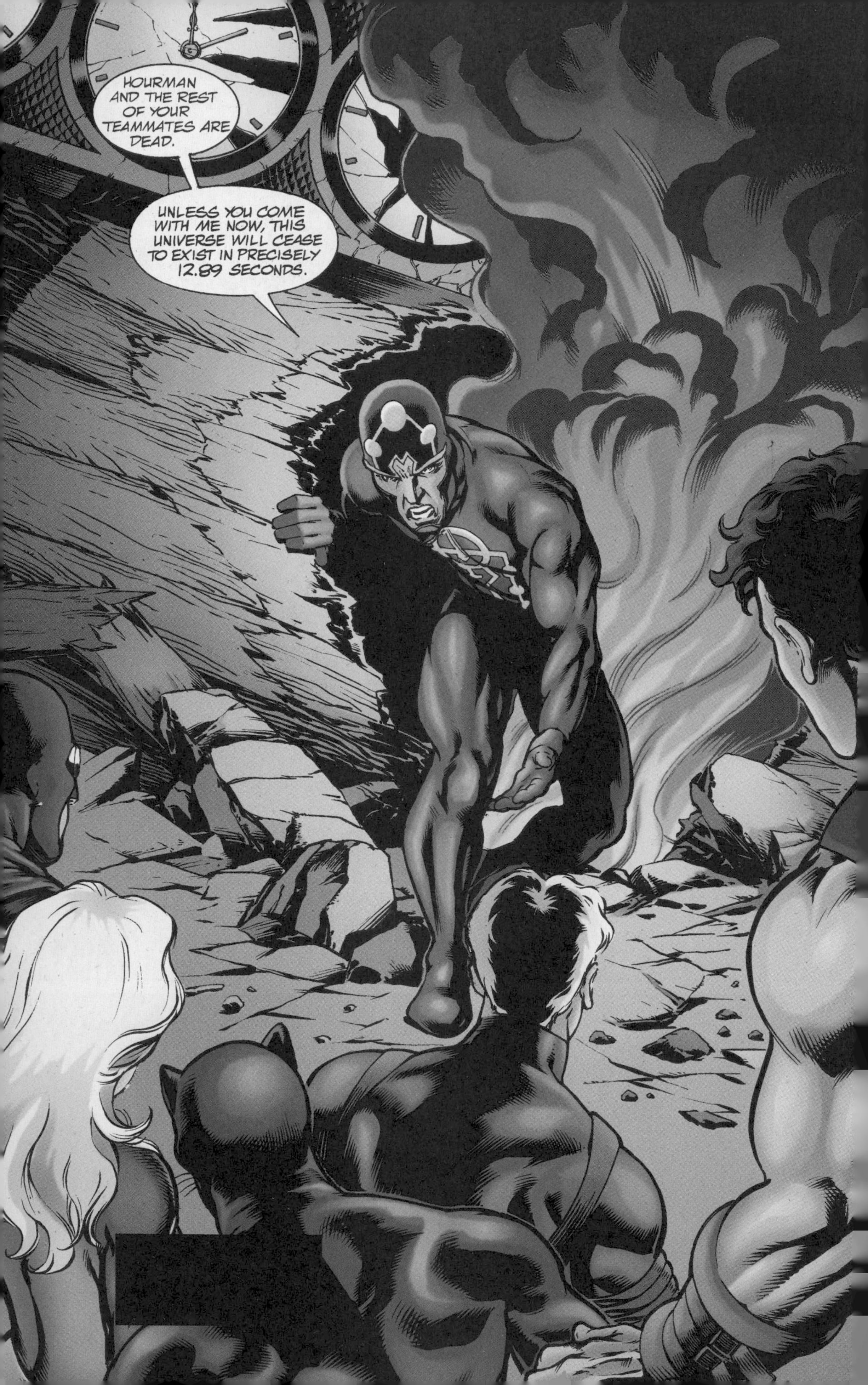
HOURMAN AND THE REST OF YOUR TEAMMATES ARE DEAD.
UNLESS YOU COME WITH ME NOW, THIS UNIVERSE WILL CEASE TO EXIST IN PRECISELY 12.89 SECONDS.
[redacted]

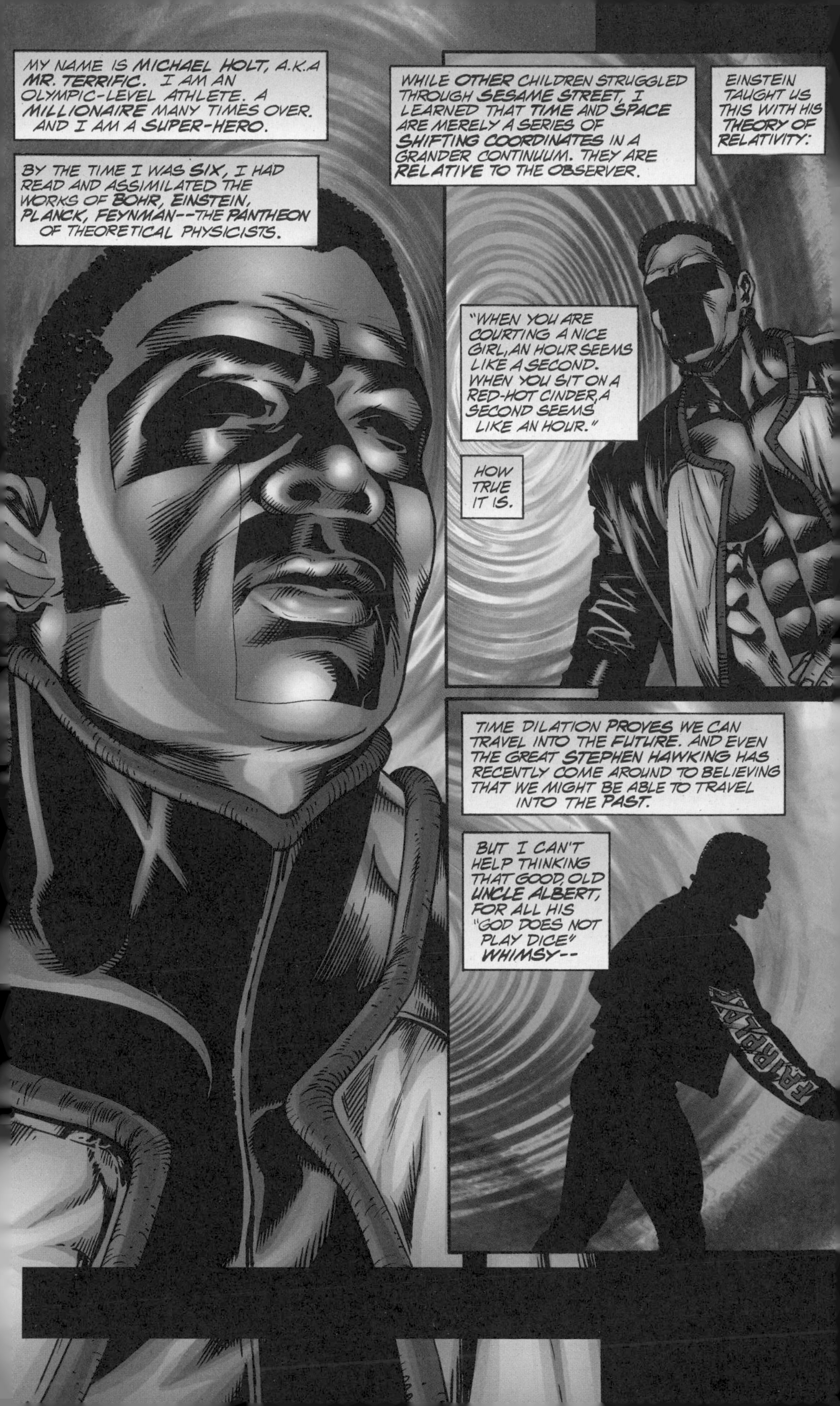
MY NAME IS MICHAEL HOLT, A.K.A MR. TERRIFIC. I AM AN OLYMPIC-LEVEL ATHLETE. A MILLIONAIRE MANY TIMES OVER. AND I AM A SUPER-HERO.
BY THE TIME I WAS SIX, I HAD READ AND ASSIMILATED THE WORKS OF BOHR, EINSTEIN, PLANCK, FEYNMAN--THE PANTHEON OF THEORETICAL PHYSICISTS.
WHILE OTHER CHILDREN STRUGGLED THROUGH SESAME STREET, I LEARNED THAT TIME AND SPACE ARE MERELY A SERIES OF SHIFTING COORDINATES IN A GRANDER CONTINUUM. THEY ARE RELATIVE TO THE OBSERVER.
EINSTEIN TAUGHT US THIS WITH HIS THEORY OF RELATIVITY:
"WHEN YOU ARE COURTING A NICE GIRL, AN HOUR SEEMS LIKE A SECOND. WHEN YOU SIT ON A RED-HOT CINDER, A SECOND SEEMS LIKE AN HOUR."
HOW TRUE IT IS.
TIME DILATION PROVES WE CAN TRAVEL INTO THE FUTURE. AND EVEN THE GREAT STEPHEN HAWKING HAS RECENTLY COME AROUND TO BELIEVING THAT WE MIGHT BE ABLE TO TRAVEL INTO THE PAST.
BUT I CAN'T HELP THINKING THAT GOOD, OLD UNCLE ALBERT, FOR ALL HIS "GOD DOES NOT PLAY DICE" WHIMSY--

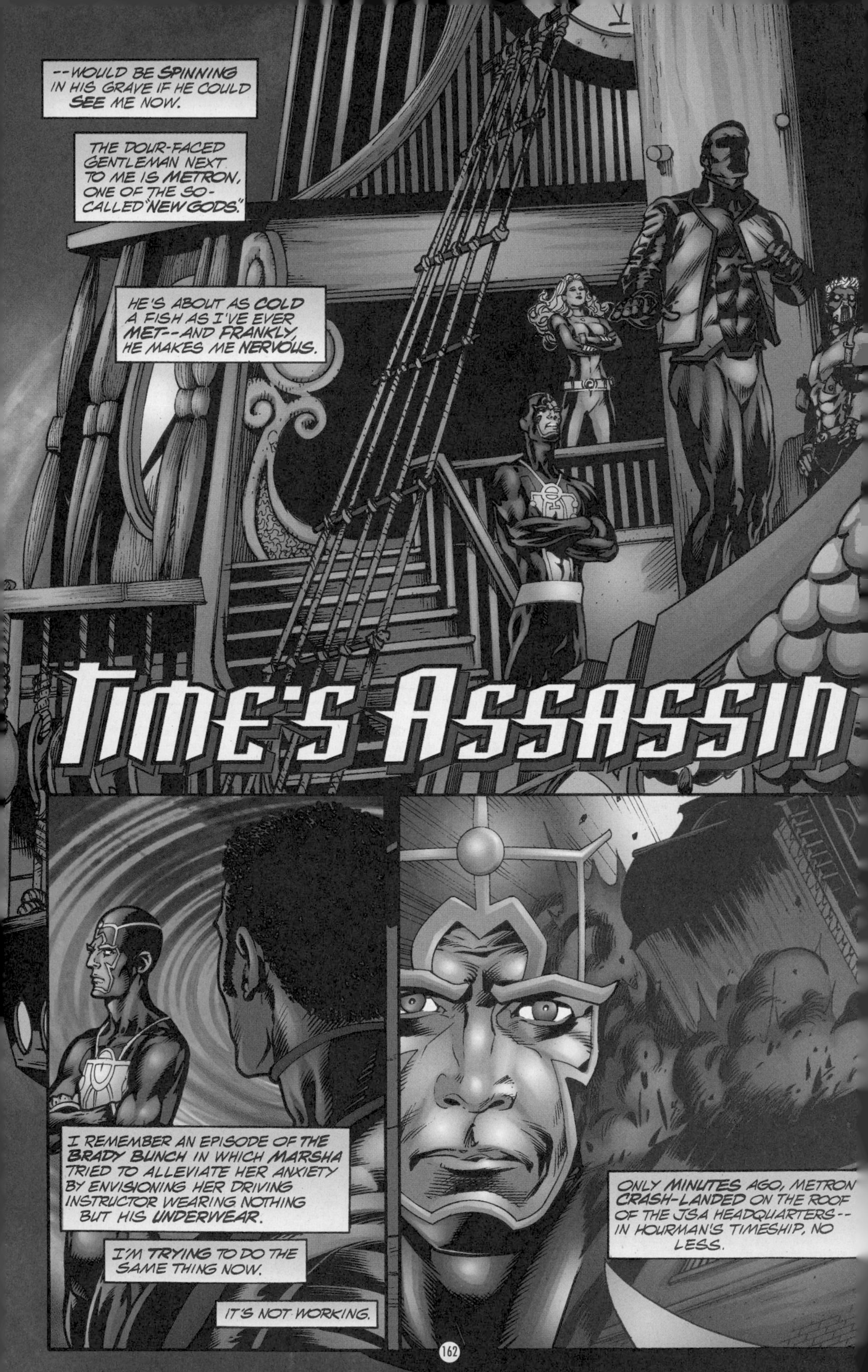
--WOULD BE SPINNING IN HIS GRAVE IF HE COULD SEE ME NOW.
THE DOUR-FACED GENTLEMAN NEXT TO ME IS METRON, ONE OF THE SO-CALLED "NEW GODS."
HE'S ABOUT AS COLD A FISH AS I'VE EVER MET--AND FRANKLY, HE MAKES ME NERVOUS.
TIME'S ASSASSIN
I REMEMBER AN EPISODE OF THE BRADY BUNCH IN WHICH MARSHA TRIED TO ALLEVIATE HER ANXIETY BY ENVISIONING HER DRIVING INSTRUCTOR WEARING NOTHING BUT HIS UNDERWEAR.
I'M TRYING TO DO THE SAME THING NOW.
IT'S NOT WORKING.
ONLY MINUTES AGO, METRON CRASH-LANDED ON THE ROOF OF THE JSA HEADQUARTERS--IN HOURMAN'S TIMESHIP, NO LESS.

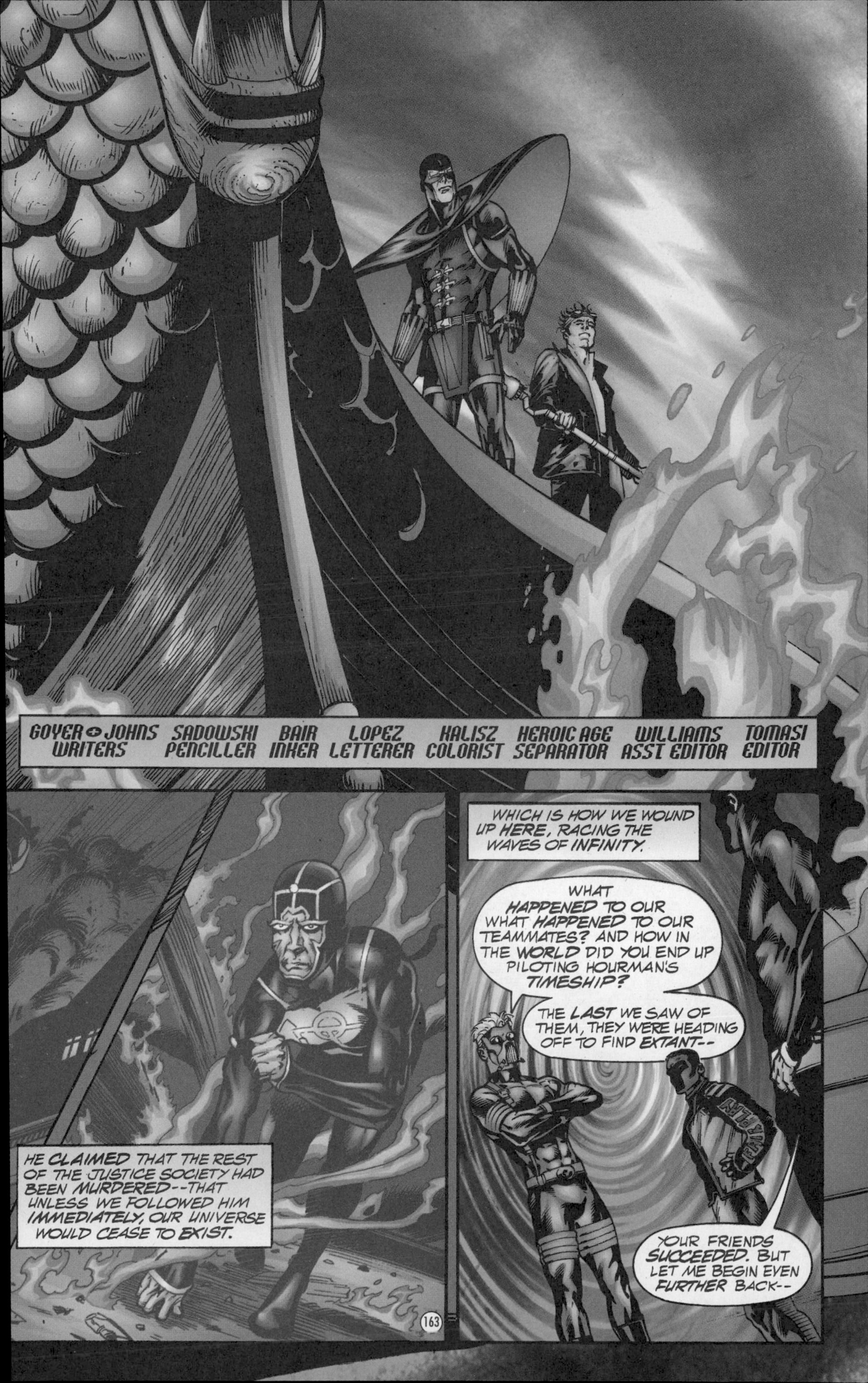
GOYER + JOHNS WRITERS
SADOWSKI PENCILLER
BAIR INKER
LOPEZ LETTERER
KALISZ COLORIST
HEROIC AGE SEPARATOR
WILLIAMS ASST EDITOR
TOMASI EDITOR
HE CLAIMED THAT THE REST OF THE JUSTICE SOCIETY HAD BEEN MURDERED--THAT UNLESS WE FOLLOWED HIM IMMEDIATELY, OUR UNIVERSE WOULD CEASE TO EXIST.
WHICH IS HOW WE WOUND UP HERE, RACING THE WAVES OF INFINITY.
WHAT HAPPENED TO OUR WHAT HAPPENED TO OUR TEAMMATES? AND HOW IN THE WORLD DID YOU END UP PILOTING HOURMAN'S TIMESHIP?
THE LAST WE SAW OF THEM, THEY WERE HEADING OFF TO FIND EXTANT--
YOUR FRIENDS SUCCEEDED. BUT LET ME BEGIN EVEN FURTHER BACK--

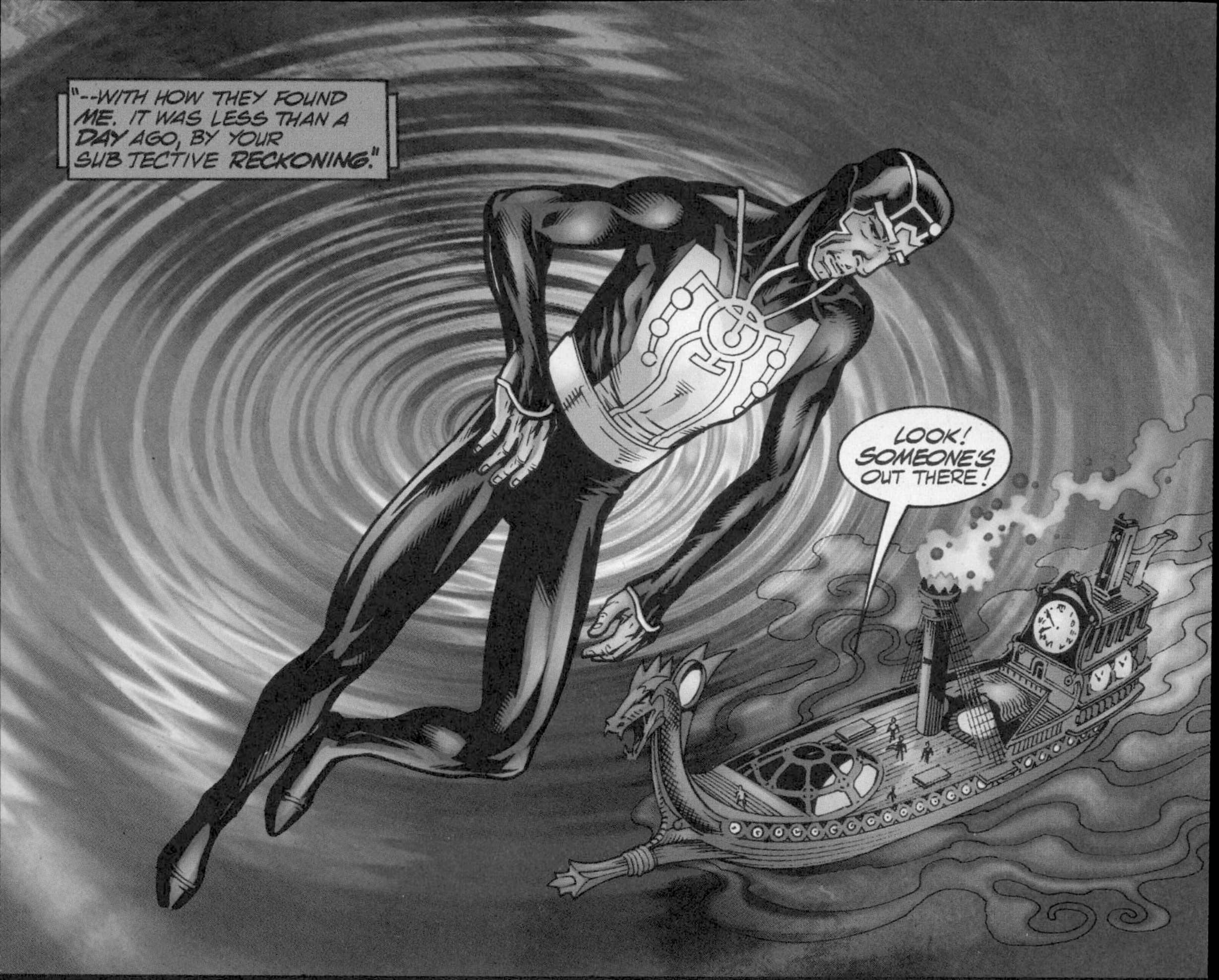
"--WITH HOW THEY FOUND ME. IT WAS LESS THAN A DAY AGO, BY YOUR SUBJECTIVE RECKONING."
LOOK! SOMEONE'S OUT THERE!

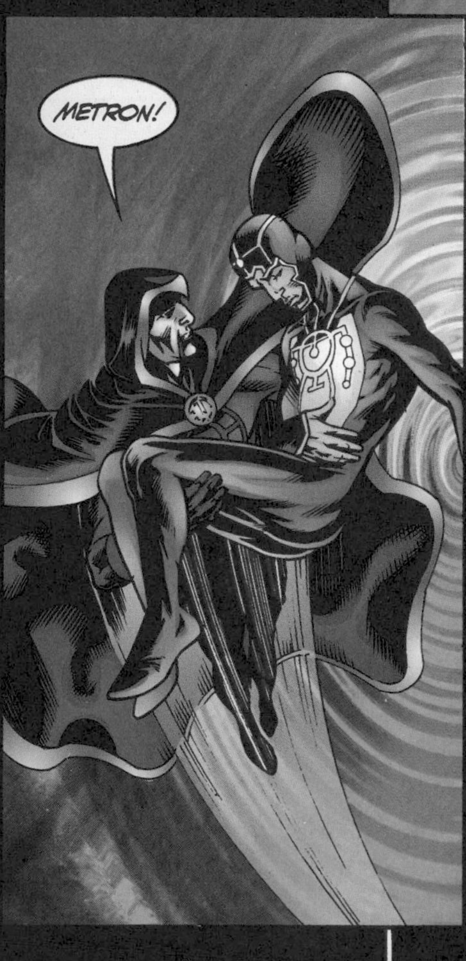
METRON!

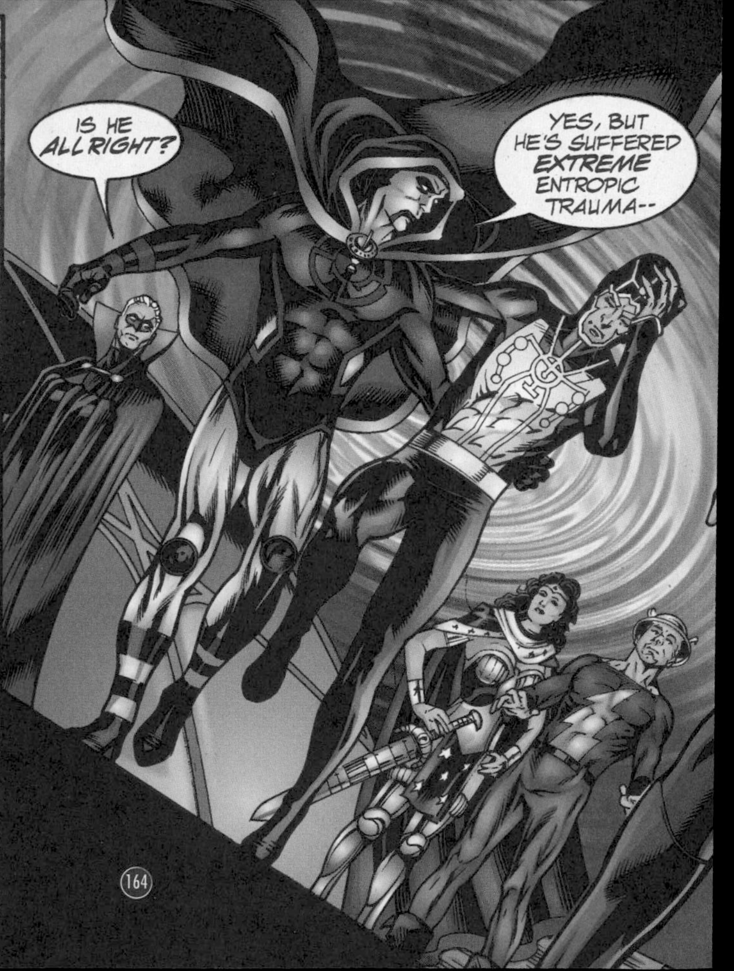
IS HE ALL RIGHT?
YES, BUT HE'S SUFFERED EXTREME ENTROPIC TRAUMA--

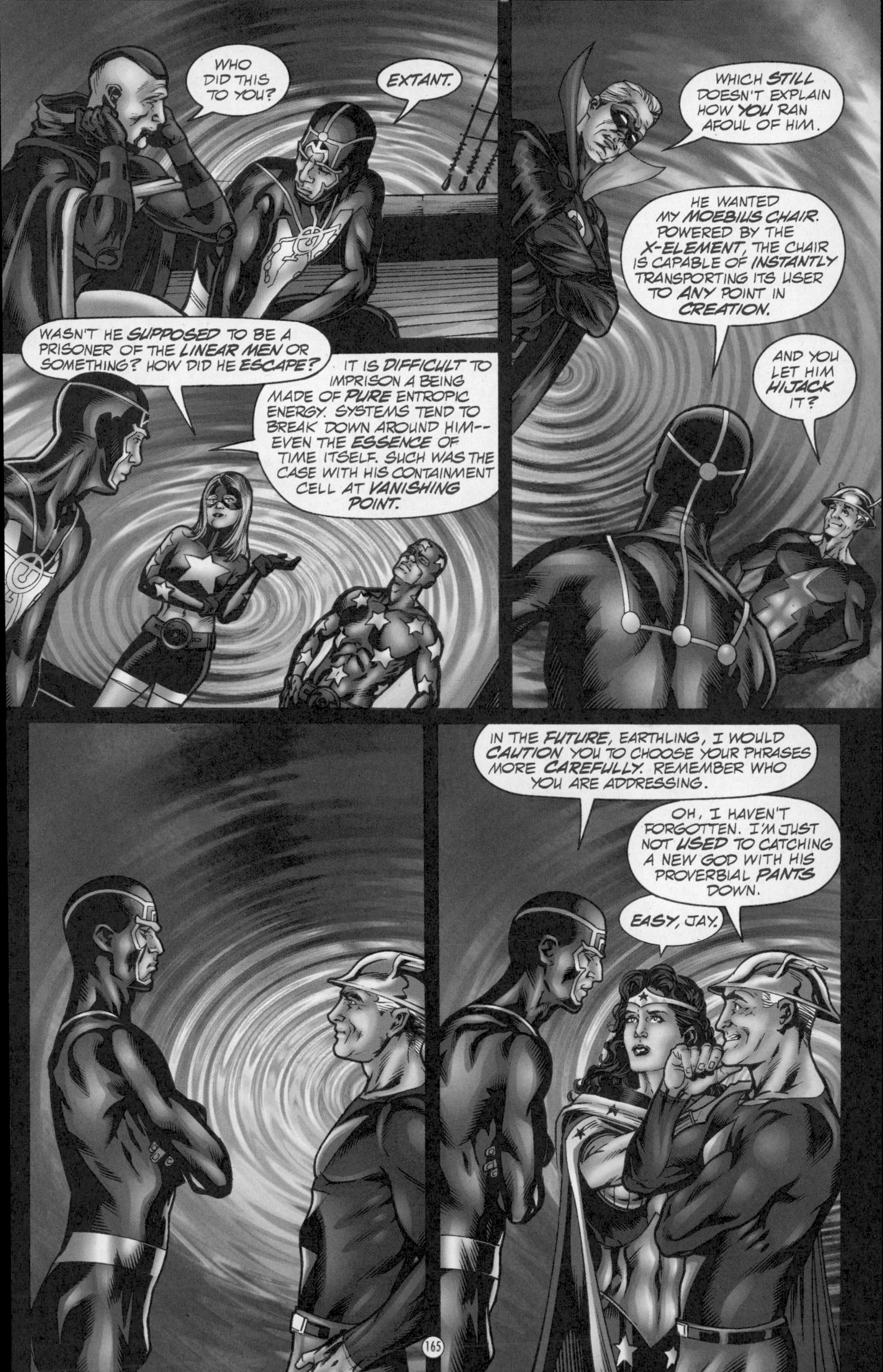

WHO DID THIS TO YOU?
EXTANT.
WHICH STILL DOESN'T EXPLAIN HOW YOU RAN AFOUL OF HIM.
HE WANTED MY MOEBIUS CHAIR. POWERED BY THE X-ELEMENT, THE CHAIR IS CAPABLE OF INSTANTLY TRANSPORTING ITS USER TO ANY POINT IN CREATION.
WASN'T HE SUPPOSED TO BE A PRISONER OF THE LINEAR MEN OR SOMETHING? HOW DID HE ESCAPE?
IT IS DIFFICULT TO IMPRISON A BEING MADE OF PURE ENTROPIC ENERGY. SYSTEMS TEND TO BREAK DOWN AROUND HIM-- EVEN THE ESSENCE OF TIME ITSELF. SUCH WAS THE CASE WITH HIS CONTAINMENT CELL AT VANISHING POINT.
AND YOU LET HIM HIJACK IT?
IN THE FUTURE, EARTHLING, I WOULD CAUTION YOU TO CHOOSE YOUR PHRASES MORE CAREFULLY. REMEMBER WHO YOU ARE ADDRESSING.
OH, I HAVEN'T FORGOTTEN. I'M JUST NOT USED TO CATCHING A NEW GOD WITH HIS PROVERBIAL PANTS DOWN.
EASY, JAY.

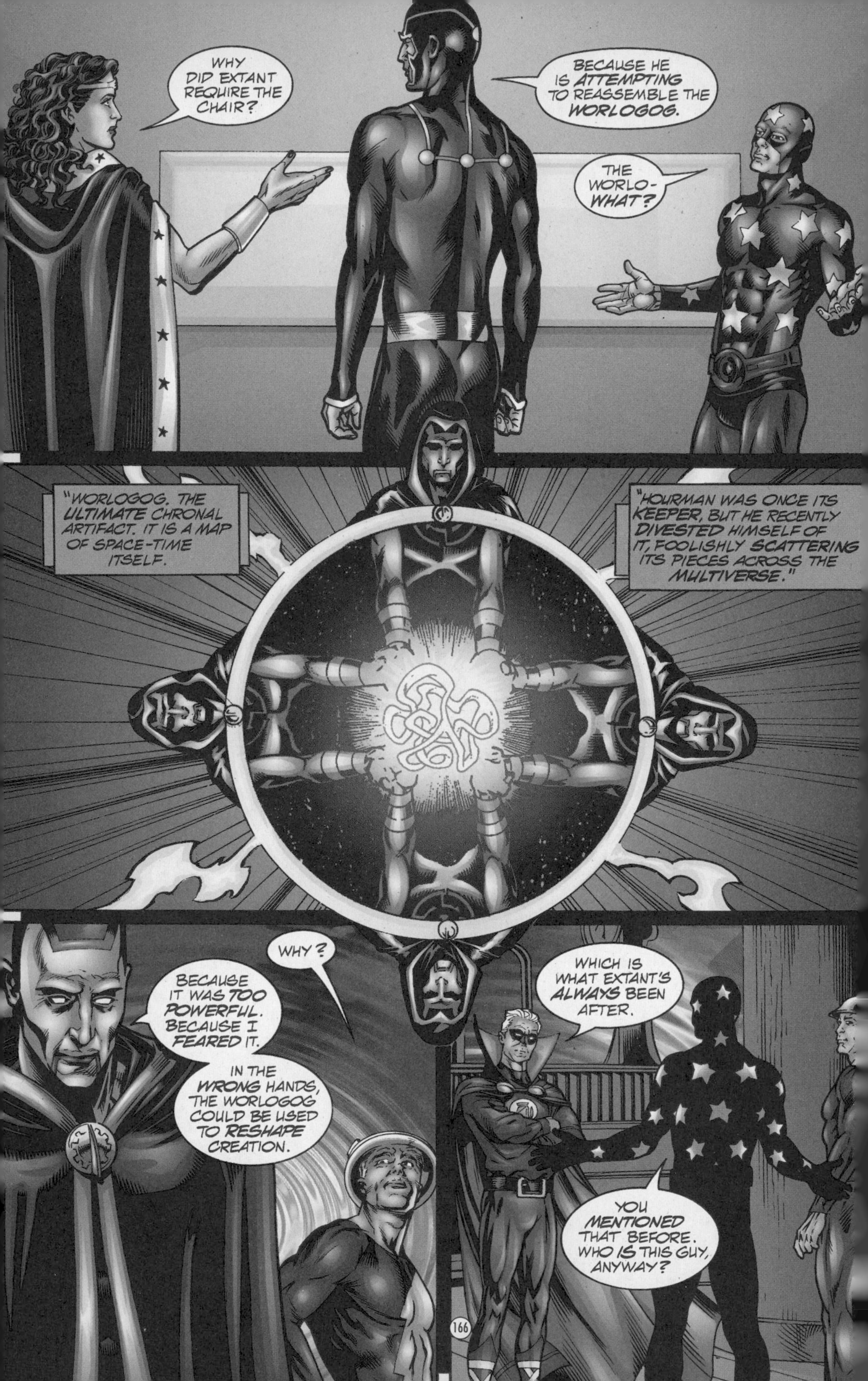
WHY DID EXTANT REQUIRE THE CHAIR?
BECAUSE HE IS ATTEMPTING TO REASSEMBLE THE WORLOGOG.
THE WORLO-WHAT?
"WORLOGOG. THE ULTIMATE CHRONAL ARTIFACT. IT IS A MAP OF SPACE-TIME ITSELF.
"HOURMAN WAS ONCE ITS KEEPER, BUT HE RECENTLY DIVESTED HIMSELF OF IT, FOOLISHLY SCATTERING ITS PIECES ACROSS THE MULTIVERSE."
WHY?
BECAUSE IT WAS TOO POWERFUL. BECAUSE I FEARED IT.
IN THE WRONG HANDS, THE WORLOGOG COULD BE USED TO RESHAPE CREATION.
WHICH IS WHAT EXTANT'S ALWAYS BEEN AFTER.
YOU MENTIONED THAT BEFORE. WHO IS THIS GUY, ANYWAY?

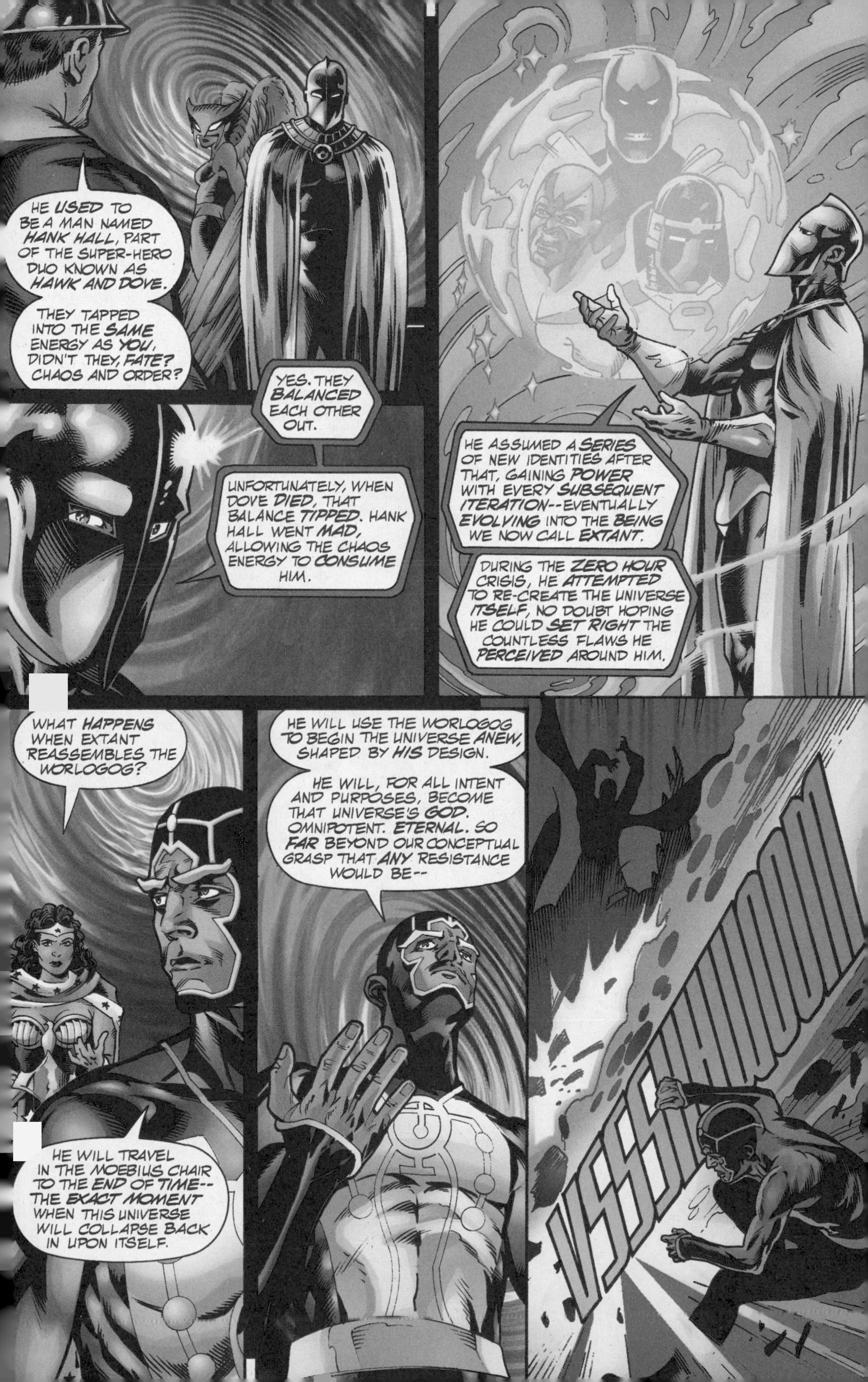
HE *USED* TO BE A MAN NAMED *HANK HALL*, PART OF THE SUPER-HERO DUO KNOWN AS *HAWK AND DOVE*.
THEY TAPPED INTO THE *SAME* ENERGY AS *YOU*, DIDN'T THEY, *FATE?* CHAOS AND ORDER?
YES. THEY *BALANCED* EACH OTHER OUT.
UNFORTUNATELY, WHEN DOVE *DIED*, THAT BALANCE *TIPPED*. HANK HALL WENT *MAD*, ALLOWING THE CHAOS ENERGY TO *CONSUME* HIM.
HE ASSUMED A *SERIES* OF NEW IDENTITIES AFTER THAT, GAINING *POWER* WITH EVERY *SUBSEQUENT ITERATION*--EVENTUALLY *EVOLVING* INTO THE *BEING* WE NOW CALL *EXTANT*.
DURING THE *ZERO HOUR* CRISIS, HE *ATTEMPTED* TO RE-CREATE THE UNIVERSE *ITSELF*, NO DOUBT HOPING HE COULD *SET RIGHT* THE COUNTLESS FLAWS HE *PERCEIVED* AROUND HIM.
WHAT *HAPPENS* WHEN EXTANT REASSEMBLES THE WORLOGOG?
HE WILL TRAVEL IN THE *MOEBIUS CHAIR* TO THE *END OF TIME*-- THE *EXACT MOMENT* WHEN THIS UNIVERSE WILL COLLAPSE BACK IN UPON ITSELF.
HE WILL USE THE WORLOGOG TO BEGIN THE UNIVERSE *ANEW*, SHAPED BY *HIS* DESIGN.
HE WILL, FOR ALL INTENT AND PURPOSES, BECOME THAT UNIVERSE'S *GOD*. OMNIPOTENT. *ETERNAL*. SO *FAR* BEYOND OUR CONCEPTUAL GRASP THAT *ANY* RESISTANCE WOULD BE--
VSSSHHOOOM

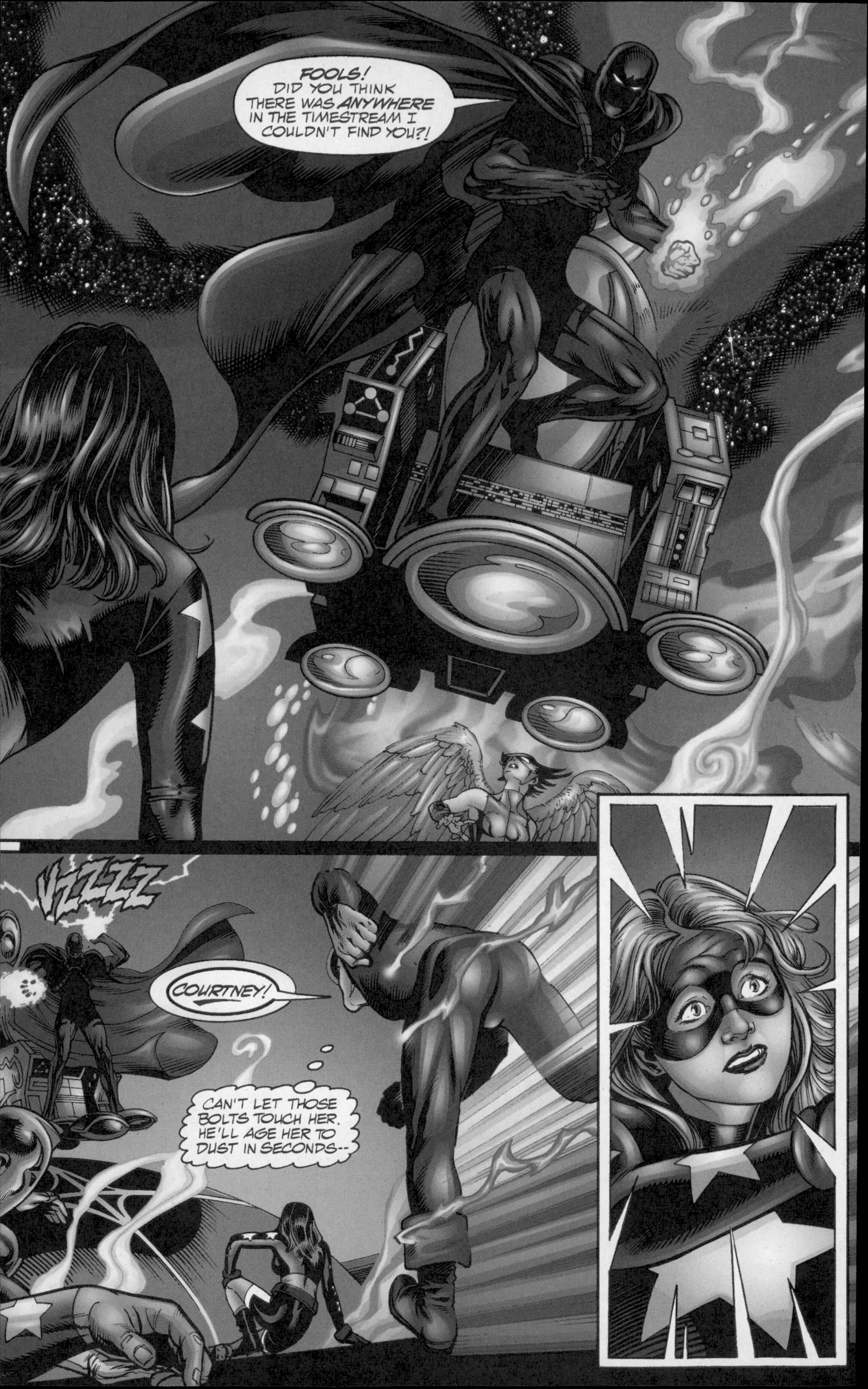

FOOLS! DID YOU THINK THERE WAS ANYWHERE IN THE TIMESTREAM I COULDN'T FIND YOU?!
VZZZZZ
COURTNEY!
CAN'T LET THOSE BOLTS TOUCH HER. HE'LL AGE HER TO DUST IN SECONDS--

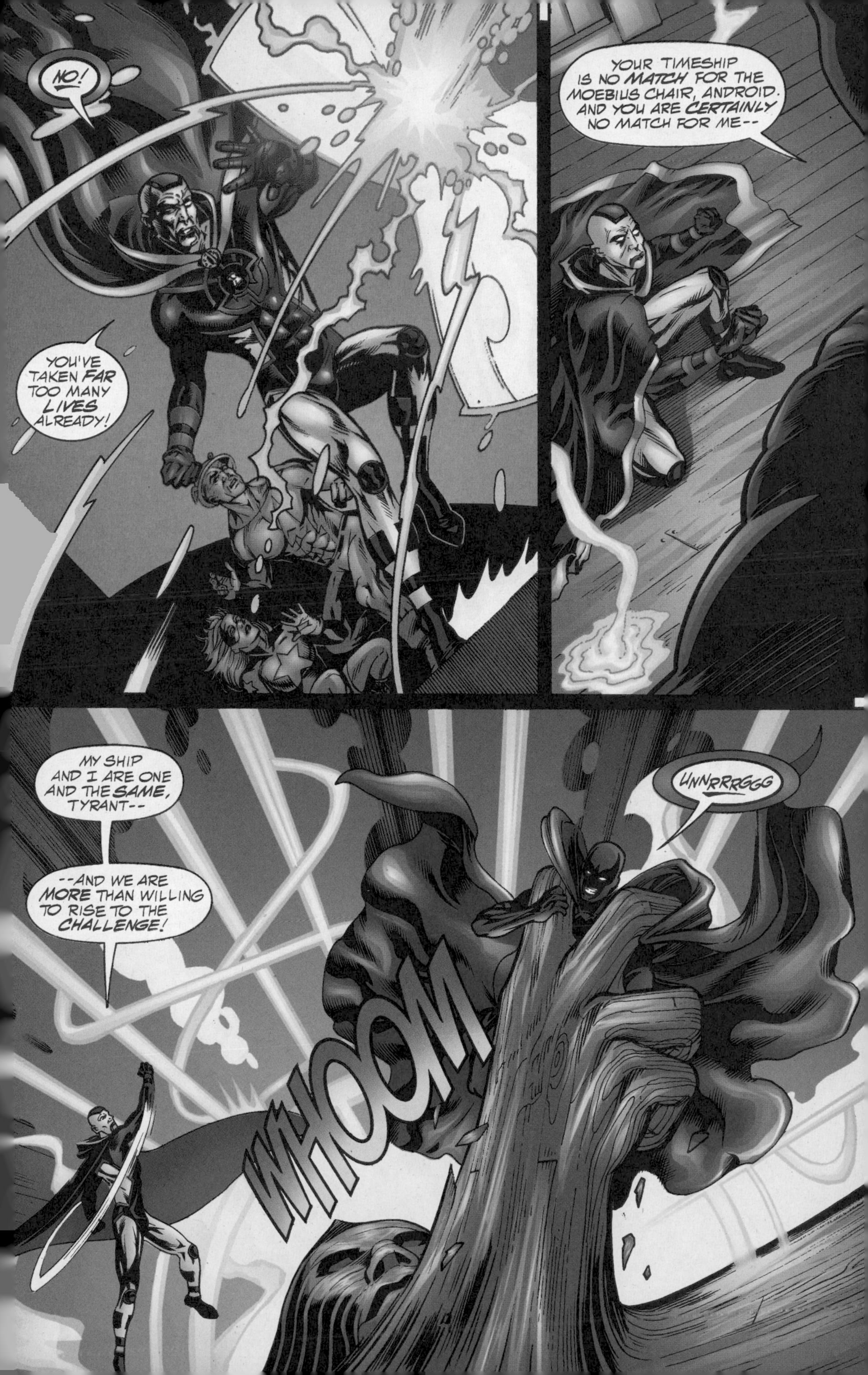
NO!
YOU'VE TAKEN FAR TOO MANY LIVES ALREADY!
YOUR TIMESHIP IS NO MATCH FOR THE MOEBIUS CHAIR, ANDROID. AND YOU ARE CERTAINLY NO MATCH FOR ME--
MY SHIP AND I ARE ONE AND THE SAME, TYRANT--
--AND WE ARE MORE THAN WILLING TO RISE TO THE CHALLENGE!
UNNRRRGGG
WHOOM

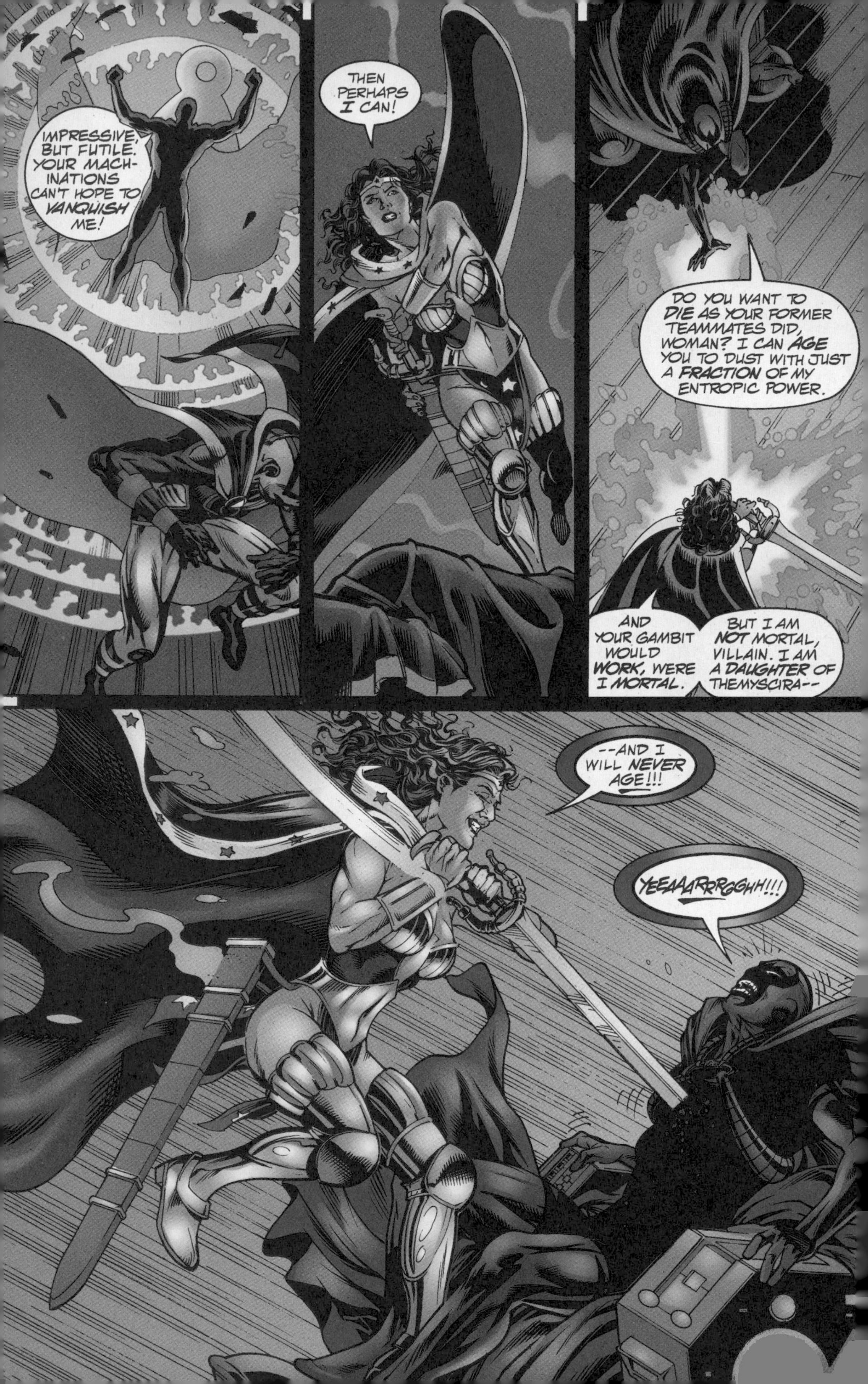
IMPRESSIVE, BUT FUTILE. YOUR MACH-INATIONS CAN'T HOPE TO VANQUISH ME!
THEN PERHAPS I CAN!
DO YOU WANT TO DIE AS YOUR FORMER TEAMMATES DID, WOMAN? I CAN AGE YOU TO DUST WITH JUST A FRACTION OF MY ENTROPIC POWER.
AND YOUR GAMBIT WOULD WORK, WERE I MORTAL.
BUT I AM NOT MORTAL, VILLAIN. I AM A DAUGHTER OF THEMYSCIRA--
--AND I WILL NEVER AGE!!!
YEEAAARRRGGHH!!!

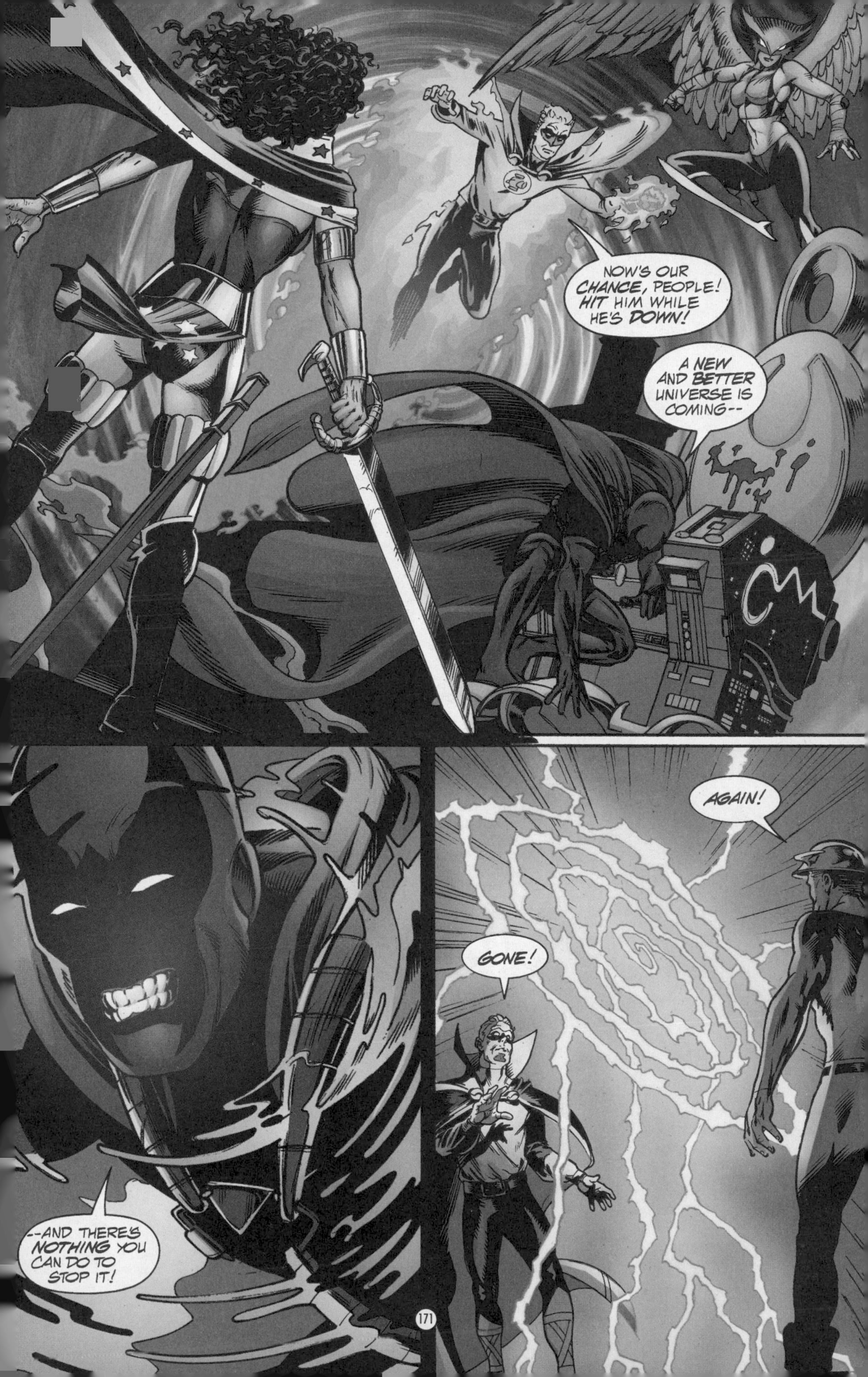
NOW'S OUR CHANCE, PEOPLE! HIT HIM WHILE HE'S DOWN!
A NEW AND BETTER UNIVERSE IS COMING--
--AND THERE'S NOTHING YOU CAN DO TO STOP IT!
AGAIN!
GONE!

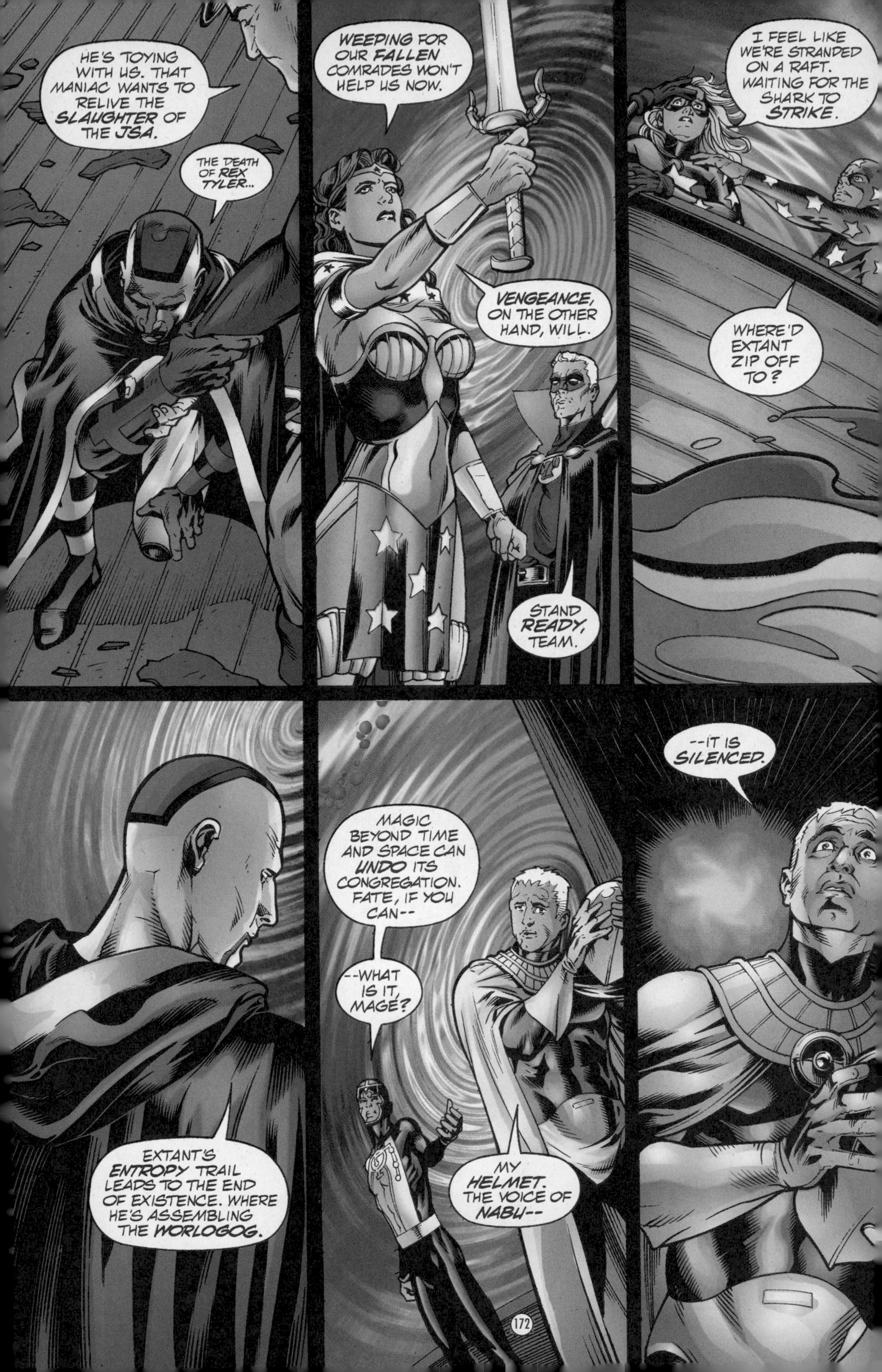
HE'S TOYING WITH US. THAT MANIAC WANTS TO RELIVE THE SLAUGHTER OF THE JSA.
THE DEATH OF REX TYLER...
WEEPING FOR OUR FALLEN COMRADES WON'T HELP US NOW.
VENGEANCE, ON THE OTHER HAND, WILL.
STAND READY, TEAM.
I FEEL LIKE WE'RE STRANDED ON A RAFT. WAITING FOR THE SHARK TO STRIKE.
WHERE'D EXTANT ZIP OFF TO?
EXTANT'S ENTROPY TRAIL LEADS TO THE END OF EXISTENCE. WHERE HE'S ASSEMBLING THE WORLOGOG.
MAGIC BEYOND TIME AND SPACE CAN UNDO ITS CONGREGATION. FATE, IF YOU CAN--
--WHAT IS IT, MAGE?
MY HELMET. THE VOICE OF NABU--
--IT IS SILENCED.

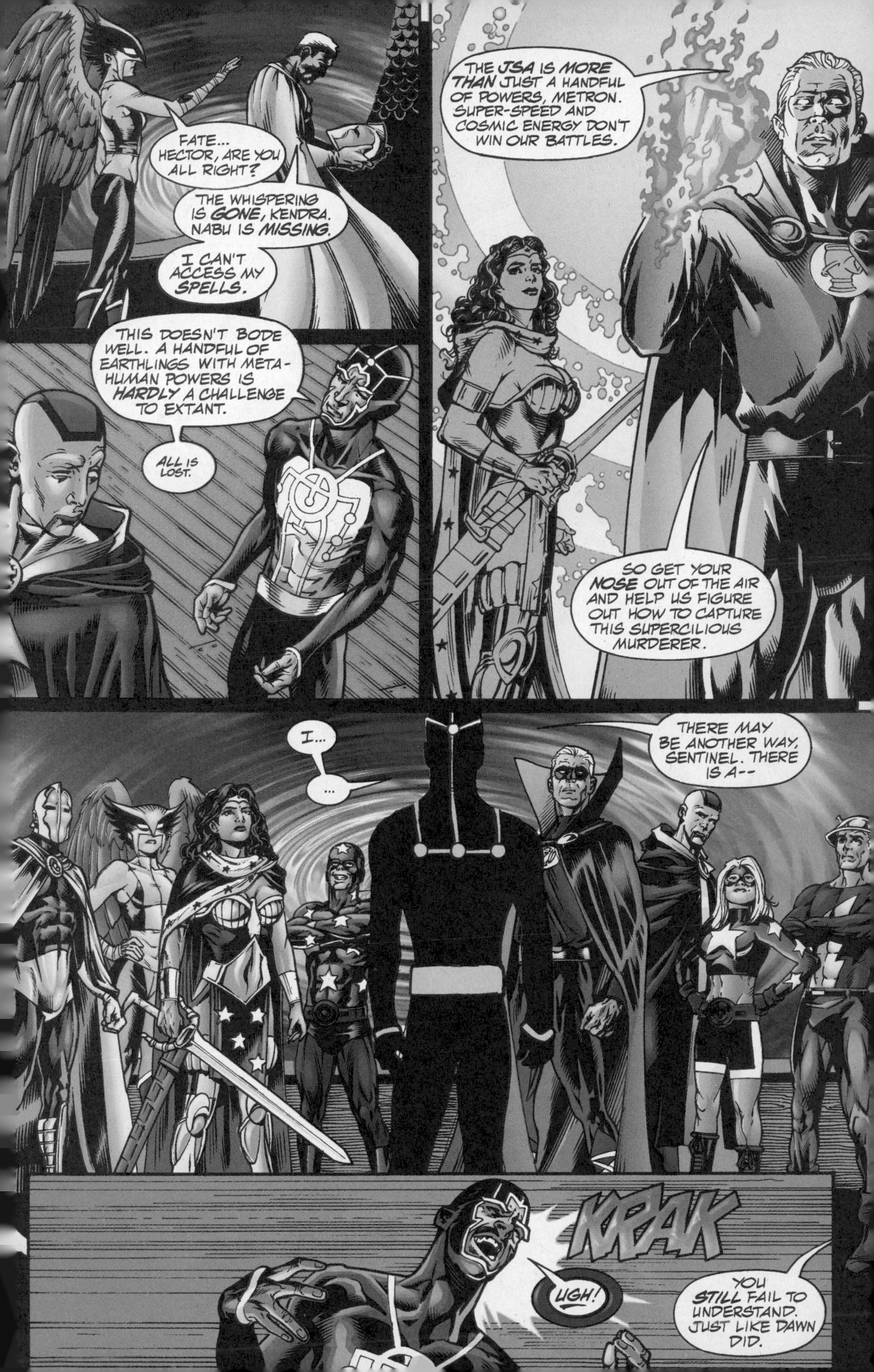

FATE... HECTOR, ARE YOU ALL RIGHT?
THE WHISPERING IS GONE, KENDRA. NABU IS MISSING.
I CAN'T ACCESS MY SPELLS.
THE JSA IS MORE THAN JUST A HANDFUL OF POWERS, METRON. SUPER-SPEED AND COSMIC ENERGY DON'T WIN OUR BATTLES.
THIS DOESN'T BODE WELL. A HANDFUL OF EARTHLINGS WITH META-HUMAN POWERS IS HARDLY A CHALLENGE TO EXTANT.
ALL IS LOST.
SO GET YOUR NOSE OUT OF THE AIR AND HELP US FIGURE OUT HOW TO CAPTURE THIS SUPERCILIOUS MURDERER.
I...
...
THERE MAY BE ANOTHER WAY, SENTINEL. THERE IS A--
KRAK
UGH!
YOU STILL FAIL TO UNDERSTAND. JUST LIKE DAWN DID.

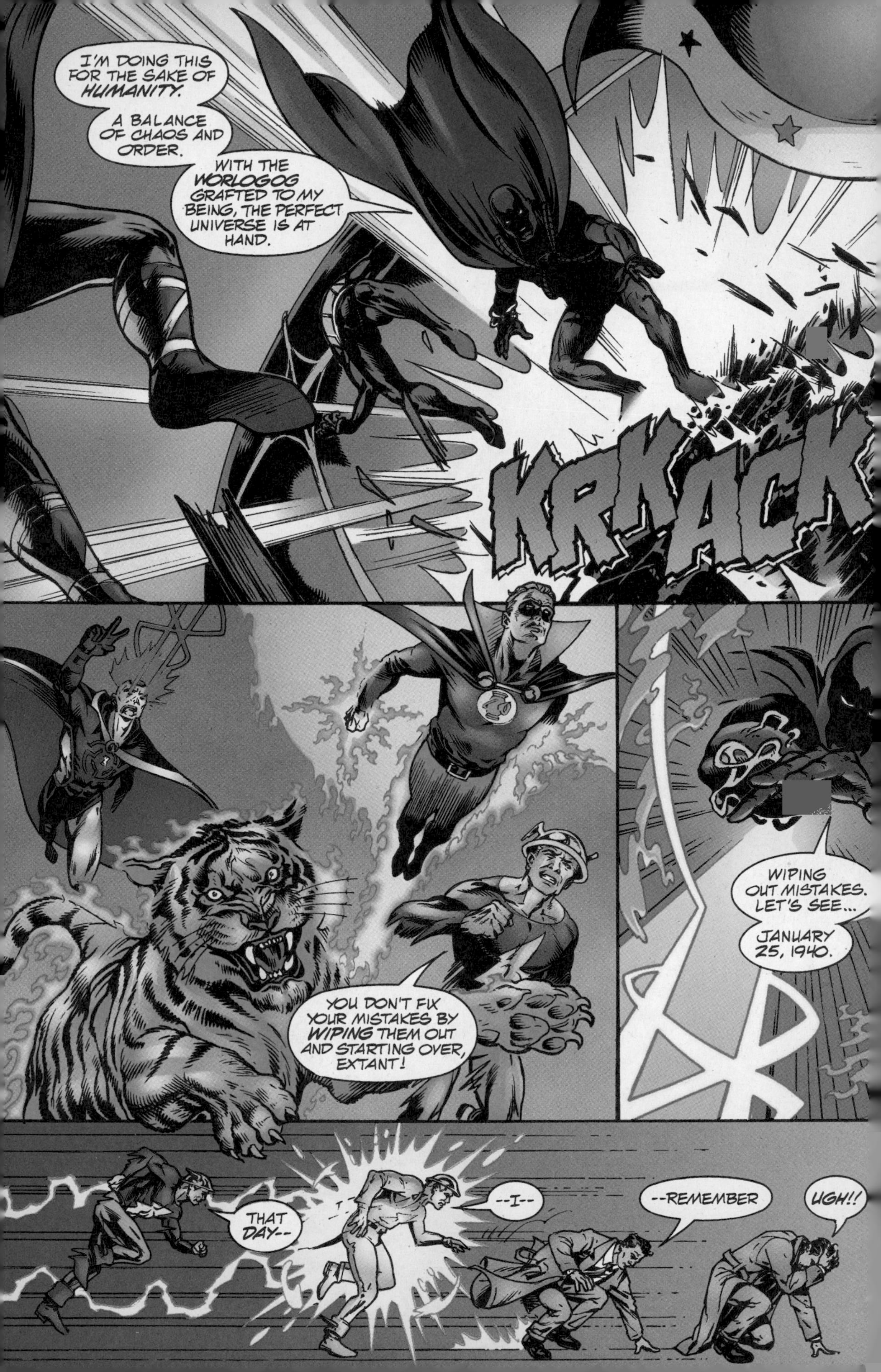
I'M DOING THIS FOR THE SAKE OF HUMANITY.
A BALANCE OF CHAOS AND ORDER.
WITH THE WORLOGOG GRAFTED TO MY BEING, THE PERFECT UNIVERSE IS AT HAND.
KRKACK
YOU DON'T FIX YOUR MISTAKES BY WIPING THEM OUT AND STARTING OVER, EXTANT!
WIPING OUT MISTAKES. LET'S SEE...
JANUARY 25, 1940.
THAT DAY--
--I--
--REMEMBER
UGH!!

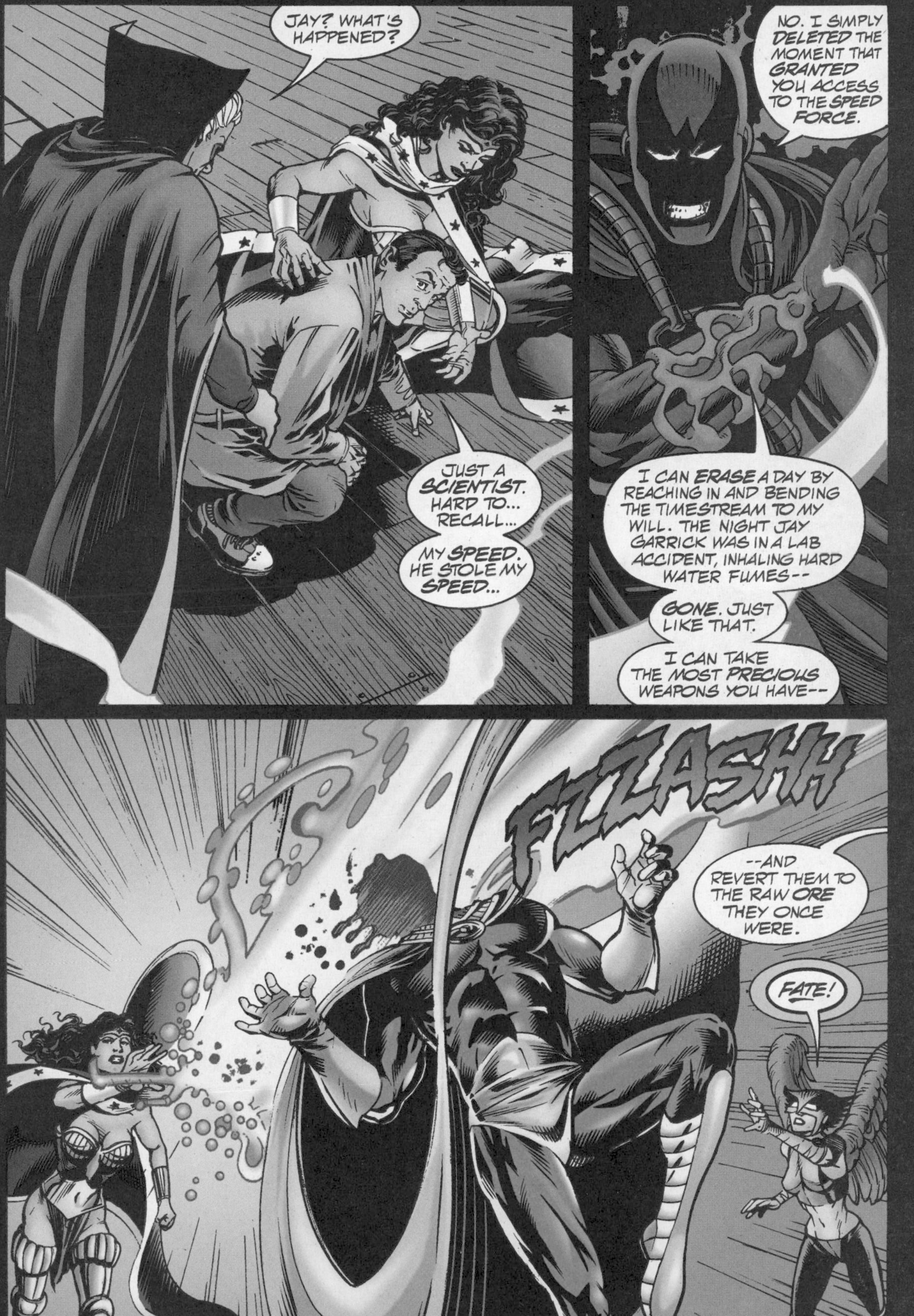
JAY? WHAT'S HAPPENED?
JUST A SCIENTIST. HARD TO... RECALL...
MY SPEED. HE STOLE MY SPEED...
NO. I SIMPLY DELETED THE MOMENT THAT GRANTED YOU ACCESS TO THE SPEED FORCE.
I CAN ERASE A DAY BY REACHING IN AND BENDING THE TIMESTREAM TO MY WILL. THE NIGHT JAY GARRICK WAS IN A LAB ACCIDENT, INHALING HARD WATER FUMES--
GONE. JUST LIKE THAT.
I CAN TAKE THE MOST PRECIOUS WEAPONS YOU HAVE--
FZZASHH
--AND REVERT THEM TO THE RAW ORE THEY ONCE WERE.
FATE!

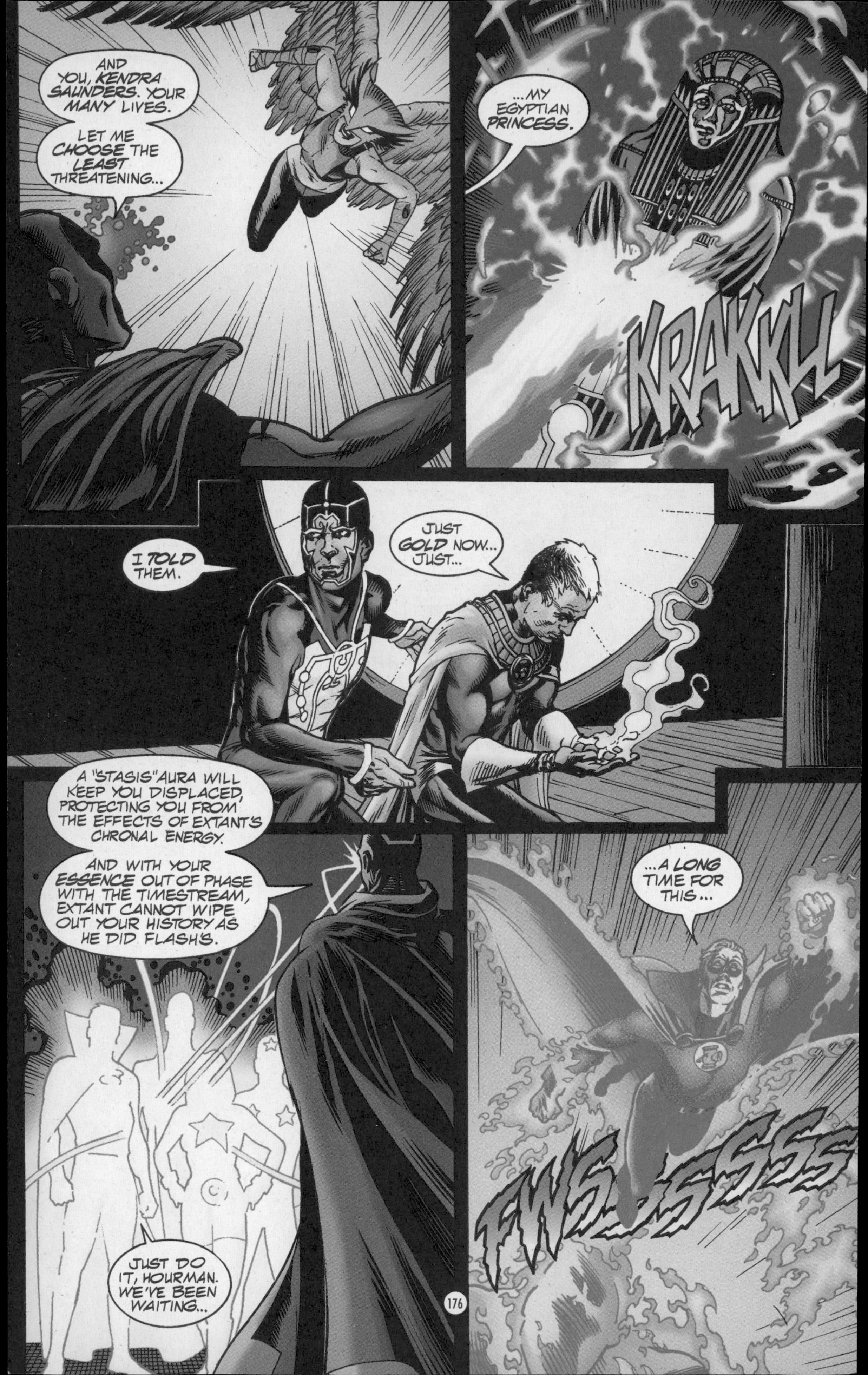
AND YOU, KENDRA SAUNDERS. YOUR MANY LIVES.
LET ME CHOOSE THE LEAST THREATENING...
...MY EGYPTIAN PRINCESS.
KRAKKH
I TOLD THEM.
JUST GOLD NOW... JUST...
A "STASIS" AURA WILL KEEP YOU DISPLACED, PROTECTING YOU FROM THE EFFECTS OF EXTANT'S CHRONAL ENERGY.
AND WITH YOUR ESSENCE OUT OF PHASE WITH THE TIMESTREAM, EXTANT CANNOT WIPE OUT YOUR HISTORY AS HE DID FLASH'S.
JUST DO IT, HOURMAN. WE'VE BEEN WAITING...
...A LONG TIME FOR THIS...
FWSSSSSS

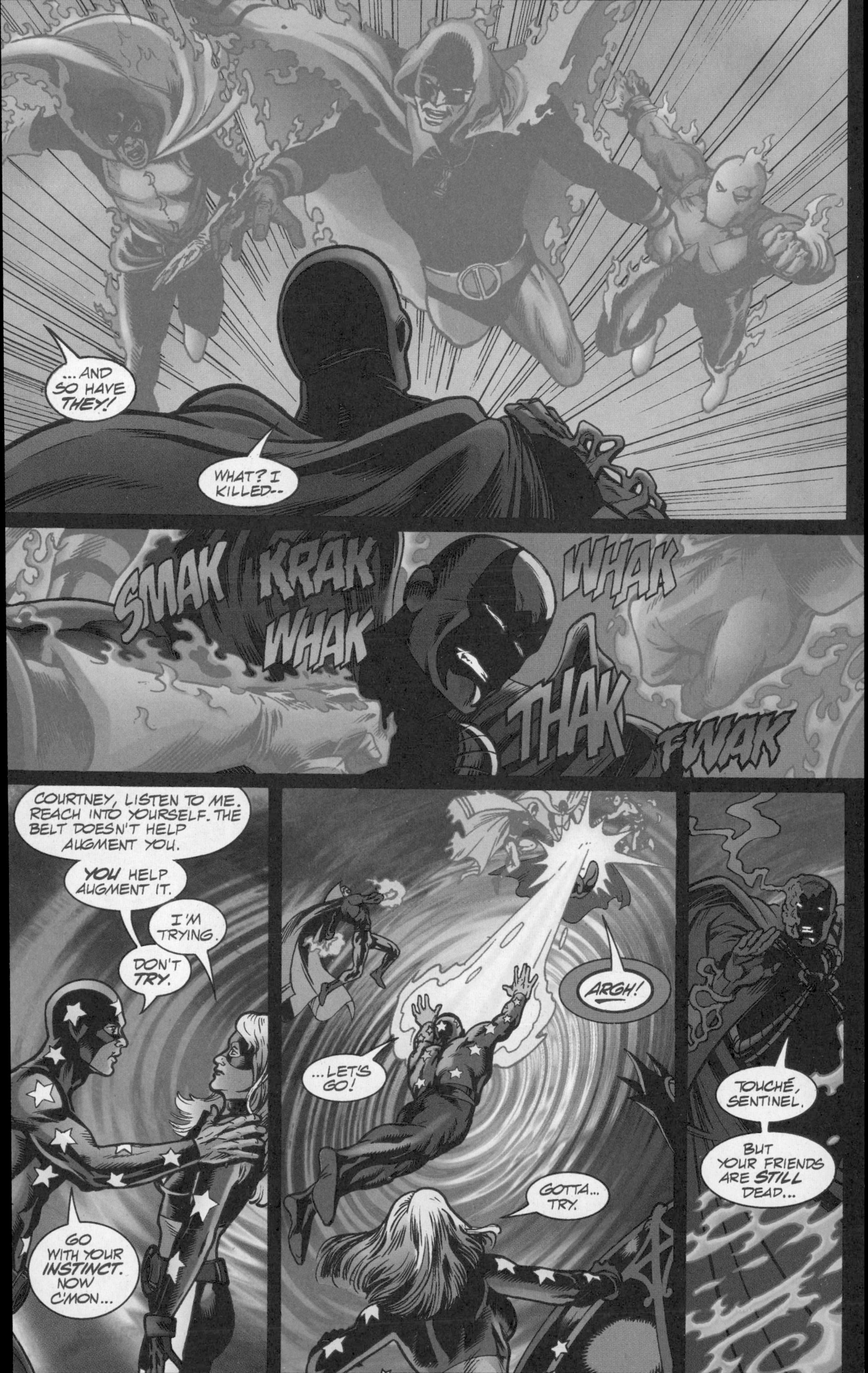
...AND SO HAVE THEY!
WHAT? I KILLED--
SMAK
KRAK
WHAK
WHAK
THAK
FWAK
COURTNEY, LISTEN TO ME. REACH INTO YOURSELF. THE BELT DOESN'T HELP AUGMENT YOU.
YOU HELP AUGMENT IT.
I'M TRYING.
DON'T TRY.
GO WITH YOUR INSTINCT. NOW C'MON...
ARGH!
...LET'S GO!
GOTTA... TRY.
TOUCHÉ, SENTINEL.
BUT YOUR FRIENDS ARE STILL DEAD...

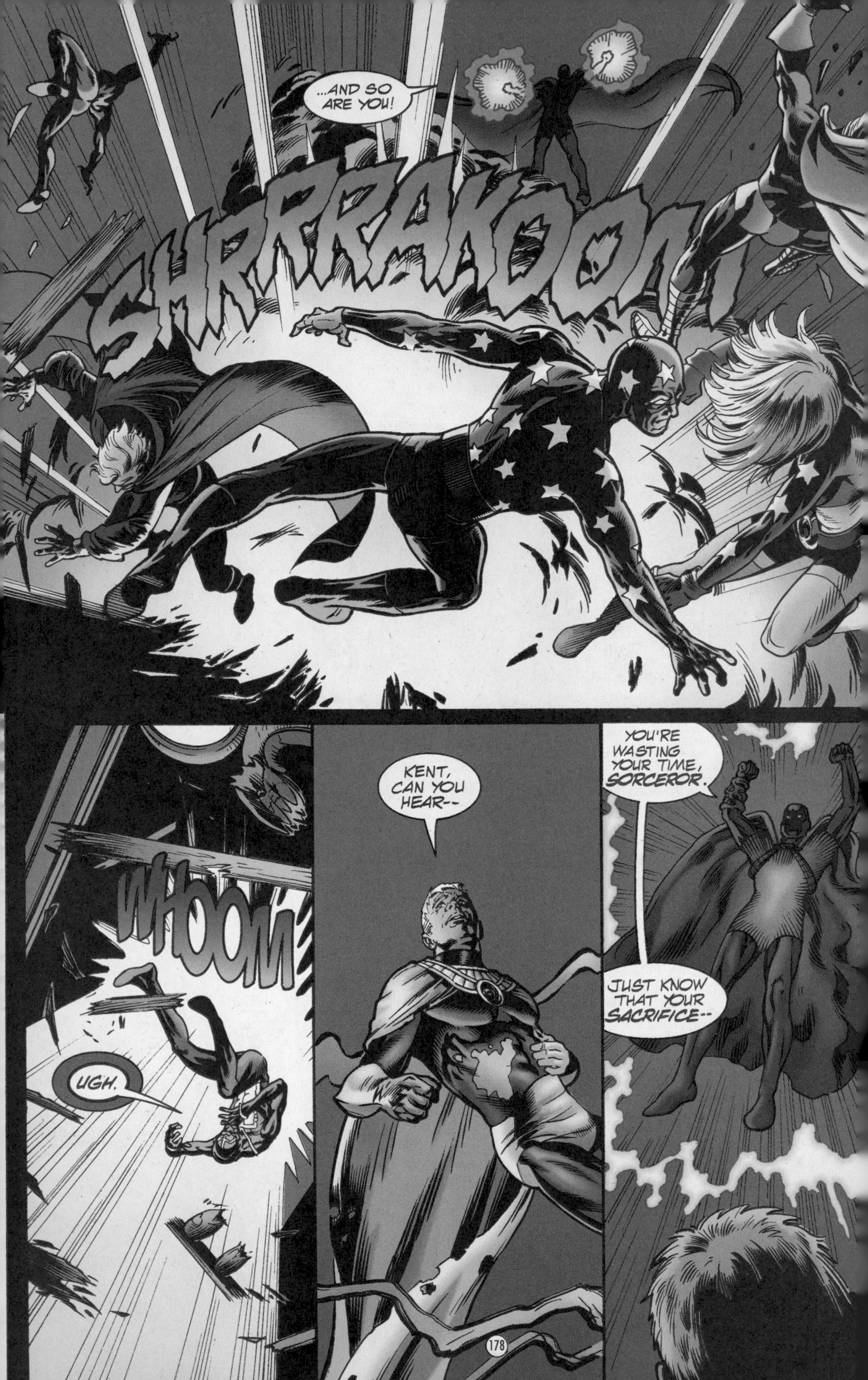
...AND SO ARE YOU!
SHRRRAKOOM
WHOOM
UGH.
KENT, CAN YOU HEAR--
YOU'RE WASTING YOUR TIME, SORCEROR.
JUST KNOW THAT YOUR SACRIFICE--

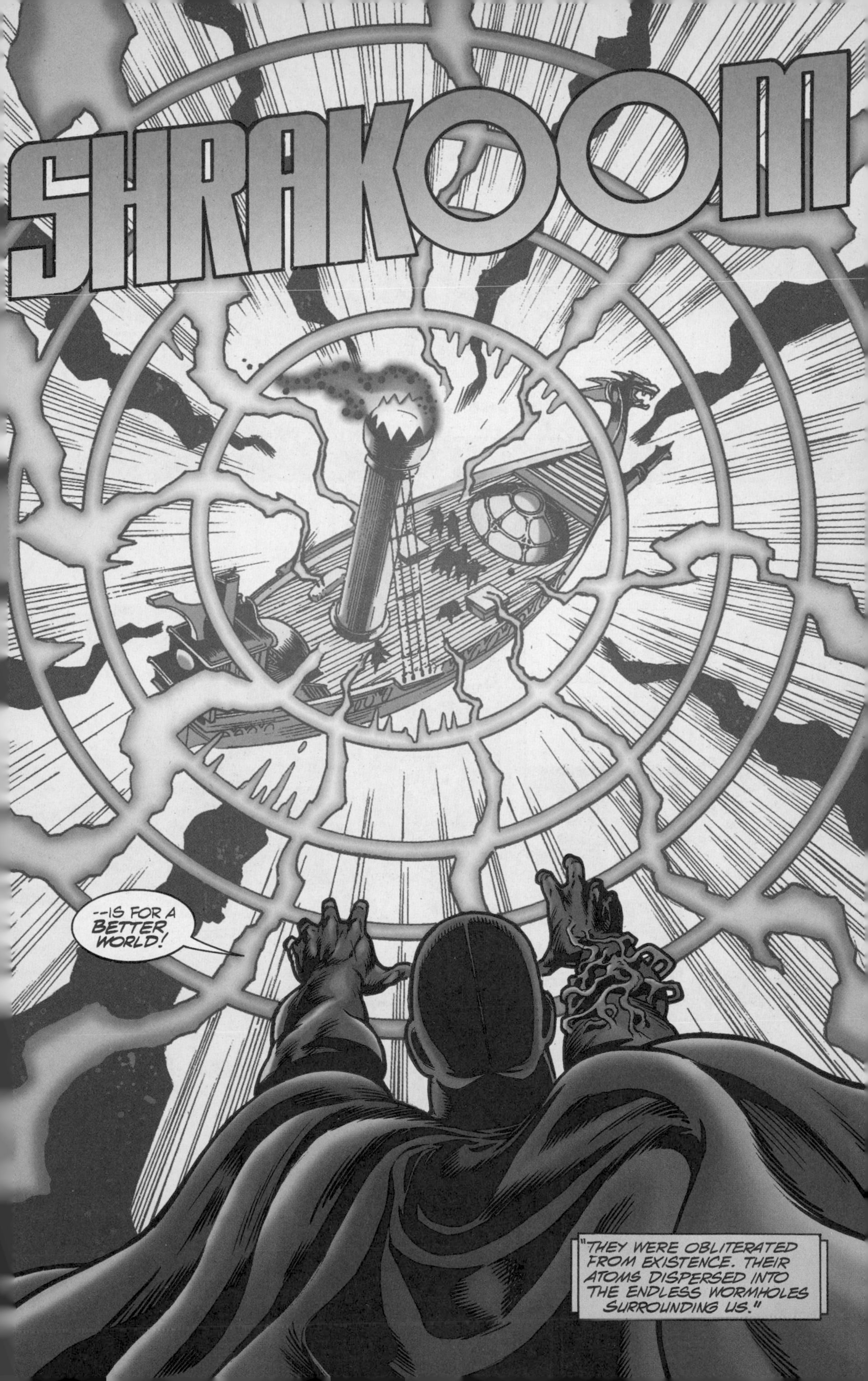
SHRAKOOM
--IS FOR A BETTER WORLD!
"THEY WERE OBLITERATED FROM EXISTENCE. THEIR ATOMS DISPERSED INTO THE ENDLESS WORMHOLES SURROUNDING US."

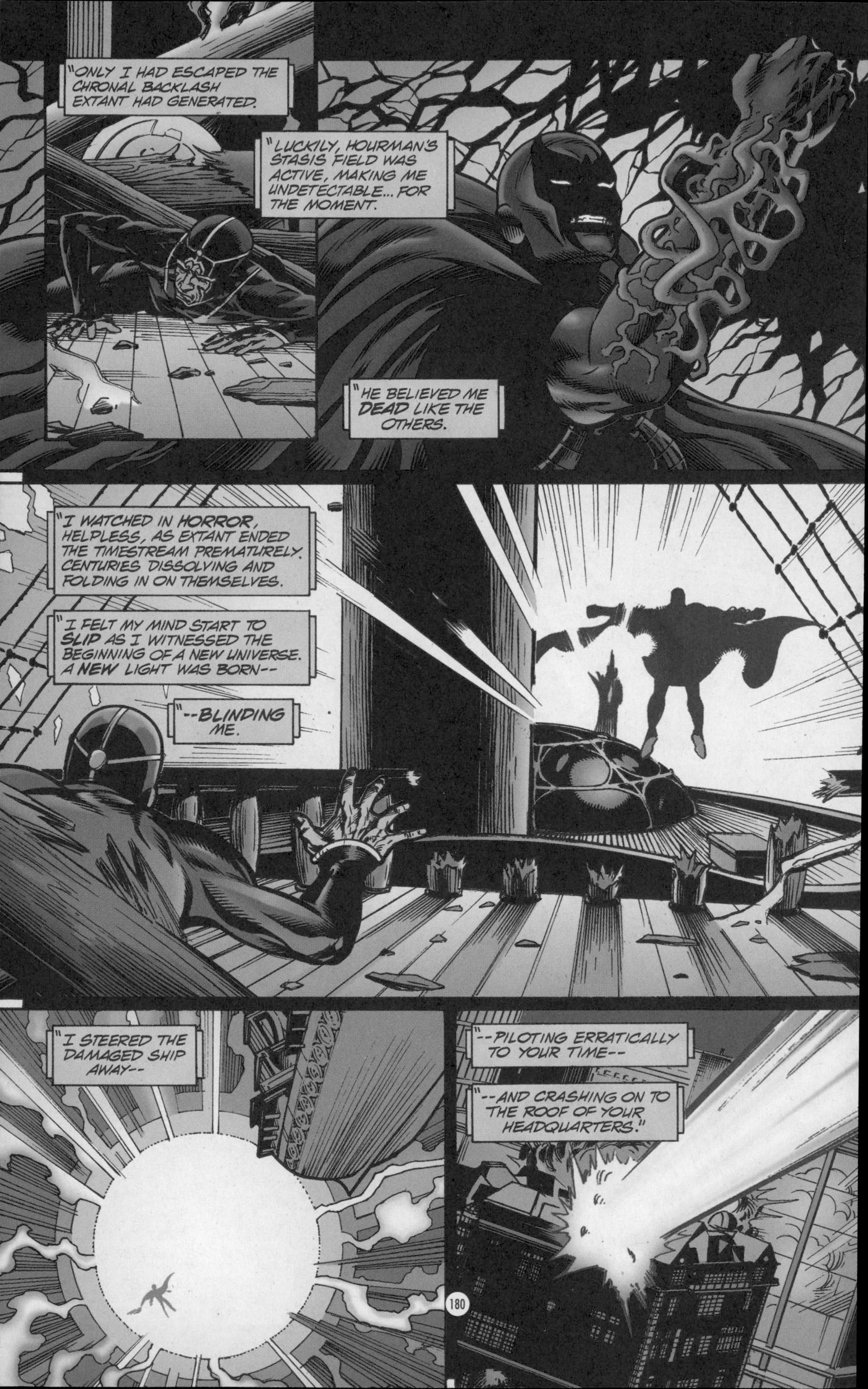
"ONLY I HAD ESCAPED THE CHRONAL BACKLASH EXTANT HAD GENERATED.
"LUCKILY, HOURMAN'S STASIS FIELD WAS ACTIVE, MAKING ME UNDETECTABLE... FOR THE MOMENT.
"HE BELIEVED ME DEAD LIKE THE OTHERS.
"I WATCHED IN HORROR, HELPLESS, AS EXTANT ENDED THE TIMESTREAM PREMATURELY. CENTURIES DISSOLVING AND FOLDING IN ON THEMSELVES.
"I FELT MY MIND START TO SLIP AS I WITNESSED THE BEGINNING OF A NEW UNIVERSE. A NEW LIGHT WAS BORN--
"--BLINDING ME.
"I STEERED THE DAMAGED SHIP AWAY--
"--PILOTING ERRATICALLY TO YOUR TIME--
"--AND CRASHING ON TO THE ROOF OF YOUR HEADQUARTERS."

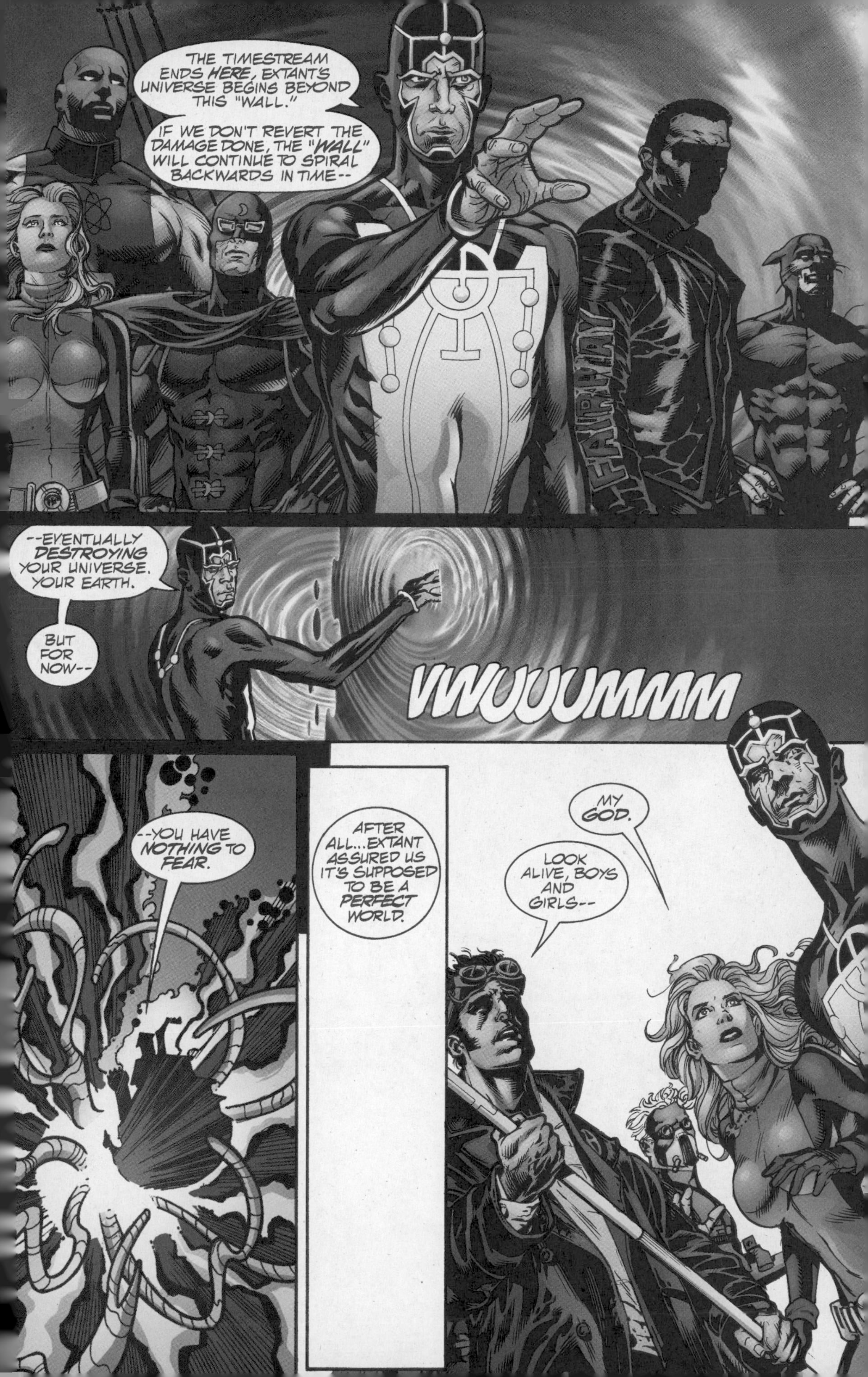
THE TIMESTREAM ENDS HERE, EXTANT'S UNIVERSE BEGINS BEYOND THIS "WALL."
IF WE DON'T REVERT THE DAMAGE DONE, THE "WALL" WILL CONTINUE TO SPIRAL BACKWARDS IN TIME--
--EVENTUALLY DESTROYING YOUR UNIVERSE. YOUR EARTH.
BUT FOR NOW--
VWUUUMMM
--YOU HAVE NOTHING TO FEAR.
AFTER ALL...EXTANT ASSURED US IT'S SUPPOSED TO BE A PERFECT WORLD.
MY GOD.
LOOK ALIVE, BOYS AND GIRLS--

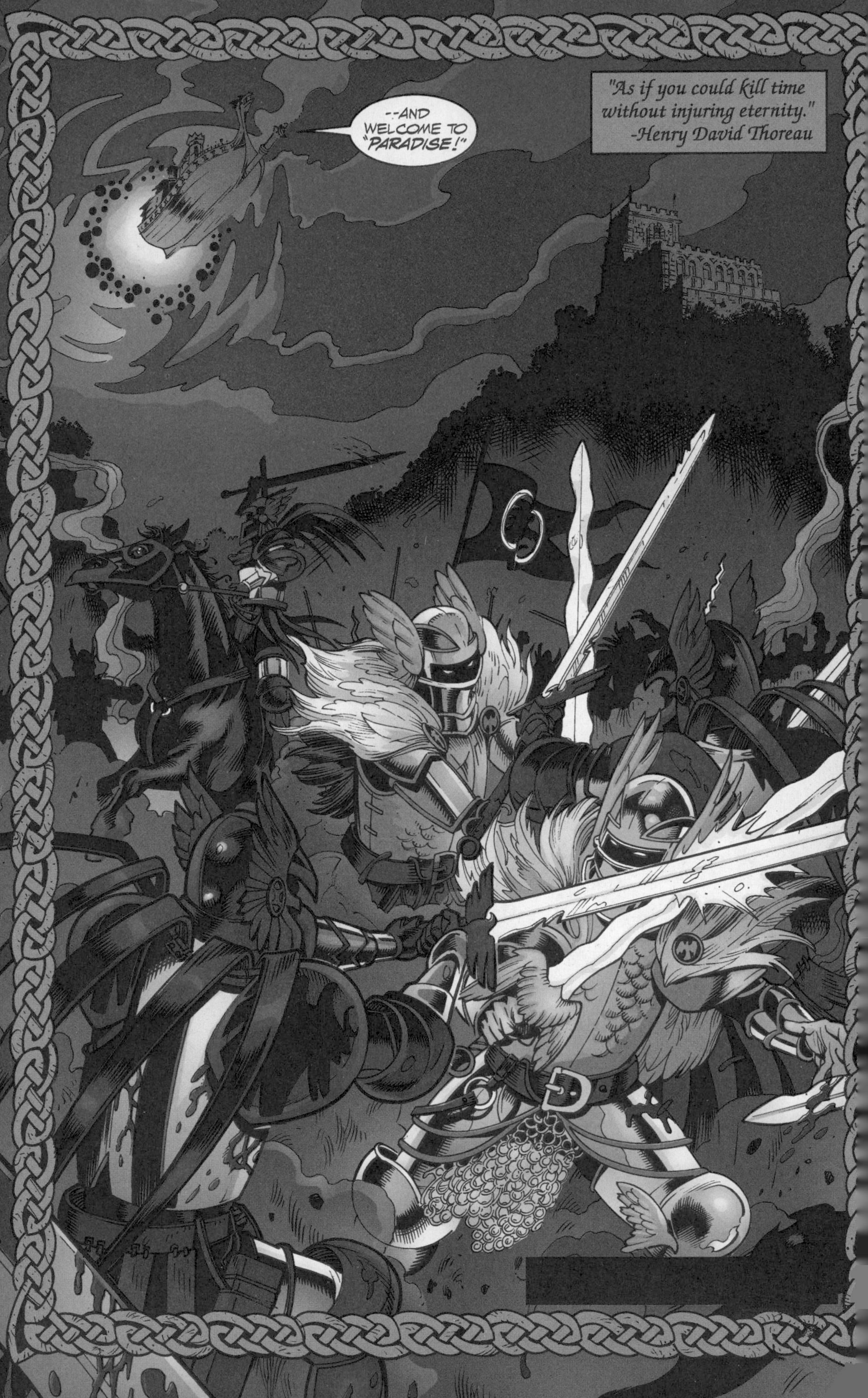
"As if you could kill time without injuring eternity." -Henry David Thoreau
--AND WELCOME TO "PARADISE!"
[redacted]

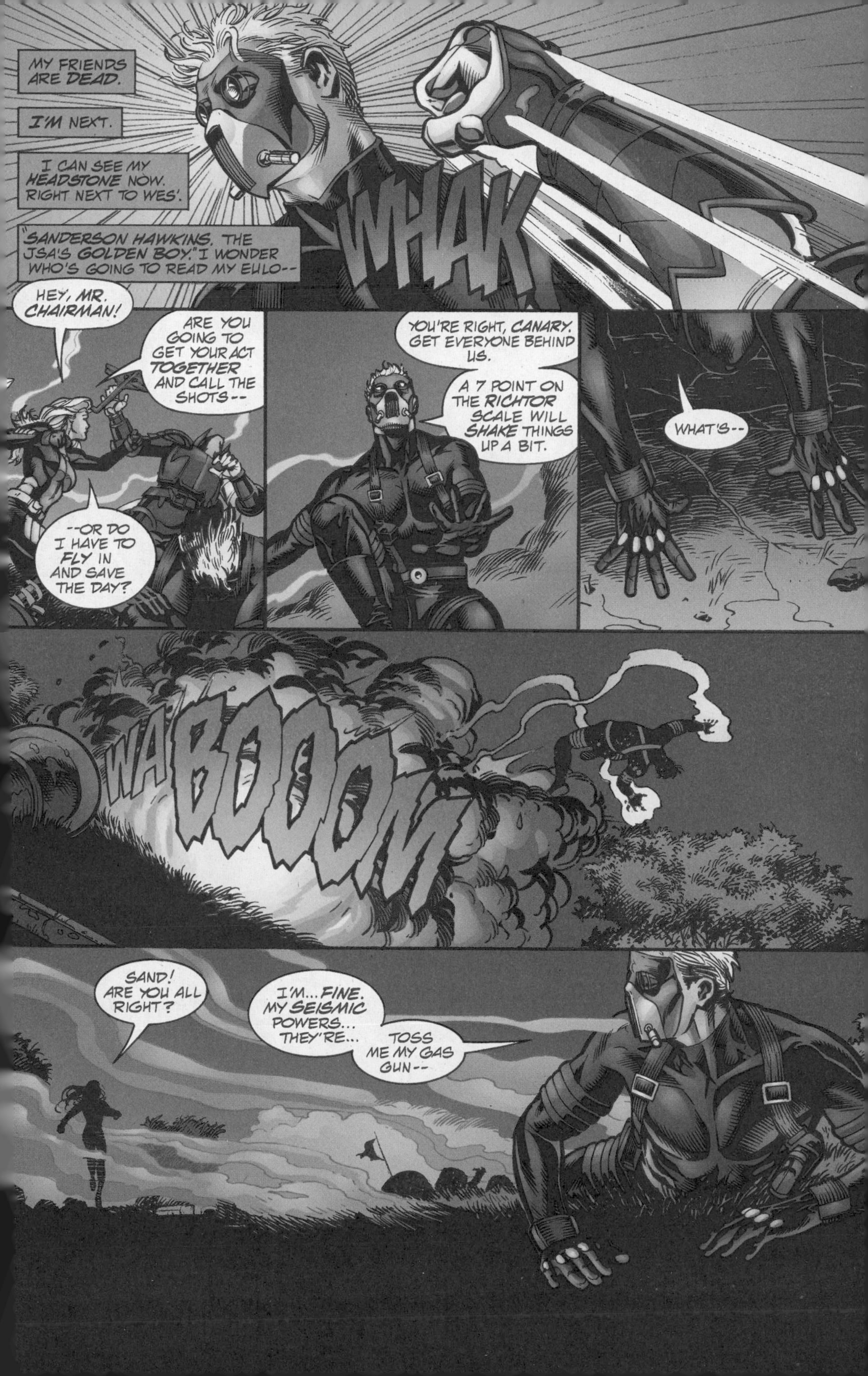
MY FRIENDS ARE DEAD.
I'M NEXT.
I CAN SEE MY HEADSTONE NOW. RIGHT NEXT TO WES'.
"SANDERSON HAWKINS. THE JSA'S GOLDEN BOY." I WONDER WHO'S GOING TO READ MY EULO--
WHAK
HEY, MR. CHAIRMAN!
ARE YOU GOING TO GET YOUR ACT TOGETHER AND CALL THE SHOTS--
--OR DO I HAVE TO FLY IN AND SAVE THE DAY?
YOU'RE RIGHT, CANARY. GET EVERYONE BEHIND US.
A 7 POINT ON THE RICHTOR SCALE WILL SHAKE THINGS UP A BIT.
WHAT'S--
WABOOOM
SAND! ARE YOU ALL RIGHT?
I'M... FINE. MY SEISMIC POWERS... THEY'RE...
TOSS ME MY GAS GUN--

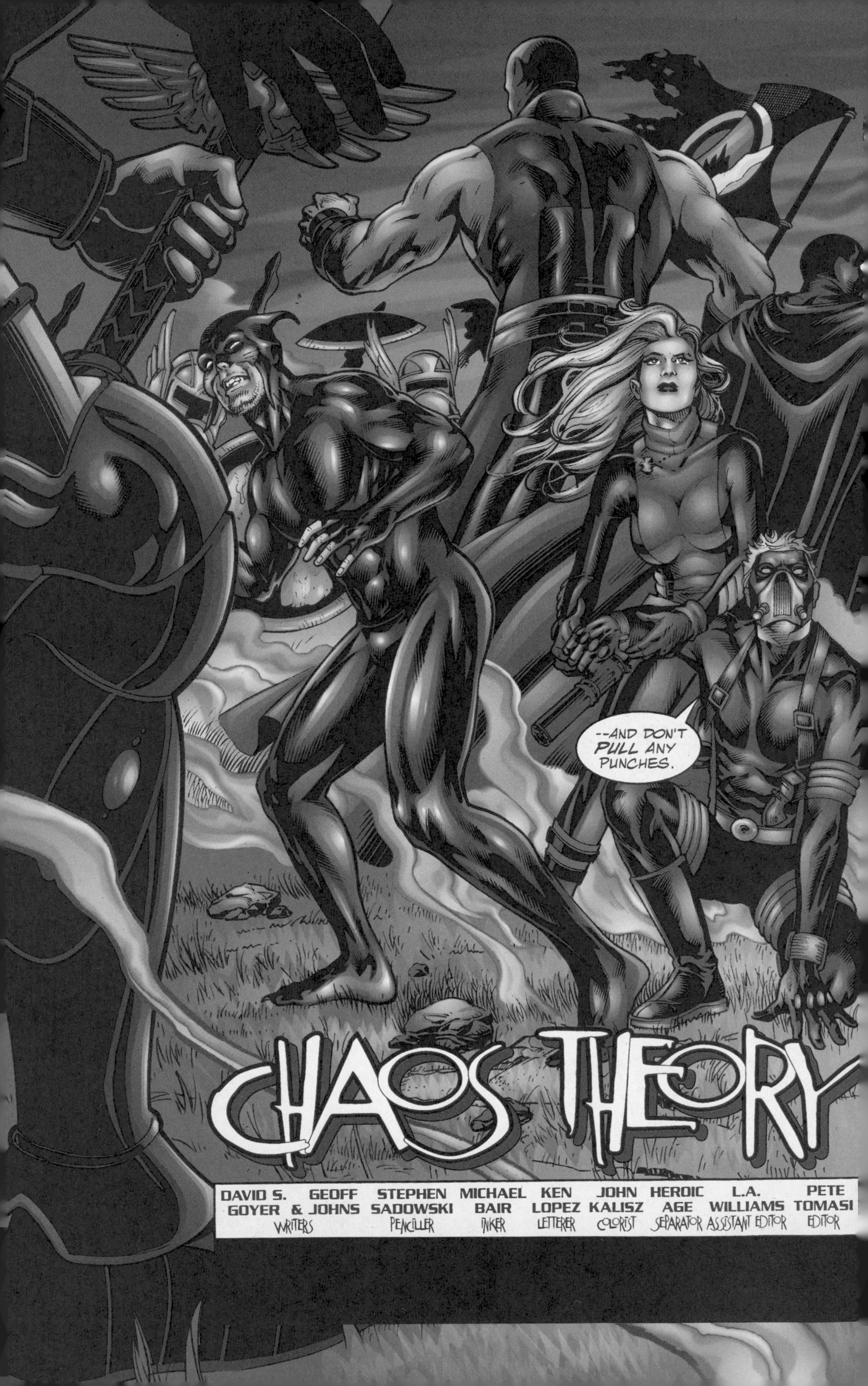
--AND DON'T PULL ANY PUNCHES.
CHAOS THEORY
DAVID S. GOYER & GEOFF JOHNS WRITERS
STEPHEN SADOWSKI PENCILLER
MICHAEL BAIR INKER
KEN LOPEZ LETTERER
JOHN KALISZ COLORIST
HEROIC AGE SEPARATOR
L.A. WILLIAMS ASSISTANT EDITOR
PETE TOMASI EDITOR

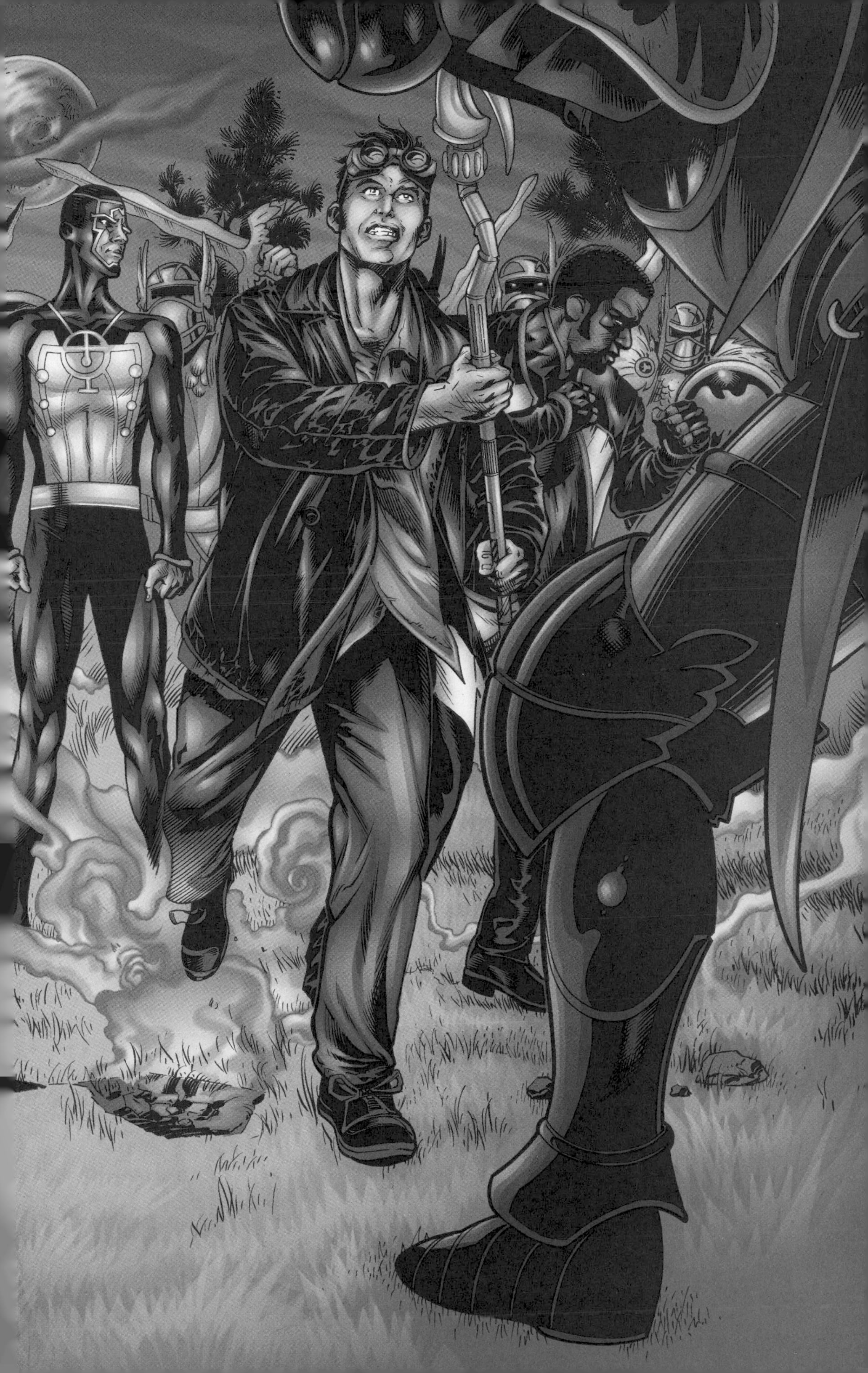

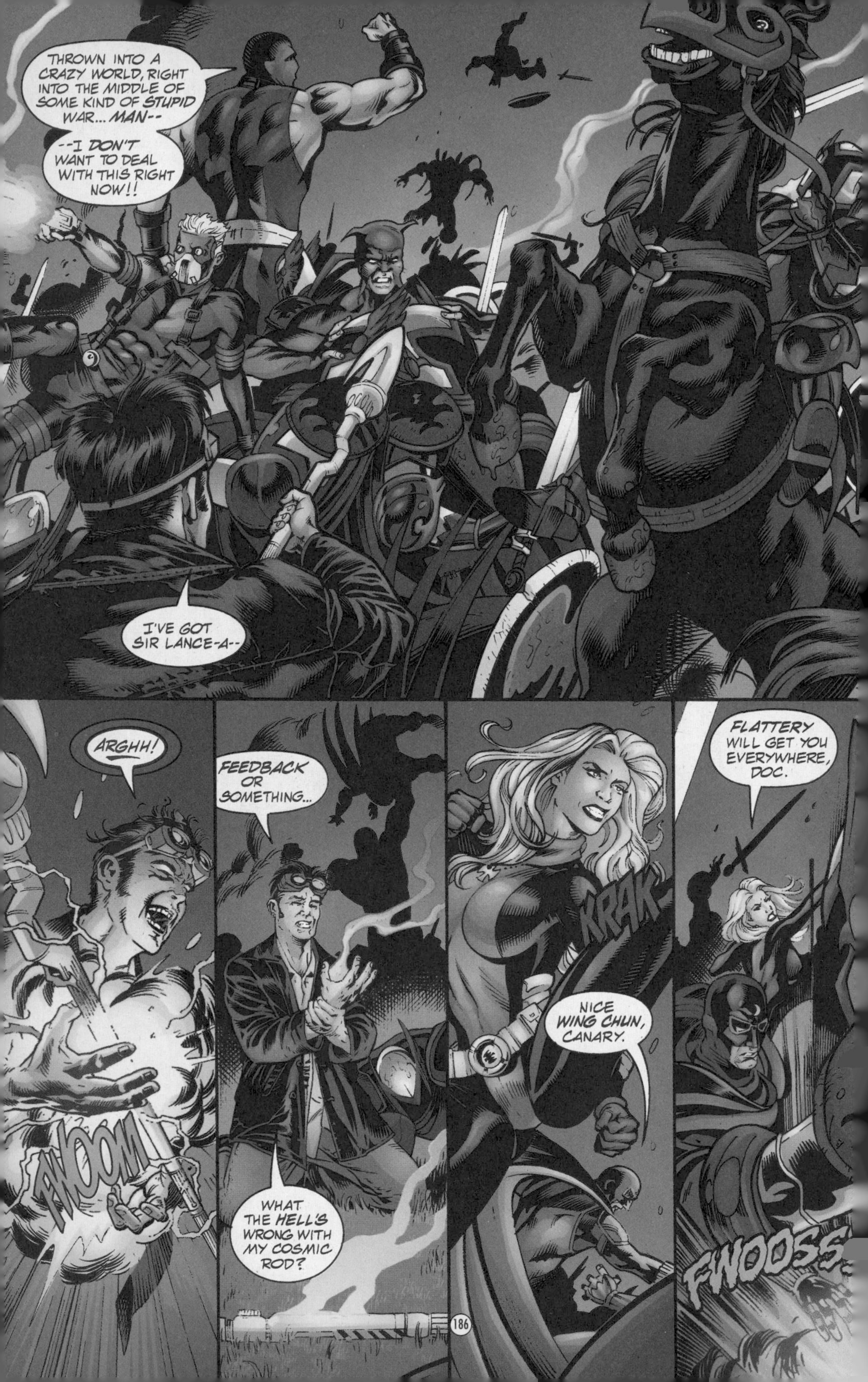
THROWN INTO A CRAZY WORLD, RIGHT INTO THE MIDDLE OF SOME KIND OF STUPID WAR... MAN--
--I DON'T WANT TO DEAL WITH THIS RIGHT NOW!!
I'VE GOT SIR LANCE-A--
ARGHH!
FWOOM
FEEDBACK OR SOMETHING...
WHAT THE HELL'S WRONG WITH MY COSMIC ROD?
KRAK
NICE WING CHUN, CANARY.
FLATTERY WILL GET YOU EVERYWHERE, DOC.
FWOOSS

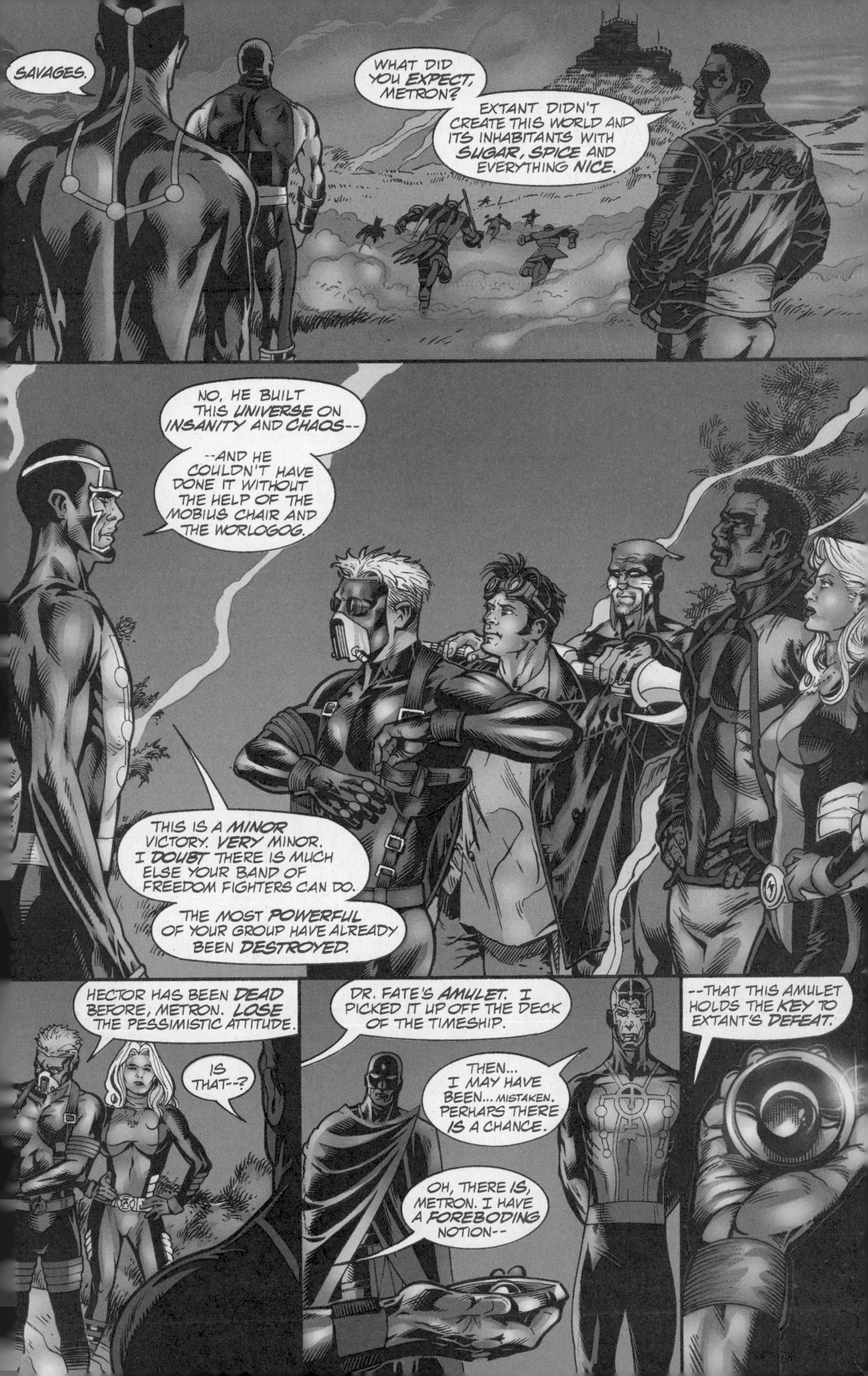
SAVAGES.
WHAT DID YOU EXPECT, METRON?
EXTANT DIDN'T CREATE THIS WORLD AND ITS INHABITANTS WITH SUGAR, SPICE AND EVERYTHING NICE.
NO, HE BUILT THIS UNIVERSE ON INSANITY AND CHAOS--
--AND HE COULDN'T HAVE DONE IT WITHOUT THE HELP OF THE MOBIUS CHAIR AND THE WORLOGOG.
THIS IS A MINOR VICTORY. VERY MINOR. I DOUBT THERE IS MUCH ELSE YOUR BAND OF FREEDOM FIGHTERS CAN DO.
THE MOST POWERFUL OF YOUR GROUP HAVE ALREADY BEEN DESTROYED.
HECTOR HAS BEEN DEAD BEFORE, METRON. LOSE THE PESSIMISTIC ATTITUDE.
IS THAT--?
DR. FATE'S AMULET. I PICKED IT UP OFF THE DECK OF THE TIMESHIP.
THEN... I MAY HAVE BEEN... MISTAKEN. PERHAPS THERE IS A CHANCE.
OH, THERE IS, METRON. I HAVE A FOREBODING NOTION--
--THAT THIS AMULET HOLDS THE KEY TO EXTANT'S DEFEAT.

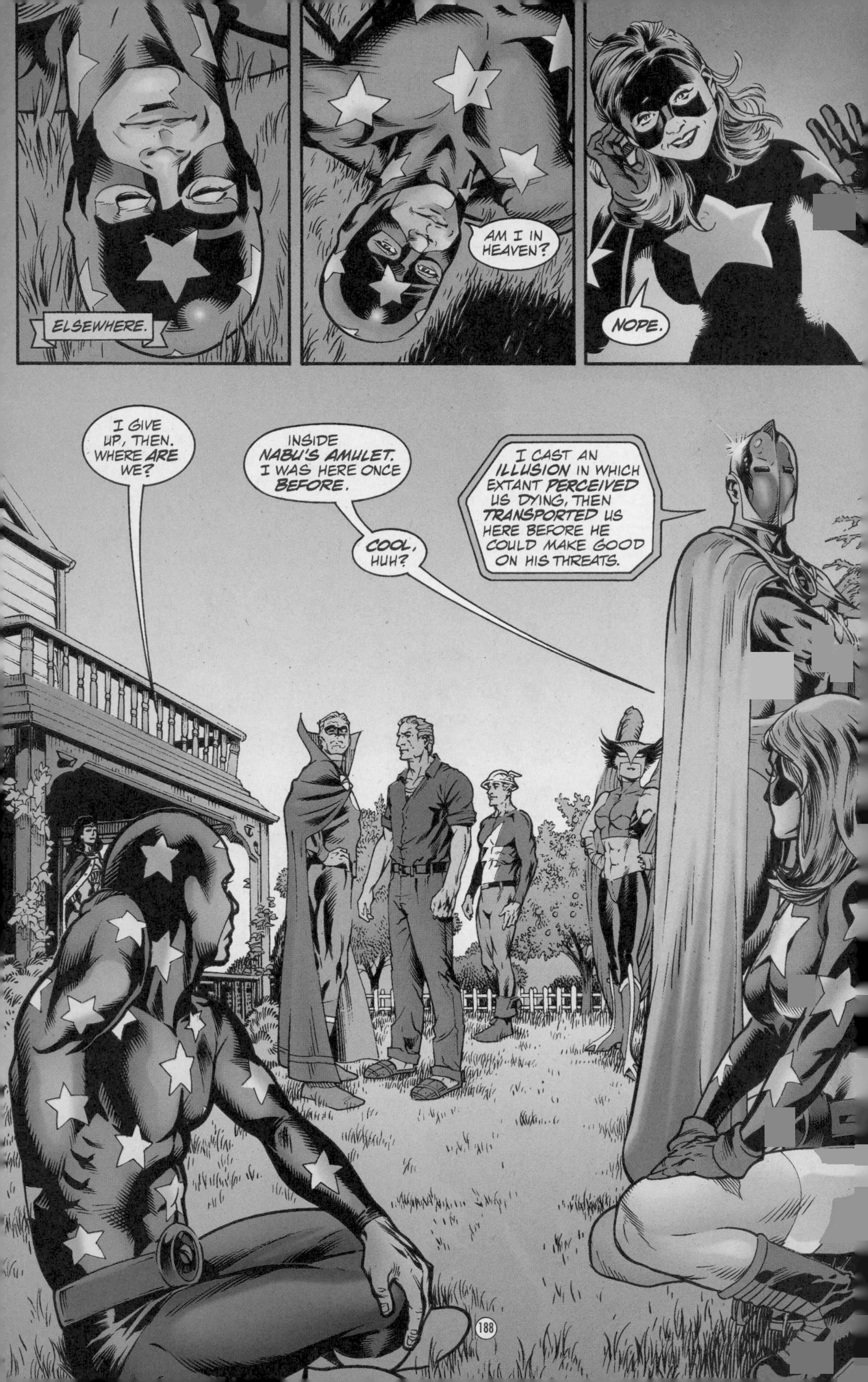
ELSEWHERE.
AM I IN HEAVEN?
NOPE.
I GIVE UP, THEN. WHERE ARE WE?
INSIDE NABU'S AMULET. I WAS HERE ONCE BEFORE.
COOL, HUH?
I CAST AN ILLUSION IN WHICH EXTANT PERCEIVED US DYING, THEN TRANSPORTED US HERE BEFORE HE COULD MAKE GOOD ON HIS THREATS.

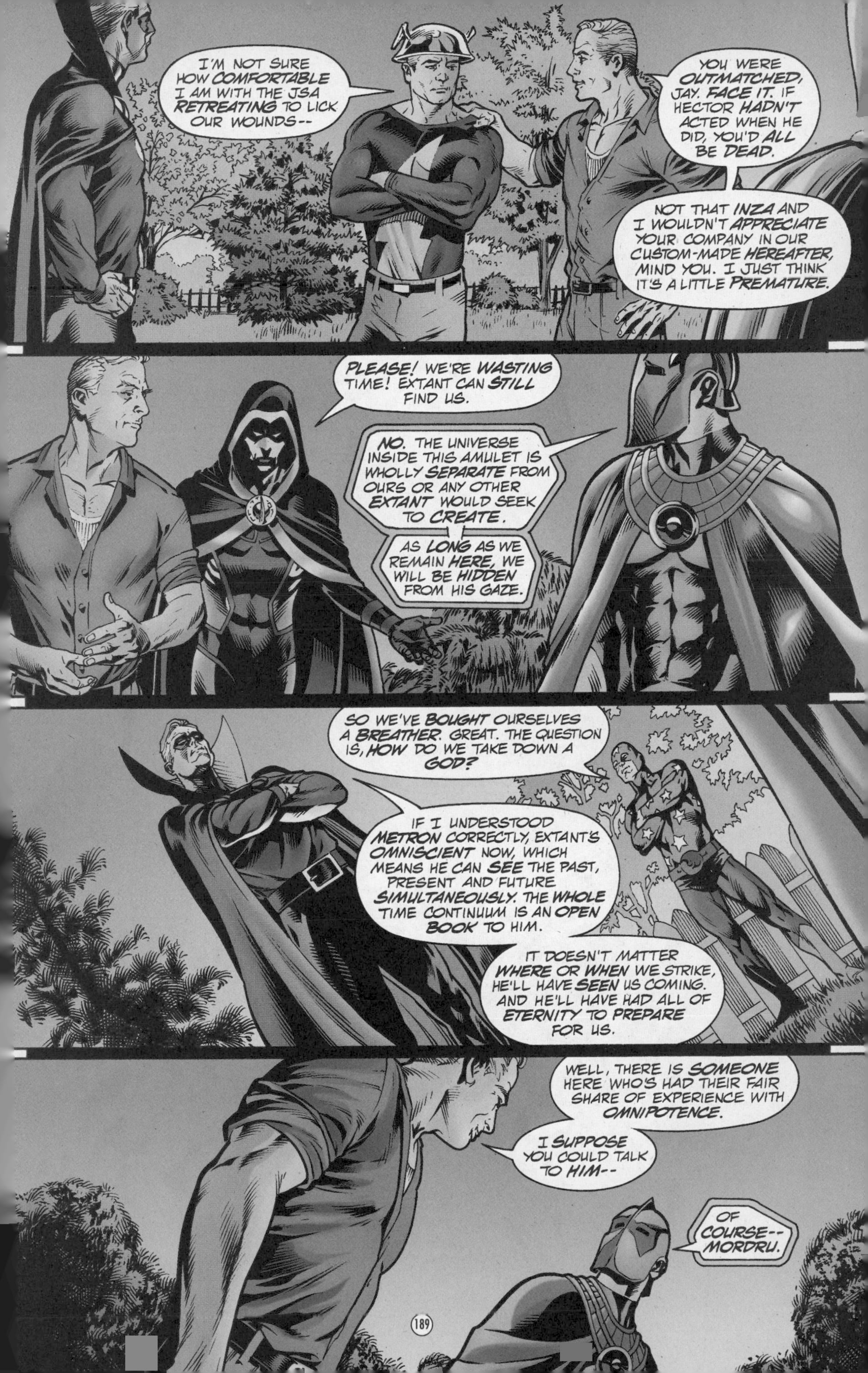
I'M NOT SURE HOW COMFORTABLE I AM WITH THE JSA RETREATING TO LICK OUR WOUNDS--
YOU WERE OUTMATCHED, JAY. FACE IT. IF HECTOR HADN'T ACTED WHEN HE DID, YOU'D ALL BE DEAD.
NOT THAT INZA AND I WOULDN'T APPRECIATE YOUR COMPANY IN OUR CUSTOM-MADE HEREAFTER, MIND YOU. I JUST THINK IT'S A LITTLE PREMATURE.
PLEASE! WE'RE WASTING TIME! EXTANT CAN STILL FIND US.
NO. THE UNIVERSE INSIDE THIS AMULET IS WHOLLY SEPARATE FROM OURS OR ANY OTHER EXTANT WOULD SEEK TO CREATE.
AS LONG AS WE REMAIN HERE, WE WILL BE HIDDEN FROM HIS GAZE.
SO WE'VE BOUGHT OURSELVES A BREATHER. GREAT. THE QUESTION IS, HOW DO WE TAKE DOWN A GOD?
IF I UNDERSTOOD METRON CORRECTLY, EXTANT'S OMNISCIENT NOW, WHICH MEANS HE CAN SEE THE PAST, PRESENT AND FUTURE SIMULTANEOUSLY. THE WHOLE TIME CONTINUUM IS AN OPEN BOOK TO HIM.
IT DOESN'T MATTER WHERE OR WHEN WE STRIKE, HE'LL HAVE SEEN US COMING. AND HE'LL HAVE HAD ALL OF ETERNITY TO PREPARE FOR US.
WELL, THERE IS SOMEONE HERE WHO'S HAD THEIR FAIR SHARE OF EXPERIENCE WITH OMNIPOTENCE.
I SUPPOSE YOU COULD TALK TO HIM--
OF COURSE-- MORDRU.

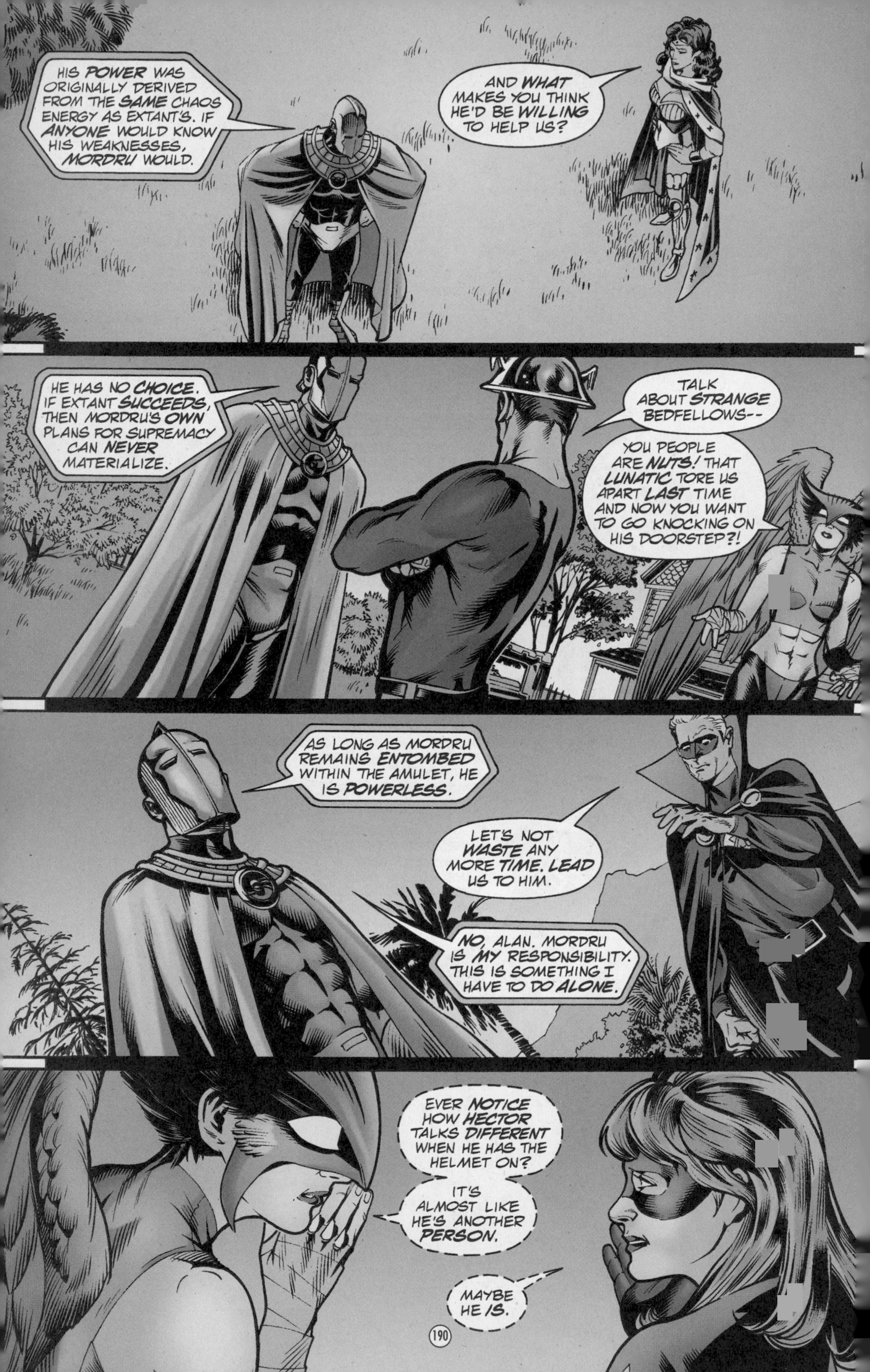
HIS POWER WAS ORIGINALLY DERIVED FROM THE SAME CHAOS ENERGY AS EXTANT'S. IF ANYONE WOULD KNOW HIS WEAKNESSES, MORDRU WOULD.
AND WHAT MAKES YOU THINK HE'D BE WILLING TO HELP US?
HE HAS NO CHOICE. IF EXTANT SUCCEEDS, THEN MORDRU'S OWN PLANS FOR SUPREMACY CAN NEVER MATERIALIZE.
TALK ABOUT STRANGE BEDFELLOWS--
YOU PEOPLE ARE NUTS! THAT LUNATIC TORE US APART LAST TIME AND NOW YOU WANT TO GO KNOCKING ON HIS DOORSTEP?!
AS LONG AS MORDRU REMAINS ENTOMBED WITHIN THE AMULET, HE IS POWERLESS.
LET'S NOT WASTE ANY MORE TIME. LEAD US TO HIM.
NO, ALAN. MORDRU IS MY RESPONSIBILITY. THIS IS SOMETHING I HAVE TO DO ALONE.
EVER NOTICE HOW HECTOR TALKS DIFFERENT WHEN HE HAS THE HELMET ON?
IT'S ALMOST LIKE HE'S ANOTHER PERSON.
MAYBE HE IS.

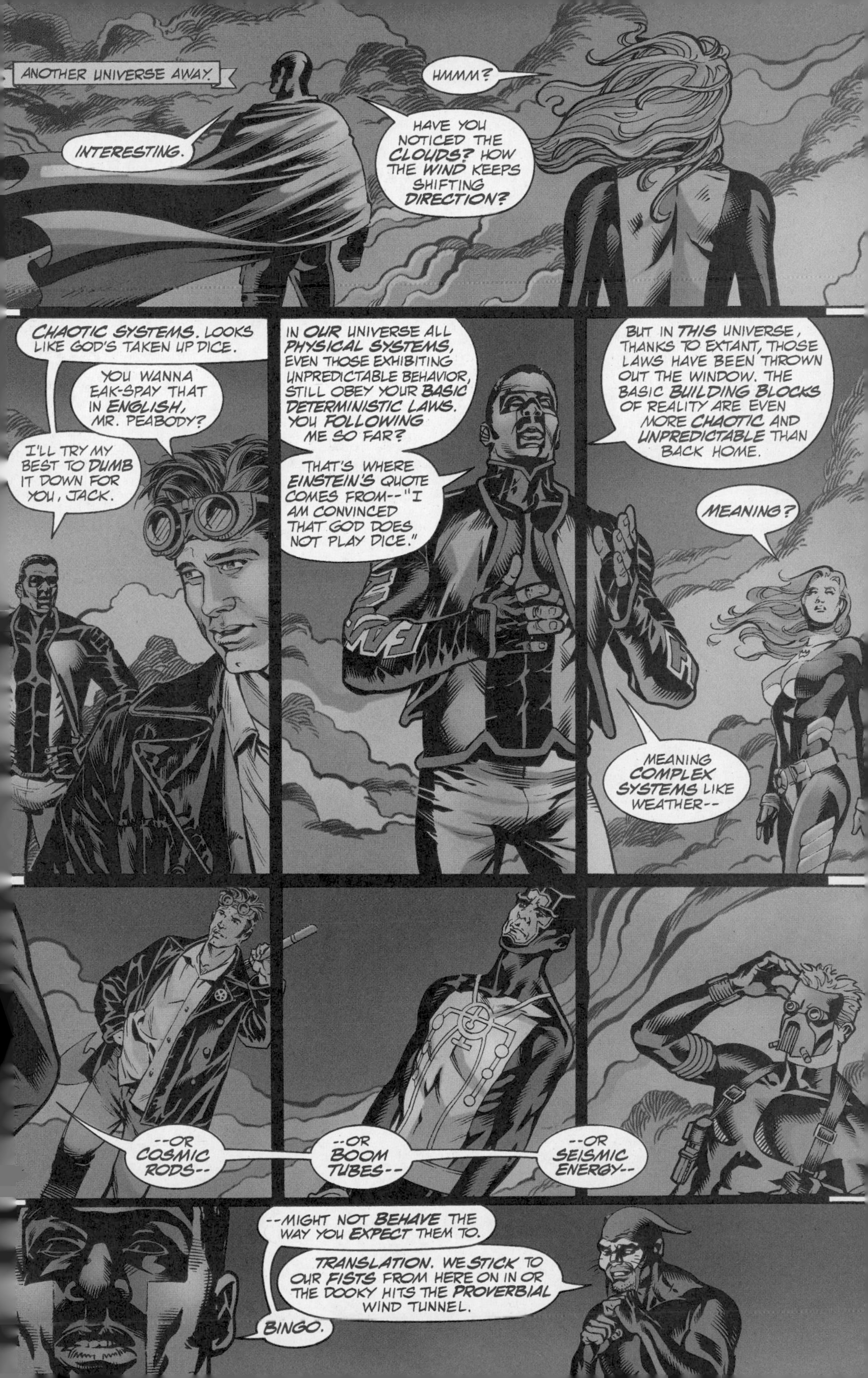
ANOTHER UNIVERSE AWAY.
INTERESTING.
HMMM?
HAVE YOU NOTICED THE CLOUDS? HOW THE WIND KEEPS SHIFTING DIRECTION?
CHAOTIC SYSTEMS. LOOKS LIKE GOD'S TAKEN UP DICE.
YOU WANNA EAK-SPAY THAT IN ENGLISH, MR. PEABODY?
I'LL TRY MY BEST TO DUMB IT DOWN FOR YOU, JACK.
IN OUR UNIVERSE ALL PHYSICAL SYSTEMS, EVEN THOSE EXHIBITING UNPREDICTABLE BEHAVIOR, STILL OBEY YOUR BASIC DETERMINISTIC LAWS. YOU FOLLOWING ME SO FAR?
THAT'S WHERE EINSTEIN'S QUOTE COMES FROM--"I AM CONVINCED THAT GOD DOES NOT PLAY DICE."
BUT IN THIS UNIVERSE, THANKS TO EXTANT, THOSE LAWS HAVE BEEN THROWN OUT THE WINDOW. THE BASIC BUILDING BLOCKS OF REALITY ARE EVEN MORE CHAOTIC AND UNPREDICTABLE THAN BACK HOME.
MEANING?
MEANING COMPLEX SYSTEMS LIKE WEATHER--
--OR COSMIC RODS--
--OR BOOM TUBES--
--OR SEISMIC ENERGY--
--MIGHT NOT BEHAVE THE WAY YOU EXPECT THEM TO.
TRANSLATION. WE STICK TO OUR FISTS FROM HERE ON IN OR THE DOOKY HITS THE PROVERBIAL WIND TUNNEL.
BINGO.

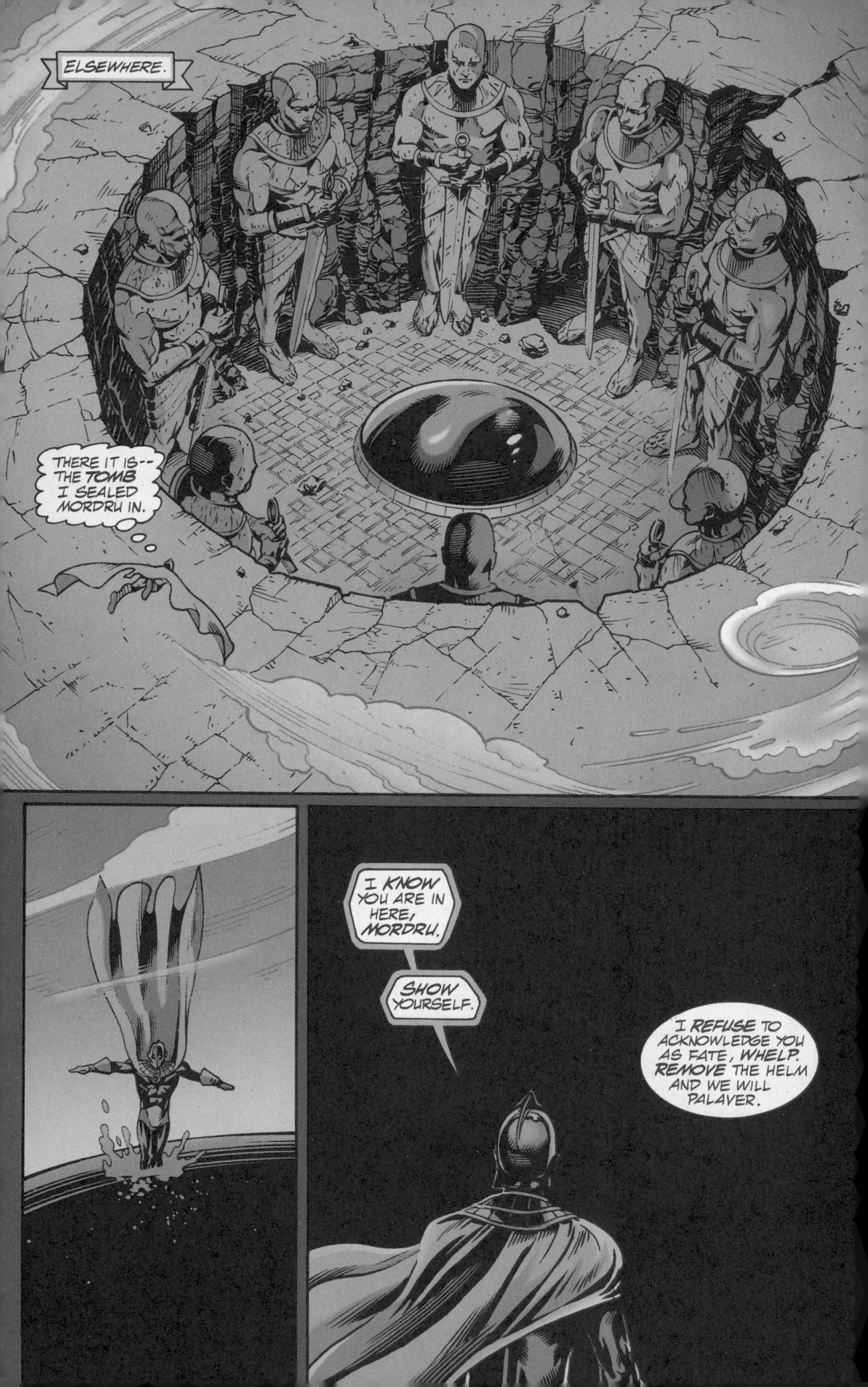
ELSEWHERE.
THERE IT IS-- THE TOMB I SEALED MORDRU IN.
I KNOW YOU ARE IN HERE, MORDRU.
SHOW YOURSELF.
I REFUSE TO ACKNOWLEDGE YOU AS FATE, WHELP. REMOVE THE HELM AND WE WILL PALAVER.

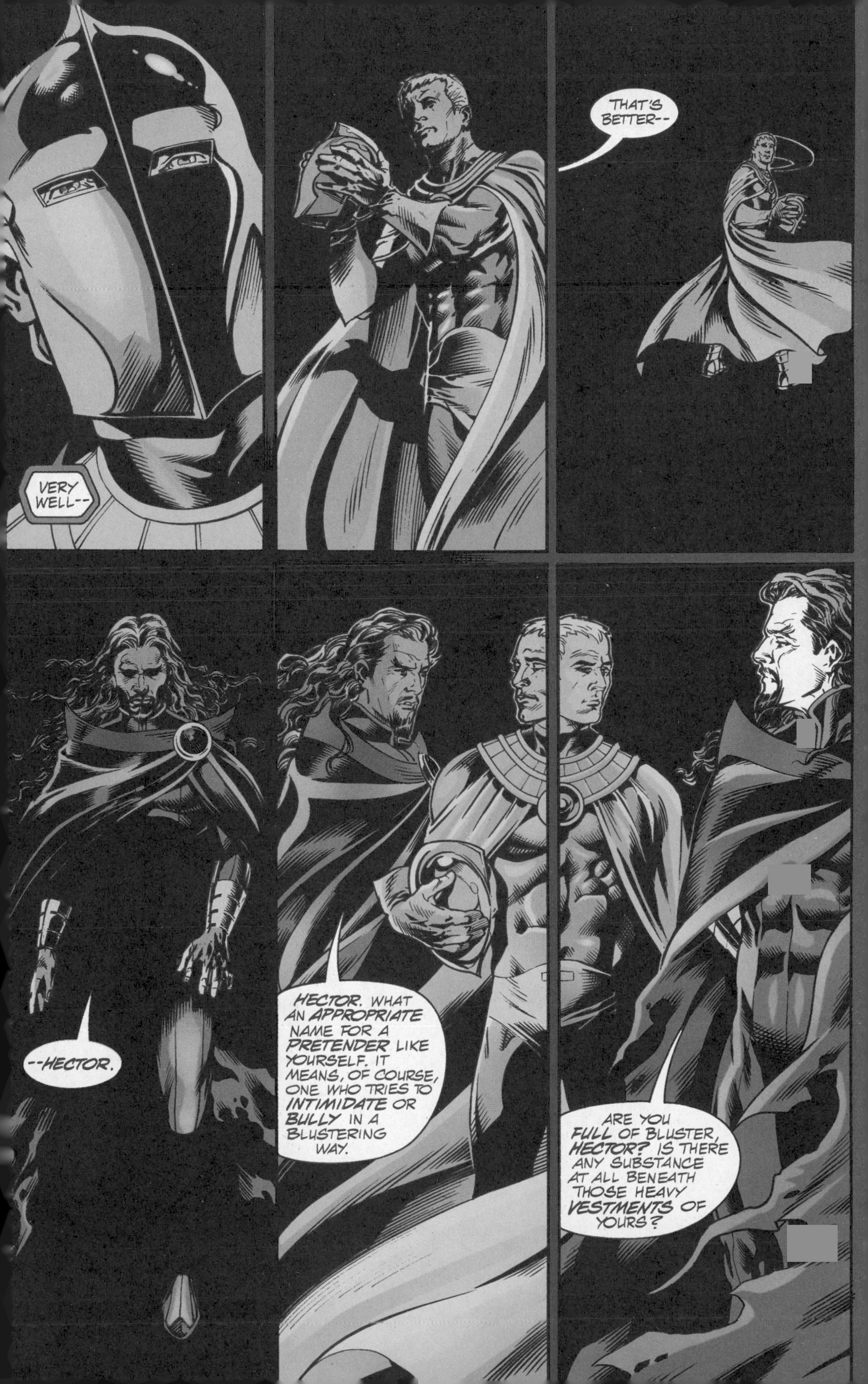
VERY WELL--
THAT'S BETTER--
--HECTOR.
HECTOR. WHAT AN APPROPRIATE NAME FOR A PRETENDER LIKE YOURSELF. IT MEANS, OF COURSE, ONE WHO TRIES TO INTIMIDATE OR BULLY IN A BLUSTERING WAY.
ARE YOU FULL OF BLUSTER, HECTOR? IS THERE ANY SUBSTANCE AT ALL BENEATH THOSE HEAVY VESTMENTS OF YOURS?

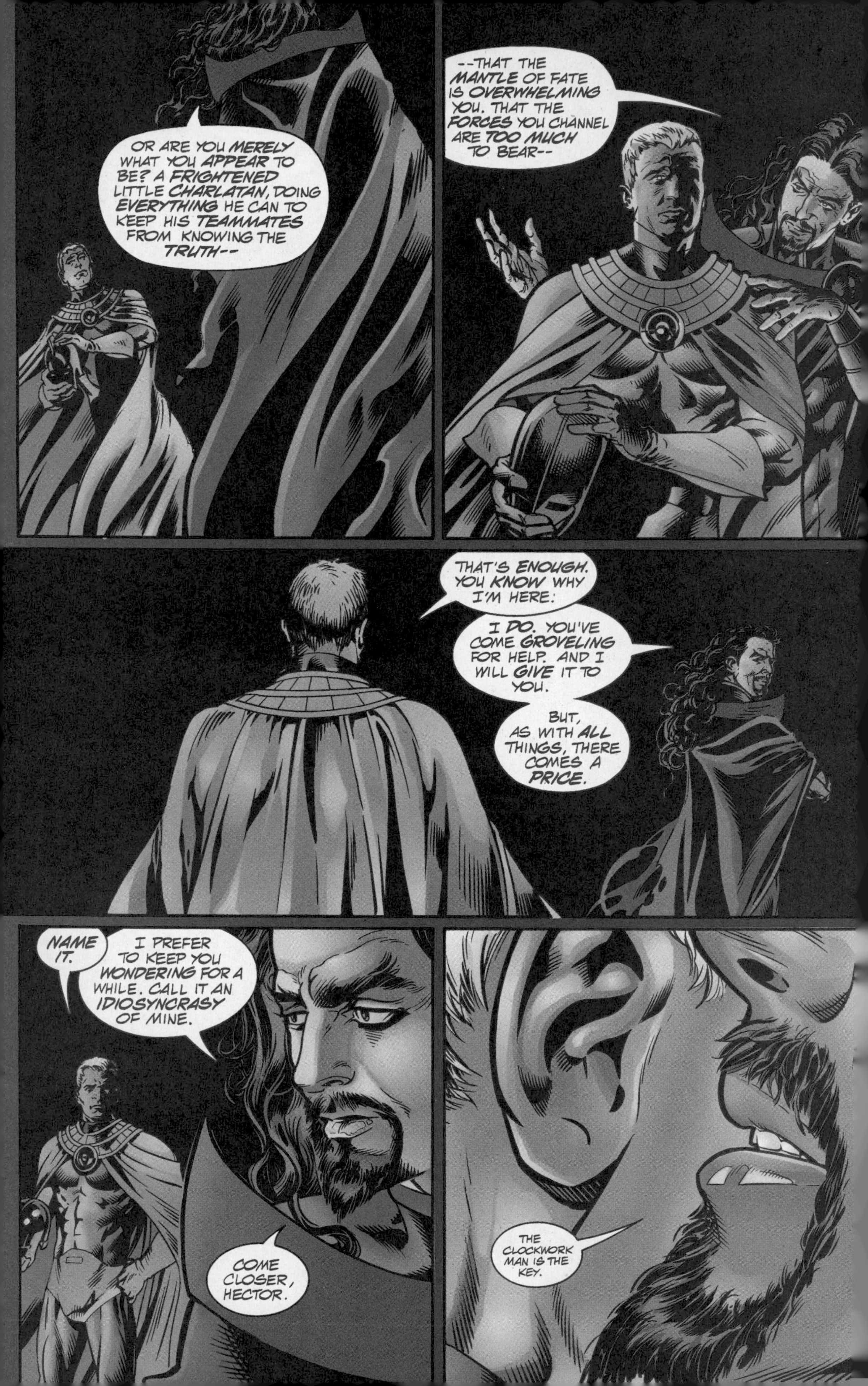
OR ARE YOU MERELY WHAT YOU APPEAR TO BE? A FRIGHTENED LITTLE CHARLATAN, DOING EVERYTHING HE CAN TO KEEP HIS TEAMMATES FROM KNOWING THE TRUTH--
--THAT THE MANTLE OF FATE IS OVERWHELMING YOU. THAT THE FORCES YOU CHANNEL ARE TOO MUCH TO BEAR--
THAT'S ENOUGH. YOU KNOW WHY I'M HERE.
I DO. YOU'VE COME GROVELING FOR HELP. AND I WILL GIVE IT TO YOU.
BUT, AS WITH ALL THINGS, THERE COMES A PRICE.
NAME IT.
I PREFER TO KEEP YOU WONDERING FOR A WHILE. CALL IT AN IDIOSYNCRASY OF MINE.
COME CLOSER, HECTOR.
THE CLOCKWORK MAN IS THE KEY.

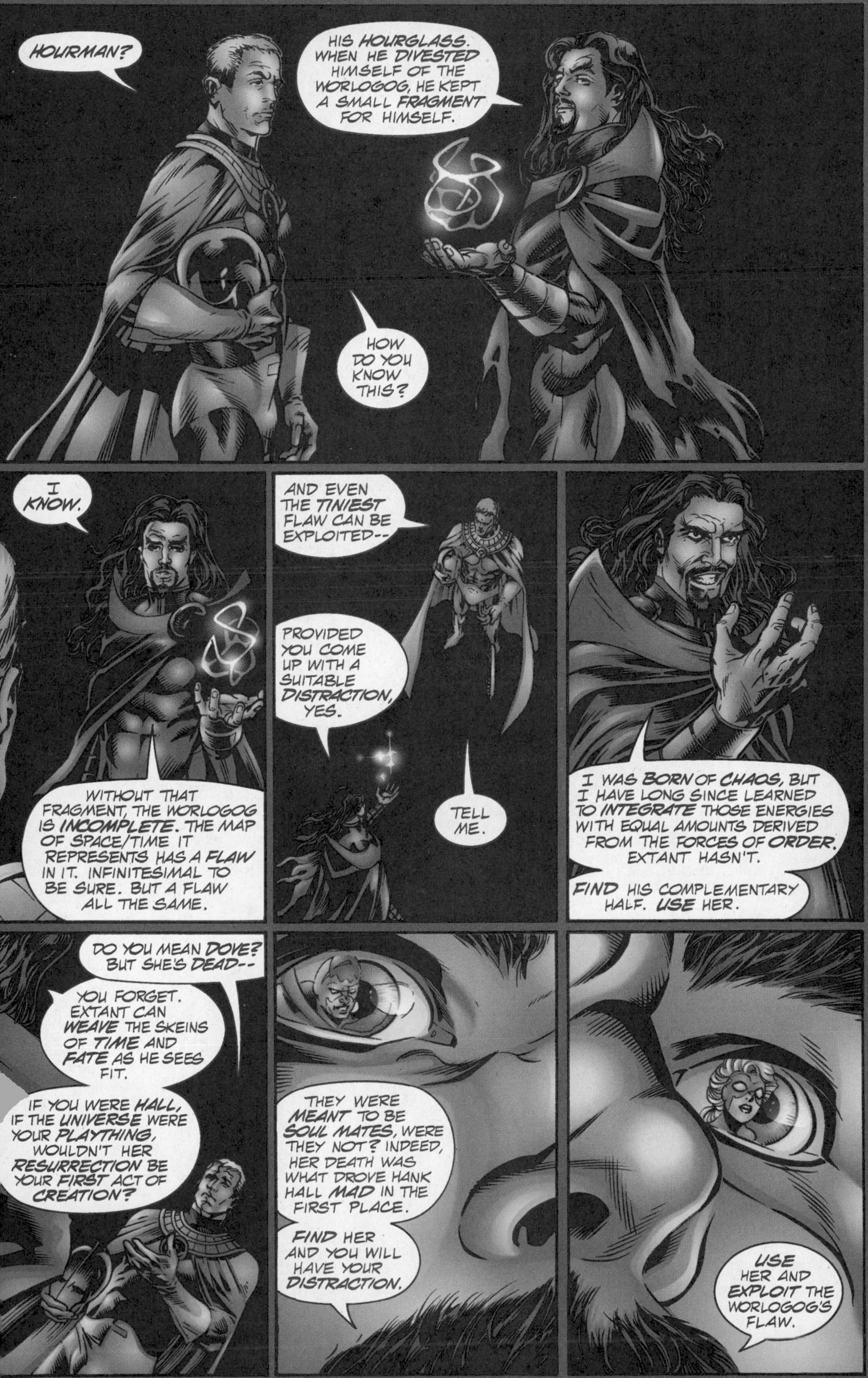
HOURMAN?
HIS HOURGLASS. WHEN HE DIVESTED HIMSELF OF THE WORLOGOG, HE KEPT A SMALL FRAGMENT FOR HIMSELF.
HOW DO YOU KNOW THIS?
I KNOW.
WITHOUT THAT FRAGMENT, THE WORLOGOG IS INCOMPLETE. THE MAP OF SPACE/TIME IT REPRESENTS HAS A FLAW IN IT. INFINITESIMAL TO BE SURE. BUT A FLAW ALL THE SAME.
AND EVEN THE TINIEST FLAW CAN BE EXPLOITED--
PROVIDED YOU COME UP WITH A SUITABLE DISTRACTION, YES.
TELL ME.
I WAS BORN OF CHAOS, BUT I HAVE LONG SINCE LEARNED TO INTEGRATE THOSE ENERGIES WITH EQUAL AMOUNTS DERIVED FROM THE FORCES OF ORDER. EXTANT HASN'T.
FIND HIS COMPLEMENTARY HALF. USE HER.
DO YOU MEAN DOVE? BUT SHE'S DEAD--
YOU FORGET. EXTANT CAN WEAVE THE SKEINS OF TIME AND FATE AS HE SEES FIT.
IF YOU WERE HALL, IF THE UNIVERSE WERE YOUR PLAYTHING, WOULDN'T HER RESURRECTION BE YOUR FIRST ACT OF CREATION?
THEY WERE MEANT TO BE SOUL MATES, WERE THEY NOT? INDEED, HER DEATH WAS WHAT DROVE HANK HALL MAD IN THE FIRST PLACE.
FIND HER AND YOU WILL HAVE YOUR DISTRACTION.
USE HER AND EXPLOIT THE WORLOGOG'S FLAW.

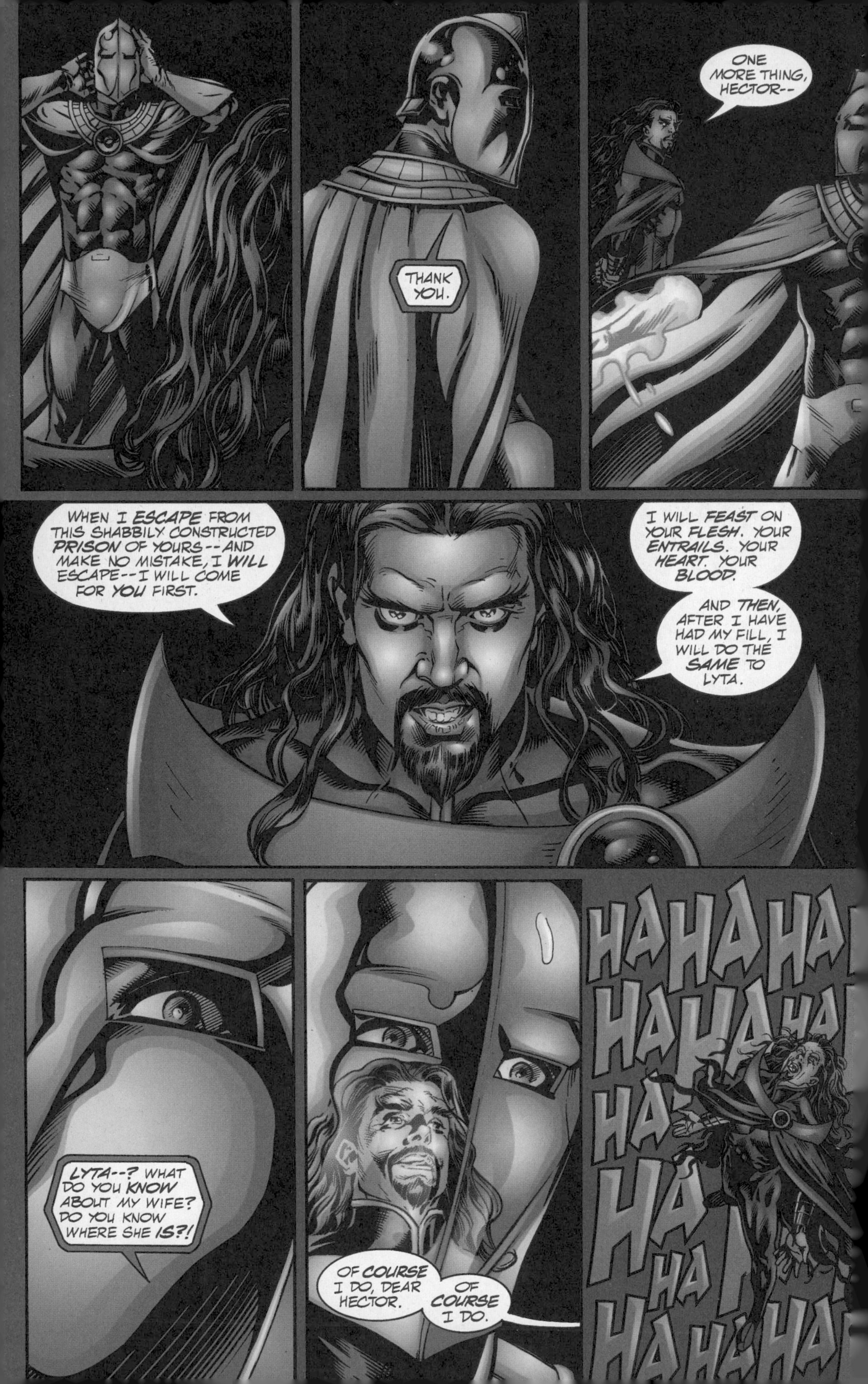
THANK YOU.
ONE MORE THING, HECTOR--
WHEN I ESCAPE FROM THIS SHABBILY CONSTRUCTED PRISON OF YOURS--AND MAKE NO MISTAKE, I WILL ESCAPE--I WILL COME FOR YOU FIRST.
I WILL FEAST ON YOUR FLESH. YOUR ENTRAILS. YOUR HEART. YOUR BLOOD.
AND THEN, AFTER I HAVE HAD MY FILL, I WILL DO THE SAME TO LYTA.
LYTA--? WHAT DO YOU KNOW ABOUT MY WIFE? DO YOU KNOW WHERE SHE IS?!
OF COURSE I DO, DEAR HECTOR.
OF COURSE I DO.
HAHAHAHA HAHAHAHA HA HA HA HA HAHAHAHA

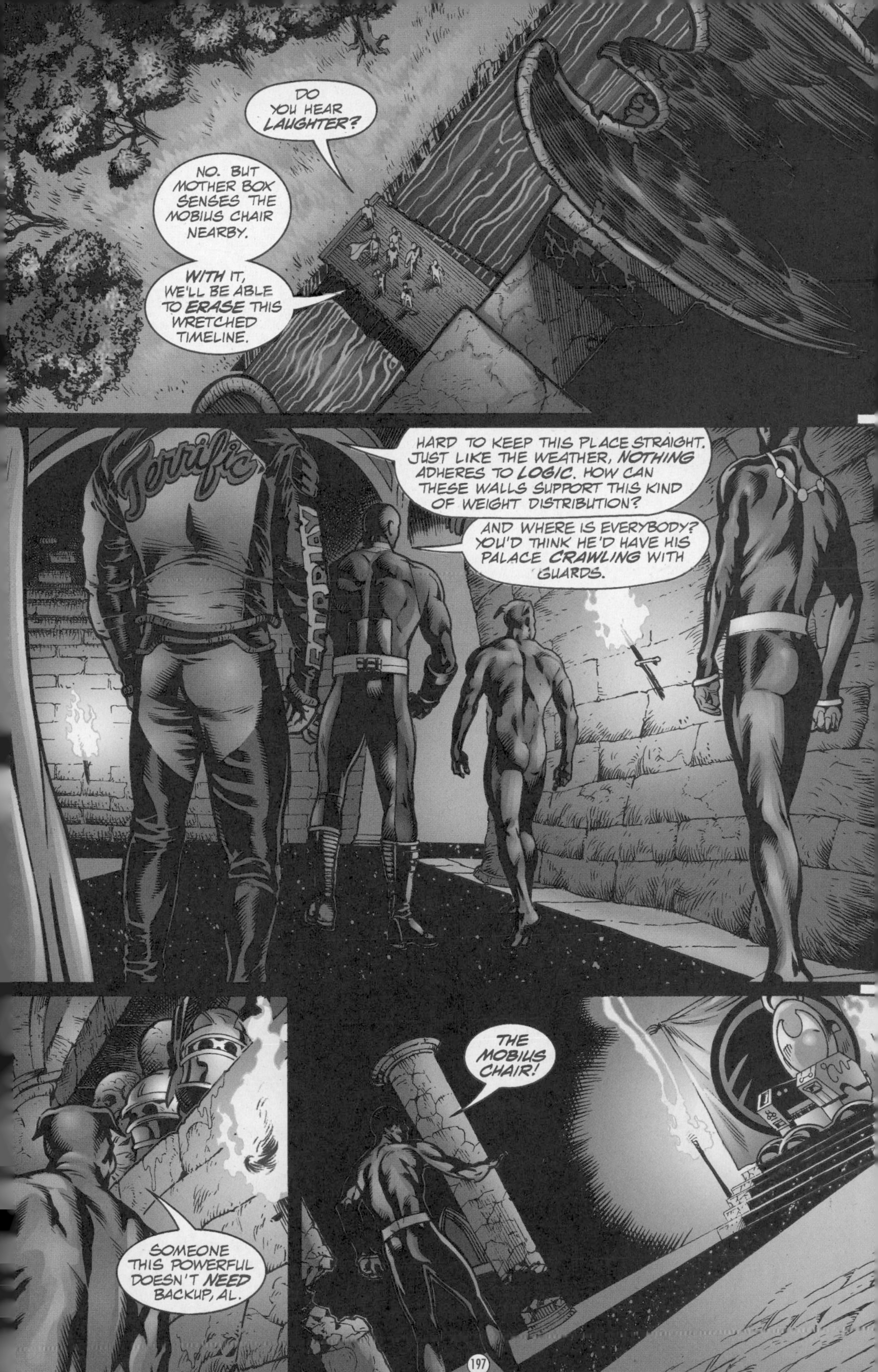
DO YOU HEAR LAUGHTER?
NO. BUT MOTHER BOX SENSES THE MOBIUS CHAIR NEARBY.
WITH IT, WE'LL BE ABLE TO ERASE THIS WRETCHED TIMELINE.
Terrific
HARD TO KEEP THIS PLACE STRAIGHT. JUST LIKE THE WEATHER, NOTHING ADHERES TO LOGIC. HOW CAN THESE WALLS SUPPORT THIS KIND OF WEIGHT DISTRIBUTION?
AND WHERE IS EVERYBODY? YOU'D THINK HE'D HAVE HIS PALACE CRAWLING WITH GUARDS.
SOMEONE THIS POWERFUL DOESN'T NEED BACKUP, AL.
THE MOBIUS CHAIR!

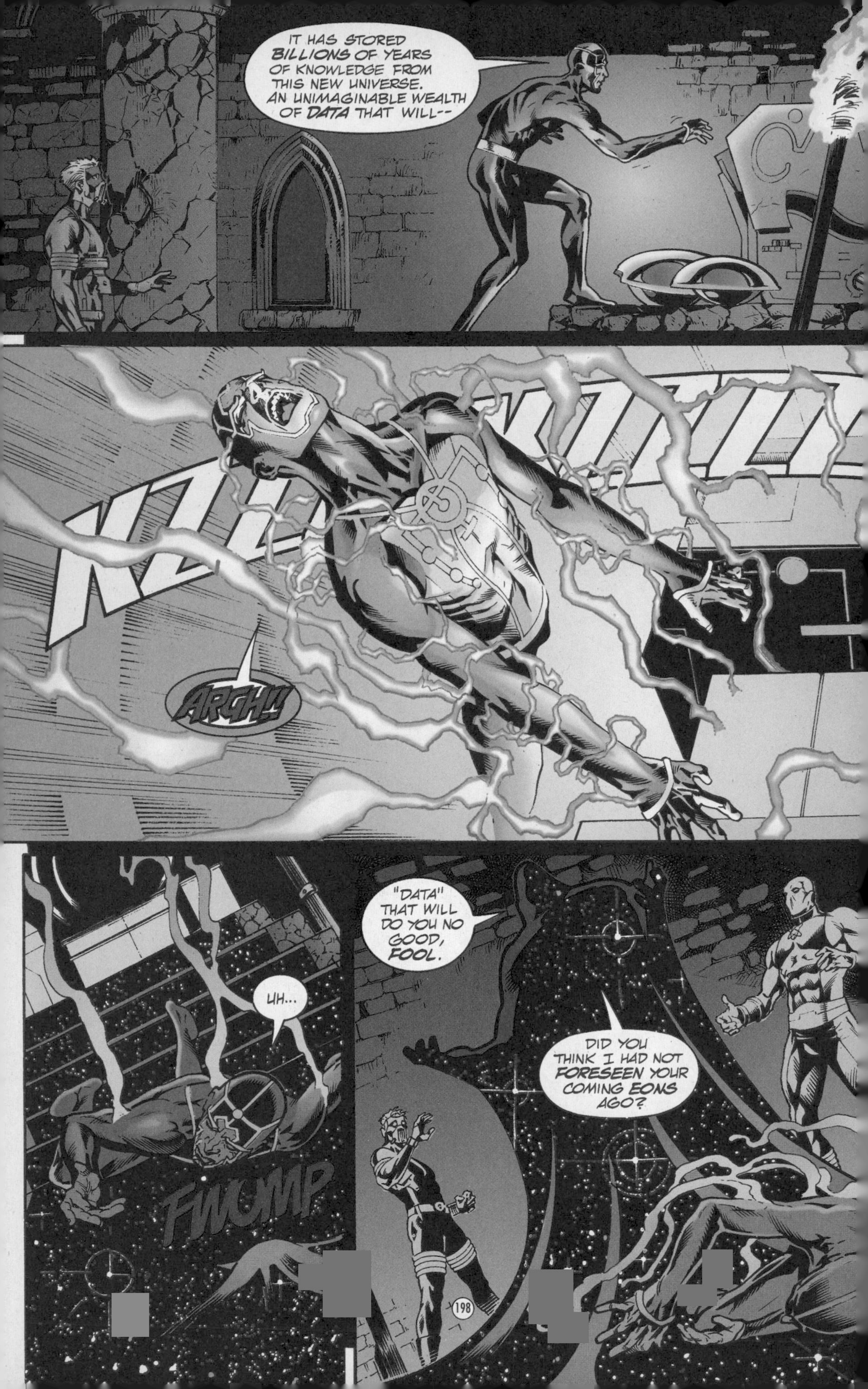
IT HAS STORED BILLIONS OF YEARS OF KNOWLEDGE FROM THIS NEW UNIVERSE. AN UNIMAGINABLE WEALTH OF DATA THAT WILL--
ARGH!!
UH...
FWOMP
"DATA" THAT WILL DO YOU NO GOOD, FOOL.
DID YOU THINK I HAD NOT FORESEEN YOUR COMING EONS AGO?

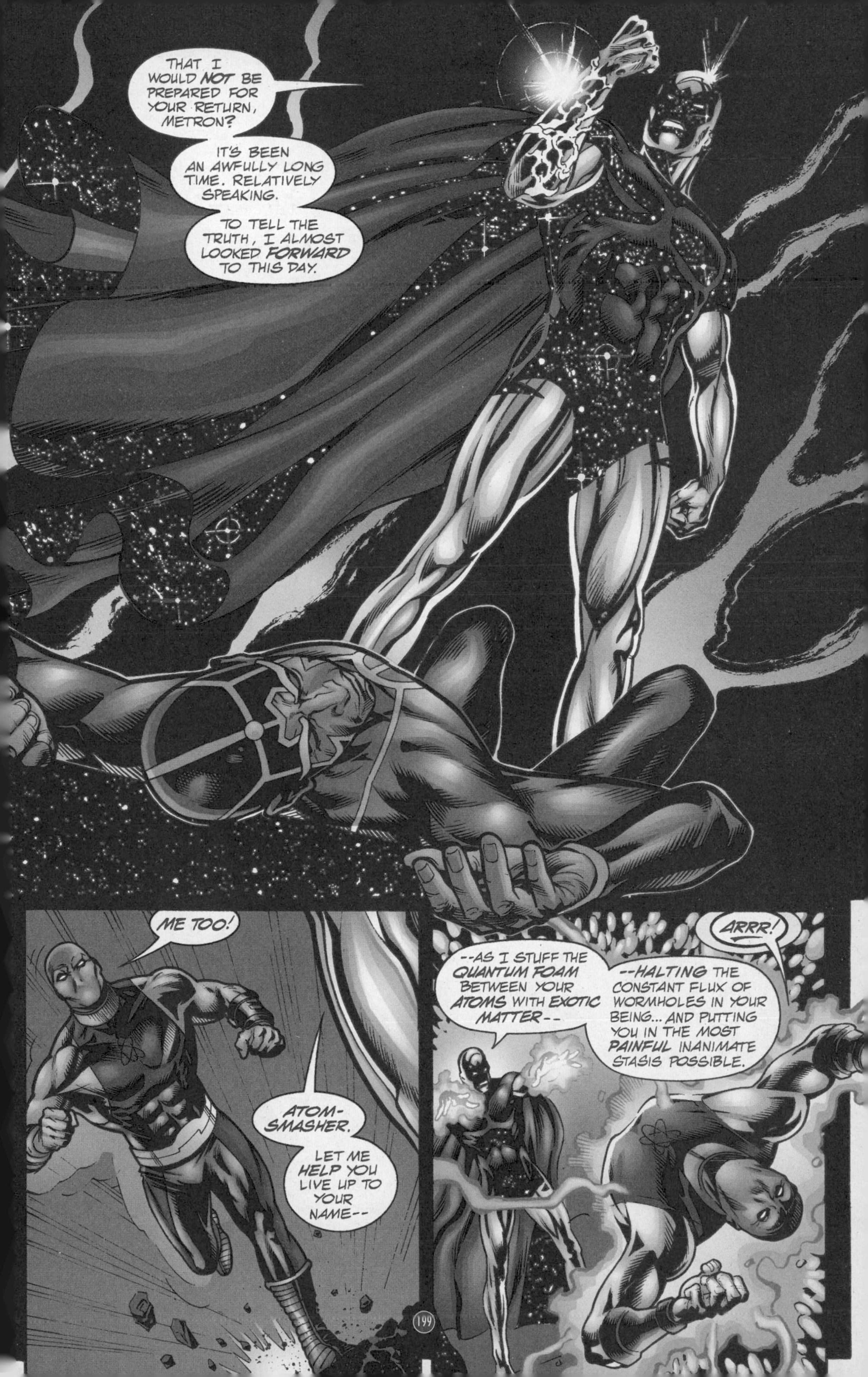
THAT I WOULD NOT BE PREPARED FOR YOUR RETURN, METRON?
IT'S BEEN AN AWFULLY LONG TIME. RELATIVELY SPEAKING.
TO TELL THE TRUTH, I ALMOST LOOKED FORWARD TO THIS DAY.
ME TOO!
ATOM-SMASHER.
LET ME HELP YOU LIVE UP TO YOUR NAME--
--AS I STUFF THE QUANTUM FOAM BETWEEN YOUR ATOMS WITH EXOTIC MATTER--
--HALTING THE CONSTANT FLUX OF WORMHOLES IN YOUR BEING... AND PUTTING YOU IN THE MOST PAINFUL INANIMATE STASIS POSSIBLE.
ARRR!

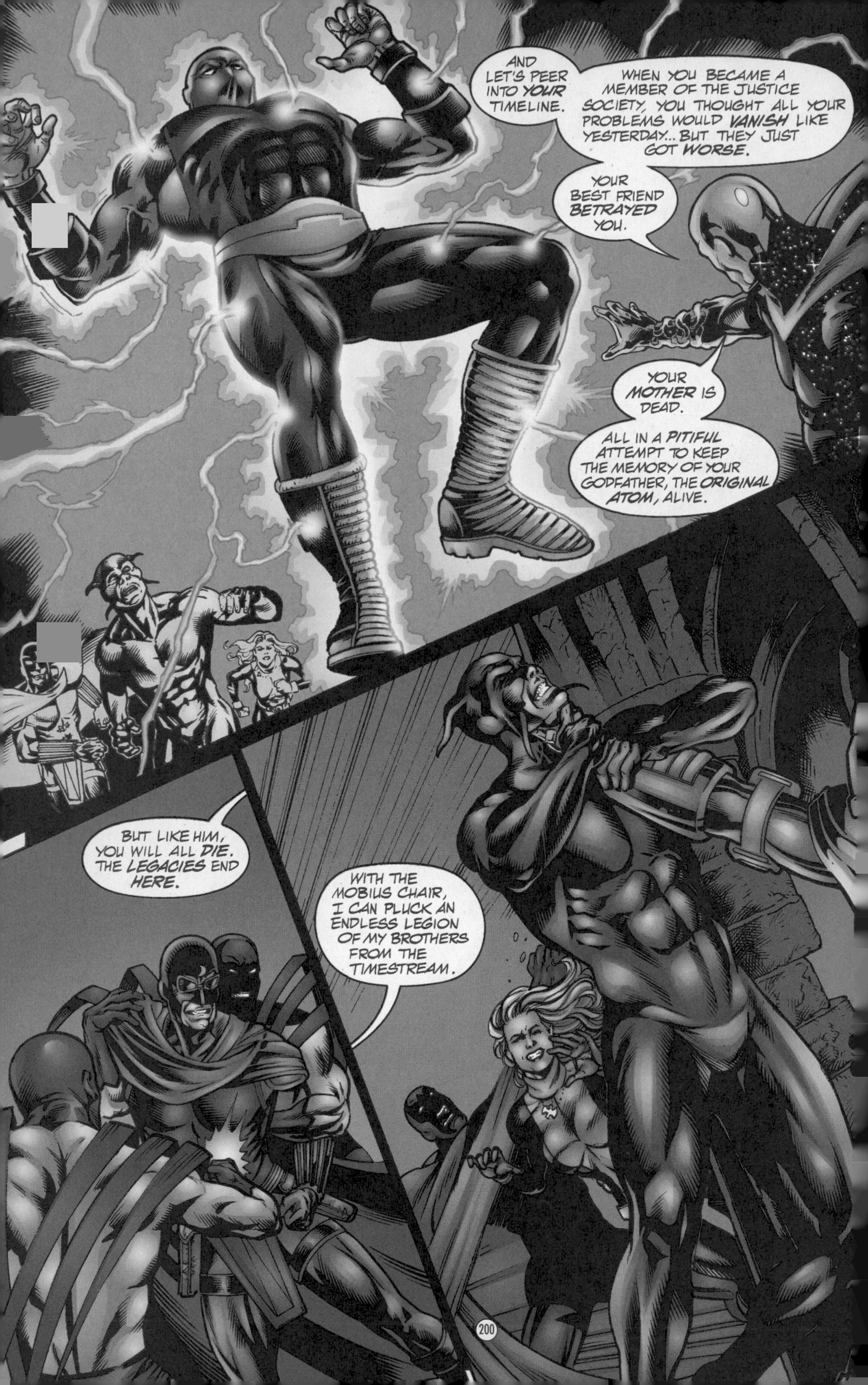
AND LET'S PEER INTO YOUR TIMELINE.
WHEN YOU BECAME A MEMBER OF THE JUSTICE SOCIETY, YOU THOUGHT ALL YOUR PROBLEMS WOULD VANISH LIKE YESTERDAY... BUT THEY JUST GOT WORSE.
YOUR BEST FRIEND BETRAYED YOU.
YOUR MOTHER IS DEAD.
ALL IN A PITIFUL ATTEMPT TO KEEP THE MEMORY OF YOUR GODFATHER, THE ORIGINAL ATOM, ALIVE.
BUT LIKE HIM, YOU WILL ALL DIE. THE LEGACIES END HERE.
WITH THE MOBIUS CHAIR, I CAN PLUCK AN ENDLESS LEGION OF MY BROTHERS FROM THE TIMESTREAM.

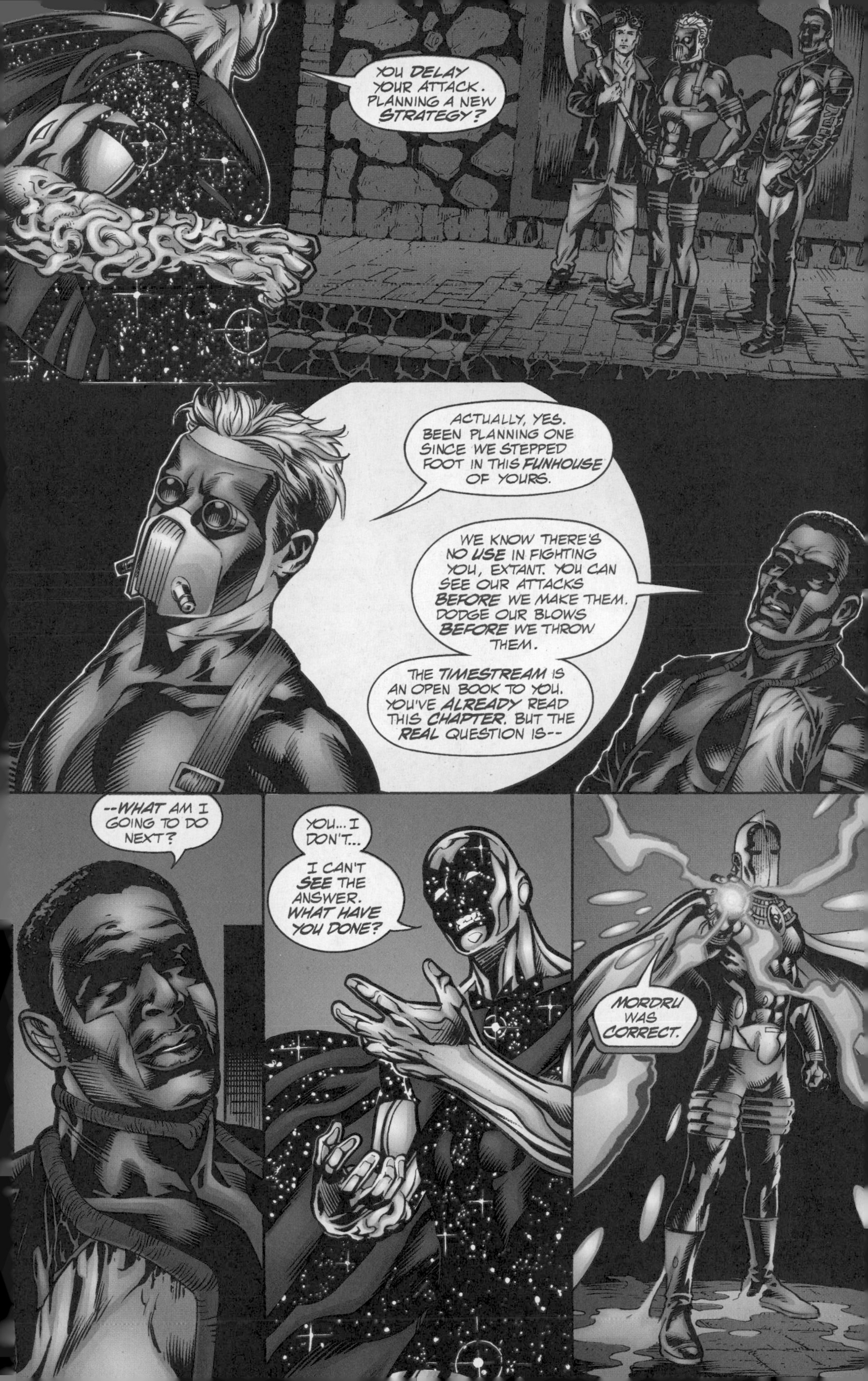
YOU DELAY YOUR ATTACK. PLANNING A NEW STRATEGY?
ACTUALLY, YES. BEEN PLANNING ONE SINCE WE STEPPED FOOT IN THIS FUNHOUSE OF YOURS.
WE KNOW THERE'S NO USE IN FIGHTING YOU, EXTANT. YOU CAN SEE OUR ATTACKS BEFORE WE MAKE THEM. DODGE OUR BLOWS BEFORE WE THROW THEM.
THE TIMESTREAM IS AN OPEN BOOK TO YOU. YOU'VE ALREADY READ THIS CHAPTER. BUT THE REAL QUESTION IS--
--WHAT AM I GOING TO DO NEXT?
YOU... I DON'T...
I CAN'T SEE THE ANSWER. WHAT HAVE YOU DONE?
MORDRU WAS CORRECT.

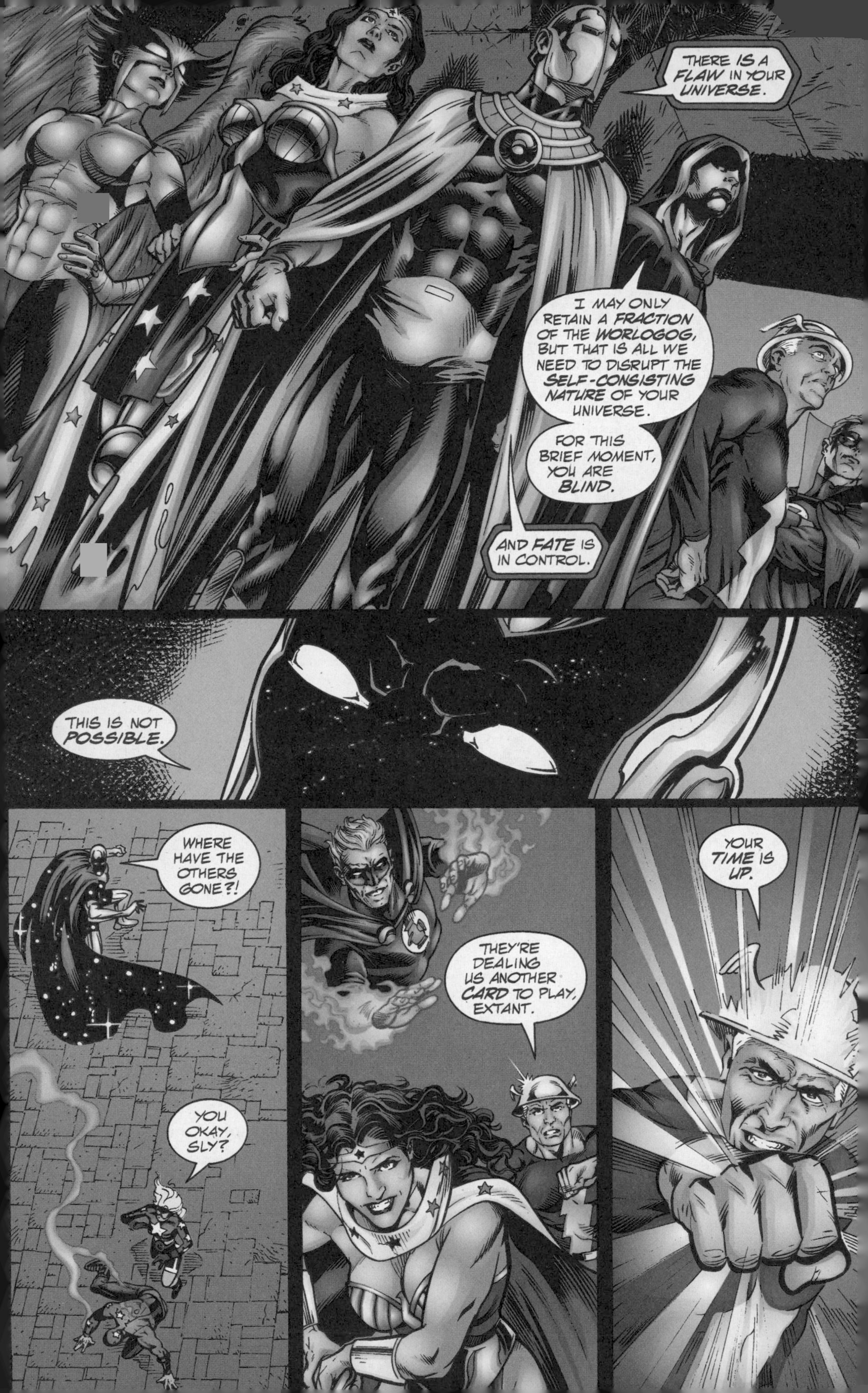

THERE IS A FLAW IN YOUR UNIVERSE.
I MAY ONLY RETAIN A FRACTION OF THE WORLOGOG, BUT THAT IS ALL WE NEED TO DISRUPT THE SELF-CONSISTING NATURE OF YOUR UNIVERSE.
FOR THIS BRIEF MOMENT, YOU ARE BLIND.
AND FATE IS IN CONTROL.
THIS IS NOT POSSIBLE.
WHERE HAVE THE OTHERS GONE?!
YOU OKAY, SLY?
THEY'RE DEALING US ANOTHER CARD TO PLAY, EXTANT.
YOUR TIME IS UP.

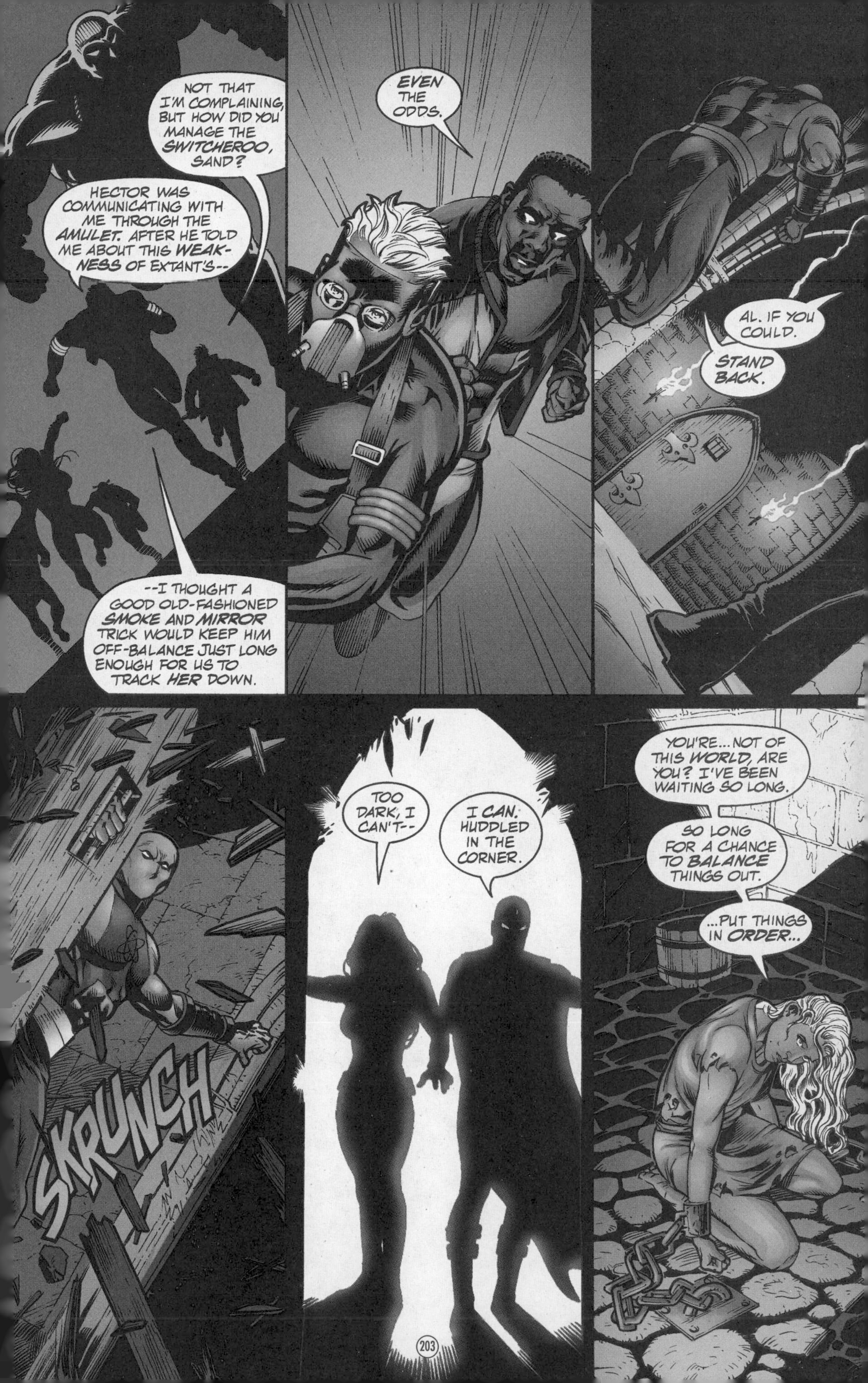
NOT THAT I'M COMPLAINING, BUT HOW DID YOU MANAGE THE SWITCHEROO, SAND?
HECTOR WAS COMMUNICATING WITH ME THROUGH THE AMULET. AFTER HE TOLD ME ABOUT THIS WEAK-NESS OF EXTANT'S--
--I THOUGHT A GOOD OLD-FASHIONED SMOKE AND MIRROR TRICK WOULD KEEP HIM OFF-BALANCE JUST LONG ENOUGH FOR US TO TRACK HER DOWN.
EVEN THE ODDS.
AL. IF YOU COULD.
STAND BACK.
SKRUNCH
TOO DARK, I CAN'T--
I CAN. HUDDLED IN THE CORNER.
YOU'RE... NOT OF THIS WORLD, ARE YOU? I'VE BEEN WAITING SO LONG.
SO LONG FOR A CHANCE TO BALANCE THINGS OUT.
...PUT THINGS IN ORDER...

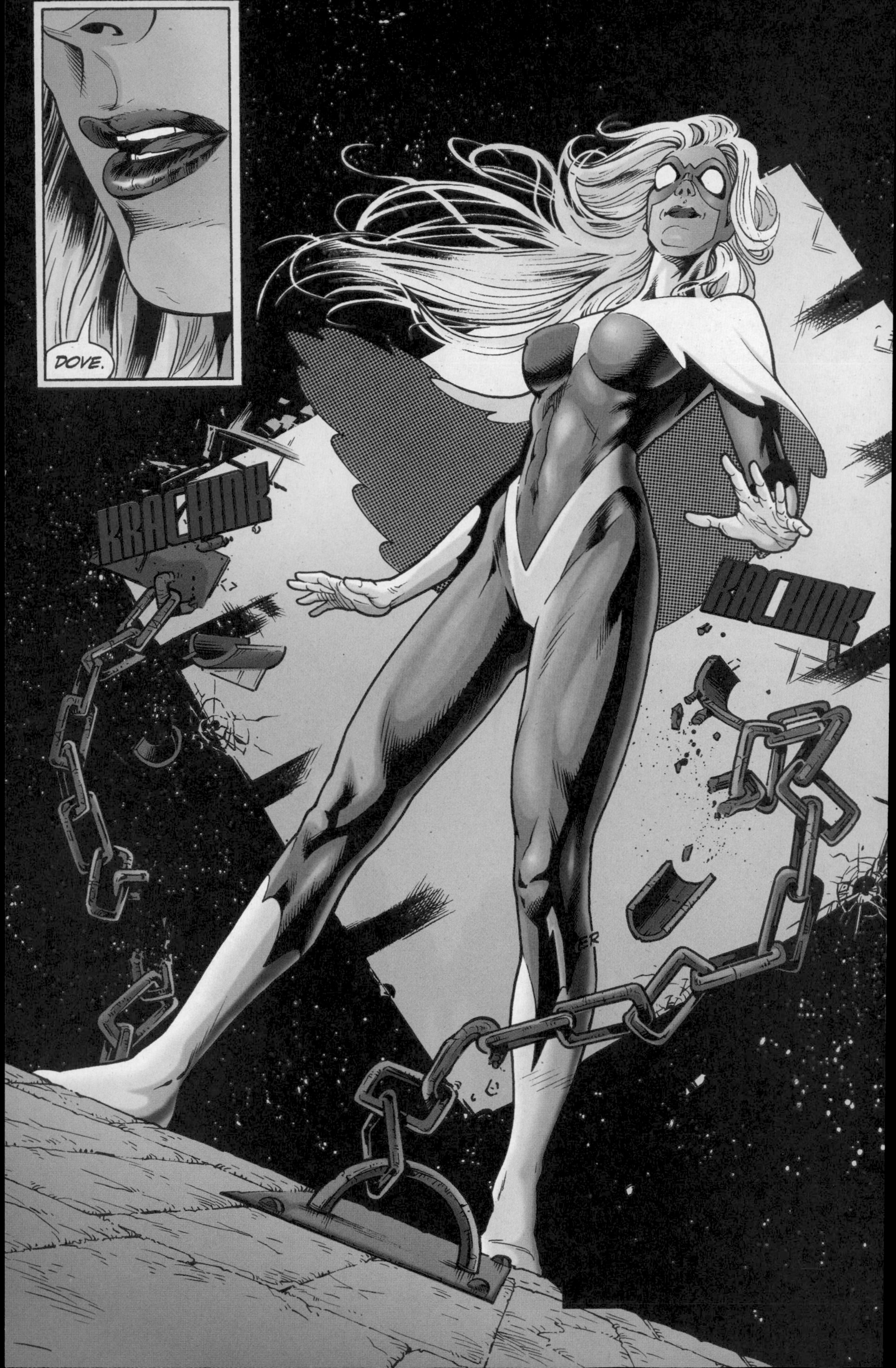
DOVE.
KRACHINK
KRACHINK

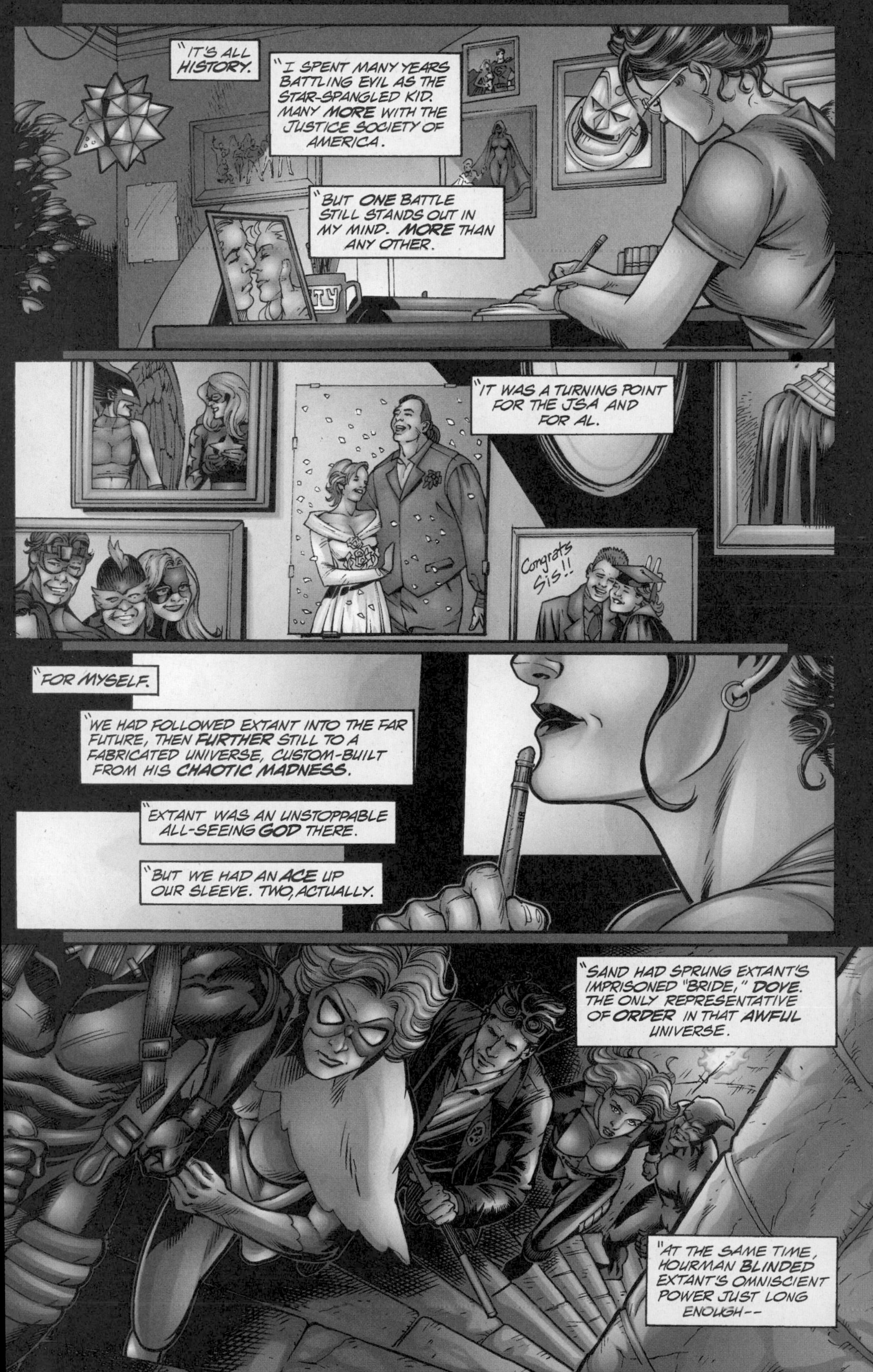
"IT'S ALL HISTORY.
"I SPENT MANY YEARS BATTLING EVIL AS THE STAR-SPANGLED KID. MANY MORE WITH THE JUSTICE SOCIETY OF AMERICA.
"BUT ONE BATTLE STILL STANDS OUT IN MY MIND. MORE THAN ANY OTHER.
"IT WAS A TURNING POINT FOR THE JSA AND FOR AL.
Congrats Sis!!
"FOR MYSELF.
"WE HAD FOLLOWED EXTANT INTO THE FAR FUTURE, THEN FURTHER STILL TO A FABRICATED UNIVERSE, CUSTOM-BUILT FROM HIS CHAOTIC MADNESS.
"EXTANT WAS AN UNSTOPPABLE ALL-SEEING GOD THERE.
"BUT WE HAD AN ACE UP OUR SLEEVE. TWO, ACTUALLY.
"SAND HAD SPRUNG EXTANT'S IMPRISONED "BRIDE," DOVE. THE ONLY REPRESENTATIVE OF ORDER IN THAT AWFUL UNIVERSE.
"AT THE SAME TIME, HOURMAN BLINDED EXTANT'S OMNISCIENT POWER JUST LONG ENOUGH--

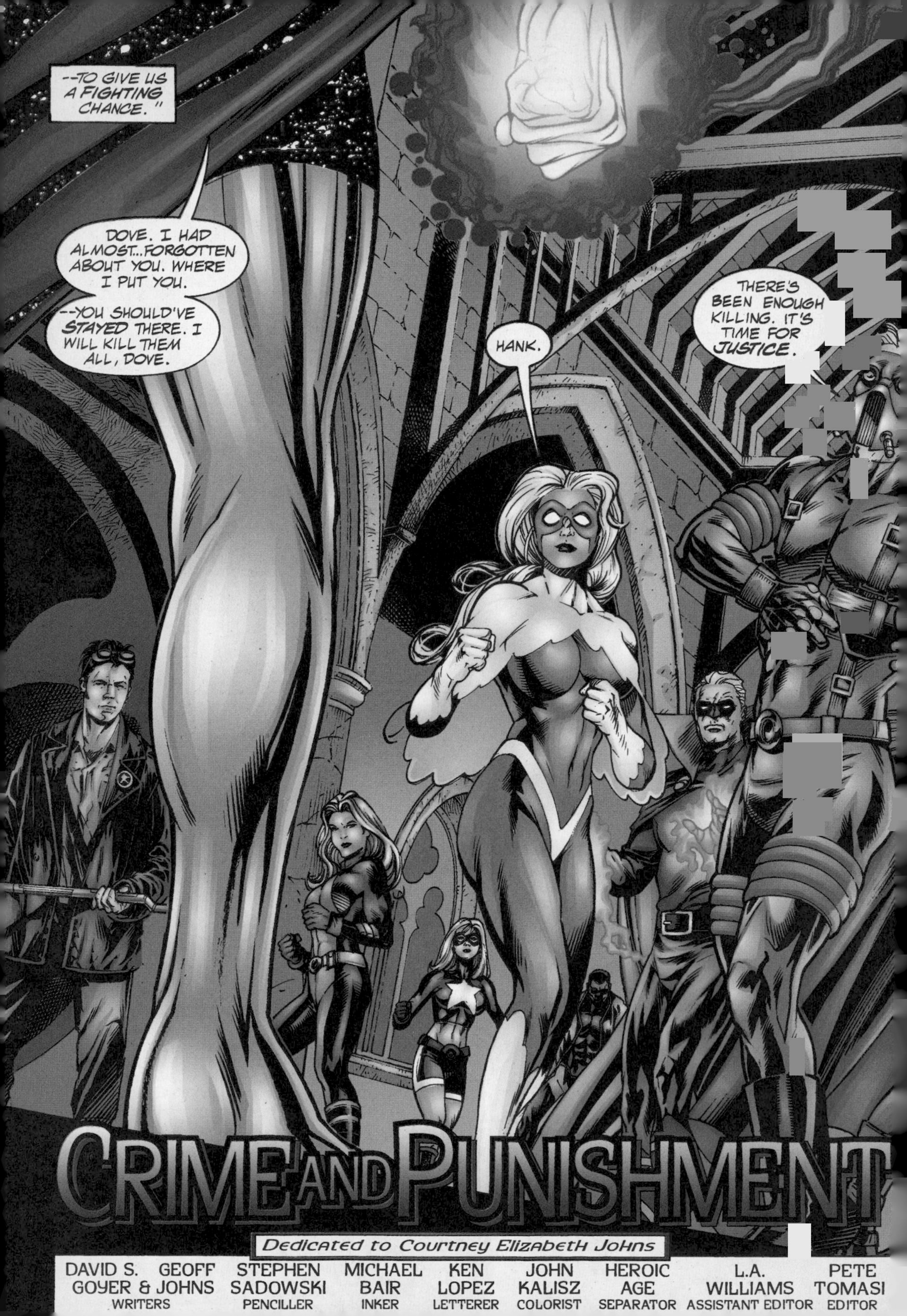
--TO GIVE US A FIGHTING CHANCE."
DOVE. I HAD ALMOST...FORGOTTEN ABOUT YOU. WHERE I PUT YOU.
--YOU SHOULD'VE STAYED THERE. I WILL KILL THEM ALL, DOVE.
HANK.
THERE'S BEEN ENOUGH KILLING. IT'S TIME FOR JUSTICE.
CRIME AND PUNISHMENT
Dedicated to Courtney Elizabeth Johns
DAVID S. GOYER & GEOFF JOHNS WRITERS
STEPHEN SADOWSKI PENCILLER
MICHAEL BAIR INKER
KEN LOPEZ LETTERER
JOHN KALISZ COLORIST
HEROIC AGE SEPARATOR
L.A. WILLIAMS ASSISTANT EDITOR
PETE TOMASI EDITOR

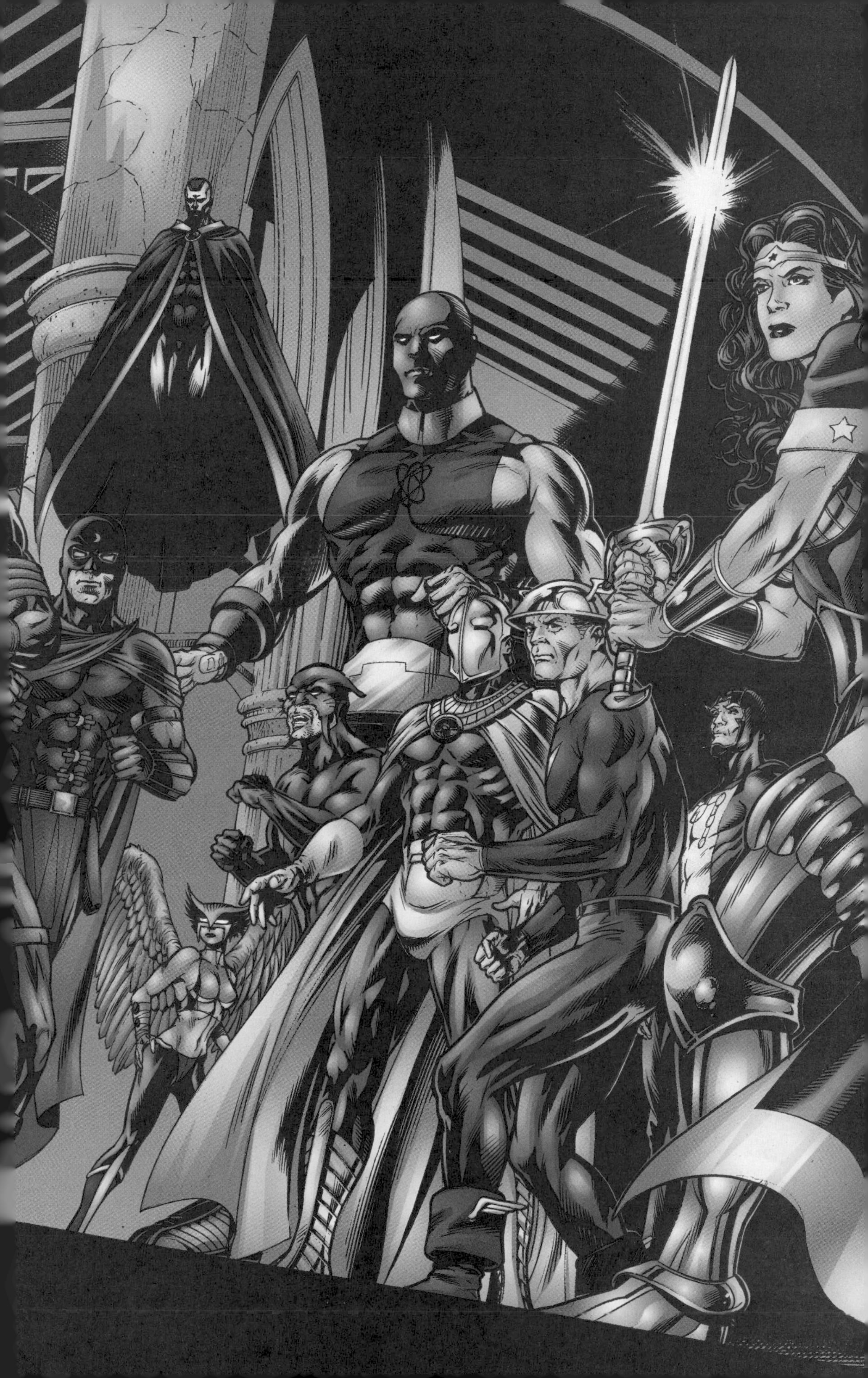

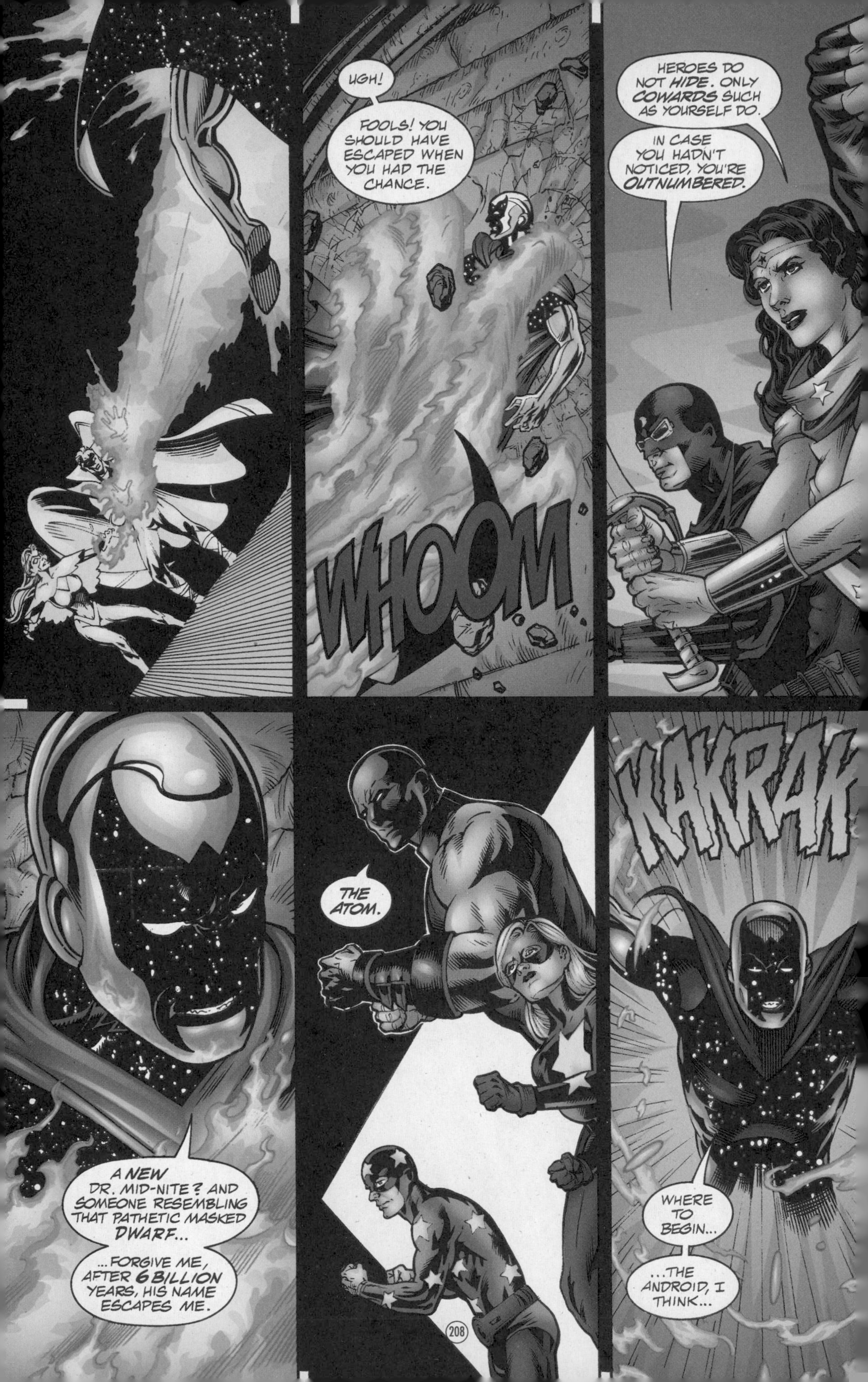
UGH!
FOOLS! YOU SHOULD HAVE ESCAPED WHEN YOU HAD THE CHANCE.
WHOOM
HEROES DO NOT HIDE. ONLY COWARDS SUCH AS YOURSELF DO.
IN CASE YOU HADN'T NOTICED, YOU'RE OUTNUMBERED.
A NEW DR. MID-NITE? AND SOMEONE RESEMBLING THAT PATHETIC MASKED DWARF...
...FORGIVE ME, AFTER 6 BILLION YEARS, HIS NAME ESCAPES ME.
THE ATOM.
KAKRAK
WHERE TO BEGIN...
...THE ANDROID, I THINK...

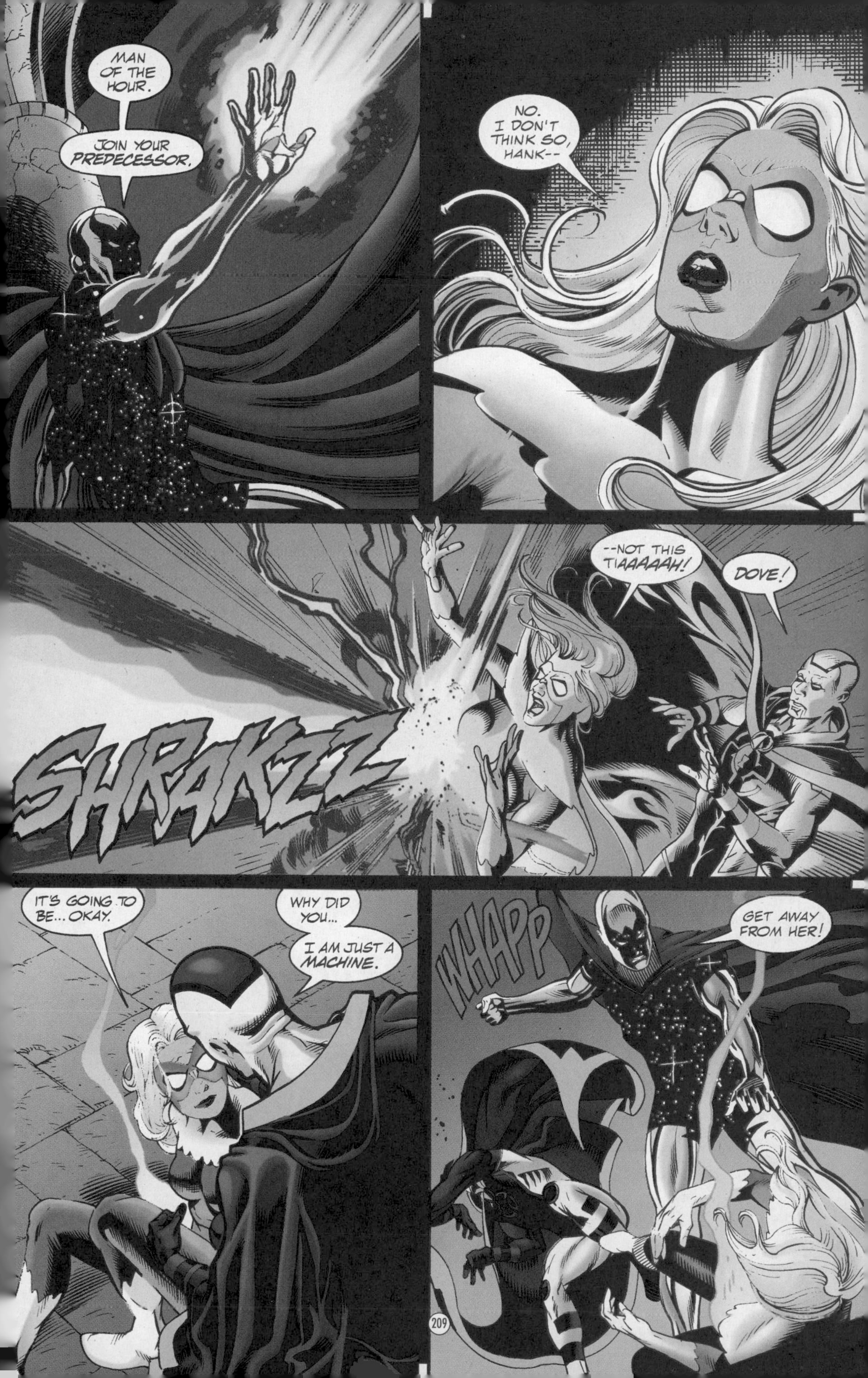

MAN OF THE HOUR.
JOIN YOUR PREDECESSOR.
NO. I DON'T THINK SO, HANK--
--NOT THIS TIAAAAAH!
DOVE!
SHRAKZZZ
IT'S GOING TO BE... OKAY.
WHY DID YOU...
I AM JUST A MACHINE.
WHAPP
GET AWAY FROM HER!

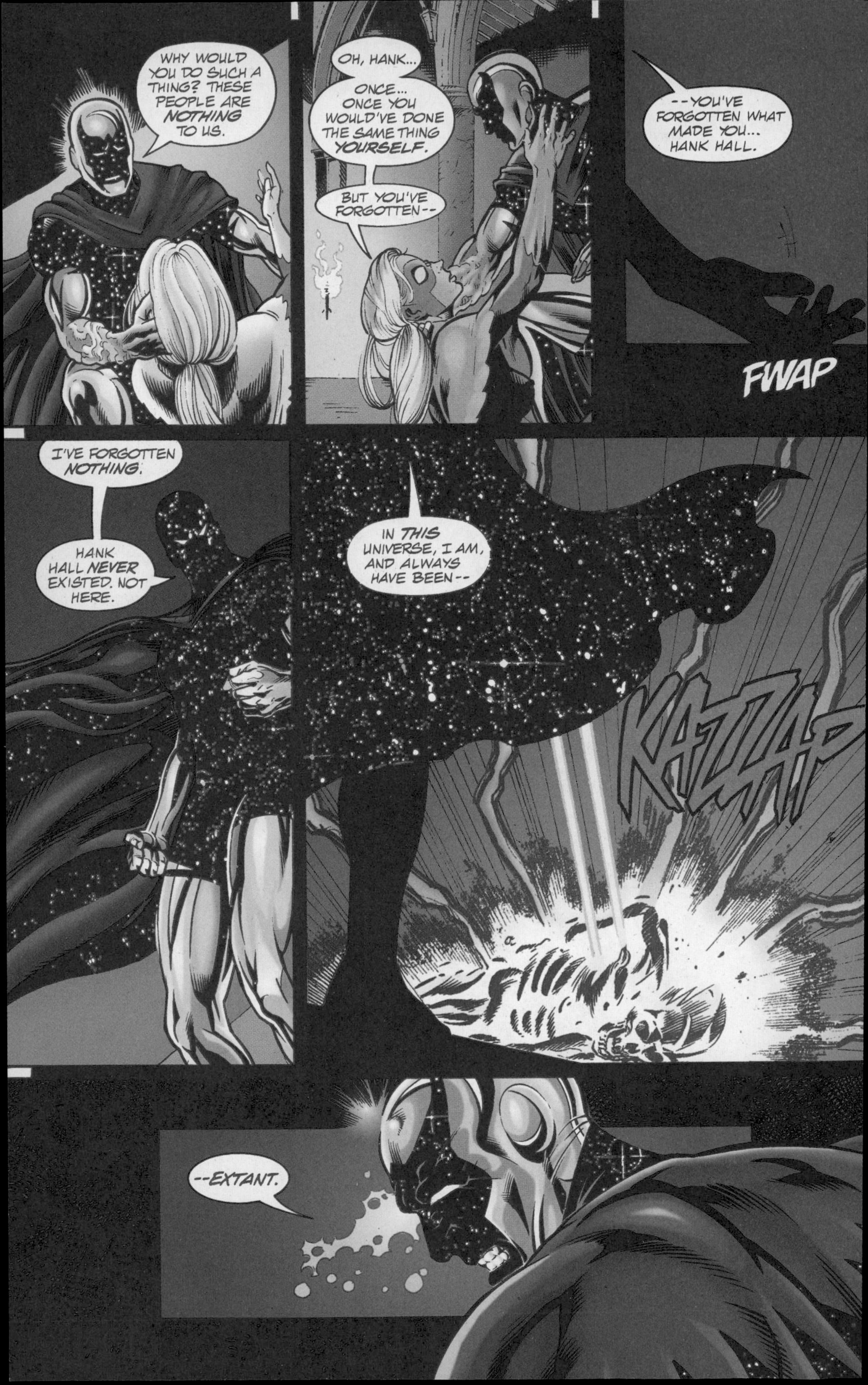
WHY WOULD YOU DO SUCH A THING? THESE PEOPLE ARE NOTHING TO US.
OH, HANK...
ONCE... ONCE YOU WOULD'VE DONE THE SAME THING YOURSELF.
BUT YOU'VE FORGOTTEN--
--YOU'VE FORGOTTEN WHAT MADE YOU... HANK HALL.
FWAP
I'VE FORGOTTEN NOTHING.
HANK HALL NEVER EXISTED. NOT HERE.
IN THIS UNIVERSE, I AM, AND ALWAYS HAVE BEEN--
KAZZAP
--EXTANT.

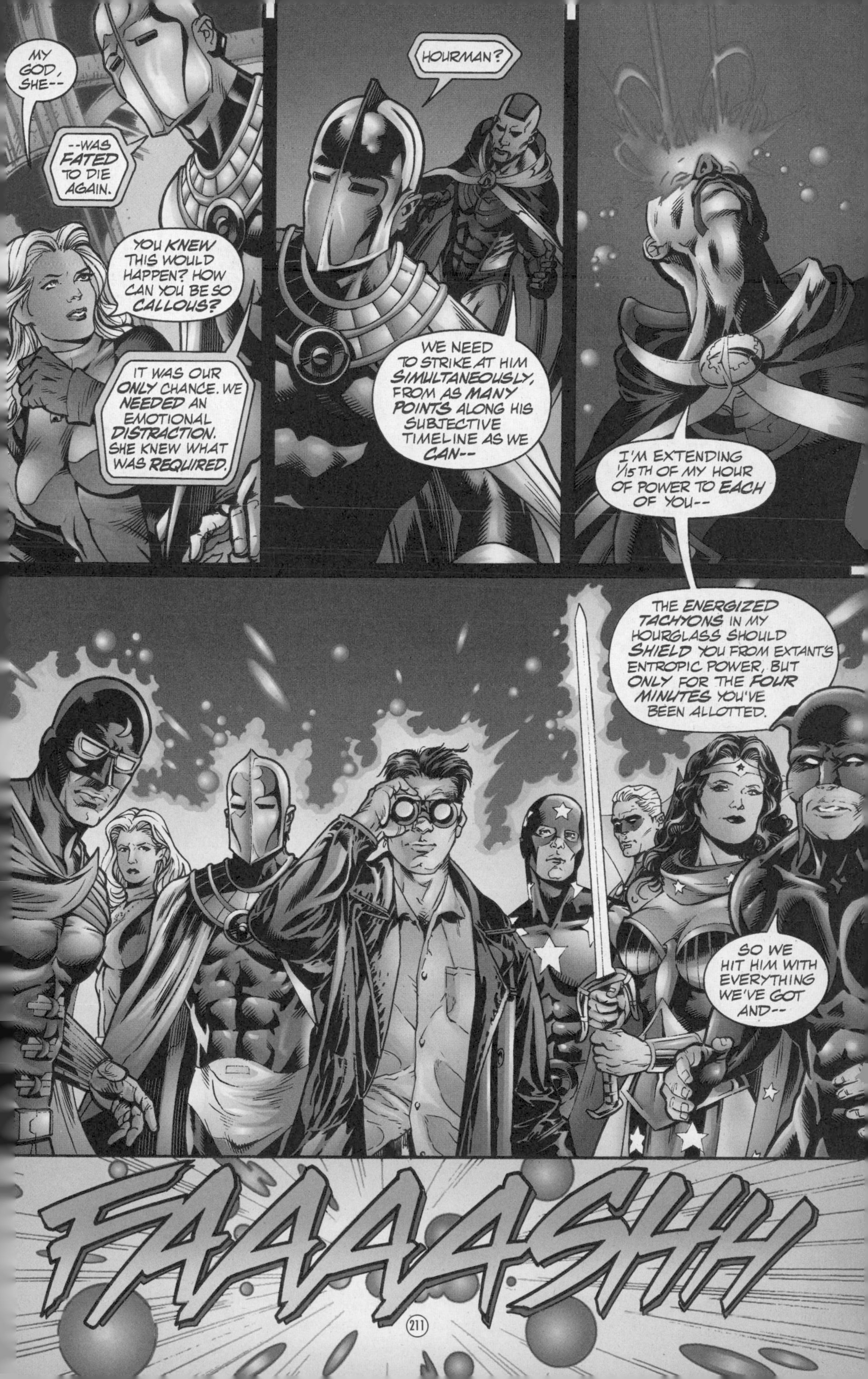
MY GOD, SHE--
--WAS FATED TO DIE AGAIN.
YOU KNEW THIS WOULD HAPPEN? HOW CAN YOU BE SO CALLOUS?
IT WAS OUR ONLY CHANCE. WE NEEDED AN EMOTIONAL DISTRACTION. SHE KNEW WHAT WAS REQUIRED.
HOURMAN?
WE NEED TO STRIKE AT HIM SIMULTANEOUSLY, FROM AS MANY POINTS ALONG HIS SUBJECTIVE TIMELINE AS WE CAN--
I'M EXTENDING 1/15TH OF MY HOUR OF POWER TO EACH OF YOU--
THE ENERGIZED TACHYONS IN MY HOURGLASS SHOULD SHIELD YOU FROM EXTANT'S ENTROPIC POWER, BUT ONLY FOR THE FOUR MINUTES YOU'VE BEEN ALLOTTED.
SO WE HIT HIM WITH EVERYTHING WE'VE GOT AND--
FAAAASHH

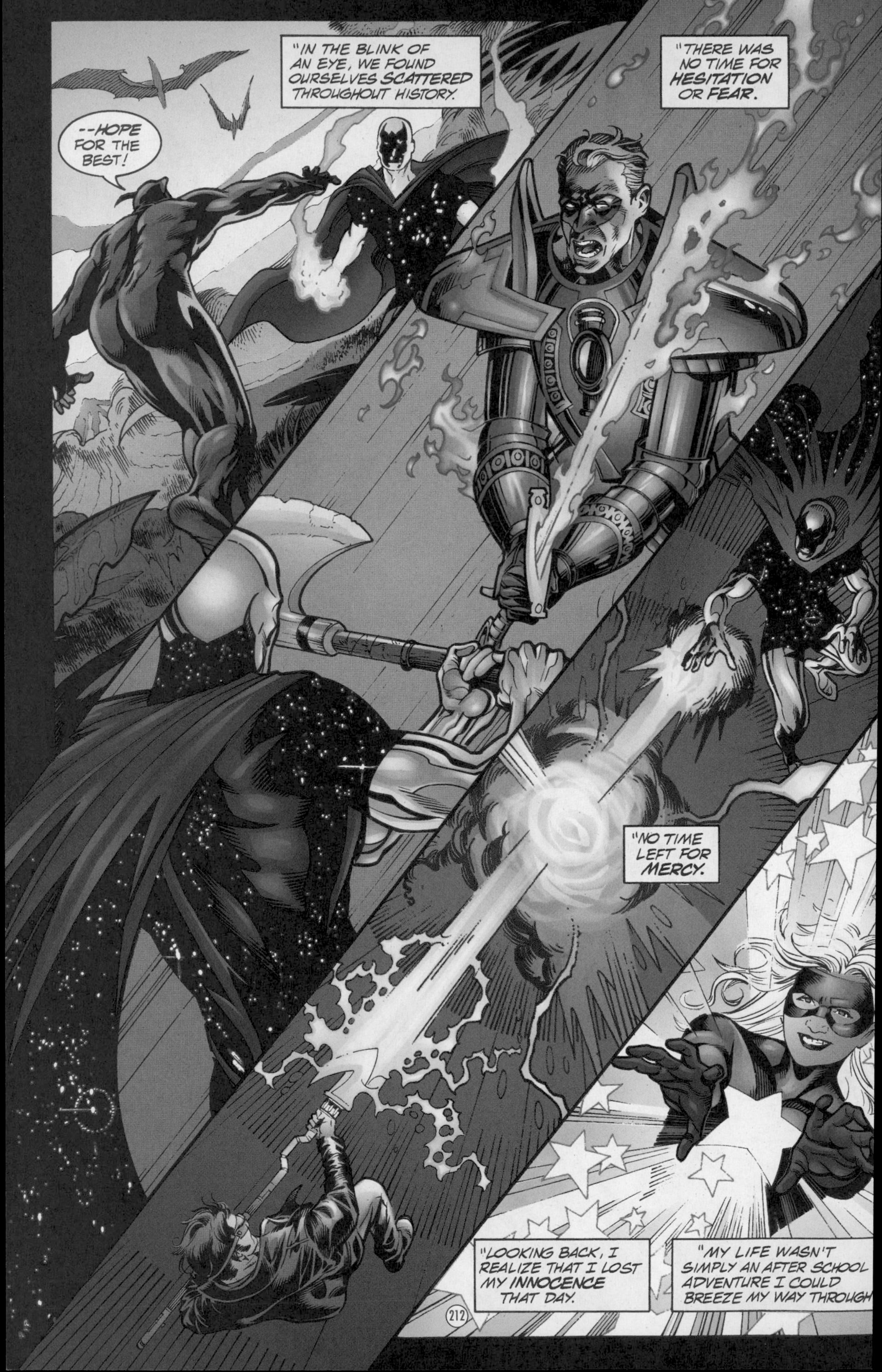

"IN THE BLINK OF AN EYE, WE FOUND OURSELVES SCATTERED THROUGHOUT HISTORY.
--HOPE FOR THE BEST!
"THERE WAS NO TIME FOR HESITATION OR FEAR.
"NO TIME LEFT FOR MERCY.
"LOOKING BACK, I REALIZE THAT I LOST MY INNOCENCE THAT DAY.
"MY LIFE WASN'T SIMPLY AN AFTER SCHOOL ADVENTURE I COULD BREEZE MY WAY THROUGH

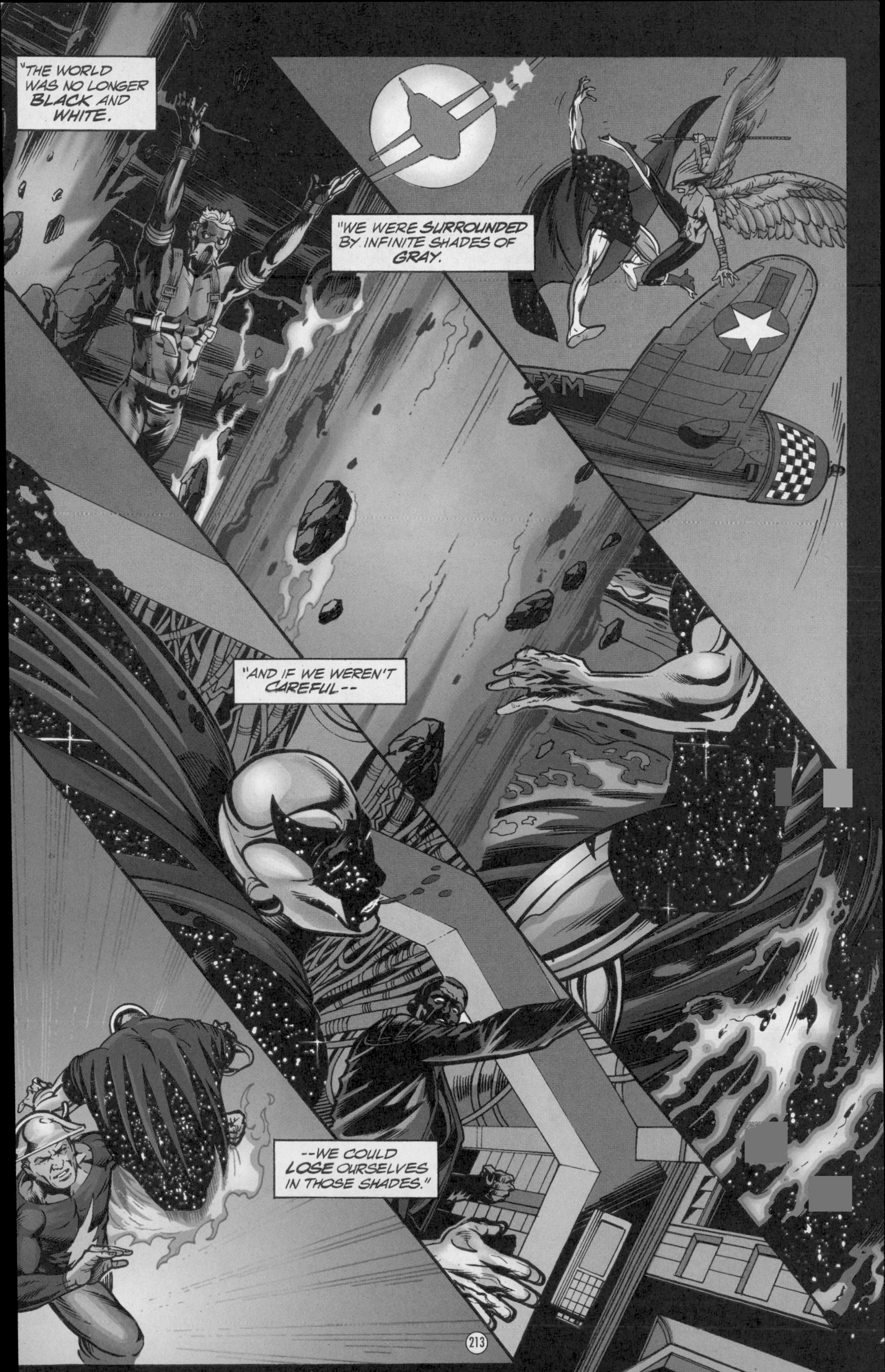
"THE WORLD WAS NO LONGER BLACK AND WHITE.
"WE WERE SURROUNDED BY INFINITE SHADES OF GRAY.
"AND IF WE WEREN'T CAREFUL--
--WE COULD LOSE OURSELVES IN THOSE SHADES."

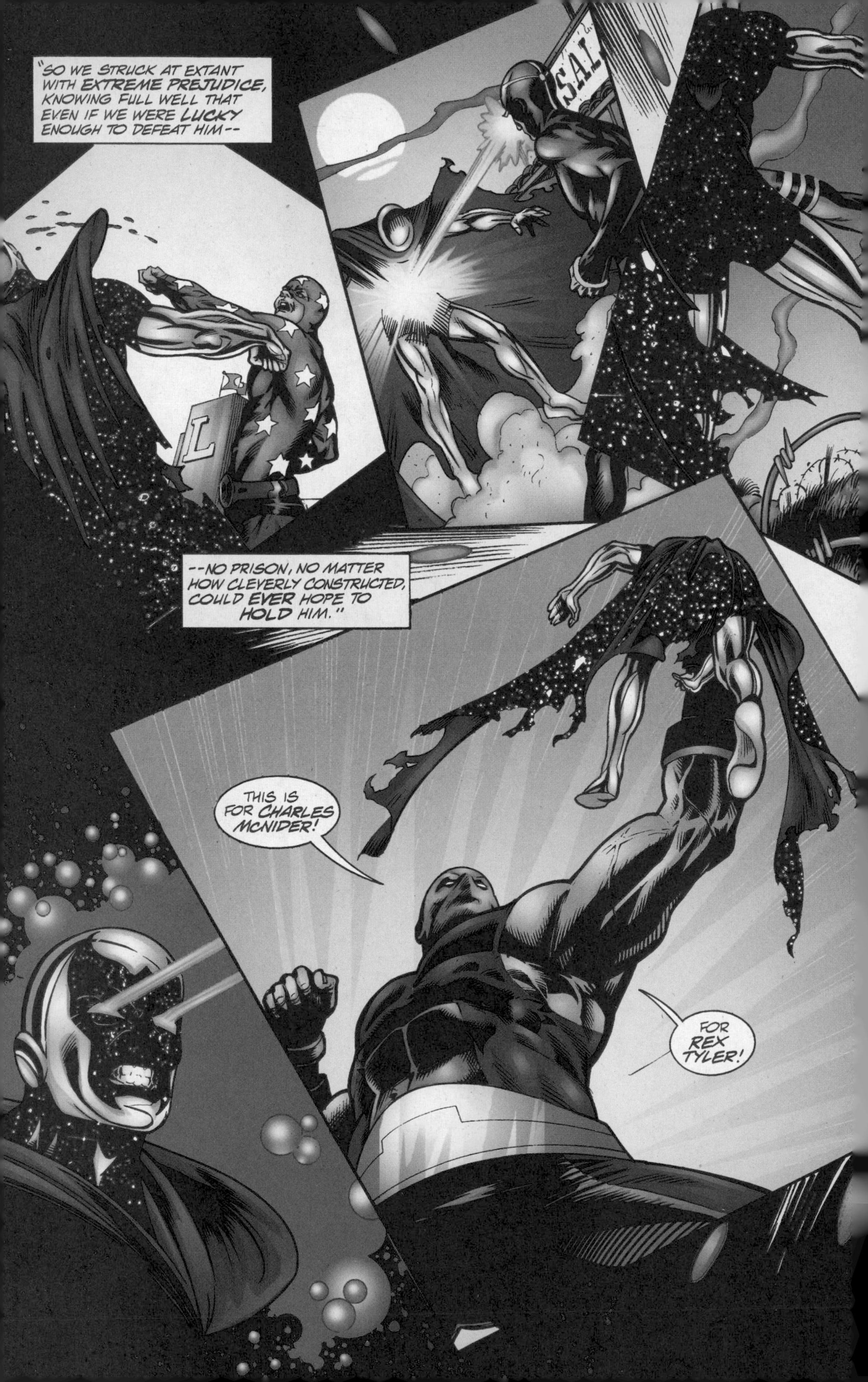
"SO WE STRUCK AT EXTANT WITH EXTREME PREJUDICE, KNOWING FULL WELL THAT EVEN IF WE WERE LUCKY ENOUGH TO DEFEAT HIM--
SAL
--NO PRISON, NO MATTER HOW CLEVERLY CONSTRUCTED, COULD EVER HOPE TO HOLD HIM."
THIS IS FOR CHARLES MCNIDER!
FOR REX TYLER!

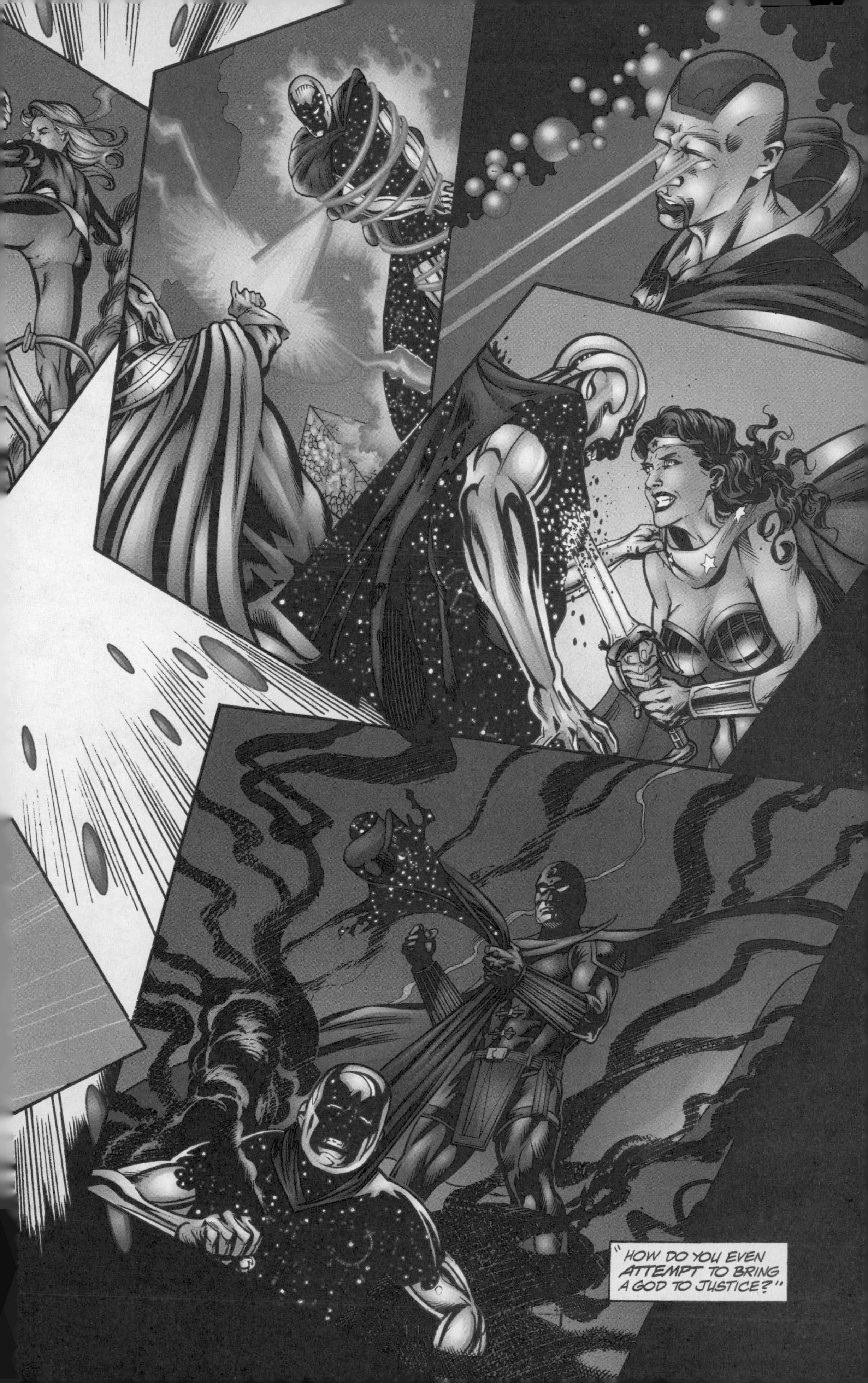
"HOW DO YOU EVEN ATTEMPT TO BRING A GOD TO JUSTICE?"

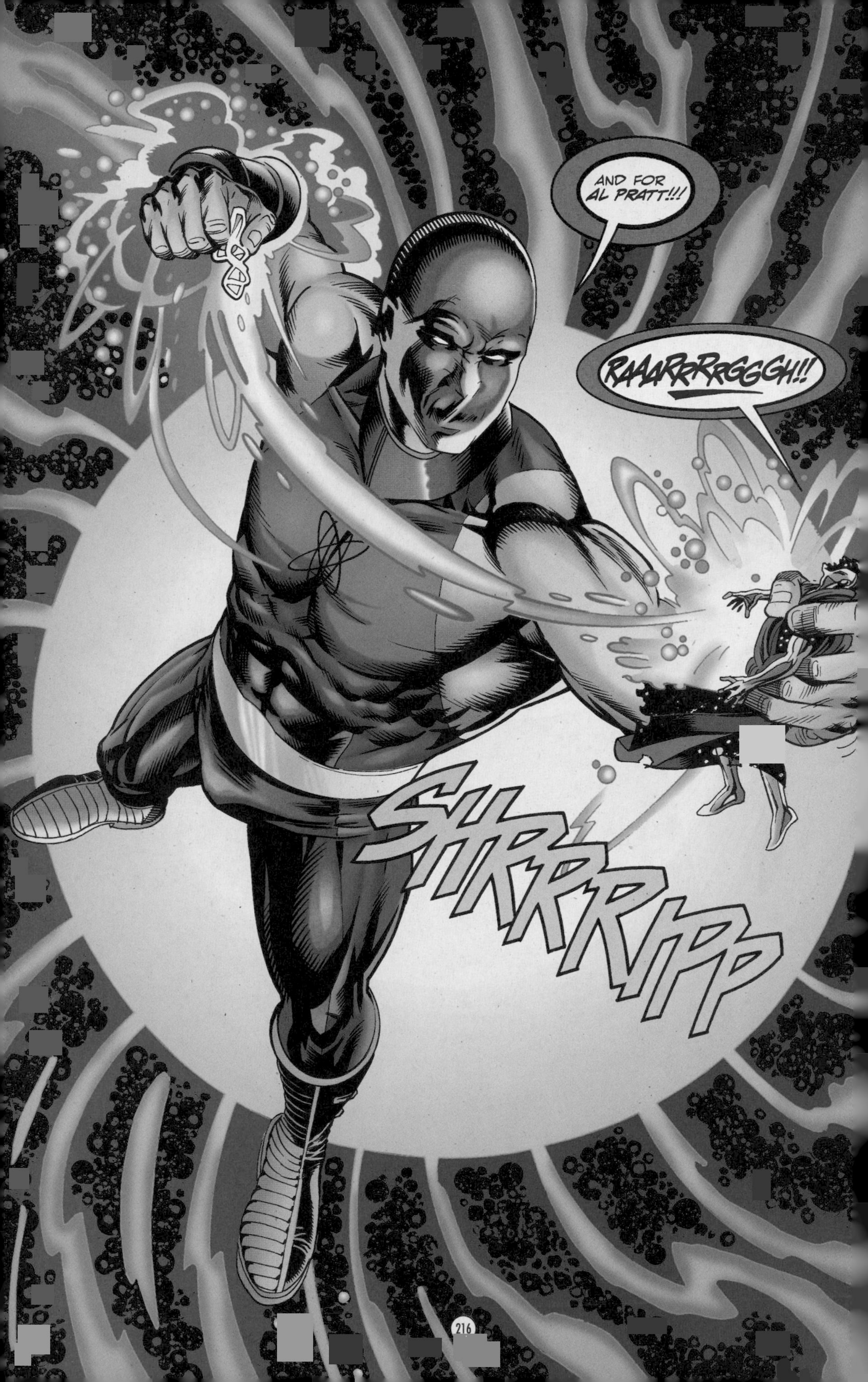
AND FOR AL PRATT!!!
RAAARRRRGGGH!!
SHRRRIPP

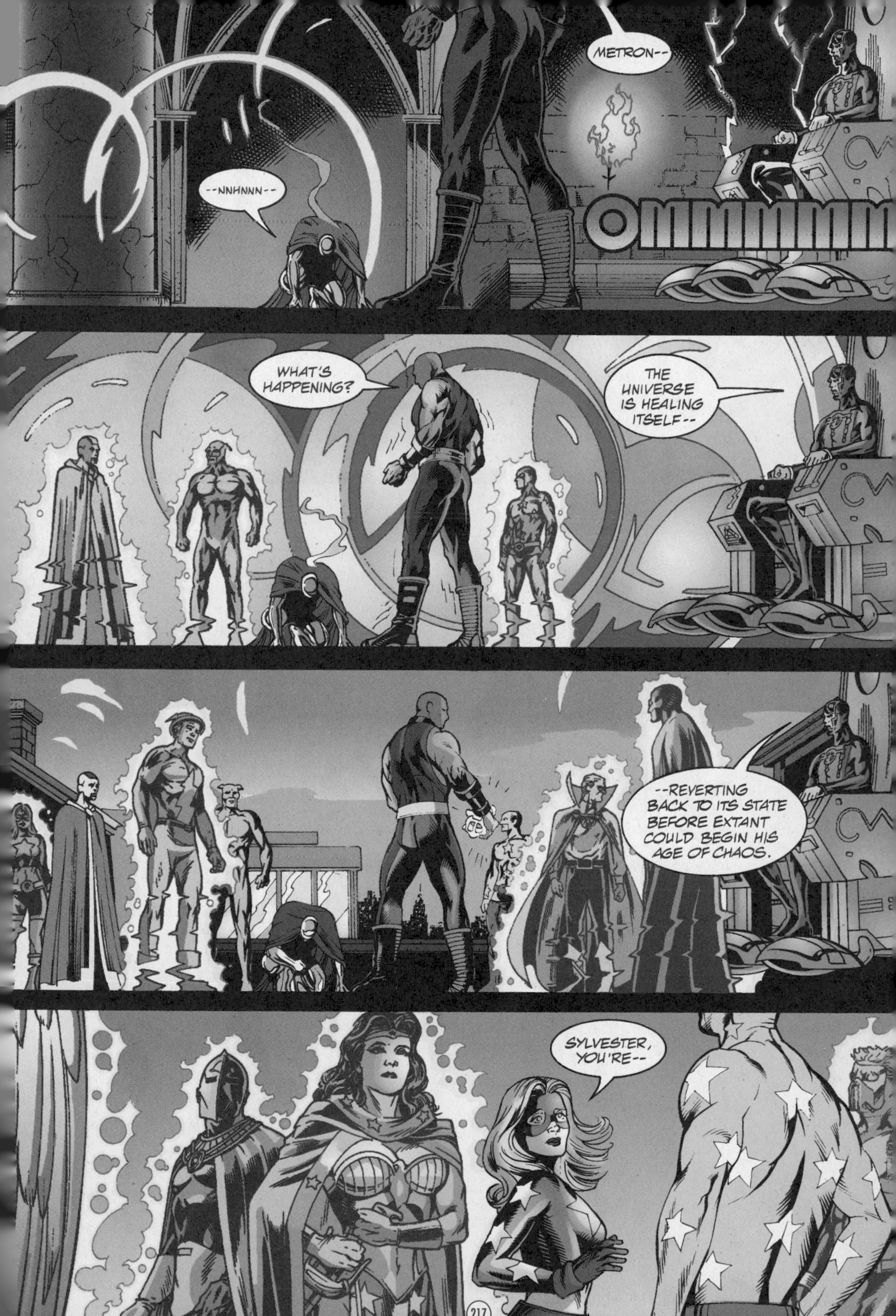
METRON--
--NNHNNN--
OMMMMMM
WHAT'S HAPPENING?
THE UNIVERSE IS HEALING ITSELF--
--REVERTING BACK TO ITS STATE BEFORE EXTANT COULD BEGIN HIS AGE OF CHAOS.
SYLVESTER, YOU'RE--

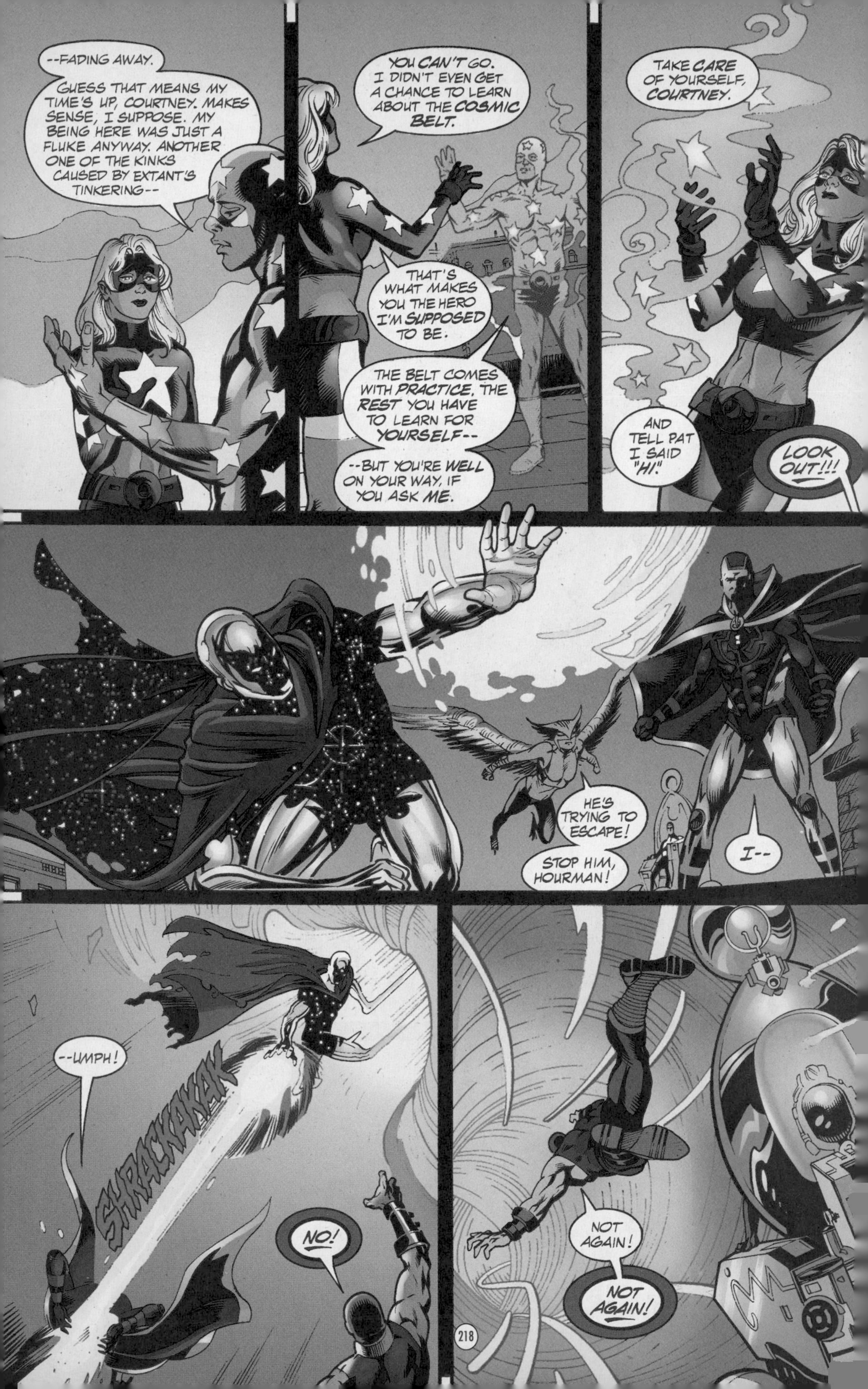
--FADING AWAY.
GUESS THAT MEANS MY TIME'S UP, COURTNEY. MAKES SENSE, I SUPPOSE. MY BEING HERE WAS JUST A FLUKE ANYWAY. ANOTHER ONE OF THE KINKS CAUSED BY EXTANT'S TINKERING--
YOU CAN'T GO. I DIDN'T EVEN GET A CHANCE TO LEARN ABOUT THE COSMIC BELT.
THAT'S WHAT MAKES YOU THE HERO I'M SUPPOSED TO BE.
THE BELT COMES WITH PRACTICE. THE REST YOU HAVE TO LEARN FOR YOURSELF--
--BUT YOU'RE WELL ON YOUR WAY, IF YOU ASK ME.
TAKE CARE OF YOURSELF, COURTNEY.
AND TELL PAT I SAID "HI."
LOOK OUT!!!
HE'S TRYING TO ESCAPE!
STOP HIM, HOURMAN!
I--
--UMPH!
SHRACKAKAK
NO!
NOT AGAIN!
NOT AGAIN!

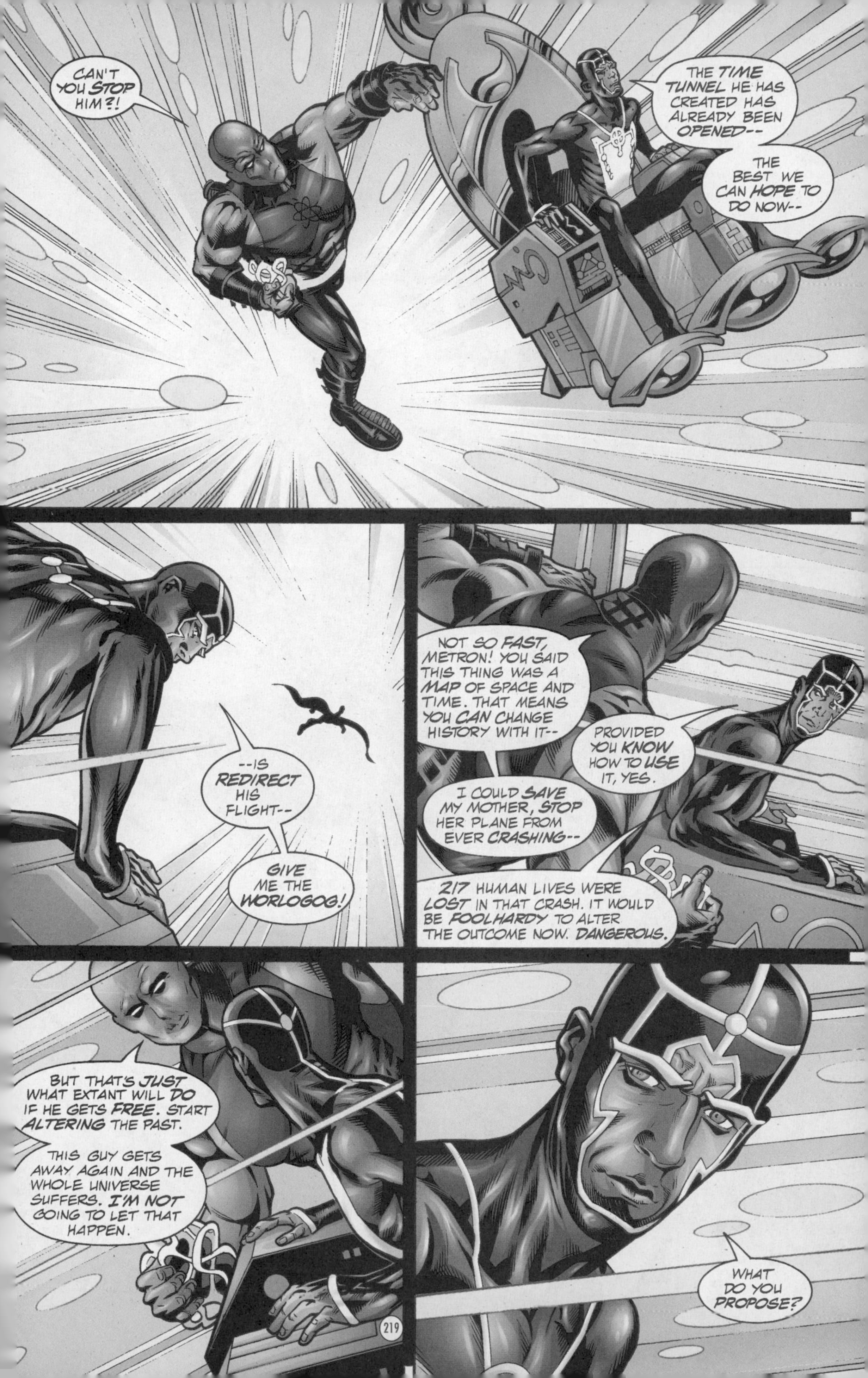
CAN'T YOU STOP HIM?!
THE TIME TUNNEL HE HAS CREATED HAS ALREADY BEEN OPENED--
THE BEST WE CAN HOPE TO DO NOW--
--IS REDIRECT HIS FLIGHT--
GIVE ME THE WORLOGOG!
NOT SO FAST, METRON! YOU SAID THIS THING WAS A MAP OF SPACE AND TIME. THAT MEANS YOU CAN CHANGE HISTORY WITH IT--
PROVIDED YOU KNOW HOW TO USE IT, YES.
I COULD SAVE MY MOTHER, STOP HER PLANE FROM EVER CRASHING--
217 HUMAN LIVES WERE LOST IN THAT CRASH. IT WOULD BE FOOLHARDY TO ALTER THE OUTCOME NOW. DANGEROUS.
BUT THAT'S JUST WHAT EXTANT WILL DO IF HE GETS FREE. START ALTERING THE PAST.
THIS GUY GETS AWAY AGAIN AND THE WHOLE UNIVERSE SUFFERS. I'M NOT GOING TO LET THAT HAPPEN.
WHAT DO YOU PROPOSE?

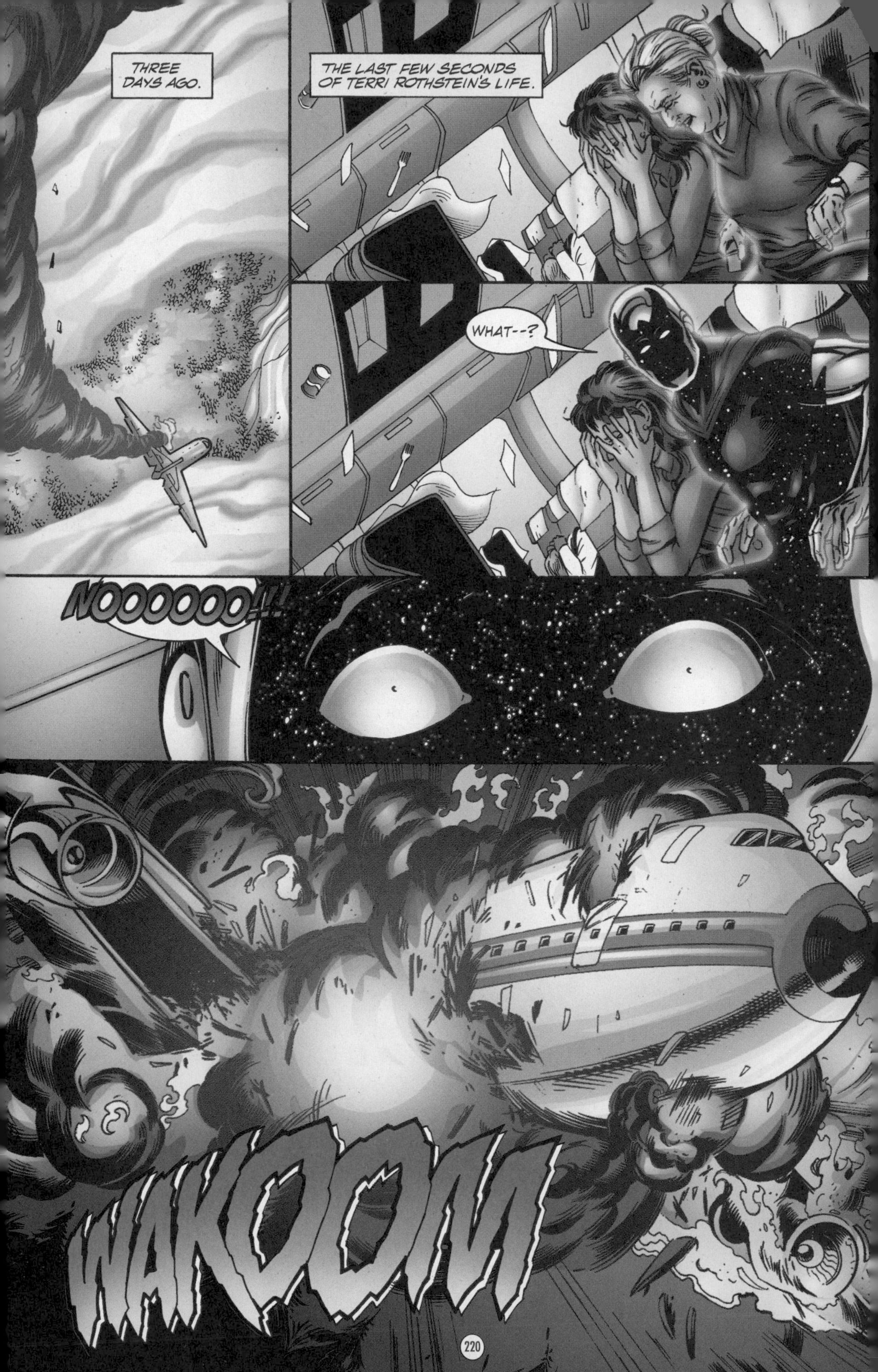
THREE DAYS AGO.
THE LAST FEW SECONDS OF TERRI ROTHSTEIN'S LIFE.
WHAT--?
NOOOOOO!!!
WAKOOM

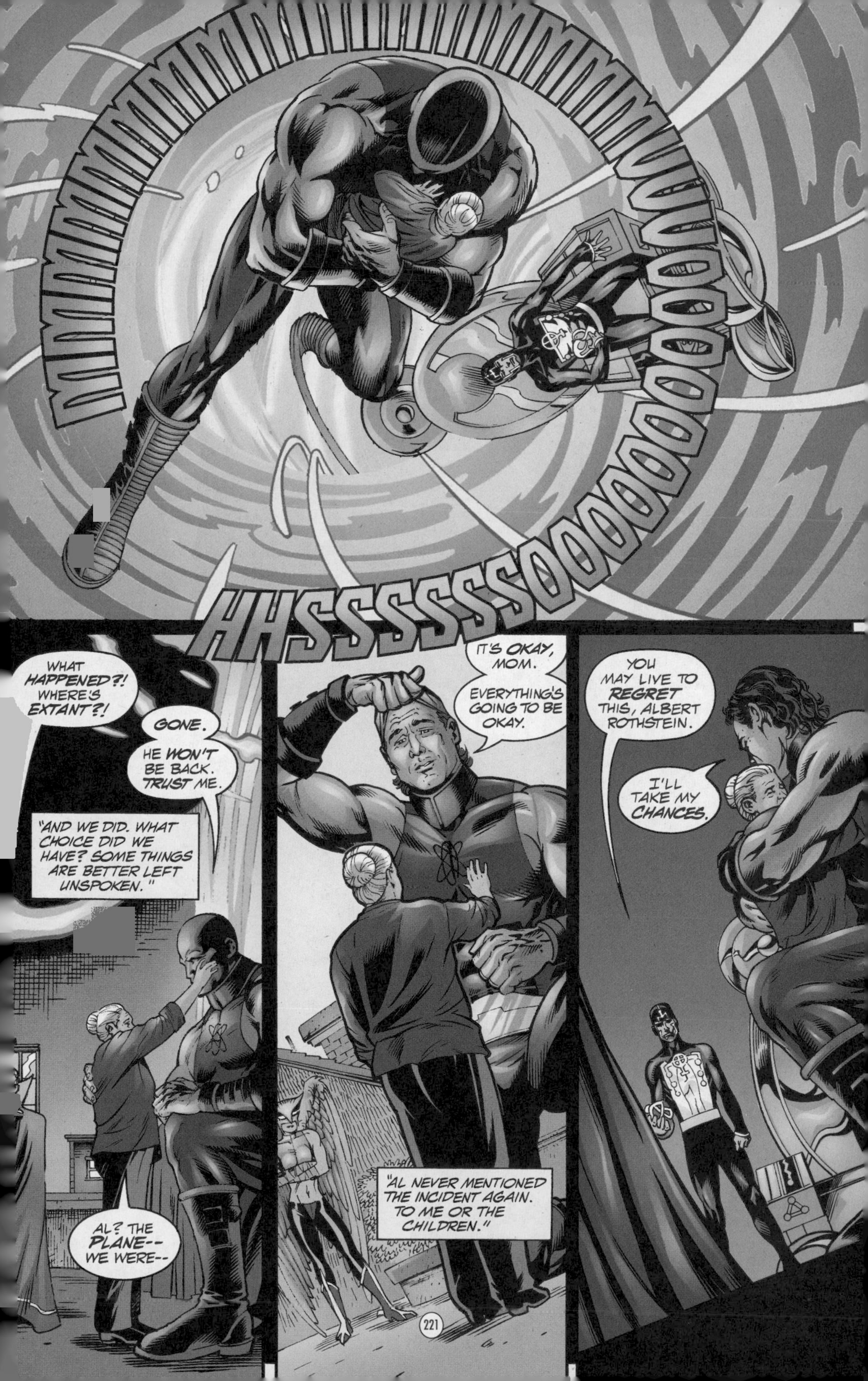
MMMMMMMMMMMMMMMMMMMMMMMMMOOOOOOOOOOOOSSSSSSHH
WHAT HAPPENED?! WHERE'S EXTANT?!
GONE.
HE WON'T BE BACK. TRUST ME.
"AND WE DID. WHAT CHOICE DID WE HAVE? SOME THINGS ARE BETTER LEFT UNSPOKEN."
AL? THE PLANE-- WE WERE--
IT'S OKAY, MOM.
EVERYTHING'S GOING TO BE OKAY.
"AL NEVER MENTIONED THE INCIDENT AGAIN. TO ME OR THE CHILDREN."
YOU MAY LIVE TO REGRET THIS, ALBERT ROTHSTEIN.
I'LL TAKE MY CHANCES.

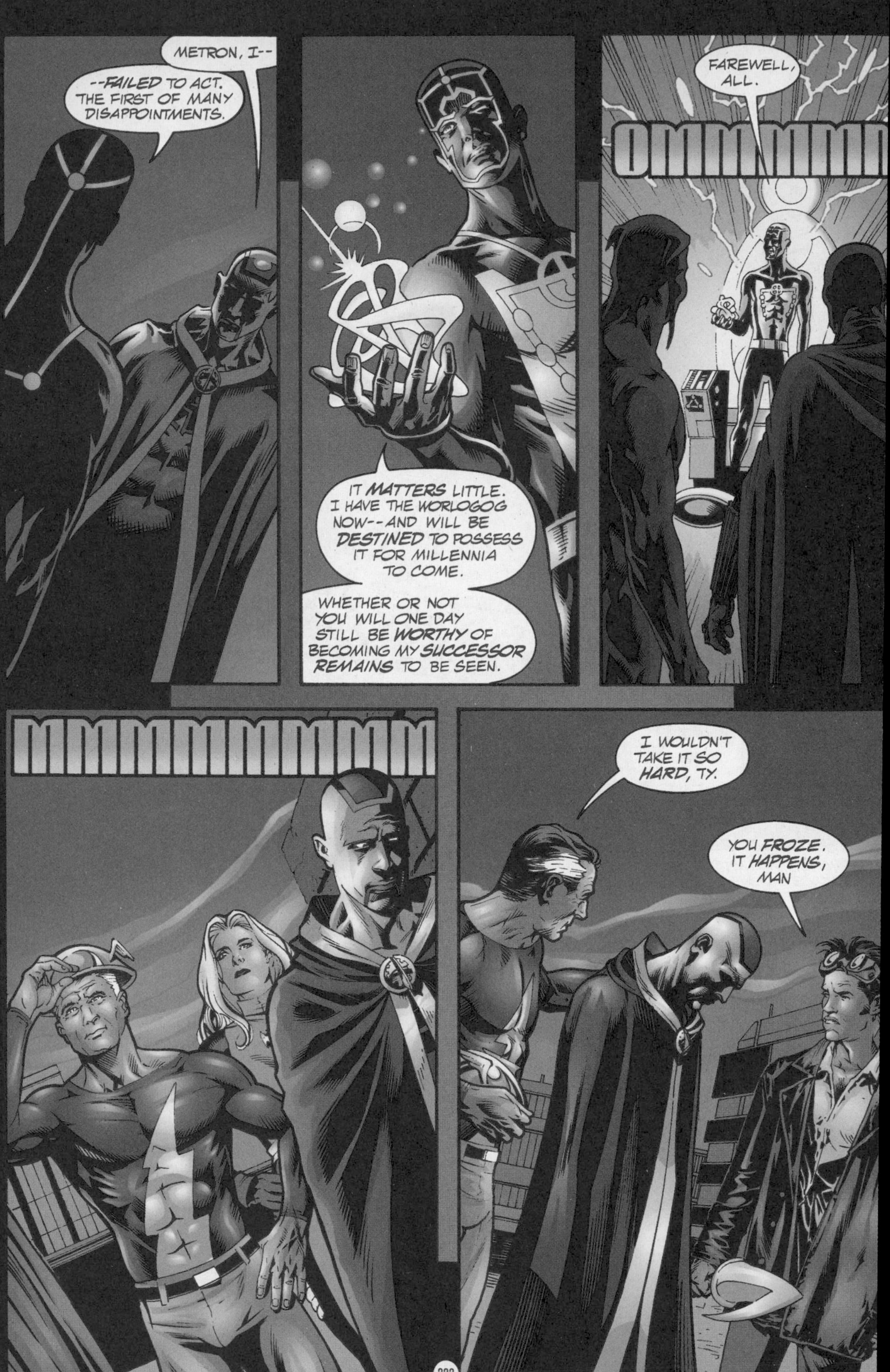
METRON, I--
--FAILED TO ACT. THE FIRST OF MANY DISAPPOINTMENTS.
IT MATTERS LITTLE. I HAVE THE WORLOGOG NOW--AND WILL BE DESTINED TO POSSESS IT FOR MILLENNIA TO COME.
WHETHER OR NOT YOU WILL ONE DAY STILL BE WORTHY OF BECOMING MY SUCCESSOR REMAINS TO BE SEEN.
FAREWELL, ALL.
OMMMMMM
MMMMMMMMM
I WOULDN'T TAKE IT SO HARD, TY.
YOU FROZE. IT HAPPENS, MAN

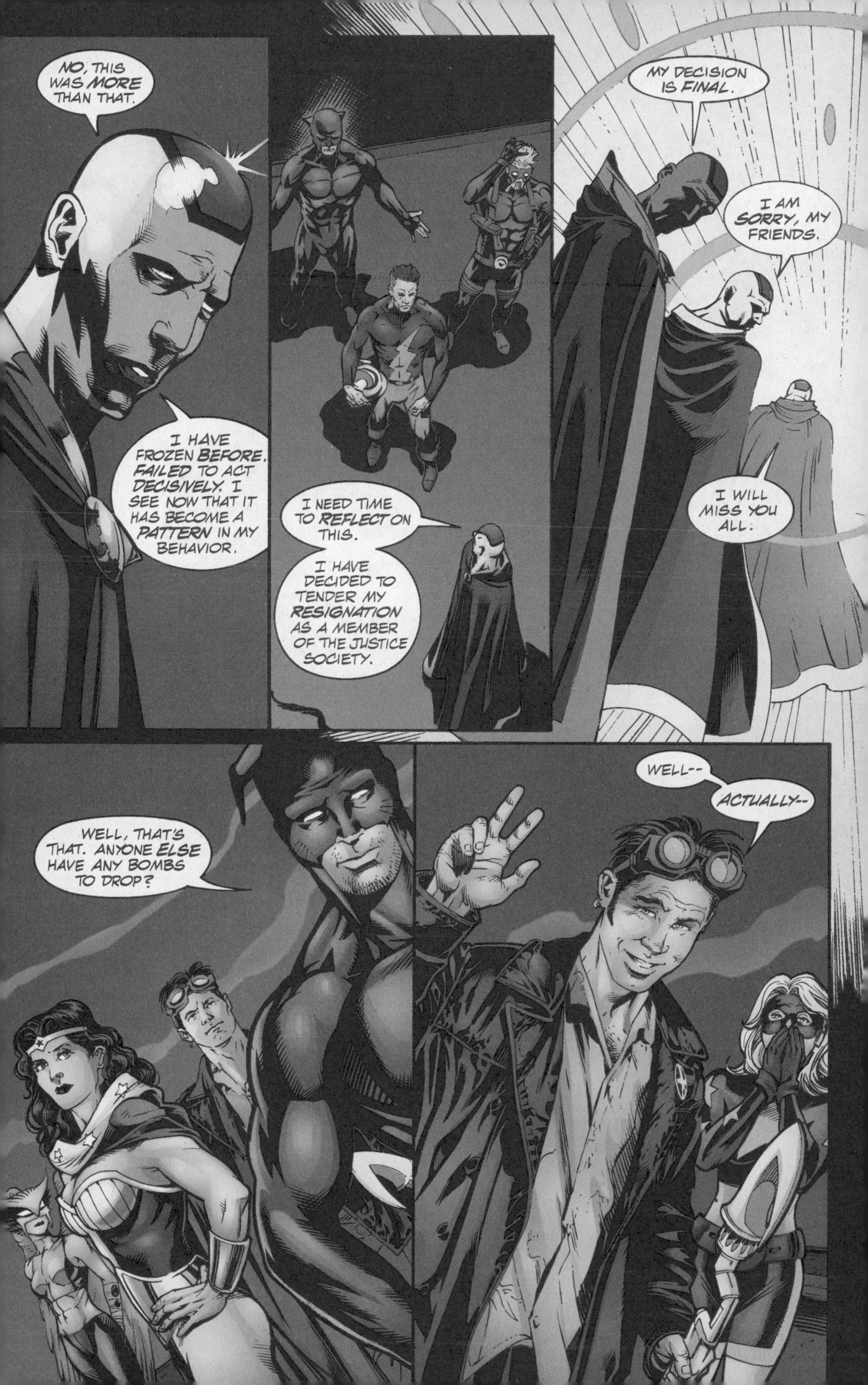
NO, THIS WAS MORE THAN THAT.
I HAVE FROZEN BEFORE. FAILED TO ACT DECISIVELY. I SEE NOW THAT IT HAS BECOME A PATTERN IN MY BEHAVIOR.
I NEED TIME TO REFLECT ON THIS.
I HAVE DECIDED TO TENDER MY RESIGNATION AS A MEMBER OF THE JUSTICE SOCIETY.
MY DECISION IS FINAL.
I AM SORRY, MY FRIENDS.
I WILL MISS YOU ALL.
WELL, THAT'S THAT. ANYONE ELSE HAVE ANY BOMBS TO DROP?
WELL--
ACTUALLY--

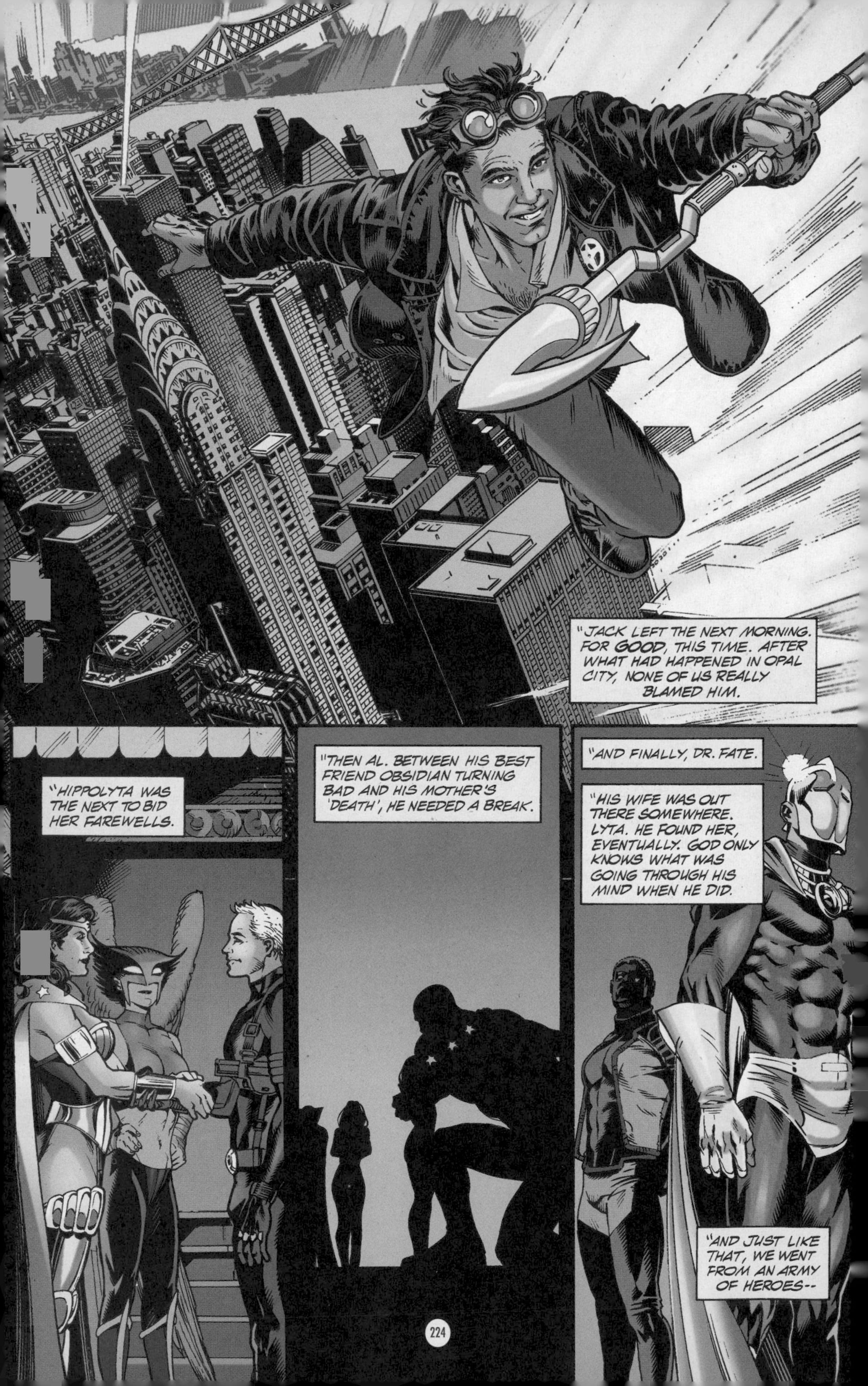
"JACK LEFT THE NEXT MORNING. FOR GOOD, THIS TIME. AFTER WHAT HAD HAPPENED IN OPAL CITY, NONE OF US REALLY BLAMED HIM.
"HIPPOLYTA WAS THE NEXT TO BID HER FAREWELLS.
"THEN AL. BETWEEN HIS BEST FRIEND OBSIDIAN TURNING BAD AND HIS MOTHER'S 'DEATH', HE NEEDED A BREAK.
"AND FINALLY, DR. FATE.
"HIS WIFE WAS OUT THERE SOMEWHERE. LYTA. HE FOUND HER, EVENTUALLY. GOD ONLY KNOWS WHAT WAS GOING THROUGH HIS MIND WHEN HE DID.
"AND JUST LIKE THAT, WE WENT FROM AN ARMY OF HEROES--

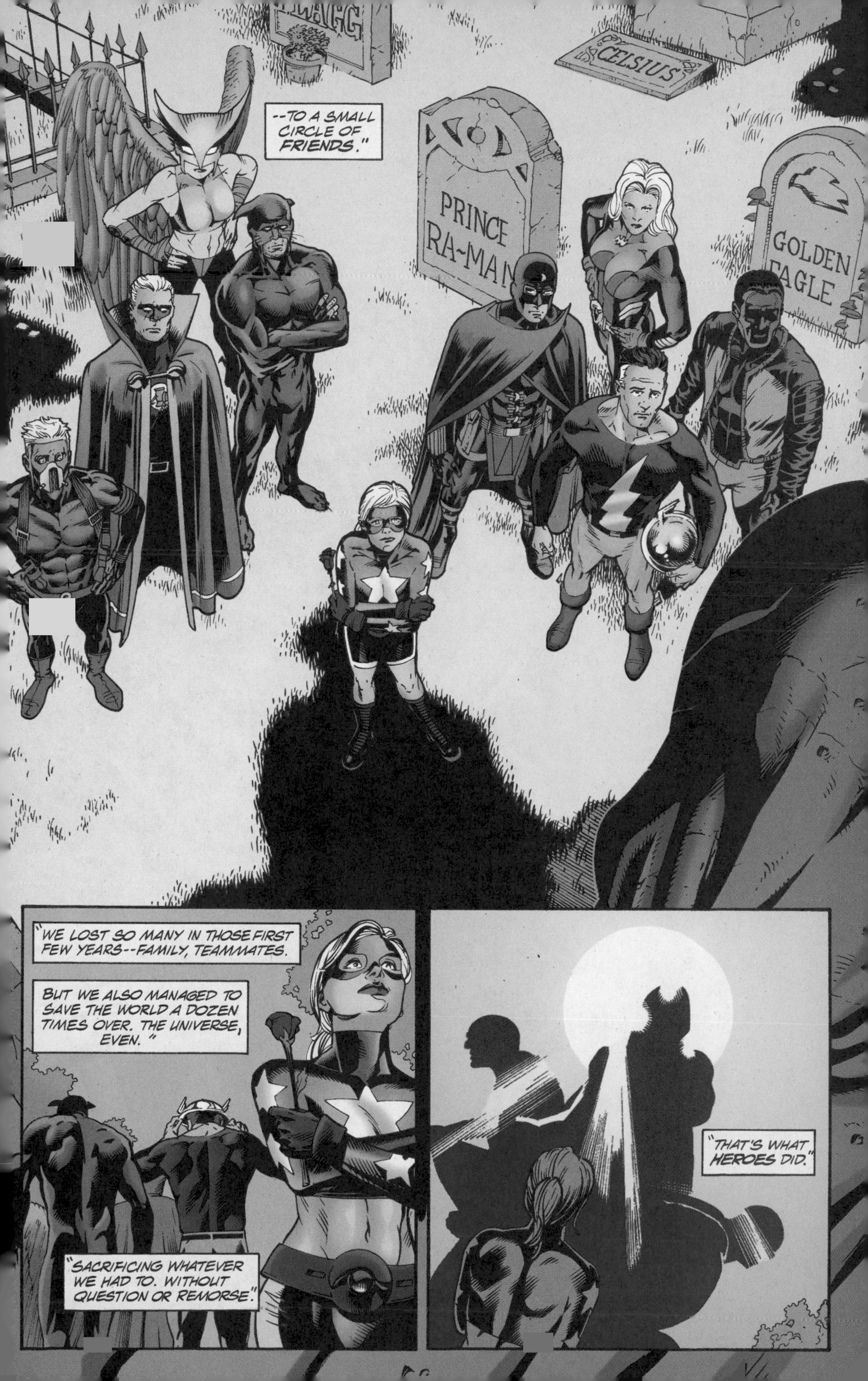
CELSIUS
--TO A SMALL CIRCLE OF FRIENDS."
PRINCE RA-MAN
GOLDEN EAGLE
"WE LOST SO MANY IN THOSE FIRST FEW YEARS--FAMILY, TEAMMATES.
BUT WE ALSO MANAGED TO SAVE THE WORLD A DOZEN TIMES OVER. THE UNIVERSE, EVEN."
"SACRIFICING WHATEVER WE HAD TO. WITHOUT QUESTION OR REMORSE."
"THAT'S WHAT HEROES DID."

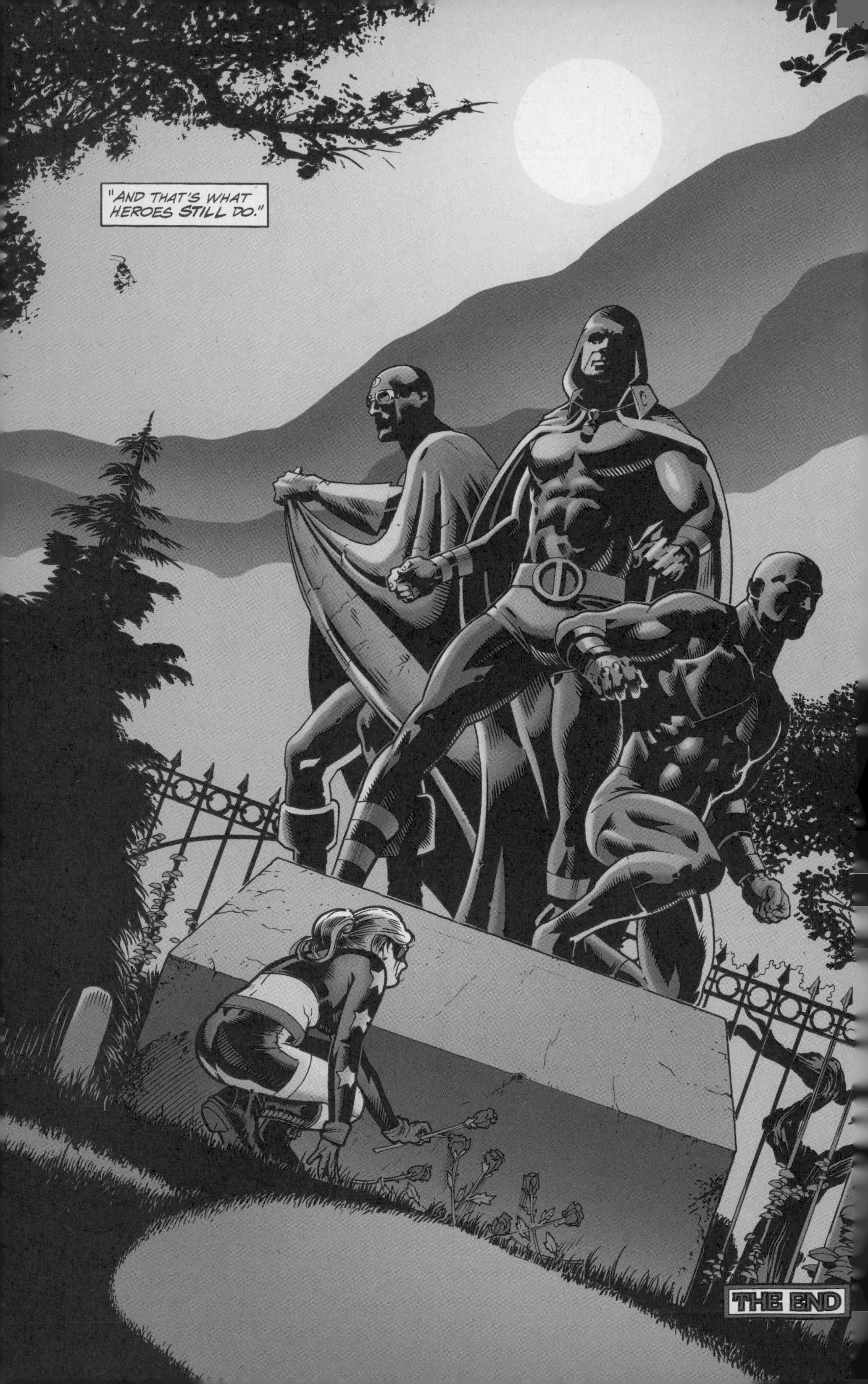
"AND THAT'S WHAT HEROES STILL DO."
THE END

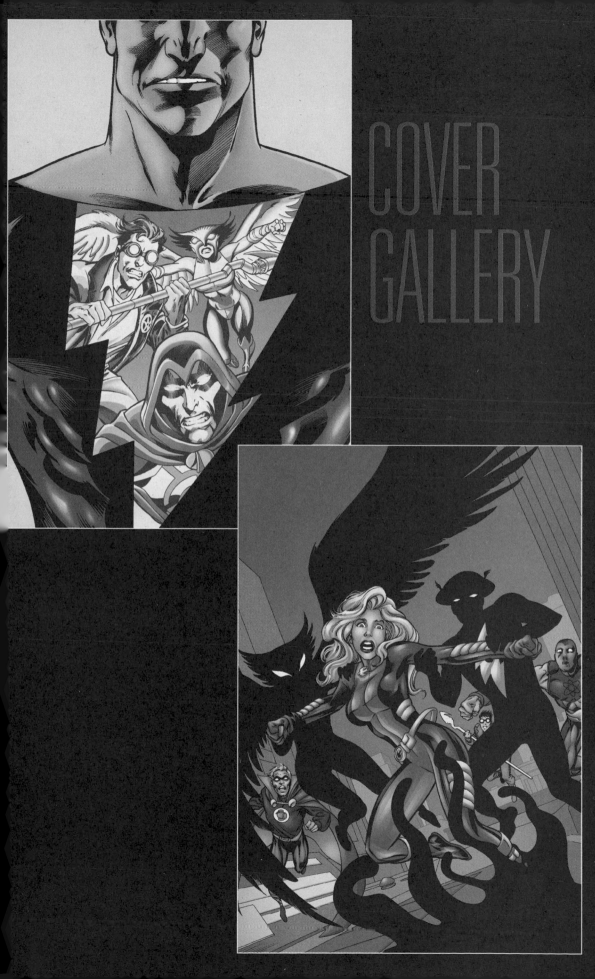

COVER GALLERY

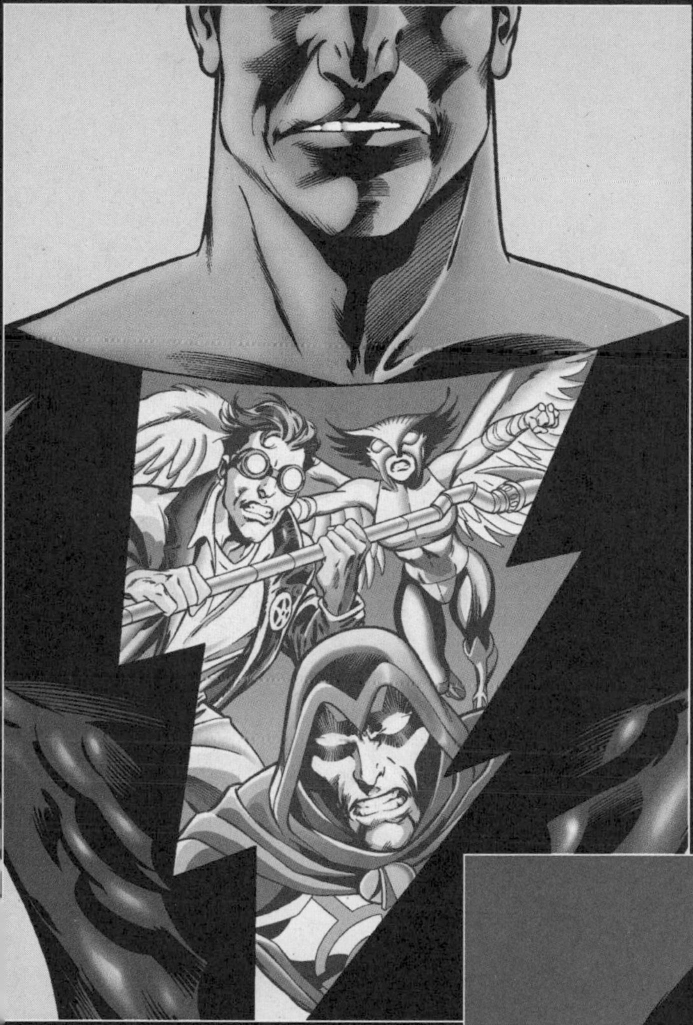

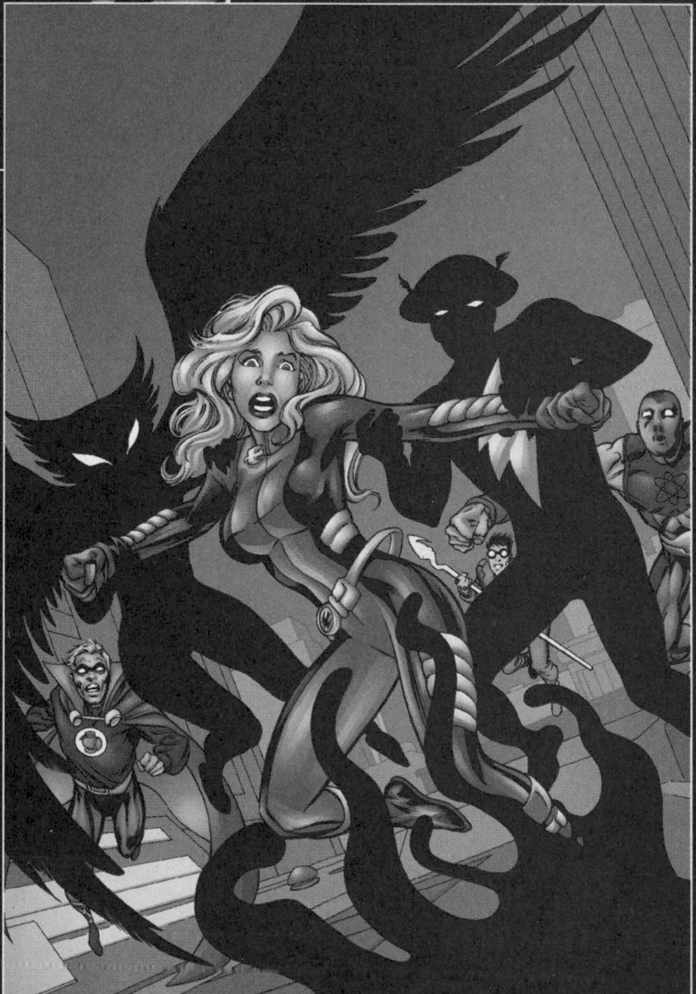

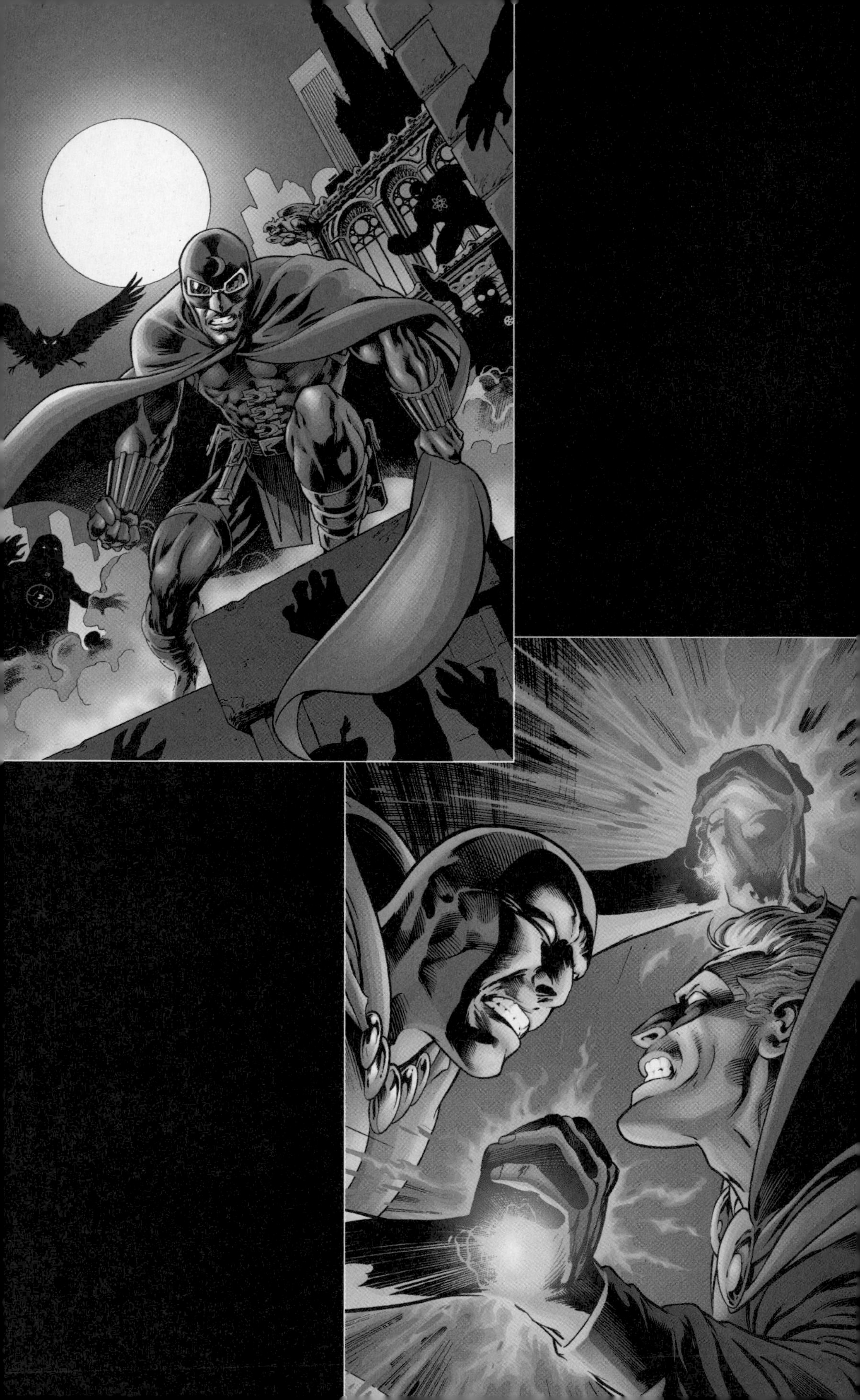

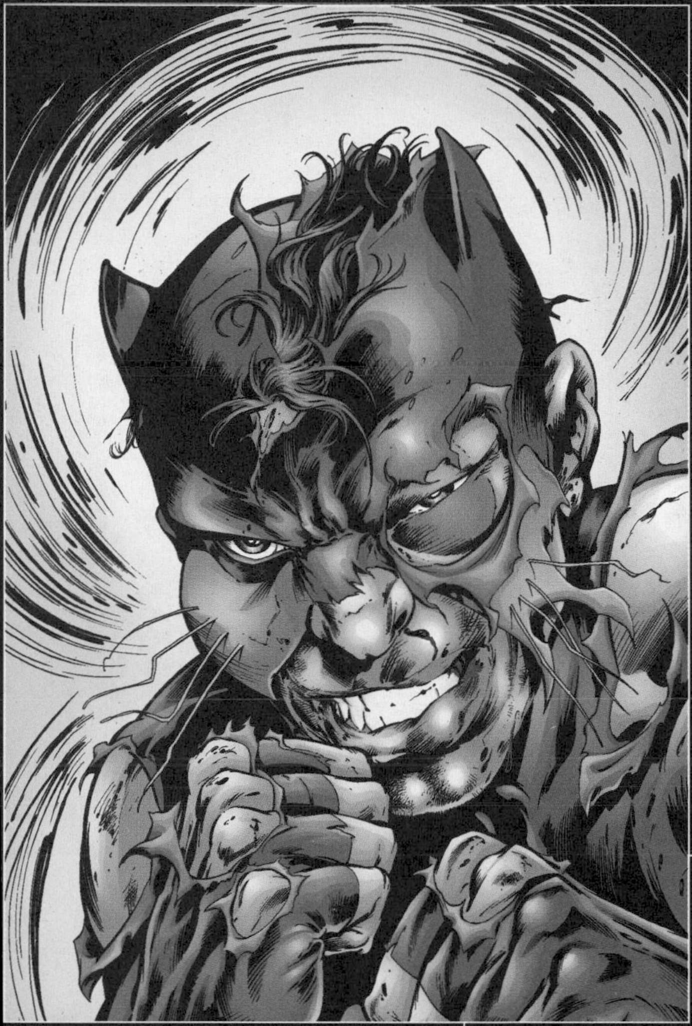

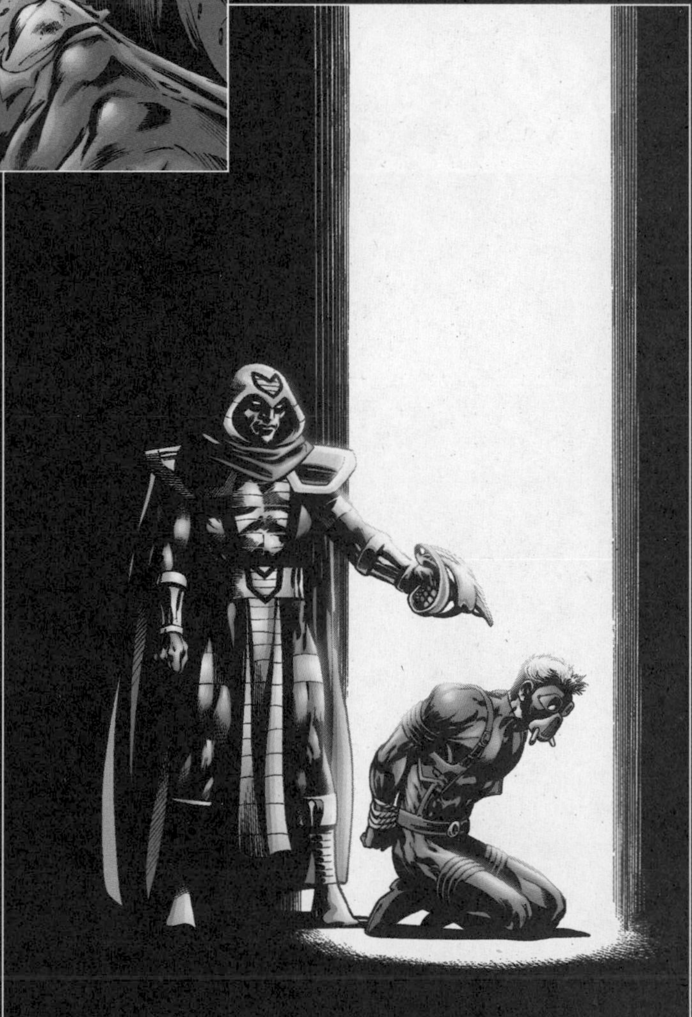

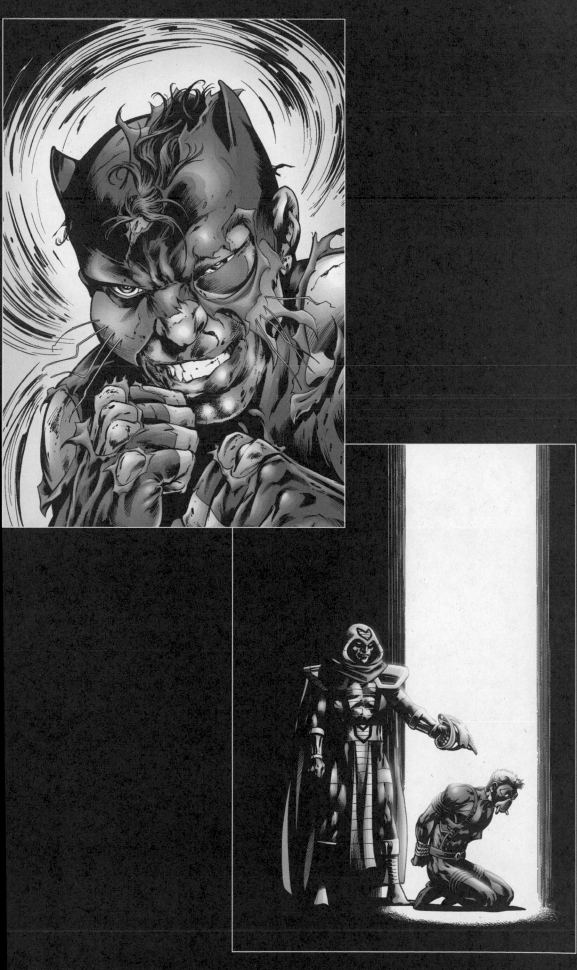

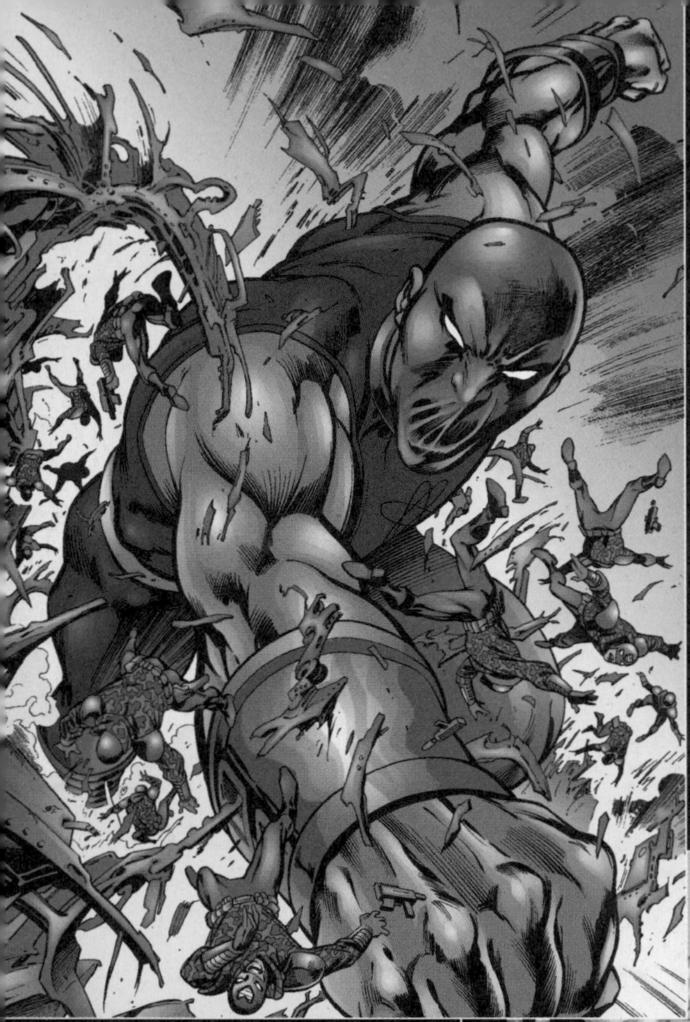

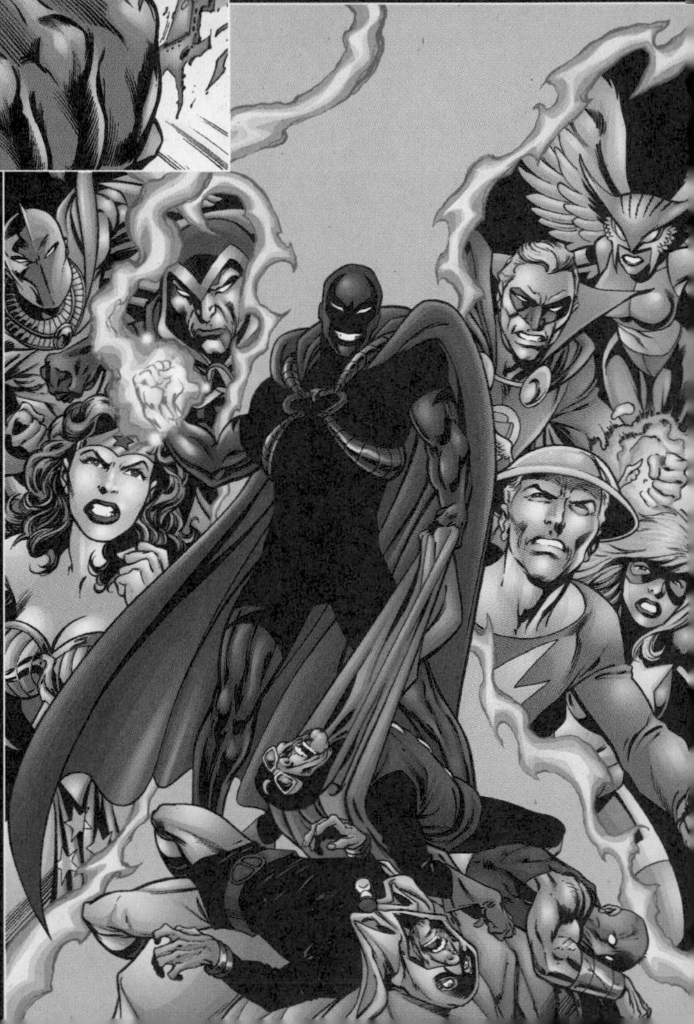

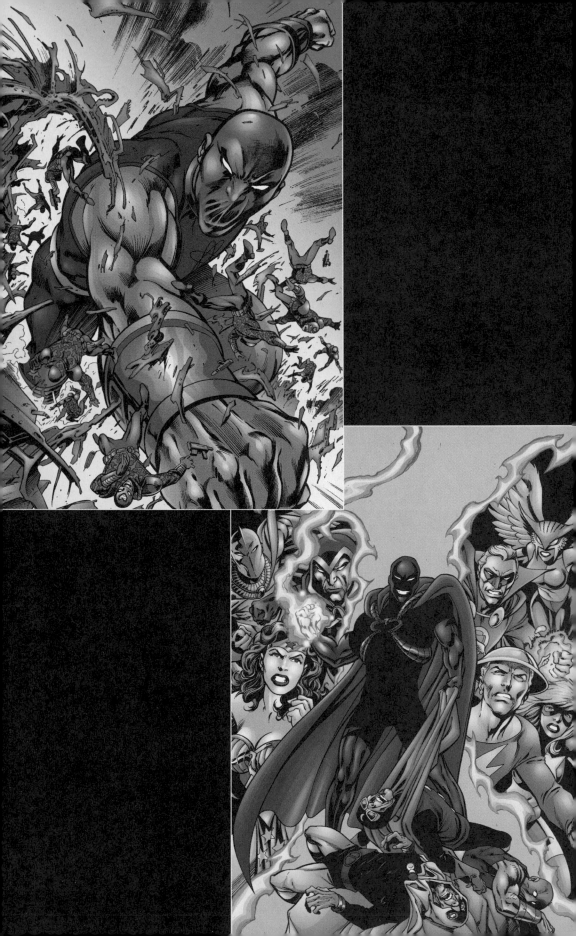

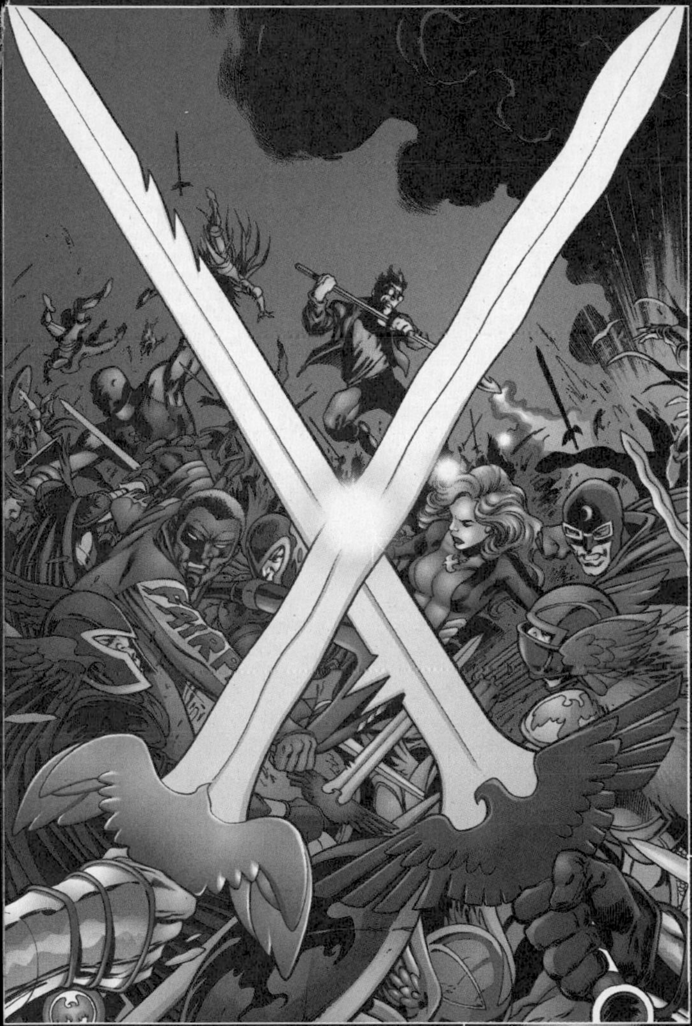

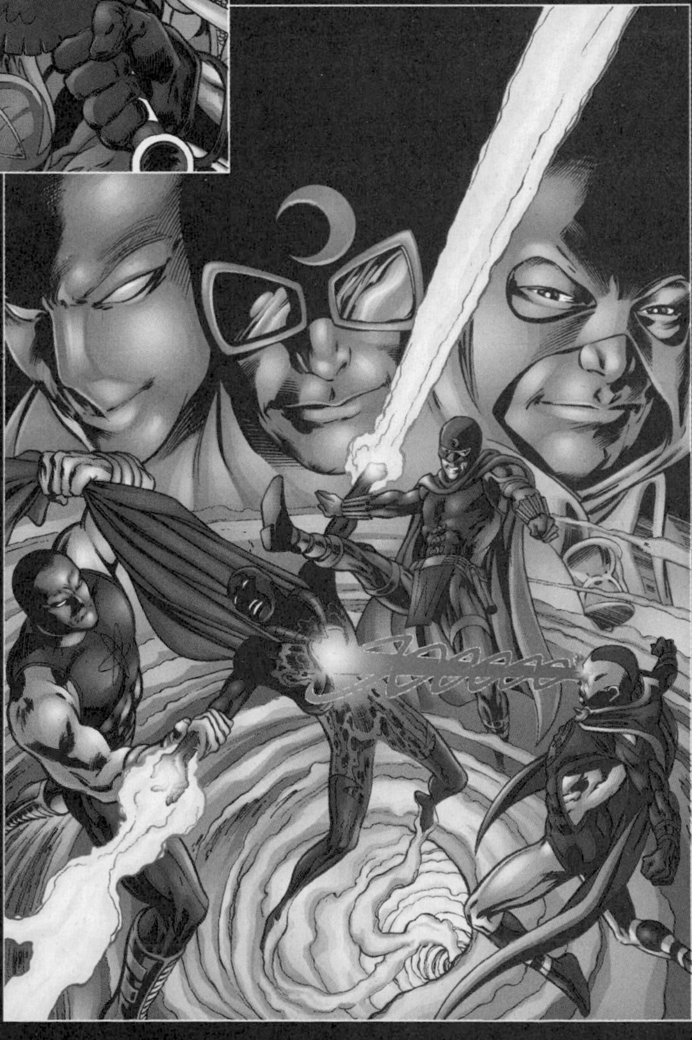

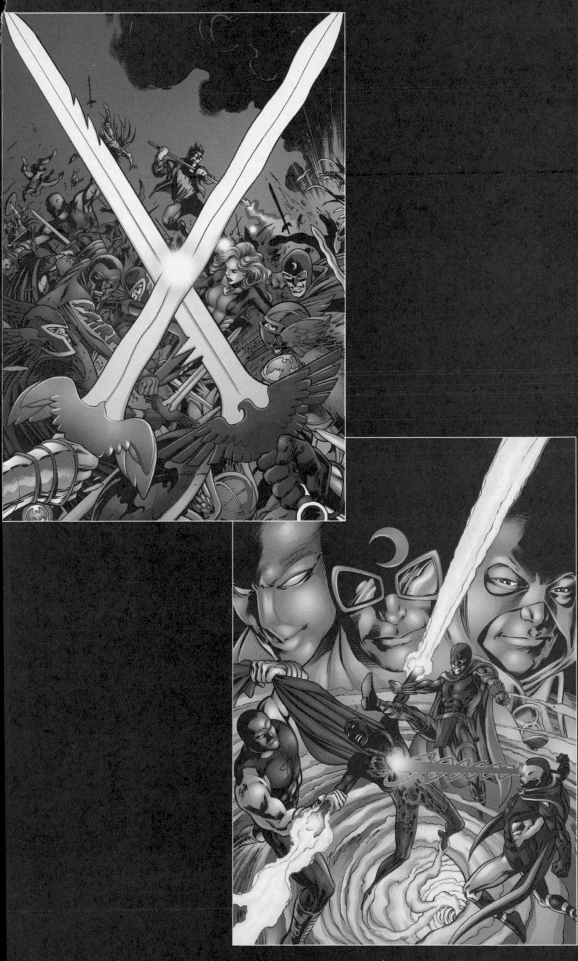

THE STARS OF THE
DC UNIVERSE
CAN ALSO BE FOUND IN THESE BOOKS:

GRAPHIC NOVELS

ENEMY ACE: WAR IDYLL
George Pratt

THE FLASH: LIFE STORY OF THE FLASH
M. Waid/B. Augustyn/G. Kane/
J. Staton/T. Palmer

GREEN LANTERN: FEAR ITSELF
Ron Marz/Brad Parker

THE POWER OF SHAZAM!
Jerry Ordway

WONDER WOMAN: AMAZONIA
William Messner-Loebs/
Phil Winslade

COLLECTIONS

THE GREATEST 1950s STORIES EVER TOLD
Various writers and artists

THE GREATEST TEAM-UP STORIES EVER TOLD
Various writers and artists

AQUAMAN: TIME AND TIDE
Peter David/Kirk Jarvinen/
Brad Vancata

DC ONE MILLION
Various writers and artists

THE FINAL NIGHT
K. Kesel/S. Immonen/
J. Marzan/various

THE FLASH: BORN TO RUN
M. Waid/T. Peyer/G. LaRocque/
H. Ramos/various

GREEN LANTERN: A NEW DAWN
R. Marz/D. Banks/R. Tanghal/
various

GREEN LANTERN: BAPTISM OF FIRE
Ron Marz/Darryl Banks/
various

GREEN LANTERN: EMERALD KNIGHTS
Ron Marz/Darryl Banks/
various

HAWK & DOVE
Karl and Barbara Kesel/
Rob Liefeld

HITMAN
Garth Ennis/John McCrea

HITMAN: LOCAL HEROES
G. Ennis/J. McCrea/
C. Ezquerra/S. Pugh

HITMAN: TEN THOUSAND BULLETS
Garth Ennis/John McCrea

IMPULSE: RECKLESS YOUTH
Mark Waid/various

JACK KIRBY'S FOREVER PEOPLE
Jack Kirby/various

JACK KIRBY'S NEW GODS
Jack Kirby/various

JACK KIRBY'S MISTER MIRACLE
Jack Kirby/various

JUSTICE LEAGUE: A NEW BEGINNING
K. Giffen/J.M. DeMatteis/
K. Maguire/various

JUSTICE LEAGUE: A MIDSUMMER'S NIGHTMARE
M. Waid/F. Nicieza/J. Johnson/
D. Robertson/various

JLA: AMERICAN DREAMS
G. Morrison/H. Porter/J. Dell/
various

JLA: JUSTICE FOR ALL
G. Morrison/M. Waid/H. Porter/
J. Dell/various

JUSTICE LEAGUE OF AMERICA: THE NAIL
Alan Davis/Mark Farmer

JLA: NEW WORLD ORDER
Grant Morrison/
Howard Porter/John Dell

JLA: ROCK OF AGES
G. Morrison/H. Porter/J. Dell/
various

JLA: STRENGTH IN NUMBERS
G. Morrison/M. Waid/H. Porter/
J. Dell/various

JLA: WORLD WITHOUT GROWN-UPS
T. Dezago/T. Nauck/H. Ramos/
M. McKone/various

JLA/TITANS: THE TECHNIS IMPERATIVE
D. Grayson/P. Jimenez/
P. Pelletier/various

JLA: YEAR ONE
M. Waid/B. Augustyn/
B. Kitson/various

KINGDOM COME
Mark Waid/Alex Ross

LEGENDS: THE COLLECTED EDITION
J. Ostrander/L. Wein/J. Byrne/
K. Kesel

LOBO'S GREATEST HITS
Various writers and artists

LOBO: THE LAST CZARNIAN
Keith Giffen/Alan Grant/
Simon Bisley

LOBO'S BACK'S BACK
K. Giffen/A. Grant/S. Bisley/
C. Alamy

MANHUNTER: THE SPECIAL EDITION
Archie Goodwin/Walter Simonson

THE RAY: IN A BLAZE OF POWER
Jack C. Harris/Joe Quesada/
Art Nichols

THE SPECTRE: CRIMES AND PUNISHMENTS
John Ostrander/Tom Mandrake

STARMAN: SINS OF THE FATHER
James Robinson/Tony Harris/
Wade von Grawbadger

STARMAN: NIGHT AND DAY
James Robinson/Tony Harris/
Wade von Grawbadger

STARMAN: TIMES PAST
J. Robinson/O. Jimenez/
L. Weeks/various

STARMAN: A WICKED INCLINATION...
J. Robinson/T. Harris/
W. von Grawbadger/various

UNDERWORLD UNLEASHED
M. Waid/H. Porter/
P. Jimenez/various

WONDER WOMAN: THE CONTEST
William Messner-Loebs/
Mike Deodato, Jr.

WONDER WOMAN: SECOND GENESIS
John Byrne

WONDER WOMAN: LIFELINES
John Byrne

DC/MARVEL: CROSSOVER CLASSICS II
Various writers and artists

DC VERSUS MARVEL/ MARVEL VERSUS DC
R. Marz/P. David/D. Jurgens/
C. Castellini/various

THE AMALGAM AGE OF COMICS: THE DC COMICS COLLECTION
Various writers and artists

RETURN TO THE AMALGAM AGE OF COMICS: THE DC COMICS COLLECTION
Various writers and artists

OTHER COLLECTIONS OF INTEREST

CAMELOT 3000
Mike W. Barr/Brian Bolland/
various

RONIN
Frank Miller

WATCHMEN
Alan Moore/Dave Gibbons

ARCHIVE EDITIONS

THE FLASH ARCHIVES Volume 1
(FLASH COMICS 104, SHOWCASE
4, 8, 13, 14, THE FLASH 105-108)
J. Broome/C. Infantino/J. Giella/
various

THE FLASH ARCHIVES Volume 2
(THE FLASH 109-116)
J.Broome/C. Infantino/J. Giella/
various

GREEN LANTERN ARCHIVES Volume 1
(SHOWCASE 22-23,
GREEN LANTERN 1-5)

GREEN LANTERN ARCHIVES Volume 2
(GREEN LANTERN 6-13)
All by J. Broome/G. Kane/
J. Giella/various

SHAZAM ARCHIVES Volume 1
(WHIZ COMICS 2-15)

SHAZAM ARCHIVES Volume 2
(SPECIAL EDITION COMICS 1,
CAPTAIN MARVEL ADVENTURES 1,
WHIZ COMICS 15-20)
All by B. Parker/C.C. Beck/
J. Simon/J. Kirby/various

THE NEW TEEN TITANS Volume 1
(DC COMICS PRESENTS 26,
THE NEW TITANS 1-8)
Marv Wolfman/George Pérez/
various

TO FIND MORE COLLECTED EDITIONS AND MONTHLY COMIC BOOKS FROM DC COMICS,
CALL 1-888-COMIC BOOK FOR THE NEAREST COMICS SHOP OR GO TO YOUR LOCAL BOOK STORE.

Visit us at www.dccomics.com